MANUFACTURING ARCHITECTURE

— — — — — — — — — — — — — —

An Architect's Guide
to Custom Processes,
Materials, and Applications

Dana K. Gulling

Laurence King Publishing

MANUFACTURING ARCHITECTURE

An Architect's Guide
to Custom Processes,
Materials, and Applications

LAURENCE KING

Published in 2018 by
Laurence King Publishing Ltd
361–373 City Road, London,
EC1V 1LR, United Kingdom
T +44 (0)20 7841 6900
F + 44 (0)20 7841 6910
enquiries@laurenceking.com
www.laurenceking.com

This book was produced by
Laurence King Publishing Ltd, London

A catalogue record for this book
is available from the British Library.

ISBN: 978-1-78627-133-4

Design: Alexandre Coco

Printed in China

To my Family—
my supportive husband and my sparkling daughter

are of aspirational architectural designs. Some of the case studies are architectural installations, such as Bioform by Murmur, made from super-plastic formed aluminum for an exhibition at Artists Space in New York. However, most of the case studies are completed buildings located around the world. These include the slumped glass windows for the Gores Group Headquarters by Belzberg Architects in Los Angeles, California; the spun metal domes for the Eemhuis by Neutelings Riedijk Architects in Amersfoort, the Netherlands; and the extruded plastic siding for the El Batel Auditorium by selgascano in Cartagena, Spain.

Finally, this book only includes repetitive manufacturing processes. These processes make repeated use of their tooling (e.g. jigs, patterns, and molds) in the production of similar units. The repetitive manufacturing processes included in this guide are limited to those processes that, in some way, outperform computer-aided manufacturing (CAM). For example, CAM is more efficient for processes such as drilling, punching, carving, and lathing than any repetitive manufacturing process. Outperformance may be measured in terms of better finishes, less waste, wider range of materials, faster production times, or lower costs.

The book's first chapter discusses the current landscape of repetitive manufacturing in architecture. It describes its relationship with CAM, identifies the type of architectural components that have customized repetitive processes, and suggests how architects may work with repetitive manufacturers. Subsequent chapters are grouped into sections by similar manufacturing processes. The sections are: "Manipulating Sheet," "Continuous Shaping," "Making Thin or Hollow," and "Forming Solid." Each section's heading defines the group and describes the similarities and differences between the manufacturing processes within it.

The subsequent chapters introduce the manufacturing process and materials with narrative texts and diagrams. Also included are standard available building products that are made by the manufacturing process, tooling requirements, environmental impacts, and similar manufacturing processes. Case studies are provided for most of the materials within a manufacturing process. Each chapter includes design parameters for a given material and process, to help architects get started with their designs. The parameters are compiled from a variety of sources (e.g. books, industry standards, conversations with manufacturers); a particular manufacturer may have capabilities beyond those listed. Always collaborate with a manufacturer directly before finalizing the design of any component.

Manufacturing Architecture gives architects the tools to customize repetitive manufacturing process for architectural application. This could include the design for new building products, architectural installation, or the design of custom components for a particular project. My hope is that with this book, architects will no longer be limited to standard building products, designed by others outside of the profession. Instead, with the tools provided here, architects will be able to design all scales of architecture—from a building's massing down to its components—thereby expanding their design role within the built environment.

Precast concrete walls, cast inside of a custom plywood mold, at the Crematorium Heimolen, designed by KAAN Architecten

Introduction

In architecture, **COMPUTER-AIDED MANUFACTURING (CAM)** has revolutionized the relationship between design and production. It has allowed **COMPUTER NUMERIC CONTROLLED (CNC) EQUIPMENT** to make individual and unique architecture components that are not prohibitively expensive.[1] Simultaneously, CNC machines have made it more affordable to customize the tools in repetitive manufacturing processes. CNC equipment has reduced **TOOLING** costs so that large production runs are no longer necessary to offset those costs. Now repetitive manufacturing can be cost effective for small-volume productions. For select applications, it has the benefits of being faster, having a wider range of materials and finishes, producing less waste, and being less expensive than typical CAM processes. In recent years, architects have focused on CAM's direct effects on contemporary design and construction, while ignoring its indirect potential for customizing repetitive manufacturing for architectural application.

There are two concepts architects should be aware of to pursue customized repetitive manufacturing: 1) they should develop designs that are easy to manufacture, and 2) they should select manufacturers that are responsive to the needs of designers. Developing designs in conjunction with understanding manufacturing methods proactively addresses issues of materials and making, and helps to control costs. At the same time, most architects have little experience with repetitive manufacturers and may not know the available options. Because of this, I recommend that architects seek out manufacturers with experience in collaborating with the design team.

There are a number of examples of architects customizing repetitive manufacturing processes for architectural application. *Manufacturing Architecture* includes case studies where architects have done this, either for an architecture prototype or for a particular building. The case studies include a mix of practices, including high-profile firms such as Foster + Partners, Machado Silvetti, Benthem Crouwel Architects, and Neutelings Riedijk Architects; local experimental practices such as 5468796 Architecture, Hierve Diseñeria, 6a Architects, and Miniwiz; and design-build prototypes housed in an academic institution such as the University of Arizona or the University of Stuttgart. The case studies are located around the world and demonstrate a global application of this approach.

COMPUTER-AIDED MANUFACTURING (CAM) manufacturing that uses computer numerical controlled (CNC) equipment for production

COMPUTER NUMERICAL CONTROLLED (CNC) EQUIPMENT equipment that uses a computer software to drive the machine tools for shape making

TOOLING manufacturing aides for forming units; examples of tooling include molds, dies, patterns, jigs, plugs, and masters

MANUFACTURING to make from raw materials by hand or by machinery, especially when carried out systematically

FORMING a single manufacturing process that transforms unformed or raw materials into the unit's final form

BLANK a flat sheet of metal already cut to the appropriate size and shape

BILLET a length of metal with either a round or square cross-section; it is a semi-finished product that is produced in a mill for transportation before being processed into the final profile of the component

PRODUCTION RUN the number of similar units or components manufactured from one tool

REPETITIVE MANUFACTURING repeated use of tools for the production of similar units

---

1   Branco Kolarevic. *Architecture in the Digital Age: Design and Manufacturing.* New York: Spon Press, 2003. Print.

DEFINING REPETITIVE MANUFACTURING

MANUFACTURING is "to make from raw materials by hand or by machinery … especially when carried on systematically with division of labor."[2]

In this context, manufacturing refers to the **FORMING** of raw materials into the components' final form. This can include techniques such as contact molding fiberglass to make a boat hull, or casting molten metal to make a lever door handle. Also included in this definition is the deformation and transformation of a raw material into another form. For example, stamping a metal **BLANK** into a car hood, extruding aluminum **BILLET** to make window mullions, or laminating layers of wood veneers into a curve to create bent plywood furniture. The cut sheet metal, billets, or wood veneers are not complete on their own; they are for the manufacturing ease of the subsequent processes—stamping, extruding, and bending laminates. In the context of this book, manufacturing refers to a single process—such as contact molding, casting, stamping, extruding, or laminating. In industrial contexts, manufacturing can refer to post-production processes—such as cutting, joining, and finishing, or product assembly.

Using this definition, manufacturing does not necessarily favor mechanized or industrialized processes, and can include nonindustrialized and handcrafted processes. For example, processes such as wood molding, hand-blowing glass, or metal casting can be considered manufacturing when done systematically. Manufacturing by hand is viable where labor costs are low and where there is little capital to purchase large equipment. Architectural examples of these labor-intensive manufacturing processes include the wood-molded, blown-glass spheres manufactured by craftsmen in Guadalajara, Mexico, for the Hesiodo by Hierve Diseñeria in Mexico City, and new concrete masonry units (CMUs) manufactured on a concrete block hand press that were made for MR 299 by HGR Architects with Ariel Rojo, also in Mexico City.

Conversely, processes such as extruding aluminum, hydroforming metal, extruding stiff mud, or pultruding fiber-reinforced plastics (FRPs) are mechanized. Often this is done with processes that have high capital costs and may include specialized equipment or tooling. For example, extruding stiff mud requires large batch or tunnel kilns to fire the materials. Production orders are most likely large so that the kilns are filled, with little downtime between shapes. Additionally, extruding aluminum requires large equipment to force the metal billet though expensive and heavy dies made of tool steel. Large **PRODUCTION RUNS** are necessary to offset the equipment costs and because changing dies may be difficult.

REPETITIVE MANUFACTURING makes repeated use of its tooling (e.g. jigs, patterns, molds, or dies) for the production of similar units. [1, 2, 3] Production runs for repetitive manufacturing can be varied, ranging from prototypes and small-batch productions to production runs over one million units. For example, because of the low costs to make a wood pattern, sand casting can be used for small batches. Conversely, plastic blow molds fabricated from hardened tool steel are appropriate for larger production runs. Large production runs are necessary to offset high mold costs. For example, if a mold costs $50,000 but produces 100,000 units, the added cost of a custom mold would be just 50 cents per unit.

1 Repetitive manufacturing tooling. Mold half for plastic blow molding

2 Repetitive manufacturing tooling. Trim die for plastic blow molding

3 Repetitive manufacturing tooling. Steel die for extruding aluminum

2   *Webster's Ninth New Collegiate Dictionary*. Springfield, MA: Merriam-Webster Inc., 1988. Print.

In repetitive manufacturing a particular tool is used for a particular shape. Processes can be customized or adjusted to introduce differences in the components produced. For example, tools may be adjusted or partitioned in such a way that portions of the tool form different shapes. This allows for some variation while still making repeated use of the tooling. Architectural examples of this practice include the bladder inflation molded exterior louvers for the Walbrook Office Building by Foster + Partners in London (Chapter 3.2). For that project, the manufacturer used one mold to make multiple lengths of louvers by lining only part of the mold with the fiber and resin layup. Additional manufacturing adjustments can be made through manufacturing speeds, conditions, or changes in media.

REPETITIVE MANUFACTURING IN AN AGE OF COMPUTER-AIDED MANUFACTURING

Although repetitive manufacturing often uses computers to run the machinery, it is distinct from CAM. In CAM, CNC equipment uses computer-controlled tooling to directly shape the manufactured item. Once programmed into the computer, alternative shapes do not necessarily slow down a CNC machine or alter its operation. CNC equipment has made some manufacturing processes more efficient even when producing repeatable objects. Examples such as drilling, rolling, routing, and cutting are often more efficient when completed by a CNC mill than by hand or repetitive means. Conversely, some repetitive manufacturing processes outperform CAM: material selection, material finish, and production speeds may be better. For example, plastic extruding through a die produces a component that is stronger, with a smoother surface, and at a faster rate than CNC milling or **RAPID PROTOTYPING (RP)** the same shape. Additionally, for some processes, repetitive manufacturing has less production waste and lower costs per unit than CAM. At the same time, repetitive manufacturing still dominates the production of architecture components. Products such as brick, metal hardware, CMUs, and bathroom fixtures are all repetitively manufactured.

In recent years, **MASS CUSTOMIZATION** and CAM technologies have transformed design and off-site building component fabrication. CNC equipment is used directly or indirectly to fabricate building components. Directly, CNC equipment has fabricated the granite stone panels for the Guangzhou Opera House by Zaha Hadid Architects in Guangzhou, China, **[4]** the structural members for the Great Court at the British Museum by Foster + Partners, **[5]** and the copper screen for the de Young Museum by Herzog & de Meuron in San Francisco, California. Indirectly, CNC equipment has fabricated individual molds to form unique architecture components. Examples of this approach include the BMW Bubble by FRANKEN \ ARCHITEKTEN at the International Motor Show in Frankfurt, Germany, and

the Nordpark Railway Stations by Zaha Hadid Architects in Innsbruck, Austria. **[6]** In these examples, there is little to no repeatability in the panel shapes, and therefore most of the molds that formed each of the panels were disposed of after a single use.[3]

At the same time, CAM's CNC machines have reduced tooling costs for repetitive manufacturing. CNC milling machines, electrical discharge machining (EDM), and hot-wire foam cutters are used to create molds and patterns for repetitive manufacturing. Since tooling costs for repetitive manufacturing are amortized over the number of units a tool produces, reduced tooling costs in turn reduces the production run necessary to off-set those costs. This means that CNC technologies have enabled smaller production runs for repetitive manufacturing, which allows the possibility of architects customizing repetitive manufacturing on a per-project basis. In *Manufacturing Architecture,* the phrase **CUSTOMIZED REPETITIVE MANUFACTURING (CRM)** refers to this type of work.

In contrast to using CNC equipment to make disposable molds for unique components, CRM requires that its tools produce multiple units. Making tools from durable materials and producing multiple components per mold results in less manufacturing waste. Today, many repetitive manufacturers use tools made by CNC equipment. Contact fiberglass molders and plastic

---

3   The BMW pavilion used polyurethane foam molds to fabricate each of the unique, double-curved acrylic panels.

RAPID PROTOTYPING (RP) CNC equipment that adds layers of media together to create an object; examples include selective laser sintering (SLS) and stereolithography (SLA), also known as 3D printing

MASS CUSTOMIZATION a consumer's ability to customize or partially customize a product; the financial cost increase for mass customization is not considered a deterrent for most consumers

CUSTOMIZED REPETITIVE MANUFACTURING (CRM) repetitive manufacturing with low tooling costs that accommodates small production runs with limited additional costs

4 Zaha Hadid Architects, Guangzhou Opera House (2010), Guangzhou, China. CAM made possible the fabrication of the granite panels

5 Foster + Partners, Great Court at the British Museum (2000), London, UK. CAM made it possible to fabricate unique pieces for each of the joints of the lamella structure

6 Zaha Hadid Architects, Nordpark Railway Stations (2007), Innsbruck, Austria. CNC equipment was used indirectly to fabricate the unique molds for each of the panels

7 Foster + Partners, Walbrook Office Building (2010), London, UK. There was a cost saving made by switching from CAM to CRM

However, CRM has a number of valuable benefits. First, CRM reuses jigs, molds, or patterns during production. Depending on the mold, the process, and the medium, a mold can produce up to 500,000 units. Second, repetitive manufacturing typically only uses as much material as the mold, pattern, or jig needs. By reusing tools and reducing raw material requirements, CRM can have little to no production waste. Third, manufacturing tolerances for most of these processes are high and have the potential to rival the tolerances of CNC equipment. Fourth, because each unit uses the same design, the **SOFT COSTS** associated with design will likely be lower than CAM.[6] Fifth, because of low capital costs, designers can customize the molds, patterns, or jigs with limited additional costs. Finally, there is a large range of shapes, finishes, and materials that are available for customized repetitive manufacturing. For example, processes such as pressing glass, slumping clay, blowing glass, and contact molding FRPs are all done with a mold.

There are environmental costs associated with **SUBTRACTIVE CNC EQUIPMENT**, or machines that subtract material to create the desired object. Examples of subtractive CNC equipment include routers, drills, presses, EDMs, lathes, milling machines, hot-wire foam cutters, surface grinders, and plasma, water-jet, laser, and knife cutters. Depending on the material and the process, three things can happen to the waste that CNC equipment generates: it can be recycled, **DOWNCYCLED**, or sent to a landfill. For some CAM processes and materials, the manufacturer can do nothing with the waste generated. Although the wood shavings and dust from a CNC router may be directly downcycled into particle or medium-density fiberboards, the plywood that is left over between the router cuts cannot be recycled and can only be reprocessed for downcycling. Shop coordinators and architectural instructors are familiar with this problem of waste. The leftover plywood scraps often line the hallways and fill the waste bins of architectural shops. If students do not use the scraps, the coordinators send them to landfill. This is so much of a problem that instructors have been giving students the design problem of creating something using CAM equipment that produces as little waste as possible.[7]

In addition to environmental costs, CAM equipment often has higher soft costs than CRM. Proponents of CAM may argue that the CNC machine "does not care" if it is making unique or repetitive pieces. However, there are the soft costs of designing and drafting each of the shapes and programming them into the machine. Time spent designing individual pieces and

thermoformers use CNC-milled, high-density foam for their tooling. CNC routers, CNC millers, and EDM wire and spark machines fabricate hardened-steel molds for injection, compression, and transfer moldings, and dies for extrusion and pultrusion. Meanwhile, new developments in **RAPID TOOLING (RT)** have been promoting the use of rapid prototyping (RP) equipment to create tooling. For example, sand casters can use FDM and SLA printed patterns for small production runs,[4] and manufacturing production researchers are investigating the use of metal laser sintering to make molds for injection molding plastic.[5]

Using CNC equipment to make tooling for repetitive manufacturing creates tension between CAM and CRM. Repetitive manufacturing is dependent on the technology of CAM in order to reduce tooling costs. But at the same time, CRM is a competitor to CAM, as it produces components in shapes, materials, finishes, and at a cost that CAM cannot. Conversely, CAM has some advantages over CRM. These include direct design to manufacturing with the digital files, the ability to make free forms and unique components, and shorter **LEAD TIMES** to prototyping. Additionally, for additive RP processes no tooling is required, reducing manufacturing waste and costs.

4   Plastic patterns in sand casting tend to wear out faster than wood or cast aluminum patterns and can be used for production runs under 50 units.

5   Hongbo Lan. "Web-based Rapid Prototyping and Manufacturing Systems: A Review." *Computers in Industry*. June 2009. Combrink, J. et al. "Limited Run Production Using Alumide Tooling for the Plastic Injection Moulding Processes." *South African Journal of Industrial Engineering*. Online.

6   Frank T. Piller, et al. "Does Mass Customization Pay? An Economic Approach to Evaluate Customer Integration." *Production Planning & Control: The Management of Operations*. 2004. Online.

7   When I was an assistant professor at the University of New Mexico School of Architecture and Planning, Matt Gines, shop coordinator and instructor, gave an assignment that specifically targeted eliminating waste from the laser cutter (2010). Frank Jacobus, University of Idaho Assistant Professor, writes that eliminating waste is an assignment parameter ("The 2to3. Chairs: An Exploration of CNC Assemblies." *Assembling Architecture: 2009 BTES Conference Proceedings*. 2010: 225–232). Mark N. Carbinha, Cal Poly, San Luis Obispo Assistant Professor, also acknowledges this point and shifts his assignments in order to reduce waste ("Material Imagination in Digital Culture." *Made: Design Education and the Art of Making*. School of Architecture, The University of North Carolina at Charlotte. 2011: 85–92).

8 Hierve Diseñeria, Hesiodo (2005), Mexico City, Mexico. A 27,000ft² apartment building with 7,723 custom, wood-molded blown glass spheres

RAPID TOOLING (RT) using rapid prototyping (RP) equipment to fabricate tooling

LEAD TIME the time between the start and finish of a production

SOFT COSTS the indirect costs associated with a project, including design and management or service fees

SUBTRACTIVE CNC EQUIPMENT CNC equipment that manufactures its components by removing materials; examples includes CNC routers, hot-wire foam cutters, and laser cutters

DOWNCYCLE to reuse a material or object to make another material or object with a lesser quality that the original

programming the machines represents a cost passed onto the consumer, which can be significant. For example, Gehry Partners has pioneered streamlining the process between design and fabricator, but its projects' costs can greatly exceed the industry standard. According to *Wired* magazine, Gehry Partners' Stata Center "came to $400 per square foot, $650 when you include design costs. The industry average for *design and construction* [author emphasis] of a new science facility is $260 a square foot."[8]

Production cost comparisons between CAM and CRM vary based on materials, desired shapes, and tooling. CNC equipment can save money when compared to traditional machining, especially in places where labor costs are high. This is particularly true when the architect has designed a building with a number of complex and unique components. However, in some cases, repetitive manufacturing can save production costs. According to *Detail*, Foster + Partners investigated using CAM technology to manufacture the Walbrook Building's (Chapter 3.2) exterior fiberglass louvers, **[7]** but the design team discovered that repetitive manufacturing would be less expensive than CAM.[9] Foster's team members did two things: 1) they altered their designs slightly to make repeated use of the mold, and 2) they designed a single mold that could be partitioned to make the different lengths needed.

CRM is a necessary alternative to CAM for the manufacturing of architecture components; since it is defined by a customized and yet repetitive manufacturing process, the manufacturing processes included in CRM must make repeated use of the tooling in the production of the component. In other words, architecture components must be designed to be used in multiples. At the same time, the production runs with CRM are relatively small, as they may only be used to create components of a particular building's design. CRM allows for customization from the designer, while balancing the need for repetition in order to remain cost effective. This balance makes CRM easily applicable for the custom design of architecture components.

Architects are most likely to use customized repetitive manufacturing on a building-by-building basis, so *Manufacturing Architecture* includes those processes that can have production runs under 10,000 units. In architecture, 10,000 units may seem high, but if you consider exterior-facing materials such as brick, terra cotta tiles, or metal panels, 10,000 units is easily achieved. For example, Hierve Diseñeria designed a 27,000ft² (2,500m²) apartment building in Mexico City with a decorative screen made from 7,723 custom, wood-molded, blown-glass spheres (Chapter 3.5); **[8]** and over 24,000 aluminum domes were spun for the Eemhuis by Neutelings Riedijk Architects in Amersfoort, the Netherlands (Chapter 1.7). **[9]**

8   Jessie Scanlon. "Frank Gehry for the Rest of Us." *Wired.* November 2004. http://www.wired.com/wired/archive/12.11/gehry.html. Accessed 9 July 2012.

9   Markus Gabler. "The Walbrook London – Façade in Glass-Fibre-Reinforced Polymer." *Detail.* June, 2008. Online.

9 Neutelings Riedijk Architects, Eemhuis (2014), Amersfoort, the Netherlands. Over 24,000 metal spun domes were produced

Throughout this book are case studies of architectural projects that have used customized repetitively manufactured components. All have been completed since CAM was a readily available option for manufacturing custom components. Examples include Studio Gang's bent laminated structure for the Lincoln Park Zoo Education Pavilion (2010) in Chicago, Illinois (Chapter 1.4); the stamped aluminum screen on Benthem Crouwel's Mall Forum Mittelrhein (2012) in Koblenz, Germany (Chapter 1.5); the pressed clay tiles for Machado Silvetti's Asian Art Study Center at the Ringling Museum of Art (2015) in Sarasota, Florida (Chapter 4.6); and the precast composite cladding for ACME's Victoria Gate Arcades (2016) in London (Chapter 4.1). The gathered case studies demonstrate the relevance of customized repetitive manufacturing for today's building design.

DESIGN FOR MANUFACTURING | MANUFACTURING FOR DESIGN

To pursue CRM, there are two concepts of which architects should be aware: design for manufacturing, and manufacturing for design. **DESIGN FOR MANUFACTURING (DFM)** is standard in industrial design and engineering; products are designed that are easy to manufacture. Simultaneously, manufacturers also have to be responsive to the designer's needs. Architects should seek out manufacturers willing to explore the limits of the manufacturing equipment, and flexible enough to complete small production runs. This is the idea behind **MANUFACTURING FOR DESIGN (MFD)**. Both DFM and MFD are important concepts for architects in the design of components within the context of CRM.

The goal of DFM is to seek design and production problems early in the design process, when mistakes are easier and less costly to correct. DFM is important for repetitive manufacturing processes, particularly those with high tooling costs; in repetitive manufacturing, any mistakes in the tool are duplicated throughout all produced units. Mistakes that are not realized and fixed

10 A toolmaker at Superior Tooling in Wake Forest, North Carolina, which makes tools on contract for injection plastic molders

before the tools are fabricated can be quite expensive to remedy. Produced units are then discarded, and the tool must be repaired or replaced. Designers therefore need to consider manufacturing parameters while making design decisions. For example, they may start designing, then investigate possible manufacturing processes, then revise the design based on the manufacturing process capabilities. The qualifications for a design's easy manufacturing depend on issues such as production run, finishes, tolerances, and necessary skills.

Architects are familiar with the concept of DFM. Today, as a result of integrated design practices, many architects work with general contractors or construction managers early in the design process to control costs and ensure greater quality control. Similar to prototyping products, some architecture projects may have portions of a building built (i.e. mocked up) for quality assurance. At the North Carolina Museum of Art by Thomas Phifer and Partners (Chapter 3.1), the contractor constructed two structural bays, complete with the exterior cladding, interior coffers, skylights, and finishes. The mock-up was for quality control and assurance for both the building's construction and design. It demonstrated both the contractor's construction abilities and the anticipated quality of the interior lighting to the client. Just as with making a prototype, any design changes would have been easier to change with the mock-up than with the full building.

Architects interested in CRM must consider the manufacturing process, what can be done within process, and the restrictions *before* starting the design process. They must be willing to balance capital costs with production runs, mold complexity with manufacturing parameters, and dimensional restrictions with the manufacturer's ability and equipment. In subsequent chapters of *Manufacturing Architecture* different design parameters for each process are listed by manufacturing media or by mold material, where appropriate. These parameters are a starting point during initial design, and any design development should be done in collaboration with a manufacturer.

DFM is especially important to CRM. Unlike CAM, where the computer controls the tooling, the tooling in repetitive manufacturing is static. Any tooling mistake that is not discovered prior to a production run will be repeated on all items in the run. This would, in turn, increase the cost and waste to fix the mistake. In order to comply with DFM, some manufacturers may make their tools a little smaller in critical locations during prototyping. This is particularly true with machined molds made by subtracting material from a solid block—such as CNC-milled metal, wood, or foam molds. Making the tool smaller in some locations allows a **TOOLMAKER** to remove material from the area for minor adjustments, without needing to make another tool. **[10]** For tools made by assembly or additive methods—such as plywood boxes for casting concrete, or built-up molds for bending laminate—additional materials can be added to a mold.

The goal for MFD is to find manufacturers that will be responsive to a designer's needs. If architects are interested in pursuing CRM for their projects, they will need to consider how to select manufacturers that will meet their needs; CRM requires manufacturers to be higher-tier suppliers or contract manufacturers. The tier of the manufacturer is counted from the **ORIGINAL EQUIPMENT MANUFACTURER (OEM)** to the manufacturers of the smaller components. OEMs are those manufacturers that make the final product and may be primarily responsible for the final assembly of multiple parts. This would include automobiles, light fixtures, and computers. Higher-tier suppliers hold contracts with lower-tier suppliers to make the components that get sent to the OEM. For example, in automobile manufacturing, the casing for a side mirror is made by a contract manufacturer or tier 2 supplier that does plastic compression molding. The tier 2 supplier sends the casing to a tier 1 supplier, who assembles the casing with a mirror, gears, and electronics. The tier 1 supplier then sends the mirror to the OEM, who in turn places it onto the automobile. Some OEMs have the capacity to manufacture components

directly—in the automobile manufacturing example, the car hood may be metal stamped at the OEM. Although the OEM may do metal stamping, they have their own orders to fill and are unlikely to do custom metal stamping for someone else.

Some product manufacturers do not use a manufacturing supply chain and manufacture their own products. Like OEM, they are filling their own orders and cannot do custom manufacturing. For example, because of the abundance of clay in North Carolina, there is a concentration of brick manufacturers. Most are high-capacity plants and produce particular brick products that they sell to the customer. These manufacturers have automated their facilities with robots and other equipment to efficiently produce, package, and ship their products. These companies are reluctant to accept custom brick orders. Conversely, one brick plant in North Carolina, Taylor Clay Products, has distinguished itself from its competition by promoting its ability to produce specialty clay products. Taylor Clay has reduced automation in its facility in order to increase its flexibility in production and with clients. Taylor Clay produces a limited number of its own products and, instead, has concentrated on small production runs of custom fired-clay products.

CONTRACT MANUFACTURERS hold contracts with a variety of clients and, in turn, manufacture a variety of items. Contract manufacturers work on a **PULL SYSTEM** of manufacturing. That is, they manufacture items as their clients place orders. Today, because of lean manufacturing, most contract manufacturers do not hold inventory of their produced items. This reduces capital cost because less storage space is needed and less money is tied up in inventory that has not yet been bought. To be responsive to their clients' schedules, contract manufacturers need manufacturing equipment on which it is easy to change the tooling: tooling is changed often, production runs are smaller, and production lines flexible.

With the recent economic challenges, in order to diversify and develop other income streams, some manufacturers are both OEMs and contract manufacturers; they continue to produce components for other manufactures, but they also produce their own product lines. For example, Jeannette Specialty Glass in Jeannette, Pennsylvania, manufactures pressed borosilicate glass. It makes lenses, shades, and diffusers on contract for lighting manufacturers, as well as its own product lines of spa sinks and foot basins. Similarly, Penguin LLC in Sturgis, Michigan blow molds and injection molds plastic. It makes kayaks and plastic landscape drains on contract. It also has its own line of plastic folding tables, in which the tabletop is blow molded in plastic, and the table legs are shaped and assembled using steel tubing, which is then powder coated. Penguin has a few specific blow-molding lines that are dedicated to manufacturing the tabletops, so it is easily able to accommodate contract orders for other blow-molded components. However, all of its steel tube forming lines

DESIGN FOR MANUFACTURING (DFM)
designing products so that they are easy to manufacture

MANUFACTURING FOR DESIGN (MFD)
manufacturing that responds to the need of the designer

TOOLMAKERS those who make tooling (e.g. jigs, dies, patterns, molds, etc.) for manufacturing; the toolmaker may or may not be the manufacturer

ORIGINAL EQUIPMENT MANUFACTURER (OEM) refers to a company that makes the final product for the consumer

CONTRACT MANUFACTURERS manufacturers that manufacture on contract; they are not dedicated to one product or one company

PULL SYSTEM the concept where production is pulled through the line; orders are placed first, and production happens second

are dedicated to Penguin's own product, and the manufacturer cannot accommodate custom orders to bend steel tubes.

For MFD, manufacturers should be flexible with their use of tooling media, in order to reduce capital costs. Typically, tooling costs directly correlate to production runs. A more expensive tool has the capacity for a higher production run; lower tooling costs allow for a smaller production run. Sand cast iron can use three different **PATTERN** materials—cast aluminum, wood, and plastic—to form the sand molds. Each of three materials has a certain number of cycles that can be run before the pattern degrades. Aluminum patterns are for high-production runs over 50,000 units, wood patterns are for production runs of fewer than 1,000 units, and plastic patterns are for runs of fewer than 50 units. The correct tooling material should be matched with the intended production run. Manufacturers must be willing to work with all levels of tooling in order to meet the needs of designers.

Manufacturers should also be flexible enough with their processes to modify them to further reduce tooling costs. In selgascano's El Batel Auditorium in Cartagena (Chapter 2.1), two different plastics were required for use in the building's interior and exterior, and the practice wanted the same profile for both plastics. Typically, extrusion dies are made specific to the extruding plastic, meaning that although the profiles were the same, two different dies would be typically required. Polimer Tecnic, the plastic extruder for the project, developed a special die with moveable modifications so that one die could be used for the two different plastics. For Foster + Partners' Walbrook Office Building in London (Chapter 3.2), Foster and FIBER-TECH Group GmBH (the manufacturer of the bladder-inflated, contact molded louver) collaborated closely to balance the design team's intentions with the reduced costs associated with repetition. Toward that end, Fiber-Tech partitioned the molds in such a way that they could be used to produce louvers of different lengths and curves.

Architects should seek out manufacturers who value the design process. For many of the case studies, the architects and the manufacturers developed close relationships with one another through this process. For King Roselli Architetti's Sheraton Milan Malpensa Airport Hotel and Conference Center (Chapter 2.2), the relationship between the pultrusion manufacturer, Progettazione Costruzione Ricerca (PCR) and the architect was one of mutual respect. According to an industry publication on pultrusion, the manufacturer stated that one of its goals was to "make the architect smile."[10] From its experience on that project, PCR developed a new department, Artex, dedicated to providing a service for creative design.[11] Similarly, 5468796 Architecture has developed a close relationship with KlarTech, the fabricator for the custom extrusion aluminum screen for the OMS Stage in

Winnipeg, Canada (Chapter 2.1). KlarTech and 5468796 have worked closely together over the years; at a recent exhibition of the firm's work, KlarTech had collaborated with 5468796 for nine out of ten projects displayed.

In addition to contract manufacturers, there are also smaller workshops run by craftspeople or artisans, which can also produce CRM components. These facilities are often able to manufacture components on a much smaller scale than their industrialized counterparts, including contract manufacturers. For example, the blown glass spheres for the Hesiodo by Hierve Diseñeria were made in a workshop in Guadalajara, Mexico (Chapter 3.5) that was able to produce over 7,700 glass spheres, whereas a small production run for mechanized glass blowing could be 25,000–50,000 units. Oftentimes, the cost per piece with a workshop may be higher than with a manufacturer, but if the production run is small, there might not be a manufacturer willing to take the contract. The advantage of the workshop is therefore its small scale. Most workshops do only custom work, are highly flexible, and are enthusiastic to collaborate. For example, for Hariri Pontarini Architects' Bahá'í Temple in Chile (Chapter 4.3), the architect collaborated with Jeff Goodman Studio over years to develop a cast glass panel that had the layered look of stone and could be slumped over a mold. **[11]** The Goodman Studio's commitment to the project was so strong, that it custom-made six kilns in order to manufacture the cast glass panels.

COMPONENT DESIGN, (NOT) PRODUCT DESIGN

History has demonstrated that the role of the architect is broad. Vitruvius wrote that architects could plan cities, military camps, and buildings. In the Middle Ages, architects were master masons. During the Renaissance, architects were artists and engineers. At the turn of the century, with influence from the Bauhaus, architects continued to broaden the field beyond that of building design—so much so that many of the well-known modernist architects—Ludwig Mies van der Rohe, Eileen Gray, Charles and Ray Eames, and Marcel Breuer—are known as much for their furniture designs as they are for their architecture.[12] For some architects, their success in product design even surpassed their success in building design. For example, architects Michael Graves and Philippe Stark might be better known to the public through their product lines, offered through retailers such as Target.

Although there are similar issues between the design and manufacturing of products and architecture components, there are distinct differences. In product design, consumers choose where to place the product, and the product can be relatively easily moved to another location. In other words, the product is siteless. Conversely, architecture components have a place, physically

10   Donna Dawson. "Hotel Wrap: Cuvilinear Pultrusions." *Composites Technology*. 30 June 2010. www.compositesworld.com/articles/hotel-wrap-curvilinear-pultrusions. Accessed 25 March 2015.

11   Progettazione Costruzione Ricerca website. http://www.pcr-srl.it/about-us/?lang=en. Accessed 30 March 2015.

12   In 1974, *Fortune* magazine estimated that Charles and Ray Eames earned $15,000 dollars per month in royalties for their furniture sales.

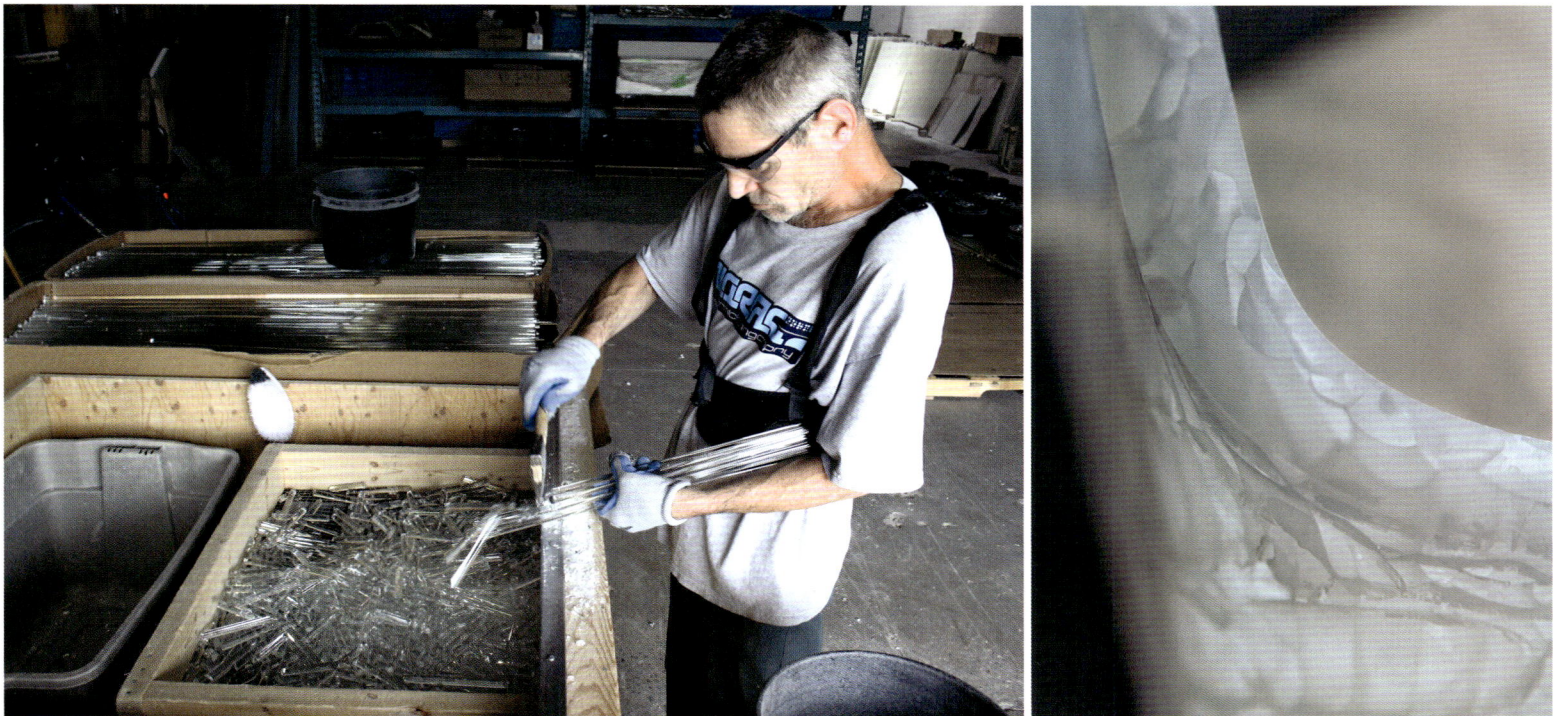

11 Jeff Goodman Studio developed the method, manufactured all of the glass panels, and slumped some of the panels for Hariri Pontarini Architects' Bahá'í Temple for South America (2016), outside of Santiago, Chile

attached to a building. Once attached, the component is more difficult to relocate than a product. Architecture components include door hardware, window assemblies, exterior cladding materials, and structural components.

Generally, architects have not designed many of the architecture components that we use for buildings.[13] The goal of *Manufacturing Architecture* is to be a resource guide for architects who are interested in CRM for customizing building components. This includes custom components as a new architecture product, an architecture prototype, or a custom component for a particular building. For each of these applications, there are different criteria that an architect should consider in the repetitive manufacturing for the component.

ARCHITECTURE PRODUCTS

Architecture products are architecture components designed by architects and available for mass consumption. Examples include Zaha Hadid's ZH Duemilacinque doorknobs for Valli & Valli, and Robert A.M. Stern's Rhythm light fixtures for Philips Lightolier. Architecture products are the most similar to product design. The architecture product is a stand-alone object and the competency of the design is not dependent on its context. In other words, the design of Hadid's doorknobs is not dependent on the door on which it is placed, nor the design of the room in which it

is located. Unlike product design, architecture products are physically attached to the building and are a part of the architecture.

Architecture products are closer to a push model in both design and manufacturing terms. In a **PUSH SYSTEM**, the product is being pushed to the consumer, and there is an inherent need to advertise it. The producer must educate the customer that a product exists to create a demand so that the product will be purchased. Even before the building has been designed, the architecture product has been designed. Before building construction starts, the product is manufactured. Architecture products are most similar to product or industrial design and many of the manufacturing processes for these products can be found in industrial design texts; however, I have chosen to include

PATTERN tooling that is used to form a temporary or sacrificial mold

PUSH SYSTEM a concept in which production is pushed through a line; the products are being produced before an order is placed

---

13   Dana K. Gulling. "Mobile Home Breakdown: A Study of Building Product Design Lineage." Association for the Collegiate Schools of Architecture (ACSA) NE Regional Conference: *Urban/Suburban Identity* (2010). Conference proceedings.

12 The plywood panels for the Dragon Skin Pavilion (see pages 82–85) were not trimmed post-shaping

only one architecture product in *Manufacturing Architecture*. POLLI-Brick, originally custom designed and manufactured for EcoARK (Chapter 3.5), has since become an architecture product available to the mass market. Although this book's case studies of architecture products are limited, architects can use the book to aid in architecture product design.[14]

Manufacturing architectural products will restrict the types of repetitive manufacturing processes that can be used. First, depending on their perceived popularity, architecture products may have large production runs. With larger production runs, manufacturers can support manufacturing processes with higher tooling costs. For example, processes such as plastic blow molding (Chapter 3.5) could be considered. Second, typically when an architect-designed product is available to the mass market, a high level of finish is required, as there are high expectations of quality. This may mean using manufacturing processes with tighter tolerances, and surface finishes that are more refined. For example smooth, high-gloss finishes are available in cast metal through lost-wax casting, but not sand casting. Third, architecture products are often certified. That may include Underwriters Laboratory (UL) certification for light fixtures, and American Society of Testing and Materials (ASTM) certification for hardware. The certification standards may affect the materials, tolerances, finishes, and designs of the products. Finally, an architecture product manufacturer may contract out the sub-components to a tier 1 or tier 2 manufacturer. For example, the Stern light fixture is made with a slump glass diffuser and spun metal base, both of which could be made by a contract manufacturer. This means that an OEM manufacturer, such as Lightolier, may distance architects from the contract manufacturers, thus limiting possible collaborations.

14   Architects interested in designing architecture products should also make use of other industrial design books, such as Chris Lefteri's *Making It: Manufacturing Techniques for Product Design* (London: Laurence King, 2007) and Rob Thompson's *Manufacturing Processes for Design Professionals* (London: Thames & Hudson, 2007).

ARCHITECTURE PROTOTYPES

Architecture prototypes are forward-thinking architectural explorations at full scale, and may be parts or pieces of a building that an architect intends to apply to future buildings. Examples include Bioform by Murmur (Chapter 1.2), the Dragon Skin Pavilion for the Hong Kong and Bi-City Biennale of Urbanism/Architecture by LEAD and EDGE (Chapter 1.4), and the 2012 ICD/ITKE Research Pavilion at the University of Stuttgart (Chapter 3.3). Both Bioform and the Dragon Skin Pavilion were studies into material and making processes for architectural application, whereas the 2012 Research Pavilion looked at the relationship between biology, architecture, and structure. Architecture prototypes bridge the gap between architecture product design and architecture building design. Like products, prototypes are built at full scale; unlike products, they are not available for mass consumption.

CRM for an architecture prototype will also restrict the manufacturing processes. First, in order to reduce costs, the architect (or other, less-skilled labor) often makes the prototype. For example, the student designers of the Dragon Skin Pavilion manufactured all of the building's post-formable plywood scales. **[12]** Second, manufacturing processes with easily accessible equipment are more likely to be selected for production. Most prototype designers have easy access to thermoforming, contact molding, and plywood bending equipment, so these processes are often selected for architecture prototypes. For example, both the Dragon Skin Pavilion and the 2012 Research Pavilion were made by equipment that their associated universities already owned. Third, to reduce costs, architecture prototypes may have to modify their design to work with a manufacturer's existing tooling. For Bioform, Murmur designed the tile so that it could be made in one of Superform's existing air chambers. Finally, because production runs are low, manufacturing processes with low capital costs may are required. Production runs for prototypes may easily be fewer than 50 units; therefore manufacturing processes such as extrusion or compression molding may not be financially feasible.

CUSTOM COMPONENTS

Custom components are designed by architects on a per-project basis. Custom components are developed because mass-market components either do not meet the design intent or are not cost effective. Customized components are a design response to a particular building context. They allow for customization from the designer while balancing the need for repetition in order to remain cost effective. Examples include Renzo Piano's custom sand-cast ductile iron truss members for the Menil Collection (1987) in Houston, Texas, **[13]** and Kraaijvanger Urbis's explosive formed metal panels for the Castellum Theater (2005) in Rotterdam, the Netherlands. **[14]**

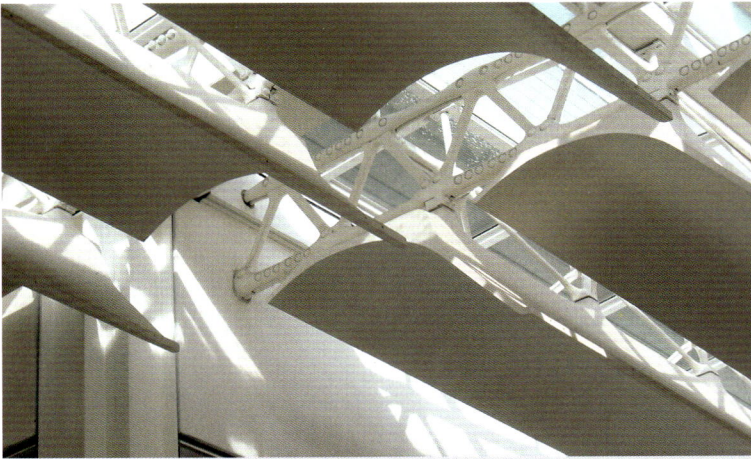

13 Renzo Piano Building Workshop, Menil Collection (1987), Houston, Texas. Sand-cast ductile iron truss members are part of the building's high-tech structural expression

14 Kraaijvanger Urbis, Castellum Theater (2005), Rotterdam, the Netherlands. Explosive formed metal panels depicting waves of the adjacent Rhine River

In many ways, custom components are the most interesting examples of architects using CRM for the design of architecture components. They are unique to a building, are unattainable for the masses, and demonstrate a holistic design approach. Custom components are typically pursued by architects and building designers who are concerned with building details. As shown by the two examples above, the custom components help complete the vision of the project. The truss members of the Menil Collection are part of the building's high-tech structural expression, and the ornamental wave detail of the Castellum Theater's metal panels references the building's location next to the Rhine River.

Custom components affect the types of repetitive manufacturing processes that architects can select. First, production runs for custom components can vary based on design. There are only nine repeated slumped glass shapes for the Bahá'í Temple, whereas there are over 310,000 extruded stiff mud bricks on the Yale University Health Services Building by Mack Scogin Merrill Elam Architects (2010) in New Haven, Connecticut. Therefore architects have to consider production run at the same time as building design. Second, since custom components are done on a building-by-building basis, architects may not have prior experience with their selected repetitive manufacturing processes. This requires architects to educate themselves about the processes and find manufacturers willing to collaborate to develop the design.

CONCLUSION

CAM and CNC equipment have transformed design and off-site building component fabrication. Proponents argue that CAM reconnects architects directly to the craft of making and recasts the architect in the role of master builder.[15] Additionally, they say that CNC equipment has made repetitive manufacturing obsolete, as CNC equipment operation does not depend on repeatability. At the same time, CNC equipment has also reduced the tooling costs for repetitive manufacturing, as CNC equipment such as routers, EDM, and 3D printers now make the tools for repetitive manufacturing. This has made it easier for architects to customize repetitive manufacturing processes and thus increased repetitive manufacturing's impact on architectural design.

Repetitive manufacturing can offer lower production and design costs, less production waste, more selection of materials and finishes, and faster production times than CAM. *Manufacturing Architecture* demonstrates the importance of CRM in architecture, and the case studies throughout this book include a range of approaches. The case studies also illustrate a range of different relationships between manufacturer and architect. Through the case studies, I found that the experience for CRM improved when the architect considered the manufacturing process during the beginning of a component's design and when the architect found a manufacturer who was willing to collaborate.

Manufacturing Architecture is a reference guide for architects for customizing repetitive manufacturing. Each chapter provides the architect with information about the process, current products, available media, design parameters, and examples. With the information provided, perhaps architects may be more confident in exploring architecture component design by designing architecture products, architecture prototypes, or custom components. My hope is that this book inspires architects, building designers, and students to explore more potential opportunities for architectural design.

---

15   This argument is presented by both Stephen Kieran and James Timberlake. *Refabricating Architecture: How Manufacturing Methodologies are Poised to Transform Building Construction*. New York: McGraw-Hill, 2004; and Branko Kolarevic. *Architecture in the Digital Age: Design and Manufacturing*. New York: Spon Press, 2003. Print.

1

Manipulating Sheet

1.1 Slumping / 1.2 Thermoforming / 1.3 Explosive
Forming / 1.4 Bending Plies / 1.5 Stamping
1.6 Hydroforming / 1.7 Spinning

Included in this section are manufacturing processes that deform previously manufactured sheet goods (e.g. plastic sheets, glass panes, or metal blanks) into another shape. Deformations happen with added heat, pressure, force, or a combination of any of these. Because these processes start with a flat sheet, the final manufactured components will be limited in how far the material can be moved out of its original plane without tearing or incurring other damage.

For manufacturing processes in this section there is a wide range of equipment, tooling costs, and facilities. Some processes, such as slumping glass and clay (Chapter 1.1), require no special equipment to deform the materials other than kilns. Tooling costs are minimal and molds can be made from refractory plaster for glass and canvas, or newspaper for clay. Other processes, such as stamping (Chapter 1.5) and hydroforming (Chapter 1.6), require large presses and expensive dies made from tool-hardened steel. Meanwhile explosive forming (Chapter 1.3) requires inexpensive tools made from fiber-reinforced plastic (FRP) or concrete, but also requires remote worksites for detonations and cranes for the large components often formed with this process.

For all of these processes, the surface area of the components will be significantly larger than their cross-sectional thickness. In most cases, the material deformation strengthens the material compared with its strength in its original sheet form. As the sheet deforms over the mold it can thin in some areas, causing tears or holes to the medium. Tools should have a small radius at entry corners to help ease the material flow around the tool, and draw angles are often required so that the component can be removed from the tool without damage.

1.1 Slumping

INTRODUCTION

Slumping is a passive manufacturing process that uses gravity to pull a softened medium into a desired shape. The makers have little to no direct physical contact with the medium. Typically, slumping forms large, gently curving surfaces, and can be used for single or complex curves. Slumping can also be used to form small surface textures. Surface texture is typically limited to the mold side of the component as textures often do not transfer to the face that is not in contact with the mold. Most slumping media cannot accommodate material bends of 90° or less. The component face in contact with the mold is the surface that will be more dimensionally precise. Surface quality and tolerances can range from fair to very good, depending on the manufacturer's capabilities.

A sheet of the slumping medium is placed onto the mold. Depending on the slumping medium, heat may be added to soften the sheet. Under the force of gravity the sheet begins to sag, or slump. The amount of slump is dictated by the length of cycle time, as the longer the cycle time, the deeper the slump. If using a partial mold, the slumping sheet material takes on a natural catenary curve, and the cycle time will be carefully controlled to ensure the correct slumping depth. If using a full mold (see figure 1.1.10), then the shape and depth are less dependent on time. After slumping is completed, the medium is hardened through cooling or drying, so that it is stiff enough to retain its shape once removed from the mold.

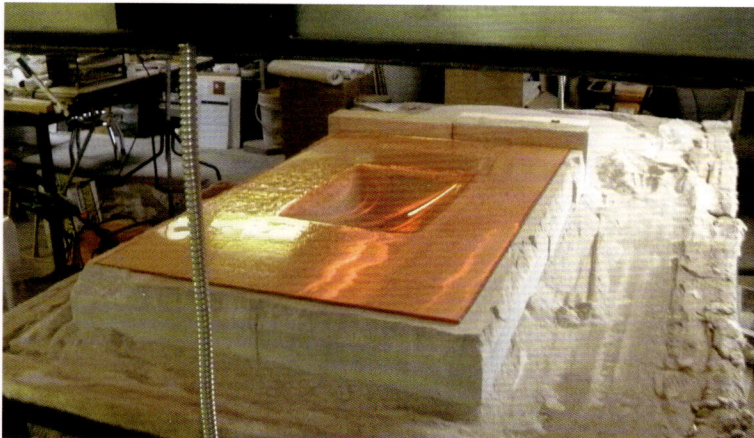

1 Large kiln used for slumping glass sink and integrated counter on a sand mold

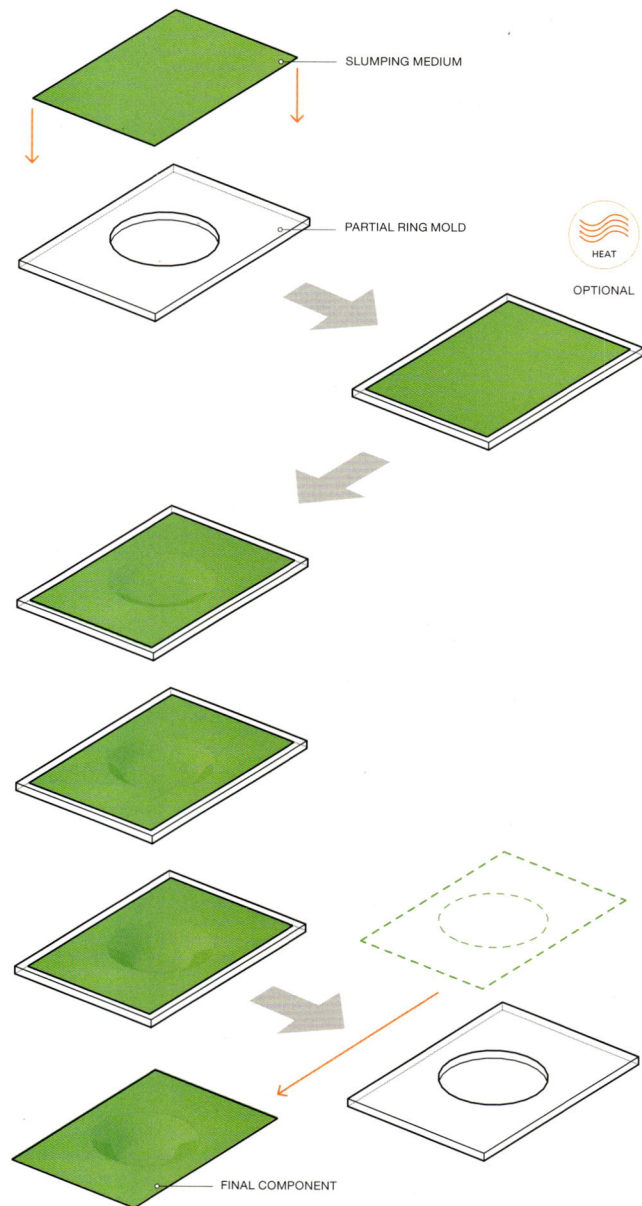

SLUMPING MEDIUM

PARTIAL RING MOLD

HEAT

OPTIONAL

FINAL COMPONENT

Slumping can be used for any sheet material that can be softened, including glass, plastic, and clay. This chapter looks at glass and clay, as both materials have been slumped for custom architectural applications. Glass is softened using heat from a kiln, whereas clay is softened by moisture content, additives, and temperature. More viscous media, such as glass and plastic, may flow during the slumping process, causing a thicker cross-section in valleys and a thinner cross-section at peaks. The depth of the slumping therefore depends on the material, its thickness, its viscosity, its self-weight, and the amount of time it is allowed to slump. Almost all slumping is time intensive, as gravity, rather than active presses or vacuums, pulls the medium into shape.[1] Cycle times for slumping are long, and multiple molds may be used for parallel productions to speed up production times.

Slumping can be mechanized for high-volume production runs, or can be done by hand for small production runs or prototypes. The manufacturer's equipment will affect the quality and size/capacity of the slumped units. For slumping glass, a kiln is typically required to heat the sheet to a softened state; therefore the size of the maker's kiln can limit the size. [1] Conversely, clay is slumped at room temperature and often requires no specialized equipment to soften the medium. The size limits for clay are dictated by the kiln size available for firing. High-volume manufacturers may have large tunnel kilns for continuous production, thus accommodating large production runs with short schedules. A craftsperson's workshop will typically include a smaller batch kiln, which often limits component size and production schedules.

High-volume slumping manufacturers are highly automated and may be less able to take custom orders than smaller producers or craftspeople. High-volume manufacturers often use large equipment, machinery, or robots, which make it difficult to quickly change tooling or handle a variety of differently shaped components. This often restricts them to larger production runs than smaller producers, and runs of similarly shaped components. However, high-volume manufacturers may be better able to comply with industry standards such as those set by the ASTM, and more able to produce items with predictable quality. Products such as car windshields tend to be made by high-volume manufacturers.

Conversely, smaller producers and craftspeople may not be able to produce components with quality as predictable as the high-volume manufacturers. However, the fact that smaller facilities are often not highly mechanized means that they can produce smaller production runs, and runs of differently shaped items. They may be more experimental, perhaps by modifying typical manufacturing processes to accommodate a particular design. For example, the Vakko Fashion Center by REX (2010), in Istanbul, Turkey, has slumped glass windows for its exterior curtain wall. To slump the large panels, the manufacturer did not slump the glass in a kiln, but instead used a combination of localized and generalized heat to soften the glass. [2] A craftsperson's production work may offer the advantage of qualifying as a local building product, or it could qualify as part of a project's commitment to including public art. For example Laurel Porcari, a glass artist working in New Orleans, Louisiana, designed and made The Beacon, a private dining room in L'Auberge Casino and Hotel in Baton Rouge. [3, 4, 5] The room is made complete by the slumped glass formed in her New Orleans studio.

BUILDING PRODUCTS

There are a few commercially available building products that are made by slumping. Slumping may be used to create sink bowls, glass or plastic bathroom counters with integrated sinks, curved glass shower doors, or curved glass for light fixture shades and diffusers. Textured glass can be made by taking a sheet of standard float glass, reheating it, and slumping it against a mold.[2] This is done by slumping when the texture is too deep to be applied to the glass surface with a patterned roller. Commercial extruded terra cotta rainscreen components can be formed into a gentle arc with slumping; however, the curved pieces are typically custom-made for a particular building.

TOOLING

Most often, slumping tooling includes the mold, and in some cases a clamp to hold the medium in place. Because gravity forms the medium, there is little pressure on the mold itself; therefore molds can be made from a wide range of materials. For slumping glass, steel and cast iron molds are used for high-volume productions, whereas refractory plaster or concrete, ceramic, clay slip, or sand are used for small-volume productions or prototypes. [6] For glass slumping with a sand mold, the tooling typically includes a pattern pressed into the sand bed, which then forms the desired shape. [7, 9, 8] The pattern can be made of a variety of materials, such as high- or low-density foam, MDF, or plywood, and usually made by CNC millers.

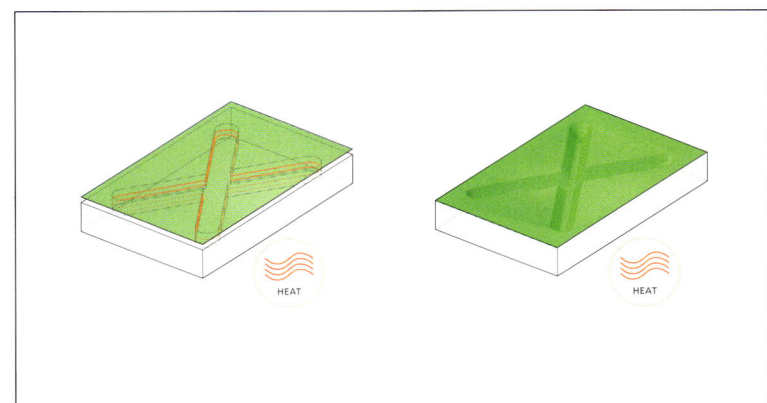

2 Localized heat is used to deform only part of the glass

3 Laurel Porcari, architectural art glass in The Beacon, a private dining room in L'Auberge Casino and Hotel, Baton Rouge, Louisiana. Made with fused art glass, slumped on a plaster mold and a custom stainless steel armature

For manufacturing slumped clay, molds can be made from steel, bisque-fired clay, plaster, wood, wood products, or Styrofoam. For prototypes, almost any material can be used, including draped canvas and wadded newspaper. For manufacturing slumped clay, steel is rarely used; although it is durable, it is the most expensive mold material, and production runs for slumping clay are often small. Generally, bisque-fired clay and plaster molds are the best for clay slumping, as those tooling materials absorb water from the clay, thereby decreasing the drying time necessary to stiffen the clay. This decreases the manufacturer's production time. Typically, molds for glass slumping are more expensive than those of clay slumping, because they need to withstand the high temperatures of the glass kiln.

The molds for slumping are open and may be partial or full. A partial mold does not fully support the slumping medium during the manufacturing process. Instead, the medium is allowed to deform under gravity into a natural catenary curve. Partial molds depend on a combination of time, self-weight, and material viscosity to determine the depth of the drape. Partial molds work better with glass than clay, because glass will behave consistently at particular temperatures. For example, curved car windshields can be slumped using a partial ring mold, which only supports the glass along its edges. Within these parameters, the glass can be slumped to particular curves at a high tolerance.

4 Close-up of the glass

5 Laurel Porcari shaping the plaster mold to be used in the kiln

6 Slumped glass pieces and their molds

Glass slumping is best done in a partial mold when an architect desires visual clarity, as both sides are exposed to heat, giving the glass a flame polish.

In a full mold, the slumping medium deforms until it is in complete contact with the mold's surface. The mold's surface will directly transfer to the face of the slumped medium; therefore care must be taken to properly prepare the mold surface. Full molds can be symmetrical or asymmetrical, and either male or female. [10] If the full mold is a female mold, then ventilation holes must be added to avoid trapping air as the slumping medium fills the mold. [11] Slumping molds can be fairly intricate; however, the more intricate the mold the more difficult it is to slump the material. If the mold is too intricate, it can place stress on the medium as the medium shrinks, resulting in cracks. To avoid cracking, intricate molds should incorporate expansion joints, or be made from a flexible medium such as sand. [12]

Steel ring or partial molds are often fabricated by hand, but full, more complex tooling may be machined by CNC millers or spark or wire EDMs. Molds such as clay, plaster, or concrete are most often cast against hand-made or CNC-milled molds, but can also be made directly by CNC milling, or by hand pressing or other build-up methods. Wood molds can be fabricated by hand or CNC mills, and foam molds can be made by hand, CNC mill, or CNC hot-wire cutting.

7 CNC-milled pattern

8 The resulting slumped glass panel

9 Sand bed and kiln. The pattern is pressed into the sand bed, deforming the sand into the shape of the pattern. The sheet of glass is carefully placed onto the sand, and then the kiln is closed for heating

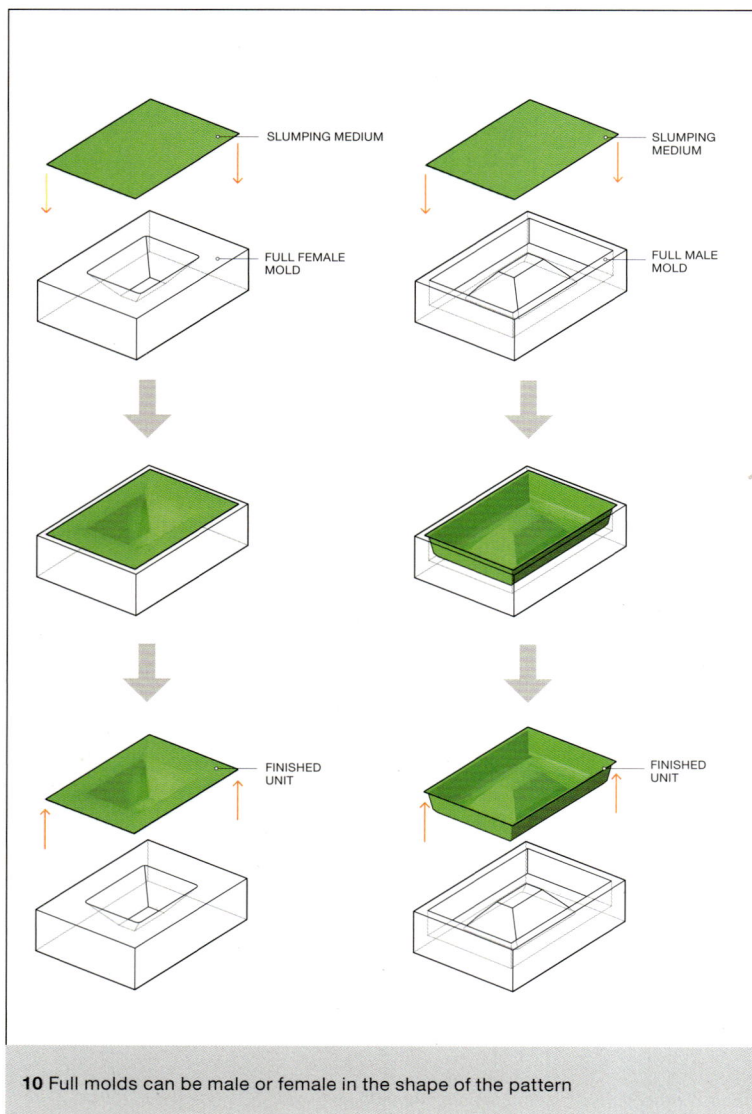

SLUMPING MEDIUM

FULL FEMALE MOLD

SLUMPING MEDIUM

FULL MALE MOLD

FINISHED UNIT

FINISHED UNIT

10 Full molds can be male or female in the shape of the pattern

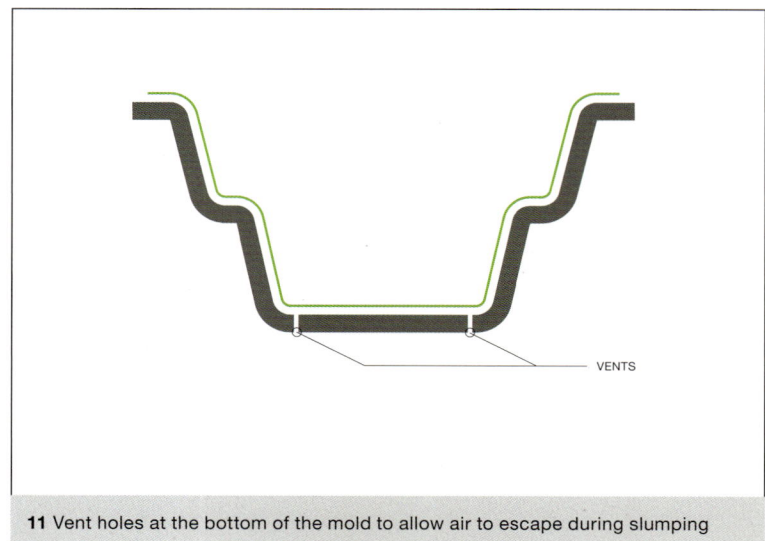

VENTS

11 Vent holes at the bottom of the mold to allow air to escape during slumping

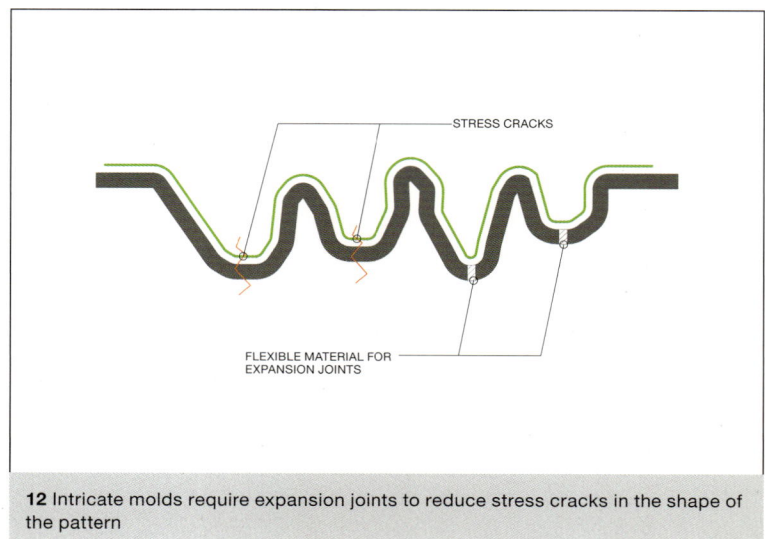

STRESS CRACKS

FLEXIBLE MATERIAL FOR EXPANSION JOINTS

12 Intricate molds require expansion joints to reduce stress cracks in the shape of the pattern

ENVIRONMENTAL IMPACT

Little energy is used in this forming process. No energy is required for the forming itself, as gravity deforms the material; however, energy is required for processing both glass and clay. With glass slumping, kiln temperatures are lower than glass casting and glass blowing, but there will be post-forming annealing, or tempering. With clay slumping, no heat is required for deforming clay; however, it is required for firing the clay after forming.

Generally, glass scrap from post-production trimming may be recycled. All clay that is discarded during trimming can be put back into the pug mill and directly reused on site.

MATERIAL CONSIDERATIONS + DESIGN PARAMETERS

GLASS

Glass is viscous when heated, so it flows across the sheet during the heating process. This may make the wall thickness inconsistent across the component's cross-section, and can often lead to the two components' faces being different. The side that is not in contact with the mold surface will be smoother and less exact than the mold face. Ideally the slumping process should take long enough for the glass to make full contact with the mold, but no longer than that.[3] Often, a craftsperson relies on observation during the slumping process to achieve consistency, whereas a manufacturer will primarily rely on time and temperature measurements. Full and intricate slumping glass molds may make it difficult for a craftsperson to see the flow of the glass; therefore it may be difficult to gauge the time required without multiple attempts.

Slumped glass may also be known by other names, including bent, curved, sagged, draped, or kiln-formed glass. Slumping can be done with single or multiple sheets. For large, stacked glass sheets, if the kiln's temperature is high enough, then glass pieces will fuse to each other as the sheets are slumping. For small glass pieces, the maker may consider a two-step process— first fusing the glass together, then cooling it and finally slumping. Different types of glass have different coefficients of thermal expansion; therefore when combining glass for slumping, the process will be less predictable than when slumping a single, homogenous sheet. Alternatively, multiple glass sheets can be stacked with a chemical barrier between them, which allows for them to be slumped simultaneously without fusing. This is often done to make curved safety glass or insulated glass panels.

In general, slumping glass increases the bending strength. As with bent sheet metal, slumped glass panels have higher moment of inertia than standard annealed glass. This increases bending and shear strength and decreases deflection. Slumped glass can be further strengthened through tempering, enabling it to be used in virtually any architectural application in the same way as sheet glass.

SIMILAR PROCESSES

Glass slumping is not similar to other glass-shaping processes. The component size in slumping is much larger than what is available in pressed glass. Shapes similar to those attained with slumped glass can be achieved by other glass-working techniques, but without the consistency in shape making.

COATINGS

Note that some glass coatings, such as tints, metallic, or low E coatings, may not work with slumped glass. If architects are interested in using coated glass for slumping, then they should speak with the manufacturer.

CORNERS

Rounded corners are the easiest and most predictable to slump, as the glass can flow.

Angled corners and square mold shapes sometimes result in uneven distribution of the component medium, which often results in a thickening at the corners.

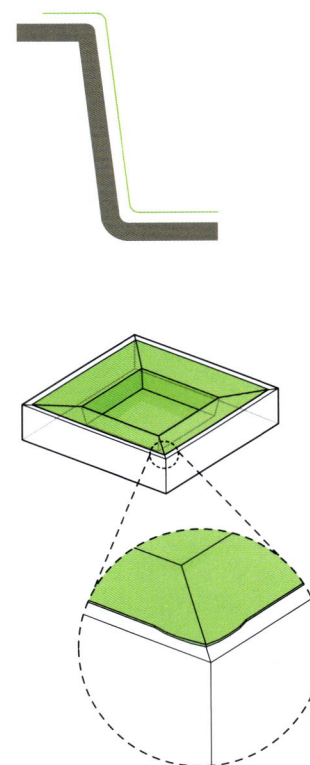

DRAFT ANGLES

Generally, the draft angles for full molds should be 7° or more. Typically, draft angles for ring molds are not necessary.

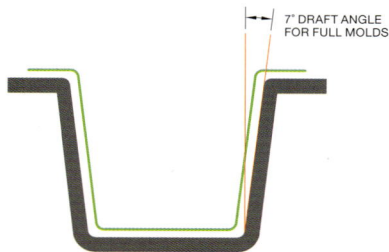

7° DRAFT ANGLE FOR FULL MOLDS

Draft angles are required and are a function of the time allocated to slumping, the draw depth, and the mold material. The steeper the draft angle, the more time is required for slumping. The greater the draw depth, the more friction there will be between the component and the mold faces, and the greater the chance of breaking the glass or the mold when stripping the component. Because of the high temperatures associated with glass slumping, the coefficient of thermal expansion of the mold should be compared to that of the glass. The greater the difference between the two, the greater the draft angle required.

DRAW DEPTH

The draw depth for this process is approximately 16–18in (400–460mm), depending on the thickness of the glass, the size of the glass sheet relative to the mold, and the size of the mold opening (particularly for ring molds).

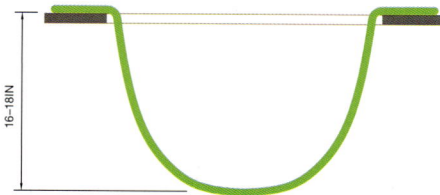

16–18IN

FINISH

If using a partial or ring mold, the glass will have a flame finish on both surfaces. If using a full mold, the glass surface in contact with the mold will pick up the finish from the mold and will likely not remain clear. If a flame finish is desired on all surfaces, this can be done by flame finishing as a postproduction process.

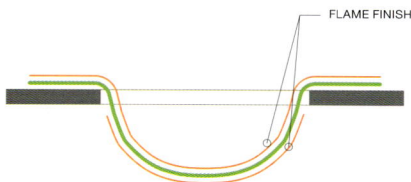

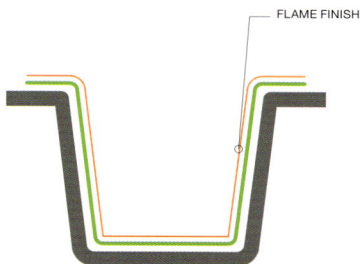

FLAME FINISH

FLAME FINISH

INSERTS

Inserts are not recommended with this manufacturing process. As a result of the high temperatures, material movement, and differential expansion and contraction rates, it is best to place inserts using a post-production process.

JOINING

During the slumping process, different glass pieces can be joined together by kiln fusing. This is done naturally under heat and gravity pressure if there is no inhibitor placed between the sheets of glass.

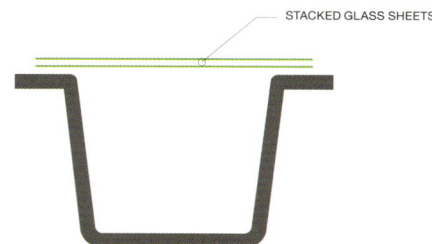

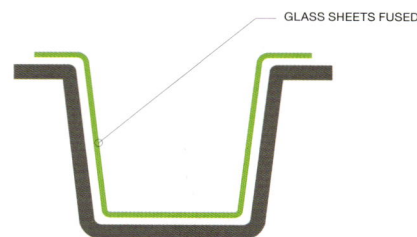

STACKED GLASS SHEETS

GLASS SHEETS FUSED

POST-PRODUCTION PROCESSING

Post-production processing is often limited to cutting the slumped components to size or placing any side-wall holes that may be needed.

PRODUCTION SPEED

Slumping is a cyclical process and production speeds can be slow. The manufacturer must wait for gravity to deform the glass into the correct shape. After slumping, the glass needs to be annealed and may be subsequently tempered, further increasing production time.

PRODUCTION VOLUME

Generally, production volumes for this process are low and may range from one-offs to batches of 500–1,000 units. For commercial applications such as automobile windshields, the batch sizes can reach 10,000 units; however, the manufacturers of these types of products are highly mechanized and cannot accommodate custom shapes.

SINK MARKS

Sink marks do not typically form with this process.

SHAPES

Bowl shapes with rounded corners are the easiest and fastest glass shapes to slump, but almost any shape can be slumped. The more complex the shape the longer the slump time required, thus decreasing production speed.

In addition, rims or collars are preferred on the molds, as it helps locate the glass and form an even slump. Rims or collars should be 1–1.5in (25–40mm) wide. After slumping the rim or collar may be cut or removed.

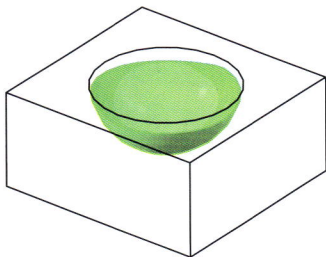

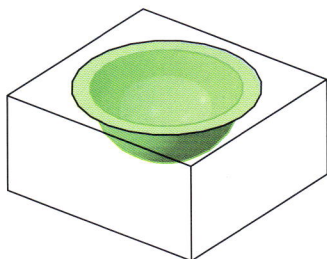

SIZE LIMITS

The kiln is the limiting size for glass slumping. The glass sheet is often sized slightly smaller than the mold, which allows the glass to expand during heating without overflowing the mold.

TOOLING COMPLEXITY

Generally, tools are very simple with no moving parts. Tools can be made in multiple pieces to accommodate expansion joints, but this is unusual.

TOOLING COSTS

Tooling costs are very low, depending on the material used.

TOLERANCES

The tolerances for slumping should be 0.12–0.25in (3–6mm) for high-volume manufacturers, and in the range of 0.25–0.38in (6–10mm) for craftspeople. Generally, tolerances are easier to maintain in full molds rather than partial molds.

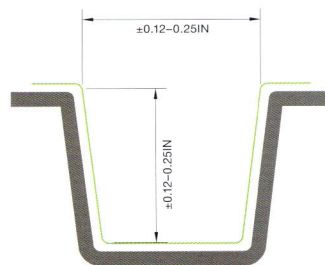

UNDERCUTS

Undercuts are not permissible.

VENTS

Vents are required for any female mold, or mold cavities. Typically, the vents do not leave a mark on the component.

WALL THICKNESS

The minimum wall thickness is 0.12in (3mm) to avoid distortions or tears. Multiple sheets can be simultaneously fused and slumped, making components that are 4in (100mm) thick.

Because the glass flows during slumping, constant wall thicknesses are difficult to maintain for deep slumps.

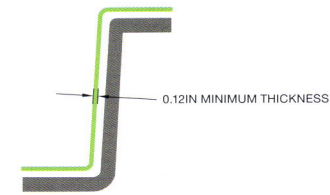

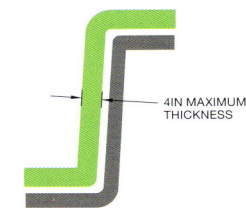

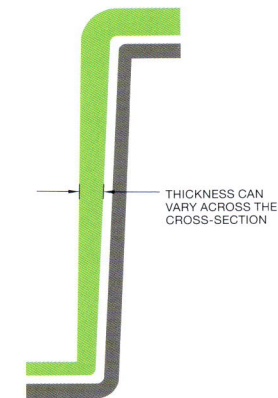

SLUMPING: GLASS

EXTERIOR GLASS PANELS
GORES GROUP HEADQUARTERS
Belzberg Architects
Los Angeles, California

Belzberg Architects was commissioned to design and to produce construction documents for the renovation, addition, and new exterior skin of an existing 1960s Los Angeles office building, which was completed in 2014. **[13, 14]** The project's original client had been a law firm; however, the Gores Group bought the building after the building permit had been obtained and construction begun. In the interest of continuing to work on the project, Belzberg Architects contacted Alec Gores—founder, chairman, and chief executive officer of the Gores Group—to show him designs and mock-ups for the exterior glazing system. The new owner required some changes, but most of the original design of the building's exterior remained. The addition

13
Gores Group Headquarters by Belzberg Architects, Los Angeles, California. Wilshire Boulevard façade

14
Façade detail

15

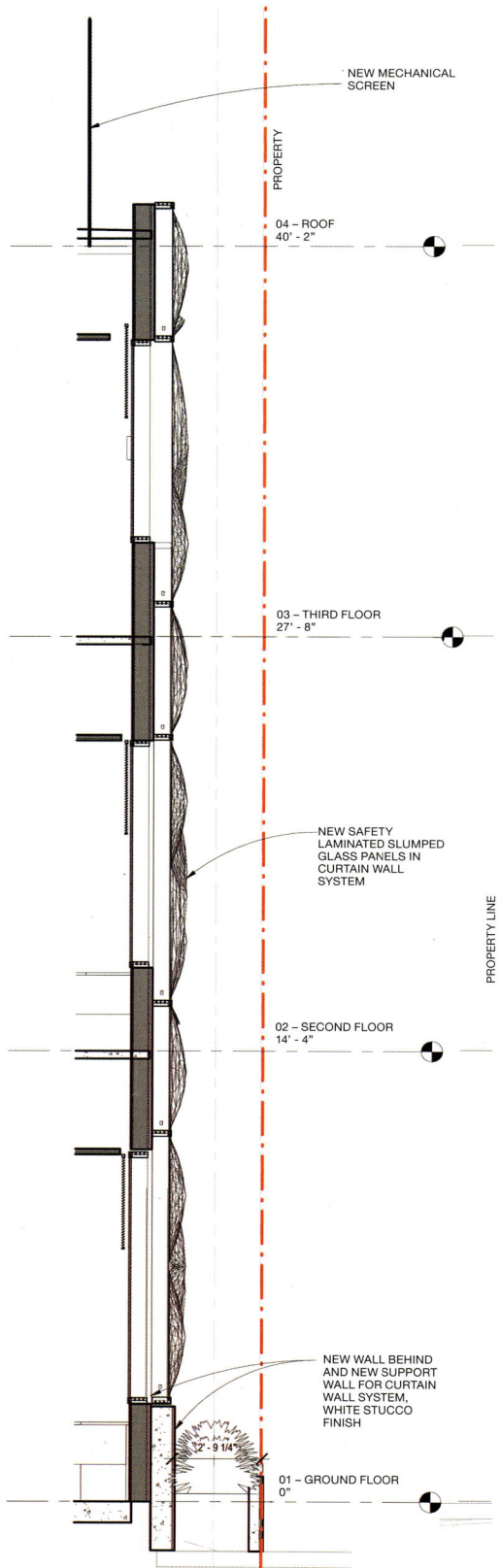

NEW MECHANICAL
SCREEN

PROPERTY

04 – ROOF
40' - 2"

03 – THIRD FLOOR
27' - 8"

NEW SAFETY
LAMINATED SLUMPED
GLASS PANELS IN
CURTAIN WALL
SYSTEM

PROPERTY LINE

02 – SECOND FLOOR
14' - 4"

NEW WALL BEHIND
AND NEW SUPPORT
WALL FOR CURTAIN
WALL SYSTEM,
WHITE STUCCO
FINISH

12' - 9 1/4"

01 – GROUND FLOOR
0"

16

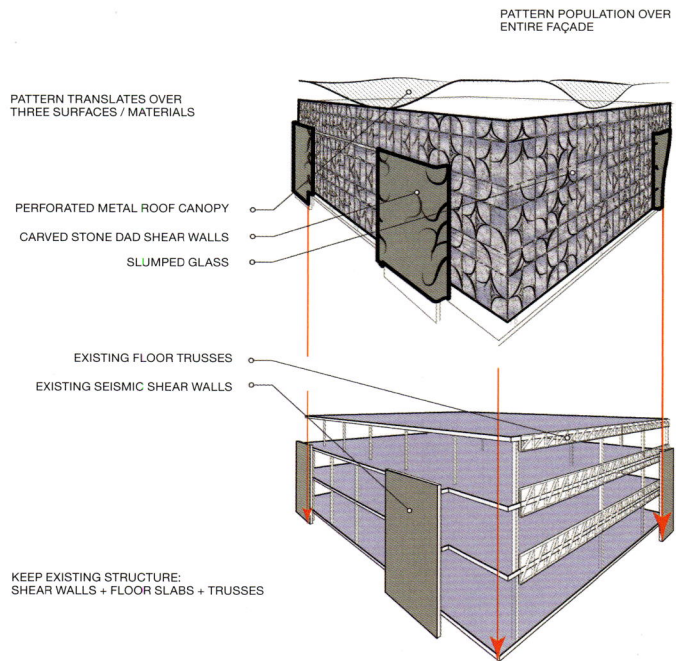

PATTERN POPULATION OVER
ENTIRE FAÇADE

PATTERN TRANSLATES OVER
THREE SURFACES / MATERIALS

PERFORATED METAL ROOF CANOPY

CARVED STONE DAD SHEAR WALLS

SLUMPED GLASS

EXISTING FLOOR TRUSSES

EXISTING SEISMIC SHEAR WALLS

KEEP EXISTING STRUCTURE:
SHEAR WALLS + FLOOR SLABS + TRUSSES

17

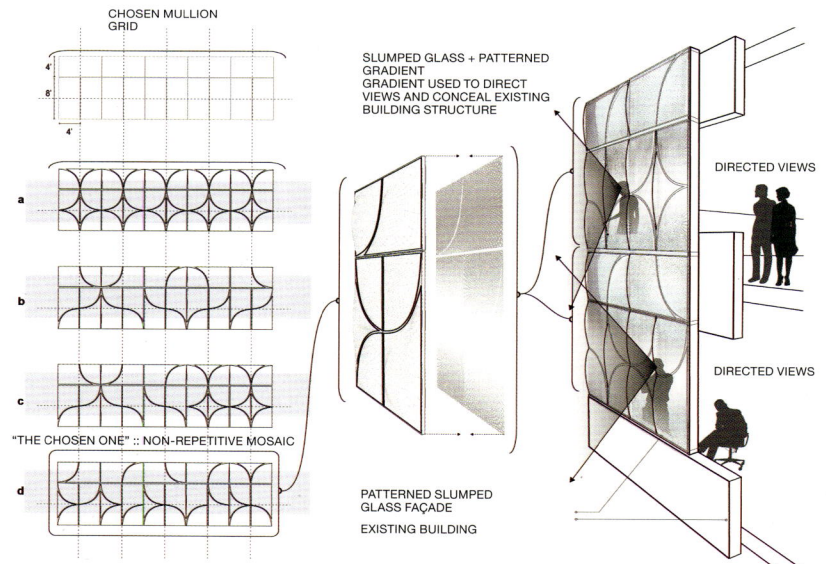

CHOSEN MULLION
GRID

4'

8'

4'

a

b

c

"THE CHOSEN ONE" :: NON-REPETITIVE MOSAIC

d

SLUMPED GLASS + PATTERNED
GRADIENT
GRADIENT USED TO DIRECT
VIEWS AND CONCEAL EXISTING
BUILDING STRUCTURE

DIRECTED VIEWS

DIRECTED VIEWS

PATTERNED SLUMPED
GLASS FAÇADE

EXISTING BUILDING

is a separate volume from the original building, and a bridge connects the two. To unify the 135,000ft² (12,500m²) project, Belzberg Architects used the same materials of stone, perforated metal, and slumped glass on both the renovation and addition.

The slumped glass panels form the exterior layer of a two-layer building enclosure, with the interior layer of the building consisting of stucco, concrete, and storefront glazing. [15] The slumped glazing is made from two laminated glass sheets with a custom-printed design to change the opacity of the polyvinyl butyral (PVB) inner layer. There are three custom slumped glass shapes, and four different designs printed on the PVB layer, resulting in twelve different glass panels. The transparent PVB designs are at eye height, while opaque patterns are reserved for hiding building elements such as vertical shafts, shear walls, and plenum space between the ceiling and the floor. [16]

Pulp Studio, located in Los Angeles, had the technology to print a custom-designed pattern on the PVB layer. California Glass Bending Corporation (CGB), located in Wilmington, California, manufactured the slumped glass panels. In 2012, Pulp Studio bought CGB, which streamlined the manufacturing for this project. Each of the three slumped glass panels measures over 4ft × 8ft (1,220mm × 2,440mm) and has a slump of approximately 5in (130mm) from the original face of the glass sheet. Each layer of glass is 0.15in (4mm) thick, with a PVB layer of 0.06in (1.5mm).

DESIGN CONSIDERATIONS

For this project, Belzberg Architects was interested in making the skin the primary expression of the building. The firm had investigated different methods for achieving this, including curving the curtain wall's aluminum extrusions and slumping the glazing. According to Cory Taylor, the project manager and the firm's managing principal, they believed that curving the aluminum extrusions would be cost prohibitive, so they limited their designs to curving the glass.[4]

Belzberg Architects did initial design research with Rayotek Scientific Inc., a San Diego company that does a wide variety of specialty glass manufacturing and fabrication, including molding and slumping glass, for optic, reflective, and window applications. Rayotek's clients have included the National Aeronautics and Space Agency (NASA), Sandia National Laboratories, and Apple, as well as some specialty art-glass applications in architecture. Rayotek and Belzberg collaborated to make initial prototypes. As the project moved forward, its required production exceeded Rayotek's manufacturing capabilities and Belzberg Architects contacted CGB for the manufacturing.

Belzberg Architects did many design studies of the building skin. To keep production costs down, the design team members limited themselves to using only three different slumped glass shapes. They investigated a number of pattern options with the three panels, and in the end selected a non-repetitive arrangement of the panels. [17] With the three shapes, the four patterns on the PVB layer, and the seemingly random organization of the panes on the façade, it is difficult to discern that the component is repetitively manufactured.

15
Wall section, showing new curtain wall over existing building conditions

16
Curtain wall panels over existing building conditions

17
Functional patterning, design studies that examine PVB, and slumped glass patterns over the façade

18 Fabrication kiln, where glass panels were heated for slumping

19 Fabrication formwork. Steel frame (i.e. open mold) used to slump glass

20 Vacuum forming inner layers. Laminating two sheets of glass together with a PVB inner layer

MANUFACTURING CONSIDERATIONS

The manufacturing of this component was challenging. In addition to the custom-printed PVB, there were cost restrictions, and the glass needed to be thin to reduce shipping costs. CGB's kiln size dictated the size of the glazing panels, as their kilns could only accept glass sheets up to 4ft × 8ft (1,220mm × 2,440mm) in size. [18] Similar to a ring mold, the Gores Group mold used a steel frame to partially support the glass while it was in the kiln. The glass slumped into a catenary curve, between the frame pieces. [19, 20] Using a steel frame instead of a full mold reduced the mold's material and fabrication costs. It also provided a flame finish to both sides of the glass, reducing postproduction finishing.

For these components, CGB and Pulp Studio developed and used a number of proprietary manufacturing processes. Because of this, Pulp Studio limited Belzberg Architects' visits to CGB and the photographs they could take. A number of prototypes and mock-ups were made as part of this project's design process. Belzberg had access to these, and used them to evaluate the design and manufacturing quality for the slumped glass. [21, 22] The design team had to rely on the parameters established by the CGB and Pulp Studio, with little negotiation.

OTHER CONSIDERATIONS

Initial design prototypes had 8–10in (200–250mm) of slumping depth. This was a deeper slump than CGB could manufacture; although the glass could slump that deep, the inner PVB layer could not without compromising the lamination. Belzberg Architects wanted to use laminated glass for its strength, safety in breaking, and the ability to print a custom pattern on the inner layer. In turn, this required Belzburg to reduce the slumping depth.

LESSONS LEARNED

The chief lesson learned was around the difficulty in ensuring quality control. First, there was a high breakage rate of 10–20% for the glass panels.[5] Second, Acadia Group held the contract for the project's curtain wall. In order for it to warrant the performance of the curtain wall assembly, the company required that the glass panes' edges be flat on all four sides where the panes met the curtain wall's aluminum mullions. [23, 24] The design shape of these panels often resulted in the edges being somewhat curved, which meant that the contractor rejected a number of the slumped panels. Taylor estimated that over 500 panels were made and 330 used. This is similar to the challenges faced at the Vakko Fashion Center by REX (see figure 1.1.2), which resulted in the slumped shape being isolated to the middle of the glass plane.

21 Finished glass test panels. Mock-up used to evaluate curtain wall panels

22 Test sample studies, used to evaluate the process

23

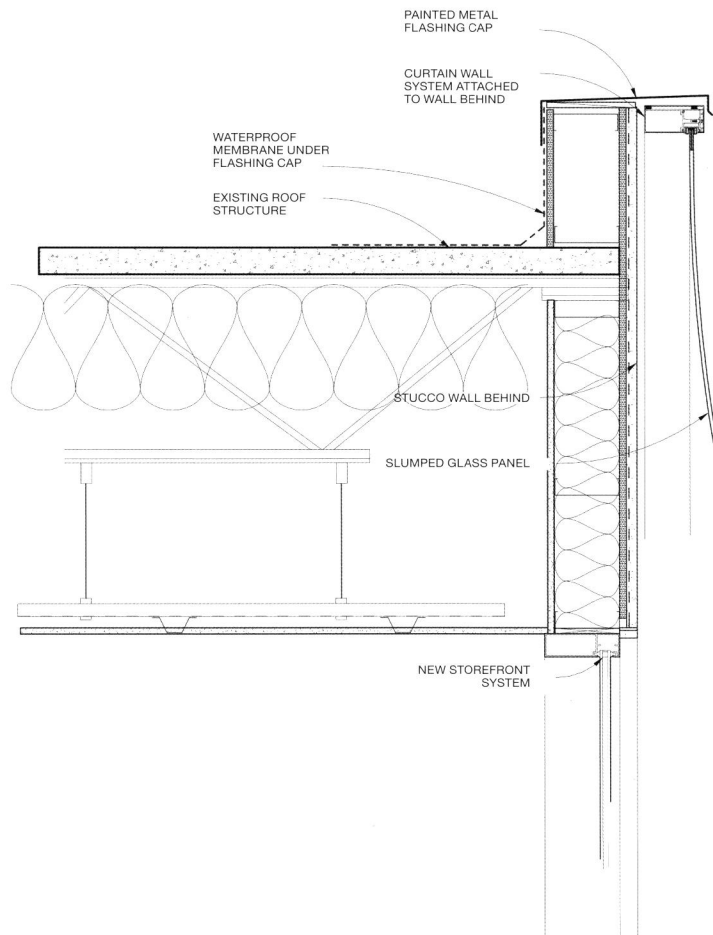

PAINTED METAL
FLASHING CAP

CURTAIN WALL
SYSTEM ATTACHED
TO WALL BEHIND

WATERPROOF
MEMBRANE UNDER
FLASHING CAP

EXISTING ROOF
STRUCTURE

STUCCO WALL BEHIND

SLUMPED GLASS PANEL

NEW STOREFRONT
SYSTEM

24

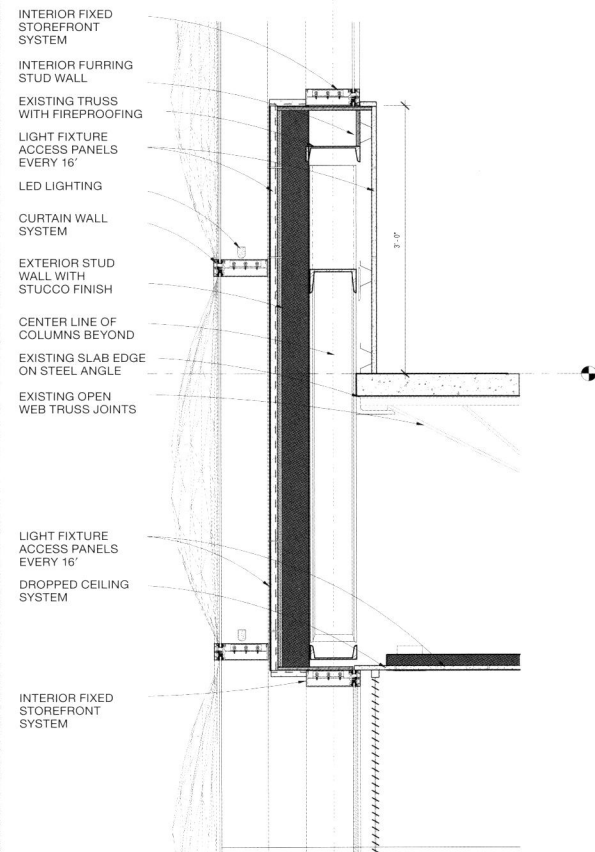

INTERIOR FIXED
STOREFRONT
SYSTEM

INTERIOR FURRING
STUD WALL

EXISTING TRUSS
WITH FIREPROOFING

LIGHT FIXTURE
ACCESS PANELS
EVERY 16'

LED LIGHTING

CURTAIN WALL
SYSTEM

EXTERIOR STUD
WALL WITH
STUCCO FINISH

CENTER LINE OF
COLUMNS BEYOND

EXISTING SLAB EDGE
ON STEEL ANGLE

EXISTING OPEN
WEB TRUSS JOINTS

LIGHT FIXTURE
ACCESS PANELS
EVERY 16'

DROPPED CEILING
SYSTEM

INTERIOR FIXED
STOREFRONT
SYSTEM

23
Section details. Note the
closeness of the glass curve with
the aluminum mullion

24
Section details

MATERIAL CONSIDERATIONS + DESIGN PARAMETERS

CLAY

Slumped clay may be known by other names, including soft-slab construction, draped clay, or humped clay. The amount of water in the clay will affect how much of a slump it can take. The clay needs enough water to be sufficiently plastic so that it can be formed. If the clay is too dry, it will deform only a little or may crack during slumping. However, if the clay is too wet, then it will move, creating an inconsistent wall thickness, or it will take too long to dry on the mold, lengthening production time.

The clay sheets are referred to as clay slabs, which are formed by slab rollers, hand rollers, or cut from a clay block with a wire cutter. Slab rollers make slabs with the most consistent thickness, while wire-cut slabs are least consistent. Unlike glass, clay is not viscous, so there is little to no material flow during the slumping process; therefore consistent slab thicknesses will result in consistent component thicknesses. Slabs can be cut to shape either prior to or after slumping. If done prior to slumping, the slabs are cut using templates made from any stiff material, such as plywood, plastic sheets, or cardstock papers. If done after slumping, the slabs can be trimmed with a putty knife or similar tool against the mold.

Clay shrinks as it dries and is fired. The shrinkage amount varies widely between clay mixtures and is often marked by the manufacturer for packaged clay and clay mixtures. Shrinking affects the type of mold and the draw depth. Deep slumps should use female molds so that the clay shrinks away from the mold as it dries.

SIMILAR PROCESSES

Clay slumping is similar to clay pressing (Chapter 4.6), but does not require the large press. Clay slumping molds may made of inexpensive materials than clay press molds, as there is little pressure on the mold.

CORNER RADII (EXTERIOR)

To prevent the clay from tearing, all exterior corners should have a radius of two to five times the thickness of the clay slab. The specific radius will depend on the plasticity of the clay used.

CORNER RADII (INTERIOR)

Interior corners do not require a radius, as the clay will not tear there; however, it is likely that with slumping the clay will not fill the corner without added pressure. This can easily be done by hand with a moist sponge.

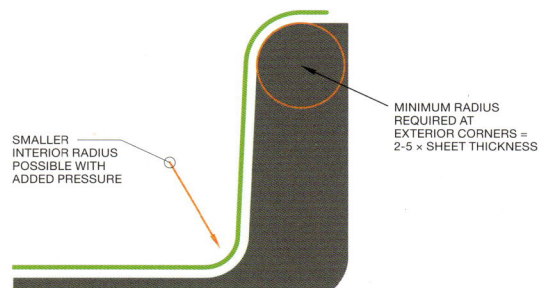

SMALLER INTERIOR RADIUS POSSIBLE WITH ADDED PRESSURE

MINIMUM RADIUS REQUIRED AT EXTERIOR CORNERS = 2-5 × SHEET THICKNESS

DRAFT ANGLES

A 1–3° draft angle is recommended for female molds, and a 7–10° draft angle for male molds. Smaller draft angles—approaching 0°—are possible with female molds, as the clay will shrink away from the mold as it cools. Greater draft angles are required for male molds, as the clay shrinks around the mold, making removal difficult. Using minimum draft angles can prematurely wear the mold and scuff the component during demolding.

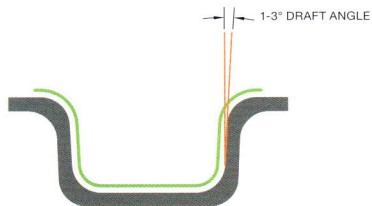

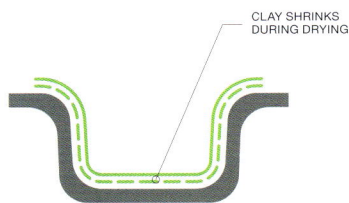

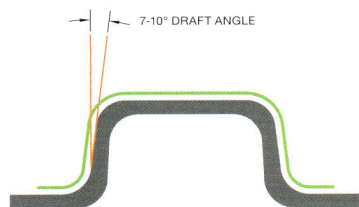

1-3° DRAFT ANGLE

CLAY SHRINKS DURING DRYING

7-10° DRAFT ANGLE

DRAW DEPTH

The draw depth can range from 2–12in (5–30cm) or more, depending on the type of clay, the shape of the mold, and the size of the component.

2–12IN

JOINING

Multiple clay slabs cannot be joined during this process.

PRODUCTION SPEED

Generally, production speed with this process is slow. Cycle times can range from 24 to 48 hours or more. Often the clay is left on the mold until it becomes leather-hard, allowing it to hold its shape when it is removed. Cycle times can be increased by using molds made of plaster or canvas, which wick away water from the clay. For large production runs, manufacturers may use multiple molds to speed up production.

PRODUCTION VOLUME

Clay slumping is best suited to small production runs under 500 units.

SHAPES

In clay slumping, shapes are typically limited to shallow and gentle curves.

SHRINKING

Clay typically shrinks in the range of 6–15% in all directions.

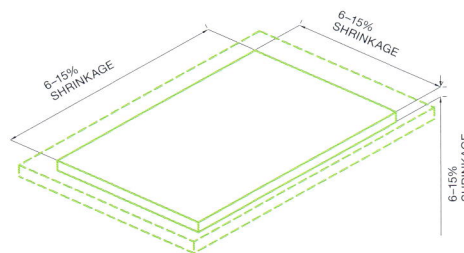

6–15% SHRINKAGE

6–15% SHRINKAGE

6–15% SHRINKAGE

SIZE LIMITS

The size of the clay slab is limited by what two people can carry. The slabs may be temporarily supported on cardboard, canvas, or plywood when transferred from the slab-rolling machine to the slumping mold.

TOOLING COMPLEXITY

Generally, tools are very simple with no moving parts. Tools can be made in multiple pieces to accommodate expansion joints, but this is unusual.

TOOLING COSTS

Tooling costs for this process are very low, and for some materials, such as canvas or newspaper, are inconsequential.

UNDERCUTS

Undercuts are not permissible, unless additional pressure is added by hand with a moist sponge. Female molds are better for undercuts, as the clay will shrink away from the mold. If a male mold is used, the mold should be disassembled in order to remove the component.

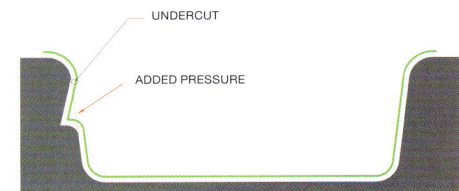

UNDERCUT

ADDED PRESSURE

VENTS

Typically, vents are not required.

WALL THICKNESS

Slumping clay is typically limited to clay sheets that are 0.12in (3mm) or thicker. For deep slumps or large components, thicker slabs will be required. If thicker slabs are required, but not desired, then the clay can be reinforced with chopped nylon fibers to increase material strength. Wall thickness will remain constant except at interior corners or where exterior pressure is exerted.

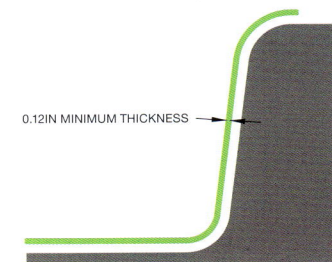

0.12IN MINIMUM THICKNESS

1.2 Thermoforming

aka vacuum forming, pressure forming, superforming [metal],
or superplastic forming (SPF) [metal]

INTRODUCTION

Thermoforming is a manufacturing process that uses sheets of materials that become pliable when heated. The heated material is placed onto a mold, and air pressure forms the heated medium to the shape of the mold. [1] Thermoformed shapes can be complex, with details such as ridges and valleys, ribs and dimples, and surface textures. [2] Surface quality is very good for the face of the sheet in contact with the mold; however, the surface not in contact with the mold can be distorted. Component dimensions should be set by the surface that contacts the mold. Thermoforming can be used with both thermoplastics and special metal alloys known as superplastic alloys, which are typically aluminum based. In thermoforming plastics, the terms thermoforming or vacuum forming may be used. In thermoforming metals, the terms superforming or superplastic forming (SPF) will be used.

In thermoforming, the mold can be made in a variety of ways and with different materials, depending on the thermoforming media. For thermoforming plastics it is made from high-density foam, MDF, or wood, and is often cut using a CNC mill. Once the mold is formed, any female cavities will require vent holes drilled through the mold. This allows the vacuum to reach the cavity to pull the manufacturing medium, or allows the air to escape in pressure forming. The mold is placed on a platen, while the manufacturing medium is placed in a clamping frame and heated until it is pliable. The clamping frame and pliable sheet are

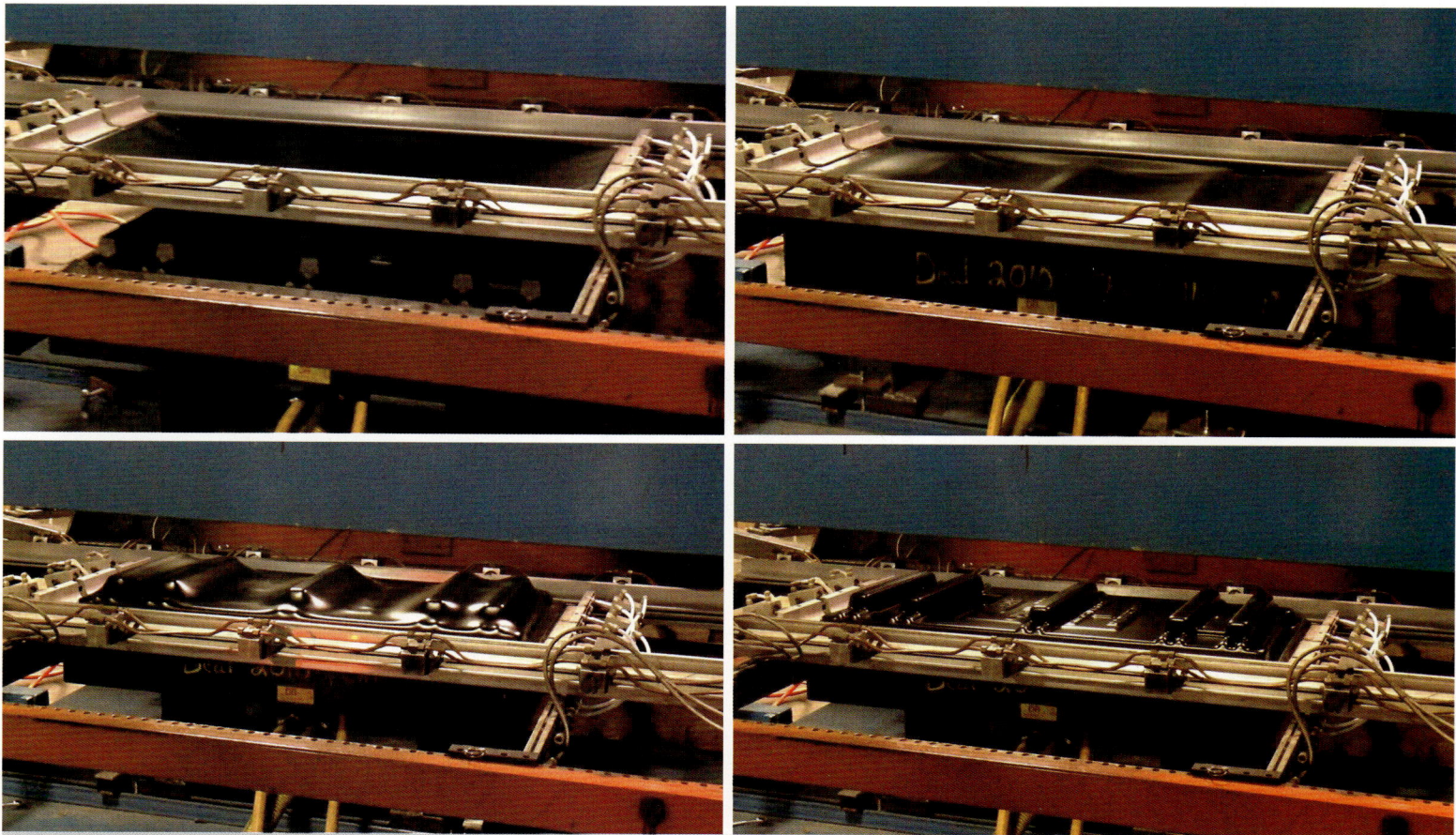

1 Still images of vacuum forming plastic

then placed over the mold. In vacuum forming, an air seal must form between the manufacturing medium, the clamping frame, and the platen. This allows the vacuum to deform the sheet to the shape of the mold. Once the component is formed, it is cooled on the mold until it can retain its shape. The component is then demolded and trimmed to its final dimensions.

There are different air pressure methods for thermoforming a sheet to the mold. [3] First, there is vacuum forming, which uses negative air pressure below the mold to pull the material onto the mold. Second, there is pressure forming, which uses positive air pressure above the sheet to push the material onto a mold. Third, thermoforming may use a combination of vacuum and pressure forming. This may be done when the parts are complex or have a deep draw. Vacuum forming is typically used for thermoforming plastic, while pressure forming is used for thermoforming metal. There are also thermoforming modifications, called assist forming, which stretch the medium prior to its contact with the mold. This includes pressure-bubble assist forming, which uses air pressure to pre-stretch the material; and plug-assist forming, which uses a plug to mechanically push the sheet into the mold. [4, 5] These process variants will affect cost, cycle times, shapes, and the thermoforming medium.

Any trimming, cutting, or hole drilling is considered a post-production process, and is often done by the thermoform manufacturer. This work can be done by hand, but most manufacturers will use a five-axis CNC router. [6] Additional tooling is required to hold the component in a consistent and fixed location so that the router can make the proper cuts. Typically, this tooling is done using an additional, perforated mold that uses a negative pressure vacuum to securely hold the blank in place during trimming. These trimming molds have soft joints at the edges and are designed in such a way that none of the actions performed by the router will break the vacuum. Rough sanding will be done on the edges, to remove any burrs or chips left by the router's cutting.

Thermoforming plastics can be done by hand in workshops, by small- and medium-sized contract manufacturers, or

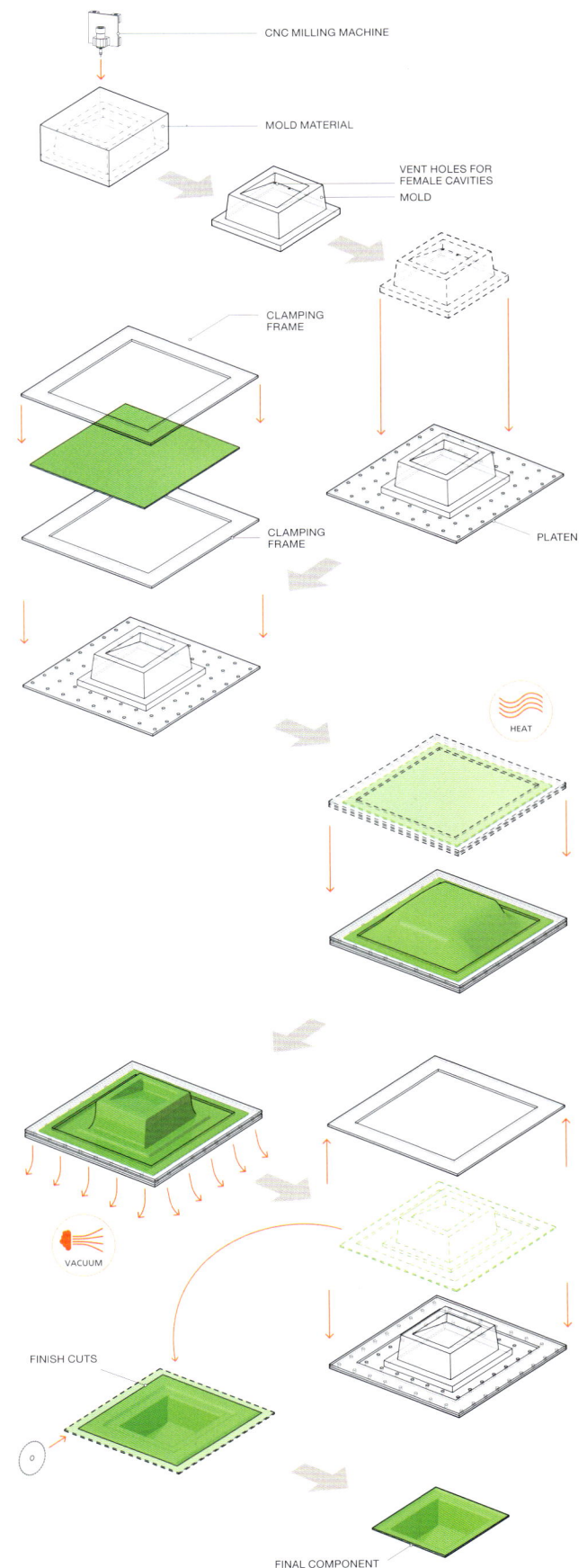

2 Complex thermoformed plastic components

CNC MILLING MACHINE

MOLD MATERIAL

VENT HOLES FOR FEMALE CAVITIES
MOLD

CLAMPING FRAME

CLAMPING FRAME

PLATEN

HEAT

VACUUM

FINISH CUTS

FINAL COMPONENT

by high-volume production manufacturers. Workshops and contract manufacturers are not highly mechanized; therefore they may be able to accommodate a range of different thicknesses of manufacturing media. Use of thicker media often results in longer cycle times, because the medium needs to be cool enough to hold its shape prior to demolding. Workshops may only have one or two machines and may be limited by the sheet sizes they can fit. Contract manufacturers may have between two and six machines that can accommodate a larger range of sheet sizes. Generally, this is a labor- and time-intensive process, with high per-piece costs. At the same time, tooling costs are low, and therefore manufacturing small production runs with this process can be cost effective.

Most high-volume manufacturers are highly mechanized, and are therefore equipped to handle only high-volume, thin-gauge thermoforming. Working with thin-gauge media decreases cooling and overall cycle times, making this process cost effective for high-volume productions. This can be seen in the thin product packaging used for clamshell containers, or other plastic product packing.

BUILDING PRODUCTS

Thermoformed plastic is used to produce a number of commercially available building products, including plastic ceiling tiles,

bath and whirlpool tubs, integrated sinks and counters, and bathtub and shower enclosures. Other thermoformed plastic products familiar to architects include the plastic liners for refrigerator doors, ice cube trays, and the exterior shells of hard hats. SPF is not often used for commercially available architecture products, but is typically used to manufacture parts for the aerospace industry or to prototype parts for the automobile industry.

TOOLING

Generally, there are two sets of tooling required for thermoforming. First is the mold, which is necessary, and gives shape and finish to the component. [7] Second is the trim die, which is optional and holds the thermoformed component for CNC trimming and drilling. [8] Molds must be able to withstand the temperature of the manufacturing medium and the pressure of forming, and cool sufficiently so the manufacturing medium sets. The more durable the mold material, the faster the cycle times and the longer the production runs. Molds will expand when heated; therefore both the mold material and the thermoforming medium's coefficient of thermal expansion should be considered when fabricating the tools.

In thermoforming plastic, temperature and pressures are generally low—around 350°F (175°C) and 10–15lb/in² (0.7–1.1kg/cm²)

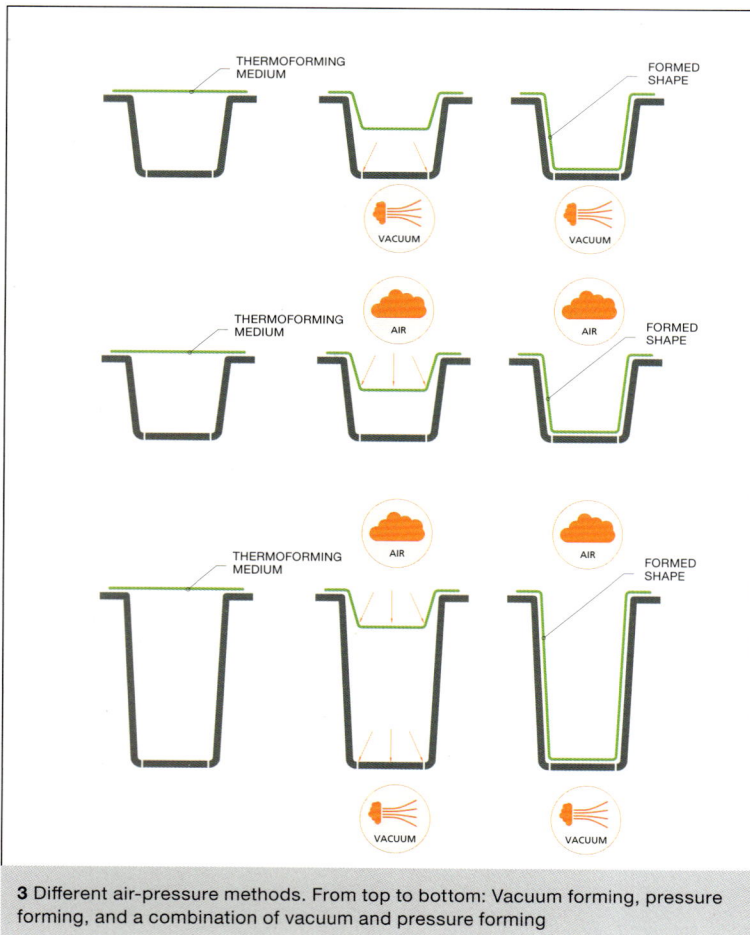

3 Different air-pressure methods. From top to bottom: Vacuum forming, pressure forming, and a combination of vacuum and pressure forming

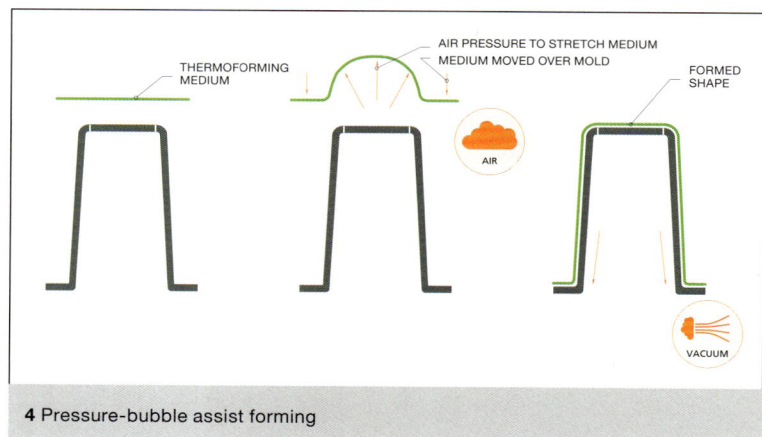

4 Pressure-bubble assist forming

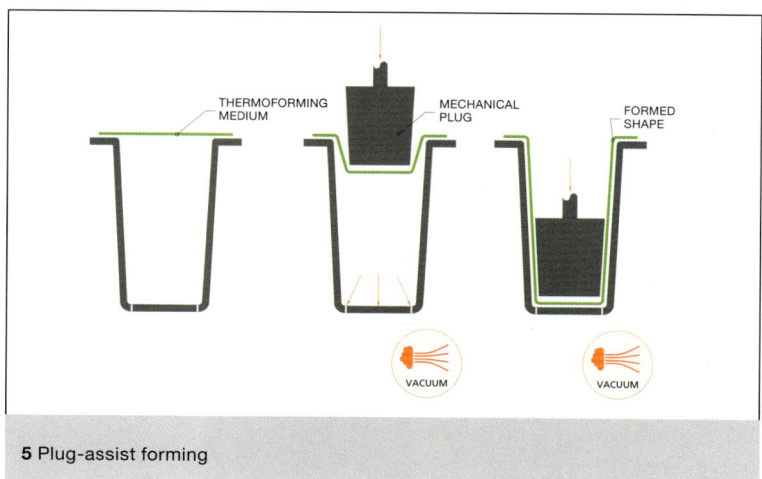

5 Plug-assist forming

for vacuum forming. This means that there is little wear on the molds during production. Thermoforming plastic molds can be made from high-density foam, wood, MDF, thermoset plastics, fiber-reinforced plastic (FRP), thermoset plastic with metal particles, plaster, or metal. The mold's temperature increases as the heated plastic comes into contact with it. Wood and MDF tend to warp and break down the fastest compared to the other tooling media. Metal molds are very durable, and are often embedded with cooling lines to actively cool the mold and the medium. The metal used is typically aluminum, as it transfers heat more efficiently than other metals; however, aluminum is softer than other metals, so care should be taken not to scratch or nick the tooling.[1] Metal molds are appropriate for high-volume productions. FRP molds are appropriate for large components such as tubs and bathroom enclosures.

For SPF, temperatures and pressures are lower than in metal casting, but higher than when vacuum forming plastic. Depending on the specific superplastic alloy, temperatures can range from 850°F (450°C) for aluminum to 1600°F (870°C) for titanium. The SPF mold should be heated to the same temperature as the heated alloy to reduce cracking due to thermal shock. SPF molds can be made from ceramic that is reinforced with steel to reduce bending loads and cracking, or metals such as steel or cast iron. With metal molds there is a danger of welding the alloy to the mold; therefore a mold-releasing agent should be used.

High-density foam, wood, MDF, and plaster molds can be CNC milled. Aluminum molds can also be CNC milled, but can also be cast (see Chapter 4.2). Steel molds may be CNC milled or cut by EDM if there are fine details. When making multiple molds for parallel productions, casting molds may be more efficient than milling, as it is easier to make multiples.

ENVIRONMENTAL IMPACT

Little energy is used in this forming process. Temperatures are generally lower than for other forming processes, as the plastic and metal are not heated to their fluid state. Generally, lots of scrap is generated as a result of post-trimming processes. Both the plastic and the metal can be recycled, but they often need to be sent back to the sheet-goods manufacturer for reforming. If working with high-volume plastic producers, the recycling may be done within the thermoforming facility. This is most likely available for packaging manufacturers and other high-volume manufacturers.

6 A five-axis CNC router, trimming thermoformed components to final shape

7 A thermoformer's collection of molds

8 A thermoformer's collection of trim dies

MATERIAL CONSIDERATIONS + DESIGN PARAMETERS

Prior to thermoforming, the plastic or metal sheets used should be of uniform thickness. This allows the material to flow over the mold. The sheets must be thick enough to allow for the material to stretch as it deforms to the mold's shape. During thermoforming, the portion of the sheet that first contacts the mold will stretch the least and will remain thick; the portion of the sheet that contacts the mold last will stretch the most and will thin. [9] If the sheet is too thin, the draw depth too deep, or the plastic too hot, tears may occur. [10] These materials may stretch as much as 1,000% without tearing. Heat is used to soften the material so it stretches, but not so much that the material melts.

Both plastic and metal have the potential to bond to other sheets during thermoforming. For example, two sheets can be placed into a closed mold and positive air pressure pushed in between the sheets. The two sheets will then bond at the mold's parting line, forming a single hollow unit. [11] In plastic, this process is called twin sheet thermoforming, and it is similar to plastic blow molding (see Chapter 4.5). In metal, this process is referred to as combined diffusion bonding and superplastic forming (DB/SPF).

THERMOPLASTIC

All thermoplastics can be thermoformed, but not all thermoplastics are suitable for thermoform manufacturing. There are two groups of thermoplastics—amorphous and crystalline. Amorphous plastics have a random molecular structure, while the molecules in crystalline plastics are ordered. Generally, amorphous thermoplastics thermoform more easily as they have a larger temperature range for heat softening. These include plastics such as polystyrene (PS), acrylonitrile butadiene styrene (ABS), polycarbonate, polyvinyl chloride (PVC), and PVC/ acrylic blends. Crystalline materials such as polyethylene, polypropylene (PP), thermoplastic olefins (TPOs), and nylon require a much more accurate temperature for thermoforming. This can increase manufacturing failure rates, decrease cycle times, and increase manufacturing costs.

The heating temperature for plastic thermoforming depends on the specific plastic used. PS is heated up to 360°F (180°C) and PP is heated up to 330°F (165°C). Some plastics have a large window for heating, such as high-impact polystyrene (HIPS), which makes it easier to thermoform. If the plastic is too hot, it will stretch too much and not maintain its surface, causing folds, bubbles, and melting. If it is heated too little, it will not stretch enough to fully take on the mold form.

SIMILAR PROCESSES

Thermoforming is used as a substitute for rotational molding, injection molding, transfer molding, compression molding, and blow molding (Chapter 3.5). Thermoforming is best for when production runs are low and cannot offset the higher tooling costs associated with those other processes. Shapes made with thermoforming are similar to those made by contact molding (Chapter 3.1); however, contact molding works with fiber-reinforced thermoset plastics while thermoforming uses thermoplastics.

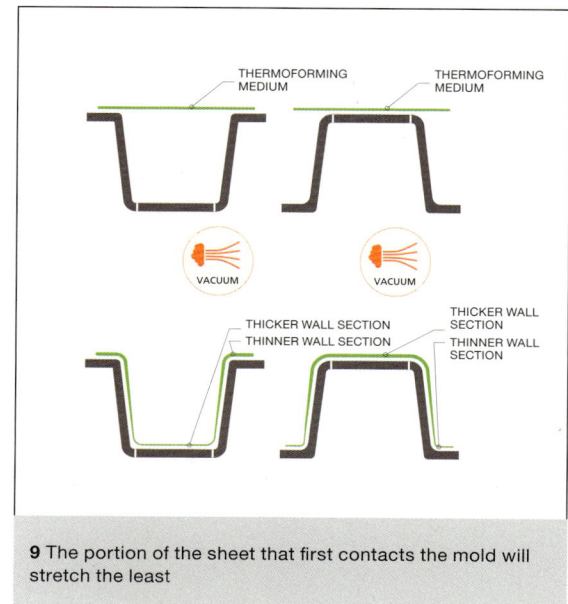

9 The portion of the sheet that first contacts the mold will stretch the least

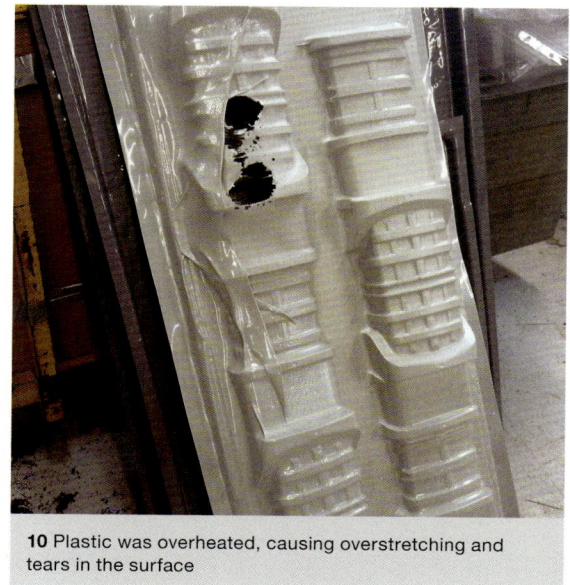

10 Plastic was overheated, causing overstretching and tears in the surface

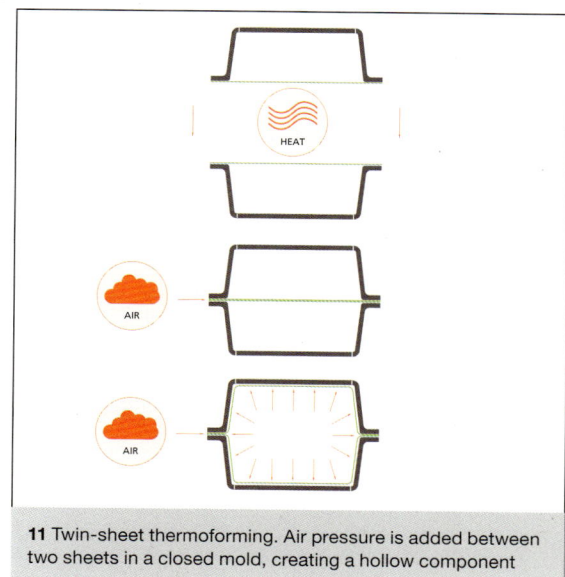

11 Twin-sheet thermoforming. Air pressure is added between two sheets in a closed mold, creating a hollow component

CORNER RADII (THREE-SIDED)

The curve radii for a three-sided corner should range from 0.015in (0.4mm) to over 0.25in (6mm), depending on the draw depth. As the plastic sheet stretches to accommodate a draw depth, it is likely to tear at sharp corners. The deeper the draw, the larger the required radius.

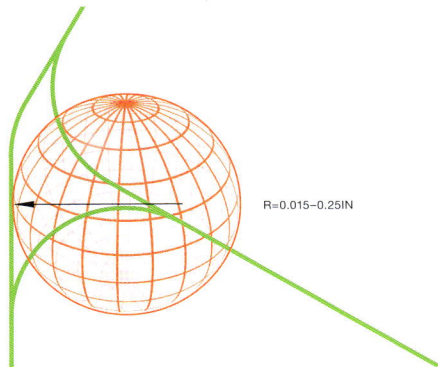

R=0.015–0.25IN

CORNER RADII

The corner radius will depend on the thickness of the plastic sheet blank and the depth of the draw. For shallow draws the radius should be the same as the sheet thickness. For deep draws the radius should be four times the sheet thickness. If a smaller radius is required, consider pressure-assisted thermoforming.

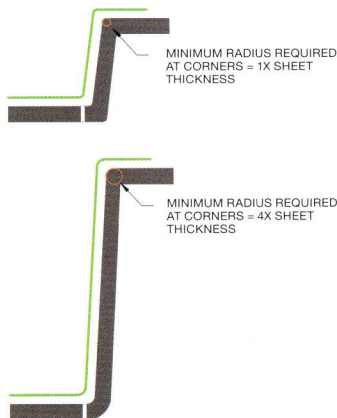

MINIMUM RADIUS REQUIRED AT CORNERS = 1X SHEET THICKNESS

MINIMUM RADIUS REQUIRED AT CORNERS = 4X SHEET THICKNESS

DRAFT ANGLES

A 3° draft angle is recommended for female molds, and a 5° draft angle for male molds. Smaller draft angles—approaching 0°—are possible with female molds, as the thermoformed component will shrink away from the mold as it cools. Greater draft angles are required for male molds; as the thermoformed material cools, it will shrink around the mold, making removal difficult.

Bear in mind that using minimum draft angles can prematurely wear the mold and scuff the component during demolding.

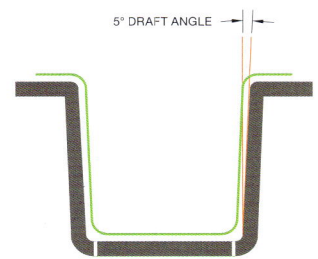

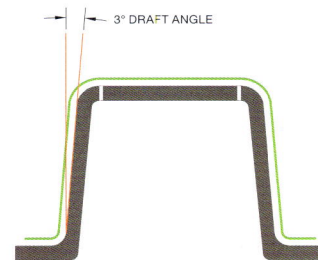

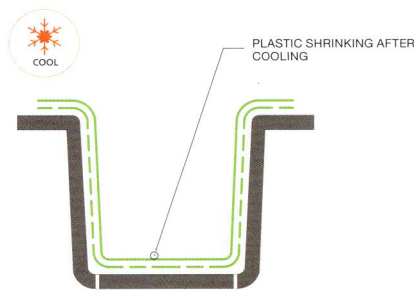

5° DRAFT ANGLE

3° DRAFT ANGLE

COOL

PLASTIC SHRINKING AFTER COOLING

DRAW DEPTH

Overall, the draw depth should be limited to the minimum width of the component. If a deeper draw is required, then a variant of thermoforming (e.g. pressure-assisted thermoforming or plug-assisted thermoforming) may be required. A variant will most likely increases costs and limit the number of manufacturers able to make the component.

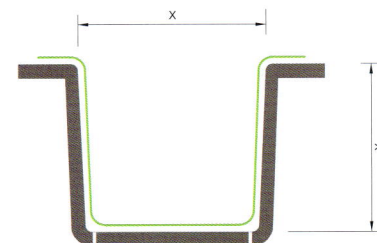

x

x

DRAW RATIO

Typically, thermoforming plastic is done to a draw ratio of 3:1; however, some manufacturers and certain plastics may be able to exceed this ratio.

Draw ratio = Surface area of final component / Projected plan of component

For example, in the diagram here, the draw ratio will be:

= 242in^2/156in^2

= 1.55

(If working in SI units, the equation for the draw ratio would remain the same, as a ratio is without units. The SI equation for the converted dimensions would be 1,561cm^2/1,006cm^2 = 1.55.)

The draw ratio can then be used to estimate the resulting wall thickness of the thermoformed component. For example, if the draw ratio is 1.55 and the starting sheet thickness is 0.25in (6mm), take 0.25/1.55 to get an average sheet thickness of 0.16in (4mm).

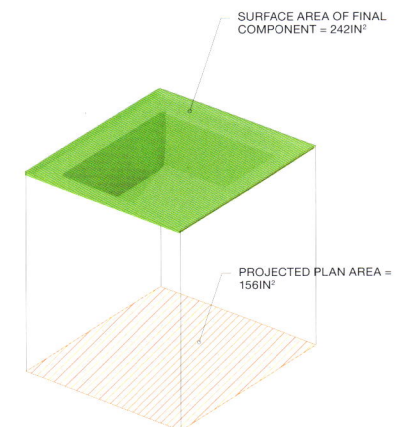

SURFACE AREA OF FINAL COMPONENT = 242IN^2

PROJECTED PLAN AREA = 156IN^2

FINISH

The finish for this process can vary from high-gloss to a fine texture. The finish will depend on the finish of the plastic sheet prior to thermoforming, and the mold medium. If properly sanded and sealed, an MDF or high-density foam mold can result in a high-gloss finish, if starting with a high-gloss plastic.

If the mold surface is rough or unfinished, or if the mold draw is too deep, there will be distortions on the component surface. The distortions will be more noticeable with a high-gloss plastic rather than a satin or textured surface.

HOLES

Holes can be made in a post-production process, either drilled by hand or CNC. If done by hand, then dimples may need to be thermoformed into the component's surface to make location easier.

INSERTS

Inserts cannot be added during the molding process. Inserts may be added in post-production with the use of targeted heat or adhesives.

JOINING

Two or more plastic sheets can be joined together in this process.

PRODUCTION RUNS

Production run lengths for thermoforming can range from prototypes and small production runs to large production runs for thin-gauge thermoformed packaging. If thermoforming thick-gauge material, production runs of fewer than 5,000 units would be best.

PRODUCTION SPEED

Cycle times for this process are long, and can range from 1 to 10 minutes, depending on size.

RIBS

Ribs can be added to the surface of a thermoformed component. Ribs help stiffen the component without increasing its wall thickness. The width of the rib should be at least 1.75 times its depth.

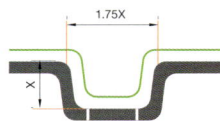

SHRINKING

The amount of shrinking will depend on the thermoplastic used. The mold should be oversized to accommodate shrinkage and should be sized to the particular plastic. Increasing cycle times will decrease shrinking; the more time the thermoformed plastic is in contact with the mold, the less shrinking will occur.

SIZE LIMITS

This largest size that can be thermoformed will be limited by the size of the oven necessary to heat the plastic, and the thermoplastic sheet sizes. Size limits for thermoforming plastic can range from small, hand-held pieces to large units approximately 6ft × 12ft (1.8m × 3.6m).

SURFACE TEXTURE

Surface textures can be pre-embossed onto the plastic sheet and can remain after the sheet is thermoformed, or the texture can be thermoformed into the component. If the plastic sheets are pre-embossed with a texture, then some of the texture may be lost as the material stretches over the mold. If the texture is thermoformed into the component, then the component's draft angle should be increased for proper mold release. In addition to the recommended draft angles, the draft should be increased by 1° for every 0.01in (0.25mm) of texture.

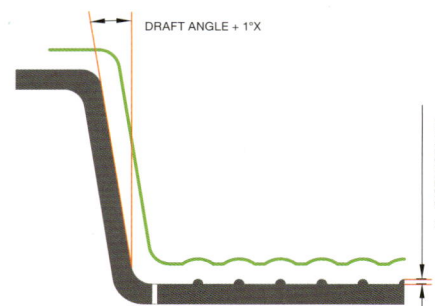

TOLERANCES

Molded dimension tolerances will range from +/– 0.01 to 0.015in (0.25–0.4mm) for the first inch (25mm) and +/– 0.001 to 0.0015in (0.025–0.04mm) for the subsequent inches. It is more difficult to maintain tolerances on female molds than male molds, because the thermoformed plastic shrinks away from the mold, making it difficult to maintain dimensions.

TOOLING COMPLEXITY

Generally, this process uses simple tools with no moving parts. High-production metal molds may have embedded cooling lines that use either oil or water to draw heat away from the component.

TOOLING COSTS

Tooling costs will depend on the tooling medium. MDF and high-density foam molds can cost as little as $100. Aluminum molds with embedded cooling lines may cost as much as $10,000. Generally, tooling costs are much lower when compared with other plastic manufacturing processes such as extrusion, compression molding, or injection molding.

UNDERCUTS

Undercuts should be limited to 0.5in (13mm) or less, and require a vent hole. If thermoforming a thin plastic, then the component may be flexible enough to remove it from a mold with a shallow undercut. If thermoforming an inflexible plastic, then a multi-part mold that breaks down into smaller pieces should be used. In most cases, undercuts are much more cost effective in thermoforming that other plastic molding processes such as injection or compression molding.

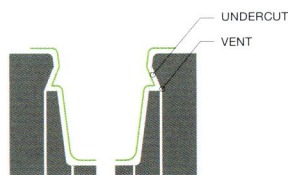

UNDERCUT
VENT

VENTS

Vents should be placed in interior corners, and at low points, ribs, undercuts, shelves, and deep surface decorations. For example, if thermoforming letters, vent holes should be used for each letter. The goal is to allow all trapped air to escape and to ensure a lower pressure between the component and the mold than atmospheric pressure.

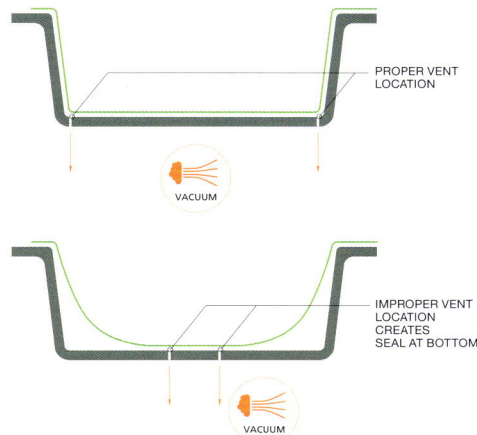

PROPER VENT LOCATION

VACUUM

IMPROPER VENT LOCATION CREATES SEAL AT BOTTOM

VACUUM

For most male molds, vent holes are not necessary, unless there are interior corners to which the plastic must form.

Vent holes can vary in size. If large, say 0.12in (3mm) diameter, then only one or two will be needed in the lowest cavities. However, the larger the hole, the more impact it will have on the component's finished surface. If small, say, 0.013in (0.3mm) diameter, then more vent holes are required, but they will only leave a mark on thin-gauge plastics.

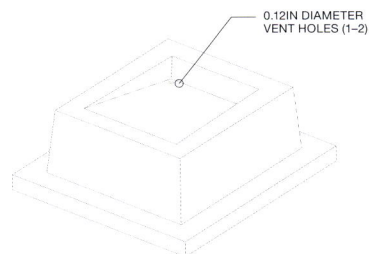

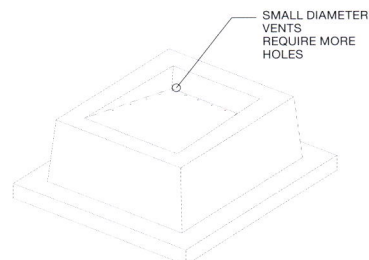

0.12IN DIAMETER VENT HOLES (1–2)

SMALL DIAMETER VENTS REQUIRE MORE HOLES

WALL THICKNESS

Wall thickness of a thermoformed component is based on the original sheet stock used for thermoforming. Standard thermoplastic sheet stock thicknesses range from 0.003in to 0.5in (0.07in–13mm), but thicker wall thickness can be thermoformed.

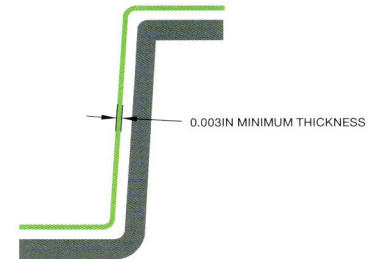

0.003IN MINIMUM THICKNESS

Since the material stretches as it forms over the mold, a component's wall thickness is difficult to control. It is typical that the part of the sheet first in contact with the mold will stretch the least, and the part of the sheet that contacts the mold last will stretch the most. Therefore if thickness is critical in certain locations, design the mold so that part of the sheet touches the mold first (see figure 1.2.9).

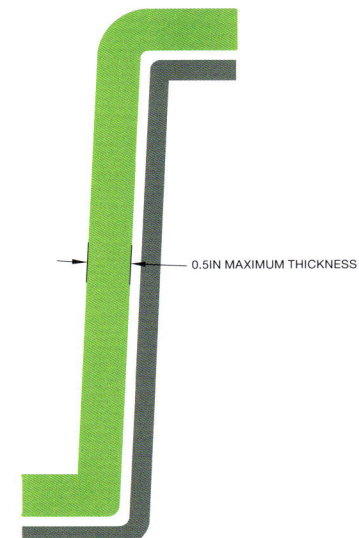

0.5IN MAXIMUM THICKNESS

THERMOFORMING: THERMOPLASTIC

WATER WALL | SEED [pod] HOUSE
University of Arizona
Washington, DC

The SEED [pod] House was the University of Arizona's submission to the United States Department of Energy's 2009 Solar Decathlon, held on the Washington, DC Mall.[2] The SEED [pod] House was prefabricated and shipped from Tucson, Arizona to Washington, DC in four modules, with a porch and deck built as an addition. The 2009 Solar Decathlon was a public exhibition and competition in which built houses were judged by a series of criteria (architecture, engineering, comfort zone, appliances, etc.). Winners were recognized in each category and scores totaled to assess that year's Decathlon winner.[3] The houses were on temporary display and were removed by the end of the exhibition.

To help regulate internal temperature, the University of Arizona team was interested in using a Trombe wall, or thermal mass. **[12, 13]** Traditionally, building materials that have a high thermal mass—such as concrete or masonry—also have high dead loads. This makes using a high thermal mass for a prefabricated, modular house too expensive to ship. The SEED [pod] House used a thermal mass of water stored in custom-made, thermoformed plastic tanks. **[14, 15, 16, 17]** Prior to shipping, the water was drained from the tanks, which were refilled once it was assembled on site. This made using a thermal mass in a prefabricated home a viable option.

The team thermoformed clear polyethylene terephthalate glycol-modified (PET-G)[4] plastic to make the front and back faces of a module. Each module measured 1ft tall by 2.5ft wide (300mm × 760mm) and approximately 2.5in (60mm) at its widest point. The two sheets of thermoformed plastic were sealed together at the edges with silicone and locked together

12
SEED [pod] House by the University of Arizona (led by Dale Clifford, Jason Vollen, Matt Gindlesparger, and Eddie Hall) for the 2009 Solar Decathlon, Washington, DC. Water wall with custom-manufactured thermoformed plastic sheets to make tanks

13
Completed water wall

14
Filmstrip of water wall's components

15
Building section with water wall on the left

16
Longitudinal section with header and sill details

17
Plan detail of water wall at mullion

14

17

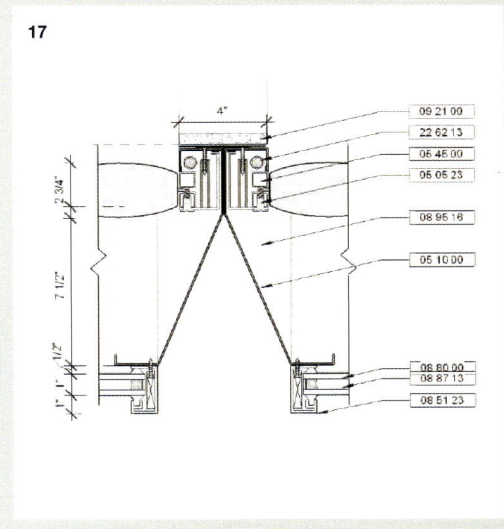

09 21 00
22 62 13
06 46 00
05 05 23
08 95 16
05 10 00
08 80 00
08 87 13
08 51 23

4"
2 3/4"
7 1/2"
1" 1" 1/2"

15

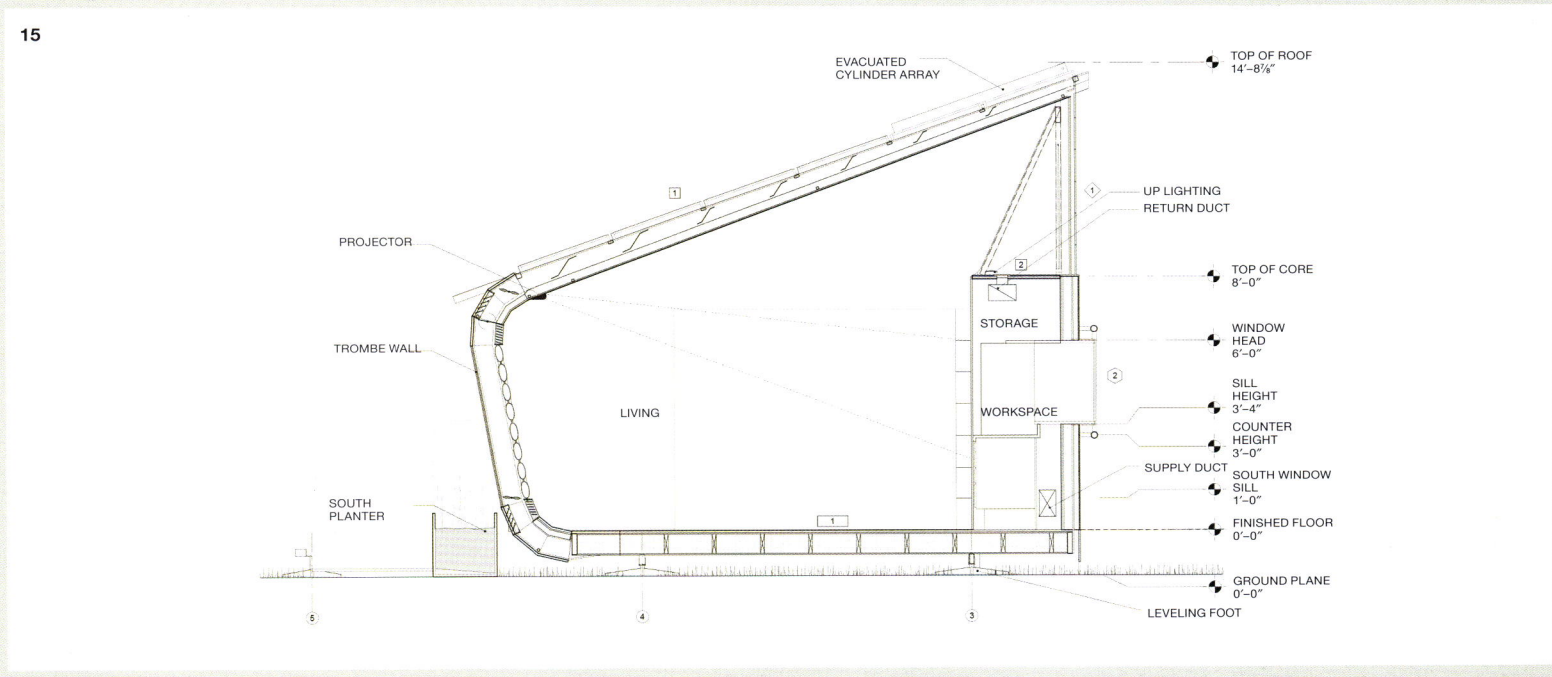

EVACUATED CYLINDER ARRAY
TOP OF ROOF 14'–8⅛"
UP LIGHTING
RETURN DUCT
PROJECTOR
TOP OF CORE 8'–0"
STORAGE
WINDOW HEAD 6'–0"
TROMBE WALL
SILL HEIGHT 3'–4"
WORKSPACE
COUNTER HEIGHT 3'–0"
LIVING
SUPPLY DUCT
SOUTH WINDOW SILL 1'–0"
FINISHED FLOOR 0'–0"
SOUTH PLANTER
GROUND PLANE 0'–0"
LEVELING FOOT

16

SOUTH WALL HEAD 4'–6"

SOUTH WALL SILL –0'–9"

with a snap connection at various points across the surface. These snap connections kept the two surfaces from bulging out under the hydrostatic pressure of the water. Ten modules (two modules wide and five modules tall) were connected to make a 40-gallon (150L) tank. The house had five tanks, one in each prefabricated section.

The plastic sheets were thermoformed in the University of Arizona College of Architecture, Planning and Landscape Architecture's fabrication shop. [18, 19, 20, 21] The thermoformed molds were fabricated at the university out of CNC-milled MDF. All of the manufacturing work was done by the students, with support by the team leaders and the fabrication shop staff. Because the two sheets snapped into one another, two slightly different molds were required for manufacturing. Fifty sheets of each shape were thermoformed.

DESIGN CONSIDERATIONS

SEED [pod]'s water wall was one of the celebrated features of the house. Its transparency allowed for more daylight to enter, and reduced the need for electrical lighting compared to a thermal mass of concrete. The interior wall's undulating surface and the resulting daylight effects dynamically affected the experience of the house's interior. The water wall's curved surface seemed to invite touch. The wall was therefore not only a component of the house's environmental performance, it was celebrated as an architectural feature.

According to Dale Clifford, University of Arizona Team Leader, there were a number of reasons why the team ended up using thermoformed plastic to make the water wall.[5] First, the team wanted transparency. In order to increase natural light in the space, they needed a clear material that could be shaped. Second, the material had to be able to conduct heat from the air to the water, in order for the wall to properly perform. Next, the material had to be strong enough to resist the hydrostatic pressure of the water. Fourth, the design team knew that in order for the tanks to work, there would need to be a lot of them. This required a manufacturing process that could accommodate repeatability. Fifth, cost was a consideration. The team investigated blow molding plastic for the wall, but discovered that tooling would be too expensive. As the University of Arizona had thermoforming equipment in its fabrication shop, this process cost the team very little. In the end, selecting thermoforming worked well for the team, as it then had unlimited access to prototypes to test the manufacturing process.

MANUFACTURING CONSIDERATIONS

Unlike the other case studies in this book, the designers for the SEED [pod] House were the thermoform manufacturers. [22] The design team was responsible for both CNC milling the MDF for the molds and for thermoforming the plastic modules for the tanks. According to Clifford, prior to this project, the team had little to no experience with the college's thermoforming equipment. Although the team's labor was unskilled, Clifford believes its inexperience gave it freedom to experiment and prototype often. As part of its prototyping process, the team investigated different shapes that could be

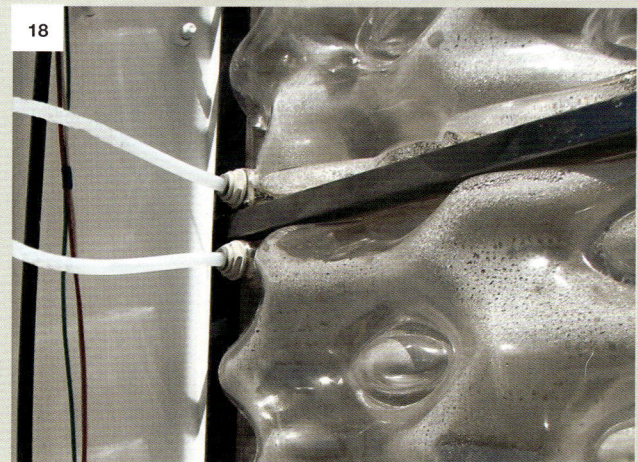

18
Early prototype of tanks, illustrating the inner workings

19
CNC milling mold from MDF

20
Completed MDF mold

made with the PET-G. Prototyping was used to evaluate both the tank's design and its performance. The team investigated different wall thicknesses, how deep those thicknesses could be drawn on to the mold, and what strength the thermoformed sheet would have in resisting the pressure of the water.

According to Clifford, production of the final fifty panels was slow and took approximately one week. However, because the team had done extensive prototyping and troubleshooting, there were no notable manufacturing problems with the panels.

OTHER CONSIDERATIONS

The team made a number of design decisions for the water wall in order to resist the lateral pressure from the water. First, in addition to the PET-G thickness, the curved geometry of the panels is based on catenary curves, which help stiffen the panel. Second, the curves' valleys snap-fit together, connecting the front sheets to the back sheets, similar to form ties used in site-cast concrete formwork. Third, once the water filled the tanks, vacuum pressure was added at the top, which helped to hold the water up and lessen hydrostatic pressure at the bottom of each tank.

As part of the design and manufacturing process, the design team made many prototypes. Most of the prototypes evaluated a number of different outcomes and tests such as aesthetics, manufacturing, and performance. There were separate tests to evaluate the different types of chemical sealers to be used to form the tanks. Clifford also noted that there is a gap between prototyping and final construction, which became evident in this project. Prototyping requires a quick sort of roughness in order to make decisions and push the project forward. On the other hand, final construction requires careful decisions about durability, craft, and how the pieces come together. After the 2009 Solar Decathlon, SEED [pod] was moved back to the University of Arizona campus where it was exhibited for over a year. It has since been dismantled and the parts salvaged.

LESSONS LEARNED

As a design-build project within an academic setting, the nature of this project was to be a learning opportunity for the design team. According to Clifford, this project's components included a number of learning discoveries for the team. The design team members learned that thermoforming the panels on their in-house vacuum former gave them control over the process. They also had the opportunity to quickly prototype, test ideas, learn about the process, and discover what was possible. Access to the manufacturing process made it safe for the students to fail, which in turn made innovation possible and facilitated rapid learning.

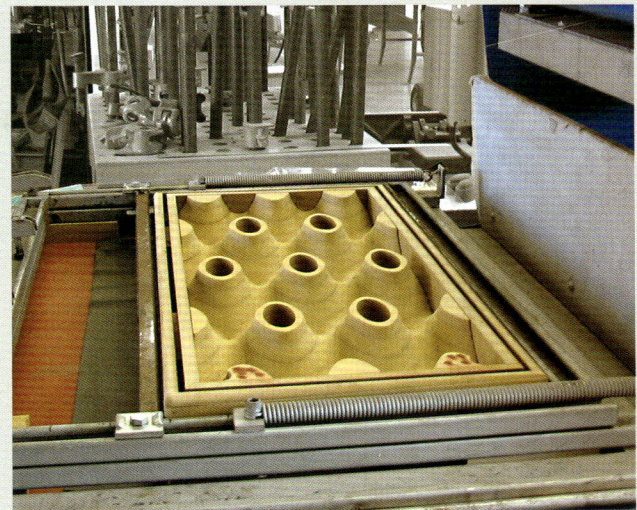

21 Thermoforming plastic in the shop's thermoformer

22 Tanks in production in the University of Arizona fabrication shop

MATERIAL CONSIDERATIONS + DESIGN PARAMETERS

METAL (SUPERPLASTIC ALLOYS)

Superplastic forming (SPF) requires a specific microstructure for the metal alloy. When superplastic alloys are heated, the material flow stress is lowered, allowing the microstructure to flow in a plastic state over the mold. The alloy must be highly ductile, and exhibit little necking when exposed to tension. [23] Superplastic alloys are specific alloys that must be processed in a particular method, and heated to a prescribed temperature range to exhibit their superplastic behavior.[6] Temperatures are maintained throughout forming. The alloys are aluminum, magnesium, or titanium based, and include AA2004, AA7075, AA8090, SUPRAL, and ICONEL alloy 718SPF. SUPRAL and ICONEL are both proprietary alloys and may not be available to third-party manufacturers. Because the superplastic alloys have been developed specifically for this manufacturing process, material costs are generally high.

Typically, SPF uses positive air pressure to form the components, as pressures are relatively high in this method. [25] SPF pressures can range from 13 to 75k/in^2 (650–3,500kPa). Air blowing is done slowly during forming to reduce material strain and rupture. Pressure varies during the cycle—depending on the alloy, the shaped formed, wall thickness, and size—and is computer controlled. Other assist-forming methods such as air-bubble assist, plunger assist, and matched die plates may be used for deep draws or complex details.

Multiple sheets can be formed together to make complex shapes with interior structure. [24] In SPF, this process is referred to as diffusion bonding (DB). The sheets are often arranged in a pattern, and a parting agent is deposited onto the sheets where no bond is wanted. When air pressure is added, the parts of the sheet without the parting agent will touch and bond, while parts with the parting agent will separate. This process is often used to create an interior ribbed structure that is helpful for making structural components for airplanes and similar applications.

SIMILAR PROCESSES

SPF is similar to other metal-sheet forming process, such as explosive forming (Chapter 1.3), stamping (Chapter 1.5), hydroforming (Chapter 1.6), and spinning (Chapter 1.7). Generally, material costs for the alloys are higher with this process than the others. Springback is less with SPF than stamping. SPF tooling costs are similar and slightly higher than that of explosive forming, but cycle times are much shorter.

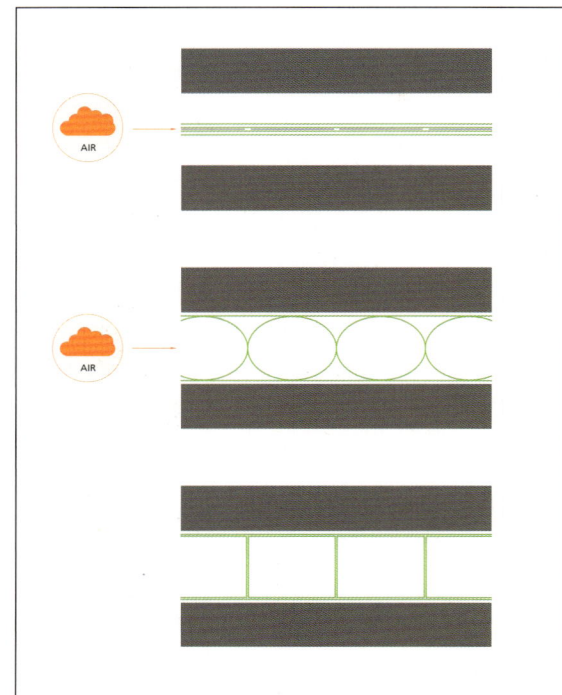

24 This process can be used to form components with complex shapes or inner structures

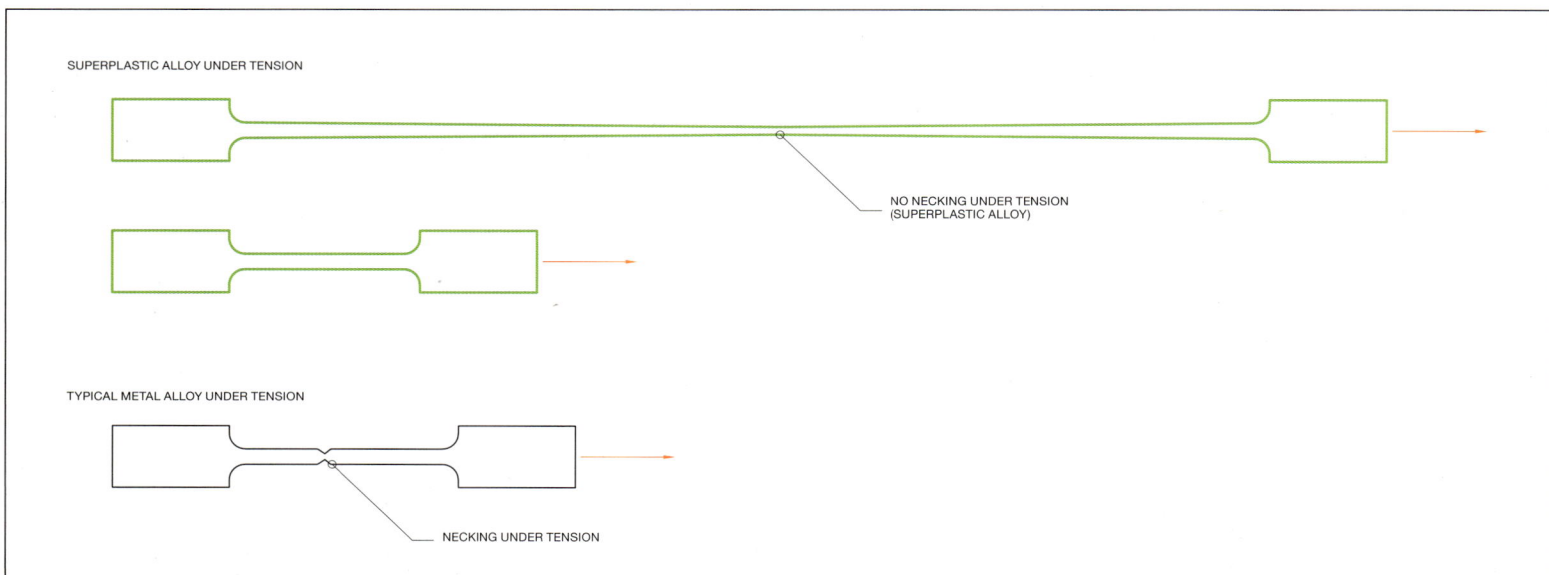

23 Superplastic deformation exhibits little necking when exposed to tension

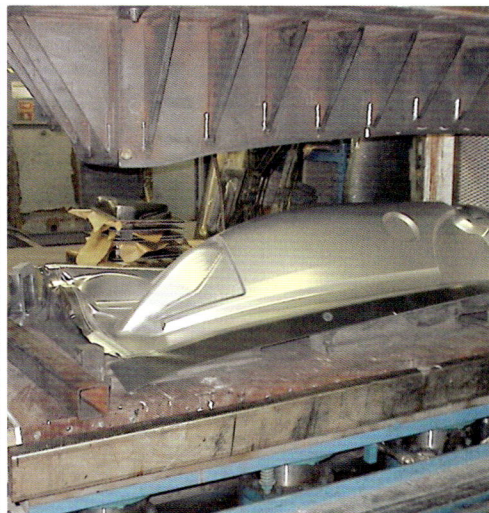

25 Little of the superplastic forming process can be seen; to achieve the air pressure necessary to deform the metal, the chamber must be closed

There are differences between SPF and other metal-sheet forming processes such as stamping (Chapter 1.5) or hydroforming (Chapter 1.6). First, SPF has longer cycle times than the other two processes as the metal is heated and needs time to flow over the mold. Second, SPF can manufacture more complex shapes and deeper drawings with a single tool when compared to stamping or hydroforming. This may reduce tooling costs and the total production time. Third, because the material is heated prior to forming, internal stresses and springback are reduced.

Generally, shape making in SPF is similar to thermoformed plastic. Many of the design parameters for plastic also apply to SPF. The advantages of SPF over plastic are the inherent strength, stiffness, fire performance, and electrical conductivity. SPF enables the exploitation of the superior properties of metals while adding a styling capability that had previously been exclusive to plastics.[7] This makes SPF a good option for architectural application.

CORNER RADII

The minimum corner radius is 0.2in (5mm).

It is recommended that the entry radius into the die be increased based on the depth of the draw, so that the ratio of radius (R) to depth (D) is 0.25in (6mm) minimum.

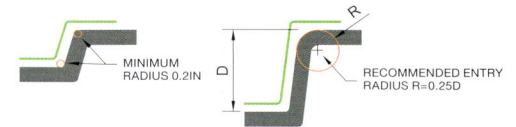

DRAFT ANGLE

It is recommended that draft angles range from 2 to 3°, depending on the alloy, tooling medium, and number of units produces. With draw depths less than 1.5in, draft angles may be 0°.

DRAW DEPTH

The draw depth can be up to 24in (600mm), depending on the alloy used and the size of the draw opening.

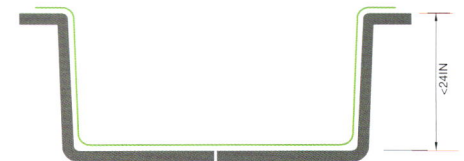

DRAW RATIO

Typically, SPF is limited to a draw ratio of 4:1, but some manufacturers and certain alloys may be able to exceed this ratio.

Draw ratio = Surface area of final component / Projected plan of component

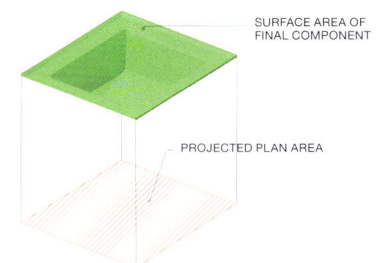

HOLES

Holes can be made in the post-production process, either drilled by hand or using CNC.

INSERTS

Inserts are not possible with this process.

JOINING

Multiple sheets of superplastic alloys can be joined together during this process. The sheets are often arranged in a pattern, and a parting agent is deposited onto the sheets where no bond is to form.

PRODUCTION RUN

SPF is best for production runs under 1,000 units, but it can be used in productions up to 20,000 units.

PRODUCTION SPEED

Cycles times can vary with this process, ranging from 1 to 30 minutes. Cycle times depend on the alloy, component size, and surface complexity. The larger the component and the more complex the surface detail, the longer the cycle times.

RIBS

Ribs are used to strengthen otherwise thin gauges of metal. The depth-to-width ratio for pultruding ribs should be 0.5, with a minimum draft angle of 55°. The depth-to-width ratio for inset ribs should be 0.4.

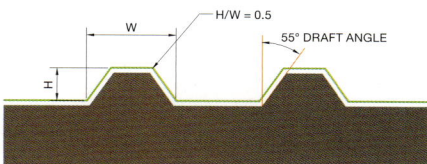

W
H/W = 0.5
55° DRAFT ANGLE
H

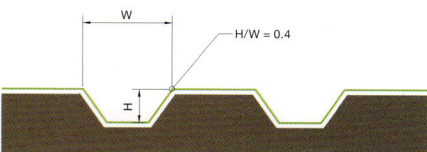

W
H/W = 0.4
H

SIZE LIMITS

The maximum size is limited to 120in × 80in (3,000mm × 2,000mm); however, finding manufacturers with equipment this large may be difficult.

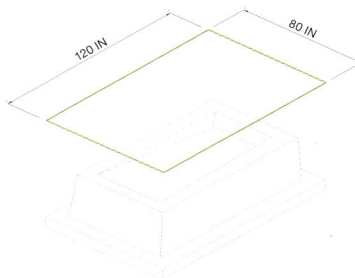

120 IN
80 IN

SURFACE DESIGNS

Fine surface designs and textures are very easy to create with this process. Because this process lends itself to thinner gauges of metal than metal stamping or spinning, most textures will translate to the surface opposite of the die.

SURFACE IMPERFECTIONS

Stress marks from deformation are less likely than with metal stamping.

TOLERANCES

Tolerances for this process can be as fine as 0.001in/in.

TOOLING COMPLEXITY

Tooling for this process is simple, with no moving parts.

TOOLING COSTS

Generally, tooling costs are very low for this process. Costs will be primarily affected by tooling materials. Ceramic will be the least expensive, while machined steel will be the most expensive.

UNDERCUTS

Generally, undercuts are not permissible with this process, as the metal is not flexible enough to be released from tools with undercuts. If undercuts are needed, then a multi-part mold should be used. This will increase manufacturing costs and cycle times.

VENTS

Vents can be located centrally, to let the air escape as the alloy is being formed. Because most SPF is done with pressure forming, the vent placement is less critical than with vacuum forming. Vent holes will leave a mark on the component.

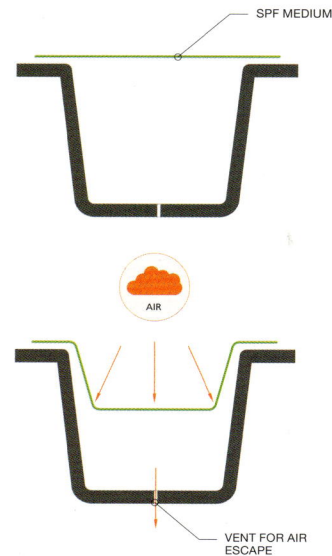

SPF MEDIUM

AIR

VENT FOR AIR ESCAPE

WALL THICKNESS

Starting sheet thickness should be less than 0.25in (6mm). Sheets will thin during forming, and it is not unusual for the SPF component to have half the wall thickness of the original sheet.

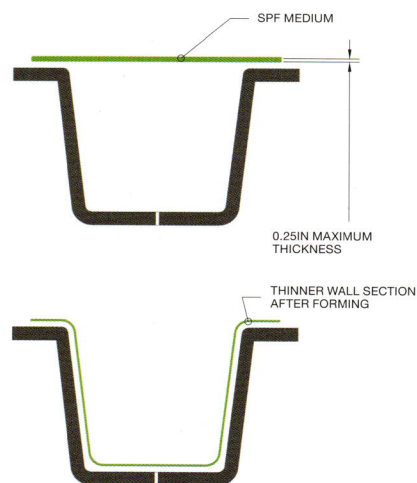

SPF MEDIUM

0.25IN MAXIMUM THICKNESS

THINNER WALL SECTION AFTER FORMING

THERMOFORMING: METAL (SUPERPLASTIC ALLOYS)

INSTALLATION WALL | BIOFORM
Murmur
New York, New York

Bioform was part of a group architecture studio exhibition titled *Matters of Sensation*, held at Artists Space in New York City in 2008. The exhibition included the work of fourteen architecture studios in the United States, among whom the use of computers created diverse sensations of space, material textures, and surfaces. Heather Roberge, Murmur's principal, developed a three-dimensional aluminum tile that would be installed as a tessellated field. [26] Bioform is made up of forty-three identical aluminum panels mounted on the wall in six different orientations. The installation measured 11ft wide and 6ft high (3.35m × 1.83m), and protruded 7in (18cm) from the wall. [27]

Bioform developed from Roberge's University of California Los Angeles (UCLA) seminar, titled "Between the Sheets." Through the seminar, Roberge introduced UCLA students to superforming metal and to the specific manufacturing process available at Superform USA's facility in Riverside, California, located just over 65 miles (100km) from the school. Through the seminar, Superform provided students with a tour of its facility, a presentation of the process, literature, and design feedback. In turn, students designed tessellated patterns for components that could be made by superforming metal. However, since the mold and material costs associated with superforming were too high for students, thermoforming plastic was used as a substitute.[8] With the three years of seminar work and the resulting relationship with Superform, it seemed natural for Roberge to approach the company for the production of Bioform.

DESIGN CONSIDERATIONS

The schedule for this project was short, and Roberge did not have a lot of time to study different forms. The organic shape of the Bioform tile was derived from interior residential designs that Murmur had been working on for a client who was interested in coral-like forms. According to Roberge, by working with this initial design, the time necessary for computer modeling was greatly reduced. Even with that reduced time, digital modeling was labor intensive, and it was difficult to work through the complex geometries in Rhinoceros (a 3D modeling program). Unlike the aerodynamically shaped aerospace or automobile parts typically manufactured by Superform, Bioform had fine

26
Filmstrip simulation of forming Bioform by Murmur for *Matters of Sensation* (2008), Artists Space, New York City

27
Image of Bioform in the exhibition

28
Detail image of Bioform

29
Detail image of Bioform in the exhibition

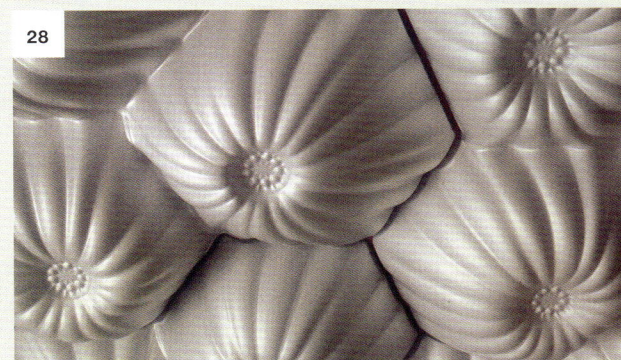

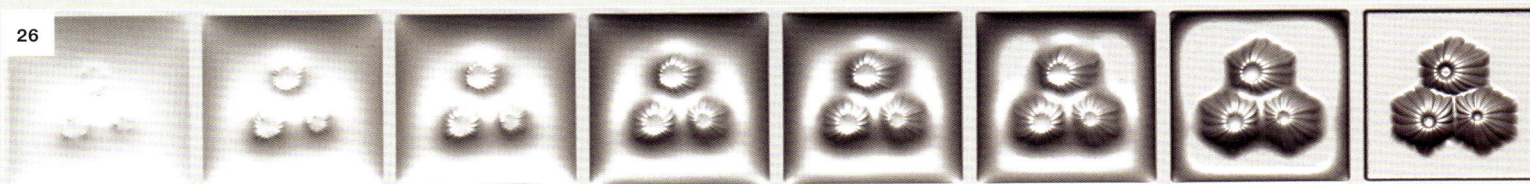

detail that the manufacturing process could replicate. To make the most of the process's capabilities, Roberge designed the Bioform tile with jewel-like details such as the small dimples at the top of each dome. [28, 29]

Within the seminar work, the students looked at different ways to resolve the joint between the tessellations. Roberge worked with students to understand how the seam between the tiles would be a part of their designs. The students investigated design options that would either embrace the seam or would minimize the seam through a larger, super-pattern. In Bioform, Roberge actually took a third approach. To disguise the seam between the units, she designed the tile unit with three smaller cells. To disguise the repeatability of the units, she then rotated each unit. [30] The idea is that the joints between the cells and the joints between the units read the same. In the final installation, however, the joints between the units ended up being larger than intended. Roberge misunderstood the tolerance level for superforming. She had planned the installation with a 0.04in (1mm) tolerance, but in the end, she found there was no dimensional difference between the units.

MANUFACTURING CONSIDERATIONS

Because Bioform had a small production run of only forty-three units, Superform's typical manufacturing process was modified. First, Superform modified an existing forming chamber, which restricted the units' size. [31] Second, Superform typically uses either cast iron or milled steel for its mold, but for this project it used a CNC-milled aluminum mold. [32, 33] Generally, aluminum is less costly than iron or steel, but produces fewer units. According to Roberge, with the units produced for Bioform, there was no notable change to the mold from the first unit to the last. Third, all post-production trimming was done by hand rather than by CNC milling, presumably because a secondary tool to hold the unit while trimming would not have been cost effective. The hand-trimmed edges were hidden by the joint between the tiles. Finally, Superform produced all of the units on a weekend so that the production did not interrupt the company's schedules. [34, 35, 36]

Cycle times for this manufacturing process were 20 minutes. According to Roberge, this is longer than is typical because of the design of the unit and its fine detail. Prior to superforming, the original aluminum sheet was 0.04in (1mm) thick; it thinned to 0.02in (0.5mm) after superforming. Thin material was selected because of high material costs and reduced cycle times. However, the combination of the thin material and the air pressure needed to push the material onto the mold caused pin holes to form the in surface of the aluminum. In the end, Roberge did not reject any panels for the installation.

OTHER CONSIDERATIONS

Initially, Roberge conceived of modifying the manufacturing process so that time would be the limiting factor. In other words, a manufacturing cycle would be cut short, before the metal was in full contact with the mold. This would provide a more draped effect between the material and the mold. She learned from Superform that this process is too difficult to control in this way and therefore could not be done.

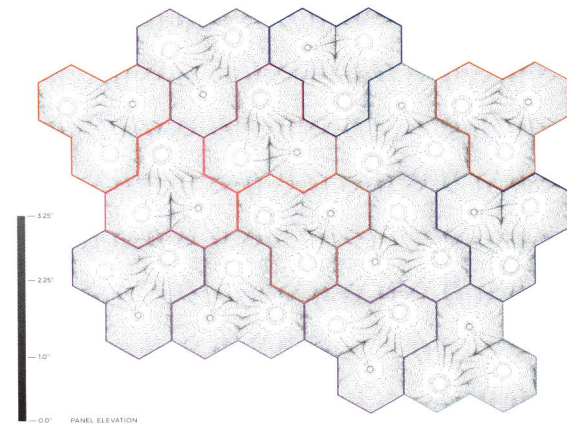

30 Contours and orientation of components

31 Tool in air chamber

32 CNC-milled aluminum mold

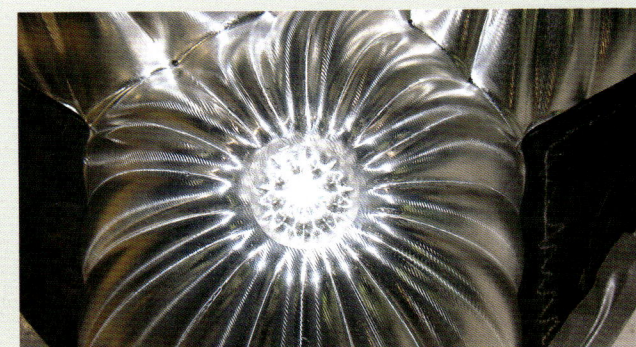

33 Detailed image of aluminum mold. Note the CNC tool marks on the surface

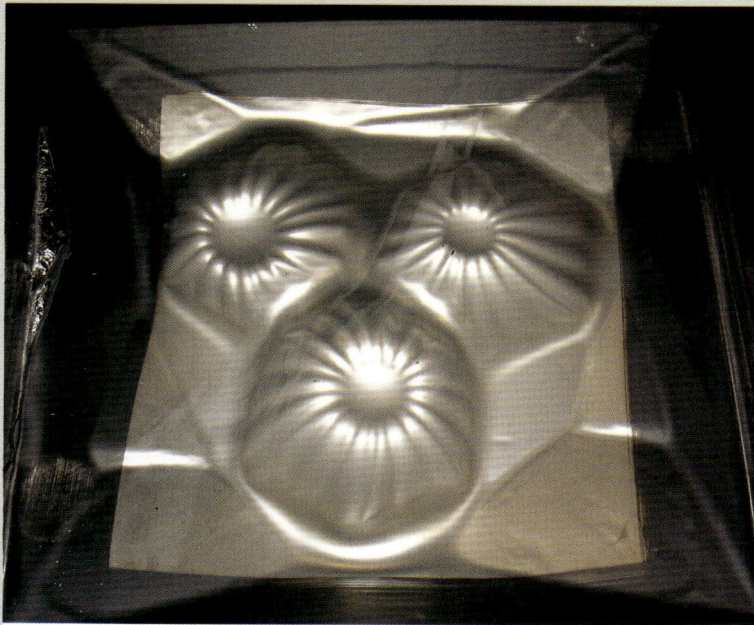

34 Superforming process, showing the component, stopped mid-cycle

36 Superforming process, showing the final component

35 Multiple units drying after cleaning

37 Surface detail of completed unit. Note residual CNC tool marks translating to the component's exterior surface

LESSONS LEARNED

A lesson that Roberge learned through this project was that is much harder to develop the digital model than she had thought. In addition, the manufacturing process was able to pick up finer features than she had anticipated. Therefore any geometric modeling issues, such as the tangency of the curves or splining, were picked up by the mold and transferred to the final component. Second, SPF is sensitive to the mold's surface. The CNC tool cuts from the mold translated from the inside face of the component (where it was in contact with the mold) to the component's outside or finish face. **[37]**

1.3 Explosive Forming

aka explosion forming, explosive working, high-energy rate
forming (HERF) or high-energy hydroforming (HEH),
high-velocity metal forming (HVMF)

INTRODUCTION

Explosive forming is a manufacturing process within a larger
group of manufacturing processes, called high-energy rate forming (HERF).[1] HERF processes apply a force at a high velocity
over a short period of time to deform a metal sheet. (For brevity, I
refer to both pure metals and metal alloys as 'metal.') In explosive
forming, the high-velocity force is from an explosion, traveling
through a medium such as water or air. [1] This causes the metal
to flow within the sheet, deforming the blank to the die. Explosive
forming is best used for large metal sheets, with deep draws and
smooth curves. Examples include large metal components for
the aerospace industry. [2] Explosive forming can also be used
to deform metal tubes or to fuse together two dissimilar metals.[2]
Both ferrous and non-ferrous metals can be shaped with this process. Surface quality and manufacturing tolerances are good with
this process.

In explosive forming, a metal sheet, called a blank, is
clamped to a die and placed inside of a protective tank. A vacuum
is used to remove any air from between the blank and the die so
that the blank can fully conform to the die shape. Then the tank
may be filled with water, to transfer the energy from the explosion
to the blank. Next, the explosive charge is placed inside the tank
and detonated. The force from the explosion and the subsequent
shock waves deform the blank to the die. The workpiece is then
removed from the tank. Any trimming or other work can then be
done through post-production processes.

Many different explosives can be used in explosive forming,
which will affect performance, shape, and distance to the blank.
Explosives—such as trinitrotoluene (TNT) and dynamite—have
different detonation velocities, pressures, and energies when detonated.[3] In turn, the explosive affects what metals, sizes, shapes,
draw depths, and thicknesses can be deformed. The explosive can
take the form of a point, ring, or line charge. [3] Ring charges help
distribute the force over a larger area than point charges. Line
charges are best for deep deformations, tube deforming, or when
two blanks are deformed in one cycle. Explosives can also be
placed in contact with the blank—called the contact method, or
they can be placed a distance from the blank—called the standoff
method. Generally, the explosives themselves are not expensive;
however, the restrictions, safety regulations, transportation, and
storage associated with using explosives can be expensive.

The standoff method is the most common method of explosive forming. The explosive is placed a predetermined distance
away from the blank, and a medium transfers the energy from
the explosive to the blank. Water is the most effective transfer

1 Explosive forming with water plume

2 Metal component for the aerospace industry, before and after forming

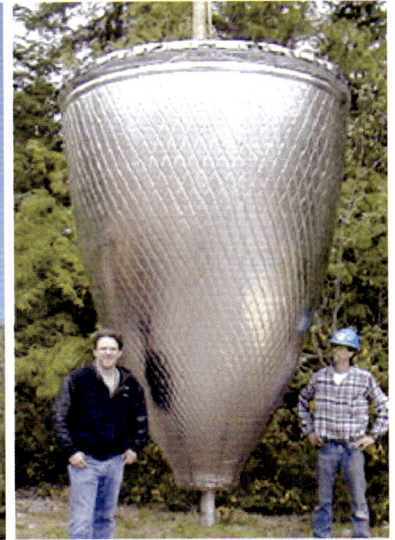

medium, but the use of air will reduce the set-up time between cycles. In the standoff method, the energy transferred from the explosive to the blank is uneven. The portion of the blank closest to the point of detonation receives the most energy, while sections farther away receive less energy. [4] Generally, the greater the distance between the explosion and the blank, the less pressure that is applied, but the more evenly it is distributed across the blank. If the explosive is too close to the blank, the metal may thin, tear, or harden in the area closest to the explosion. To make the pressure more even, explosive formers may use a plug cushion, made of a ductile material such as lead or aluminum, to distribute explosive force over a blank's face. Using the plug cushion reduces blowouts and material thinning.[4]

To contain the explosion, explosive forming may be done inside in-ground tanks, or inside a protective container above ground. It can be done with open or closed dies. The face of the workpiece that is in contact with the die is considered the finish face, and the face forced by the explosive is considered unfinished. The die shape may be simple or complex. No lubricant is required between the die and the workpiece, thus reducing costs.

Explosive forming is done by small or medium-sized contract manufacturers. It is not a highly mechanized process and there are long set-up times between cycles. This process is not

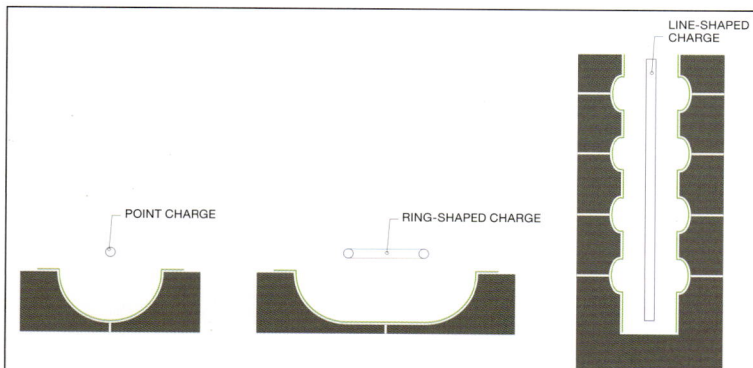

3 Different explosive charge shapes (from left to right: point, ring, and line) and their corresponding component shapes

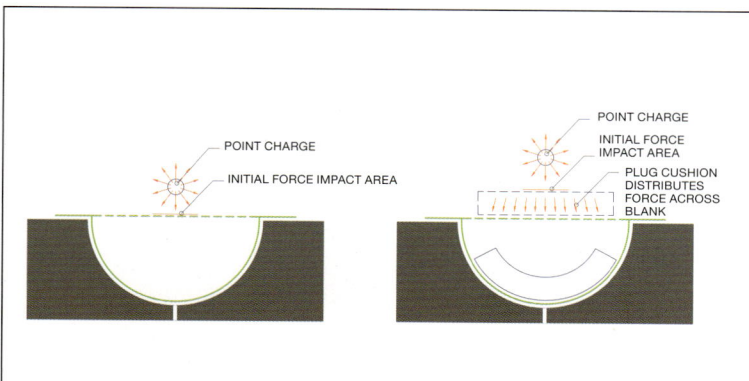

4 The portion of the blank closest to the point of detonation receives the most energy; to better distribute the force a plug cushion may be used

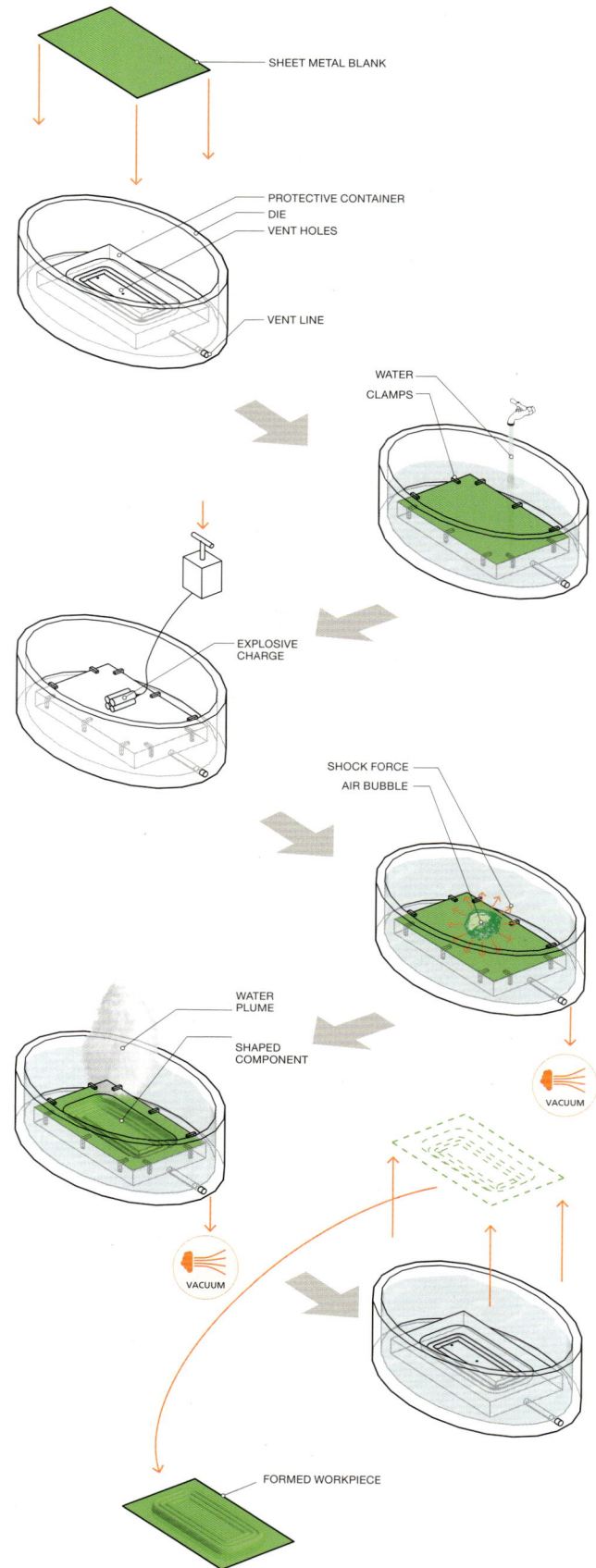

appropriate for high-volume producers. Explosive formers can require a lot of space because the components are often large, the process is noisy, and there are many safety regulations associated with using explosives; for this reason it is often done in remote locations. For example, Souriau PA&E, the only explosive former in the United States, is located on an inland peninsula in northwest Washington state and bordered by Olympic National Park. This geographic isolation increases the transportation costs associated with this process.

BUILDING PRODUCTS

There are no notable commercially available building products made by explosive forming. This process is best suited to limited production runs of large or custom components. [5]

TOOLING

The tooling includes the die, which gives the blank its form, and the hold-down ring or clamps, to prevent wrinkles during forming. The die surface should be as smooth as the desired surface of the component. Dies can be open or closed, [6, 7, 8] with open

being the most common. Open dies are most often female, to keep the transfer medium from getting between the die and the blank. If the transfer medium gets between the two, deformation of the workpiece will be reduced. Dies can be full or partial, such as a ring mold. With a full die, the full surface of the die forms the finished surface of the component, whereas a partial die only partially supports the blank during deformation. Ring molds hold the blank around the outer edge and are open in the middle; they usually produce conical or hemispherical shapes. The exact shape depends on the explosive amount, shape, and type; the standoff distance; the energy transfer medium, such as water or air; and the blank.

Generally, tooling costs associated with explosive forming are lower than other comparable manufacturing processes such as stamping (Chapter 1.5) and hydroforming (Chapter 1.6). First, unlike stamping, which requires two die halves, explosive forming dies are single-sided, reducing tooling costs by at least half. Also, unlike stamping, which uses match die halves with dimensional offsets based on the material blank thickness, in explosive forming a die can be used for any blank thickness. Second, tooling in explosive forming may be thin materials supported by a framework of structural members, or may be solid. [9] Third, explosive forming dies can be made from a variety

5 *Now* by Piotr Kowalski, located at California State University, Long Beach. The large stainless-steel parts of the sculpture were made by explosive forming

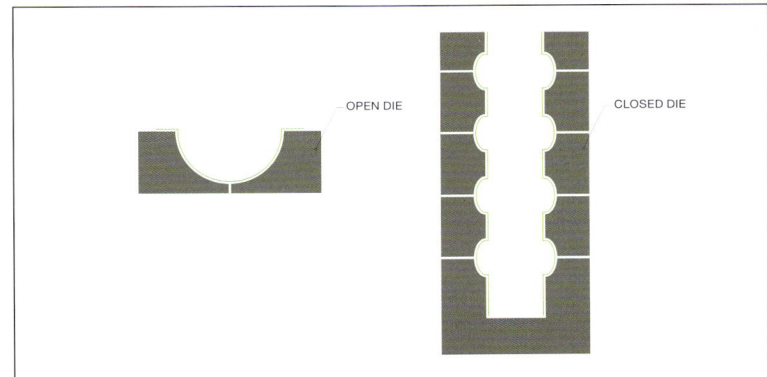

7 Dies can be open or closed

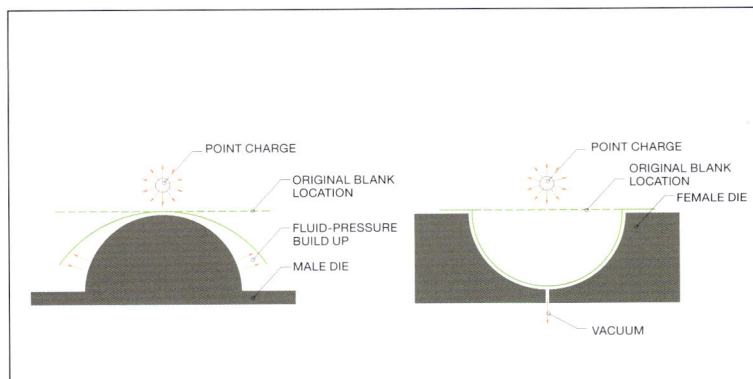

6 Open dies should be female, as they will keep fluid pressure from building up behind the workpiece

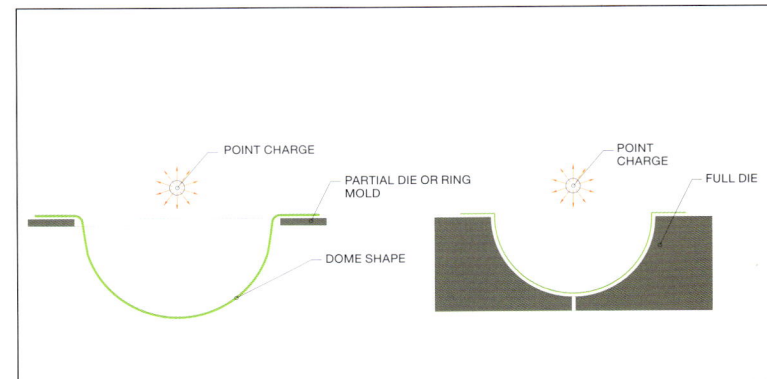

8 Full or partial dies may be used

of materials, including concrete, fiber-reinforced plastic (FRP), cast kirksite, ductile iron and steel, and machine-milled and tooled steel. Dies made from concrete, FRP, and cast metals cost substantially less than the machined steel tools required for both stamping and hydroforming.

The selection of the die material depends on how many components are to be produced from each die, the applied pressure of the explosion, and the material weight. (Because dies are often large, their weight can become a challenge and make handling them expensive.) Concrete is best for large parts formed with medium pressure and is appropriate for productions of five components or fewer. Fiberglass is best for large parts formed with low pressure, is appropriate for productions of five components or fewer, and is more easily handled than concrete. Cast kirksite is best for low pressure and can produce between ten and one hundred components. However, kirksite creeps under high pressure and impulse loads, so it is best for thin blanks.

Cast ductile iron and steel are best for high pressures and can produce up to 500 components from one mold; however, they do not give a good surface quality to the component. Machined steel is the most expensive, gives best surface quality, and will produce over 500 components.

ENVIRONMENTAL IMPACT

This process is highly energy intensive, with more energy spent in a HERF operation than on an ordinary one.[5] Although explosive forming does not require the large presses of stamping and hydroforming, cranes are often needed to maneuver components and dies in and out of tanks. Because explosive forming makes large components in remote areas, fossil fuels are required for transportation over large distances. However, there is generally little manufacturing waste with this process. Any waste that is generated by post-production trimming can be recycled off-site.

9 Molds can be made from thin materials with a supporting framework. This is an image of the mold used for *Now* by Piotr Kowalski

MATERIAL CONSIDERATIONS + DESIGN PARAMETERS

METAL

Explosive forming can be done to both ferrous and nonferrous metals, and to pure metal and metal alloys. Explosive forming works well for ductile metals and for tough metals that are difficult to form with other sheet metal processes. Metals that can be formed by this process include magnesium, aluminum, titanium, nickel, steel, and stainless steel. With explosive forming, the force exerted is high and takes place during a fraction of a second, causing more plastic deformation than stamping or hydroforming. Because of this, explosive forming can shape larger blanks, at greater thicknesses, with less springback than stamping or hydroforming. This means that explosive forming dies are designed to near net shape without allowances for over-bending.

There are other advantages to explosive forming's quickly applied force. First, little to no friction develops between die and blank, eliminating the need for lubricant. Second, this process tends to result in fewer wrinkles than stamping or hydroforming. Third, it can accommodate embossing or coining over large areas, which can give the component very fine surface decorations and textures. Fourth, it increases the metal's hardness, tensile strength, and yield stress; the amount of increase depends on the metal, the component shape, and the type of explosive. Finally, a variant of this process, EXW, may be used to bond dissimilar metals during deformation.

SIMILAR PROCESSES

Explosive forming is similar to other metal-sheet forming process, such as superplastic forming (Chapter 1.2), stamping (Chapter 1.5), hydroforming (Chapter 1.6), and spinning (Chapter 1.7). Generally, material handling costs and cycle times are higher in explosive forming than other processes, but tooling costs are lower and component size significantly larger.

CORNER RADII

The entry radius into a female die should be rounded so the metal does not tear during deformation. The minimum radius is 0.05in (1.5mm); however, 0.125in (3mm) is recommended. Generally, to prevent tearing, a larger radius is required for thinner blanks.

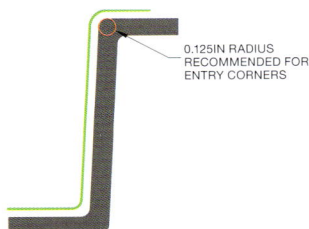

0.125IN RADIUS RECOMMENDED FOR ENTRY CORNERS

DRAFT ANGLE

The draft angle should be 1° or more for shallow draws, and 3° or more for deep draws. The greater the angle, the less wear on the die and blank.

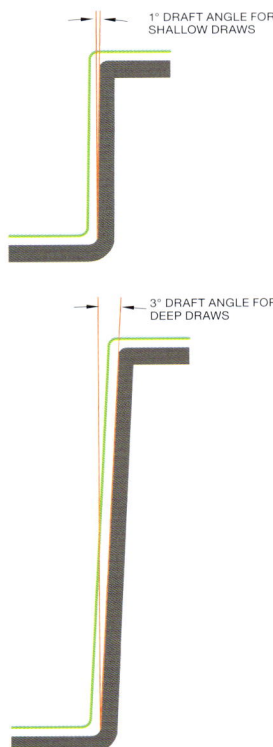

1° DRAFT ANGLE FOR SHALLOW DRAWS

3° DRAFT ANGLE FOR DEEP DRAWS

DRAW DEPTH

The draw depth will depend on the type of explosive and its shape (e.g. point, ring, line).

HOLES

Holes can be made in a post-production process, either drilled by hand or using CNC.

INSERTS

Inserts cannot be added during the molding process.

JOINING

Similar or dissimilar metals can be joined together with this process, also known as EXW. The explosive force forms a curling wavelike joint at the seam between the blanks, making a mechanical-like connection between the two.

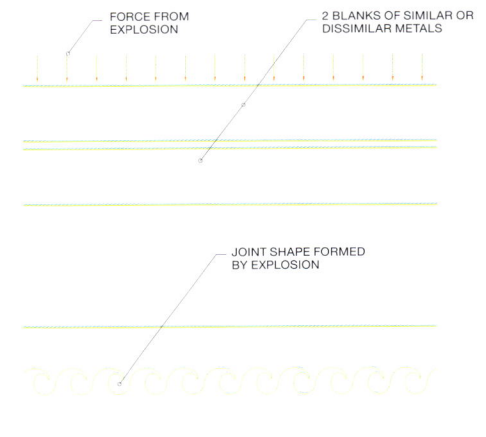

FORCE FROM EXPLOSION

2 BLANKS OF SIMILAR OR DISSIMILAR METALS

JOINT SHAPE FORMED BY EXPLOSION

LEAD TIME

Lead time should be about half of that required for metal stamping.

PRODUCTION RUNS

This process is most appropriate for small quantities, under 500 units.

PRODUCTION SPEED

Generally cycles are long, due to set-up times. The cycle times can range from about an hour to a day, depending on size and complexity.

SHAPES

Shapes can be simple or complex. Domes and cones are the most common shapes to be formed. Unlike metal spinning (Chapter 1.7) there is no requirement that shapes be axisymmetric.

SIZE LIMITS

This process is best suited to large blanks. 40ft (12m) diameter domes have been manufactured with this process.

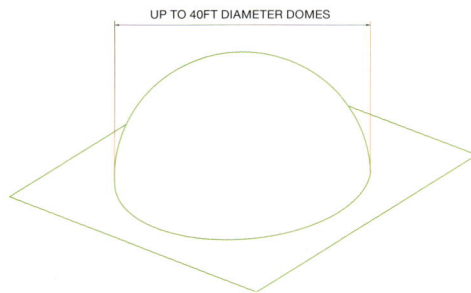

UP TO 40FT DIAMETER DOMES

SPRINGBACK

Springback is limited with this process, and may range from 0.5 to 2.5%. The amount of springback can be reduced if the draw depth is increased, or the amount of explosive increased as the standoff distance is decreased.[6]

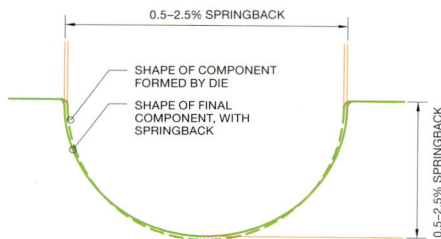

0.5–2.5% SPRINGBACK

SHAPE OF COMPONENT
FORMED BY DIE

SHAPE OF FINAL
COMPONENT, WITH
SPRINGBACK

0.5–2.5% SPRINGBACK

SURFACE TEXTURE

Fine surface designs and textures are very easy to create with this process. Generally, smooth contours are preferred, as sharp corners are susceptible to tearing.

TOLERANCES

Tolerances can range from 0.01 to 0.04in (0.025–1mm), depending on the size of the component and the mold medium.

TOOLING COSTS

Tooling costs are generally low with this process, but can be high if a large number of units are required.

TOOLING COMPLEXITY

Tools are simple and have no active or moving parts.

UNDERCUTS

Undercuts as they relate to the component's orientation are permissible, as long as their surface is accessible by the force of the explosion and the die can be taken apart for removal. For example, undercuts in a tube explosion are possible if using a line explosive. Undercuts that block the explosive force are not permissible.

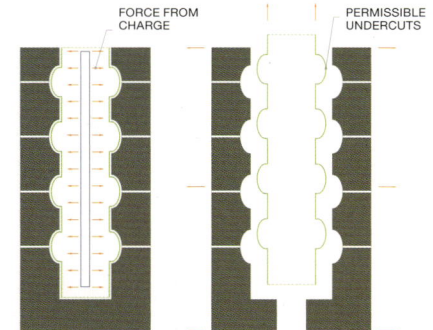

FORCE FROM
CHARGE

PERMISSIBLE
UNDERCUTS

VENTS

Vents should be located centrally, to let the air escape as the metal is being deformed. Unless the blank is very thin, it is unlikely that the vents will leave a mark on the component.

WALL THICKNESS

Material thicknesses are up to 2.25in (60mm).

Explosive forming produces components with relatively uniform wall thicknesses, depending on the draw depth. Wall thicknesses tend to be thinner nearer to the explosion. For example, when explosive forming a dome shape, the top of the dome—which had been the center of the blank—will be thinner than the edges. The manufacturer can use a plug cushion to reduce thinning of the wall.

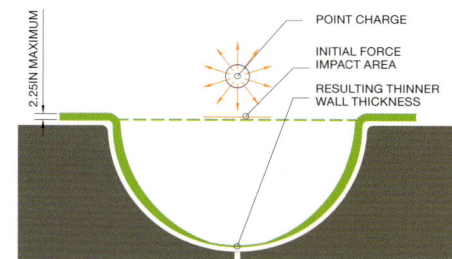

2.25IN MAXIMUM

POINT CHARGE

INITIAL FORCE
IMPACT AREA

RESULTING THINNER
WALL THICKNESS

EXPLOSIVE FORMING: METAL

EXTERIOR METAL PANELS AND ARTIST WORK | DE GRIJZE GENERAAL (THE GRAY GENERAL)
IAA Architecten with Hieke Luik
Eindhoven, the Netherlands

De Grijze Generaal, or the Gray General, completed in 2008, is a modern senior living facility, providing over 150 residential units and a variety of amenities, including a fitness center, community center, roof garden, public library, coffee house, public parking, and teaching restaurant. **[10, 11, 12]** This IAA Architecten project is the second phase of a larger masterplan and is designed to be the social link for the neighborhood.[7] The building is located just north of Eindhoven city center. It is at the corner of two four-lane divided streets, and located across from a shopping mall and a hospital.

IAA designed the building to be clad with an aluminum panels, painted in four different shades of green. **[13, 14]** Harry Abels, director at IAA, worked with the project's client, Wooninc., to include the work by Dutch artist Hieke Luik on De Grizje Generaal's main north façade. Luik works in both two and three dimensions and uses a variety of media, including watercolor, metal, and wax. IAA and Luik had collaborated previously on an apartment building.[8] According to Abels, Luik's work looks like ornament and is suited to architectural application.[9]

Luik titled her project *Swimmers*, and her inspiration for the piece came from IAA's comment that the building form was similar to a walrus. There are 106 decorated panels on the building, all made from the same mold. Most of the panels are oriented in the same direction, with only a handful rotated 180°. The relief dimensions are all the same, but the overall panel dimensions were set by the architect to fit the building elevation. 3D-Metal Forming, part of Van Campen Industries, did the explosive forming and worked directly with Luik to develop the panels.

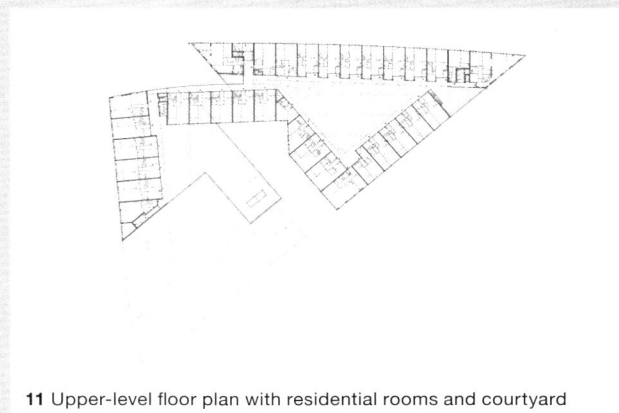
11 Upper-level floor plan with residential rooms and courtyard

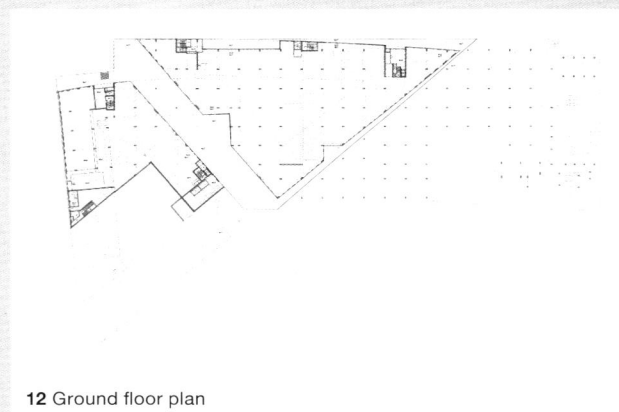
12 Ground floor plan

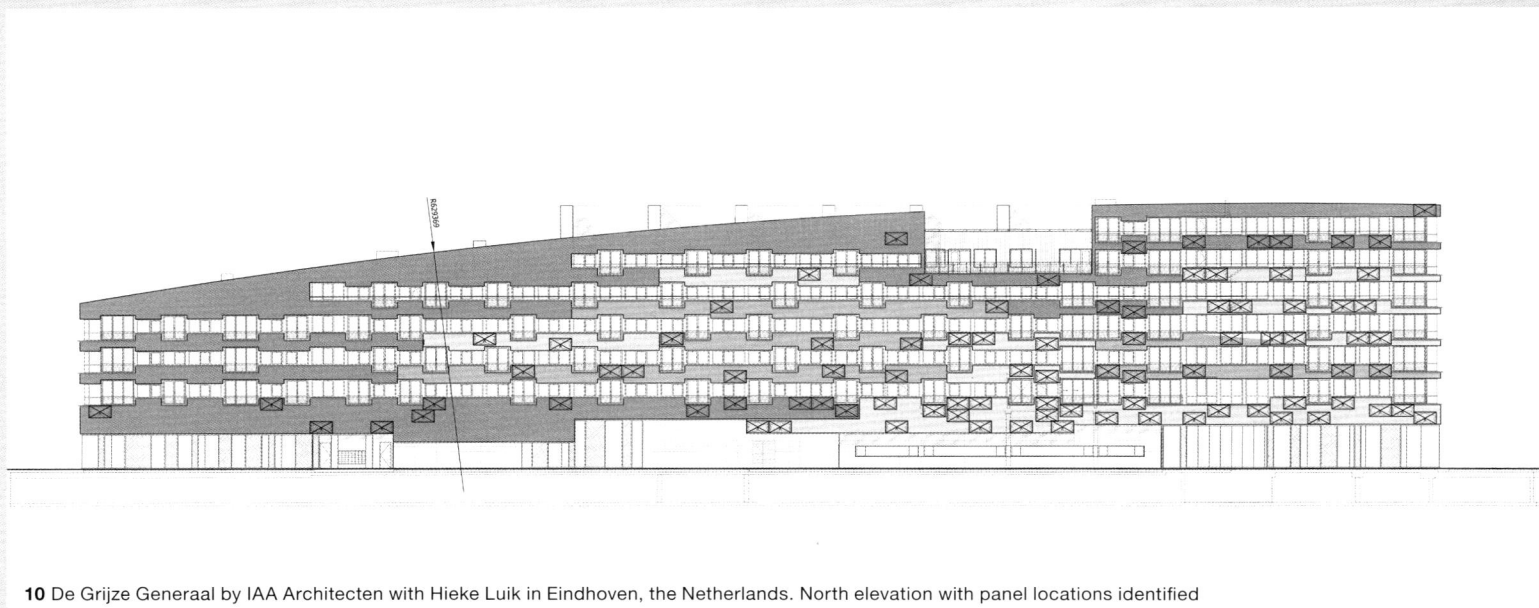
10 De Grijze Generaal by IAA Architecten with Hieke Luik in Eindhoven, the Netherlands. North elevation with panel locations identified

DESIGN CONSIDERATIONS

According to Abels, there is a history of architects and artists collaborating on building design, and he is seeing a resurgence of this tradition. Abels himself has a close relationship with artists. His mother was an artist, and Luik is an old family friend. It was happenstance that Abels had samples of Luik's work in his car when he met with the building client for De Grijze Generaal. After seeing Luik's watercolors, the client became interested in commissioning her for this project.

Luik produced a full-scale model for *Swimmers* out of three-dimensionally formed wax on a flat sheet of plywood. [15] It was painted white, splattered with black ink, and photographed from different angles. [16] Photogrammetry software analyzed the photographs in order to create a three-dimensional digital surface. 3D-Metal Forming used the digital file to predict how the aluminum would behave during the explosive forming process. Luik's original model design then had to be smoothed out, because the digital model predicted that the material would tear during forming. As a result, the draw depth was lessened and the corners rounded in order to ensure proper forming.

MANUFACTURING CONSIDERATIONS

Because the shape was digitally changed from Luik's initial physical model, the artist wanted to evaluate the quality of the final piece, and 3D-Metal Forming did not want to commit to fabricating the tool until the design was approved. Luik worked with 3D-Metal Forming to produce a smaller sculpture equivalent to *Swimmers*. The equivalent piece was made, scanned, and analyzed as the original. It was then explosive formed and analyzed again.[10] Once approved, the tooling for *Swimmers* was CNC milled from solid steel.

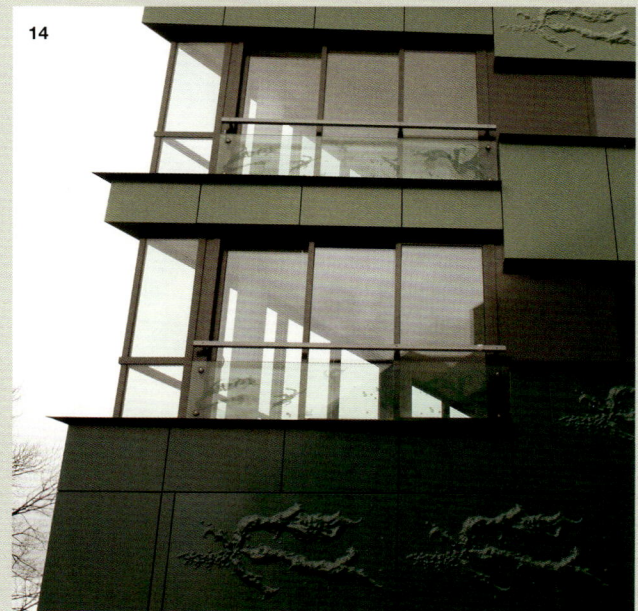

13
Photograph of north elevation

14
A close-up image of *Swimmers* by Hieke Luik on De Grijze Generaal

15 An image of Luik's studio with her a variety of her work. A watercolor of *Swimmers* can be seen on the back wall

16 The pattern was painted white, splattered with black ink, and photographed from different angles. Photogrammetry software created a 3D digital surface from the photographs

It took several months for 3D-Metal Forming to produce all of the decorated panels. Luik remembered that most of the time was spent preparing for production, rather than producing the panels themselves. The preparations must have been worth it, because in the end, Luik did not remember any panels being rejected.

OTHER CONSIDERATIONS

The project was completed in 2008, and there has been some difficulty with the panels since. **[17]** All of De Grijze Generaal's metal panels were painted, including the flat panels and the explosively formed *Swimmers*. The explosively formed panels were painted by a method and in a facility different from what was used for the flat panels. Unfortunately the paint on the *Swimmers* panels was not correctly applied, and blisters have formed. According to Abels, this is not due to 3D-Metal Forming's technique, but rather to mishandling of the paint and too much humidity when the *Swimmers* were painted.

LESSONS LEARNED

Although not a specific lesson learned as stated by Luik or Abels, I think it important to note with this case study that explosive forming requires physical isolation and additional safety precautions because of the use of explosives. Luik remembered 3D-Metal Forming doing its explosive work on a military base; although she asked, she was not permitted to see the panels being formed. In the end, it was not clear to either Luik or Abels how the manufacturing actually happened. This in turn can create distance between manufacturing and design.

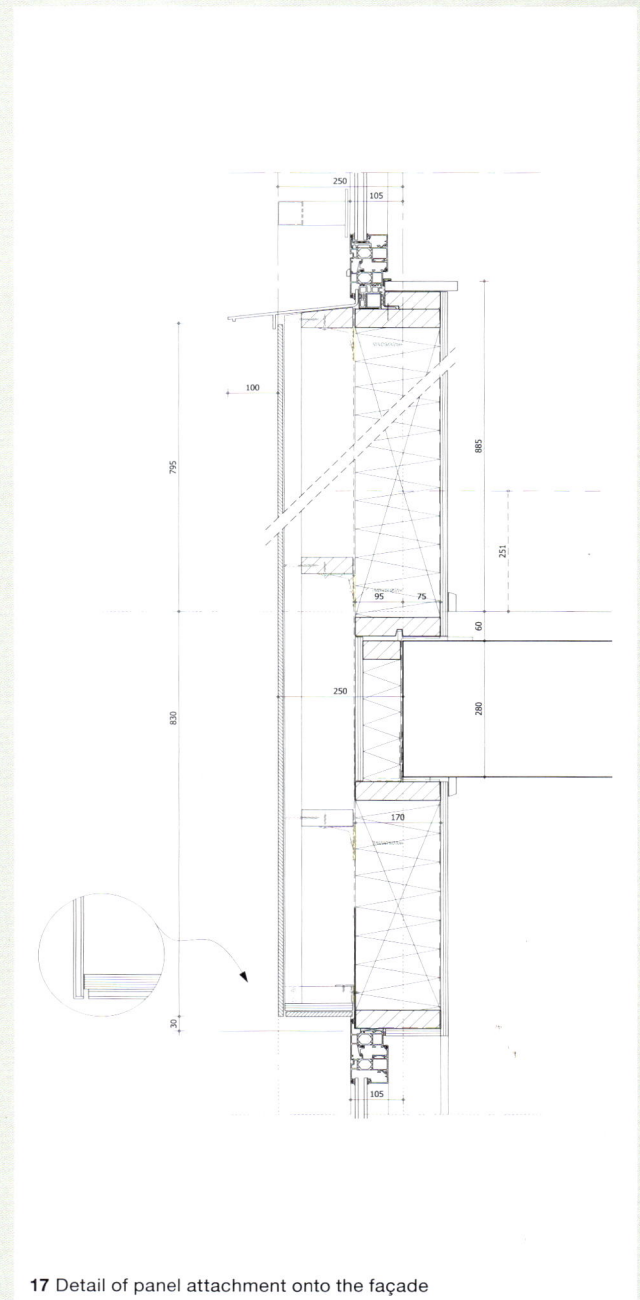

17 Detail of panel attachment onto the façade

1.4 Bending Plies
aka curving plywood, pressing plywood

INTRODUCTION

Bending plywood is a manufacturing process that presses thin, malleable cellulose-based sheets and adhesive into a shape and holds them until the adhesive sets, or cures. [1] Once the adhesive has set, the bent sheets are held in place relative to one another, retaining the shape of the mold. The shapes that can be made with bending are typically single curves, although a slight double curve with a more substantial single curve can be achieved.[1] Surface quality is very good with this process, although tolerances are difficult to maintain. Sizes range from small, hand-held pieces to large units that fit on a truck bed. This chapter includes wood veneers and post-formable plywood, but this manufacturing process can also be used to bend other laminates of cellulose-based

media—such as thin paper, chipboard, or medium-density fiberboard (MDF).

In bending plywood, a layer of adhesive is applied to thin wood sheets. The adhesive must cover the full face of each sheet and may be applied with by hand, machine roller, or with a glue curtain. [2] The wood sheets with adhesive are then stacked into what is called a layup, and the top and bottom sheets of the layup are cleaned to remove debris. Optional Mylar sheets, or polyester film, may be added on the top and bottom of the layup to keep these surfaces clean. The layup is then placed into a mold and pressure is applied evenly and consistently until the adhesive cures. After the adhesive has set, the pressure is released and the

1 A layup of wood veneers, before and after pressing

2 Adhesive applied to wood veneers by machine roller

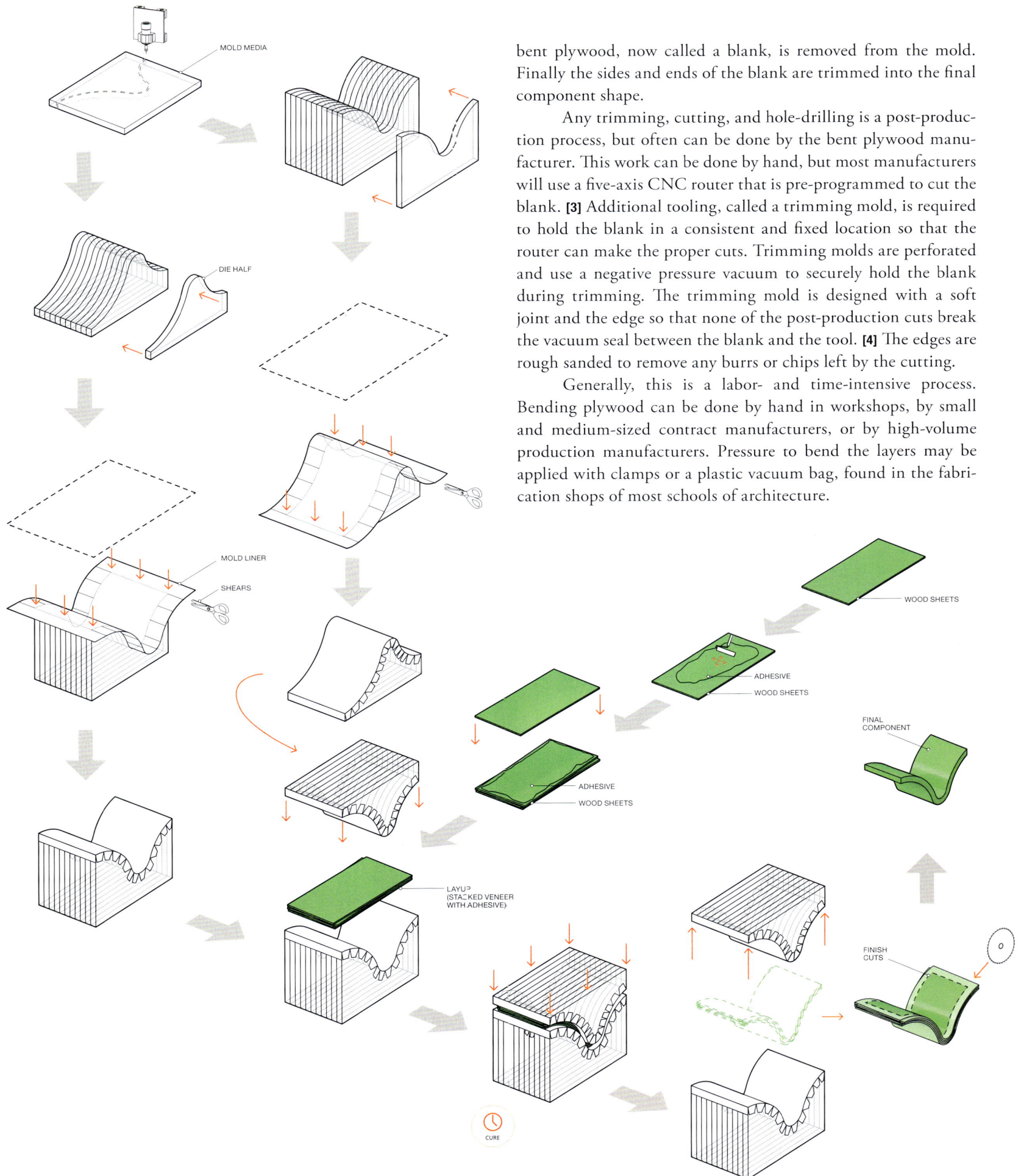

MOLD MEDIA

DIE HALF

MOLD LINER

SHEARS

WOOD SHEETS

ADHESIVE
WOOD SHEETS

ADHESIVE
WOOD SHEETS

FINAL
COMPONENT

LAYUP
(STACKED VENEER
WITH ADHESIVE)

FINISH
CUTS

CURE

bent plywood, now called a blank, is removed from the mold. Finally the sides and ends of the blank are trimmed into the final component shape.

Any trimming, cutting, and hole-drilling is a post-production process, but often can be done by the bent plywood manufacturer. This work can be done by hand, but most manufacturers will use a five-axis CNC router that is pre-programmed to cut the blank. [3] Additional tooling, called a trimming mold, is required to hold the blank in a consistent and fixed location so that the router can make the proper cuts. Trimming molds are perforated and use a negative pressure vacuum to securely hold the blank during trimming. The trimming mold is designed with a soft joint and the edge so that none of the post-production cuts break the vacuum seal between the blank and the tool. [4] The edges are rough sanded to remove any burrs or chips left by the cutting.

Generally, this is a labor- and time-intensive process. Bending plywood can be done by hand in workshops, by small and medium-sized contract manufacturers, or by high-volume production manufacturers. Pressure to bend the layers may be applied with clamps or a plastic vacuum bag, found in the fabrication shops of most schools of architecture.

In contract manufacturing, cycle times are shorter than in a fabrication shop, and a hydraulic ram is used to provide the pressure required for bending. Workers manually move the layup to the press, and for most average-sized bent plywood components this requires two people. Placing the veneer stacks on the mold before pressing is not an exact science, and is typically done by eye. Additionally, the operator can then make adjustments as the press pushes on the laminates. This is particularly useful for deep draws. Contract manufacturers also use manual labor to move the blanks from the press to the CNC router for trimming. In high-volume manufacturing, much more of this process may be mechanized, where robots are used to move the layups and the blanks to the next station. Typically, high-volume manufacturers are producing particular products and are unable to accommodate small or mid-sized production runs.

BUILDING PRODUCTS

Creating bent plywood for commercially available building products is less common than using straight or flat laminated products, such as plywood or laminated veneer lumbers (LVLs). There are a number of flexible plywood products commercially available; these include Dukta, Wacky Woods, and FlexPly. These products can be used to create bent plywood, but unless part of a glue-laminated assembly, they are not stable on their own. Historically, bent plywood has been used to form boats and airplanes, thanks to its thinness, strength-to-weight ratio, stiffness, and ability to be formed. Further research and development by architectural designers Charles and Ray Eames made bent and molded plywood suitable for high-volume productions, such as medical equipment and furniture.

TOOLING

Generally, there are two sets of tooling required for bending plywood. [5] There is the mold, which gives the shape to the component; and there is the optional trim die, which holds the blank for CNC trimming and drilling. The pressures required to manufacture bent plywood are low, ranging from 30 to 65lb/in² (5.4–11.7km/cm²); therefore molds can be made from a range of materials, including foam, chipboard, corrugated cardboard, plywood, plaster, and metal. Typically, the cost of the mold, its durability, and its potential production run are directly related. For example, corrugated cardboard molds are very inexpensive, but are damaged easily and are best for small production runs. Most contract manufacturers will make their molds from 0.75in (19mm) solid, laminated plywood.

3 Five-axis CNC machine, doing all post-production trimming, routing, and drilling

4 Trim die with soft edge for vacuum seal

5 A bent plywood manufacturer's collection of molds

Molds can be open or closed. Open, or one-sided, molds can be used with vacuum bags or clamps if the curve is slight, and an even pressure can be applied to all surfaces. If using a vacuum bag, a male mold is preferable to a female mold, as the bag can contact all surfaces with a male mold. If molding on a female mold, making a tight curve, or a deep draw, then a plug may be needed. [6] (A plug is a partial mold that can be used to place pressure on a part of the component that the bag cannot reach.) Closed molds are often used for hydraulic presses or to help the vacuum bag apply even pressure on the component's surface. Closed molds should be made so that the curves between the two halves are offset to account for the thickness of the laminates and adhesive. [7]

Molds are made bigger than the component. This allows for some adjustment of the laminate as pressure is applied, and leaves enough room so that the blank's edges can be trimmed as needed. Typically, the mold curves are tighter than the final component, as the plywood springs back when it is removed from the mold. If dimensions are critical, the mold should be designed by experienced mold makers, as they will be able to predict the material's movements and make the necessary allowances.[2]

In addition to the range of tooling media, there is a range of different constructions. First, molds may be solid: constructed of CNC-milled plywood that is laminated together. If heat induction or radio waves are used to cure the adhesive, aluminum sheets may be added to the mold surface for conduction. [8] Second, molds can also be made from a frame or closely spaced ribs, with a stiff skin such as 0.25in (6mm) Masonite or other thin bendable plywoods. Finally, a manufacturer may use jigs instead of molds. Jigs are a series of adjustable pieces that can be moved along a track to make any curve desired. Jigs are particularly useful when the width of wood laminate is narrow compared to its length.

ENVIRONMENTAL IMPACT

Little energy is used in this forming process. Equipment is typically small, as pressures are typically low so as to not damage the cell structure of the wood. Manufacturing waste is generally low. Tooling can be made from a variety of renewable materials such as cardboard and plywood. The material plies are made from wood or cellulose-based products, which have low carbon footprints and are renewable. Adhesives such as urea formaldehyde will give off volatile organic compounds (VOCs), affecting indoor air quality.

7 With closed molds, the offset between the mold halves should be determined by the thickness of the laminates. For storing molds, this manufacturer keeps a laminate between the mold halves to reduce warping

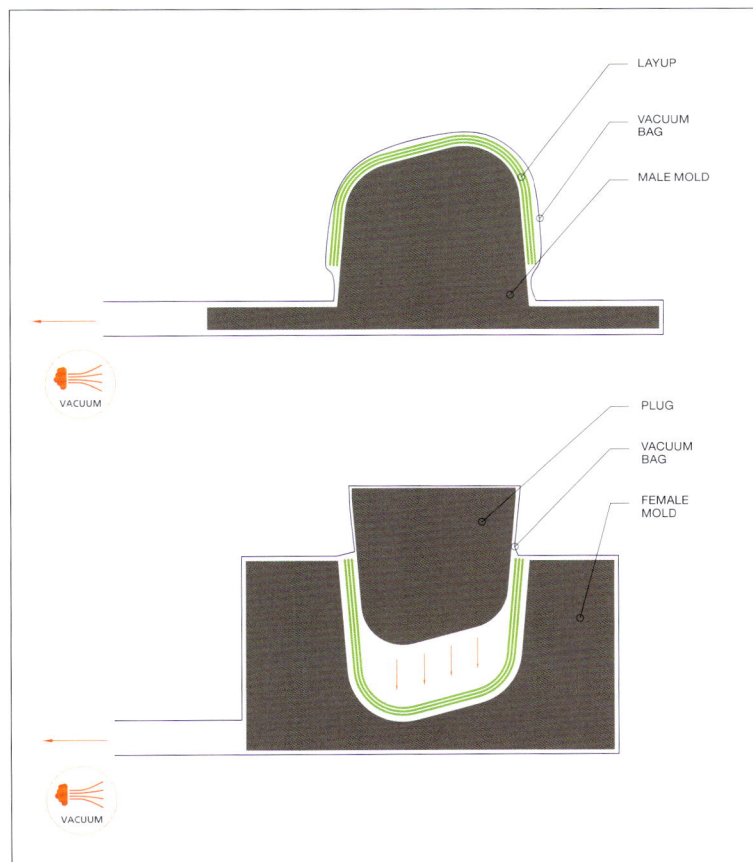

6 A plug can be used for deep draws or tight curves, where a vacuum bag may not exert enough pressure

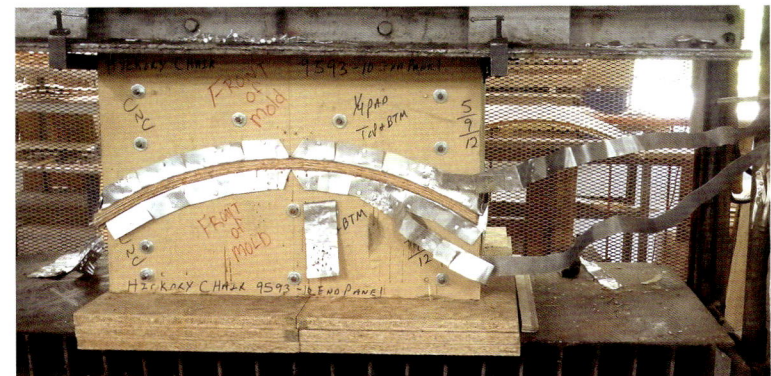

8 Aluminum strips transmit radio waves from the transmitter to the aluminum covering the mold surface

MATERIAL CONSIDERATIONS + DESIGN PARAMETERS

Bent plywood is a composite material, one in which the adhesive and the veneers work together.[3] The specific adhesive used depends on the required strength, tightness of curve, exposure to moisture, and desired cycle times. If manufactured by a craftsperson, white or yellow wood glues may be used; however, cycle times are long and creep may be an issue for tight curves. For components that are exposed to moisture or have tight curves, urea formaldehyde glue is best, although difficult to work with. Most contract manufacturers will use synthetic resins that are activated by heat induction or radio waves, and pressure. Generally, heat induction has a longer cycle time than radio frequency, but is better suited for complex parts, as it is more precise and results in less distortion.[4] After the blank is removed from the press it cools, and the adhesive continues to cure.

This chapter focuses on two different ply media—wood sheets and post-formable plywood. Wood sheets include individual sheets of wood veneers, thin plywood sheets, or bendy plywoods (e.g. Wacky Woods). With these, the wood sheets are laminated together with a wet adhesive, and are placed in the press until the adhesive cures. Post-formable plywood is a proprietary plywood that uses temperature change to loosen and set the adhesive between the layers of wood.

WOOD SHEETS

Typical wood veneers for bending plywood are Douglas fir, maple, or birch, but they can include any wood species, bendable plywood (less than 0.12in/3mm thick), or bendy plywood. If the design allows, most manufacturers will use inexpensive woods (e.g. fir or birch) or plywoods for the inner plies, while reserving the more expensive or decorative wood veneers (e.g. quartersawn mahogany or lacewood) for the face veneers. The inner layers can be in any thickness, as long as they can form the desired curve. The face veneers should be sanded prior to pressing, reducing the need for post-production sanding, which can be difficult on the curved surfaces of the bent plywood.

Wood veneers are cut thin enough for the desired curve and allowable springback, but thick enough to reduce labor costs and set-up time. Typically, the wood sheets are laminated dry, as the adhesive's moisture is enough to soften them for a little more flexibility. If the desired curve is too great or the wood sheets too thick, the sheets may be steamed or soaked in water for added flexibility. This should be avoided, though, because added moisture can thin the glue and cause delamination with some adhesives.

In layups with wood veneers, the grain direction of the wood plies may be laid parallel or perpendicular to one another. If the plies' grains are parallel, then the bent plywood is called a lamination. It will act in a similar way to solid wood, expanding and contracting along the grain width with changes in moisture. If the plies' grains are perpendicular, the bent plywood is called veneering.[5] In veneering, the changing grain direction of the plies provides stability in changing moisture conditions.

CURVE RADII

The minimum curve radius for contract manufacturers using a hydraulic press is 2in (50mm). The curve radius depends on the thickness of the veneers, the applied pressure, the moisture content of the wood, and the adhesive used. If made by a craftsperson in a workshop, you should expect a 4in (100mm) minimum radius.

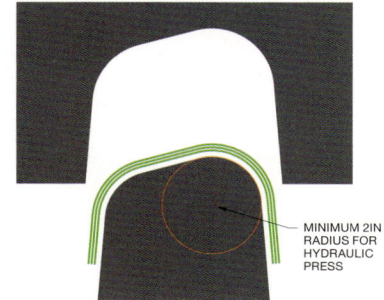

MINIMUM 2IN RADIUS FOR HYDRAULIC PRESS

DRAFT ANGLES

If the bent plywood is flexible enough, draft angles are not required. If the bent plywood will be stiff, a draft angle of 3–5° is recommended.

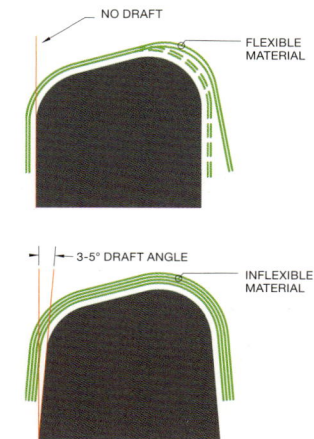

NO DRAFT

FLEXIBLE MATERIAL

3-5° DRAFT ANGLE

INFLEXIBLE MATERIAL

DRAW DEPTH

There is no limit to the draw depth to this process, as the plies can be placed as needed, even vertically, into the tooling.

PLIES PLACED IN LAYUP AS NEEDED TO MEET DEPTH

FINISH

The finish of the material depends on the finish of the face veneers rather than the mold surface. High-quality finishes should be done post-production.

INSERTS

Fastener inserts may be added between the plywood layers for the final component assemblies. Plies should be cut to hide insert flanges as necessary.

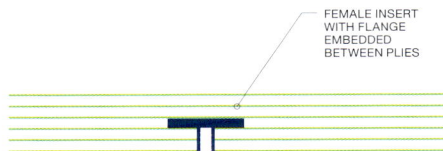

FEMALE INSERT WITH FLANGE EMBEDDED BETWEEN PLIES

JOINTS

Joints between wood plies within the layup must be offset from joints in the preceding and following layers. This will eliminate any material weakness at the joint.

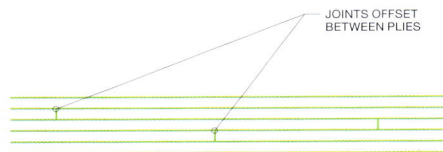

JOINTS OFFSET BETWEEN PLIES

PRODUCTION RUNS

Production run lengths will depend on the tooling media, the equipment, and the manufacturing facility. Workshops can produce prototypes and production runs of 2–50 units, with 2–25 being typical, using molds made from foam, cardboard, or plywood. Contract manufacturers can produce prototypes and production runs of up to 2,000 units.

PRODUCTION SPEED

Cycle times can be long. If manufactured in workshops, the time in the press may range from 4 to 12 hours, depending on the size of the piece, the number of plies, and the adhesive used. In contract manufacturing technologies such as heat induction or radio waves are used to speed up the adhesive curing; cycle times are typically under 20 minutes per layup. Post-production CNC trimming may take an additional 3–10 minutes per piece, depending on the cutting path.

SHRINKING

Unless moisture is added to the plies prior to bending, there is very little shrinking with this process.

SIZE LIMITS

There are almost no size limits when bending plywood. Boats, airplanes, and furniture have all been manufactured by bending or molding plywood. The component size will be limited by handling and the available equipment, such as the size limits of the hydraulic press.

SPRINGBACK

Springback of 0.06–0.12in (1.5–3mm) is normal in bending plywood, as the layers try to straighten against the curve. The amount of springback will depend on the thickness of the laminate, the type of plies, the amount of curve, and the type of glue. For example, yellow wood glue typically has more springback than urea glue. Generally, the thinner the laminates and the more plies, the less springback.

SPRINGBACK FROM MOLDED SHAPE

To counter springback, manufacturers will bend the plywood slightly tighter than desired, so that with springback the component will still meet design specifications.

TOLERANCES

Shape and curvature tolerances may be difficult to predict as a result of springback. If tolerances are an issue, prototypes should be made to predict the springback, or thinner veneers can be used. With CNC post-production trimming, tight dimensional tolerances can be maintained.

TOOL COMPLEXITY

Tools are simple, almost rudimentary. Tools can be fabricated by CNC mills, routers, wire cutters, or by hand.

TOOLING COSTS

Tooling costs for this process are quite low. A large, single-bend, closed, wood mold suitable for mid-volume production runs can range from $1,000 to $5,000.

UNDERCUTS

Typically when manufacturing, undercuts are not permissible as an undercut will keep a full mold from closing are a vacuum bag from applying ample pressure. For making prototypes with clamps or jigs, an undercut is permissible.

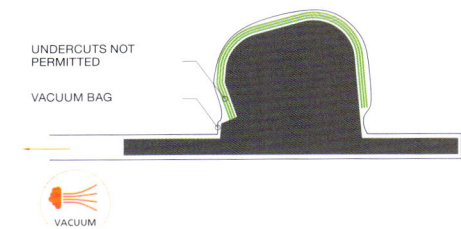

UNDERCUTS NOT PERMITTED

VACUUM BAG

VACUUM

VENTS

Vents are not required, as the press moves slowly and air can escape out of the sides of the mold.

WALL THICKNESS

Wall thicknesses typically vary from 0.12 to 1in (3–25mm).

Typically, the wall thickness needs to be consistent for the entire component. If not, then the layers of wood sheets and adhesive will be visible and will negatively affect the component's finish face. If the layers are custom cut, then they can be cut into a tapered angle. This creates a layup with a varying thickness. This technique is much more expensive, and likely will only be done by highly skilled craftspeople.

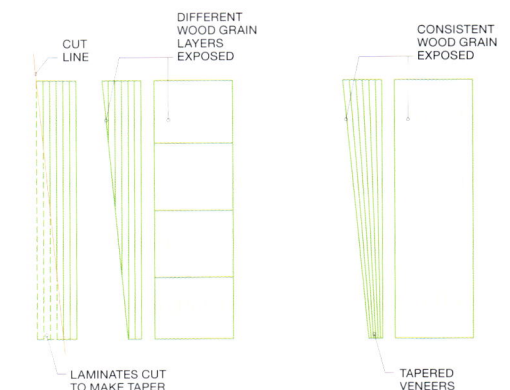

CUT LINE

DIFFERENT WOOD GRAIN LAYERS EXPOSED

CONSISTENT WOOD GRAIN EXPOSED

LAMINATES CUT TO MAKE TAPER

TAPERED VENEERS

BENDING PLIES: WOOD SHEETS

CURVED STRUCTURE | EDUCATION PAVILION AT LINCOLN PARK ZOO
Studio Gang
Chicago, Illinois

The Education Pavilion, completed in 2010, is located on the South Pond in Chicago's Lincoln Park. The pavilion is part of Studio Gang's Nature Boardwalk, a large landscape and natural infrastructure project that improves the city's hydrology, reduces drinking water waste, and provides urban residents with access to natural environments. [9] The Education Pavilion was commissioned by Lincoln Park Zoo, and serves as an outdoor, open-air classroom. The pavilion is approximately 40ft (12m) long and 16ft (5m) high.

Studio Gang designed the pavilion with a limited palette of materials: concrete for the pavilion foundation and slab, metal for the connections, fiberglass for the contact-molded fiberglass shells, and custom-manufactured, cross-laminated timbers (CLTs). The cross-laminated members are the pavilion's primary above-ground structure, and the fiberglass shells provide some protection from the weather. Studio Gang's use of wood for the structure keeps the pavilion's carbon footprint low and is in keeping with the spirit of the Nature

9
Boardwalk approach to the Education Pavilion by Studio Gang in Chicago

10
Pavilion design diagrams, illustrating the manufacturing process for the laminated wood structure

Boardwalk. The shape of the wood structure makes further connections with natural forms, as the firm looked toward structures such as milkweed pods and tortoiseshell patterns to develop the form.

All wood members have the same shape, and had two separate molding steps to make the complex curve. **[10]** The first step bent the plies to form the overall pavilion arch. In this bend, 0.75in (19mm) Douglas fir strips were laminated together to make a 15ft 3in (4.65m) radius curve. After the adhesive cured from the first bend, the curved beam was sliced into 0.25in (6mm) thick strips to accommodate a tighter bend than the first. Then the strips were laminated into a 2ft 7in (0.79m) radius curve. The final dimensions of the wood member cross-section is 3in × 15in (75mm × 380mm), with a narrower section at the ends and in the middle to accommodate a steel connecting plate.

RLD Company won the competitive bid to make the bent CLT structure, and it subcontracted the manufacturing to Shelton Lam & Deck. Both companies are located in Washington state, a region of the United States where Douglas fir is plentiful and bending plies are often used. Douglas fir was chosen for its natural decay resistance, straight grain, and its strength-to-self-weight ratio, as well as its availability. A light stain was added to the wood for further protection from weather. The stain is to be reapplied every few years and is detailed in the building's maintenance plan.

DESIGN CONSIDERATIONS

According to Todd Zima, design principal at Studio Gang, during the beginning of the design phase, the team investigated different structural systems and materials, including space-frames in steel.[6] They were interested in a material and system that could be shaped to make openings, for air-flow and views. When they moved toward wood, the design team researched different traditions of woodworking, including coopering, weaving, carving, and boat building. The material and studies into the possible shaping methods were studied simultaneously during design. **[11]** For Jeanne Gang, the material cannot be separated from how it can be shaped. In her writings about her work, she has stated that "construction materials have unique physical characteristics that are under-explored or have yet to be discovered, making it possible and exciting to work with them as generative forces for a project, rather than relying on form or imagery as a starting point."[7]

Studio Gang contacted Magnusson Klemencic Associates (MKA), a structural engineering firm, to help develop the design further. MKA has its headquarters in Seattle (with additional offices in Chicago and Shanghai, China) and has experience in designing laminated wood structures. MKA solicited Structurlam Products LP, a CLT manufacturer in British Columbia, Canada for research support. Structurlam provided information about materials and shaping capabilities for bending Douglas fir, and created prototypes for testing and design evaluations. Using the same shape for all of the wood members reduced manufacturing and testing costs, and lessened engineering fees.

Work by MKA and Structurlam re-informed the design of the components and the building. Originally, Studio Gang designed the pavilion with seven bays, but the torsional stress on the wood members was too high. To

10

1. THE FIRST LAMINATION

0.75IN PLY DOUGLAS FIR
5.5IN   0.75 IN

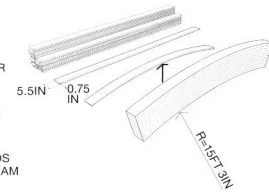

BOW IN THE WEAK AXIS

LAMINATE BENT BOARDS INTO A SINGLE BOW-BEAM

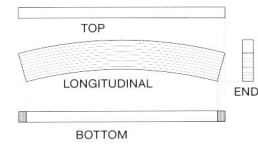

R=15FT 3IN

THIS IS THE RESULTANT STOCK FIRST LAMINATION BEAM.

TOP
LONGITUDINAL
END
BOTTOM

2. SLICE LONGITUDINALLY

STEP 1 BEAM...

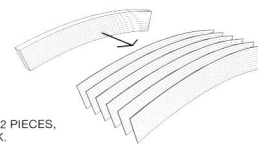

...IS SLICED INTO 12 PIECES, EACH 0.25IN THICK.

THIS CREATES STRONG THIN LAMINATES THAT CAN BE BENT IN THE WEAK AXIS FOR THE SECOND LAMINATION.

3. THE SECOND LAMINATION

STEP 2 SLICES ARE...

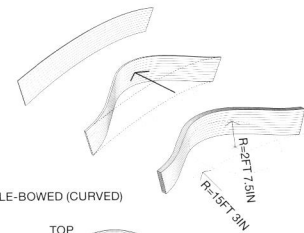

...BENT IN THE WEAK AXIS

AND LAMINATED INTO A DOUBLE-BOWED (CURVED) BEAM.

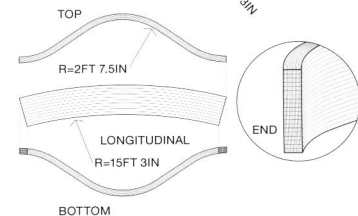

R=2FT 7.5IN
R=15FT 3IN

TOP
R=2FT 7.5IN
LONGITUDINAL
R=15FT 3IN
END
BOTTOM

THIS IS THE RESULTANT BASIC STRUCTURAL BEAM-UNIT.

4. CONSTRUCTION

THE BEAM IS MILLED

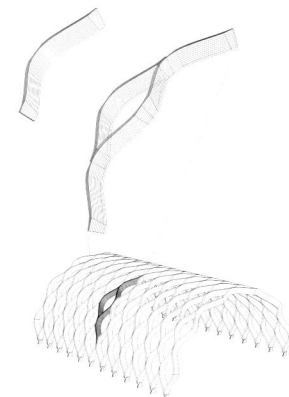

AND WHEN JOINED WITH OTHER IDENTICAL BEAMS CREATES THE BARREL VAULTED PAVILION STRUCTURE.

keep the members' cross-section to 3in x15in (75mm × 380mm), the number of bays was increased to twelve, while the overall building length remained the same. This reduced the bay width and the amount of curve required from the wood, in turn reducing the torsional stress on each member. The members are connected to one another so that the ends of one member are connected to the middle of an adjoining member. The connection between the members is simple and includes a custom-made metal splice plate and through bolts. Two people assembled the pavilion in just five days. **[21, 22, 23]**

MANUFACTURING CONSIDERATIONS]

With the design, each wood component has three different curves. **[12, 13, 14, 15]** The first curve is a 15ft 3in (4.65m) radius, formed by the overall pavilion's arch-shape. The second curve is the 2ft 7in (0.79m) radius to create the openings for the shells. The third curve was required at the end of each member to resolve the twist resulting from the first two curves. **[16]** In other words, the third curve is necessary so that the member ends and middle are flat relative to one another for the steel plate connectors. **[17]** The added complexity of three curves made the components more expensive and time-consuming to manufacture, as not all manufacturers have the capacity to make the three curves. **[18, 19]**

Both Structurlam and RLD bid for the project. Structurlam proposed using CNC equipment to carve the components into the third curve. This made its projected costs and lead times higher than those of RLD, and it lost the bid. In contrast, Shelton (through RLD) had the capacity to combine the second and third curves into one molding process; therefore it was able to make the component for the least cost.

Shelton used two custom-made steel molds to manufacture the component curves. After creating the bends, the company used post-production tools to hold the blanks for edge finishing with routers. **[20]** They also used tools to hold the blank while they pre-drilled holes for the connector plates. Shelton manufactured the components to a tight 0.03in (0.8mm) tolerance, necessary because of the number of bays and the number of connections that the pavilion required. Had the tolerance been larger, any discrepancies would quickly have added up along the building's length.

OTHER CONSIDERATIONS

First, since the components were laminated in two directions, published design values for glue-laminated structures could not be used. Regulatory agencies required proof that the structural members would perform as designed. The client paid the American Plywood Association (APA) to test prototypes made by Structurlam for shear, bending, and torsional allowable stresses. The resulting values were used in the pavilion's structural design.

Second, upkeep is an issue for this building. Although, the fiberglass shells help protect the wood from sun, rain, and snow, the wood components still require maintenance. As part of the project deliverables, Lincoln Park Zoo was issued with an owner's manual, which stated that the wood structure was to be resealed every two years. Because the pavilion is in a popular

11 Material studies of bending plywood done during initial design phases in Studio Gang's architectural office

12 Cut laminates after first bend at the manufacturer

13 Close-up of laminate after first bend

14 Using a hand roller to apply adhesive between laminates

18 Layup clamped to steel mold until adhesive cures

15 Placing layup on steel mold for complex bend

19 The second bend was able to bend the laminates in two directions, resolving the geometry in one manufacturing step

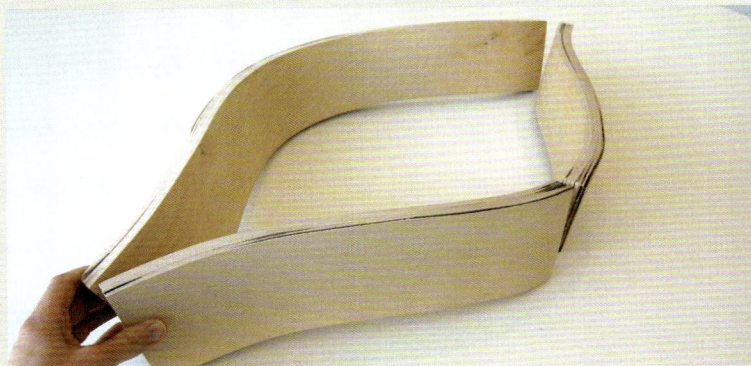

16 Pavilion design mock-up. During earlier iterations, the design team learned that a third curve was needed to resolve the geometry created by the other two curves

17 Testing to make sure that the steel connector plate between the components works

20 A post-production trim die to hold the component for edge finishing

21 Pavilion construction

22 Pavilion construction

city park, design team members often visit. **[24, 25, 26]** A few years after the project was completed, design team members noted that proper maintenance was not being performed, and contacted the client as a reminder. Shortly thereafter, the pavilion was resealed.

Third, this project required buy-in from a number of parties. MKA did a number of computer simulations to evaluate the structure and worked hard with Studio Gang to resolve some of the issues. Structurlam did initial research into the material, how it could be shaped, and how strong it could be. RLD and Shelton streamlined the manufacturing process to reduce costs. Finally, the client supported the design to build the pavilion with a unique manufacturing process, and paid for the necessary testing. This buy-in depended on trust between all parties, which may not be possible on every project.

LESSONS LEARNED

One of the lessons learned resulted from the public-bid process on this project. Typically, public projects require that construction contracts be awarded to the lowest bidder, as the intention is to avoid misuse of public funds; however, this can make collaboration between designer and contractors difficult. For this project, Studio Gang needed to consult with a manufacturer to understand the material and the manufacturing process to develop the design and for testing. Although Structurlam helped with the research and development of the bent wood structure, it did not submit the lowest bid. In the end, RLD won the bid and Structurlam was not paid for its efforts.

23 Hinge detail at the bottom of the plywood arches

24
Studio Gang's Nature Boardwalk project, with the Education Pavilion nestled on the left

25
Inside view of pavilion, looking at downtown Chicago

26
A transverse view through the pavilion

MATERIAL CONSIDERATIONS + DESIGN PARAMETERS

POST-FORMABLE PLYWOOD

Post-formable plywood is a flat, preformed plywood with alternating wood-grain veneers and a thermoplastic adhesive film between the plies. [27, 28, 29] It is a proprietary product by UPM, called Grada.[8] When Grada is heated to an internal temperature of 265°F (130°C), the thermoplastic adhesive becomes viscous, allowing the plies to slide past one another. The heated Grada is the placed onto a cool mold and bent into a simple curved shape. After Grada cools to 175°F (80°C), it holds its shape and can be removed from the mold. Heat can be applied to the entire layup for bending or can be focused on a local area for a partial bend. Because the adhesive is a thermoplastic, it does not contain any formaldehyde; therefore when the post-formable plywood reaches the end of its life, it can be recycled or safely burned.

This material eliminates much of the labor cost of applying liquid adhesive, stacking the layup, and transferring the layup to the mold. UPM promotes Grada as an alternative material for furniture making.[9] Grada comes in standard sheet sizes, and the sheets can be rough cut to the approximate component size before pressing. Grada cannot be stored at temperatures above 85°F (30°C) or with a relative humidity over 60%.

Currently, Grada uses birch veneers that are certified by the Forest Stewardship Council (FSC) or the Programme for the Endorsement of Forest Certification (PEFC), the international organization for sustainable forest management. According to the company's US patent application, the post-formable technology can work with all wood species and with wood products such as particle board, and hard- and medium-density fiberboard.[10]

The thickness of the adhesive layer will depend on the wood sheets used, and the desired properties of flexibility, strength, or stiffness. The adhesive reduces the hydrophilic nature of the wood in the plywood's plies, and the moisture take-up of Grada is only 50% of standard plywood. This makes Grada more dimensionally stable than standard plywood. Because the adhesive is a thermoplastic rather than a thermoset plastic, some creep will occur.

28 Bending test of Grada panel with three-dimensional curve in a cold press

27 Heating a Grada panel with a hot press for exact and even temperature

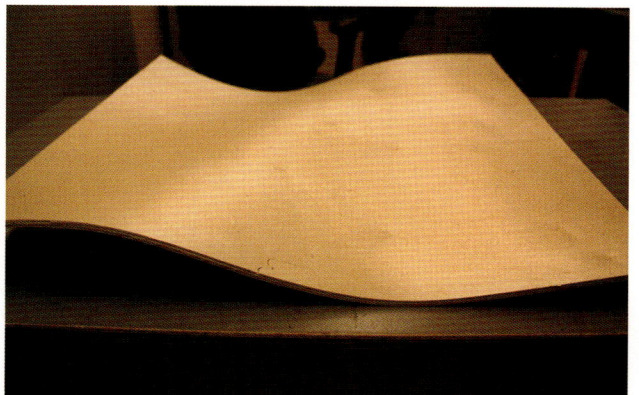

29 The resulting Grada component

POST-FORMABLE PLYWOOD

HEAT

COOL

FINISH CUTS

FINAL COMPONENT

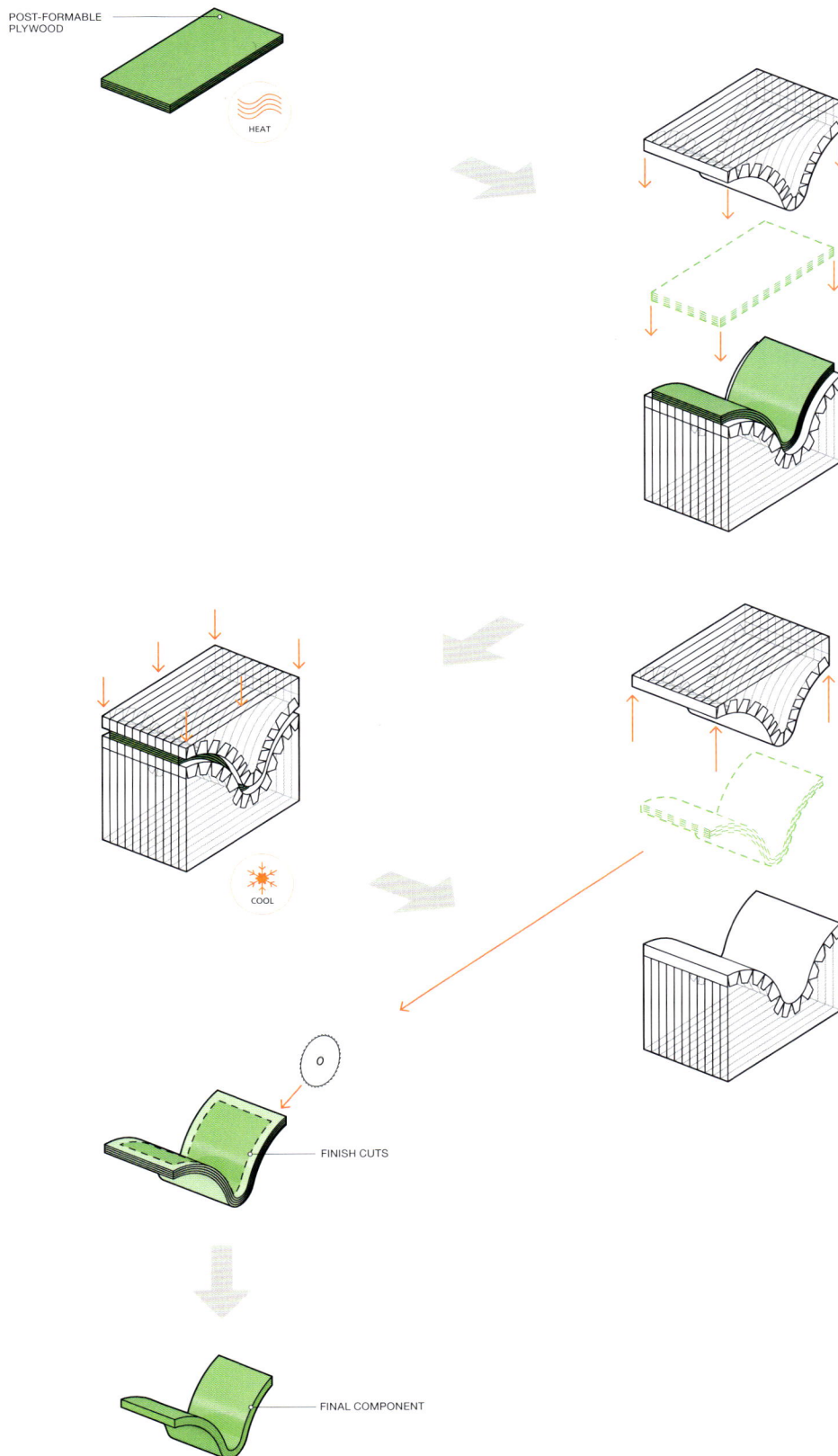

NOTE: Many of the design parameters listed for wood sheets also apply to post-formable plywood. The parameters listed below are only those that differ from the wood sheet parameters given on pages 72–73.

CURVE RADII

The minimum curve radius ranges from 1 to 2in (25–50mm), depending on thickness of the post-formable plywood.

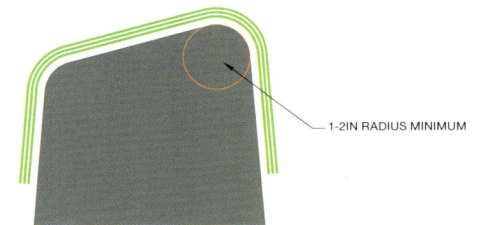

1-2IN RADIUS MINIMUM

INSERTS

Inserts cannot be added between the plywood's layers.

PRODUCTION SPEED

Production speed ranges from just over 2 minutes to 11 minutes, but depends on the thickness of the post-formable plywood. Heating times may range from 1.5 minutes for the narrowest panels to 7 minutes for the thickest panels. Similarly, cooling times range from 45 seconds to 4 minutes.

SIZE LIMITS

There are two standard panel sizes for UPM Grada: 50in × 100in (1250mm × 2500mm) and 60in × 120in (1500mm × 3000mm).

WALL THICKNESS

Grada is available in standard thicknesses of ³⁄₁₆in, ¼in, ⅜in, and ½in (4.5mm, 7mm, 10mm, and 13mm). Wall thickness cannot vary across the component, unless cut post-production.

BENDING PLIES: POST-FORMABLE PLYWOOD

STRUCTURAL SKIN | DRAGON SKIN PAVILION
Emmi Keskisarja and Pekka Tynkkynen (EDGE), and Kristof Crolla and Sebastien Delarange (LEAD)
Shenzhen Pavilion, Hong Kong, and Bi-City Biennale
of Urbanism/Architecture, Shenzhen, China

The Dragon Skin Pavilion was a temporary pavilion made for the 2012 Hong Kong and Shenzhen Bi-City Biennale of Urbanism/Architecture, and was located in the Shenzhen Pavilion of the Biennale. **[31, 32]** The Biennale occurs every two years, and architects apply to have projects accepted. It features architecture and art installations, and other exhibitors for the 2012 Biennale included Office for Metropolitan Architecture (OMA), Steven Holl, MVRDV, and Reiser + Umemoto. The pavilion's design was the result of a collaboration between Laboratory for Explorative Architecture & Design (LEAD), a young Hong Kong- and Antwerp-based architectural design and research practice founded by Belgian architect Kristof Crolla; and EDGE Research Lab at Tampere University of Technology (TUT). Founded in 2005, EDGE's goal is "to develop and dispose of funding for new research projects" for TUT.[11]

The collaboration between LEAD and EDGE was initiated by Emmi Keskisarja, a PhD candidate at TUT. Keskisarja was researching potential intersections between digital design, digital fabrication, and the Finnish wood industry.[12] As part of her work, Keskisarja invited Crolla to lead an eight-day architectural design workshop at TUT, titled "Material Design and Digital Fabrication." In this studio, students worked with Grada and parametric modeling software to design a structure from post-formable plywood.

31
Dragon Skin Pavilion by Emmi Keskisarja and Pekka Tynkkynen (EDGE), and Kristof Crolla and Sebastien Delarange (LEAD), located in Kowloon Park

32
Panels interlock with one another through slotted connections

30 Cutting figures for CNC milling. All 163 panels and their joint locations

31

32

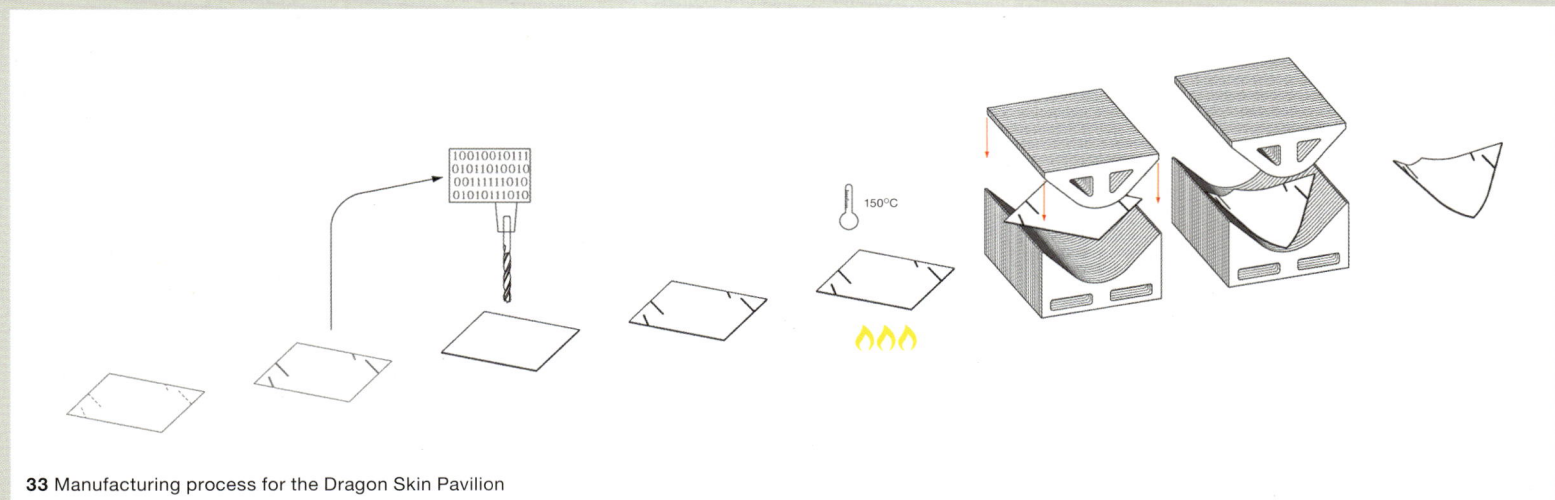

33 Manufacturing process for the Dragon Skin Pavilion

According to Keskisarja and Crolla, "The workshop version was quick and rough; in the end the structure did not stand, as it could not support its self-weight."[13] The group then had the opportunity to present at the Biennale, so they revised the prototype, optimizing the structure and components for the final version which became the Dragon Skin Pavilion.

The pavilion is made from 163 post-formable plywood components that measured approximately 2ft × 2ft (600mm × 600mm). **[30, 33]** Interlocking slots were used to connect all of the plywood components together without the use of glue or mechanical connectors. The slots are custom-located for each component and were cut with a CNC router prior to bending. All of the components were molded into the same shape. It is a single curve, placed diagonally across each square, resulting in two curved corners and two straight corners. The manufacturing of the components was done by students at the university workshop and shipped to the Biennale. The final pavilion measures 14ft 9in (4.5m) wide, 11ft 6in (3.5m) deep, and 8ft (2.5m) high, and took 6 hours to assemble on-site. **[34]**

DESIGN CONSIDERATIONS

The original TUT workshop led by Crolla investigated the integration of digital tools with physical materials. Through the workshops, participants made physical mock-ups with cardboard or other stand-in materials to understand fabrication operations. **[35]** From there, participants wrote parametric code (in Grasshopper or a similar program) for the digital design of the pavilion. The idea of the workshop was not to learn the specifics of coding, but instead to learn the logic that scripts use to generate design options. In the workshop, Crolla focused on participants understanding how their unskilled craftsmanship intersected with the precision of the digital world.

After the workshop, the design team made changes to the structure's design. First, the components were made smaller. Next, the pavilion's overall shape changed from a barrel vault to a parabolic shape, reducing its horizontal thrust and stabilizing the structure. Finally, the team relocated the slotted joints from the curved portion of the component to the flat portion. By moving the joint location, the connections between components were more consistently placed, lessening the movement between components.

34 A night view of the pavilion

35 An early cardboard prototype to test the logic of the components

36 An overview of production at the TUT shop

MANUFACTURING CONSIDERATIONS

All of the components were made at TUT and shipped to Hong Kong. **[36, 37, 38]** Unlike most of the other case studies in this book, the Dragon Skin Pavilion was self-manufactured. In other words, the designers were also responsible for making the components. This can be challenging, as the designers cannot necessarily learn from the makers. For Keskisarja, the greatest challenge was the amount of time it took to bend all of the Grada components. Each sheet was heated to the recommended temperature, pressed in the mold until it cooled, and then removed from the mold. Between two and four students molded all 163 components over three days.

OTHER CONSIDERATIONS

To make the curved forms, layers of post-formable plywood slid past one another during forming. Because the components' slotted joints were cut into the panels before forming, the plies slid past one another at the slots. Therefore the edges of the plies at the panels' slots and edges were not aligned. This reduced the bearing surface of the slots, reduced tolerances, and required looser joints for fitting. Moving the slots from the components' curved surface to the flat surface helped, but did not solve the problem. For the final design, slots were trimmed 0.08–0.12in (2–3mm) larger that the plywood's thickness to accommodate shift between the plies.

For Crolla, the project's biggest challenge was the on-site assembly. The structure was not self-supporting until all of the components were in place. The team attempted to use temporary supports during erection, but in the end depended on manual labor for support. According to the project video that documents the making of the pavilion, up to twelve people supported the structure during final assembly.[14] Once assembled, the pavilion was stable and was approved to be occupied by Biennale visitors.

The Dragon Skin Pavilion was placed in an unconditioned area of the Biennale, under a temporary structure made from bamboo and covered with a thin, translucent plastic sheet. The temperature inside the Biennale structure ranged from 68°F (20°C) to 86°F (30°C). Although the Pavilion was protected from rain, humidity levels inside the temporary structure were high. In the three months that the Pavilion was up, delamination between the plies had already occurred.

LESSONS LEARNED

This project was part of an academic investigation into a new material, digital modeling and fabrication methods, and working at full scale. In many ways the lessons learned on this project were similar to other architectural prototypes for an academic application. For Keskisarja, she learned the value of making prototypes and testing ideas during the early design phases. There were also lessons in the limitations of the computational tools relative to the actual material and the skilled labor. For Crolla, the project had an unintended lesson: the effect that the material had on the visitors. The light in the Pavilion's interior, reflected by the warmth of the wood, was something that was not predicted.

37 A step-by-step of the pressing process

38 The sliding of the veneers is visible on the plywood edges. It took between two and four students three days to mold all of the components

1.5 Stamping

INTRODUCTION

Stamping is a manufacturing process that uses a force combined with tooling to deform a sheet of metal. (For brevity, I refer to both pure metals and metal alloys as "metal.") [1] "Stamping" is a generic term that includes different processes, including blanking, punching, shearing, parting, drawing and deep drawing, bending, and forming. Blanking, punching, drawing, and deep drawing require expensive tooling or machinery and are associated with high-volume productions. Bending metal uses break presses to isolate metal deformation to a limited area and does not require customized tooling; instead the fabricator adjusts the sheets in the break press to make the custom component. In this

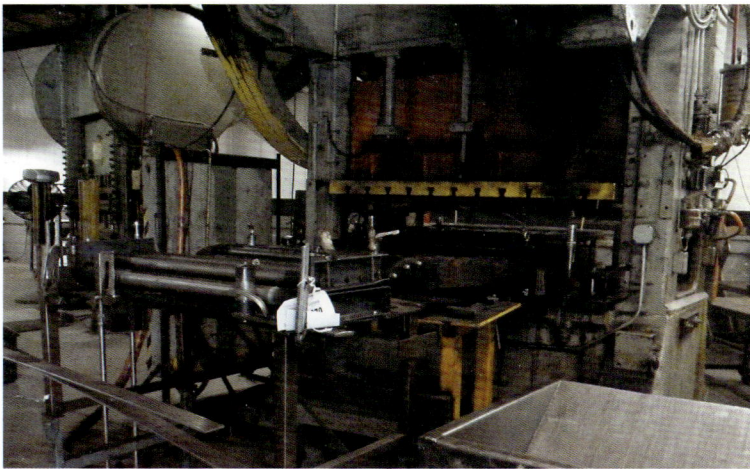

1 Large press for stamping metal

2 Mate die for large metal-stamping press

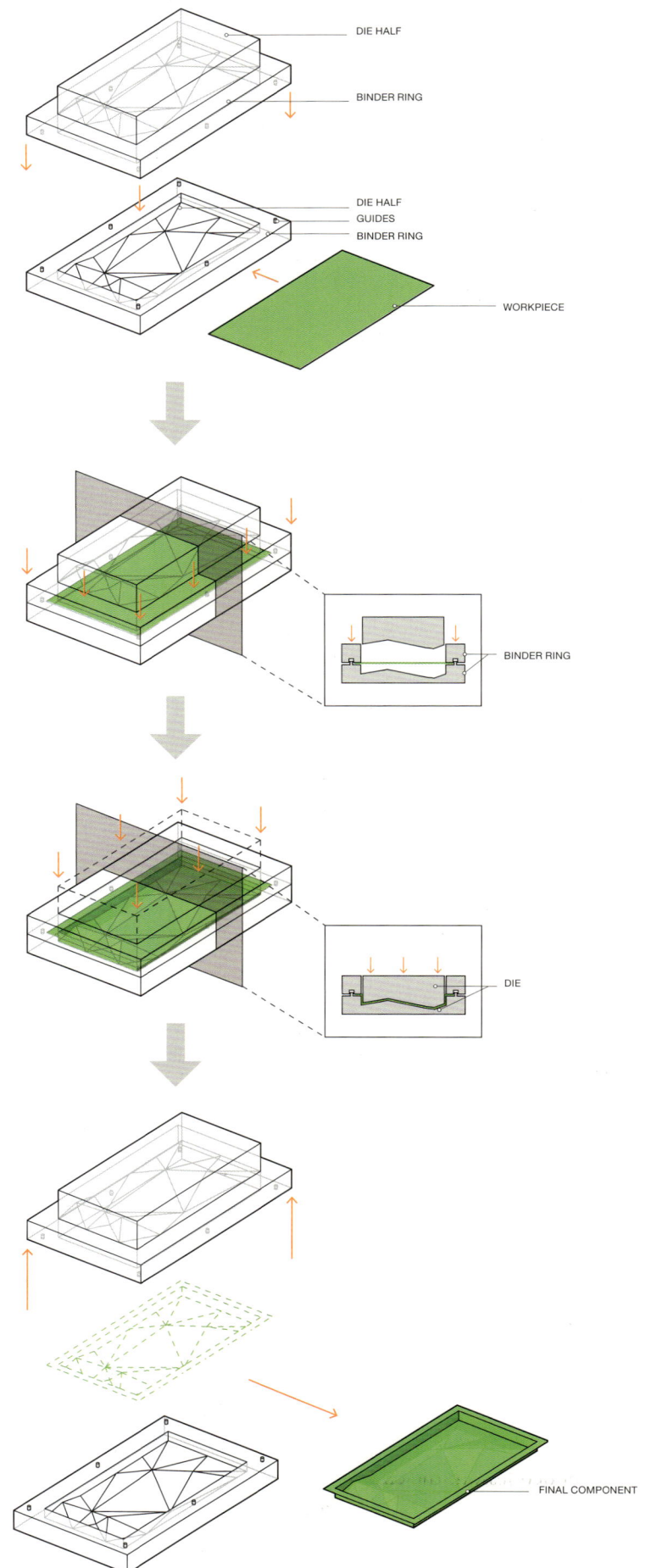

DIE HALF
BINDER RING

DIE HALF
GUIDES
BINDER RING

WORKPIECE

BINDER RING

DIE

FINAL COMPONENT

book, the focus is on stamping methods that use a mate die. [2] Mate dies include a male and a female die part that come together to deform metal into a three-dimensional form.

The force exerted by the tooling puts the metal sheet into a combination of elastic and plastic states. This causes the metal within the sheet to flow and take the shape of the tooling. Shapes can vary in metal stamping, ranging from deep, round, narrow cup-like shapes, such as aluminum cans; to large components with gentle curves, such as car hoods; to complex shapes like wall mounting brackets for flat-screen televisions, which are manufactured using multiple press actions, including punching holes, trimming, and bending within a continuous process. Both ferrous and nonferrous metals can be stamped, with aluminum, steel, and stainless steel being the most common. Surface quality can range from good to very good with this process, depending on the amount of strain on the metal during deformation. Tolerances are high with metal stamping, and sizes can range from small L-shaped brackets to large components. [3, 4]

In metal stamping a metal sheet, called a blank, is inserted into a binder ring. The binder ring is held by the press, and as the press closes, the binder ring clamps the blank in place. The die

half then moves, forcing the metal sheet to stretch as it takes the shape of the mating dies. Lubricant is used between the blank surfaces and upper and lower die halves, to reduce friction and increase the metal's flow. The die halves open and the binder ring releases the workpiece. Depending on the size of the component, this process has a short cycle time. The press operates as if it is hitting the blank rather than pressing it, and each hit is referred to as a stroke. If the shape is deep or complex, the press may need to make multiple strokes to achieve the final shape. After forming, the workpiece may undergo post-production processes, such as drilling or cutting.

Because both sides of the workpiece are in contact with the mating die, both sides are finished faces. Stamping tools are often hard, and may scratch the surface of the workpiece during the stamping process; therefore the workpiece may undergo post-production finishing such as sanding, anodizing, or painting to remove any marks. Although the metal blank stretches to form to the mating die, ideally the change in the blank's wall thickness should be kept to a minimum. If thinning is intended, this is often done in a secondary process called ironing.

The stroke force used for deformation depends on the component's shape, the type of metal, the gauge of the sheet, the surface area, and the type of lubricant. Typically, metal stamping is a cold working process, although warm and hot stamping processes are possible. Cold working increases the metal's strength and decreases the energy required for production, while increasing the press force.

Stamping can be done on presses in small workshops, by small- and medium-sized contract manufacturers, or by high-volume production manufacturers. Workshops and contract manufacturers are not highly mechanized, and depend on manual labor to move the blanks and workpieces in and out of the presses. [5] Both workshops and contract manufacturers are well suited to custom projects, or working with atypical metals such as titanium. Most high-volume manufacturers are mechanized, with complex machinery and tooling. They are likely to limit

3 A stack of final stamped components

4 Pre-cut blank

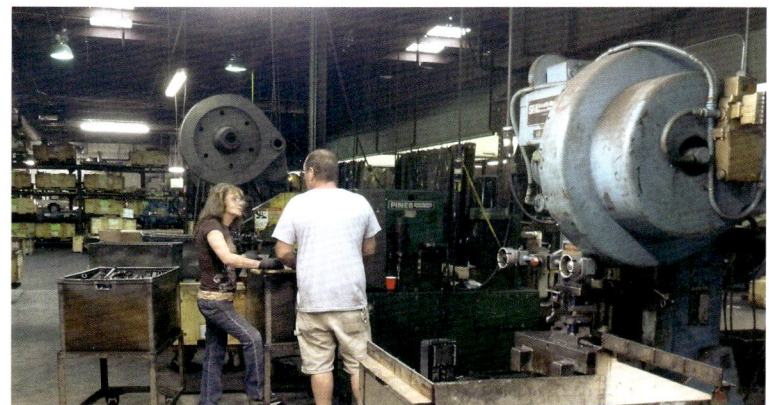

5 Two workers in a metal stamping shop, moving pieces by hand

manufacturing to high-volume productions, and may have long lead times. Generally, stamping has high tooling costs and fast cycle times. This process is suitable for larger production runs than other sheet-metal deforming processes. [6]

BUILDING PRODUCTS

There is a number of commercially available building products made from stamped metal. Most of these products are the ordinary and yet necessary parts of our buildings. Stamped products include electrical junction boxes, mounting brackets, door and window hardware, and louvered air-supply grilles. Stamped products for architectural finishes include tin ceiling tiles, metal roof tiles, and non-slip floor surfaces for mechanical areas.

TOOLING

Stamping tooling includes two halves of a mate die and a binder ring or blank holder.[1] [7] A mate die includes a female die half—referred to simply as "die," and the male die half—referred to as "punch." Mate dies are designed to accommodate a particular wall thickness of metal between the two die halves. If the die

mates are too close to one another, the metal sheet will thin too much. If the die mates are not close enough together, then the metal sheet may not deform enough.

Generally, the tooling needs to be durable enough to withstand the force exerted by the press, and strong enough to deform the blank. [8] The surface of the die should be polished and lubricated to reduce friction and increase flow, and the manufacturer may plate the die with hard chromium to further reduce friction and to protect it from wear. To hold the blank in place, draw beads may be used. A draw bead locks the blank in place so that as the blank deforms, it moves evenly in tension. [9, 10] The draw beads are often kept a distance away from the final face of the workpiece to reduce tearing and wrinkling. The marks left by the draw beads can be removed in post-production trimming.

A die with no additional moving parts that has one cavity per stamped shape is a simple die. There are also progressive dies, which have multiple steps in a single tool. With progressive dies, the metal sheet is fed into a press, and it moves from one die station to another. [12] As the press makes its stroke, each step of the die deforms the metal towards the final shape. Perforated side-walls are formed in the blank and progress the workpiece from one die station to another. Finally, there are compound dies. A compound die can accommodate sequential operations within

6 Metal stamping is suited to high-volume productions

8 A steel die in the die repair shop. Note the smooth surface and the lubricant

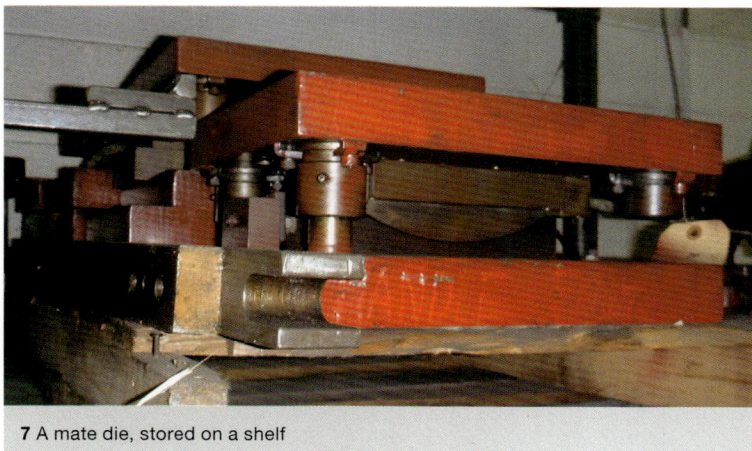

7 A mate die, stored on a shelf

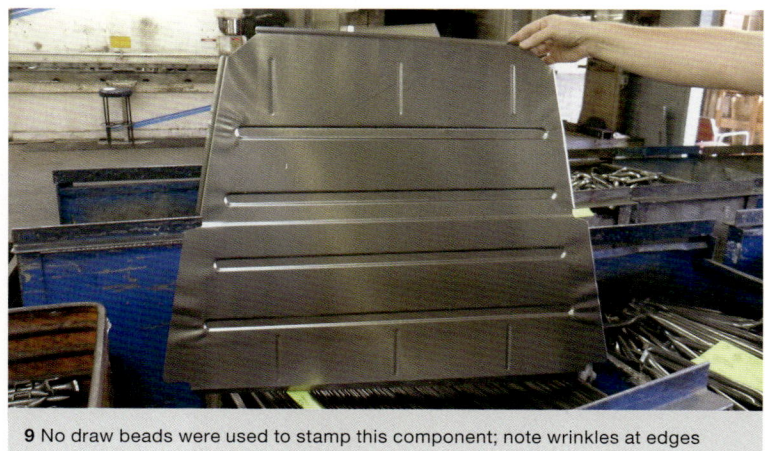

9 No draw beads were used to stamp this component; note wrinkles at edges

one cycle of the press. [11] For example it can draw a blank and, before it opens, punch the workpiece's side-walls to create holes. Compound dies require multiple moving parts and therefore increase tooling costs. They often perform only two to four operations simultaneously; if more steps are required, or if the shape is irregular, progressive dies are more suitable. As the workpiece does not move within the die, compound dies are better suited to stampings that require a high degree of tolerance.

The materials used affect the cost and durability of tooling. Hardened tool-steel dies are long-lasting and can be used for up to 500,000 strokes before repair; however, steel dies are expensive and require a long lead time to fabricate. Steel tools are machined into shape by either CNC millers or routers, or spark or wire EDMs. After shaping, they may be chrome-plated to extend their life. Some stampers use dies made of kirksite, a zinc alloy. Kirksite dies are better suited to prototyping or for production runs of under 5,000 units. Kirksite molds are cast (often by sand casting, see Chapter 4.2) to a near net shape and then CNC machined to their final shape. This reduces their fabrication time and cost.

ENVIRONMENTAL IMPACT

This process can be done so that it produces little to no manufacturing waste. Generally, metals are highly recyclable, so that any waste produced—often through post-production trimming—can be sent back to the metal sheet manufacturer for re-processing.

This process is most often done at room temperature and uses no energy to heat the medium before forming. Production cycles are shortest with this sheet-metal forming process; therefore for large production runs, this process will often have the most energy savings. The process of bending the sheets of metal increases their strength, especially when compared to similar cast or machined components. This means that less material can be used when making a component from stamped metal than with casting or machining.

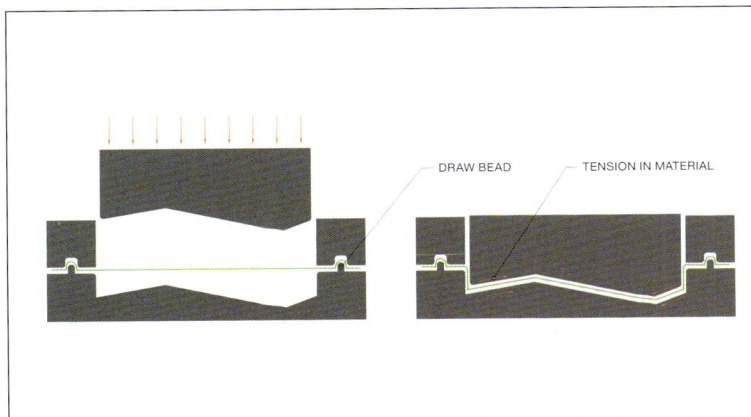

DRAW BEAD   TENSION IN MATERIAL

10 Draw beads reduce wrinkles

12 Half of a progressive die with stamped unit laying on top. This die works from right to left and forms the component in pairs. At the first station, the die punches the holes and shears the shape. At the next station, the die bends the end tabs and outside flanges up. At the third station, the die bends the inside flanges down. At the last station, the die shears the component from the side-walls

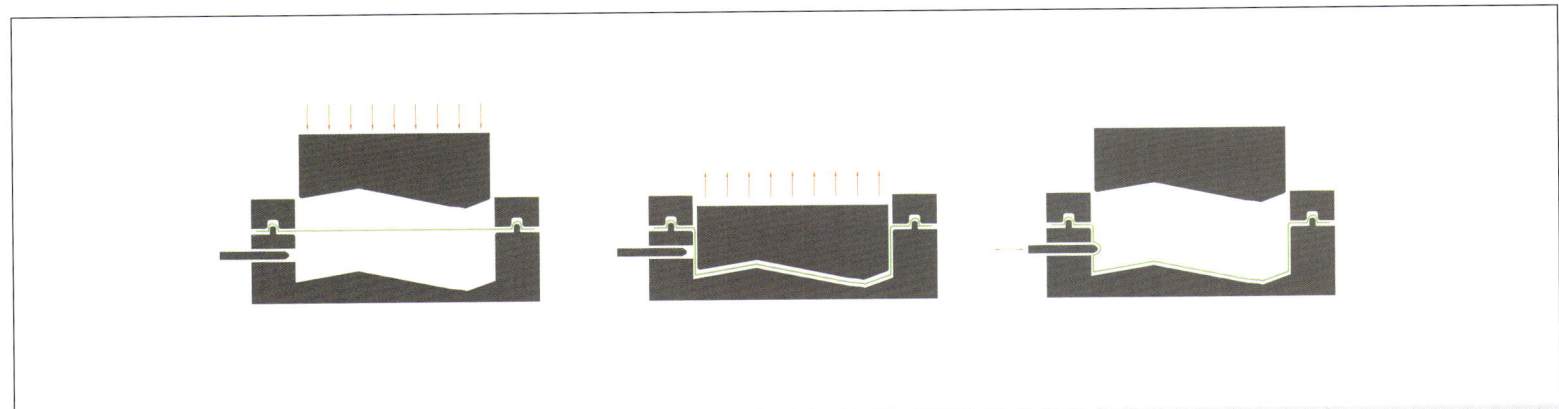

11 A compound die can accommodate sequential operations within one cycle of the press

MATERIAL CONSIDERATIONS + DESIGN PARAMETERS

METAL

Metal stamping can be done on both ferrous and nonferrous metals and on pure metal and metal alloys. The metal used in stamping has to be ductile enough to undergo permanent, or plastic, deformation; the deeper the draw, the more ductility is required. If a metal undergoes too much deformation, it will begin to harden, making further deformations more difficult. Annealing may be required between draws to counteract any hardening. Certain metals have a more pronounced grain structure than others and are more likely to tear when bent in certain directions. [13] Although bending with the grain is easier, it often results in a weaker stamping than bending against the grain.

Although plastic behavior is preferred in metal stamping, all stamping is a combination of elastic and plastic behavior. If the metal is not stressed enough past its yield point, it is more likely to return to its preformed shape. This elastic behavior is known as springback, and is often the result of cold working metals. The amount of springback depends on the type of metal, its thickness, and the type of forming operation. Generally the thicker the material, the more springback there will be. To counter springback, the metal may be bent beyond the radius or angle desired, in a process called "over-bending." [14] Other methods to reduce springback include annealing the metal prior to stamping, calibrating the press with a higher stroke force, or bending the metal in two directions; a 90° bend may be combined with a curve to form stretch flanges. [15]

Generally, the thinner the sheets, the more difficult they will be to form without tearing, wrinkling, or orange-peeling. Tears happen where the metal moves the most in the die—such as at the bottom of a drawn cup. The risk of tears can be lessened by reducing the draw depth, or rounding the entry corners into the die to enable metal flow. Wrinkling often occurs in flanges, or at the sides of a draw as a result of excessive compressive forces. Orange-peeling is when the metal loses its shiny surface, becomes dull, and in some extreme cases can become rough. It happens when the metal is over-stretched but not torn. For some components these defects may be acceptable, as the allowable defects mean lower manufacturing or material costs. To preemptively address the possibility of defects before the tools are fabricated, manufacturers can run computer-aided formability analyses to predict how the metal will behave.

SIMILAR PROCESSES

Stamping metal is similar to other metal-sheet forming processes, such as explosive forming (Chapter 1.3), hydro-forming (Chapter 1.6), and spinning (Chapter 1.7). Stamping is also similar to superplastic forming (Chapter 1.2), but with lower material costs than SPF. Generally, stamping metal has higher tooling costs, longer lead times, and shorter cycle times than the other sheet-metal forming processes. It is best suited to high-volume productions.

CORNER RADII

Corners with radii of two to three times the material thickness are preferred; however, most metals can bend with a corner radius the same as the metal thickness. If the metal is particularly ductile, half the thickness will be sufficient. An insufficient radius will tear the workpiece and prematurely wear the tool.

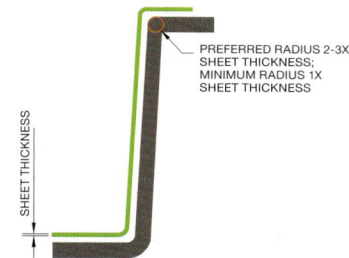

PREFERRED RADIUS 2-3X SHEET THICKNESS; MINIMUM RADIUS 1X SHEET THICKNESS

SHEET THICKNESS

DRAFT ANGLES

Minimum draft angles range from 0.5 to 2°, depending on the metal, thickness, lubricant used, and springback. Steep draft

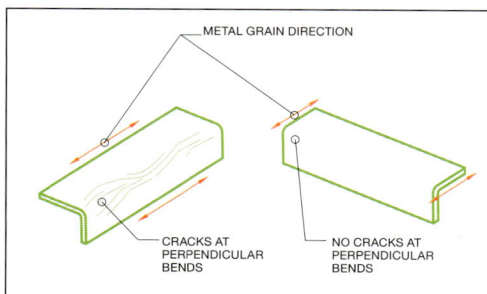

13 A metal's grain structure affects the ease and strength of the bend

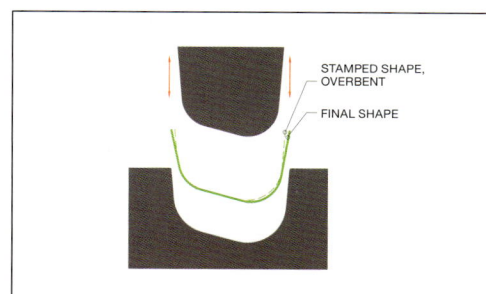

METAL GRAIN DIRECTION

CRACKS AT PERPENDICULAR BENDS

NO CRACKS AT PERPENDICULAR BENDS

14 Springback occurs in metal stamping

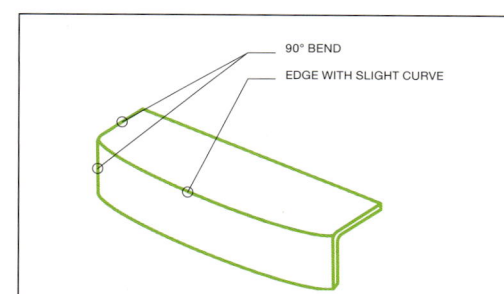

STAMPED SHAPE, OVERBENT

FINAL SHAPE

15 To reduce springback of a 90° bend, a curve—also known as a stretch flange—can be added to the angle

90° BEND

EDGE WITH SLIGHT CURVE

angles can scratch the component surface during removal, or prematurely wear the die.

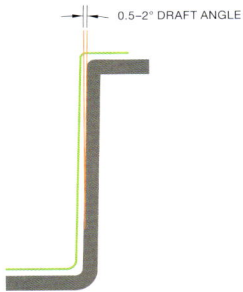

0.5–2° DRAFT ANGLE

DRAW DEPTH

The draw depth will depend on the size or width of the blank. The greater the width, the deeper the draw. If the draw depth is more than twice the minimum blank width, stamping will often be referred to as deep drawing. The draw depth depends on the metal, blank thickness, lubricant used, press force, and the number of strokes per unit.

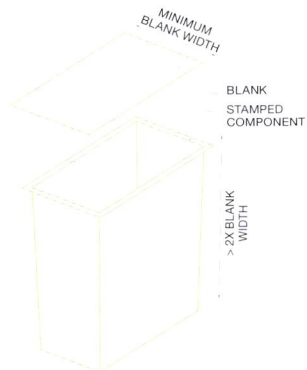

MINIMUM BLANK WIDTH
BLANK
STAMPED COMPONENT
> 2X BLANK WIDTH

HOLES

Holes, such as those for mechanical fasteners, should be made during post-production, after the workpiece has been stamped. The sheet's deformation would otherwise likely distort or move the holes from their original position. If a hole must be pre-drilled, locate it a minimum distance of 1.5 times the thickness of the metal from any bend.

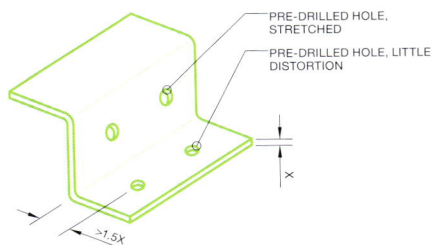

PRE-DRILLED HOLE, STRETCHED
PRE-DRILLED HOLE, LITTLE DISTORTION
>1.5X

JOINING

Metal sheets cannot be joined together during stamping.

LEAD TIME

Due to tooling fabrication time, the lead time for a stamped prototype can be six to eight weeks, or longer.

NOTCHES

If a workpiece will be subjected to too much tension or compression, consider adding notches to the area before forming. In tension, the notches will allow the metal to stretch without causing tears. In compression, the notches will allow the metal to shrink without causing wrinkles.

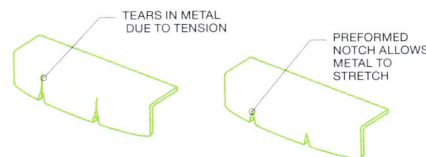

TEARS IN METAL DUE TO TENSION
PREFORMED NOTCH ALLOWS METAL TO STRETCH

Notches or cutouts are particularly needed if a bend is placed in hard metal at an abrupt change in width. If notches are not wanted, offset the bend from the change in width.

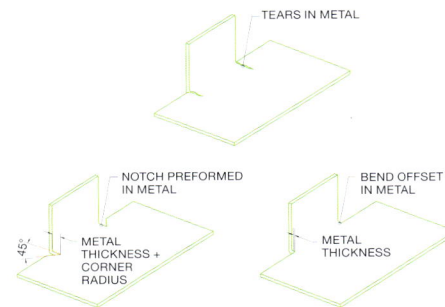

TEARS IN METAL
NOTCH PREFORMED IN METAL
BEND OFFSET IN METAL
45°
METAL THICKNESS + CORNER RADIUS
METAL THICKNESS

PRODUCTION RUNS

Metal stamping is typically appropriate for production runs of over 1,000 units, but this will depend on the size and complexity of the workpiece. If using a progressive or compound die, the production run should be over 10,000 units.

SIDE-WALL HOLES

For architectural application, punched side-wall holes are unlikely to be cost effective. If side-wall holes are required, consider drilling them post-production. Side-wall holes can also be made with a progressive or compound die.

SURFACE TEXTURE

Metal stamping can accommodate fine surface textures.

TOLERANCES

Tolerances for metal stamping can range from 0.004 to 0.03in (0.1–0.8mm). Tolerances are affected by the type of die, the component shape, and the blank size. Round, drawn shapes can have tighter tolerances than square or rectangular shapes; square or regular shapes can have tighter tolerances than irregular shapes.

Angles will be within 1°, as designed. If the bent flange is less than 1in (25mm), the angle will be within 2°.

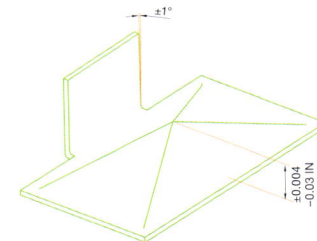

±1°
±0.004 –0.03 IN

TOOLING COSTS

Tooling costs are very high for this process. A simple matched die can cost $15,000–50,000, with progressive or compound dies costing more.

UNDERCUTS

If using a simple matched die set, this process cannot accommodate an undercut. If stamping the metal with progressive or compound dies, undercuts can be formed.

WALL THICKNESS

Sheet metal thickness ranges from 0.05 to 0.25in (1.25–6mm). As the metal moves during this process it is difficult to predict the wall thickness of the formed workpiece. For drawn parts, a deviation of 10–20% from the original blank thickness is acceptable.

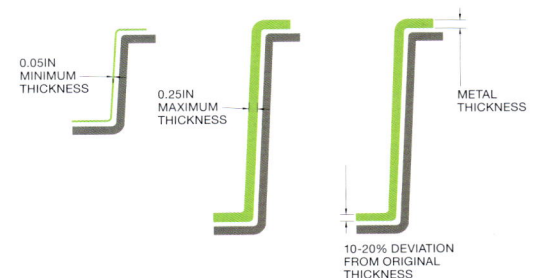

0.05IN MINIMUM THICKNESS
0.25IN MAXIMUM THICKNESS
METAL THICKNESS
10-20% DEVIATION FROM ORIGINAL THICKNESS

STAMPING: METAL

SCREEN | MALL FORUM MITTELRHEIN
Benthem Crouwel Architects

Koblenz, Germany

In 2007, Benthem Crouwel Architects won first prize in an invited competition to redesign Koblenz city center. **[16]** The project includes cultural buildings including a library and museum, a tourist information center, a public square, and a mall with parking. The Mall Forum Mittelrhein was competed in 2012 and has an area of over 450,000ft^2 (42,000m^2), with parking located on the building's top two floors. **[17, 18]** The Mall has received a gold certificate from the Deutsche Gesellschaft für Nachhaltiges Bauen (DGNB), which is Germany's Sustainable Building Council, and a Building Research Establishment Environmental Assessment Methodology (BREEAM) Excellent certificate.

The upper-level parking is screened with the "Weinlaub façade," a custom-stamped metal panel inspired by the form of grapevine. **[19]** There were 2,856 panels stamped for this building, measuring approximately 4ft × 4ft (1.25m × 1.25m), with a three-dimensional depth of almost 12in (300mm). Benthem Crouwel designed the panels to be rotated 90°, 180°, or 270°

16
A bird's-eye view of Koblenz, Germany, including the Mall Forum Mittelrhein cultural building, mall with parking, and public square between

17
Public space between the shopping mall and museum

18
Rear façade of the shopping mall

19
Detail of the stamped metal panels (from behind)

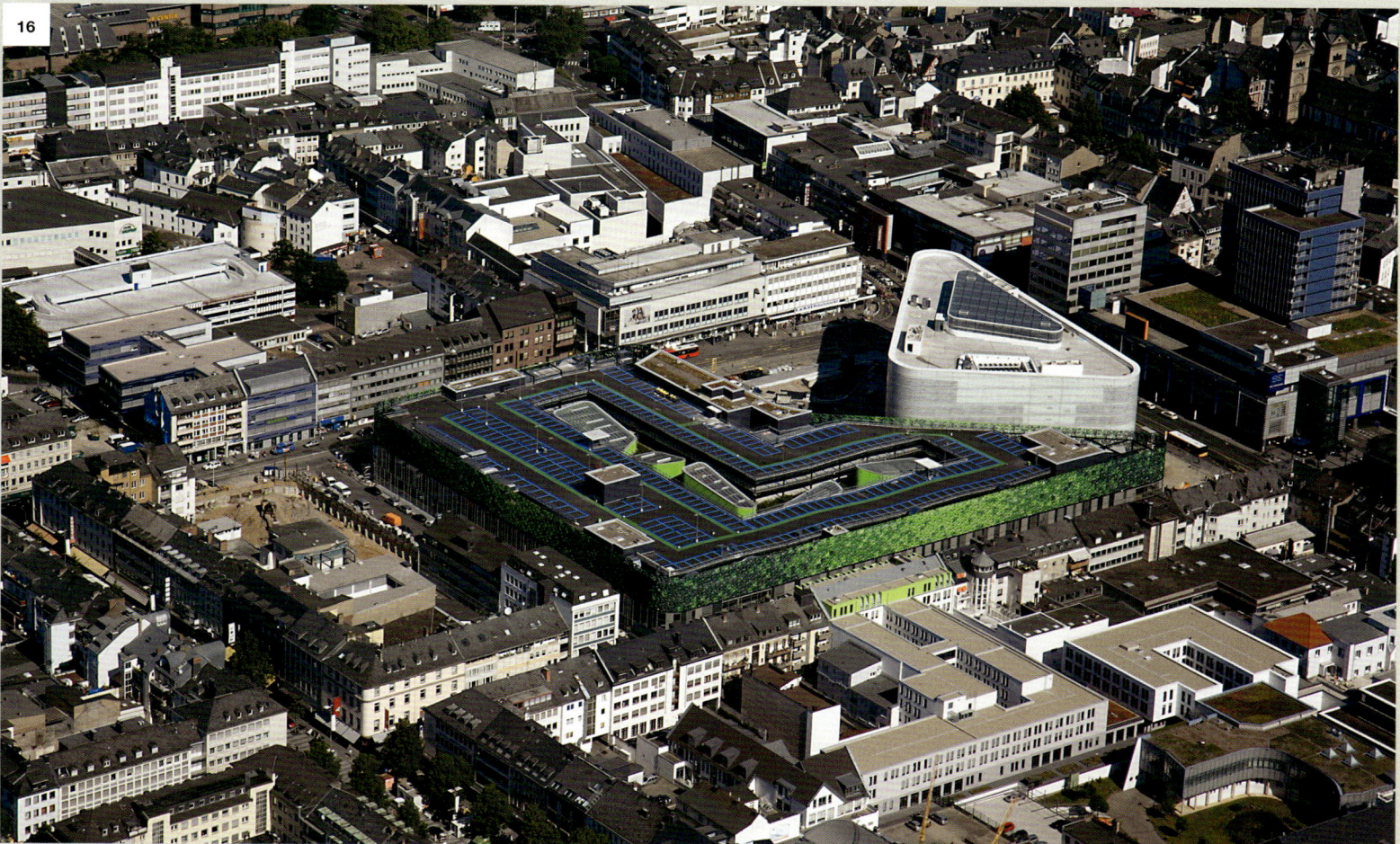

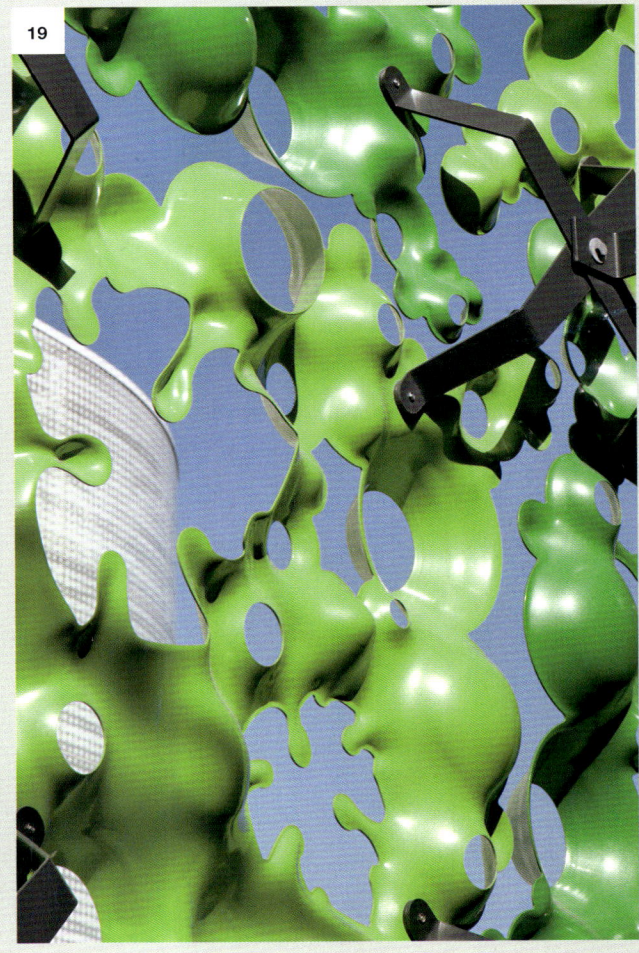

20

POSITION 1

POSITION 2

POSITION 3

POSITION 4

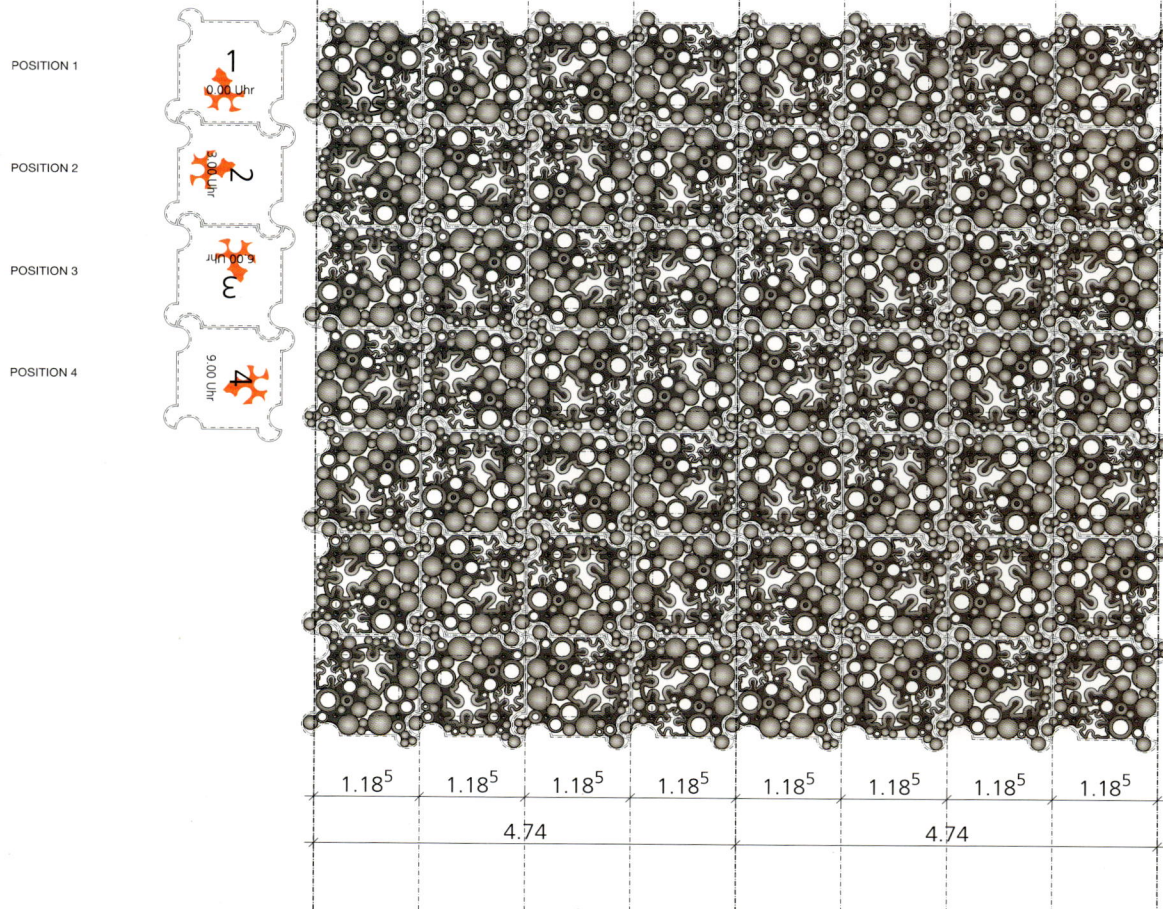

| 1.18⁵ | 1.18⁵ | 1.18⁵ | 1.18⁵ | 1.18⁵ | 1.18⁵ | 1.18⁵ | 1.18⁵ |

4.74   4.74

21

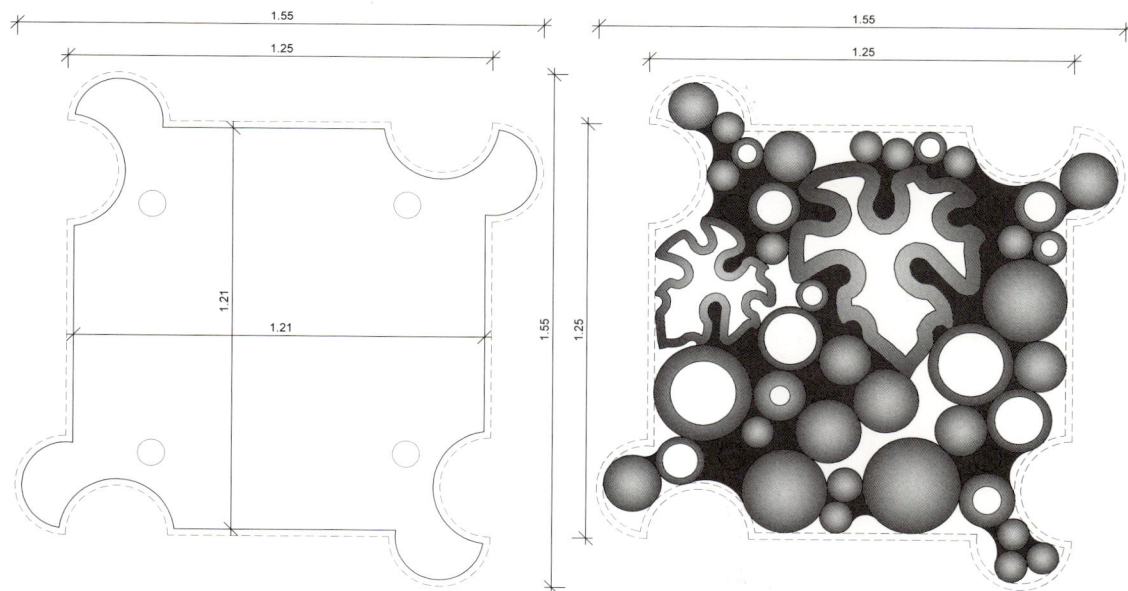

from the original to match key points without appearing repetitive. [20, 21] After forming, the tiles were painted in three different shades of green. [22] Benthem Crouwel prescribed the placement, orientation, and shade of each of the panels on the building.

The project's general contractor, Ed. Züblin AG, is a large German contractor with locations throughout Europe and the world, and was responsible for finding and selecting Seacon Umformtechnik GmbH to stamp the panels. Seacon is located only 300 miles (475km) from Koblenz and has the capacity to stamp metal panels as large as 6.5ft × 19.5ft (2m × 6m) in aluminum, steel and steel alloys, brass, and copper.[2] Seacon manufactures panels for household appliances, medical, industrial, and architectural applications.

DESIGN CONSIDERATIONS

The screen was used to visually hide the cars from the street and the public square, while properly venting the parking. In the original competition entry, the design team had proposed using live plants for screening, but through the design's development the team looked at a custom-design metal screen.

Koblenz is in the wine region of Germany and, to give the project local identity, the grapevine was the inspiration for the screen panel's design. According to project architect Cornelius Wens, Mels Crouwel did a sketch of a vine that was then translated into a three-dimensional model by computer to become the shape of the panel.[3] The computer file was then sent to the manufacturer for tooling fabrication.

MANUFACTURING CONSIDERATIONS

During design development, the team investigated a number of different manufacturing processes, including stamping, explosive forming, casting, and thermoforming plastic. To evaluate the different manufacturing processes, the design team spent two days at Züblin's Stuttgart office to meet with manufacturers. According to Wens, the design team was skeptical that explosive forming could be used to manufacture the panels. Of particular concern was explosive forming's precision and the time required to produce all of the panels required. Next, casting was rejected, as it would not give the same surface quality and thinness as manipulating the metal sheets. Finally, plastic was rejected because of flammability concerns. In the end, Benthem Crouwel believed that stamping was the best option.

The manufacturing process included cutting aluminum sheets from a large coil. The sheets were then stamped with the shaped mate die on a ten-ton press. [23, 24, 25, 26] From there, the panels were transferred to a laser cutter for trimming them to shape and cutting holes. Finally, the panels were returned to the press for a final stroke. (This process is called restriking and is used to realign the workpiece after trimming, increase metal hardness, and maintain close tolerances.[4]) After the sheets were formed, they were sent to another manufacturer for painting. [27, 28]

Fabrication of the dies was done directly from Benthem Crouwel's 3D digital file. It took the manufacturer ten months from receiving the digital file to start production. Prototypes were not made, but the manufacturer sent

22

20
Arrangement of the stamped metal component, so that there is no visible repetition on the building façade

21
Drawing of the stamped metal façade component

22
Three shades of green painted on the panels

23 Lubricants are applied by hand to each blank before stamping

25 The workpieces after their initial stamping

24 During the manufacturing process, blanks are loaded into and removed from the press by hand

26 The workpiece is cut to shape by a laser cutter

27 The components in line to be powder coated

Benthem Crouwel 3D digital images of the panels for final approval.[5] Once production started, it only took six to eight weeks to manufacture the panels.

OTHER CONSIDERATIONS

The 3D deformation of the panel surface caused material defects in the aluminum. Marks can be seen in the unpainted panel surfaces, where the material stretched beyond its limit. [29] The panels were designed to be painted, so Benthem Crouwel was not concerned with the marks. Had the panels been clear-finished, a progress die stamp could have been used, a different aluminum alloy, or an alternative manufacturing process to eliminate these marks.

For this project, there was little collaboration between the architect's office and the metal stamping manufacturer. Initially, Benthem Crouwel was concerned as it was unfamiliar with the process and worried that there were not enough panels to offset the high tooling costs. The general contractor took the lead on finding a manufacturer to make the panels. From there, Benthem Crouwel worked with the general contractor, and the contractor worked with the metal stamping manufacturer. Benthem Crouwel was happy with this arrangement and, according to Wens, the panels were manufactured as designed.

LESSONS LEARNED

Wens noted that although the panels were repetitively manufactured, there was still a lot of manual labor involved in their production. Between every step, the panels were handled by hand. This included placing each aluminum sheet into the press, removing it from the press and moving it to the laser cutter, removing it from the laser cutter back to the press for final forming, and finally removing it from the press.

28 Workpieces after painting

29 Workpiece, prior to laser cutting, with visible stress marks due to deformation

1.6 Hydroforming

aka sheet hydroforming (SHD)

INTRODUCTION

Hydroforming is a manufacturing process that uses hydraulic pressure in combination with tooling to deform metal. (For brevity, I refer to both pure metals and metal alloys as "metal.") [1] Hydroforming is a generic term, and includes tube hydroforming and sheet hydroforming. In tube hydroforming, the hydraulic fluid is pressurized inside the tube, deforming the tube's walls to the inside of a closed die. It is primarily used in the automobile industry.[1] [2] In sheet hydroforming (SHD), the hydraulic fluid is pressurized in a large bladder that pushes the sheet metal against an open die. SHD is analogous to metal stamping (Chapter 1.5) and has the most architectural application.

The force exerted by the fluid and the tooling puts the metal sheet into a combination of elastic and plastic states. This causes the metal to flow and take the shape of the tooling. Shapes can vary, from deep, narrow cup shapes; to large components with gentle curves, such as car hoods; to complex curves with multiple valleys and peaks. Both ferrous and nonferrous metals can be shaped this way, with aluminum, magnesium, and stainless-steel alloys being the most common. Surface quality is very good with this process, and tolerances are high.

In hydroforming a metal sheet, called a blank, is inserted into a binder ring held by the press. As the press closes, the binder ring clamps the blank and holds it in place. Hydraulic fluid within the press is pressurized so that the blank is pressed against the tool. If the hydraulic pressure comes from the top of the press, a rubber bladder is used to contain the fluid. The hydraulic pressure forces

1 Hydraulic press cycle

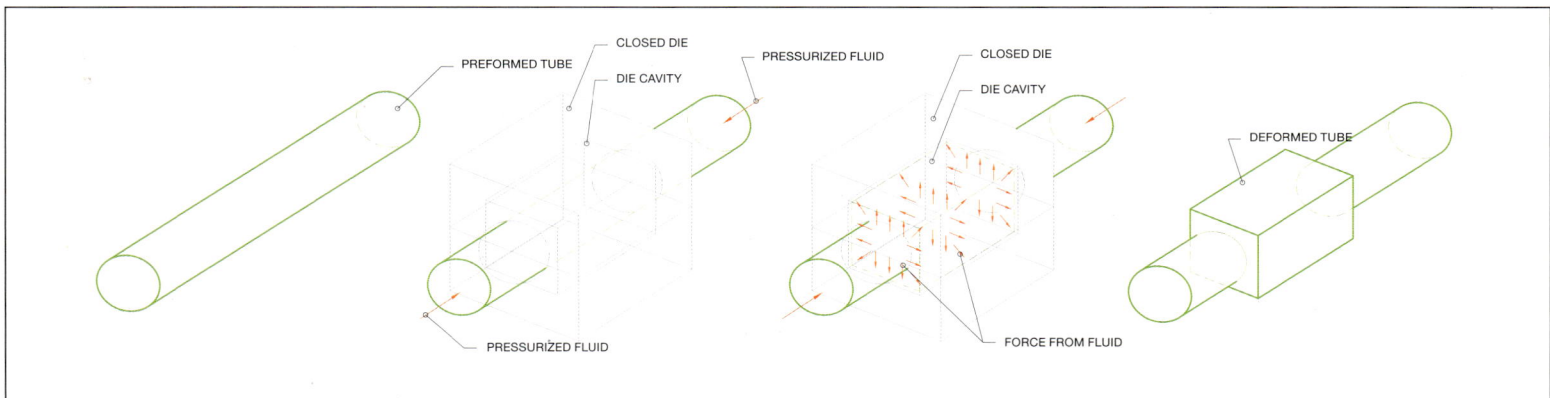

2 Tube hydroforming process

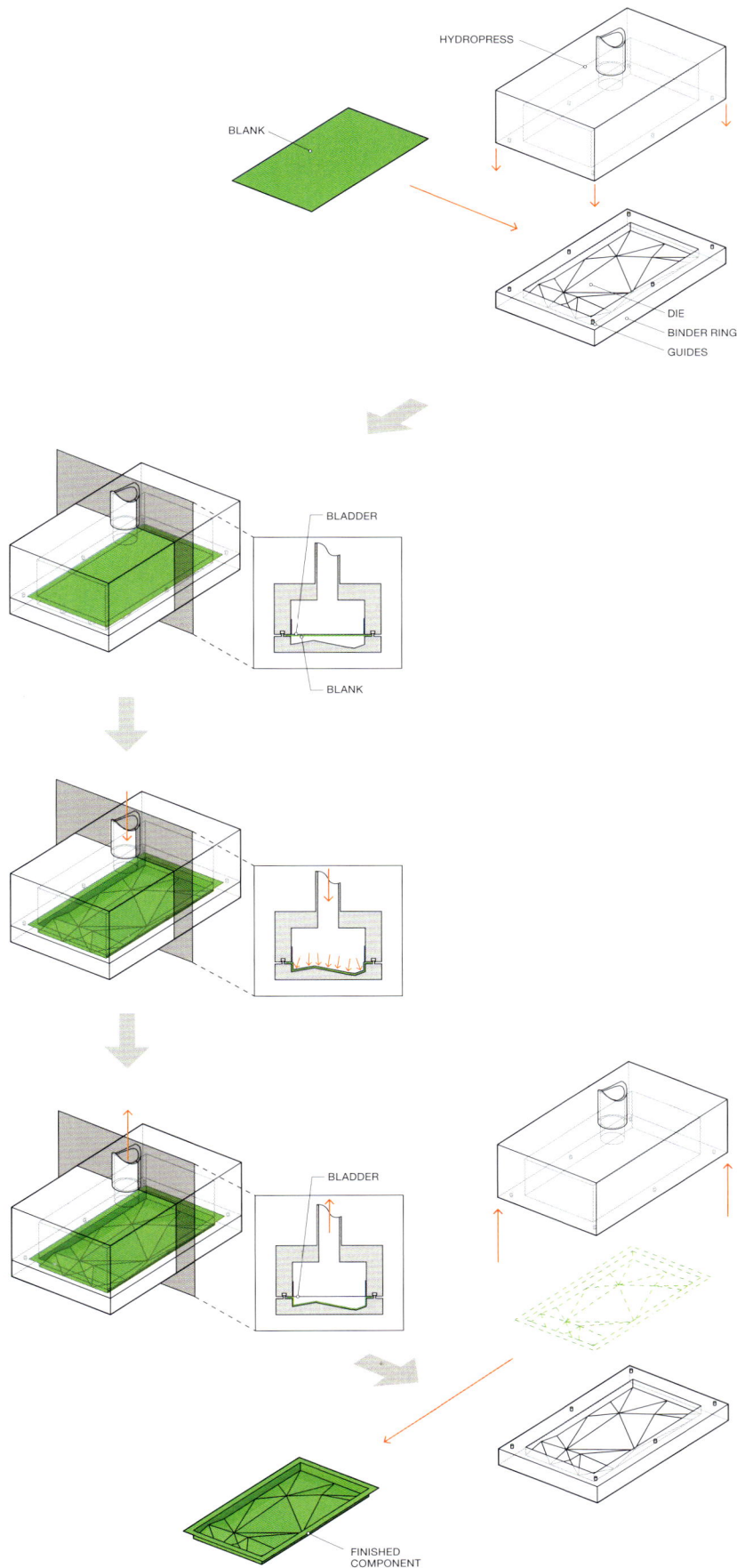

the blank to deform against the die. To reduce friction, lubricant is used between the blank and the die, and a slip sheet of a flexible material is used between the blank and the bladder. [3] The pressure in the press is then released. The die halves open and the binder ring releases the workpiece. Any post-production trimming, drilling, or finishing is carried out as required.

The face of the workpiece against the die is considered to be its finish face, as dimensions will be exact; however, the hard die may scratch the surface. The face of the workpiece in contact with the fluid-filled bladder has less dimensional accuracy, but is less prone to scratching.

There are variants of sheet hydroforming. First is hydroforming with a membrane diaphragm, which is the most common and is illustrated in the diagram on the left. Second is hydromechanical deep drawing (HMD), in which the presses have the hydraulic fluid on the bottom, without a bladder and covered by the blank. A mechanical punch is pressed into the blank, while the fluid provides

3 A person inserting a slip sheet into the press between the blank and the bladder

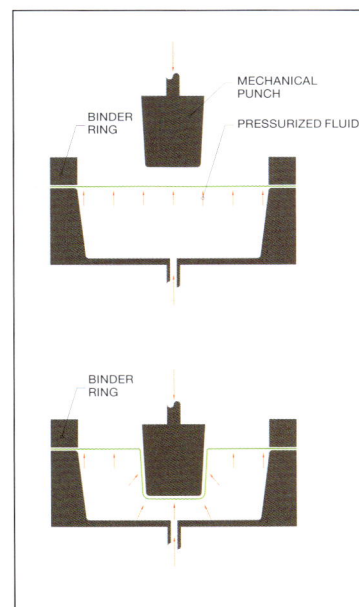

4 Hydromechanical deep drawing (HDD) process

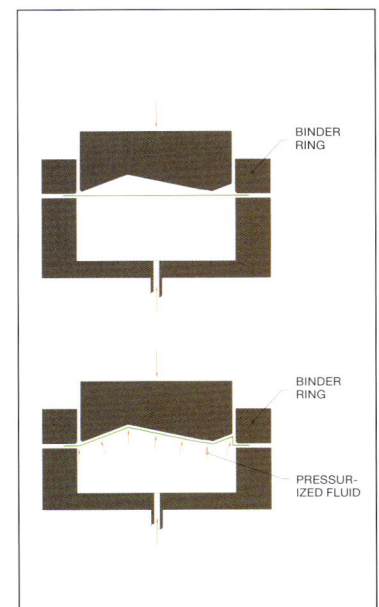

5 Hydraulic stretch forming (HSF) process

enough resistance. [4] Third is hydraulic stretch forming (HSF), which also has the fluid at the bottom of the press, but without a bladder. With HSF the fluid is pressurized so that it pre-stretches the blank before forming it to the tooling. [5] Fourth is dual sheet hydroforming, which starts with two stacked metal blanks placed within a closed die. [6] The hydraulic fluid is injected between the two sheets, pressing each to the inside face of the closed die. This process can be used to make tanks or other hollow components.

During the cycle, the pressure of the fluid is controlled by computer. [7, 8] Often the pressure is varied as the metal deforms, to obtain the best flow at all times. The controlled flow rate of the metal results in more precise forming with fewer defects and less springback than metal stamping. Hydroforming has a longer cycle time than metal stamping, and may last up to 3 minutes or more, depending on the medium, the sheet thickness, and the shape. This means the process is not often used by high-volume production manufacturers. Hydroforming can be done on presses by small- and medium-sized contract manufacturers. Because of the presses, small workshops and craftspersons do not have access to this process.

BUILDING PRODUCTS

Tube hydroforming is used to make plumbing components, such as faucets, as it can form flares for the faucet end, complex curves, and bulges in the pipes. Sheet hydroforming can produce similarly shaped building products in the same way as metal stamping (Chapter 1.5), but is often not used for high-volume products such as electrical junction boxes, mounting brackets, or window

hardware. Single sheet hydroforming includes decorative metal panels with an embossed surface. Surface patterns include waves, bubbles, or anything else that might have universal architectural appeal. Examples include the Borit by Leichtbau-Technik GmbH and the TECU_shape by KME. Depending on the manufacturer and the panel's specifications, these panels can be used for interior or exterior applications.

TOOLING

A sheet hydroforming tooling set includes a steel die, and may include a rubber bladder, a blank holder, inserts if needed, and a trim die. [9, 10, 11, 12] The die is often made from hardened tool steel and may be a female die (or cavity) or a male die (or punch). The bladder corresponds to the blank size, and is purchased by the hydroformer as part of the manufacturing tool package. For some

7 The fluid pressure changes during the cycle and is controlled by computer

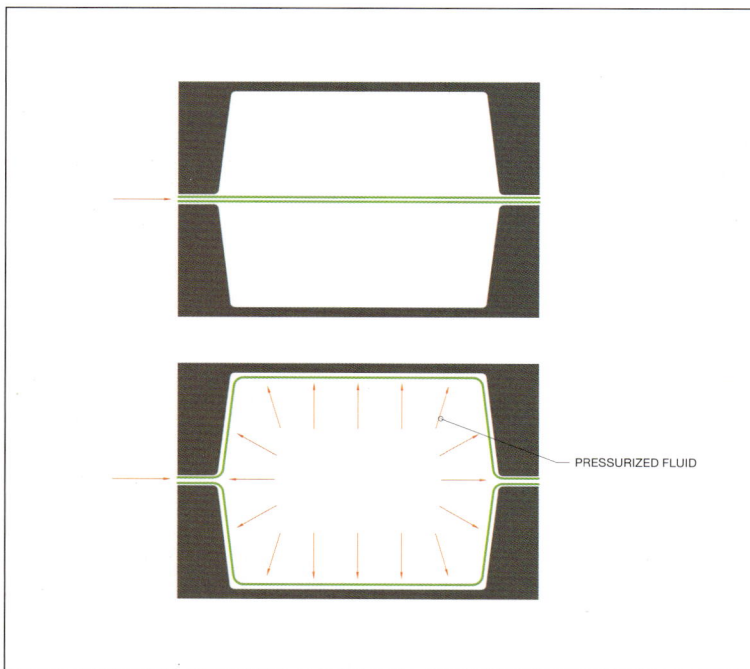

6 Dual-sheet hydroforming process

PRESSURIZED FLUID

8 Hydraulic presses can be large and costly

9 Steel die for a hydraulic press

10 Rubber bladder

11 Optional rubber inserts for deep, narrow crevices

12 Trim dies

13 Trim die on a five-axis CNC router

components, the bladder can act as a blank holder; however, if no bladder is used, a separate blank holder is fabricated from tool steel. Inserts make small modifications between cycles without the need to exchange the die, and help the bladder apply pressure in narrow crevices. [12] The trim die holds the workpiece for post-production trimming and drilling with a CNC router. [13]

Generally, a hydroforming tool needs to be strong enough to withstand the pressure exerted by the fluid to deform the blank. The die surface should be polished and lubricated to reduce friction and to increase flow. The manufacturer may consider plating a die with hard chromium to further reduce friction and to protect the tool's structure from wear. The bladder needs to be flexible enough that it can deform to the shape of the die, strong enough that is can resist fluid pressure, and durable enough to be used for multiple cycles. Bladders can last between 500 and 1,500 cycles before deteriorating.

Hydroforming tools are typically made from hardened tool steel and are machined into shape by either CNC millers or routers, or spark or wire EDMs. Steel dies are long-lasting and can be used for up to 500,000 cycles before repair; conversely, they are expensive and require a long lead time to fabricate. The advantage of hydroforming over metal stamping is that only one die half is required (versus the two mated dies for stamping). This results in a lower tooling cost and shorter lead time than metal stamping.

ENVIRONMENTAL IMPACT

This process can be done so that it produces little to no manufacturing waste. Generally, metals are highly recyclable, so that any waste that is produced—often through post-production trimming—can be sent back to the metal sheet manufacturer for re-processing.

This process is most often done at room temperature and so uses no energy to heat the medium before forming. The bending process increases the strength of the metal sheets, especially when compared to similar cast or machined components. This means that less material is used when making a component with hydroforming than with casting or machined metals.

MATERIAL CONSIDERATIONS + DESIGN PARAMETERS

METAL

Hydroforming can be done on both ferrous and nonferrous metals and on pure metal and metal alloys. Material characteristics for hydroforming metals include ductility, uniform elongation, high strain hardening, low anisotropy, and good surface quality. The blank surface should be free from scratches and burred edges to protect the bladder surface. Generally, all metals that are good for stamping are good for hydroforming. Hydroforming is well suited to lightweight metals such as aluminum and magnesium because fluid pressure can vary during cycles, reducing defects due to deformation. Steel and aluminum alloys are the main metals used in sheet hydroforming, but in hydroforming tubes for the piping and sanitary industries, copper and brass are often used. Some alloys have been specifically developed for hydroforming to achieve a particular strength, stiffness, and lightness—primarily in the automobile industry, where lightweight, stiff materials are developed to reduce vehicle weight.

With the pressure exerted by the fluid, hydroforming places a higher and more uniform pressure on the blank than metal stamping. Lubricants are important to hydroforming to enable the metal to slide across the die. The draw depth in hydroforming is 1.5 times deeper than an equivalent piece made by metal stamping. Hydroformed components also have a more consistent wall thickness than those manufactured by stamping. Springback is not as much of a concern in hydroforming as it is in metal stamping; therefore over-bending is not typical to this process. There also appear to be fewer defects such as tearing and orange-peeling in hydroforming than with metal stamping.

Before production begins, a manufacturer may run a finite element analysis (FEA) on a design in order to predict how a sheet of metal will behave during forming. If an area of the sheet demonstrates concentrated stress, the design or the fluid pressure can be adjusted.

SIMILAR PROCESSES

Hydroforming metal sheets is similar to other metal-sheet forming processes, such as explosive forming (Chapter 1.3), stamping (Chapter 1.5), and spinning (Chapter 1.7). Hydroforming is also similar to superplastic forming (Chapter 1.2), with lower material costs than SPF. Generally, hydroforming metal has higher tooling costs, longer lead times, and shorter cycle times than explosive forming and spinning; but lower tooling costs, shorter lead times, longer cycle times, and less springback than stamping. This process is best suited to mid-volume productions.

CORNER RADII

The inside corner radius for a female die depends on the material, the material thickness, and the pressure exerted by the hydroforming press. Aluminum requires a radius range of 0.5–2 times the blank thickness. Stainless steel requires a radius range of 3–7.5 times the blank thickness. Generally sharp corners and edges should be avoided, as they are hard on the bladder and will cause premature wear.

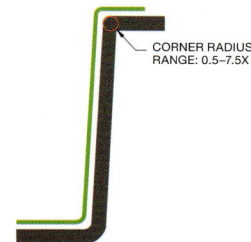

CORNER RADIUS
RANGE: 0.5–7.5X

DRAFT ANGLES

The draft angle should be a minimum of 1°. The greater the angle, the less wear on the die and bladder.

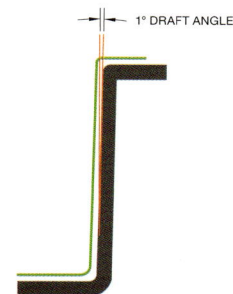

1° DRAFT ANGLE

DRAW DEPTH

The draw depth ranges from 5 to 12in (127–300mm), depending on the material, its thickness, and the component's shape. Deeper draws are achieved through hydroforming in multiple molds with increasing depths, and annealing the metal between each pressing.

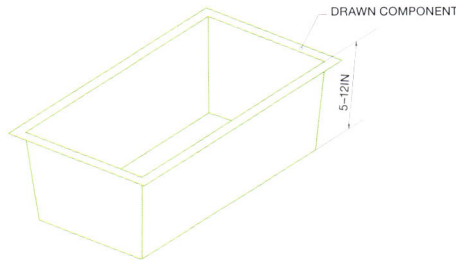

DRAWN COMPONENT

5–12IN

HOLES

Holes should be made during post-production. The blank's deformation will most likely distort or move the holes from their original position.

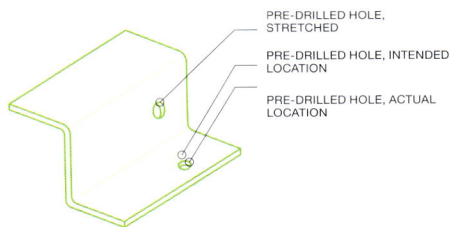

PRE-DRILLED HOLE, STRETCHED

PRE-DRILLED HOLE, INTENDED LOCATION

PRE-DRILLED HOLE, ACTUAL LOCATION

LEAD TIME

Due to tooling fabrication time, the lead time for a hydroformed prototype can be four to six weeks or more.

PRODUCTION RUNS

Hydroforming is appropriate for production runs over 500 units, but it will depend on the size and complexity of the workpiece.

PRODUCTION SPEED

The production speed for hydroforming ranges from 20 to 90 cycles per hour. The cycle time will depend on the size, material, shape, thickness of the component, and the press.

SIZE LIMITS

Hydroforming can deform sheets as long as 20ft (6m), but there are few manufacturers with this capability. A sheet size of 24 × 72in (600 × 1,825mm) is reasonable for most hydroformers.

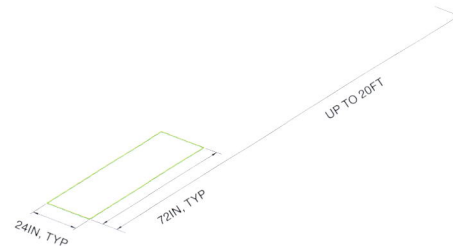

UP TO 20FT

24IN, TYP

72IN, TYP

TOLERANCES

Hydroforming can produce components within 0.002in (0.5mm) tolerances.

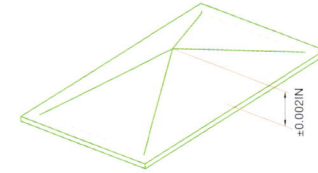

±0.002IN

TOOLING COSTS

Tooling costs can range from $10,000 to $25,000, and depend on the shape and size of the component to be manufactured. Tooling costs are slightly more than half of those associated with metal stamping.

UNDERCUTS

Hydroforming cannot form undercuts.

WALL THICKNESS

Hydroforming produces components with uniform wall thicknesses.

HYDROFORMING: METAL

LOUVERS | LALUX ASSURANCES HEADQUARTERS
Atelier d'Architecture et de Design Jim Clemes S.A.
Leudelage, Luxembourg

Through a 2007 architectural competition, Atelier d'Architecture et de Design Jim Clemes was awarded the commission to design a new company headquarters building for La Luxembourgeoise (LALUX), an insurance company. **[15, 16, 17]** The original LALUX headquarters had been located in the city center of Luxembourg, but was difficult for customers to access.[2] The location of the new building is southwest of Luxembourg City center, in an industrial zone in Leudelage. The Jim Clemes design stands out from the neighboring industrial park buildings, and overlooks the surrounding countryside to the west. When Jim Clemes was awarded the commission, LALUX disclosed that it had already sold its downtown headquarters and required that the project move quickly. Construction started in January 2009 and was completed in November 2011.

LALUX's new headquarters has many sustainable features. The building includes solar collectors for heating water, heat exchangers, and thermal mass to reduce energy use. The building collects gray water for toilet and urinal flushing, and has a filtering system to make drinking water. The building is organized in five, 41ft (12.5m) wide, three-story high office bars atop a wide base. These bars have continuous bands of horizontal windows, giving workers access to daylight. The building is equipped with dimmers and daylight sensors to reduce its use of artificial light, and motorized exterior blinds to reduce glare. LALUX's 350 employees occupy three of the five bars. The building is over 210,000ft^2 (19,690m^2) and includes leasable office space in the remaining two bars, a shared lobby and reception area, training classrooms, a cafeteria, restaurant, and gym, a 172-seat auditorium accessible from the building's base, and three stories of below-grade parking.

Dispersed over the five three-story office bars are 2,500 vertically mounted aluminum louvers. **[14]** The louvers are folded into a box shape, with the two broadest sides having a custom-designed, three-dimensional

14
LALUX Assurances Headquarters by Atelier d'Architecture et de Design Jim Clemes S.A. in Leudelage, Luxembourg. Building section between bars and through bridge. Note that each louver color and angle is labeled

15
Façade overlooking open field

16
Detail image of louvers

17
Street façade showing louvered three-story bars sitting atop base

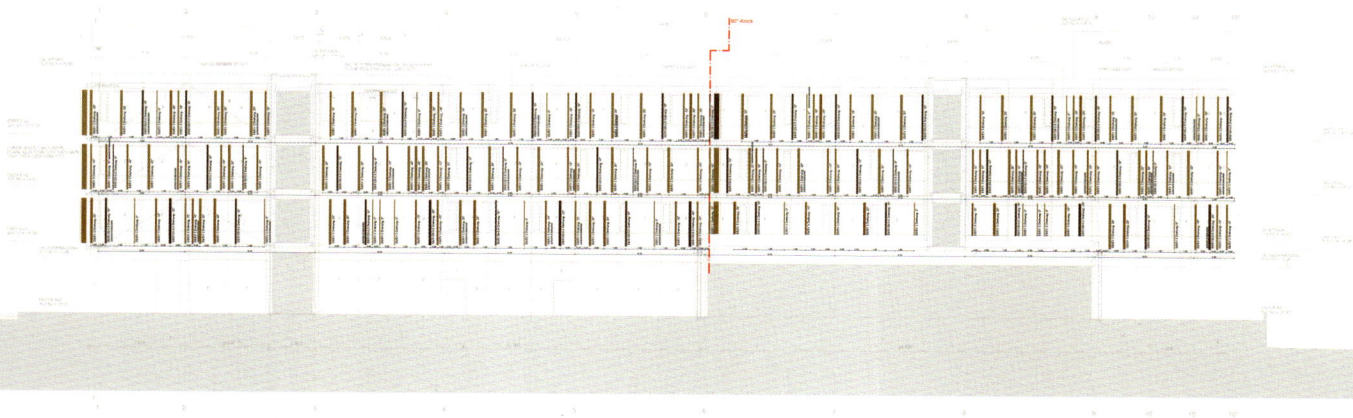

14

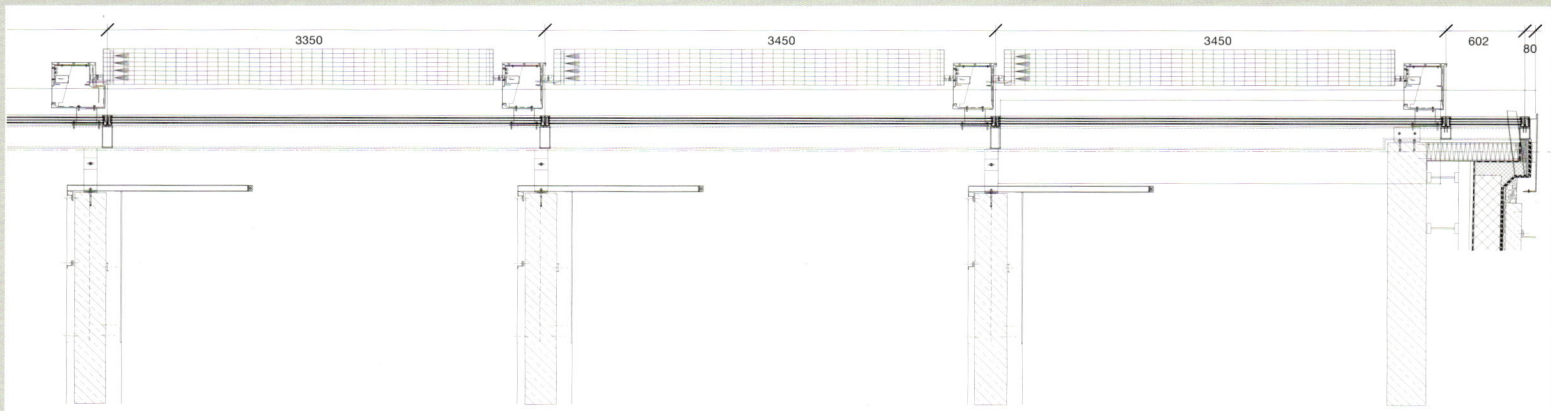

18 Tender drawing of the façade

pattern of squares made from hydroforming. Five hundred of the louvers are formed from perforated metal (instead of solid) and are internally lit by LEDs at night. All of the louvers are just over 9.5ft (2.9m) tall and just under 20in (500mm) wide. The louvers are oriented at five different angles and are coated in three different colors—gold, brown, and bronze. Schindler Fenster + Fassaden GmbH was the façade contractor, Fielitz hydroformed and bent the louvers into their box shape, and HD Wahl was responsible for the louvers' color coatings.[3]

DESIGN CONSIDERATIONS

According to Ingbert Schilz, Jim Clemes director/partner, the introduction of the louvers was in response to the programmatic needs of the client.[4] To meet LALUX's requirements for flexibility, the building required horizontal bands of windows. To reduce the horizontality of the windows, Jim Clemes added the vertical louvers. As the design team members developed the louver design, they investigated materials, what the louvers' function and use could be, and whether they would be static or moveable. They believed that the louvers should be lightweight, as they did not want to add additional weight and structure to the building. The firm also wanted the louvers to be constantly presenting the image of the company; therefore the louvers could not weather or change over time. With these considerations, they decided on a box aluminum component.

The placement and angles of the louvers is intentional and set by the interior use of the building. The louvers provide the iconic image of the building; their embossed surface design is derived from the graphic inset cubes of the LALUX logo, and as Schilz stated, they permanently connect LALUX to the building. Jim Clemes took the logo, modified it digitally, and used Rhinoceros to develop the pattern. The color coatings are based on the company color, orange, while also reflecting the building's site next to the countryside. The color and angle of each louver were prescribed by the architect's drawings. **[18]**

The iconic function of the louvers was heightened by making 20% of them perforated, and placing LEDs inside them. Instead of placing the lights on the ground and shining them up to illuminate the building at night, LALUX is illuminated by louvers spread across the façade. In 2010–2011,

19 At night, the building is lit by LEDs on 500 perforated louvers on the façade, reducing electricity use

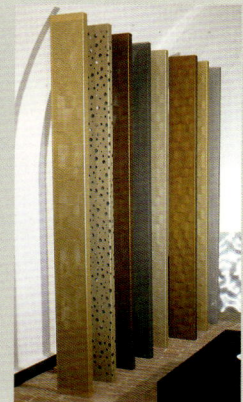

21 Samples of sheet hydroforming

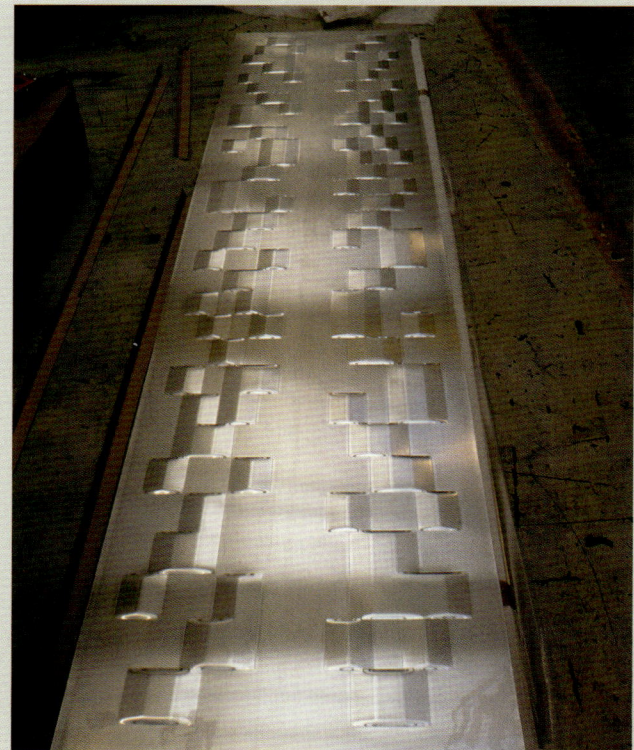

20 Louver surface, after hydroforming

LEDs were in early development, and a special lens was used to cast the LED light the length of the fin. Prototypes were made of the lights to verify that they would work as intended. Those louvers were then distributed intuitively across the building's upper levels. The use of the LEDs and the scattered distribution meant that the building's energy consumption and light pollution were reduced compared with standard building lighting schemes. [19]

MANUFACTURING CONSIDERATIONS

As Jim Clemes worked on the louvers' design, the firm's team was invited to Fielitz's showroom to better understand the manufacturer's capabilities, how hydroforming worked, and the finishes available. [20, 21] From that visit, the design team developed the louvers in collaboration with Fielitz, establishing size restrictions, draw depth, and deformation. Schilz stated that at the time, Fielitz was limited to hydroforming panel lengths up to 9.7ft (2.95m), so that set the length of the louvers. Fielitz was also limited to a minimum width of 19.7in (500mm) for bending the metal to make the box, which set the width for the louvers.

Fielitz folded the louvers to a tolerance of less than 0.02in (0.5mm), and left the seam between the two open. [22] The façade contractor attached an aluminum trim piece on the inside of the box to connect the two sides.

OTHER CONSIDERATIONS

Jim Clemes and Fielitz worked closely during the design phases. Fielitz produced a small mock-up of a louver section for evaluation, but did not commit to a full-size prototype until the contract was awarded. Because schedule and quality were issues for this project, Jim Clemes worked with the client to identify five façade contractors that were qualified to bid the project. Each contractor was then required to work with Fielitz to manufacture the louvers. [23, 24]

LESSONS LEARNED

With this project and the collaboration with Fielitz, Jim Clemes realized how 3D metal panels can be formed, as well as the process's limits, constraints, possibilities, and what kind of budget is required. The firm has since used that knowledge and applied it to a new design project at the University of Luxembourg.

22 Inside of louvers, after folding

23 Mock-up façade. Inside view of louvers and window, looking out

24 Mock-up façade. Detail at bottom of louver. Louvers are fixed and cannot rotate

1.7 Spinning

aka metal spinning, metal turning, spin forming

INTRODUCTION

Spinning is a manufacturing process that pushes a sheet of metal against a mandrel, while both the mandrel and the sheet spin at high speeds. (For brevity, I will refer to both pure metals and metal alloys as "metal.") [1] The plastic nature of the metal combined with the pushing force causes the metal to flow in a cold state to take the shape of the mandrel. The force can be applied by either hand or CNC machine, and often a number of passes are needed to fully shape the metal to the mandrel. The shapes that are made with this process are typically axisymmetric; examples include bowls, cones, and urn shapes. Both ferrous and nonferrous metals can be shaped this way, with copper, aluminum, brass, and stainless steel being the most common. Surface quality and tolerances are very good. Component sizes can range from small connectors and caps [2] to large components up to 15ft (4.6m) in diameter.

There are two types of spinning—conventional and shear spinning. [3]. In conventional spinning, the blank is pushed onto the mandrel with an unintentional change in the metal's thickness. This means that the metal's thickness may change while it is being spun, but this not intentional nor within the control of the spinner. Conversely, in shear spinning, a thick metal blank is placed at the end of the mandrel. As the metal is spun, it is purposefully thinned as it moves down the mandrel. This makes the component's base thicker than the walls. Shear spinning is also known

1 A craftsperson metal spinning a small copper bowl

2 Small caps made from spun aluminum

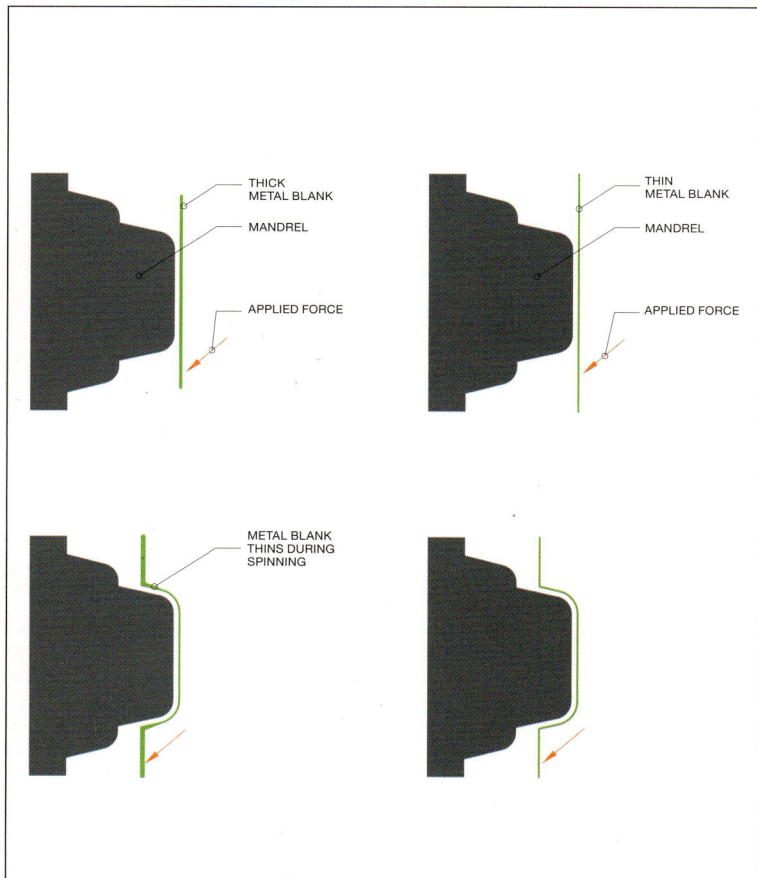

THICK METAL BLANK

MANDREL

APPLIED FORCE

THIN METAL BLANK

MANDREL

APPLIED FORCE

METAL BLANK THINS DURING SPINNING

3 Shear spinning (left) versus conventional spinning (right)

as flow turning, shear forming, and spin forging. Conventional spinning is more frequently done, and is the focus of this chapter.

In spinning, a circular sheet of metal, called a blank, is placed on the end of a mandrel and clamped with a follower block. The blank may have a centering hole or not, but the follower block exerts enough pressure to hold the sheet in place during spinning. The spindle, mandrel, blank, and follower block all rotate with the same number of revolutions per minute (RPM). Lubricant is placed on the outer surface of the sheet metal to reduce friction between the shaping tool and the metal sheet. As it spins, a shaping tool forces the metal onto the mandrel. The shaping tool works from the center to the outer edge of the blank. This processes often takes several passes, depending on the component's shape, details, and depth. Once the component has formed to the mandrel, the spinning is stopped. The follower block and the component are then removed.

The inside of spun metal is in contact with the mandrel and is considered to be the component's finished face. The exterior surface of a spun component is formed by the spinner's tools. Depending on the depth of any details, some mandrel details may not translate to the exterior surface of the component. [4] After forming, workpieces can be trimmed and the surface finished. Finishes may be brushed, sanded, or highly polished.

4 Interior details do not fully translate to exterior

5 Leveraging spinning tool against fulcrum for pressure against workpiece

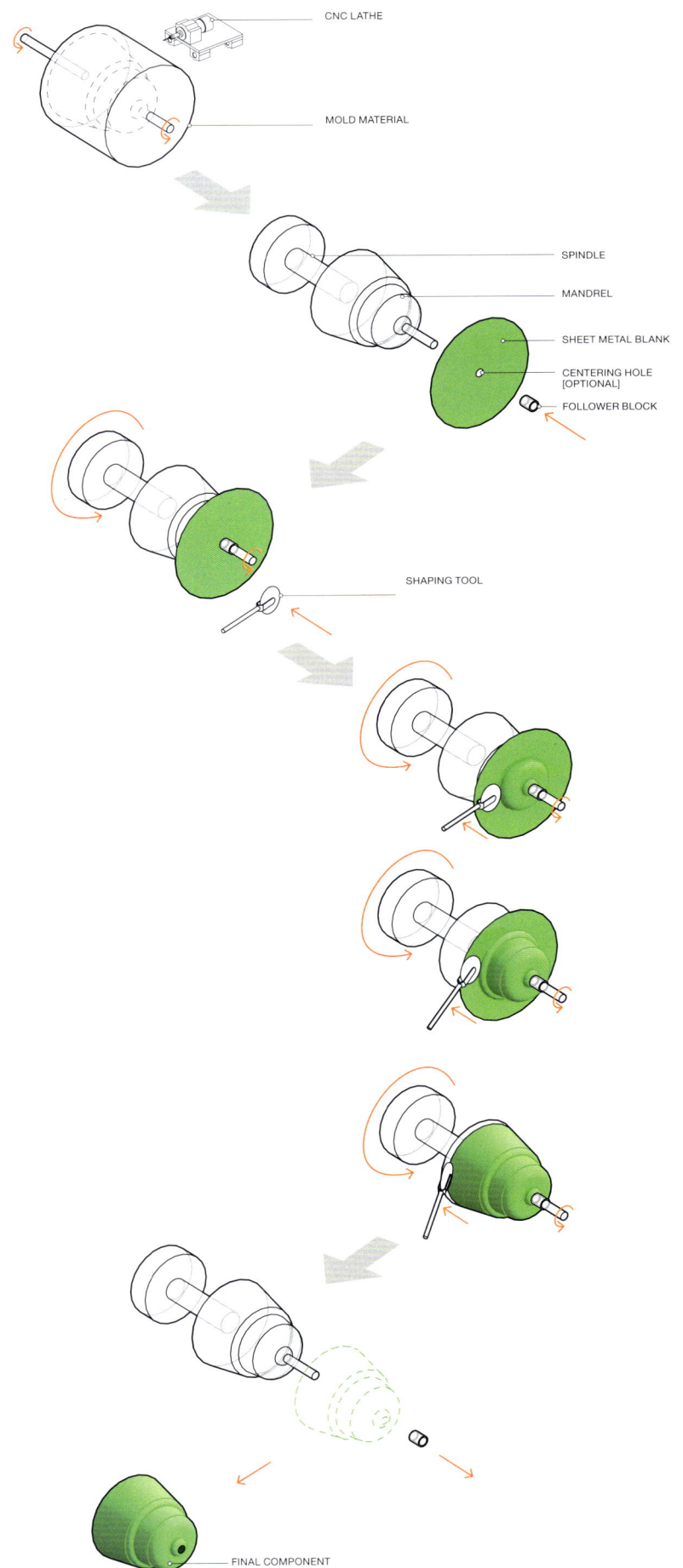

CNC LATHE

MOLD MATERIAL

SPINDLE

MANDREL

SHEET METAL BLANK

CENTERING HOLE [OPTIONAL]

FOLLOWER BLOCK

SHAPING TOOL

FINAL COMPONENT

The force needed to push the blank onto the mandrel varies based on metal strength, gauge of metal, size of spinning, and spinning speed. The larger the blank, the more pushing force will be needed. To apply pressure to the blank, a fulcrum is used to push the metal with less effort. [5]. As the metal flows down the mandrel, the fulcrum is adjusted so that it is within 1–3in (25–76mm) of the area being worked. As the mandrel and blank spin, various shaping tools are used to push the metal onto the mandrel. Wood push sticks are good for soft metals such as aluminum, as they do not dent the surface. Metal or wood push sticks are common for smaller pieces; however, wheels or rollers are required for larger pieces because they reduce friction between the shaping tool and the workpiece. [6, 7]

The spinner moves the tool slowly down the workpiece; if the tool is held in one place for too long, the metal will begin to harden. The spinner places even pressure on the workpiece as it moves down the mandrel. If too much pressure is applied, the metal may thin to the point of rupture. Wrinkles may form on the outer edge of the blank as it is pushed onto the smaller diameter of the mandrel. This is most likely to happen if the deformation is not gradual and the metal does not properly flow. The deeper and narrower the component, the more prone it is to wrinkles forming. Once wrinkles form, they are difficult to remove.

Spinning metal is a balance between craft, art, and manufacturing. Skilled metal spinners can spin a variety of shapes, including deep and narrow, without many problems. Less skilled spinners can make shallow and wide components. Expert spinners prefer to use the highest spinning speed possible. Metal flows more easily at higher speeds, less pressure is needed to push the blank onto the mandrel, and production speeds are faster.

The least expensive shapes to make with metal spinning are axisymmetric and can include either convex shapes such as bowls, or concave forms such as tulip shapes. For manufacturing ease, the mandrel's profile is smallest nearest to the blank and largest farther away. This creates a draft and allows the spun workpiece to be removed from the mandrel. Modifications to this process standards are possible. First, spun metal can have shallow surface details that are not radial, including surface patterns or ribs. Second, the workpiece can be worked over multiple mandrels with multiple centers, creating geometries with shifting centers. Third, some highly skilled metal spinners have the ability to spin non-axisymmetric, oval shapes up to a 1:2 ratio.[1]

For most of the spinning process, the metal blank is pushed onto a mandrel; however, spinners can modify the workpiece without it being in contact with the mandrel. This is called spinning "on air," and may happen when the spinner changes the tooling from a larger-diameter mandrel to a smaller-diameter mandrel and part of the workpiece that is being work is unsupported. This can be done

6 Spinner's tools

7 Spinner's tools

8 Folded edge of light fixture shade

in order to produce an undercut, or finishing edges such as beads and folded edges to give a finished quality to the component. [8, 9]

Generally, metal spinning is a labor- and time-intensive process. Spinning metal can be done by hand or by CNC machine that stands in for the spinner. If done by hand, the spinner must be trained and skilled. If done by machine, it will require programming to reflect the material properties and the component shape. CNC machine is more appropriate for large-volume productions than hand spinning. Cycle times between hand and CNC spinning are comparable. In most cases tooling costs are low, therefore metal spinning is best for small-batch productions. Most facilities that do metal spinning are highly flexible and can produce a variety of items for different clients.

BUILDING PRODUCTS

There are a number of building products available that use metal spinning. As spinning is usually associated with axisymmetric shapes, spun components are most often found in lighting, and can include light reflectors, mounting rings, housings, and trim rings. Other metal spun components include parts for decorative steeples, roof drain covers, and round door knobs.

Not attached to a building, yet designed by an architect—a chair made from spun steel and copper has been designed by Thomas Heatherwick, principal at Heatherwick Studio in London. The Spun Chair is a limited-edition chair, produced for Heatherwick's second solo exhibition in 2009 at the Haunch of Venison, a contemporary art gallery in London. [10]

TOOLING

The tooling required to spin metal is the mandrel and the follow block. The mandrel is what gives the blank its shape as it is being spun, and it is most often referred to as a chuck, or sometimes a form or buck. The follow block clamps the blank in place during spinning. Follow blocks come in a range of sizes, and can be used for multiple mandrel shapes. They may be flat or convex, forming a concave surface on the bottom of the spun component. [11] Spinning tools are wood and metal tools that the spinner uses to center, form, and trim the blank. They are selected by the spinner, and are interchangeable. There are also specialty tools to add threads or rolled edges to a workpiece.

Mandrels can made of a variety of materials, including hardwood, plastic, cast iron, or steel. [13] Wood molds are the least expensive and the most common. Hardwoods such as maple are preferred over soft woods at they can resist the heat and pressure associated with metal spinning. The wood used should have a close grain structure so the pattern does not transfer to the inside of the metal.[2] Wood

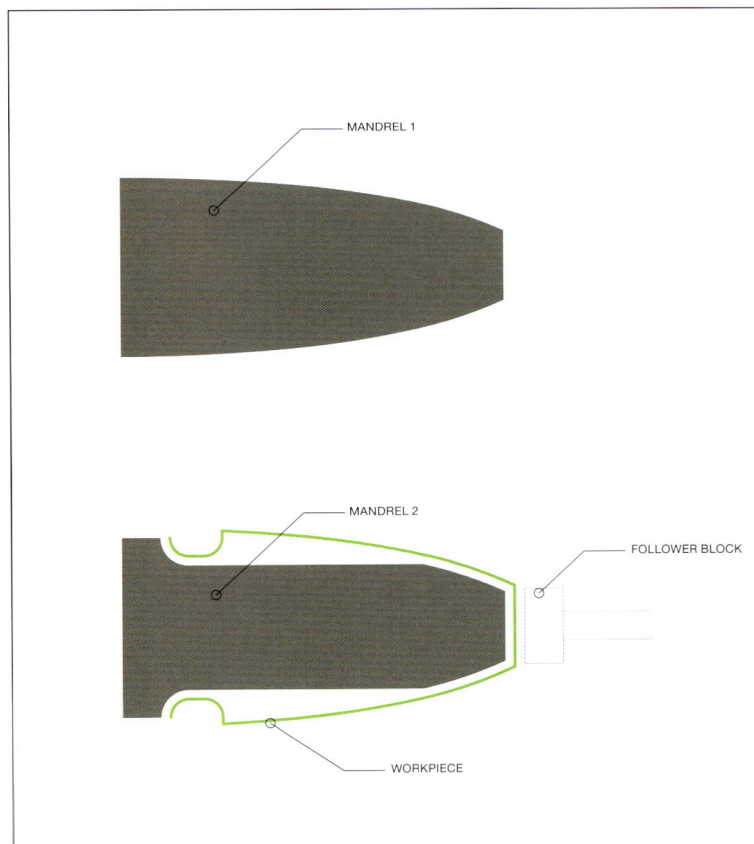

9 Workpiece is started on mandrel one and moved to mandrel two. On mandrel two, the workpiece is spun on air to make an undercut

10 The spun chair, Thomas Heatherwick

mandrels may warp and split over time. [14] This causes a wobble in the turning, which can be dangerous to the spinner and will affect the quality of the spinning. A maple mandrel can produce up to 75–100 components before wearing down and is easily repaired. To extend the life of a wood mandrel, it can be covered with a spun metal sheet for future spinnings.

The mandrel material selection depends on production run length or the duration of time over which components will need to be produced. For example, if a few components will be produced over a number of years, wood may not be the best choice, as it breaks down with moisture. Cast iron and steel are the most durable, but also the most expensive. Metal mandrels work well for large production runs, for components with tight tolerances, or for components that will be made over a number of years. Iron and steel may oxidize over time, and should be cleaned before spinning. Due to the brittle nature of cast metals, cast iron mandrels should have more rounded corners compared with steel. This will keep corners from breaking from the pressure exerted by the spinner. Plastic mandrels are the least used. They are best suited to prototypes, and do not offer significant cost savings compared to wood.

If a component's draw is deep or the draft angles are steep, vent holes should be added to prevent a vacuum from forming

13 A variety of spinning mandrels in wood and metal

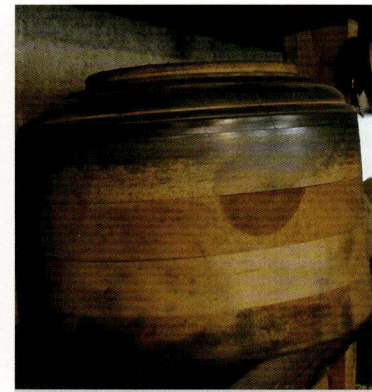

14 A large maple mandrel with cracks

between the workpiece and the mandrel. Compressed air may be blown into the hole to help remove the tool. If components have undercuts, necks, or negative draft angles, mandrels can also be made collapsible or with off-center cores so that the mandrel can be removed. [12] If the neck is very narrow or the component shape complex, the mandrel may be sacrificed. The mandrel may be left permanently inside the workpiece after spinning, or destroyed in order to remove it.

Wood mandrels can be made either by hand or on a CNC lathe. If made by hand, most metal spinners will make the mandrel themselves. Plastic or steel mandrels can be fabricated by hand, but are most likely to be machined by CNC millers, CNC lathes, or EDM (if metal). Cast iron molds will be cast in a foundry, typically by gravity casting.

ENVIRONMENTAL IMPACT

Spinning metal has little environmental impact. Generally, there is a high material utilization in forming the blank onto the mandrel and therefore there is little manufacturing waste. What little there is comes primarily from cutting the round blanks from square stock, with some minor waste if trimming during spinning. Any manufacturing waste of the metal is highly recyclable, and can be sent back to the sheet stock producer. Little energy is required for spinning, with most of the work being done by the spinner. The highest environmental impact associated with the process comes from the energy embodied in the metal.

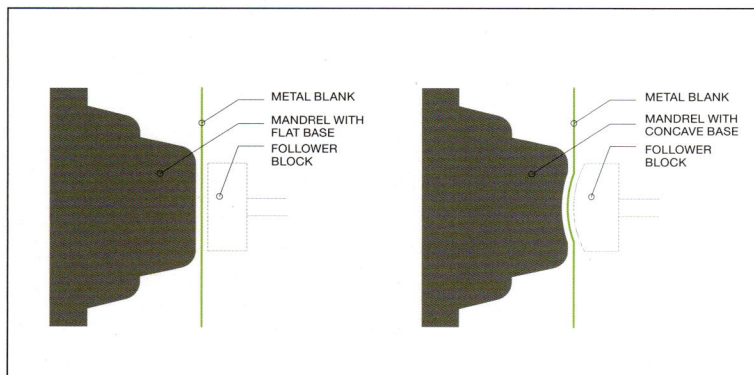

11 Shape of follower block to form bottom of component

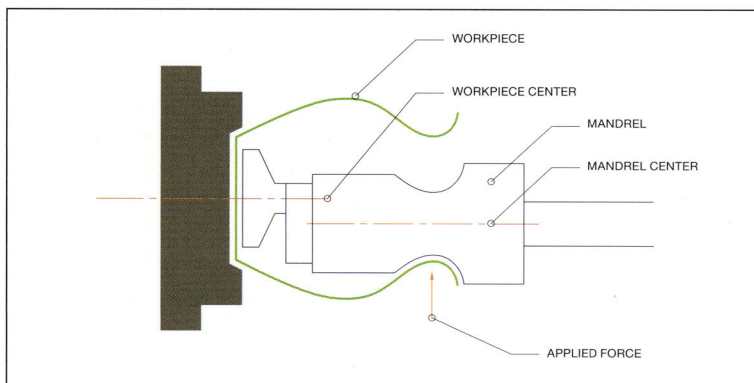

12 Mandrel made with an off-center core. This allows for undercuts to be made

MATERIAL CONSIDERATIONS + DESIGN PARAMETERS

METAL

Metal spinning is typically a cold forming process, done at room temperature. During spinning, the metal's molecules flow, moving and realigning themselves to take on the three-dimensional shape of the mandrel. Thicker-gauge material is easier to spin than thinner-gauge metals, as the thicker gauges are less likely to tear and wrinkle.

Spinning metal can be done with both ferrous and nonferrous metals, including copper, brass or bronze, aluminum, and steel and stainless steel.[3] Typically, the ferrous metals have to be thinner than the nonferrous metals, because of the additional force needed to get the metal to flow properly. Low-carbon steels (0.05–0.2% carbon) are best for spinning.

The mechanical working of the metal during the spinning process gives the metal a strengthened grain structure so that, for many metals, annealing is not necessary after spinning.[4] That said, brass should be annealed when spun, and copper should be annealed when drawn deeply.

SIMILAR PROCESSES

Metal spinning is similar to other metal-sheet forming processes, such as superplastic forming (Chapter 1.2) explosive forming (Chapter 1.3), stamping (Chapter 1.5), and hydroforming (Chapter 1.6). Metal spinning can make components with deeper draws than explosive forming or hydroforming. It can make components with the same draws as spinning, but tooling costs will be much higher. Generally, tooling costs for metal spinning are the lowest out of all of the sheet forming processes, but labor costs are high.

CORNER RADII

No corner radii are required for the mandrel; however, due to metal flow, a small radius may develop in the workpiece on the face not in contact with the mandrel.

SMALL RADIUS FORMS ON OUTSIDE FACE OF WORKPIECE AT INTERIOR CORNERS

DRAFT ANGLES

No draft angles are possible, but will require collapsible, off-center, or sacrificial mandrels. For standard mandrels, a draft angle of 5° is recommended.

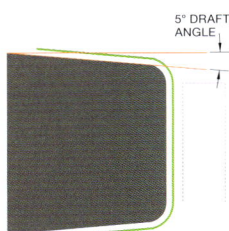

5° DRAFT ANGLE

FINISH

Surface finishes for spun components can range from a tooled or brushed finish to a bright, mirror-like finish. Surface finishing—including brushing, polishing, and buffing—is often done while the component is still on the lathe.

INSERTS

Inserts cannot be formed with this manufacturing process. If inserts are required, then they should be placed post-production.

JOINING

Metals cannot be joined during this process.

LEAD TIME

The lead time for a spun prototype is estimated to be one to two weeks.

PRODUCTION RUNS

Typically, this manufacturing process is best for production runs of 1,000 units or fewer, and for prototypes; however, the process can be used for large production runs. Actual production runs will depend on the tooling.

PRODUCTION SPEED

Cycle times for this manufacturing process may range from 2 to 10 minutes. Cycle times are directly related to the size and draw of the component being spun, so that longer cycle times are required for larger components.

SHAPES

Straight-walled shapes such as cylinders and cups are the most difficult shapes to spin. Stepped, convex, or concave curves will make the spinning process easier. Generally, the spun components are axisymmetric, but ovals up to a 1:2 ratio can be spun.

SIZE LIMITS

Blank diameters can range from 0.25in (6mm) up to 15ft (4.5m). Components larger than 5ft (1.5m) in diameter will be made in specialty shops.

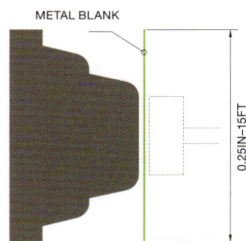

METAL BLANK

0.25IN–15FT

SPINNING RATIO

The spinning ratio (β) is a function of the original blank diameter (D) and the diameter of the spun component (d). So that:

β = D/d

The maximum spinning ratio for each metal and metal alloy is different. Steel's spinning ratio ranges from 1.2 to 2; aluminum and aluminum alloys is 1.5–1.6; nickel is 1.2–1.3; and copper and copper alloys is 2. To achieve higher spinning ratios, the metal needs to be annealed between spinnings.

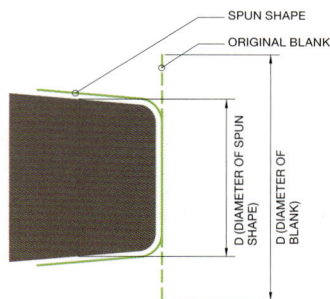

SPUN SHAPE
ORIGINAL BLANK
D (DIAMETER OF SPUN SHAPE)
D (DIAMETER OF BLANK)

SURFACE TEXTURE

Surface textures are easiest if they are axisymmetric, such as concentric rings. However, this process can accommodate shallow, non-concentric surface textures such as stippling, dents, or ribs. These textures are more difficult to spin, and may prematurely wear a spinner's tools and the mandrel.

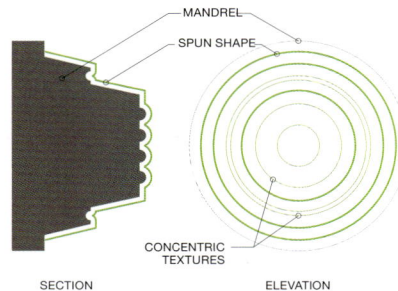

MANDREL
SPUN SHAPE
CONCENTRIC TEXTURES
SECTION   ELEVATION

TOLERANCES

Tolerances for this process may range from 0.01 to 0.015in (0.25–0.4mm) for CNC spinning and approximately 0.03in (0.8mm) for hand spinning. Smaller tolerances are possible, but with added cost.

TOOL COMPLEXITY

Mandrels are very simple and have few to no moving parts.

TOOLING COSTS

Tooling cost for this process are low, but depend on size and material. A wood mandrel can cost less than $250, whereas cast iron and steel tools may be about ten times that cost.

TOOL MARKS

A spinner's tools, such as spoons, sticks, and rollers, will leave marks on the outside of a spun component. These marks are concentric and similar to those made by a potter on a wheel-thrown pot.

UNDERCUTS

If using a solid mandrel, undercuts are not permissible. Undercuts are permissible when using an off-center core, a collapsible mandrel, a sacrificial mandrel, or spinning on air.

VENTS

Vents may be drilled along the length of the mandrel to prevent a vacuum when removing the workpiece. If the vent is located where the blank is not worked, it will not leave a mark on the component.

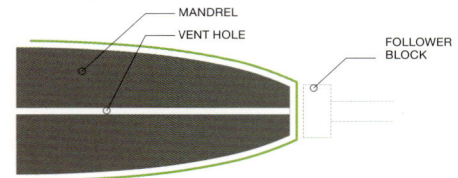

MANDREL
VENT HOLE
FOLLOWER BLOCK

WALL THICKNESS

This process works best for thin-walled components. 0.004in (0.1mm) is the thinnest material to spin. 0.25in (6mm) is the maximum thickness for spinning by hand, and 3in (75mm) for spinning by CNC machine. Although the intention of spinning is to produce components with a consistent wall thickness, there is some thickening of the metal at interior corners, and thinning at exterior corners.

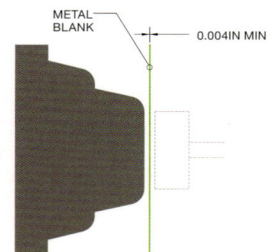

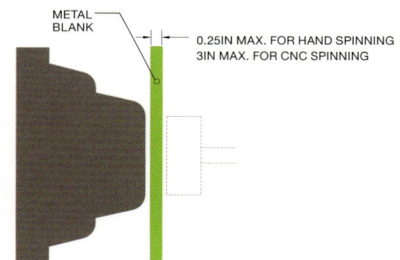

METAL BLANK
0.004IN MIN

METAL BLANK
0.25IN MAX. FOR HAND SPINNING
3IN MAX. FOR CNC SPINNING

SPINNING: METAL

EXTERIOR SKIN | EEMHUIS
Neutelings Riedijk Architects
Amersfoort, the Netherlands

The Eemhuis, or Cultural House, was part of a larger masterplan developed by Bolles + Wilson and commissioned by the City of Amersfoort. The site is next to the Amersfoort historic city center, with the Eem River to the north and railway tracks to the east. The masterplan provides public access through a courtyard to the Eem River, and includes cultural, leisure, and residential buildings. Neutelings Riedijk Architects was among six architectural practices to work on buildings within the masterplan. The Eemhuis provides separation between the courtyard and the railway tracks. The building program combines a number of different Amersfoort cultural institutions, including the city library, an exhibition center, heritage archives, and a school of dance, music, and visual arts. **[15]** The building also includes public amenities such as a café, shop, and underground parking for 375 cars.

The Eemhuis was completed in 2014. It is four stories tall and contains over 161,000ft^2 (15,000m^2) of floor area. The building has a lower base made of brick, which grounds it to the site. Three volumes, which houses the art school's three different departments, hover above the base, and are clad with metal to further differentiate them from the base. The metal cladding is made from a pattern of flat panels and two sizes of spherical-shaped spun domes, making a building skin that has been compared to medieval armor.[5] **[16, 17]**

There are 24,000 spun aluminum components in total. The large domes are approximately 11in (300mm) in diameter and the small ones are approximately 4in (100mm) in diameter. The spun components give relief and tactility to the surface, as well as concealing mechanical connectors, and provide housing for utilities such as light fixtures.[6] **[18, 19, 20]** In some of the spun components, different-sized holes were added for fixture openings or for drainage if mounted to a horizontal surface on the building's exterior.

15
Longitudinal section through the library in Eemhuis by Neutelings Reidijk Architects in Amersfoort, the Netherlands

16
Detail elevation of upper two floors

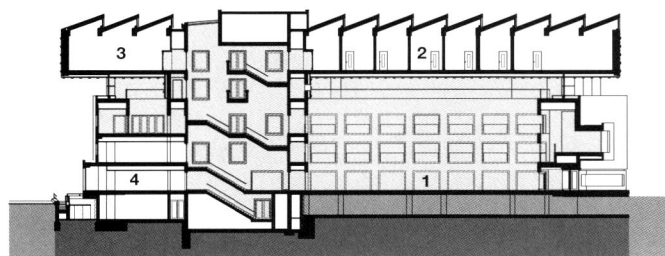

15

SECTION DD

0 5 10 15 20 25 m

LEGEND

1. LIBRARY
2. HERITAGE ARCHIVES
3. ARTS SCHOOL
4. EXHIBITION CENTER

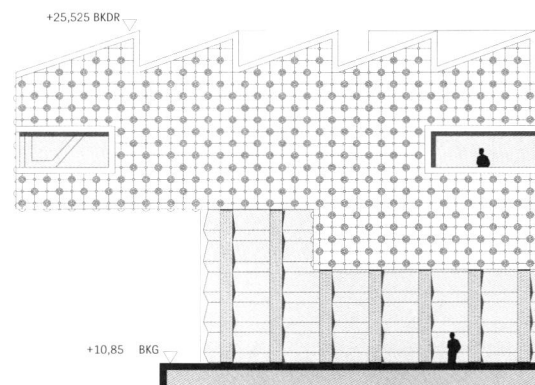

16

+25,525 BKDR

+10,85 BKG

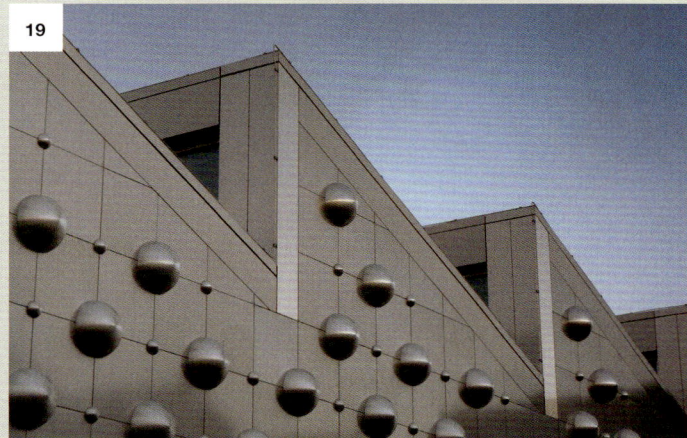

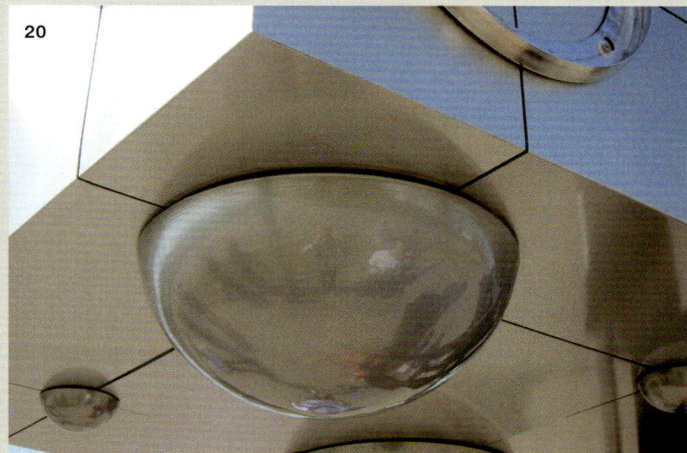

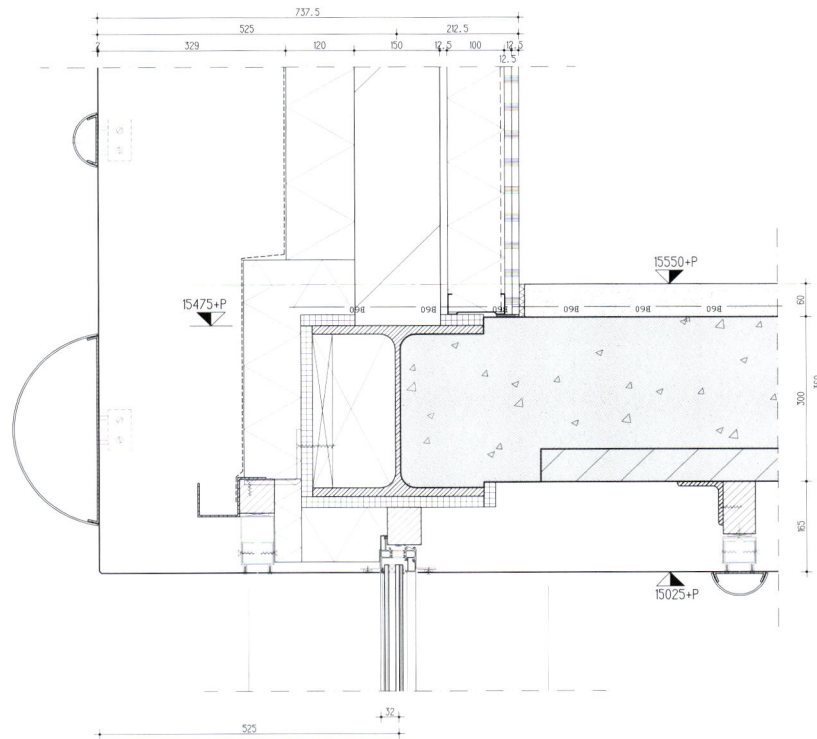

17
View of the Eemhuis from public square

18
Domes inside of library

19
Detail image of spun component and flat panels

20
Detail image of light fixture

21 Technical detail

ABT was contracted by Neutelings Riedijk to help with the project's technical details. **[21, 22]** According to Eric Thijssen, Neutelings Riedijk project leader, ABT was responsible for the Eemhuis plan and construction development.[7] Dura Vermeer was the project general contractor, and Leebo Intelligent Building Systems was the façade contractor. Leebo subcontracted the manufacturing of the domes to another company.[8]

DESIGN CONSIDERATIONS

When Bolles + Wilson completed the masterplan, they set the goal of the Eemhuis building to be a shimmering crown or jewel-like building. **[16]** Neutelings Riedijk also wanted to separate the Eemhuis from the surrounding commercial buildings. Neutelings Riedijk's buildings are known for their use of ornament, for example, the cast metal hands on the exterior of the Museum Aan de Stroom (MAS) in Antwerp or the letters applied to the exterior of the Veenman Printshop. Generally, Neutelings Riedijk does a large amount of design work for public buildings. Toward that end, Thijssen states that the firm likes to design buildings that are unique and have never been seen before. Similar to the Eiffel Tower, over time, the uniqueness of a single building can form part of a city's identity.

The design of the façade derived from the firm's initial studies of pattern making. The design team developed a system of panels and domes that were large enough to give the building a texture, even from a distance.

22 Mock-up panel. Mounting rings for spun components are located at corners of square panels, hiding their mechanical fasteners

According to Thijssen, the domes reference the city's history in literature and landscape, and relate to boulders found in and around Amersfoort.

The metal cladding system wraps the three volumes, extending into the building's interior and creating the ceiling surface of the Eemhuis library. The large domes house the library's light fixtures. [23] The domes are threaded on the interior, so that they twist onto the panels. For the spheres that are accessible to people, a small set screw was added for security.

MANUFACTURING CONSIDERATIONS

As with most of Neutelings Riedijk's work, this was a public bid project, in which construction contracts were awarded to the lowest bidder. Because of this, Neutelings Riedijk had little to no control over the selection of the contractor or the manufacturing of the spheres. Instead, Neutelings Riedijk provided the design, and Leebo subcontracted out the making of the domes. Prototypes of the domes were sent to the architect for selection and approval. Neutelings Riedijk had not specified if the spheres were to be made by stamping, hydroforming, or spinning. When reviewing the prototypes, the design team liked tooling lines that formed on the dome's exterior, as it gave them further texture. [24, 25]

Neither Thijssen nor Leebo were able to confirm why metal spinning was used instead of another sheet-metal forming process. Thijseen assumed that metal spinning must have been the most economical method, because of the public-bid process.

OTHER CONSIDERATIONS

Tolerances for the metal panels were tighter than the tolerances to which the Eemhuis was built. The joint widths between the panels were adjusted to accommodate any dimensional discrepancies. Thijssen stated that in the end, it would have been helpful if special end units had been made to help resolve the dimensional issues.

LESSONS LEARNED

Thijseen finds that these public bid projects are difficult, as the firm does not work directly with the manufacturers to develop the component. If Neutelings Riedijk does work with a manufacturer, it might just be to ask general questions about what is possible; it then develops the component as far as possible based on that knowledge. In the contract documents, Neutelings Riedijk asks the contractor to provide mock-ups and models so the architects can evaluate the quality of the component. For some projects, such as the cast hands on MAS, the firm works with artists. For that project, the contractor was given basic construction instruction, but then had to go back and make any necessary changes once the art installation was complete.

23
Interior of Eemhuis library. Note that the library's recessed lights are located within the spun components

24
Two different sizes of metal spinners

25
Inside of large dome

2

Continuous Shaping

2.1 Extrusion / 2.2 Pultrusion

Included in this section are processes that form consistent cross-sections along the component length. Unlike the other processes in this book, which are cyclical, these processes are essentially continuous, and the only limiting factors affecting component length are the manufacturing facility and transportation restrictions. There are only two processes in this section—extrusion and pultrusion. Extrusion pushes the medium out of the die, and includes materials such as clays, aluminum, or other metals, and thermoplastics. Pultrusion pulls a composite medium out of the die, and is typically limited to fiber-reinforced thermoset plastic, but can also include fiber-reinforced concrete and plaster.

Generally, extrusion and pultrusion use equipment that is not available to craftspeople and in workshops, and therefore necessitate working with manufacturers. The exception is extrusion of clay, which can be done using a die attached to a pug mill for small extrusions with low volume. Equipment for extruding aluminum and other metals can be very large and expensive, and is therefore reserved for larger companies with a lot of capital and longer lead times. Other companies, such as stiff-mud extruders, may produce high volumes of their own products (e.g. bricks) and so are less likely to accept custom orders.

Both extrusion and pultrusion can be used to manufacture cross-sections that are simple or complex, and are solid, semi-hollow, or hollow. If the manufacturing process is fast, such as extrusion of plastic and aluminum, the wall thickness should be consistent across the profile to ensure constant material flow through the die. If the manufacturing process is slow, such as extrusion of clays and pultrusion, then constant wall thicknesses do not need to be maintained, as differential material flow through the die is less likely. For almost all processes, the cut face of the component is different than the die-formed profile. Tolerances and surface finish qualities on the die face are generally better than the cut face.

2.1 Extrusion

INTRODUCTION

Extrusion is a manufacturing process that pushes a medium through a die to create a continuous cross-sectional shape. The process is similar to squeezing toothpaste from a tube. Extrusion can produce components with simple or complex cross-sections, and components that are solid, semi-hollow, or hollow. Extrusion results in good surface quality and typically requires little to no post-production surface refinishing. Theoretically, extrusion can produce components of infinite length, but length is often restricted by the size of the manufacturing facility, the method in which the medium is fed into the extrusion barrel, and transportation regulations. [1, 2, 3] If the extruded shape is flexible enough to be rolled, it can be continuously rolled while it is being extruded. [4] Extruded components are often linear, but cross-sectional shapes can be cut into small widths. [5]

The extruding medium is placed inside of an extrusion barrel, which can be vertically or horizontally oriented, with horizontal extrusion being more common. Typically, a force pushes on the medium, squeezing it toward a die opening; heat may be added to facilitate the medium's flow. The die opening shapes the medium as it exits the extruder. The extrudate, as it is now called, is cut into rough lengths as it exits the die, allowing this process to easily accommodate custom lengths of an extruded profile. The ends are then trimmed to their final length.

The extrusion faces that are in contact with the die are considered the component's finished face, whereas the trimmed edge is unfinished, and often hidden. As the extrusion exits the die, some post-production may be necessary. For example, differential

1 Extruding stiff mud at a brick-making facility

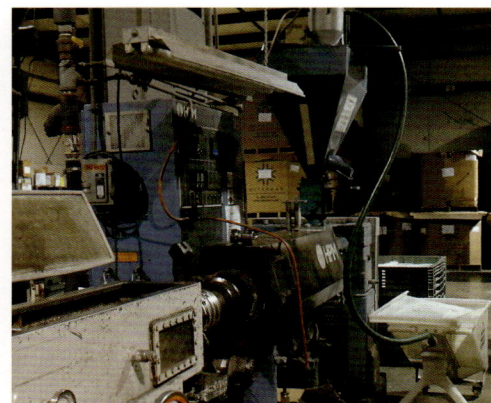
3 Plastic extruder

2 Stiff aluminum extrusions limited by length of equipment and manufacturing facility

4 Flexible aluminum tube, continuously rolled after extrusion

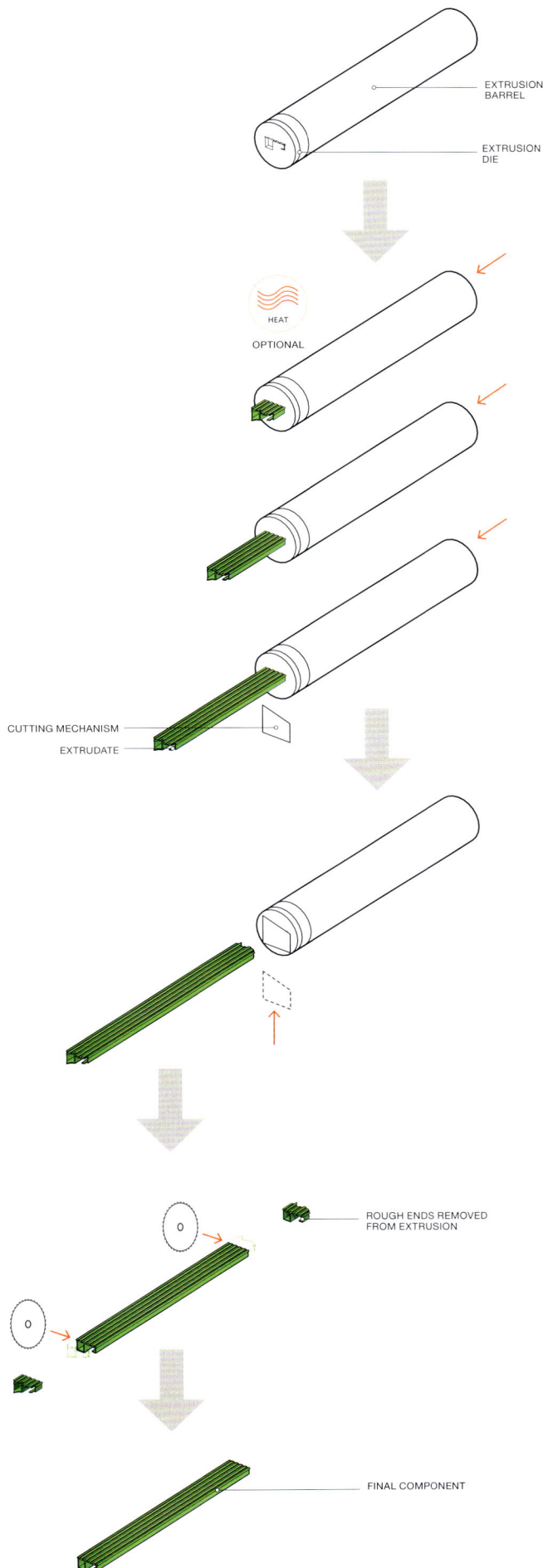

EXTRUSION
BARREL

EXTRUSION
DIE

HEAT
OPTIONAL

CUTTING MECHANISM

EXTRUDATE

ROUGH ENDS REMOVED
FROM EXTRUSION

FINAL COMPONENT

flow in the cross-section can cause the linear extrusion to develop a slight curve. The longer the piece, the more pronounced the curve. This can be particularly noticeable when extruding aluminum, and stretchers may be used to help straighten the extruded component. [6] In plastic extrusion, the medium exits the die near its melting temperature. Because of this, sizers may be added to the process to help the material maintain its shape as it enters the cooler, which uses air, water, or water mist to cool the extruded component. [7] When extruding stiff mud, additional finishing rollers may also be used to smooth or pattern the surface. [8]

Extrusion is considered to be a continuous process, with no defined cycle times. Some media, such as clay, stiff mud, and plastic, are fed into the extrusion barrel continuously, while the extrudate exits the die. In comparison, metals such as aluminum are loaded into the extrusion machine in the form of billets, or fixed-length cylinders, [10] which are then forced through the die by a ram. When the billet is almost spent, a new billet is loaded into the barrel, and a cold joint forms where the metal from two billets meets.

Extrusion can be highly mechanized for some media. The more that automation is associated with a plant, the less likely it can accommodate custom extrusions. Stiff mud, especially in the making of bricks, is highly mechanized because of the inherent manufacturing volume associated with the product, and robots

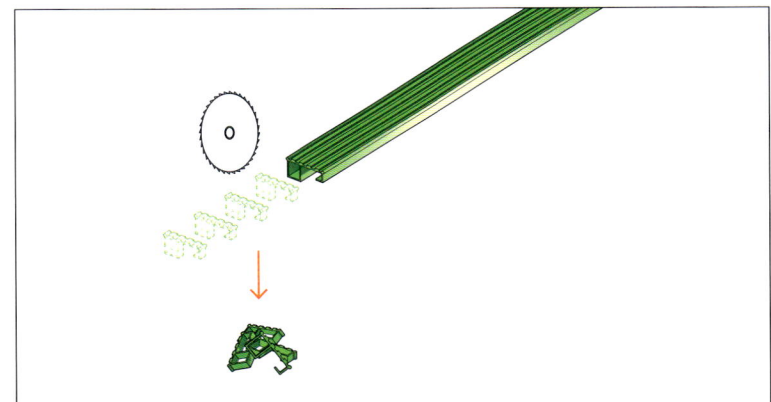

5 Extruded components cut into short widths

6 Stretching aluminum after extruding to straighten components

7 Extruded plastic exiting die and entering cooler with water bath

10 Aluminum billet

8 In-line finishing roller for extruding stiff mud

9 Robots used for large productions of similar products

may be used for packaging. [9] Extruding aluminum requires large equipment, due to the high compression forces need to push the material though the die, but it is not highly mechanized, allowing plants to accommodate a variety of extruded profiles and lengths. [11] Plastic extruding equipment is often large, and the process requires greater operating skill for maintaining quality than extruding stiff mud or aluminum. This means that plastic extruding is often not highly mechanized. Craftspeople with small presses can extrude clay; however, their equipment will limit the component size and production volume. [12]

BUILDING PRODUCTS

Numerous commercially available building products are made by extrusion. Extruded stiff mud is used to make bricks, including thin-set bricks, modular bricks, and pavers. Extruded clay can be used to make terra cotta rainscreen panels, louvers, architectural moldings, and textured tiles. Extruded plastic can be used for exterior window and door frames, vinyl siding, plumbing piping, and electrical conduit. Extruded aluminum is most commonly used for storefront and glass curtain wall mullions, and can be used for aluminum structural components, and handrail and guardrail assemblies.

TOOLING

The tooling required to extrude is the die and optional sizers, rollers, or stretchers used for post-extrusion finishing. The die channels the medium to the die opening, and gives the extrusion its profile. The edge of the die profile affects the exterior surface of the extruded component. As the extruding medium passes through the die, the die edges become worn. Dies must therefore be resistant to wear, maintain hardness when heated by manufacturing or friction, and be thermally conductive so that they

11 Large aluminum extruders

13 Plastic die (left) with associated sizers (right)

12 Small pug mill in clay workshop facility

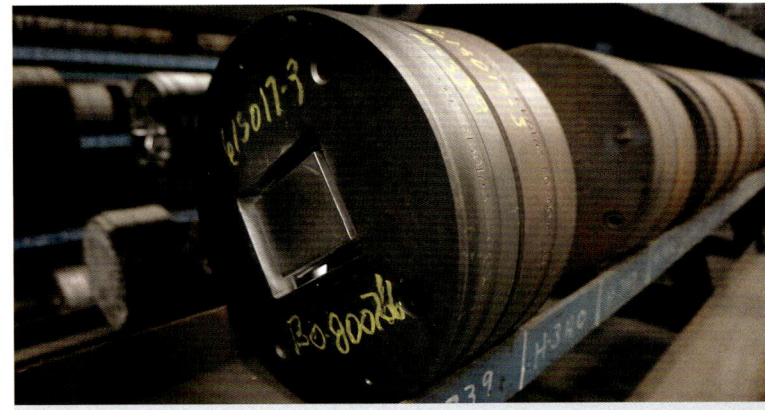

14 Aluminum extruding dies made from tool steel

draw heat away from the extruding medium. In extruding, the die is separate from the extruding barrel so that it can be changed without moving the machinery. In plastic extruding, sizers are part of the tooling package, and are made to the shape of the component. [13]

Dies are typically made from tool steel, regardless of the extruding medium. [14, 15] In some processes, such as cold extruding aluminum, additional cemented carbide may be added to reinforce the die edges. For small productions from clay-working craftspeople, the die can be make from plywood, acrylic sheets, or sheet metal. Generally, tolerances with these materials are not good, and extrudate will wander as it leaves the die opening.

Die profiles can make solid components, finely detailed elements, semi-hollow openings, and hollow openings. The shape and complexity of the die will affect the force required to push the medium through it. In extrusion, it is important that all of the extrudate emerges from the die at the same rate. For media that is extruded at a fast rate, such as aluminum and plastic, it is recommended that the component be designed with a consistent wall thickness across the cross-section, as the medium will flow faster through a narrow opening than a wider opening. Dies

can be designed to control flow rates so that upstream of the die opening, more extruding medium is directed to wider sections of the profile. This allows the medium to exit the die at a more consistent flow rate. [16] Adjusting the die in this manner will increase complexity and costs.

Although the tool steel used for dies is expensive, the technology to shape the die typically is not. Extruding dies are less expensive than other types of manufacturing equipment. Dies do not have any moving parts, and are fairly simple to fabricate. Most dies are CNC milled or wire cut by an EDM, both of which are efficient production methods.

ENVIRONMENTAL IMPACT

Generally, extrusion uses little energy and produces little manufacturing waste. Because of the inherent softness of the material, extruding clay uses the least energy; however, the firing of clay in a kiln is very energy intensive. Tunnel kilns use less energy than batch kilns of a comparable size. They control when they open and close, reducing the potential for heat loss. Additionally, many clay extruders will use residual heat from the kiln to dry the clays before they go into the kiln. Hot extruding aluminum will be the

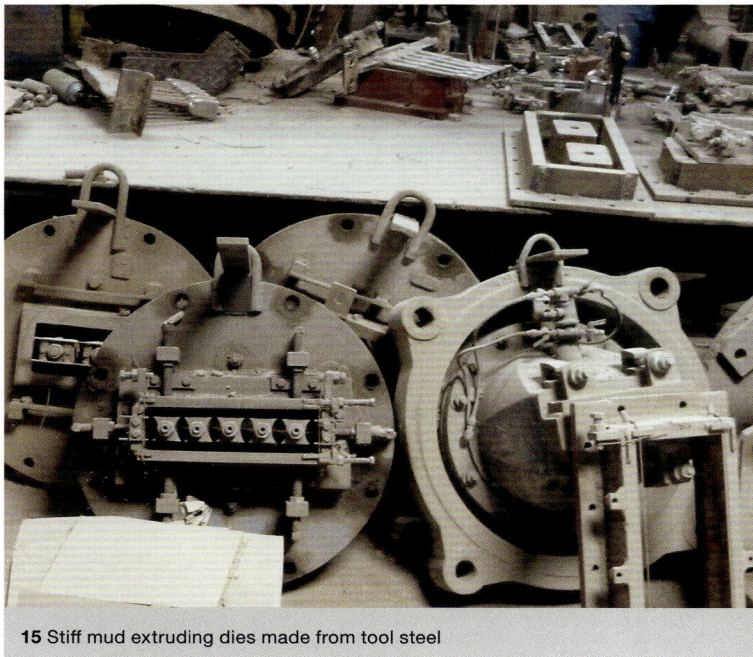

15 Stiff mud extruding dies made from tool steel

most energy intensive, as extruding metal requires the most force and the billet must be heated to 1,200–2,000°F (650–1,100°C) prior to extrusion.

Clay and plastic extrusion produces almost no manufacturing waste, and any material waste is typically recycled back directly into the pug mill or reground and put into the hopper. Aluminum extruding does result in production waste, as the end of the billet (or butt) is not extruded, and profile ends are damaged during stretching. Aluminum production waste is often shipped back to the billet manufacturer, where it is reprocessed into another aluminum billet. Thermoplastic, used for extruding plastic, may be reground and fed back into the hopper as feedstock.

Plastic extrusion can result in emissions of toxic or volatile organic compounds (VOCs) during extrusion, and plastic extruders must be properly ventilated. No harmful gases are released when extruding clays, or during cold or warm aluminum extruding.

16 Two photographs of the same die. The smaller openings are the downstream, or exit, face of the die; the larger opening is the upstream face of the die. The larger opening is shaped so that the plastic flows at a consistent speed when exiting the die

MATERIAL CONSIDERATIONS + DESIGN PARAMETERS

Materials that are best for extruding will withstand compression and shear stress, but not tension stress. This chapter includes ceramics like clay and stiff mud, aluminum, and plastic, as those have the most architectural applications. Other materials, such as lead and copper, and foodstuffs (e.g. pasta), can also be extruded. The extruding medium will affect the temperature at which the medium is extruded. For example, clay and stiff mud are extruded at room temperature; aluminum may be cold (e.g. room temperature), warm, or hot extruded; and plastic is melted into a liquid before extrusion.

All extruding media must be homogeneous as they exit the die; because a lesser-mixed, or heterogeneous mixture will cause an uneven flow rate as the material exists the die. This in turn causes internal shear stresses across the extrudate's cross-section, affecting the strength and surface quality of the extrusion. As the medium flows through the die, friction develops between the face of the extrusion and the edge of the die. This friction slows down the flow of the medium at the extrudate surface, while the medium in the center flows faster. [17] This differential friction can cause surface irregularities and tears in the extrusion. Friction can be minimized by improved die design, increased material viscosity, and slowing extruding speeds.

CLAY

Clay is a dry dust made of plate-shaped particles. Adding water allows the plates to slide past one another to make a plastic-like, shapeable material. Too little water and the particles cannot slide past one another, causing cracking as the clay is worked; too much water and the particles slip freely past one another, keeping the clay from holding a shape. For extruding, dry clay will cause cracks and ragged surfaces while wet clay will deform under its own weight. Generally, clay is more plastic than stiff mud, and can be shaped into complex and thin-walled profiles. Stiff mud contains larger particles and must be extruded at higher pressures than clay, resulting in rougher surfaces and thicker walls than clay.

Clay is mixed in a pug mill, which mechanically consolidates the clay mixture. In the pug mill, the clay will be mixed with water or dry clay to achieve the correct moisture content. Pug mills can also be used to recycle unfired clay scraps into the extruding medium. In workshops, the extruding die can be attached directly to the pug mill for small extrusions. [18] Unfortunately, as pug mills mix the clay air bubbles may be trapped, which decreases material strength, reduces surface quality, and increases likelihood of breakage during kiln firing. A vacuum may be added to the pug mill to reduce the air bubbles.

Extruded ceramic components are dried after extruding in a controlled or semi-controlled environment until the clay is leather-hard. Moisture and temperature are regulated during this process, allowing the ceramic to shrink slowly, which reduces stress cracks. When sufficiently dried, the ceramic is placed in a kiln to be fired. Kilns can be either tunnel or batch kilns. [19, 20] Tunnel kilns are expensive, and are space and energy intensive, but provide a consistent temperature and therefore a consistent quality component. They are also appropriate for high-volume productions. Batch kilns are less expensive, but wear out faster due to temperature

SIMILAR PROCESSES

There are no processes similar to extruding clay. For some shapes, such as roof tiles, ram-pressing can be substituted for extrusion; however, ram-pressing cannot produce the hollow cross-sections that extrusion can.

17 Friction between the die edge and the outside of the extrudate can cause the middle of the cross-section to flow faster than the edges

18 Die attached to pug mill opening

19 Small-batch kiln in workshop

20 Brick pallet awaiting loading into the tunnel kiln

21 Thin-walled, extruded plastic clay components. Note the die finish on the linear edge and the exposed aggregate on the cut edges

22 Thicker-walled, plastic clay components with some solid parts of the cross-section. Notice that the ends of the solid parts have been shaped post-production

fluctuations. They are less consistent in their firing temperatures. The temperature of the kiln and the amount of oxygen available during firing will affect the color of the ceramic component.

PLASTIC CLAY

When clay is plastic, it is a soft, malleable material that can be formed without rupturing or cracking, but is stiff enough to retain its shape and not collapse under its own weight. Plastic clay can be easily formed by hand, with little pressure. Clay is free of large stones, debris, and organic materials, but it may include small particles of grog (unfired, dried clay) as filler. Crushers and screens are often used before mixing the clay with water to ensure that particle sizes are small and will not be exposed on the component surface during extruding.

Clay can be used to create solid cross-sections, but is most suitable for hollow cross-sections with thin walls. The thinner the walls of the extruded profile, the more careful the manufacturer must be when mixing the clay that air bubbles are not formed, as they may be exposed on the component surface during extruding. **[21, 22]**

CORNER RADII

A small radius of 0.03–0.06in (0.8–1.6mm) is used for all die-formed corners. No corner radius is required at the cut edges of the extrusion.

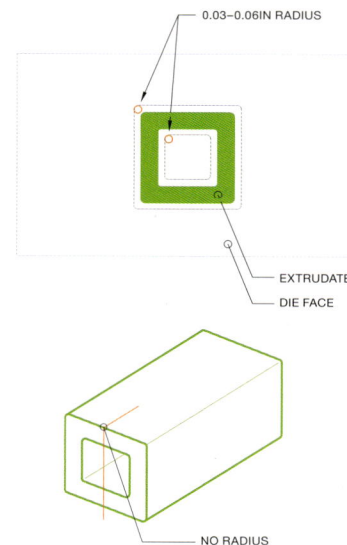

FINISH

The surface formed by the die is smooth. The cut ends are typically cut with wire, which may leave cut marks on the surface and will expose grog or other fine particulates in the clay. Extruded clay can be glazed with flat, semi-gloss, or gloss finishes, in a range of colors and opacities.

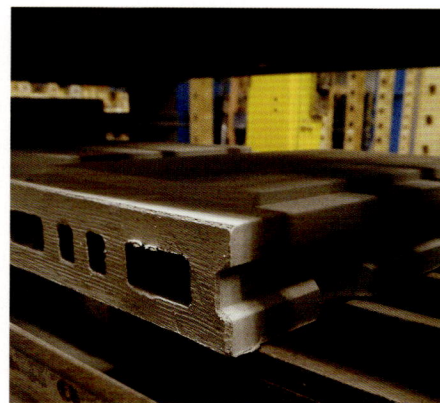

HOLLOW

Most extruded clay components are extruded as hollow elements, made up of a series of thinner walls. The hollow portions of any shape need to be carefully considered. Too many holes: the clay will not support itself during extruding, and the more expensive the die required. Too few holes: air bubbles will likely be trapped, causing breaking during firing.

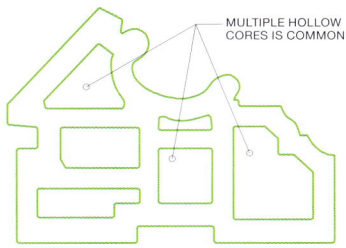

MULTIPLE HOLLOW CORES IS COMMON

JOINING

Joints cannot be made during the extrusion process; however, while the clay is green, two clay extrusions can be joined together. Joining components is done by hand and is labor intensive. Often, it is done to fabricate special corner units.

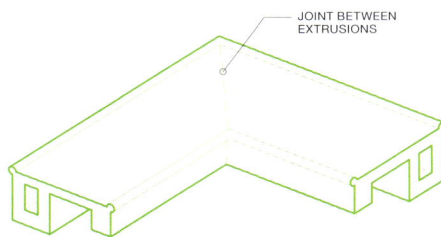

JOINT BETWEEN EXTRUSIONS

SHAPES

Extruded clay profiles can be simple or complex, with the same cross-sections extruded along the length of the profile. Modifications to the cross-section can be made along the length, but this is done off-line and by hand.

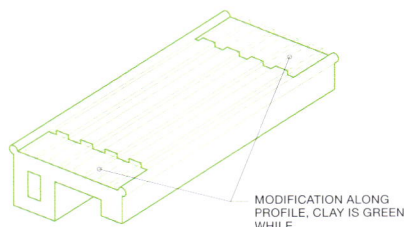

MODIFICATION ALONG PROFILE, CLAY IS GREEN WHILE

This process is best used to make cross-sections that are thin and wide. Profiles of extruded plastic clay can range from square and near-square shapes to wide, flat rectangles with height-to-width ratios of 1:15 or more.

SHRINKING

Most clay shrinks 6–10% after firing, due to water loss.

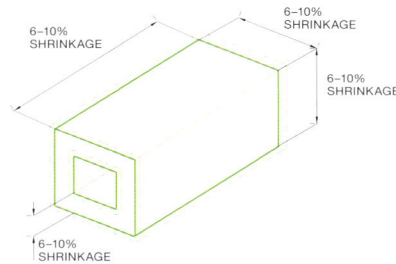

6–10% SHRINKAGE
6–10% SHRINKAGE
6–10% SHRINKAGE
6–10% SHRINKAGE

SIZE LIMITS

Extrusion widths are limited to 36in (920mm) or less, but there are few manufacturers with this size capability. Widths of 18in (460mm) or less are typical. Most clay extruders are limited by their extruding volume per minute, so the wider the clay component, the longer manufacturing will take.

SURFACE DESIGNS

There are a variety of surface designs and textures available with this process. It readily accommodates textures and designs that run the length of the component, as they can be added to the die edge. Intermittent designs and textures can be done in-line, but post-extruding. For example, patterned rollers or wire brushes can be rolled onto the extrudate surface to get nonlinear patterns.

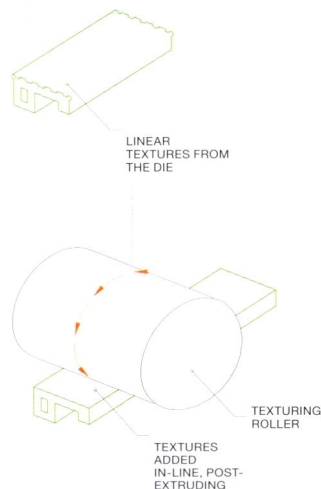

LINEAR TEXTURES FROM THE DIE

TEXTURING ROLLER

TEXTURES ADDED IN-LINE, POST-EXTRUDING

TOOLING COMPLEXITY

Tools are simple for this process and have no moving parts.

TOOLING COSTS

Tooling costs are low, with production-quality steel molds ranging from $5,000 to $15,000. Prototype dies made from plastic or plywood can be less than $200.

TOLERANCES

The tolerance of the component's die faces is 0.06–0.15in (1.6–4mm), depending on dimensions. The tolerance of the cut lengths of the extrudate is 0.03–0.13in (0.8–3.2mm), depending on total length.

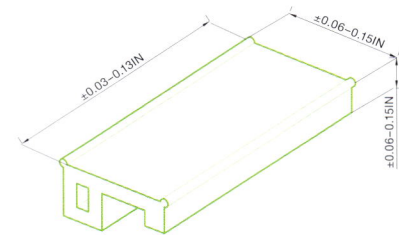

±0.03–0.13IN
±0.06–0.15IN
±0.06–0.15IN

WALL THICKNESS

Wall thicknesses can vary across the cross-section, and should be a minimum of 0.37in (9.5mm). Thicker wall thicknesses will be required as the size of the cross-section increases, as the wall needs to support the clay while it is still green.

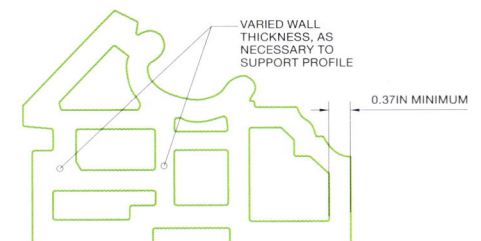

VARIED WALL THICKNESS, AS NECESSARY TO SUPPORT PROFILE

0.37IN MINIMUM

WARPING

Extruded components may warp or twist along their length. The twist should be limited to 0.005in/in (0.127mm/mm) along the length of the extrusion.

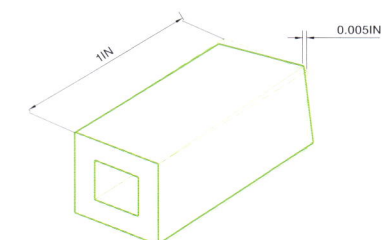

1IN
0.005IN

EXTRUSION: CLAY

COLUMN CLADDING | SPANISH EXPO PAVILION
Mangado y Asociados
Zaragoza, Spain

From June 14 to September 14, 2008, Zaragoza, Spain hosted an international exposition with the title of "Water and Sustainable Development." Francisco Mangado of Mangado y Asociados designed the expo's Spanish Pavilion in keeping with this theme. **[23, 24]** The Spanish Pavilion collects water from the building's roof and uses water for passive cooling. The building also uses recycled and recyclable materials of glass, ceramic, steel, wood, and cork as its primary materials. Finally, Mangado designed the building with a dry assembly system so that it could be deconstructed and reconstructed at a new location.

The building is a forest of vertical members that connect the pool at the base of the building to the thin roof at its top. **[25, 26, 27]** Some of the members are structural, while others serve as drainpipes from the roof. Each vertical member is clad in custom-extruded terra cotta components. There are two different diameters of extrusions—approximately 12in and 8in (300mm and 200mm)—used to clad a variety of different-sized downspouts and columns. 28,000 components were made for this project—approximately 20,000 of the 8in (200mm) diameter and 8,000 of the 12in (300mm) diameter. All extruded components were cut while green, by a steel cable, into 35in (900mm) lengths.

After initial design drawings, Mangado approached ASCER (the Spanish Association of Ceramic Tiles and Pavements), which represents almost all of Spain's ceramic manufacturers, for support.[1] From there, two companies, Ceramica Cumella and Decorativa, came together to form Decorativa-Cumella. Ceramica Cumella, founded in 1880, is located in Barcelona, and the company prides itself on collaborating with architects at a project's conception.[2] Decorativa, founded in 1862, is located in Valencia and has offices in France and Italy, and develops high-quality terra cotta in many colors. Together, Decorative-Cumella developed Mangado's design and managed material development and production.

DESIGN CONSIDERATIONS

According to Francisco Mangado, he wanted to use terra cotta as the Pavilion's exterior material because it is capable of expressing a tradition in Spanish architecture while interpreting a contemporary aesthetic.[3] Extrusion was selected as a manufacturing process, as it could produce the 28,000 units economically, practically, and within the desired time frame.

Color was one of the more difficult challenges with this component. Mangado wanted the terra cotta to be unglazed with its natural kiln finish. He also wanted the color of the terra cotta to vary across the component

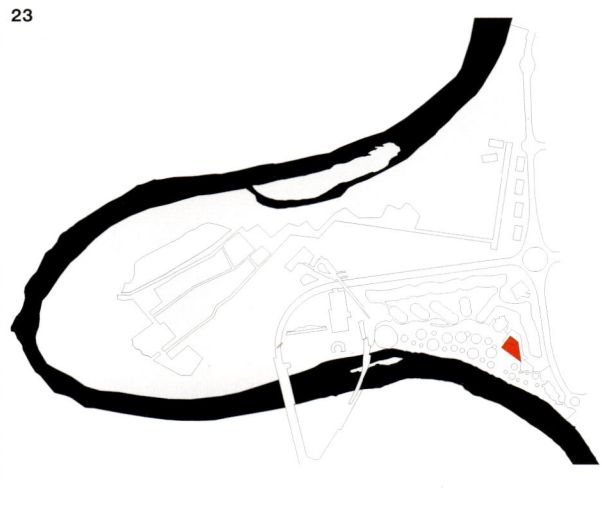

23

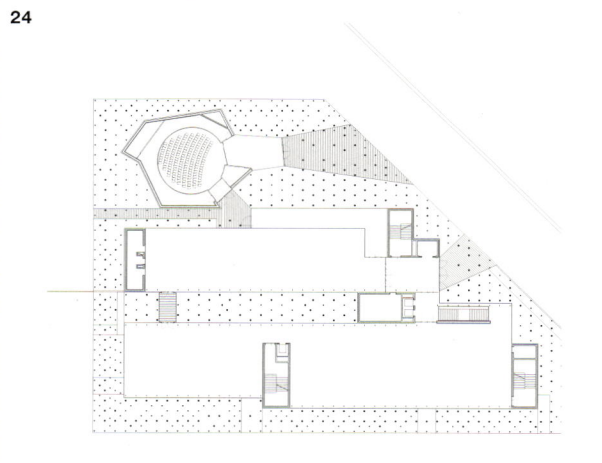

24

23
Site plan of expo with
Spanish Pavilion highlighted in red

24
Ground floor plan

25
View of building exterior

26
Dry fitting of terra cotta cladding over
steel column during construction

27
Natural color variations of the
terra cotta cladding

25

26

27

28 Extrusion process

and between components, but keep within the same tonality. Color variation was achieved by baking the components at different temperatures, ranging from 1830 to 2200°F (1000–1200°C). The colors give a natural variety to a beautiful material and reconnects the material with Spanish tradition, as temperature control and firing cycles were difficult to maintain with precision in old brick kilns.

Decorativa-Cumella made many prototypes to determine colors and color variants. Different pieces were made to determine how the color varied when baking at different temperatures. Early iterations had less heat getting into the grooves of the components, leaving the grooves redder than the ridges. This was considered undesirable by the team. The manufacturer also tested to see whether the different firing temperatures affected the components' mechanical properties and physical behavior, such as thermal expansion. According to Mangado, prototypes were made on different dies and extruders than the final produced components.[4]

MANUFACTURING CONSIDERATIONS

After Mangado's initial sketches, the design and manufacturing teams collaborated intensely to develop the component. According to Mangado, they often discussed "how to produce the pieces with maximum quality and in the shortest time possible, and about how using several small artisanal workshops simultaneously could guarantee maximum quality. We also very diligently studied the different technical details involved in the actual construction site."[5] To Mangado, this collaboration between architect and manufacturer is understood as a learning opportunity, useful to his creative process, and results in architecture that is both innovative and attractive.

The terra cotta components were extruded with a temporary internal structure intended to support the round shape as it exited the extruder, and during firing. **[28, 33]** A small neck was formed in the connection between the internal support and the interior face of the component, to facilitate breaking with little to no damage to the component. Internal pockets were formed on the inside face, along the length of the extrusion. These pockets were for construction purposes, as they fit over pin connectors attached to the columns' supporting brackets, keeping the components in place. **[29, 30]**

The manufacturer produced 100 units a day—approximately 2,750 units or 8,120ft (2,500m) per month. The units were cut to length with a wire as they came out of the extruder. This was done while the clay was still green, which caused some damage to the components' ends. Post-production trimming was required to make the ends of the units square, so that they sat properly on their supports. **[31, 32]**

COLUMN TYPE 1

1

5

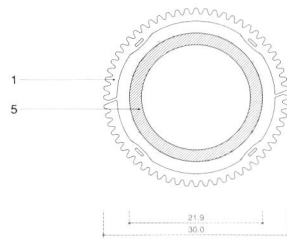

21.9
30.0

COLUMN TYPE 2

3

4

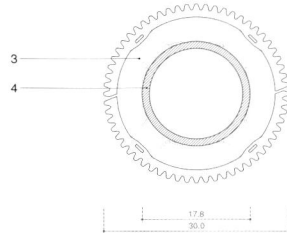

17.8
30.0

COLUMN TYPE 3

2

6

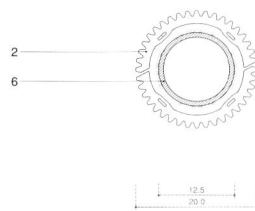

12.5
20.0

COLUMN TYPE 4

1

4

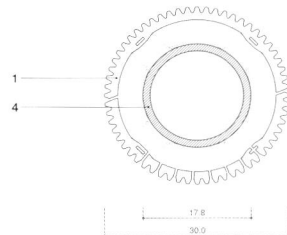

17.8
30.0

COLUMN TYPE FOR
RAINWATER DOWNPIPE

7

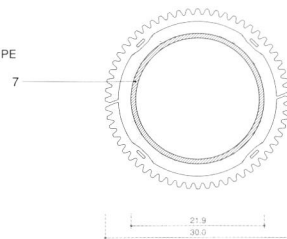

21.9
30.0

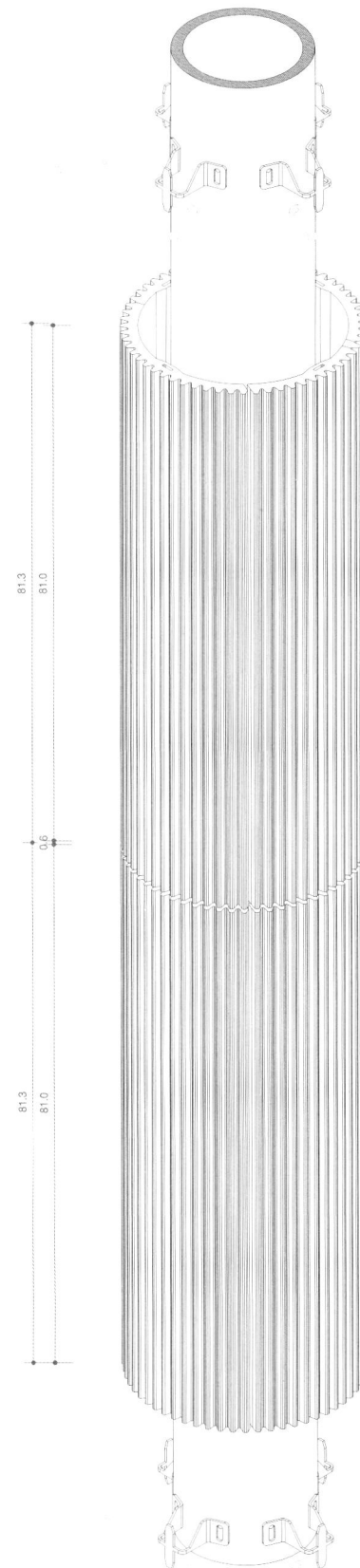

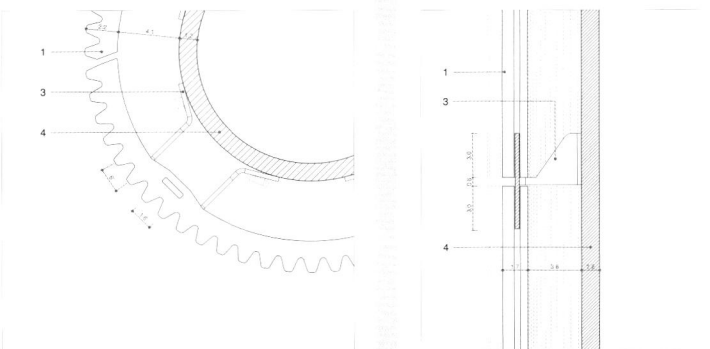

29 Detail drawing of columns, terra cotta types, and method of support

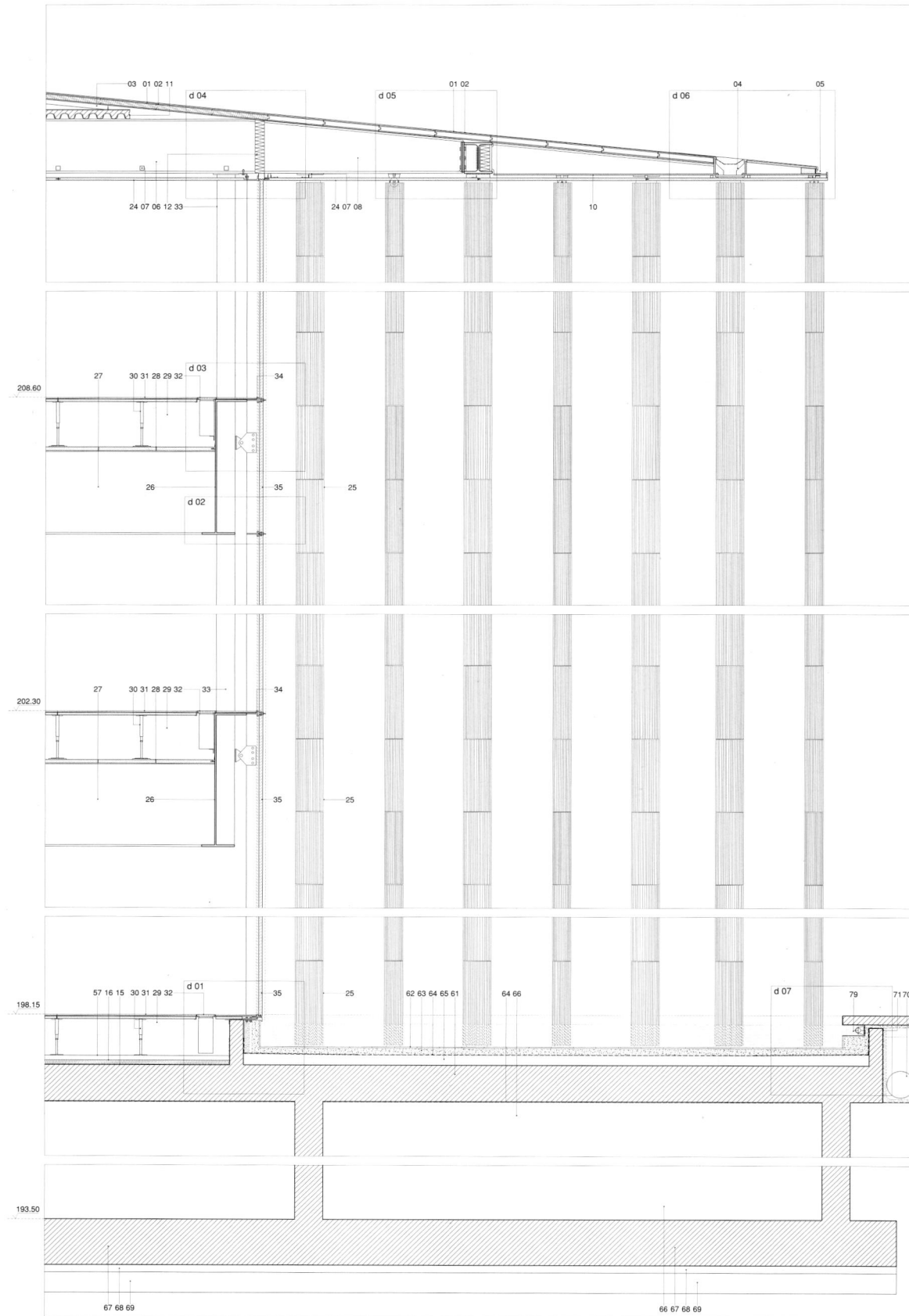

30 Construction section of building

OTHER CONSIDERATIONS

The terra cotta pieces have proved to be quite durable. It was predicted that as many as 10% of the 28,000 pieces would break, but only 1% actually did.[6] Years later, Mangado finds that the terra cotta is still in perfect condition and has even improved with age.

LESSONS LEARNED

For this project, Mangado learned the importance of collaboration and the value of a strong relationship between the architect and the manufacturer. Mangado believes that constant communication from the very beginning made the process much easier. He felt that the working relationship between his office and the manufacturer was positive and enthusiastic, and if there were any difficulties they were addressed easily. Overall, Mangado learned a lot about collaboration from this project. He wrote, "It could also well be the one [building] I have most learned from. It is now completely autonomous, but each and every piece of it, each joint, each sequence, continues to tell me that architects cannot cease to be constructors. We cannot accept administrative impositions of the separation of project and construction work."[7]

31
Terra cotta components, after firing

32
Terra cotta components on kiln cart, after firing

33
Detail image of terra cotta profile, before firing

MATERIAL CONSIDERATIONS + DESIGN PARAMETERS

STIFF MUD

Stiff mud includes clay, larger particles such as sand, feldspar, and grog, and just enough moisture and plasticity to be extruded with moderate pressure. [34] Stiff mud has less water and larger particles than extruded clay, making its surface rougher, while it shrinks, warps, and cracks less than clay. Because of the higher speed and added friction of extruding stiff mud, dies are lubricated with oil, water, or steam. [35]

When the stiff mud exits the die, it is known as a slug. It is approximately 8ft (2.4m) in length, and is then cross-cut with wires to make the bricks' height. Often the ends of the slug are damaged due to cutting with the flying saw, and are recycled back into the pug mill. [37, 38] As when extruding other materials, the cut length of the extrusion can be easily customized.

Dies for extruding stiff mud are made of tool steel. The die gives a smooth finish to the extruded stiff mud, known as die finished. Post-extrusion surface treatments are sometimes done in-line after the stiff mud exits the die. These may include wire cutting or wire brushing, and sawdust or mineral coatings may be added to the face of the units. Other post-production finishing is done off-line, and may include tumbling the brick or knocking it in molds. If there are a small number of specialty shapes required, a manufacturer may choose to remove a slug from the production line and run it through a smaller hand extruder in order to change the profile of the component. [36]

Dies are relatively simple, inexpensive, and easy to change, which allows for customization. Be aware, though, that many brick manufacturers have dedicated production lines for particular products, and may operate on a "push" system of manufacturing a product before orders are placed. Many brick plants are also highly mechanized, using robots to do brick stacking before firing and packing the brick post-firing. These automations and production processes, although they reduce product costs, will affect whether or not a stiff mud extruder is able to accommodate small, custom orders.

SIMILAR PROCESSES

Like clay, there are no similar processes to extruding mud. Molds can be used to make bricks, however, interior holes cannot be made and die and wire-cut finishes are not available.

36 Small hand extruder for bullnose profile. Done off-line with green brick

37 Bricks are cross-cut with wires

34 Stiff mud has less water and larger particles than plastic clay

35 Stiff mud coming out of the extruder with lubrication lines attached

38 Ends of slugs are damaged, cut off, and returned to the pug mill

CORNER RADII

Corner radii are not required.

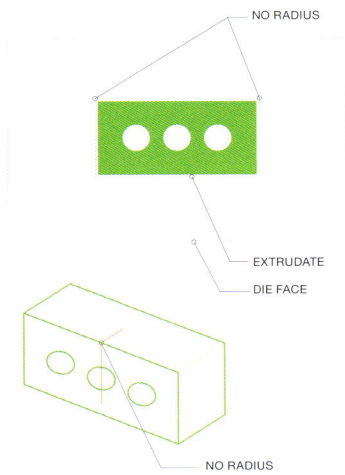

NO RADIUS

EXTRUDATE
DIE FACE

NO RADIUS

FINISH

The surface formed by the die is smooth, although particles may be visible. The cut ends are typically cut with wire, which may leave cut marks on the surface and will expose grog or other fine particulates in the clay. Extruded stiff mud can be glazed with flat, semi-gloss, or gloss finishes, in a range of colors and opacities.

HOLLOW

Most extruded stiff mud components are extruded with holes, which lighten the brick and help it bond to mortar.

JOINING

Units cannot be joined during the extrusion process, and with its low water content, stiff mud cannot be joined post-production. Instead, any corner or specialty pieces will need to be molded or carved by hand.

SHAPES

Extruded stiff mud profiles are often simple, as the material cannot pick up fine details. Complexity is often limited to the center core, where breaks and other defects do not affect the component.

Cross-sectional shapes are extruded along the length of the profile. Modifications to the cross-section may be made along the length, but brick producers may be reluctant to do this as it requires the slug to be taken off-line.

SHRINKING

Most mud shrinks 4–5% after firing.

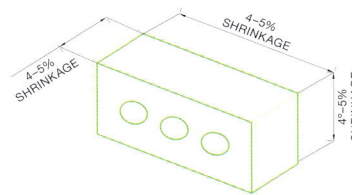

4–5% SHRINKAGE
4–5% SHRINKAGE
4–5% SHRINKAGE

SIZE LIMITS

Generally, stiff mud extrusion widths are 16in (400mm) or less and their heights are 8in (200mm) or less.

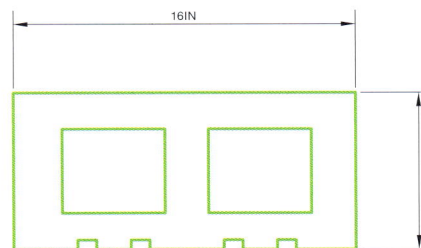

16IN

8IN

SURFACE DESIGNS

This process can accommodate textures and designs that run the length of the component, but they will not be as fine as those for plastic clay. Wire can be added to the die, to give a wire-cut finish to the components. Intermittent designs and textures can be done in-line, or post-extrusion with patterned rollers or wire brushes.

TOOLING COMPLEXITY

Tools are simple for this process, and have no moving parts.

TOOLING COSTS

Tooling costs are low, with production-quality steel molds ranging from $1,000 to $15,000.

TOLERANCES

For a modular brick the tolerances are around 0.08–0.12in (2–3mm).

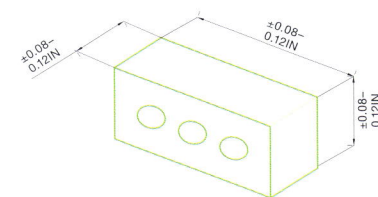

±0.08–0.12IN
±0.08–0.12IN
±0.08–0.12IN

WALL THICKNESS

Wall thicknesses can vary across the cross-section, and should be a minimum of 0.38in (9.5mm).

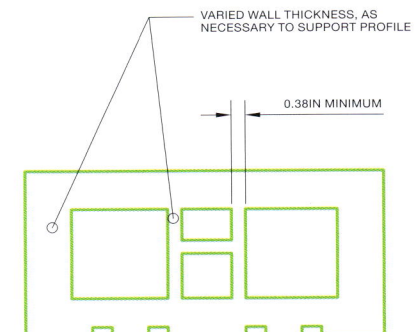

VARIED WALL THICKNESS, AS NECESSARY TO SUPPORT PROFILE

0.38IN MINIMUM

STIFF MUD

BRICK VENEER | YALE UNIVERSITY HEATH CENTER
Mack Scogin Merrill Elam Architects
New Haven, Connecticut

Designed by Mack Scogin Merrill Elam Architects (MSME), the Health Center for Yale University, completed in 2010, maintains a central location for Yale University Health Services. **[39]** It is located blocks away from other notable Yale buildings, such as the Ingalls Rink by Eero Saarinen, the Kline Biology Tower by Philip Johnson, and the Beinecke Library by Skidmore, Owings & Merrill. The new Health Center provides 147,000ft^2 (13,657m^2) of space, including approximately 850 rooms with inpatient facilities, administrative offices, a pharmacy, and meeting facilities. It serves the medical needs of all Yale's students, the majority of Yale's faculty and staff, and university retirees.

The design for this building started from an invited site design competition. Yale provided a site that was triangular-shaped and challenging. Located behind the Yale University Police Building on Locke Street, the site was bordered by the Grove Street Cemetery and the Farmington Canal Greenway. According to Merrill Elam, other invited firms had more health building experience, so MSME teamed up with Perkins + Will Atlanta, formerly Nix, Mann and Associates.[8]

The brick on this project is a dark ironspot brick with a custom, bull-nose profile and dovetail key as the mortar lock. The bricks are die-finished, meaning that the inside surface of the steel die provides a smooth surface for the brick's exterior. The brick manufacturer was Endicott, and it produced over 310,000 custom bricks for the Health Center. The custom brick coursing

39
Yale University Heath Center by Mack Scogin Merrill Elam Architects in New Haven, Connecticut. East elevation, facing a pedestrian trail

40
Detail image of exterior brick during construction

41
West-facing elevation at main building entrance

42
Initial competition drawing

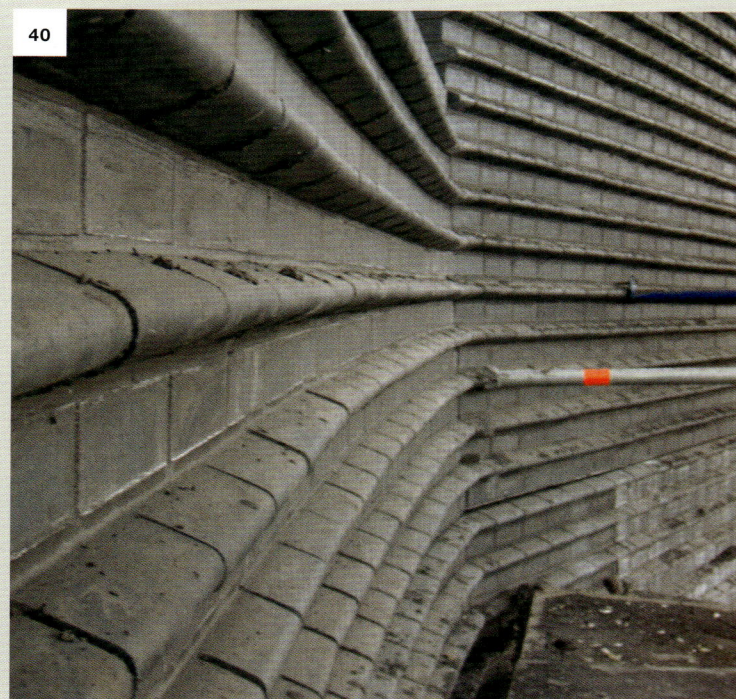

is alternated with a standard modular brick of the same color, creating deep shadow lines on the façade. The head joints between the bullnose bricks are raked back to the surface of the flat bricks and their bed joints were struck flush. **[40]**

DESIGN CONSIDERATIONS

According to Elam, the design team did not select brick as the building material until the schematic design stage. The choice of using a custom brick was the result of a number of different considerations. First, Yale University has a long history of using brick on its buildings. Second, MSME's competition drawings had illustrated a building with strong horizontal lines, and so the design team wanted to maintain that detail in order to unify the building façade. **[41, 42]** Third, the team had prior experience working with Endicott on developing a custom brick profile. MSME first found Endicott when doing the design research for WQXI Headquarters and Radio Broadcasting Facility.[9] The radio facility was never built, but the office used its design research with Endicott to design and manufacture a custom brick for a house in Brookline, Massachusetts, completed in 1999.

MSME adapted the brick and its details from the Brookline house to the Yale Health Center. For the Brookline house, the custom brick's profile is an angled beveled edge. The brick is laid in a running bond pattern, and it is used for almost all of the house's brick surfaces. In contrast, the alternating courses of bullnose and flat bricks at the Yale Health Center adjusted the scale of the brick pattern from that of a house to the larger scale of an institutional project. In addition, the majority of the walls of the Yale Health Center are angled in section 95–70° from horizontal.

According to Elam, in-house models were made out of foam to evaluate the design of the brick profile. A technical mock-up of the exterior wall assembly was also done to test the angled walls, the brick shape, the brick assembly, and the construction craft. After the mock-up, the design team brought in Ryan-Biggs Associates, a façade engineer, to help resolve the technical issues. From this experience, the brick design was changed so that the core holes were removed. This shifted the brick's center of gravity toward the back of the brick, so that its weight would be carried by the course below. Dovetails were also added to the custom brick's profile. **[43, 44]** The dovetails allowed for a better mechanical connection between the custom brick and the mortar. A brick tie could also be recessed into the dovetail so that the bricks rather than the mortar could be tied back to the light-gauge steel supports. The dovetails were hidden by the courses above and below, are not visible on the façade, and were easily accommodated by the extrusion process.

MANUFACTURING CONSIDERATIONS

The house in Brookline's custom brick was designed and manufactured with a beveled profile on its exposed leading edge. From its experience with manufacturing and shipping the Brookline brick, when Endicott was approached with manufacturing another custom brick, it recommended the use of a bullnose profile rather than a bevel. This softened the edge of the brick and helped protect it from damage during handling.

OTHER CONSIDERATIONS

When asked if liability was ever a concern, Elam answered that the firm believes that you can solve any challenge with the right people. Technical mock-ups were made and testing was done to make sure that the wall would perform as needed.

43 Custom brick as it exits extruder. In-line texture added to help bond to mortar bed

44 Final brick

MATERIAL CONSIDERATIONS + DESIGN PARAMETERS

METAL (ALUMINUM)

Metals such as aluminum, copper, magnesium, zinc, tin, and their alloys can be extruded. **[45]** This book will focus on extruded aluminum and aluminum alloys, as they are most often used in architecture. (For brevity, I will refer to both pure metals and metal alloys as "metal," and both aluminum and aluminum alloys as "aluminum.")

Aluminum is extruded cold, warm, or hot. The higher the temperature of the billet, the less force is required to push the metal through the die. Both cold and warm extrusion works the metal, improves its strength, and produces components with the best surface quality. In cold extrusion, the tolerances are highest, compared to either warm or hot extrusion. Hot extrusion involves heating of the metal billet to a temperature just above the metal's recrystallization temperature. This heat decreases the metal's strength, reduces tolerances and finish surface quality, and increases ductility.

There are two main types of metal extrusion—direct extrusion and indirect extrusion. Direct extrusion (sometimes referred to as forward extrusion) is when the metal is pushed through a static die. Indirect extrusion (sometimes referred to as reverse or backward extrusion) is when the metal is static and the die is pushed against it. **[46]** In direct extrusion, friction develops between the metal and the extrusion barrel, increasing the pushing force required and overheating the medium. In indirect extrusion little to no friction develops between the medium and the walls of the extrusion barrel; therefore the required pushing force is lower than with direct extrusion. A drawback of indirect extrusion is that as the die moves into the barrel, the extruding medium must move around the die ram. This limits the extrusion's length and makes it difficult to support the extrusion during the process.

Compared to the continuous process of extruding clay or plastic, extruding aluminum is a discrete manufacturing process. The ultimate length of the extrusion is a function of the volume of the component cross-section in relation to the volume of the billet. A new billet can be loaded into the extruder before the profile is cut, forming a cold joint in the profiles where the two billets meet. This cold joint is a point of weakness in the extrusion, and is typically cut from the extruded component.

For almost all metal extruding, the components come out of the extruder slightly warped, and components are stretched to increase straightness. Clamps are applied to the ends of the extrusion in order to stretch it, but they damage the surface, and the ends are cut off and recycled. **[47]** After being stretched the component is cut to its final dimensions.

45 Aluminum extruder with barrel (right) and plunger (left)

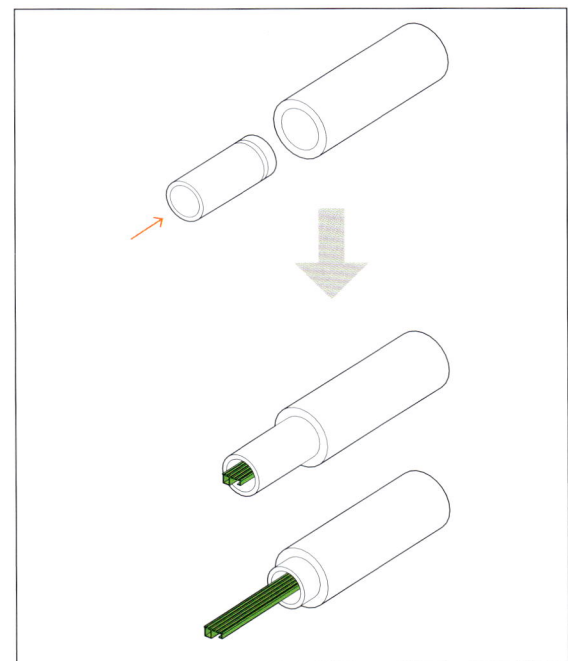

46 Indirect or backward extrusion

47 Damage to extrusion end, due to stretching

CORNER RADII

Corner radii are not required.

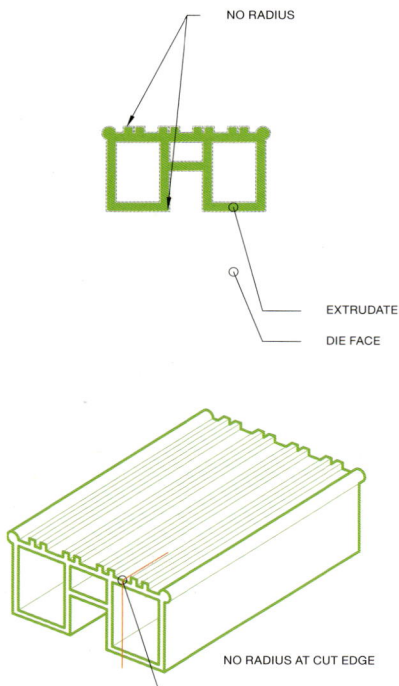

NO RADIUS

EXTRUDATE

DIE FACE

NO RADIUS AT CUT EDGE

FINISH

The surface formed by the die is smooth, with long mill lines running the length of the component. Post-production finishing can be done to achieve satin, grit, or polished surfaces.

HOLLOW

Most extruded aluminum components are hollow, as material costs are high; however, solid components can be extruded.

JOINING

Units cannot be joined during the extrusion process. Any joining of components is done post-production, and is often mechanical, as aluminum is difficult to weld.

SHAPES

Extruded shapes have the same profile along their length. Extruded aluminum can be simple or complex, as the material can pick up fine details.

SIZE LIMITS

Extruded aluminum components are limited to 30in (120mm) in diameter.

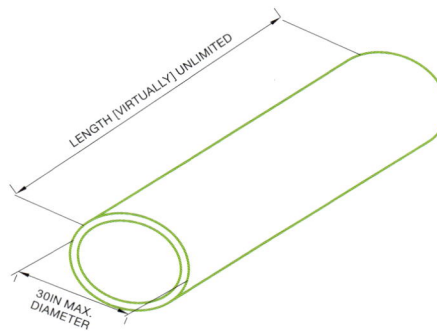

LENGTH (VIRTUALLY) UNLIMITED

30IN MAX. DIAMETER

SURFACE DESIGNS

This process accommodates fine textures and designs that run the length of the component. It does not accommodate in-line patterns or textures.

SYMMETRY

Generally, symmetrical shapes are easier to extrude. Asymmetric shapes will affect the consistency of metal flow through the die. This can cause cracks and rips in the extruded component. The die can be designed to make the flow more consistent, which will increase costs.

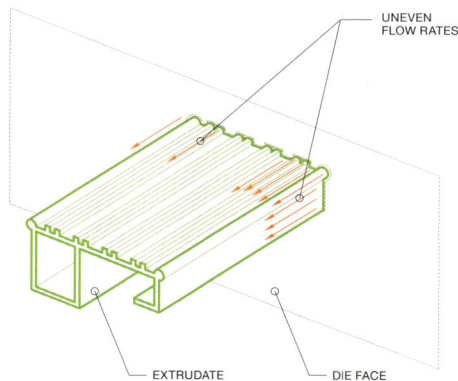

UNEVEN FLOW RATES

EXTRUDATE

DIE FACE

TOOLING COMPLEXITY

Tools are simple for this process and have no moving parts.

TOOLING COSTS

Tooling costs are moderate, due to the amount of steel necessary to resist the pressures of extrusion. Aluminum-extruding dies often start at $10,000, and the cost increases with complexity.

TOLERANCES

Profiles are commonly held to 0.01in–0.02in (0.25–0.5mm), but tighter tolerances are possible. Cut tolerances are more difficult to maintain than extruded tolerances, and can be 0.2in (5mm).

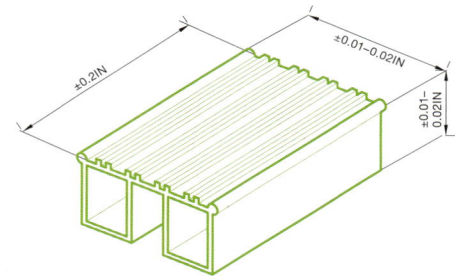

±0.2IN

±0.01–0.02IN

±0.01–0.02IN

WALL THICKNESS

It is best to design profiles with a consistent wall thickness, or transitions between one thickness and another. Profiles with an inconsistent wall thickness can be extruded, but there is increased difficulty in machine operation and die design. Metal flows slower through thicker-wall areas than thinner-wall areas, causing cracks and rips in the extruded component. This can be partially fixed by the die's design, but this will increase costs.

Minimum wall thicknesses can range from 0.04 to 0.2in (1–5mm), depending on the size of the component, the cross-sectional area, and the particular aluminum alloy.

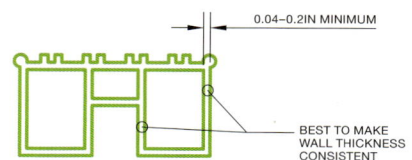

0.04–0.2IN MINIMUM

BEST TO MAKE WALL THICKNESS CONSISTENT

METAL (ALUMINUM)

CURTAIN | OMS STAGE

5468796 Architecture
Winnipeg, Canada

The city of Winnipeg held an open competition to design a bandshell for Old Market Square (OMS) in Winnipeg's Historic Exchange District. **[48, 49]** The new structure was to replace an original bandshell, which was used only fifteen times per year. According to the architect's website, the design of the OMS Stage was a response to the traditional bandshell, which looks forlorn throughout Canadian long winters.[10] 5468796 Architecture's winning submission was for a building that would serve as a public stage, with a private stage on the second level, a pavilion, a projection screen, and a beacon, allowing it to be used year round. The private stage is accessed from an internal concrete stair, and is open to the sky. **[50, 51]** The building, completed in 2010, is unconditioned, but fully wired with sound, lights, and interior projection.

5468796 designed the OMS Stage as a cube, draped with a flexible curtain made from custom-manufactured aluminum extrusions. Similar to chain mail, two sides of the cube's curtain can be drawn back with a winch,

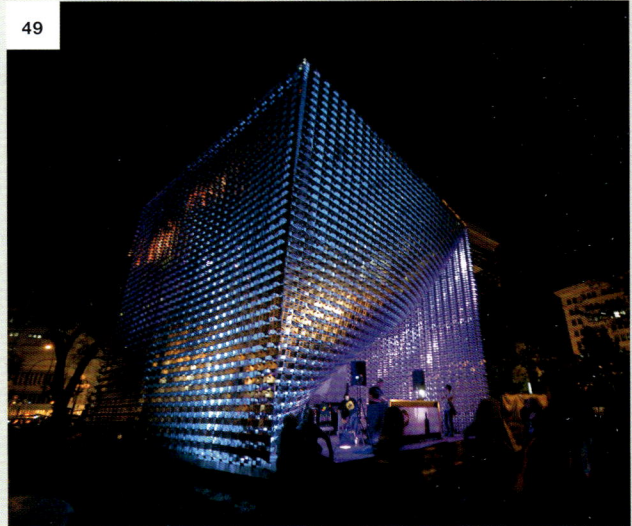

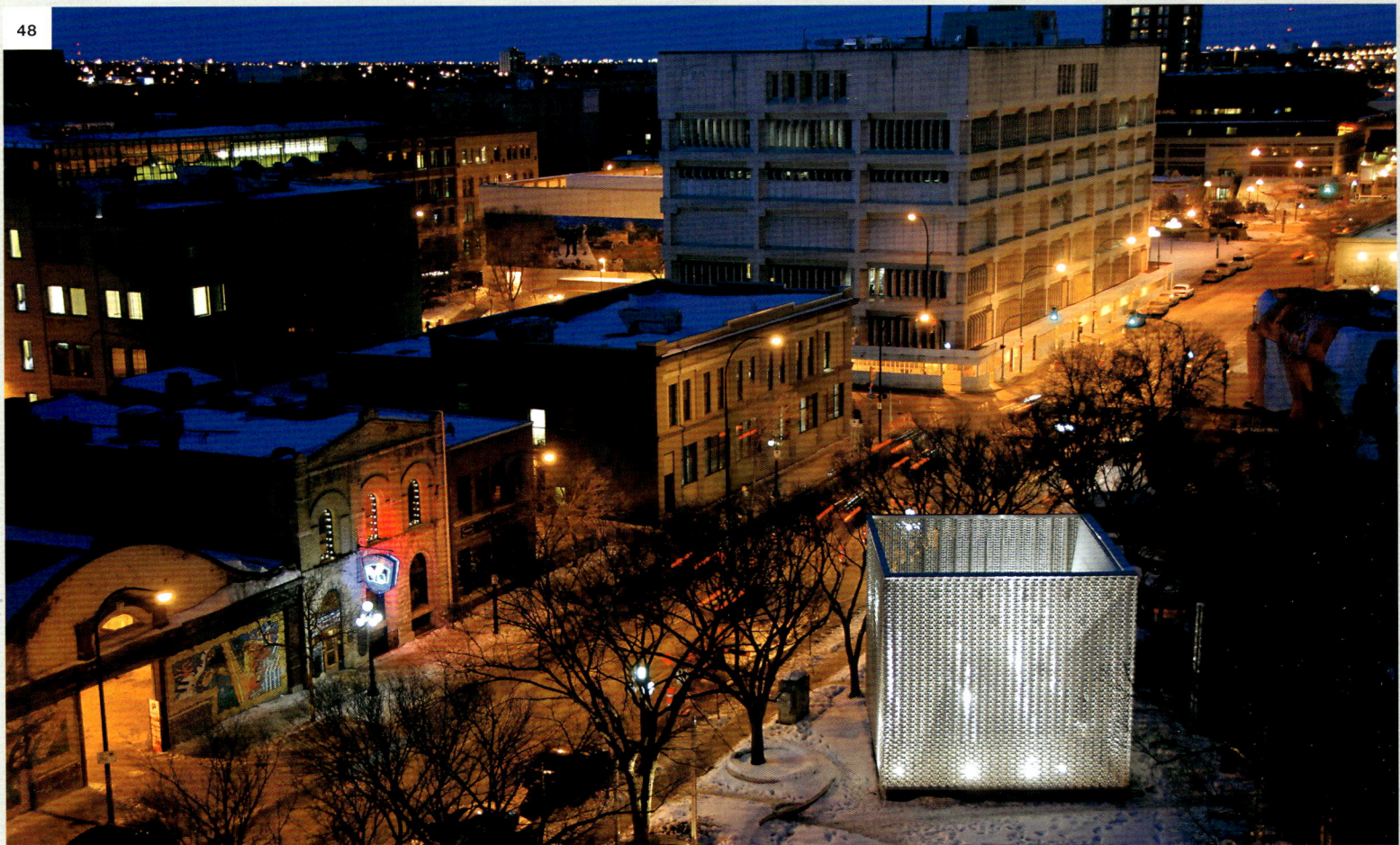

SECTION A–A'

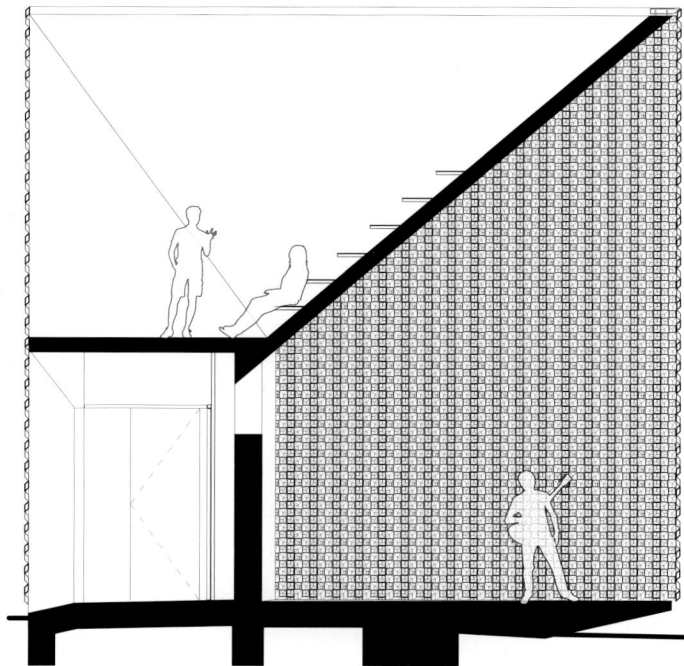

SECTION B–B'

50 Building sections

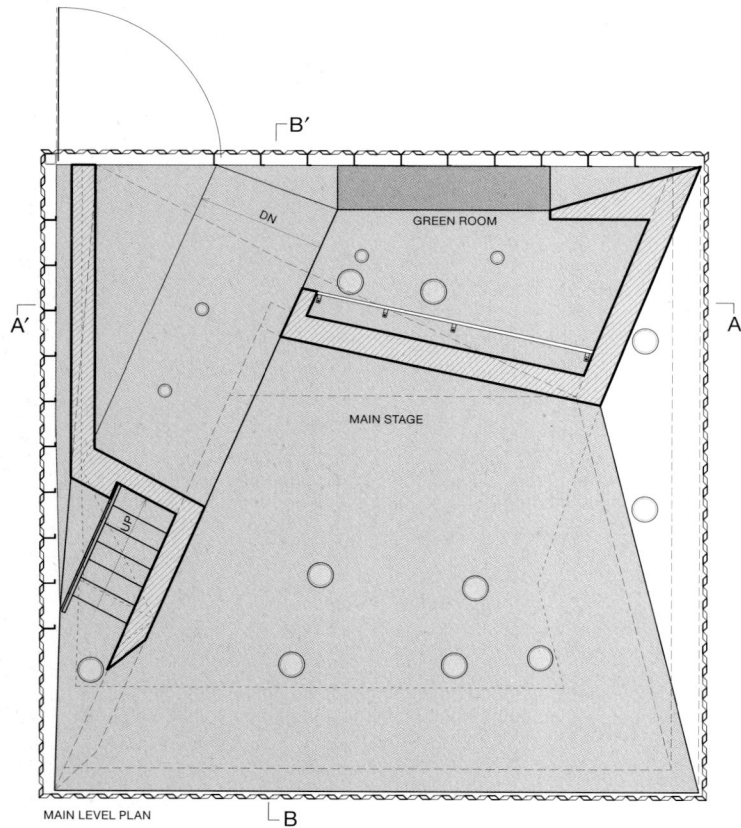

MAIN LEVEL PLAN

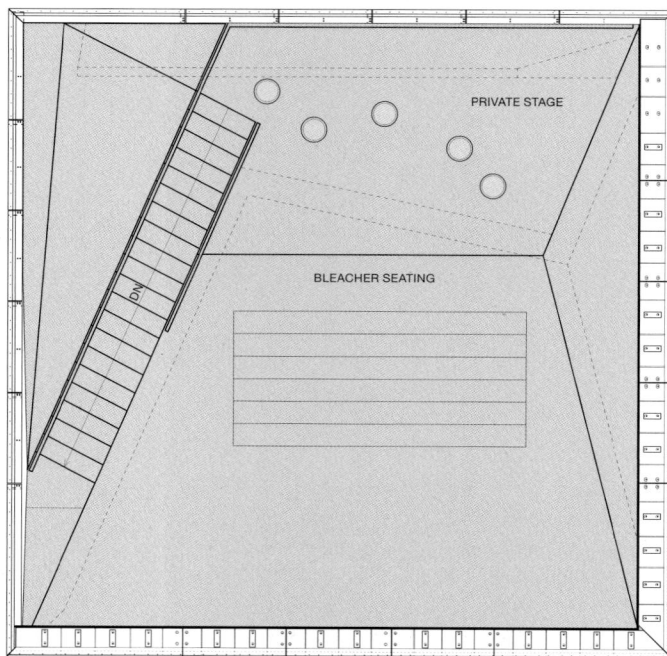

ROOF PLAN

51 Building plans

to reveal the public stage within the cube. **[52]** When not in use, the curtain falls vertically, and can be fastened to the bottom of the cube to secure the equipment inside. The extrusions are shaped so that images projected on the curtain's interior surface are reflected on the outside of the cube. When the OMS Stage is not in use for concerts or weddings, it is lit with colors and patterns for different holidays, such as green for St. Patrick's Day and a heart for Valentine's Day.

The OMS Stage has 20,000 identical extruded aluminum components, with their edges cut at the same angle and polished. **[53]** The extrusion cross-sections are rhomboid, with corners of 60° and 120°, sides that are 4in × 4in (100mm × 100mm), with a wall thickness of 0.2in (5mm). Each extrusion is then cut at a 45° angle from the longitudinal axis of the extrusion. The individual pieces are then threaded together with a cable and every third component is riveted together. This allows the curtain to be flexible, and it forms a catenary curve when opened.

The OMS Stage contractor was Green Seed Development Corporation. KlarTech was the metal fabricator for the project. In contrast to the other case studies in this book, for the OMS Stage, 5468796 maintained a close and contractual relationship with KlarTech, the fabricator, and had no communication with the aluminum extruder. It was KlarTech that subcontracted the manufacturing of the custom aluminum extrusions from the extruder and then did all the post-production cutting, trimming, polishing, drilling, and riveting of the components together.

DESIGN CONSIDERATIONS

According to Saša Radulović, co-founder of 5468796, when they submitted its design for the competition, all they knew was that the stage was going to be a cube.[11] The firm wanted the OMS Stage to be alive, and for the light to come from within the building rather than being projected onto the building. 5468796 noticed that as light passes through a thick, perforated screen, the edges of the screen light up. However, they wanted an exterior material that was sufficently flexible to wrap around the corners of the cube without disruption. The design team investigated shapes, testing models to see what could work. With little refinement, they approached KlarTech for further support with development.

KlarTech made initial prototypes of the shapes from bent metal sheets. Original shapes were made from square cross-sections with ends cut on 45° angles; however, it was KlarTech that discovered that the cross-section needed to be a rhomboid to properly reflect the light through the component. The benefit of working with bent sheet metal is that it kept KlarTech from investing too much money into tooling costs, before it had proof of concept. No computer modeling was done for the component's development; it was done by hand and by physical mock-up. With all of the development of the component shape, approximately 30% of the total project costs were directed toward the research, manufacturing, and installation of the screen.[12]

In addition to reflecting light, the curtain can be used to reflect sound. The concrete at the back of the stage reflects low-frequency sounds, and the draped curtain, if pulled behind the musicians, will reflect high-frequency

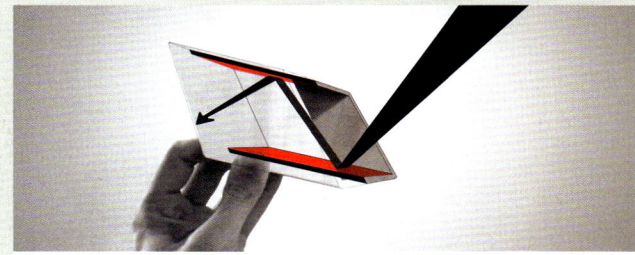

52 Reflection through component

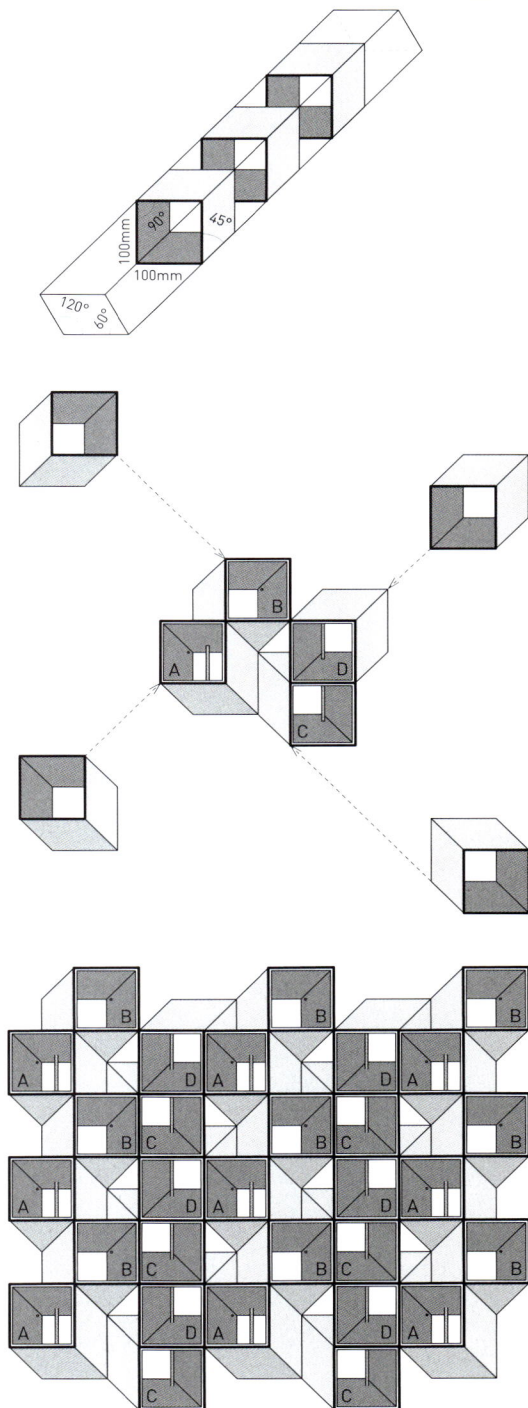

53 Module explosion

sounds. The curtain is hung from the cable and is supported every 5ft (1.5m) by a threaded stop. The stops and the cable tension can both be adjusted, allowing the curtain to be fine-tuned as it settles. The new OMS Stage is now used for concerts seventy-five days a year; an improvement over the previous structure's bookings.

MANUFACTURING CONSIDERATIONS

The commission was awarded in April 2009, and the building was to be completed by April 2010. [54, 55, 56] The schedule to make the components was also compressed. According to Radulović, the design and fabricator teams developed the curtain with little certainty of funding. It was not until February 2010 that funds were released and manufacturing of the components could begin. To complete the project on time, KlarTech had to buy equipment that could work unmanned and overnight to meet the deadline.

OTHER CONSIDERATIONS

The collaborative relationship between 5468796 and KlarTech is unusual because of its length, intimacy, and how fruitful it has been for both companies.[13] About ten years ago, 5468796 approached KlarTech for help with a design of a recycling container. KlarTech had been making agricultural equipment, and this was the first time it had worked with an architecture office. After the initial collaboration, 5468796 asked KlarTech to help develop and fabricate a metal structure for a kiosk out of slotted plates.[14] KlarTech ended up assembling the plates on site. Since then, Radulović estimated that KlarTech has worked on almost every project with the firm and has become an integral part of the practice.

Radulović asserts that all of the innovation that made the OMS Stage possible was due to KlarTech. Collaborating with the fabricators early in a project keeps the architecture firmly grounded, ensuring that architectural ideas are possible to build. It is KlarTech's expertise that has supported 5468796's interest in innovation and creating building components that are not available commercially. [57, 58] 5468796 has KlarTech do initial reviews of the designs to give an idea of price, time, labor, and scope. According to Radulović, the head of KlarTech calls the office multiple times a day to discuss ongoing projects; Radulović visits KlarTech six to seven times a year to see what it is currently working on. At a University of Manitoba exhibition in 2010, ten projects by 5468796 were on display, and nine of them were collaborations with KlarTech.

Other architectural practices have begun to partner with KlarTech. Radulović estimates that since 5468796 first worked with KlarTech architecture fabrication occupies 40% of KlarTech's work. Most of its fabrication work is CNC routing, which Radulović believes is a waste of the company's abilities and knowledge. Also over the years, 5468796 has convinced KlarTech to buy equipment to serve the company for future projects. For the OMS Stage, KlarTech bought a polishing machine and a riveting press to make connections between the aluminum components. [59, 60] Next they plan to add a cold-rolling machine to produce custom metal profiles.

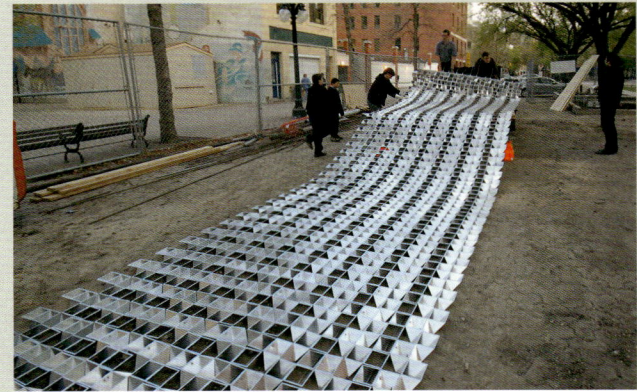
54 Ganged modules in curtain

55 Curtain being hung

56 OMS Stage, during construction

LESSONS LEARNED

According to Radulović, it was by doing this project that 5468796 gained confidence to do the extraordinary. Generally, the firm values architectural risk and has found that the greater the risk, the greater the reward. It was after this project that the firm starting asking itself on every project, "Have we taken enough risk?" Through this project, the firm learned the importance of priorities, making prototypes, and relying on the knowledge of the fabricator. According to Radulović, projects like the OMS Stage are rare—a project about innovation, ingenuity, but with a lack of complexity. It would have been a higher risk for the practice had it remained conventional.

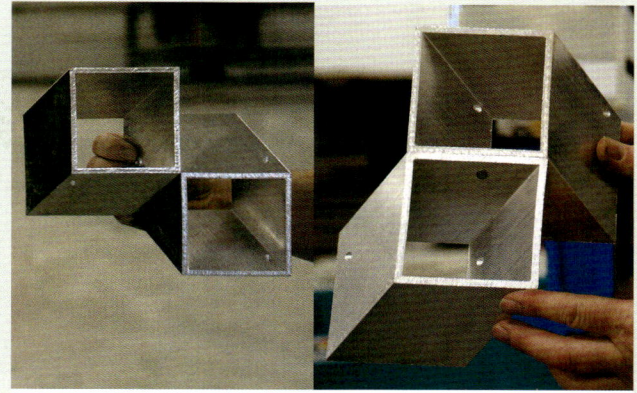

59 Rivets between modules

57 KlarTech post-extrusion cutting

58 Detail of components being cut

60 Polisher and polishing process

MATERIAL CONSIDERATIONS + DESIGN PARAMETERS

PLASTIC

In extruding, plastic is the most challenging medium. During the process the material goes through a phase change, from solid to liquid and back to solid. Generally, extruding plastic is limited to thermoplastics. Thermoplastics expand and contract more with temperature and humidity levels than thermoset plastics, therefore interior air conditions will affect the extruding process. When the plastic exits the die, it is still soft. The component's shape is maintained by sizers, and it is actively cooled by running it through a water tank or a water spray, or by air cooling. [62] After cooling it passes through pullers, which match the extruding speed. [63] This is necessary, as when it exits the die the plastic is still liquid and cannot carry the compression forces necessary to move it through the water tank.

When extruding plastic, feedstock in either pellet or powder form is added to a hopper and is gravity fed into the extruding barrel. [64] As long as the hopper is kept full of feedstock, extruding plastic is a continuous process. The extruding barrel is heated to liquefy the polymer, and additional heat develops through friction between the plastic and the inside of the extruding barrel. Extruding plastic uses a screw instead of a ram to move the melted plastic toward the die. The cross-section of the screw varies along the extruder barrel length, heating and compressing the plastic. [61]

Before the plastic melt enters the die, the plastic flows through a breaker plate. The breaker plate filters contaminants or unmelted plastic from the feed, builds pressure in the metering section of the screw, and straightens the plastic's flow from the circular action developed by the screw.

Die design for extruding plastic is more complicated than those for clays or aluminum. Because plastic is extruded as a liquid, the die must be designed to maintain proper flow of the liquid to the die opening. Therefore the die angle is shallow, and plastic extruding dies tend to be quite long. Additionally, each thermoplastic has its own characteristics, requiring a unique die design. Finally, plastic undergoes die swell when being extruded, meaning the plastic swells after leaving the die, resulting in a cross-sectional shape that is larger than the die opening.[15]

SIMILAR PROCESSES

Pultrusion (Chapter 2.2) is a process similar to extruding plastic, but is reserved for fiber-reinforced plastics, particularly thermoset plastics. Die costs between the two are comparable; however, plastic is extruded at a much higher speed than it can be pultruded.

62 Sizers before water-cooling tank help maintain component shape

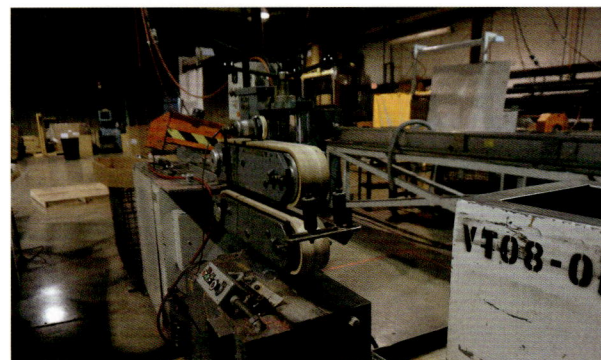

63 Pullers after cooling tank help maintain the speed of the extrudate

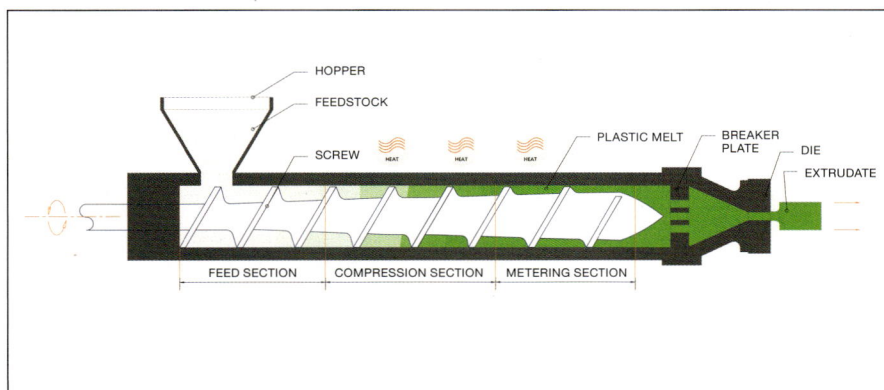

61 Longitudinal section through plastic extruder

64 Plastic extruder

CORNER RADII

Corner radii are not required.

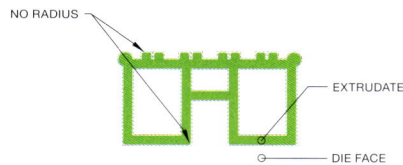

NO RADIUS

EXTRUDATE

DIE FACE

FINISH

The surface formed by the die is smooth. Finishes can range from high-gloss to flat, depending on the type of plastic and the production speed.

HOLLOW

Most extruded plastic components are hollow, particularly those used in the building industry, but solid components are possible.

JOINING

Joining can include heat bonding or mechanical connections and is done post-production.

PRODUCTION RATES

Production rates can range from 200ft/min (60m/min) to 16ft/min (5m/min), depending on the size, proportion, complexity, and type of plastic. For faster productions, a die can have multiple cavities so that multiple profiles are run at one time.

SHAPES

Extruded shapes have the same profile along their length. Extruded plastic profiles can be simple, but are most often complex, as the material can pick up fine details.

SIZE LIMITS

The smallest diameter that can be extruded is 0.04in (1mm); the largest is 45in (1,150mm).

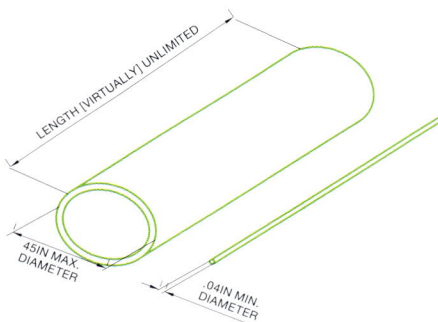

LENGTH (VIRTUALLY) UNLIMITED

45IN MAX. DIAMETER

.04IN MIN. DIAMETER

SURFACE DESIGNS

This process easily accommodates textures and designs that run the length of the component, as textures can be added to the die edge. Intermittent designs and textures can be done in-line, but post-extrusion. For example, patterned rollers can be rolled onto the extrudate surface to get non-linear patterns.

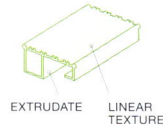

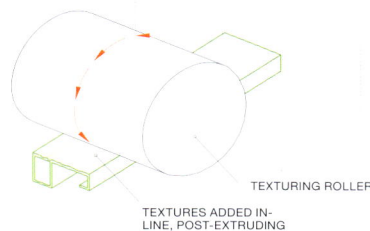

EXTRUDATE   LINEAR TEXTURE

TEXTURING ROLLER

TEXTURES ADDED IN-LINE, POST-EXTRUDING

SURFACE IMPERFECTIONS

Surface imperfections in extruded plastic are common.

SYMMETRY

Generally, symmetrical shapes are easier to extrude. Asymmetric shapes will affect the consistency of plastic flow through the die. This can cause cracks, rips, warping, or twisting in the extruded component. The die can be designed to make the flow more consistent, which will increase costs.

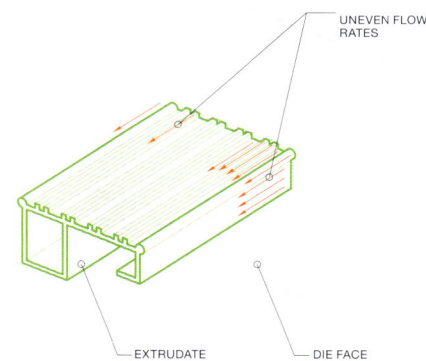

UNEVEN FLOW RATES

EXTRUDATE   DIE FACE

TOOLING COMPLEXITY

Tools are simple for this process and have no moving parts.

TOOLING COSTS

Tooling costs are moderate, as tooling includes both the die and the sizers. Tooling packages can start at $15,000, and will increase with size and complexity.

TOLERANCES

The tolerances for the extruded profile are 0.004in per 0.04in (0.1mm per 1mm) up to 0.4in per 20in (1mm per 500mm). Tolerances for the cut edge can range from 0.06 to 0.12in (1.6–3mm).

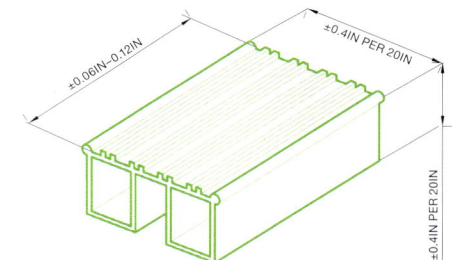

±0.06IN–0.12IN

±0.4IN PER 20IN

±0.4IN PER 20IN

WALL THICKNESS

Consistent wall thicknesses are preferred, as they help ensure consistent flow of plastic through the die. Die angles can be adjusted to help give a more consistent material flow to areas with inconsistent thicknesses, but this will increase the cost of the die. The minimum wall thickness is 0.015in (0.4mm) and the maximum wall thickness is 6in (150mm).

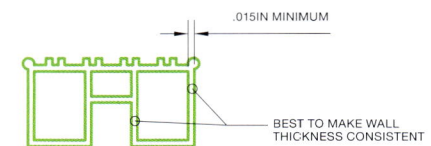

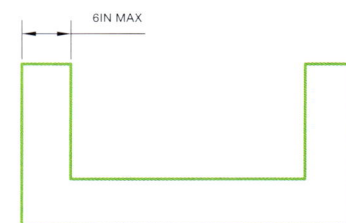

.015IN MINIMUM

BEST TO MAKE WALL THICKNESS CONSISTENT

6IN MAX

PLASTIC

RAINSCREEN | EL BATEL AUDITORIUM
selgascano
Cartagena, Spain

In 2001, selgascano won a competition to design a new auditorium on the site of the old El Batel beach in Cartagena, Spain. **[66]** El Batel Auditorium, or ElB, is part of a redevelopment on Cartagena Bay that includes restaurants, a café, a yacht club, and the National Museum of Underwater Archaeology. ElB's almost 200,000ft² (18,500m²) program includes both a small and large auditorium (seating 500 and 1,500, respectively) with below-ground rehearsal space, four conference halls, a restaurant, an exhibition hall, a café, and ample lobby and circulation spaces. **[67]**

ElB is a long, linear building that responds to the long lines of the site, including the pier edge, the docks, and the edge of the calm bay. To contrast with the site and the building massing, selgascano wanted an exterior material that would be delicate, light, and aquatic in nature. The firm designed the building exterior with custom-extruded plastic profiles, which provide a shimmering skin that both reflects and transmits light.

ElB has three different custom plastic extrusion profiles. One is a ribbed, round tube with a diameter of almost 2in (50mm) and a wall thickness of 0.08in (2mm). **[65]** The tubes cover the building's opaque building program elements and are a horizontal shading device for the exterior terrace. The other two profiles, named A and B, are flat, wide, and simple in shape, with two different projecting depths. Both profiles, A and B, are 8.6in (218mm) wide, with a wall thickness of 0.25in (6mm). These profiles are primarily transparent, with streaks of color, and are used to transfer light into the building's interior spaces.

The general contractor was a joint venture company formed by Dragados and Intersa. Polimer Tecnic—an international plastic manufacturer, with five divisions focusing on signage, industry, architecture, commercial products, and machinery—manufactured the custom plastic extrusions. Polimer Tecnic offers a wide range of materials and plastic-forming equipment, with the ability to manufacture skylights, awnings, exterior furniture, dropped ceilings, aquariums, and guardrails.

DESIGN CONSIDERATIONS

During design, selgascano researched the transparency of plastics, and believed that an "extruded plastic screen was the only way to achieve large areas of transparent façades."[16] Rejected by many architects as flimsy and cheap, plastic was embraced by selgascano. The firm wrote, "Our approach to materials is always related to economy. In our opinion, the best material is the cheapest, hence our interest in looking for alternative materials to the ones on the market. We are also interested in vernacular architecture, which is a way of working with the simplest things or whatever you have on hand."[17] The clear plastic allows for a high amount of light transmittance,

65

65
Custom, round extruded plastic tubes installed during construction of El Batel Auditorium

66
Building façade along pier edge

67
View of lobby interior, looking at extruded plastic wall

68

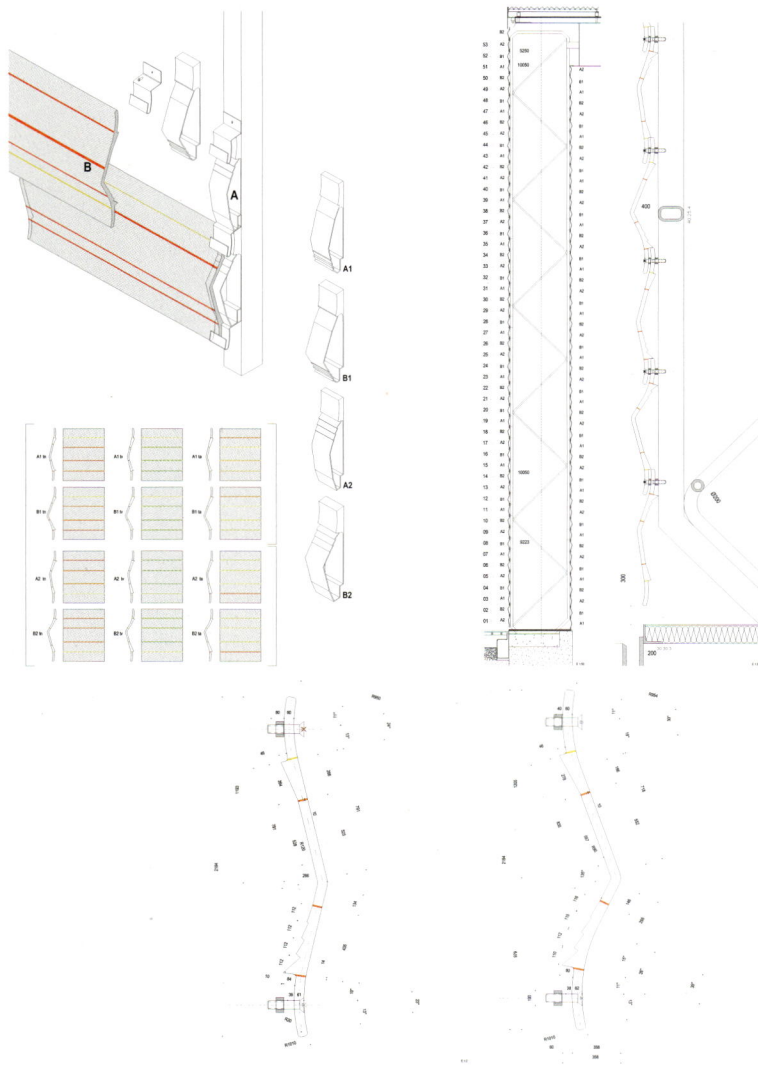

70

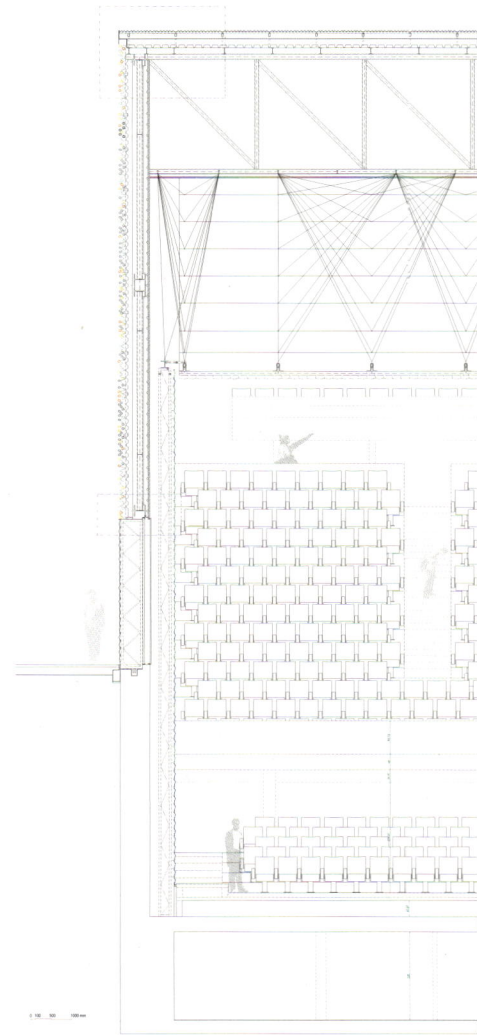

69

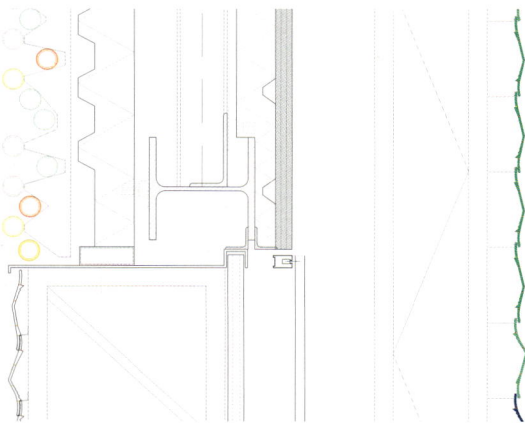

71

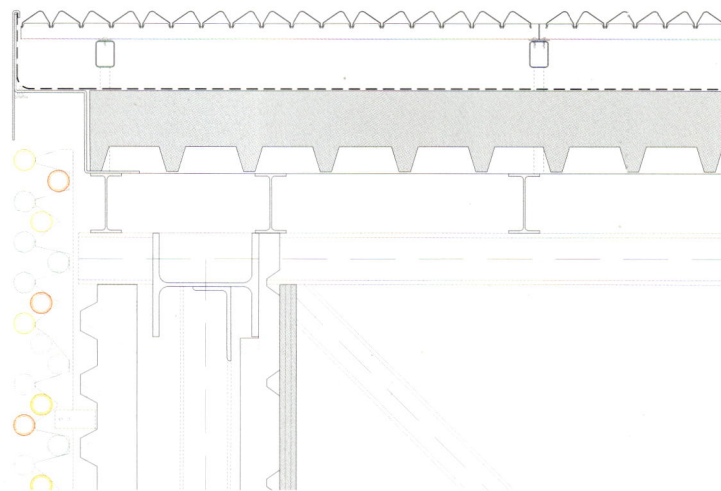

while the ribs in all three profiles cause a blurring of any images through the surface. To increase the complexity of the façade, selgascano designed both profiles to be installed with either long edge facing up, giving the two different profiles the look of four. The color and the opacity of the plastic in the three different profiles change, depending on use and location. The tubes are colored throughout the profile, and come in clear as well as colours including clear blue, white, clear yellow, and opaque yellow. On the building exterior, profiles A and B are clear, with streaks of red, yellow, orange, and green at key locations within the profiles. Inside the building, profiles A and B are through-colored with white or blue. **[68, 69, 70, 71]** Polimer Technic made prototypes to evaluate color, transparency, and material strength.

72 Extrusion of component. Note co-extruders (for color) on each side of plastic die

MANUFACTURING CONSIDERATIONS

For selgascano, communication and cooperation with Polimer Tecnic during all the processes were important to this project's success. As a plastic manufacturer, Polimer Tecnic had more knowledge and resources about extruding plastic than selgascano. That was of help as the designs were developed. Polimer Technic fabricated the extrusion dies itself, using a five-axis CNC mill and EDM. It took a few months to produce all of the extruded components. **[72, 73]**

Polimer Tecnic extruded the tubes at almost 500ft/hour (150m/hour); however, extruding profiles A and B was much slower at 90ft/hour (28m/hour). To make the internal color stripes on profiles A and B, colored plastic was injected during the extrusion process. **[74, 75]** According to Polimer Tecnic, this was done with a co-extruder in which small lateral extruders fed the colored material into the inner channels of the die.[18] The slower extruding for profiles A and B was necessary, as those extrusions required a high amount of accuracy to maintain a uniform and stable extrudate. In the opinion of selgascano, the co-extrusion process was the most difficult challenge in the manufacturing of the plastic profiles.

73 Cut-off saw

OTHER CONSIDERATIONS

Two different plastics needed to be used for the A and B extrusions. Methacrylate was used for the exterior components, because of its resistance to ultraviolet rays emitted by the sun. Unfortunately, acrylic does not meet Spain's regulations for interior finishes; therefore polycarbonate was used for the profiles of the building's interior. Typically, a different die is required for each type of plastic extruded, regardless of whether the shape is the same. This is because each plastic has its own characteristics, including flow rates and die swell. However, one of the Polimer Tecnic technicians proposed making a movable modification to the die that could accommodate both plastics. Without this movable modification, Polimer Tecnic would have to permanently modify the die with CNC machining; however, by temporarily modifying the die, Polimer Tecnic could extrude one type of plastic, then the other, and then return to the first plastic. This reduced costs, increased Polimer Tecnic's manufacturing flexibility, and reduced the need to extrude extra plastic other than that needed in case of replacement.

68
Details of two extrusion profiles (A and B) with different co-extrusion colors and two different mounting directions. Aluminum mounting brackets with a custom profile were made to match the two extrusion profiles and mounting direction

69
Technical detail where two different extrusion systems meet

70
Technical wall section of auditorium

71
Technical detail of roof

74 Edge detail of extrusion, during construction

75 Interior of building during construction, looking out

LESSONS LEARNED

The size and lightness of the components allowed the façades to be installed quickly by hand, without much construction equipment. Although a manufactured product, the extruded profiles were never perfect—pieces were never curved in the same way. There was a degree of imprecision with the material that selgascano embraced and understood as a positive. The firm wrote, "This is probably the best lesson we learn[ed] with Cartagena … We think that this is the beauty of working with this sort of material, as if it were hand made."[19]

2.2 Pultrusion

INTRODUCTION

Pultrusion is manufacturing process that pulls a composite medium through a die to create a continuous cross-sectional shape. [1, 2, 3] The word "pultrusion" comes from combining the word "pull" and "extrusion." Similar to extrusion, pultrusion produces linear elements with simple or complex cross-sections that can be solid, semi-hollow, or hollow. Pultrusion results in good surface quality and typically requires little to no post-production surface refinishing. Different than plastic extrusion, which uses thermoplastics, pultrusion typically combines fibers such as fiberglass, carbon fibers, or natural fibers and a resin such as thermoset plastic, concrete, or plaster. Unlike extrusion, pultrusion can easily accommodate inconsistent wall thicknesses across the cross-section and asymmetric profiles.

1 Pultrusion creel, guide plates, and wet-out

In pultrusion, continuous rolls of reinforcing fiber strands and often woven fiber mat are organized on a rack, or creel. Next, the fibers are pulled through a series of guide plates to position the strands and mats in the component's cross-section. The fibers are then pulled through a resin bath for full impregnation. Veils may be added to the pultruded component after the reinforcing fibers are impregnated, but before the composite enters the die. Veils improve the surface quality of the pultruded component by reducing transference of the fiber textures to that surface. Next, there is an optional pre-die former, which gradually shapes the profile close to the final shape. The pre-die former adds pressure to the medium, pushing the resin farther into the fibers. Then the medium passes through the die, where the final cross-sectional shape is formed, and heat is added to cure the resign. Finally, the component passes through the machine's pullers (e.g. rollers or walkers) that impart the tension force needed to pull the pultruded component through the machine. The component's length is cut after it exits the pullers.

Because the composite is pulled throughout the process, the reinforcing fibers that run the length of the pultruded component are placed in tension before the resin sets. [4] Similar to pre-tension steel reinforcing bars in precast concrete, the pre-tensioning of the fibers pre-stresses the resin, placing the resin into compression across the component's cross-section. This results in a pultruded component having greater bending strength and

2 Pultrusion wet-out, preform die, and die

3 Pultrusion die

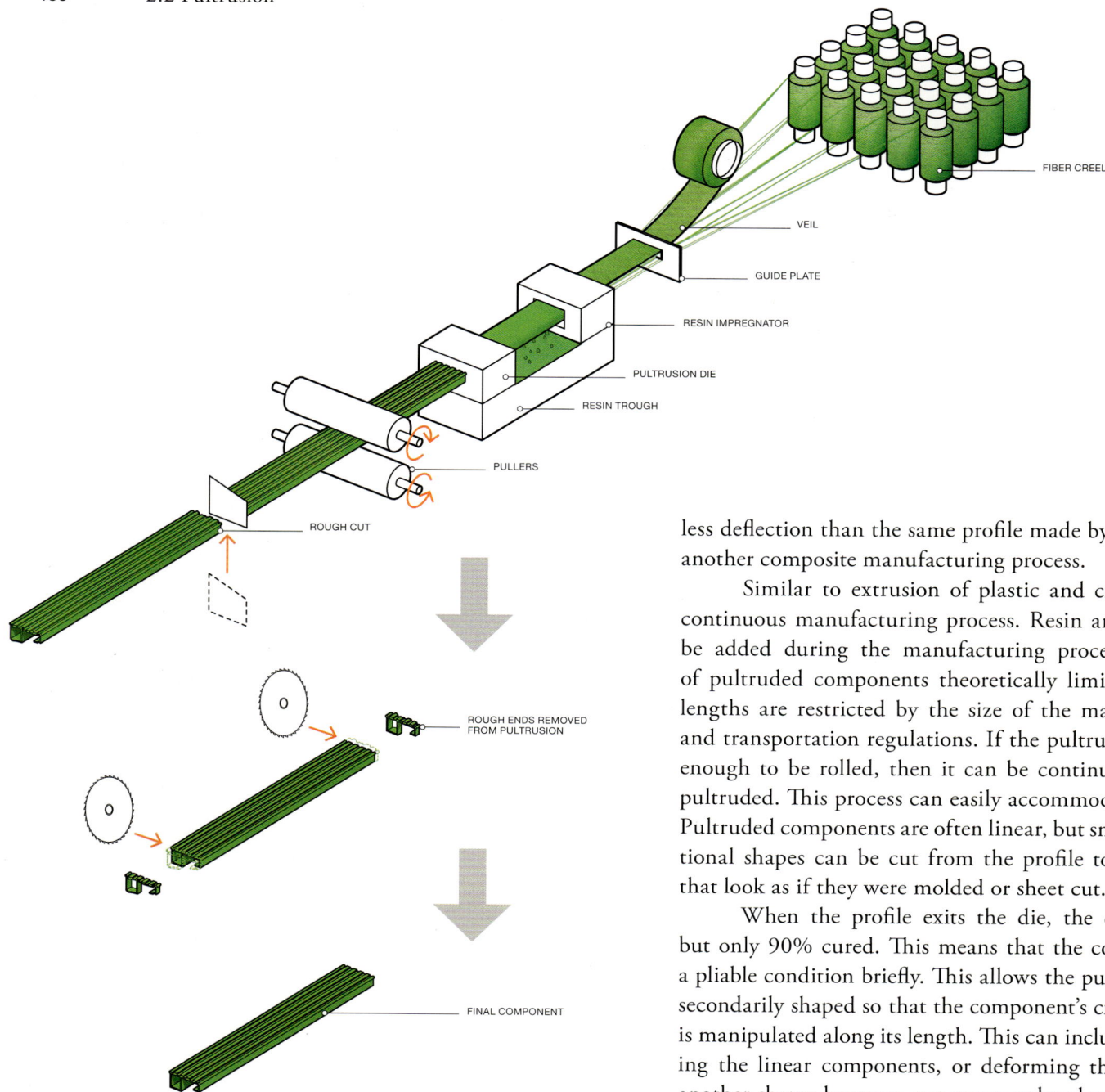

FIBER CREEL

VEIL

GUIDE PLATE

RESIN IMPREGNATOR

PULTRUSION DIE

RESIN TROUGH

PULLERS

ROUGH CUT

ROUGH ENDS REMOVED
FROM PULTRUSION

FINAL COMPONENT

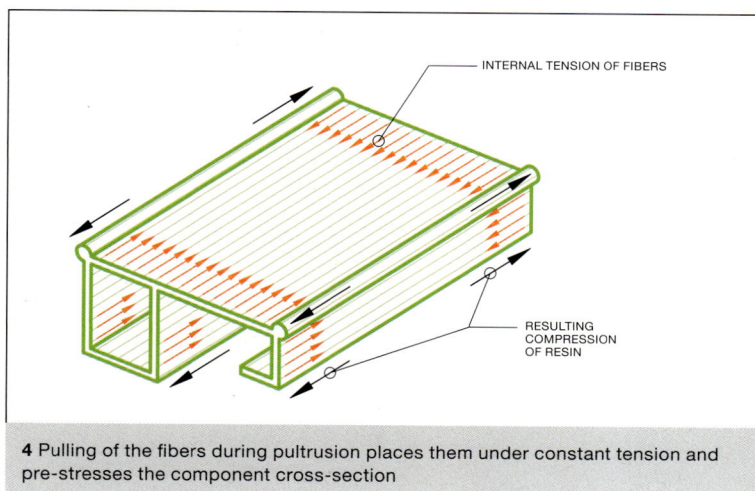

INTERNAL TENSION OF FIBERS

RESULTING
COMPRESSION
OF RESIN

4 Pulling of the fibers during pultrusion places them under constant tension and pre-stresses the component cross-section

less deflection than the same profile made by contact molding or another composite manufacturing process.

Similar to extrusion of plastic and clays, pultrusion is a continuous manufacturing process. Resin and fibers can always be added during the manufacturing process, making lengths of pultruded components theoretically limitless. In reality, the lengths are restricted by the size of the manufacturing facility and transportation regulations. If the pultruded shape is flexible enough to be rolled, then it can be continuously rolled as it is pultruded. This process can easily accommodate custom lengths. Pultruded components are often linear, but small-width cross-sectional shapes can be cut from the profile to make components that look as if they were molded or sheet cut. [5]

When the profile exits the die, the component is solid, but only 90% cured. This means that the composite remains in a pliable condition briefly. This allows the pultruded profile to be secondarily shaped so that the component's cross-sectional profile is manipulated along its length. This can include curving or twisting the linear components, or deforming the cross-section into another shape; however, not many pultruders have the capability to do this in-line. The pliability of the resin upon die exit also allows for continuous, in-line pattern rollers to emboss the surface. If tolerances are critical, a cooled aluminum block can be added to the line to hold the cross-section to the required final dimensions and shape. This is similar to sizers used in plastic extrusion.

Most manufacturers will run their machines on a twenty-four-hour cycle until the order length is filled. Typically, machines are fairly efficient to run, and only require one operator. The majority of the production time spent is in set-up, which may take a few hours, or a few days, and may require two or three operators. A typical pultruded component may have 1,500 or more rolls of fibers set up on the creel. Set-up time depends on the complexity of the shape and the required organization of the reinforcing fibers. This process is done by contract manufacturers and is not available at small workshops.

BUILDING PRODUCTS

Although pultrusion is not a process well known to architects, it is used to make a range of building products. [6] Typically, pultruded products are substituted when conventional building materials are not suitable. For example, pultruded structural sections (e.g. I-beams) may be used for bridges when moisture exposure limits the use of steel or wood. Pultruded structural sections are often used for radio towers or other structures, where steel may cause some transmission interference. There are also proprietary pultruded products, including composite decks such as GeoDeck—made from pultruded wood cellulose fibers; and plastic and composite louvers such as fibreC by Reider—a fiber-reinforced concrete louver. Both of these products are commercially available.

TOOLING

Pultrusion tooling includes the die, one or more guide plates, and the optional preform die. [7] Pultrusion dies are typically made from tool steel, are plated with chrome or ceramic to resist wear, and are heated to cure the thermoset plastic. Guide plates can be made of steel, plastic, or plywood, and are custom-made in order to organize the fibers for a particular shape. The optional preform die, which helps pre-shape the cross-section, is made from lesser-grade materials such as fluorocarbon or polyethylene. These materials are inexpensive and easy to machine, and are therefore inexpensive to customize. If a high production run is being produced, the preform die may be chrome-plated steel.

Pultruding dies are made in two or more pieces and are clamped between platens to hold them in place. This helps to reduce set-up time between production runs, as the die can be closed around the fiber strands rather than the fibers fed through the die. The die itself is not heated, but instead platens attached to the top and bottom of the die are heated and the die transfers that heat to the pultruded profile. By heating the platens rather than the die, the die can be made with simple cut-steel plates, without embedded heating lines. This means that the die can be made inexpensively, by CNC machining. The die parting line can be visible on the pultruded profile, so care should be taken to locate this joint. The multiple-part dies give some flexibility to the profile options, as a shim can be added between the plates to make different-height cross-sections. [8]

In pultruding fiber-reinforced plastic (FRP), the length of the steel die is typically 20–40in (500–1,000mm), but it can be as short as 8in (200mm) or as long as 60in (1,500mm). The die length affects production speed. If the die is short, production speed has to slow so that the resin has enough time to cure in the heated portion of the die. At the same time, because of the high cost of tool steel, the longer the die, the more expensive it is. Therefore if tooling cost is an issue and the production run is small, a manufacturer may suggest using a shorter-than-typical die length.

6 Standard pultruded profiles

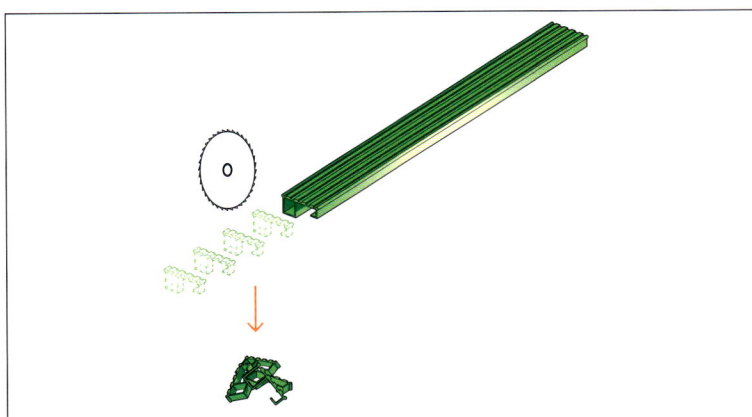

5 Short widths can be cut

7 Pultruded die and guide plates made from tool steel

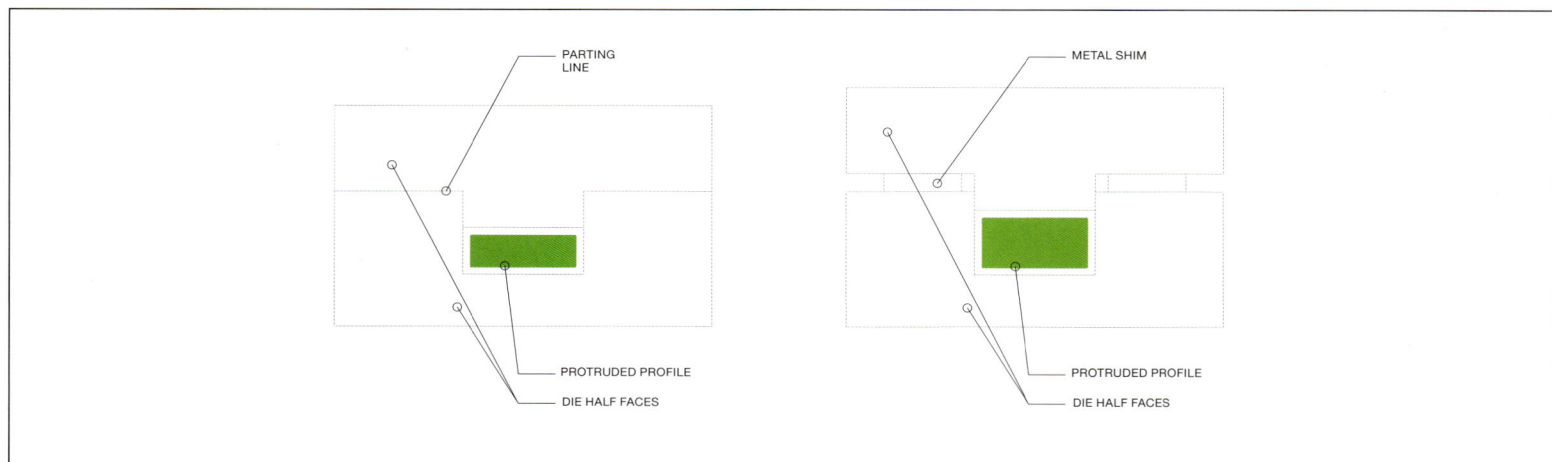

8 Shims can be added between die halves to make differently shaped cross-sections

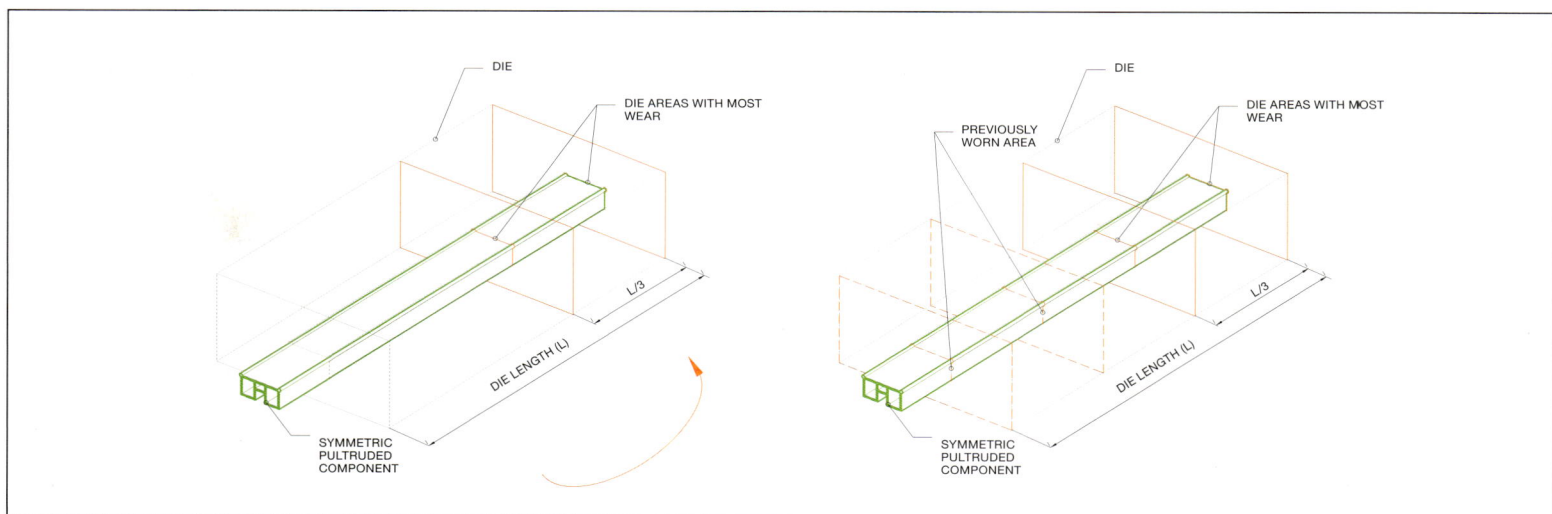

9 Die wear occurs at the die entrance and at about a third of the way along the die, where the resin cures. For symmetric profiles, dies can be rotated 180 degrees in plan to increase the production lengths between replating

Typically, the inside surface of the die is plated with chrome that is 0.001–0.003in (0.025–0.075mm) thick to extend the life of the die. The plating is sacrificial and the die can be replated when the chrome wears out. Die wear occurs primarily in two places. The first is when the fiber and resin mixture enters the die, as this area has the most friction. The second is at about one-third of the length, where the resin cures—subsequently expanding—inside the die and also creating friction. If a component's cross-section is symmetrical, manufacturers can reverse the die direction to increase the production run length between replating. [9]

Because of long set-up times, pultruding multiple profiles simultaneously, using a single die, rather than sequentially may be considered. This works well if the production run lengths for the various cross-sections are the same. A drawback is that if the die does require repair or replating for one cross-section, then production is stopped for all shapes until this is done.

ENVIRONMENTAL IMPACT

Generally, this process uses little energy for production, and any waste that is generated is through post-production cutting, trimming, or driving. However, FRPs are not environmentally friendly. Plastics have a high amount of embodied energy, and thermoset plastics cannot be recycled.

As with most plastic manufacturing, FRP releases volatile organic compounds (VOCs) and therefore affects the work environment. VOCs can be reduced by specifying low-styrene or suppressed-styrene resins, using air filters, and sufficiently ventilating the facility. After the resin cures, VOCs will continue to off-gas from the pultruded components but this will taper off over time. Using fiber-reinforced plaster or fiber-reinforced concrete instead of thermoset plastic will reduce VOC off-gassing.

Transportation distances associated with this process may be high. There are fewer FRP pultruders than plastic extruders, and even fewer manufacturers that can pultrude using concrete or plaster.

MATERIAL CONSIDERATIONS + DESIGN PARAMETERS

Typically, the resin used to impregnate the reinforcing fibers is a thermoset plastic. Pultrusion can also be done with thermoplastic, concrete, or plaster as the resin or binding agent; however, these alternatives are not produced in the same facility as thermoset pultrusions. A number of different types of reinforcing fibers can also be used. Glass and carbon fibers are the most common, but pultrusion can also be done with aramid or natural fibers such as hemp or cellulose. Fibers can be on spools—known as roving or tow; or in sheets on a roll—known as mat, fabric, or tissue. [10, 11]

The fibers give the pultruded component most of its strength and stiffness. The benefits of carbon fiber over glass fiber are greater strength and stiffness at a lower density; however, carbon fibers greatly increase material costs, as they can be two to five times the cost of glass fibers. Manufacturing costs also increase with carbon fibers. When carbon fibers are pulled during pultruding, small bits of carbon flake off. Operators must wear proper protective clothing, and the machinery's motors and pumps need to be protected as the flakes can cause electrical shorts.

The faces of the pultruded component that contacted the die are considered finished. There will be a difference in quality between the ends, which have been cut with a saw, and the faces that were in contact with the die.

FIBER-REINFORCED PLASTIC (FRP) (THERMOSET)

The specific thermoset plastic will affect production rates and the required pulling force. Some thermoset plastics are more viscous than others, requiring a greater pulling force, whereas others require more curing time, and a slower pulling speed. Inorganic filler particles, such as kaolin clay, calcium carbonate, and alumina trihydrate, can be added to improve pultrusion, reduce costs, and alter the resin's curing time. Alumina trihydrate has the added benefit of serving as a flame retardant. Additives can also be added to the plastic before curing, including color, ultraviolet light stabilizers, fire retardants, and shrinkage reducers.

SIMILAR PROCESSES

Extruding plastic (Chapter 2.1) can produce linear shapes similar to pultrusion. However, plastic extruding is limited to unreinforced thermoplastics, and is better suited for symmetric shapes with consistent wall thicknesses. Generally, production speeds are significantly slower in pultrusion than in plastic extrusion.

Contact molding (Chapter 3.1) can produce solid and semi-hollow components similar to those made by pultrusion; however, contact-molded components will have significantly less strength and slower production speeds than those made by pultrusion. Bladder inflation molding, or BIM (Chapter 3.2), can make hollow, linear components. As with contact molding, BIM components will not have the same strength as pultruded components, and the BIM profiles will be simpler than pultruded profiles.

10 Glass fiber rovings and rolls used for fibers

11 Creel of carbon-fiber rovings

CORNER RADII

Profile corners should have a minimum radius of 0.03in (0.8mm) for profiles with only fiber rovings, and a minimum radius 0.06in (1.6mm) for profiles with both fiber rovings and fiber sheets. Cut corners do not have a radius.

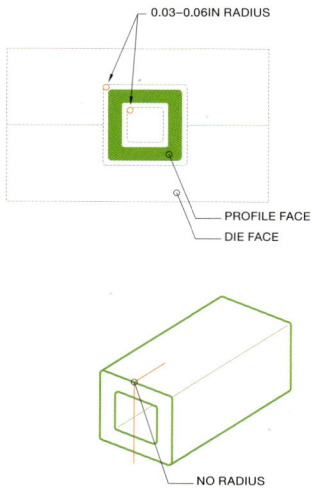

0.03–0.06IN RADIUS

PROFILE FACE
DIE FACE

NO RADIUS

FINISH

The die finish on the resin can range from matte, to satin, to high-gloss. The cut edges have a matte finish. There is some translation from the fiber mat veils to the pultruded surface, resulting in a random pattern of lines from the fibers on the surface that can be seen but not felt.

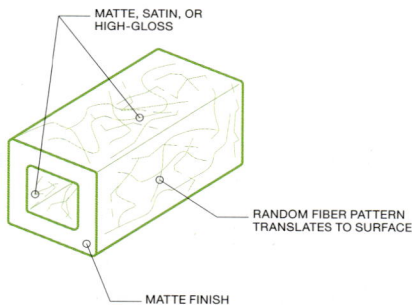

MATTE, SATIN, OR HIGH-GLOSS

RANDOM FIBER PATTERN TRANSLATES TO SURFACE

MATTE FINISH

HOLLOW

Pultruded components can be hollow, with multiple cells.

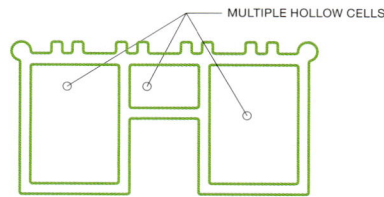

MULTIPLE HOLLOW CELLS

JOINING

Units cannot be joined during the pultrusion process. Any joining is done post-production and can include chemical bonding or mechanical connections.

PARTING LINES

Parting lines between the die halves will leave a faint line down the length of the component. They should be located just off the profile corners to avoid the corner radius.

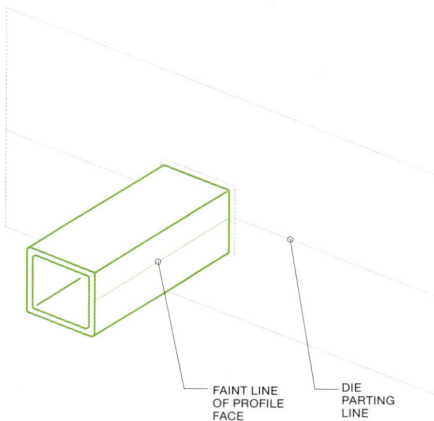

FAINT LINE OF PROFILE FACE
DIE PARTING LINE

PRODUCTION RATE

Production speed can range from 1.5 to 10ft (0.5–3m) per minute, but can be as slow as 2–5in (50–125mm) per minute if the cross-section is large and complex.

PRODUCTION RUN

A typical chrome-plated die can produce more than 100,000ft (30,000m) of pultruded length before requiring servicing. Because of long set-up times and tooling costs, orders for profiles should be over 10,000ft (3,000m) of pultruded length.

SHAPES

Pultruded shapes have the same profile along their length. They can be simple or complex; solid, semi-hollow, or hollow.

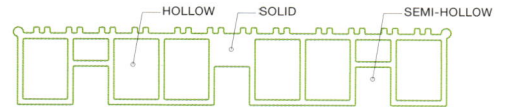

HOLLOW   SOLID   SEMI-HOLLOW

SHRINKING

Thermoset plastic can shrink up to 2% as it cures, depending on the specific plastic used.

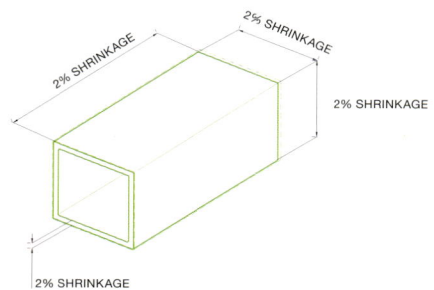

2% SHRINKAGE
2% SHRINKAGE
2% SHRINKAGE
2% SHRINKAGE

SIZE RESTRICTIONS

Maximum profile width is about 6ft (1.8m) and maximum profile depth is 1ft 8in (500mm). Profile length depends on the capacity of the manufacturing facility. If the profile is flexible enough, it can be rolled in-line, onto a spool.

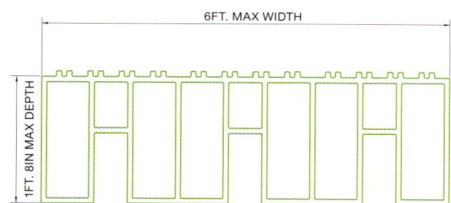

6FT. MAX WIDTH
1FT. 8IN MAX DEPTH

TOOLING COSTS

For tooling packages—including die, guide plates, and preform die—costs can range from $5,000 to $50,000.

SURFACE DESIGNS

This process easily accommodates textures and designs that run the length of the component, as textures can be added to the die edge. Intermittent designs and textures can be done in-line, after the pultruded profile leaves the die. For example, patterned rollers can be rolled onto the extrudate surface for non-linear patterns.

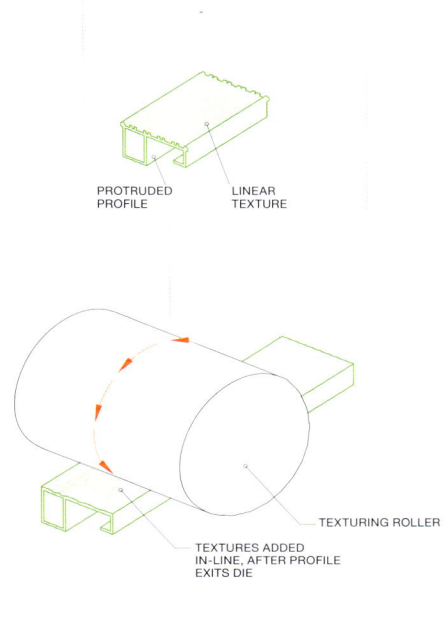

PROTRUDED PROFILE
LINEAR TEXTURE

TEXTURING ROLLER

TEXTURES ADDED IN-LINE, AFTER PROFILE EXITS DIE

SYMMETRY

Generally, symmetry is not required of pultruded profiles, as the material moves slowly and the fibers are pulled at a consistent speed through the die.

TOLERANCES

Cross-section dimensions are normally within 0.05in (1.2mm), but will be affected by the profile's shape and dimensions. Profile angles can be made within 1.5°.

The cut length tolerances may range from 0.12 to 0.5in (3–13mm).

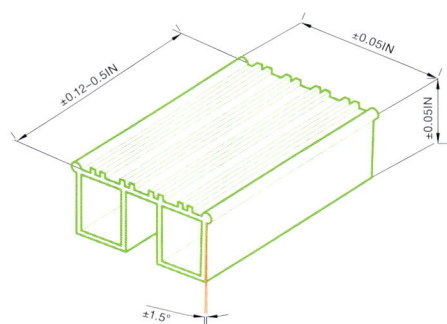

±0.05IN
±0.12–0.5IN
±0.05IN
±1.5°

WALL THICKNESS

Wall thicknesses across the cross-section can vary; however, this is only recommended if the FRP can remain a homogeneous mix of fibers and resin. At corners, it can be difficult to organize the fiber mats and rovings. Corners should not be left too sharp, nor should they be left with in interior fillet and an inconsistent wall thickness. If they are, then resin pockets, with little to no reinforcing strands, can form at the outside of the corner, causing uneven shrinking and warping.

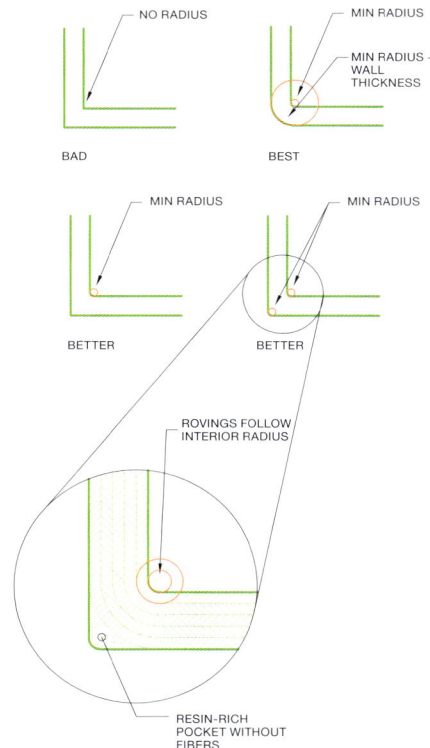

NO RADIUS
MIN RADIUS
MIN RADIUS + WALL THICKNESS
BAD
BEST

MIN RADIUS
MIN RADIUS
BETTER
BETTER

ROVINGS FOLLOW INTERIOR RADIUS

RESIN-RICH POCKET WITHOUT FIBERS

Minimum wall thickness is 0.04in (1mm) for profiles with fiber rovings only, and a minimum wall thickness of 0.06in (1.5mm) for profiles with both fiber mats and rovings. Maximum wall thickness is 3in (75mm) for profiles with fiber rovings only, and a maximum wall thickness of 1in (25mm) for profiles with both fiber mats and rovings.

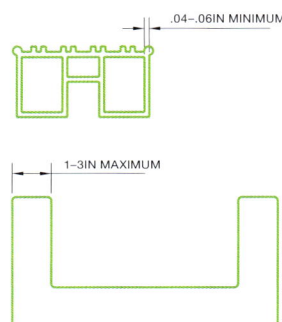

.04–.06IN MINIMUM

1–3IN MAXIMUM

WARPING

Straightness along the pultrusion length is within 0.05in/ft (4mm/m).

Twist along the pultrusion length is within 0.30in/ft (10mm/m).

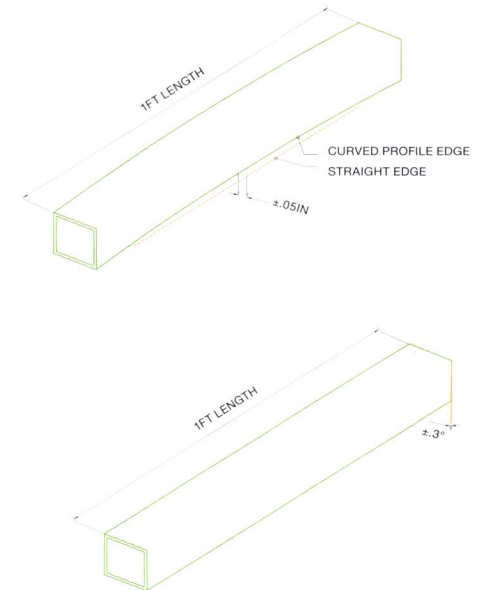

1FT LENGTH
CURVED PROFILE EDGE
STRAIGHT EDGE
±.05IN

1FT LENGTH
±.3°

FIBER-REINFORCED PLASTIC (FRP) (THERMOSET)

EXTERIOR BUILDING SKIN | SHERATON MILAN MALPENSA AIRPORT HOTEL AND CONFERENCE CENTER
King Roselli Architetti
Milan, Italy

After winning an initial design competition hosted by the Milan Airport Authority, King Roselli Architetti was commissioned to design the building massing and exterior envelope system for a Sheraton Hotel and Conference Center. [12] The competition brief asked for an architectural solution to hide the airport's Terminal 1 from a nearby highway. The new building would re-identify the airport as a gateway into Milan, the design capital of Italy, and would be a venue for tourists and business travelers visiting the city. The Sheraton is connected to the Malpensa Airport by an existing bridge, which spans the airport's ring road, and the building sits atop the airport's existing parking garage and an underground train. Completed in 2010, the building is approximately 540,000ft^2 (50,000m^2) and includes 436 guest rooms.

The Sheraton Hotel opens to the west—the primary entrance to the Malpensa Airport. Here the hotel presents a continuous linear façade, with open porches on its ends. The east elevation is articulated by seven pultruding bays, with a continuous skin that forms the roof, end walls, and underside of the building. Glass curtain walls clad the bays' north and south elevations, with the hotel rooms overlooking the U-shaped courtyards in between. [13, 14] The bays' skin is custom-designed pultruded fiberglass components that are flexible enough to bend at the building's rounded corners. The skin is supported by a substructure of standard pultruded profiles. [15, 16] The building's fascia panels, located on the north and south elevations, and the complex curved roof vents, were made using contact-molded fiberglass.

12
Façade of the Sheraton Milan Malpensa Airport Hotel and Conference Center, facing main entrance to the airport

13
View of façade facing Malpensa Airport with room bays and pultruded skin

14
Completed project

12

The design and manufacturing of all the pultruded components was done by Progettazione Costruzione Ricerca (PCR), based near Milan. The pultruded skin components are 55in (1.4m) wide and 72ft (22m) long, and there are 6 miles (9.66km) of the skin. It took 1 minute to make 12in (300mm) of skin length. Two different custom profiles were created for this project; one is located on the edge of the bays, providing a connection between the pultruded cladding and the contact-molded fascia. The other is used for the remaining skin.

DESIGN CONSIDERATIONS

The architects had originally considered titanium and then Corian as exterior cladding materials, but both were eliminated due to budgetary restrictions.[1] King Roselli selected pultrusion because it could meet the project budget. It also had the advantage over similarly priced materials, because it was waterproof, fire resistant, flexible, and lightweight. With the high amount of glass fiber relative to thermoset resin, the cladding is also dimensionally stable relative to changes in temperature. This was critical, as the airport is located near the Alps.

King Roselli wanted the building's skin to be as seamless as possible. Any horizontal seams between the component ends were hidden either on the building roof or on the underside of the bays. [17] Vertical seams connect the component edges to one another without overlaps or sealants. The joints between the components help to shed water off the building, by providing small valleys. Internal ribs and hidden fasteners connect the component's interior ribs to the pultruded substructure. [18]

MANUFACTURING CONSIDERATIONS

The relationship between the manufacturer and the architect was one of mutual respect. The architect relied on the manufacturer's knowledge of pultrusion and behavior of pultruded fiber-reinforced plastic to create a skinning system and supporting substructure that met the design needs. [19] According to an industry publication, the manufacturer has stated that one of its goals was to "make the architect smile."[2]

King Roselli had discovered PCR through some of the architecture firm's product design, and particularly noted PCR's work producing components for the interiors of cars. Prior to this project, PCR predominantly manufactured pultruded components for stock profiles, which are smaller in size and with a higher precision than that typically required for architectural application. From working with King Roselli, PCR developed a new department, Artex, which has expanded the "company's experience and profiles in the service of creative design."[3] In 2011, the company's Artex department won the international JEC Innovation Award, for its material research and innovations in the construction industry.

PCR's responsibility extended beyond manufacturing the building's skin; it also produced the finite element analysis of the force and wind loads on the pultruded substructure and skin, and specified and selected the glass fibers for the skin to address those loads. PCR worked with the King Roselli

15 Construction photograph of pultruded skin and supporting substructure

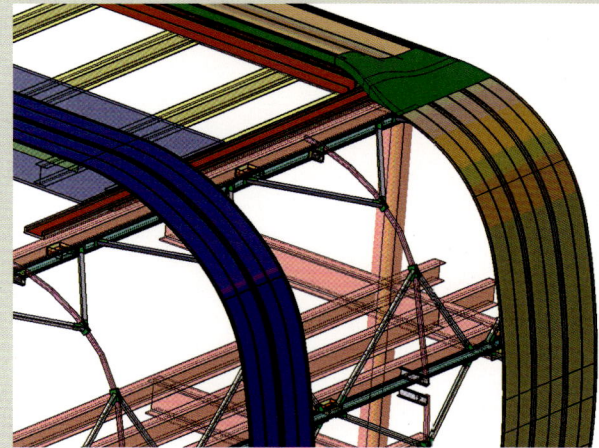

16 Shop drawing

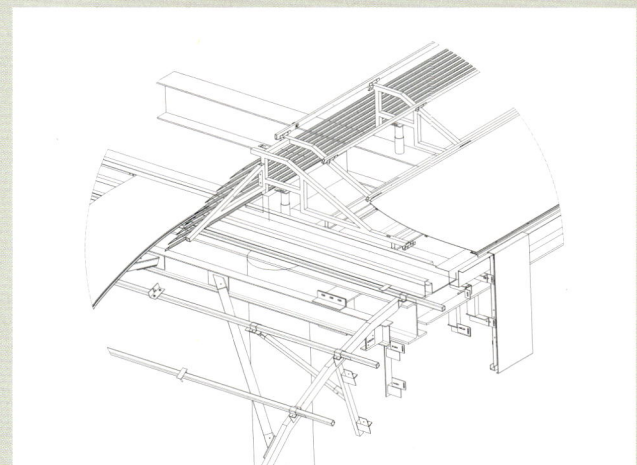

17 Construction detail at roof vent

18 Detail of pultruded component with interior ribs

19 Skin being pultruded

to keep the skin as smooth as possible. It was PCR that suggested adding a small profile at the back of the component for connection to the substructure, and to help with draining water off the flat roof.

OTHER CONSIDERATIONS

The benefits of the pultruded skin are that it is lightweight, durable, and flexible. [20] Those benefits also made the on-site assembly of the skin onto the frame difficult. Maneuvering pieces that large and light proved to be challenging. The contract restricted installation of the component on days with almost no wind so that the cladding sheets could be safely moved and secured to the structure. [21]

A non-woven surfacing veil was added to the cladding for protection from ultraviolet light. Because the architect was concerned with the possible yellowing of the white resin over time, the cladding was painted white in-line with automatic sprayers. According to Jeremy King of King Roselli, five years later the project has held up well.[4]

20 Transportation of pultruded components

LESSONS LEARNED

Through this project, King Roselli learned a lot about the manufacturing process, fiber-reinforced plastic, and what can be done with the process architecturally. King believes that there is potential for both pultrusion and FRP in the building industry. This seems to be reinforced by PCR's creation of Artex, to research the application of this process and material for building construction. According to King, the industry has continued to improve since 2010, and pultrusion holds great potential for architecture.

King Rosselli's experience, research, and knowledge gained from this project led to two additional commissions for the firm. 3B, the manufacturer of the fiberglass reinforcing strands for the pultruded FRP, commissioned the firm to design a cladding system for the company's office and research center in Batice, Belgium, and a factory in Tunis, Tunisia, for which King Rosselli completed an initial design. King Roselli also used FRP for a rainscreen in its 2011 competition submission for the Greda Factory in Carpi Modena.

21 Skin being craned into place during construction

3

Making Thin or Hollow

3.1 Contact Molding / 3.2 Bladder Inflation
3.3 Filament Winding / 3.4 Centrifugal Casting
3.5 Blow Molding

Included in this section are processes used to form thin or hollow components. For both thin and hollow items, the surface areas of the components will be significantly larger than the cross-sectional depths, and the wall thickness will vary across the cross-section. Many of the thin components produced may appear similar to those in Part 1: Manipulating Sheet. The difference is that sheet manipulation uses previously manufactured sheet goods (e.g. plastic sheets or glass panes) and reshapes them; in contrast, making thin or hollow components starts with raw or unprocessed materials and forms those into their final shape.

The manufacturing processes for making hollow components use a closed mold, and the manufacturing medium is forced against the walls of the mold cavity by gravity, air pressure, or centripetal force. The mold either hinges or disassembles to enable removal of the component without damage. Most of the manufacturing processes can accommodate multiple mold parts, which may eliminate draw angles and undercuts. There is a wide range of available media for these manufacturing processes, including fiber-reinforced plastic (FRPs), gypsum (FRG), and concrete (FRC); thermoplastic and thermoset plastic; concrete; and glass.

With most of the hollow manufacturing processes, the outer face of the component is its finished face. However, for filament winding (Chapter 3.3), it is the inside face of the component that is in contact with the tooling. Filament winders may depend on post-production processes to finish the outside face of the component. For contact molding, the component can be designed so that either surface can be finished. For some process—such as contact molding (Chapter 3.1) and bladder inflation molding (Chapter 3.2)—there is a substantial surface quality difference between the finished face and the unfinished face. For other processes—such as rotational molding and blow molding (Chapter 3.5)—there is little difference, and both faces may be exposed.

3.1 Contact Molding

INTRODUCTION

Contact molding is the manufacturing process of placing a medium of composite materials in contact with a mold. [1, 2, 3] The face of the medium in direct contact with the mold is the finished face of the component, and the component face not in contact with the mold is unfinished. Contact molding can form very large components with complex curves and some surface detail. Surface quality can range from good to very good, depending on the manufacturer's capabilities, and tolerances are acceptable. Contact molding is used for composite materials, normally fiber-reinforced plastic (FRP), but it can also be used for fiber-reinforced gypsum (FRG) and fiber-reinforced concrete (FRC).

When contact molding, typically a plug is CNC milled from foam and sprayed with a high-gloss gel-coat. For contact molding, layers are laid onto the mold. The first layer is the component's finish layer and may be a gel-coat resin, fine cement, or gypsum. Once the first layer cures, additional layers of fibers and resin are layered onto the mold. Pressure is added so that the resin fully penetrates all of the fiber layers. This can be done multiple times, until the desired thickness is reached. The component cures, and is then removed from the mold. The contact molder may use the plug directly to make the component, or may fabricate a contact-molded mold off of the plug. The plug is used for direct manufacturing if only a few components are required; otherwise, the plug is used to make a mold or multiple molds if a large production run is needed. This manufacturing process can be done using a variety of methods, including hand layup, spray-on, and pressure infusing. The hand layup method is the traditional method for contact molding and requires the least technology. Using hand layup, the worker lays alternating layers of reinforcing fibers and resin onto the mold to build up the component's cross-section. Rollers or similar tools often apply pressure to the layup to distribute the resin throughout the fibers. With the spray-on method, the worker uses a spray gun to apply a mixture of resin and fiber, also known as chop, to a mold. The spray gun has two nozzles—one for the chop, and one for the resin. The chop and the resin mix in the air before they hit the mold. Hand layup and spray-on can be done in combination, depending on the component's shape and required strength. [4] The pressure-infusing method uses hand layup, spray-on, or a

2 Cleaning up the edges of a contact-molded FRG component by hand

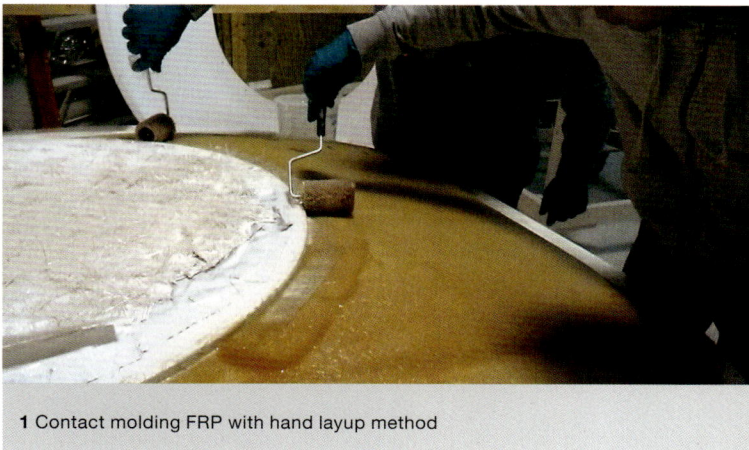
1 Contact molding FRP with hand layup method

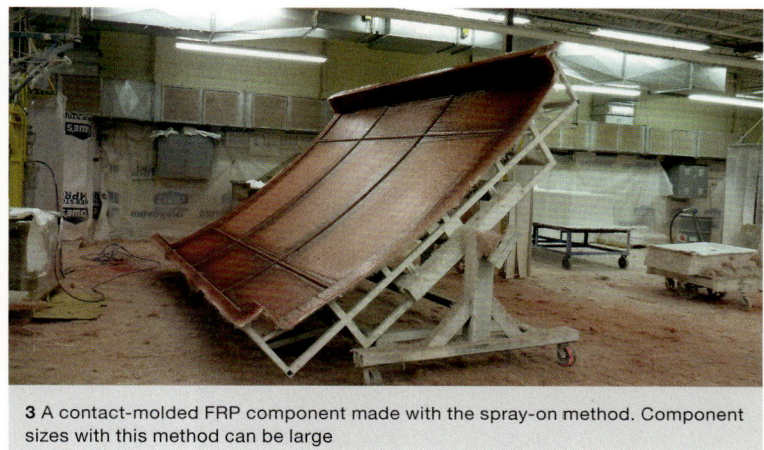
3 A contact-molded FRP component made with the spray-on method. Component sizes with this method can be large

CNC MILLING MACHINE
PLUG TO FORM MOLD

SPRAY GUN
GEL COAT

OPTIONAL FRP MOLD
FIBER WOVEN CLOTH
GELCOAT
FIBER MAT
EPOXY RESIN

OPTIONAL

CURE

FINAL COMPONENT

FRP MOLD WITH GELCOAT

HAND HELD ROLLER
GELCOAT
FIBER MAT
EPOXY RESIN
FIBER WOVEN CLOTH

CURE

FINAL COMPONENT

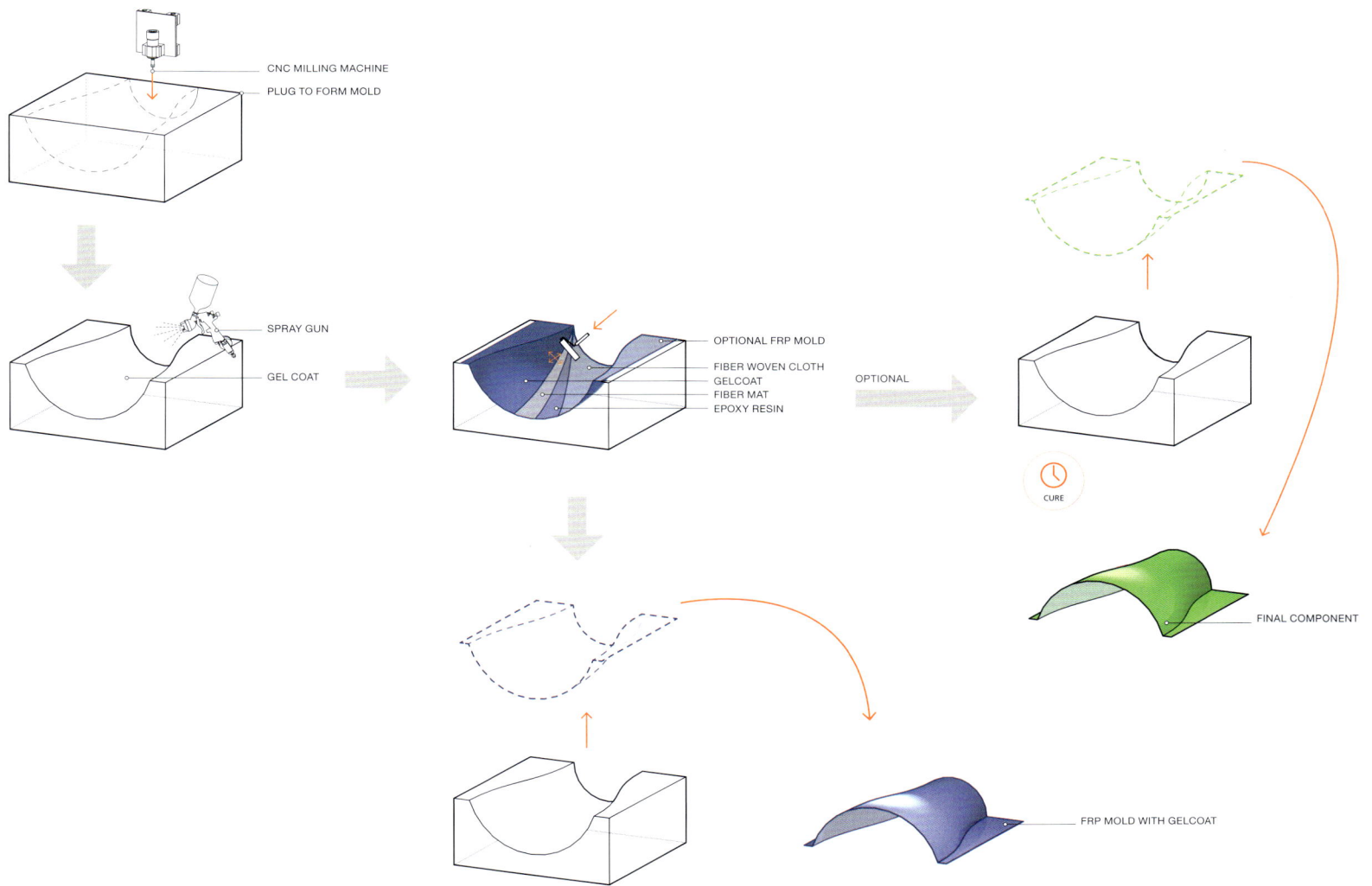

4 Hand layup combined with spray-on method. Hand layup has been used for the 90° corners. The sprayer, in the background, will be used for the rest of the layup

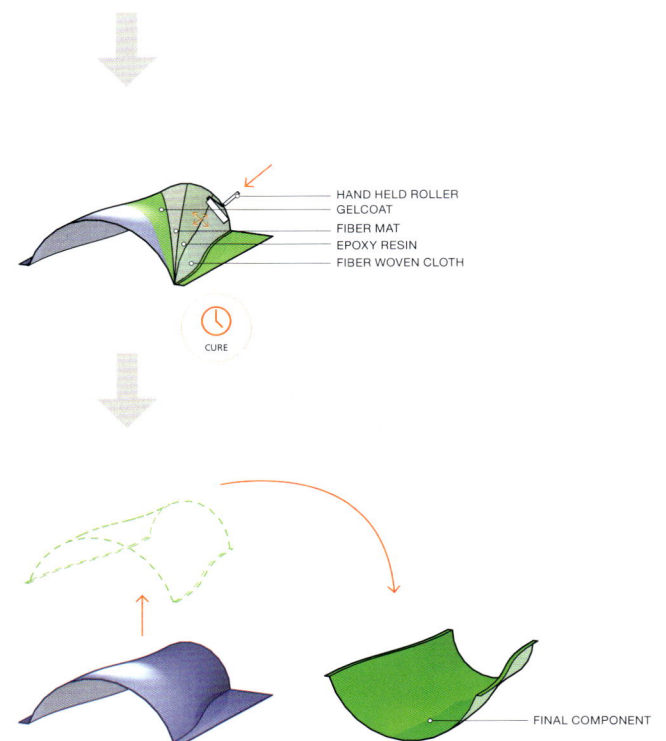

combination of the two to apply the medium to a mold. By using a vacuum, a rubber or plastic diaphragm is pulled down, placing even pressure on the composite and distributing the resin through the fibers. [5]

There is some variation in the results of the different methods. Because of the method of application, the unfinished side of a component created with the spray-on method will be rougher than with the other two methods. Because the resin is evenly distributed throughout the fibers, pressure-infused contact-molded components are typically stronger than those made by the other two methods. In addition, pressure-infused contact molding forces the medium tighter to the mold, producing components with better detail and tighter tolerances than the other two methods. All three contact molding methods are fairly labor intensive, with hand layup being the most labor intensive. [6] Because pressure infusing requires additional equipment, not all contact molders are able to offer this process.

Generally, contact molders are not highly mechanized. Most contact-molding manufacturers work on contract, are highly flexible, and are readily able to produce custom components. At the same time, this manufacturing process is not suited to high-volume production runs, and total production times may be long. To speed up production, manufacturers may run multiple molds for parallel productions. Most manufacturers will have the ability to fabricate their own molds, either by hand or by contact molding onto a plug.

Some small manufacturers will contract out the CNC milling of the plug.

There are very few size limitations associated with this manufacturing process. Sizes may be limited only by the size of the shop, the pot life of the resin, and the workers' arm lengths. [7] The resin's pot life is the amount of time before the liquid resin begins to cure and solidify, and is typically about 4 hours. To keep the component from warping during curing, it is best if all of the resin is laid at once. If this is not possible, the resin should be laid in completed layers across the component. In small shops with little to no equipment, workers' arm lengths are also limiting factors, as resin, fibers, and pressure need to be applied to all parts of the component. For some specialized shops, robotic sprayers are used for contact molding, overcoming this restriction.

BUILDING PRODUCTS

A range of commercially available building products use contact molding for their productions. Contact molding can be used for mass-produced items, such as gel-coated fiberglass shower enclosures, or for small-batch productions, such as church steeples. [8] Additional products may include commercial signage or decorative architectural components, such as brackets, balustrades, and columns.

5 The pressure-infusing method uses a diaphragm to apply consistent pressure

7 This process can manufacture large components

6 Contact molding is a labor-intensive process

8 Church steeples, made from existing molds, can be ordered through a website

9 Fiberglass mold (made by contact molding on a plug)

10 A high-density foam plug made by CNC milling with a gel-coat

11 A cast rubber mold for an FRG layup

12 A collection of plywood molds

TOOLING

Tooling for contact molding includes the mold and the optional plug to make the mold. Little pressure is applied in contact molding, therefore the mold can be made from a range of materials include gel-coated foam, plywood, FRP, rubber, or metal. However, during the resin's curing, heat is generated by the component, which in turn transfers to the mold. Because of this, foam and plywood molds tend to warp over time and break down. For repetitive productions, the components produced early on will not be the same as those produced later. Therefore foam and plywood molds are best for small production runs over a short period of time, whereas FRP and rubber molds are best for repetitive productions over a long period of time. Metal is the most durable and expensive material for molds, and is best suited to high-volume production runs, up to one million units.

If production runs are small (i.e. fewer than ten units), the gel-coated plug could be used directly for manufacturing. A foam plug can be used to create from three to ten FRP molds, allowing the contact molder to make three to ten components simultaneously. Depending on the unit's complexity, size, and details, a fiberglass mold can produce 1,000 units or more. Generally, costs for fiberglass molds are low, with a large mold costing under $6,000. **[9]**

Foam plugs or molds are often made by CNC milling. **[10]** Rubber molds can be cast against CNC-milled or hand-fabricated patterns. **[11]** Plywood molds are often fabricated by hand, with some of the more intricate details made by CNC milling. **[12]** Metal molds may be cast (Chapter 4.2), fabricated by hand, or machined by CNC millers and EDMs.

ENVIRONMENTAL IMPACT

Little energy is used in this manufacturing process, but it is labor intensive. Generally, there is little manufacturing waste with this process, as only enough composite material is made to fill the mold.

In general, plastic is not environmentally friendly, as it has a high amount of embodied energy, and thermoset plastics, specifically, cannot be recycled. As with most plastic manufacturing, contact molding FRPs releases volatile organic compounds (VOCs) and therefore should be done in a well-ventilated area. Low-styrene and suppressed-styrene resins, air filters, high-volume/low-pressure spray guns, or pressure infusing can lessen VOCs. After the FRP cures, VOCs can continue to off-gas from the produced components, but this will taper off over time. Using FRG or FRC will reduce VOC off-gassing. However, concrete also has high embodied energy, due to the process of making Portland cement. Additionally, both gypsum and concrete require water for curing.

Both plaster and concrete weigh more than plastic and will increase the component's dead load. This will increase fuel costs and, depending on shipping distances, may negate the environmental value of the gypsum over that of the plastic. In some areas, contact-molded FRP could be considered a vernacular material and manufacturing process. In coastal regions that have a heritage of boat manufacturing, contact-molding manufacturers are abundant. Many of these manufacturers build custom boats and can serve as a local manufacturer for a building located in the coastal region. For example, Fibertech, the coffer manufacturer for the North Carolina Museum of Art, is within 300 miles of Raleigh, NC.

MATERIAL CONSIDERATIONS + DESIGN PARAMETERS

Contact molding is used for composite materials, made of reinforcing fibers held in place with a binder or resin. The fibers are typically glass, but they can include carbon, steel, or natural fibers such as hemp. Carbon fibers offer the best strength-to-weight ratio but are also the most expensive. Fibers are available in either chop or mat forms for both hand layup and spray-on methods. The orientation and distribution of the fibers in mat form are more consistent than those in chop form, which often results in stronger composites. [13] The binder or resin is typically a plastic, but it can also include gypsum (FRG) or concrete (FRC).

FIBER-REINFORCED PLASTIC (FRP)

As a composite, FRP has greater strength and stiffness than plastic without reinforcing. [14] Typically, thermoset plastic is the resin used in contact-molded FRP, but thermoplastics can also be used. Generally, thermoset plastics are less susceptible to heat deformation, are more chemically resistant, and expand and contract less with temperature changes than thermoplastics. With any plastic, creep can be an issue, so manufactured components should be engineered to reduce long-term deformation.

Typically, for contact-molded FRPs, the finish is a gel-coat resin, which gives a smooth, glossy finish to the FRP, and can be matched to any custom color. [15, 16] Gel-coats cover both the molds and the produced components, helping to release the component from the mold. In production, the gel-coat is applied to the mold and allowed to cure before the fiber and resin mixture is applied. If a glossy gel-coat is not desired, then the gel-coat can be primed and painted, or additional surface materials such as thermoformed plastic can be added. If a textured surface is desired, the surface of the mold is modified with the texture. [17]

In contact molding, the spray-on method can be done in combination with the hand layup method. This is done when the mold is small, has tight internal corners, or fine details that the spray may not cover. Additional layers of composite may also be added, when additional reinforcing is required. [18, 19, 20]

SIMILAR PROCESSES
Bladder inflation molding, or BIM (Chapter 3.2) uses contact molding as part of its process; however, BIM makes hollow components in a closed mold, as opposed to thin-walled components in an open mold. Shapes made with contact molding are similar to those made by thermoforming (Chapter 1.2); however, thermoforming only uses thermoplastics.

13 Rolls of fiberglass mats. The top rack has two different woven mats, and below are chopped strand mats

14 Contact molding with FRP, using a hand layup. The precut chopped strand mat is laid onto a layer of resin. Another layer of resin is applied on the mat, and a hand roller is used to push the resin into the mat

15 Typically, the FRP finish is a high-gloss gel-coat

16 A mold with an applied white gel-coat, before the layup is done

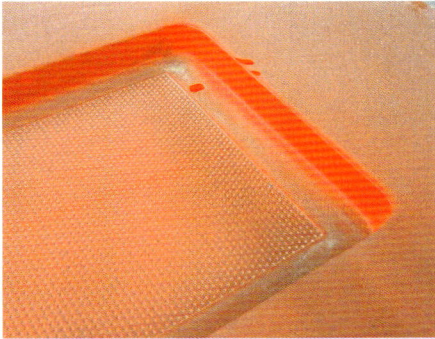

17 If a textured surface is needed—such as the anti-slip device depicted in the image—texture is added to the mold

18 Hand layup being done for the small, tight molds, as the spray will not reach all of the corners

19 Hand layup for the interior corners. This allows for a more precise application of FRP and reduces voids

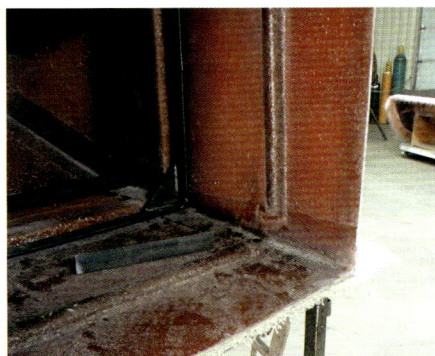

20 Hand layup and reinforcing at corners to strengthen the structure

CORNER RADII

Interior and exterior corners should have a slight radius, greater than 0.25in (6mm). This reduces stress at the corners, allows the component to be easily released from the mold, and reduces defects.

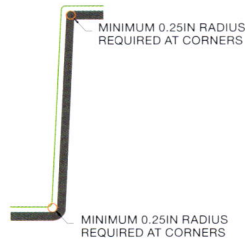

MINIMUM 0.25IN RADIUS REQUIRED AT CORNERS

MINIMUM 0.25IN RADIUS REQUIRED AT CORNERS

DRAFT ANGLES

The draft angle depends on the depth of the draw: 2–3° is required for shallow draws and 5° for deeper draws. Shallower draw angles can be used, but they will put additional wear on the molds, decreasing the potential production run.

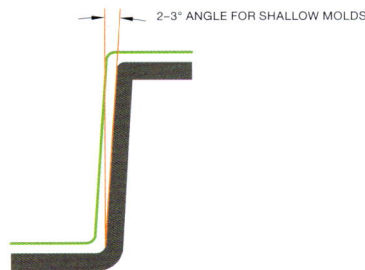

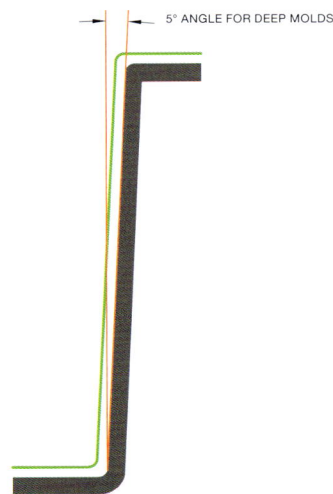

2–3° ANGLE FOR SHALLOW MOLDS

5° ANGLE FOR DEEP MOLDS

FINISH

The gel-coat layer will leave a high-gloss finish on the component. If another finish is desired, the component should be primed. Because of the difficulty of adhering the primer to the gloss finish, it is best to have the manufacturer prime the component in the factory.

INSERTS

Mechanical fasteners can be integrated into the layup.

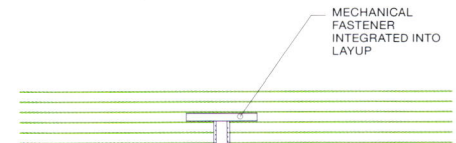

MECHANICAL FASTENER INTEGRATED INTO LAYUP

JOINTS

In hand layup, there should be a 2in (50mm) overlap between the reinforcing layers, and joints should be staggered. Although the joints will appear on the unfinished face, they will be almost imperceptible on the finished side of the component.

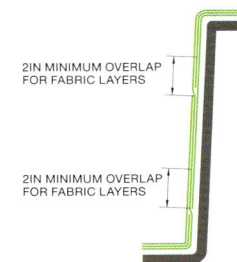

2IN MINIMUM OVERLAP FOR FABRIC LAYERS

2IN MINIMUM OVERLAP FOR FABRIC LAYERS

PRODUCTION SPEED

This process relies on the resin curing, which can take from 8 to 12 hours, depending on the size of the component. Production speed can be increased by using multiple molds for parallel productions.

PRODUCTION VOLUME

Contact molding is not typically used for high-volume productions, because it is a labor-intensive and cycle times are long. Production runs are typically fewer than 500 units.

SHRINKING

Shorter cycles are often accomplished through manufacturing at higher temperatures and the demolding of components before they have fully cooled. Both of these will increase the shrinking of the component. Each type of resin has different shrinkage rates, and molds must be oversized so that the final component size will meet the specification. If tolerances are tight, the manufacturer may consider making prototypes to verify the final mold shape.

SIDE-WALL HOLES

This process cannot accommodate side-wall holes. If they are required, they are often drilled into the component after it has been removed from the mold. To mark a consistent location for the holes, most manufacturers will place small dimples into the mold to help locate holes.

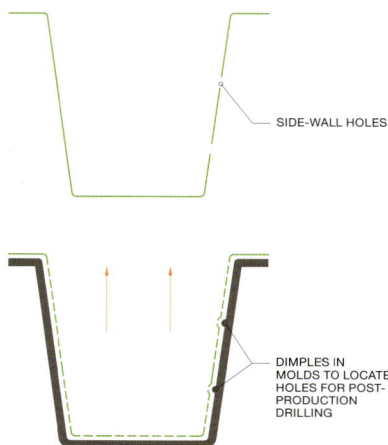

SIDE-WALL HOLES

DIMPLES IN MOLDS TO LOCATE HOLES FOR POST-PRODUCTION DRILLING

SINK MARKS

Sink marks and voids are most likely to occur in thicker sections of the component. Care must be taken to eliminate trapped air and to maintain a consistent FRP thickness.

SIZE LIMITS

Contact molding can be used to produce items of almost any size. With both spray-on and hand layup methods, size is limited by material strength, maneuverability, or transportation restrictions. In pressure infusing, the size of the produced item will depend on the size of the diaphragm.

SURFACE TEXTURE

Textures can be added to the mold and can easily be picked up by the gel-coat and the resin (see figure 3.1.17). Textures work well to provide an anti-slip surface for the high-gloss finish.

UNDERCUTS

Small undercuts are permissible. The amount of undercut will depend on the shape and angle of the undercut, the design of the mold, and how the component is removed from the mold. If the component is flexible enough, then it can be bent before removing it. Additionally, components can be slid lengthwise from the mold rather than lifted out to avoid the undercut. Keep in mind that, depending on the length of the mold, sliding a component from a mold can slow down production time and cause premature mold wear. Finally, molds can be designed with removable cores, or in multiple sections. This allows the mold to be disassembled and removed in pieces after the component has cured.

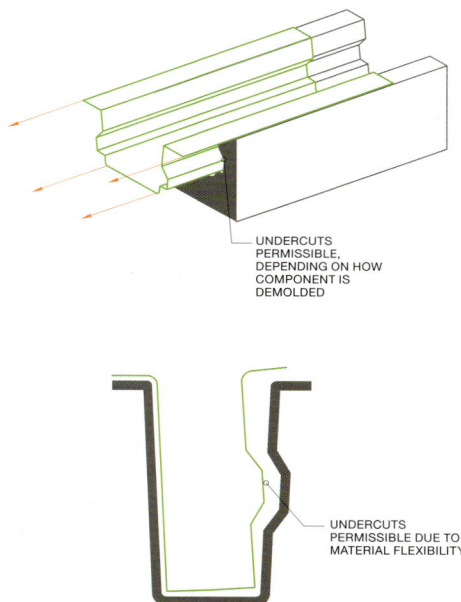

UNDERCUTS PERMISSIBLE, DEPENDING ON HOW COMPONENT IS DEMOLDED

UNDERCUTS PERMISSIBLE DUE TO MATERIAL FLEXIBILITY

WALL THICKNESS

FRP thickness can range from 0.12 to 6in (3–150mm). Thick-walled components will usually have an internal core of foam, balsa, or a honeycomb aluminum or plastic. The core helps increase the FRP's strength while decreasing the weight of the component. In both hand layup and spray-on methods a consistent cross-sectional thickness is difficult to achieve.

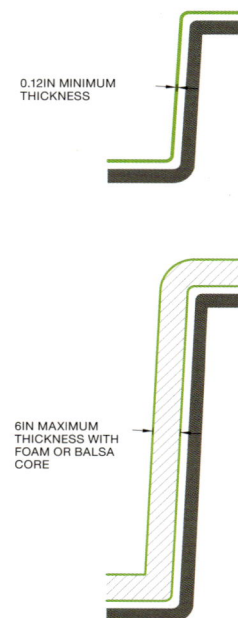

0.12IN MINIMUM THICKNESS

6IN MAXIMUM THICKNESS WITH FOAM OR BALSA CORE

WARPING

To control warping, the temperature of the component should be evenly maintained during the curing process. Toward that end, the composite should be applied in an even thickness across the unit, as greater thickness will cause more heat during curing. Cooling lines can be embedded in the mold to ensure even cooling, but this will greatly increase cost.

CONTACT MOLDING: FIBER-REINFORCED PLASTIC

CEILING COFFERS | NORTH CAROLINA MUSEUM OF ART
Thomas Phifer and Partners
Raleigh, North Carolina

In 2010, the North Carolina Museum of Art (NCMA) opened its newly constructed West Building. Designed by Thomas Phifer and Partners, the West Building provided 127,000ft² (11,800m²) of additional gallery space for the museum's collection. [21, 22, 23] Phifer designed contact-molded coffers as custom components for the building's ceiling. The coffers have a center oculus and are shaped to distribute the light evenly throughout the galleries. Each oculus has interchangeable filters and is covered by exterior, north-facing roof louvers. At the top of each coffer, below the oculus, are a concealed sprinkler head and a smoke sensor. Integrated at the bottom, between the coffers, are tracks for lighting and slot diffusers for air supply. The coffers are demountable from below for maintenance.

Fibertech, a contact molder located in Central, South Carolina, which specializes in manufacturing custom architecture components in FRP, made the coffers. [24] There are 360 coffers in the West Building, and every coffer has the same shape. [25] Each coffer is approximately 26ft (7.9m) long, 6ft (1.8m) wide, and 5ft 6in (1.7m) high. [26] The coffers are relatively lightweight, weighing approximately 400lb (180kg) each.

21
North Carolina Museum of Art by Thomas Phifer and Partners in Raleigh, North Carolina

22
Museum gallery

23
Museum gallery

24
Detail of ceiling coffers

25
Interior photograph comparing different light diffusers at the oculus between two galleries

DESIGN CONSIDERATIONS

According to Gabriel Smith, project architect, when Phifer's office originally conceived of the coffers' design, it had considered both FRP and FRC for the coffer material.[1] Due to weight, cost, and transportation issues, Phifer changed the coffers to FRP. A team at Georgia Institute of Technology engineered the coffers so that they supported their own weight and so that creep would be minimized during a forty-year term. [27]

Phifer wanted the coffers to have a low-gloss finish and opacity. Because gel-coat has a high-gloss finish, the coffers needed to be primed to accept a latex paint. The manufacturer applied a primer to the gel-coat in the factory, and the contractor applied the final coat of paint in the field. Careful testing ensured that the primer would not peel away from the gel-coat. Opacity was difficult to achieve, and Phifer's office rejected any of the submitted samples that did not meet this requirement.

During the design's mock-up process, Fibertech suggested design changes to the coffers. They proposed reducing the lip at the top of the coffer where the oculus's diffuser was mounted. By reducing the dimension of the lip, the coffers could be nested for transportation. [31] This reduced the number of trucks needed to transport the coffers and lowered construction costs.

Some research was required to ensure that the coffers complied with fire-code and flame-spread requirements. Phifer included a concealed sprinkler and a smoke sensor at the top of the coffer. [32] The coffer's shape therefore responded to the concealed sprinkler head. Both the manufacturer and Phifer's office took care to ensure that the design met clearance requirements. Phifer researched FRP and specified fire-performance criteria for the material. A thermoset plastic resin with additives was used so that the FRP would be heat- and fire-resistant.

MANUFACTURING CONSIDERATIONS

Using Rhino software, Phifer's office created a digital, three-dimensional model of the coffers for design and virtual testing of the structure. From the Rhino file, Fibertech made a mold out of medium-density fiberboard (MDF) to replicate the geometry of the model. An FRP pattern was then molded out

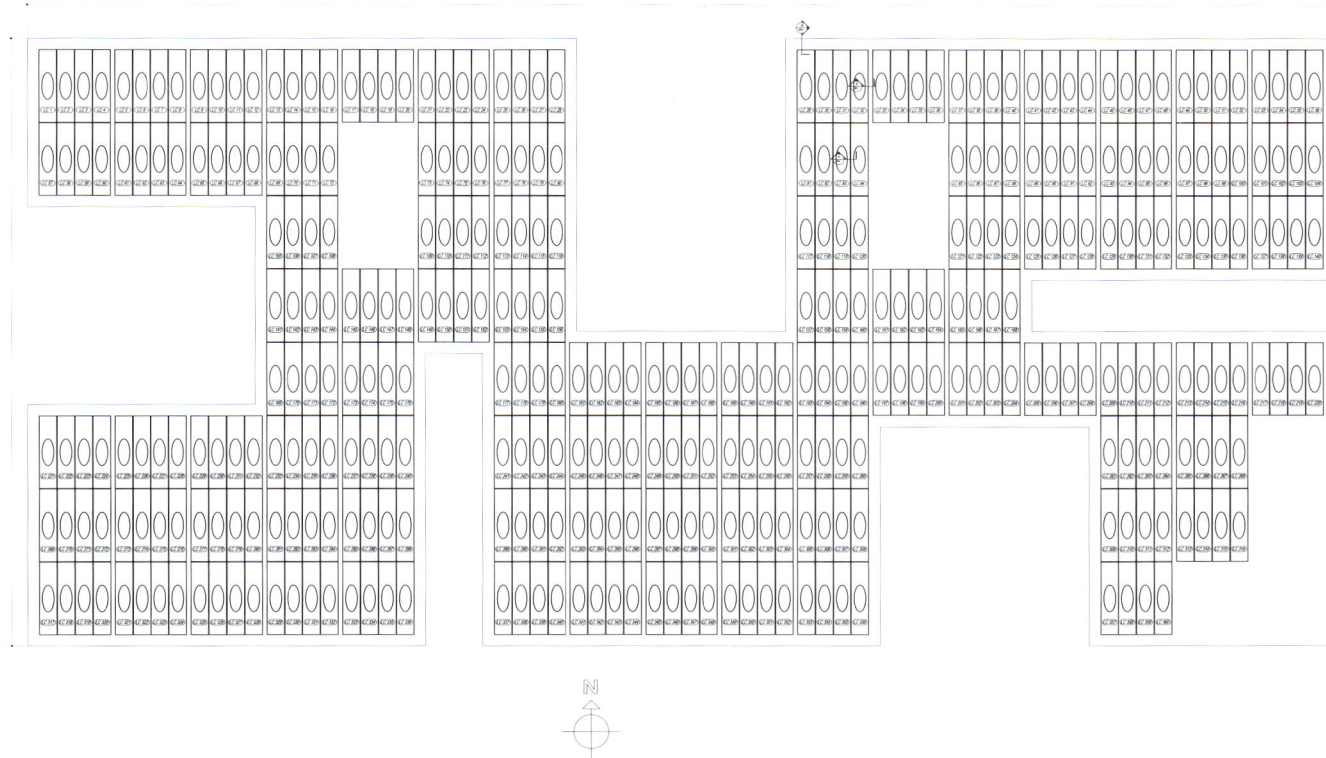

25 Fibertech shop drawing: reflected ceiling plan for the museum

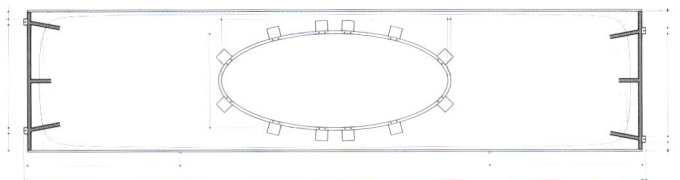

COFFER PLAN VIEW
SCALE: ¾" = 1'–0"

SECTION THROUGH COFFER
SCALE: ¾" = 1'–0"

SECTION THROUGH COFFER
SCALE: ¾" = 1'–0"

26 Fibertech shop drawing: coffer detail, reflected plan, transverse and longitudinal sections

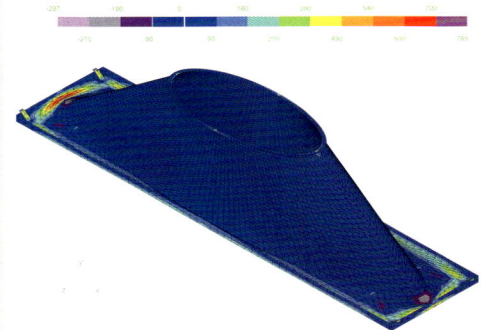

27 Stress diagram

28 Fibertech fabricating a mold out of MDF. A FRP pattern was molded off the MDF model

of the MDF mold, and then three FRP molds were made from the pattern. **[28, 29, 30]** Parallel productions were done from the three FRP molds.

Phifer designed the coffer with concealed fasteners and finished continuous edges at the bottom. **[33]** To create the finished edge, all of the coffer's sides fold back onto themselves, creating a tight space of internal corners. This space can be difficult to access with a spray gun, so the chop was not always evenly applied to the mold. This resulted in occasional irregular surfaces at the edges and corners that required post-production remediation.

OTHER CONSIDERATIONS

The NCMA was a state-funded project, and as such, the state of North Carolina required a public bid process for construction. Typically, the public bid process requires that construction contracts be awarded to the lowest bidder. The intent of the public bid process is to lessen misuse of public funds and reduce costs. However, quality of construction may be reduced as contractors and suppliers attempt to meet a low price point. For mass-produced products that are manufactured prior to construction, this is often not an issue because quality is ensured by the manufacturer prior to the contractor's purchase. For customized components that are manufactured after the contract is awarded, it may be difficult to ensure a quality product.

In order to meet the state requirements and Phifer's high standards of quality, the specifications included a pre-qualified list of contact-molding manufacturers. The specifications required that all bidders submit a 12in (300mm) square sample of the FRP for the coffers. This ensured that the bids would only be awarded to those manufacturers that could meet the design requirements.

LESSONS LEARNED

Contact molding FRP was less precise than Phifer's office had anticipated. The long edges of the coffers often bowed in plan, and sometimes entire coffers would torque. This meant that each coffer was unique in how it would attach to the supporting ceiling structure, and the attaching bolts would often force the coffer into correct alignment. **[34]** Additional rib supports were added to the bottom edge of the coffer in order to lessen bowing along the 26ft (7.9m) length.

Any number of factors could have caused the distortions. First, the resin tends to shrink during the curing process. Second, the coffer's design could have caused these distortions, because of either its large size or its open, unsupported bottom. Third, the manufacturer's use of multiple molds during production could have introduced minor inconsistencies due to discrepancies between molds.

29 FRP mold. Three FRP molds were made from the FRP pattern, for parallel productions

32 Sprinkler and smoke detector at the top of the coffer near the oculus

30 Manufactured coffer

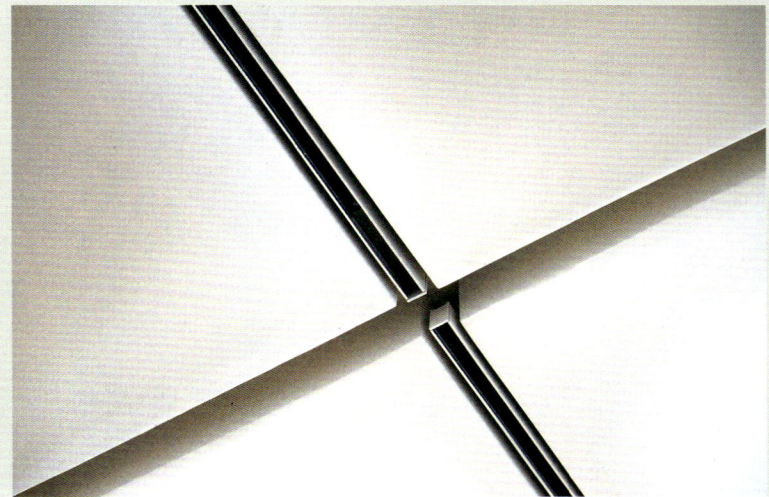

33 Detail of joints between the coffers. The sides of the coffer fold up to conceal the fasteners

31 Coffers were stacked during shipping, to save transportation costs

34 Installation of the coffers during construction

FIBER-REINFORCED GYPSUM (FRG)

As a composite, FRG has greater strength and stiffness than plaster without reinforcing, which allows FRG components to be thinner and lighter than cast plaster. [35, 36] Fibers are typically glass, can come in chop or mat form, and can be applied by spray-on or hand layup methods. FRG is for interior applications, where the material will not be exposed to moisture. The finish surface quality is good and it is easily painted.

FIBER-REINFORCED CONCRETE (FRC)

FRC is a mixture of Portland cement, fine aggregate (0.25in/6mm or smaller), water, and a maximum of 4% by weight of fibers. [37, 38, 39] Portland cement is typically a gray to buff color. If color is important, consider using a white cement and any color required as an additive, although this will increase the cost of the FRC. As with cast concrete (Chapter 4.1), post-production finishes such as acid washing and grit blasting are available with FRC. The fibers are alkali-resistant glass, and are randomly dispersed through the material. The fibers enhance the concrete's flexural, tensile, and impact strength. According to the Precast/Prestressed Concrete Institute, "The manufacture of GFRC [glass fiber reinforced concrete] products requires a greater degree of crafts-manship that other precast concrete products."[2] FRC can either be wet-cast (Chapter 4.1), hand sprayed, or troweled on to an open mold. Unlike FRG, FRC is suitable for exterior applications or where components will be exposed to moisture. The finish surface quality is good and it is easily painted.

SIMILAR PROCESSES

Contact molding FRG and FRC is a unique process. Wet-casting concrete (Chapter 4.1) can be used to cast solid FRC components, but not components with the thin walls associated with contact molding.

35 Components made with FRG

36 Large components made with FRG

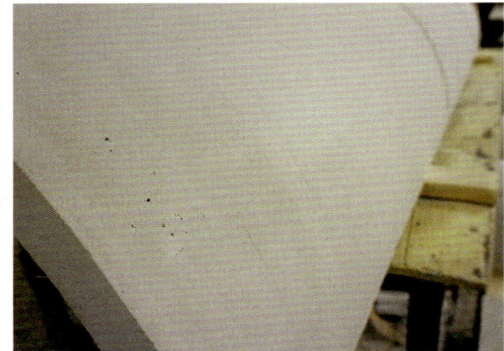

37 Detail of FRC finished surface

38 Half of a column shaft made with contact-molded FRC

39 Wood members embedded for easy handling and metal brackets inserted into layup for attachment

NOTE: The design parameters for FRG and FRC are similar, unless noted otherwise.

DRAFT ANGLES

For plywood molds, the draft angle should be 5°. For rubber molds, the draft angle can be steeper.

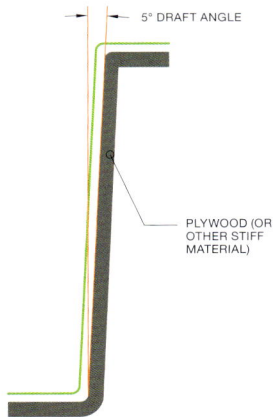

5° DRAFT ANGLE

PLYWOOD (OR OTHER STIFF MATERIAL)

INSERTS

Mechanical fasteners and attachment inserts can be integrated into the layup.

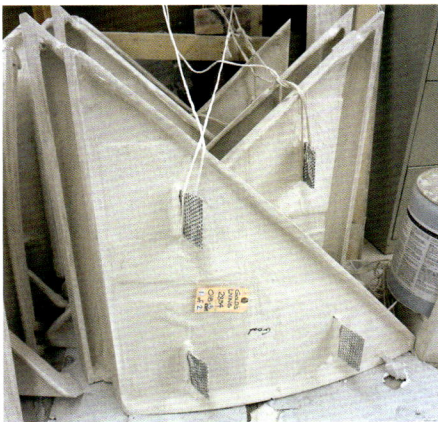

PRODUCTION RUN

Because contact molding is a labor-intensive process and cycle times are long, neither of these materials are appropriate for high-volume productions. Production runs are typically fewer than 100 units.

PRODUCTION SPEED

Production speed depends on the curing time of the plaster or concrete, as the materials will need to set before demolding.

UNDERCUTS

Undercuts are not permissible, due to material stiffness.

TOLERANCES

Industry tolerances allow for 0.06in (1.5mm) deviation within the overall width or length and 0.12in (3mm) for the overall width and length.

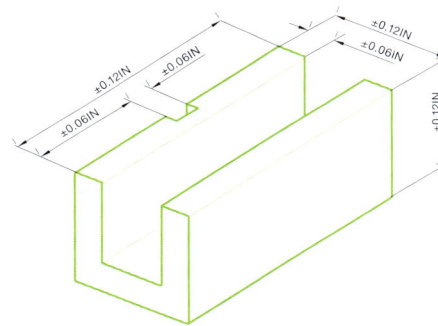

±0.12IN
±0.06IN
±0.12IN
±0.06IN
±0.12IN
±0.06IN
±0.12IN

WARPING

Industry standards allow a 0.12in (3mm) deviation within 8ft (2.5m).

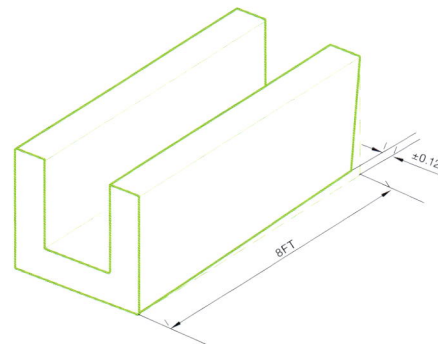

±0.12IN
8FT

WALL THICKNESS

For FRG, walls can be as thin as 0.15in (4mm), with a thickness over 0.3in (8mm) preferred.

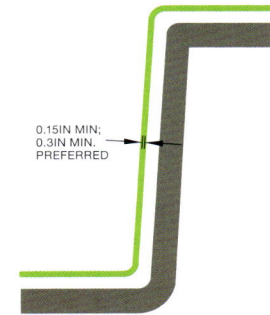

0.15IN MIN;
0.3IN MIN.
PREFERRED

For FRC, walls can be as thin as 0.5in (13mm), depending on panel size.

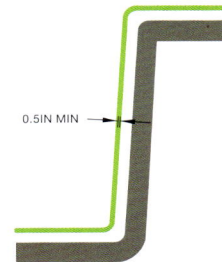

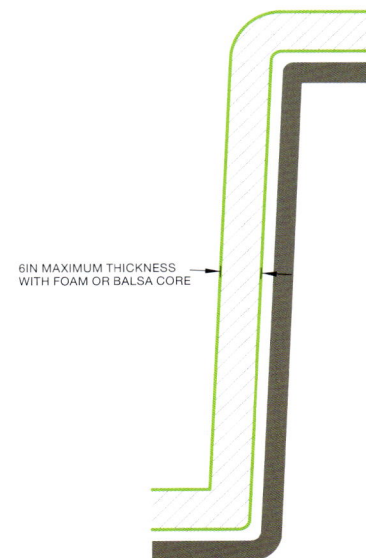

0.5IN MIN

6IN MAXIMUM THICKNESS WITH FOAM OR BALSA CORE

A consistent wall thickness is difficult to maintain with this manufacturing process.

3.2 Bladder Inflation Molding (BIM)

aka internal inflation process (IIP)

INTRODUCTION

Bladder inflation molding (BIM) is a manufacturing process that uses composite medium, a closed mold, and an internal bladder. BIM creates hollow components with complex curves. [1] The exterior face of the BIM component is in contact with the inside mold and is the component's finished face. BIM produces components with good surface quality, and to good tolerances, depending on the manufacturer's capabilities. To ensure even pressure by the internal bladder against the mold, most shapes made from BIM are rounded at the mold's parting line, and they are typically symmetrical. Any difference in shape between the two halves should be minimal.

For BIM, a composite of fiber and resin is applied to both faces of a closed mold. On at least one side of the closed mold, the FRP is laid so that it extends over the mold edges. This ensures the overlap of the two sides of the composite when the mold is closed. Before closing the mold, an internal bladder is placed inside one mold half. The bladder is slightly inflated prior to the mold being closed, to help keep the FRP in place. When closing the mold, the manufacturer should take the time to ensure that the FRP overlaps are kept inside the closed mold's cavity before fully closing the mold. This is done so that no laminate is squeezed out along the parting line, reducing the post-production finishing work. Clamps or mechanical fasteners are often used to keep the mold closed and in place. Once the mold is closed and clamped, the bladder is inflated to a prescribed pressure. The bladder is kept inflated until the resin cures. After curing, the bladder is deflated and the mold is opened. The bladder and any residual flashing are removed.

BIM is an extension of contact molding. As in contact molding, the composite medium is placed on a mold via hand layup or spray-on methods (see Chapter 3.1, Contact Molding). Hand layup is more labor-intensive than spray-on, but typically results in better consistency, allows for woven-fiber mats in the interior of the composite, and therefore has greater material strength than spray-on. In this process the two halves of the composite layup are fused together during the curing process. [2, 3] The overlap between the two halves is hidden on the inside of the hollow component. The seam is often imperceptible, and the interior overlap between the two halves ensures strength at

1 Neck support collars for race-car drivers. Made hollow with bladder inflation molding (BIM) carbon-fiber-reinforced plastic

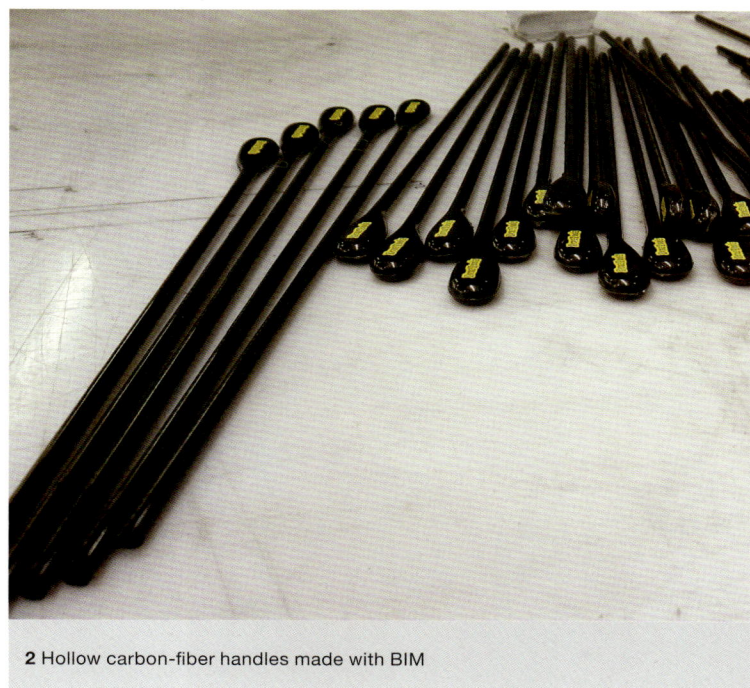

2 Hollow carbon-fiber handles made with BIM

CNC MILLING MACHINE

PLUG TO FORM MOLD

FIBER-WOVEN CLOTH
EPOXY RESIN
HAND-HELD ROLLER
FIBER MAT
GEL-COAT

GEL-COAT ON MOLD

RAISED LIP FOR OVERLAP

SPRAYER

MILLED MOLD

GEL-COAT

RAISED LIP FOR OVERLAP

RAISED LIP FOR OVERLAP

DEFLATED BLADDER

AIR VALVE

OVERLAP FORCED BY TOOL
MINIMUM 2" OVERLAP

AIR

FINAL COMPONENT

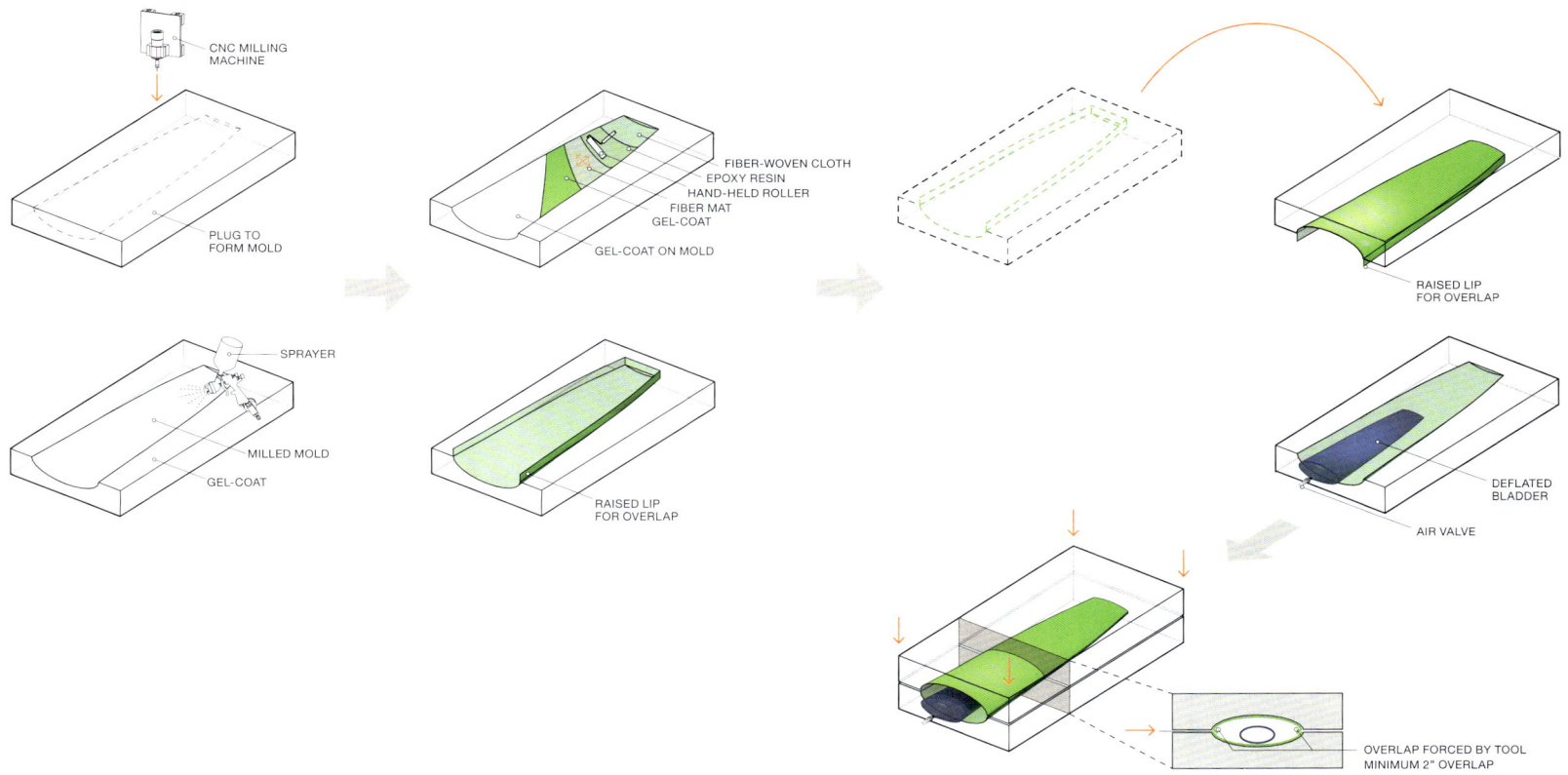

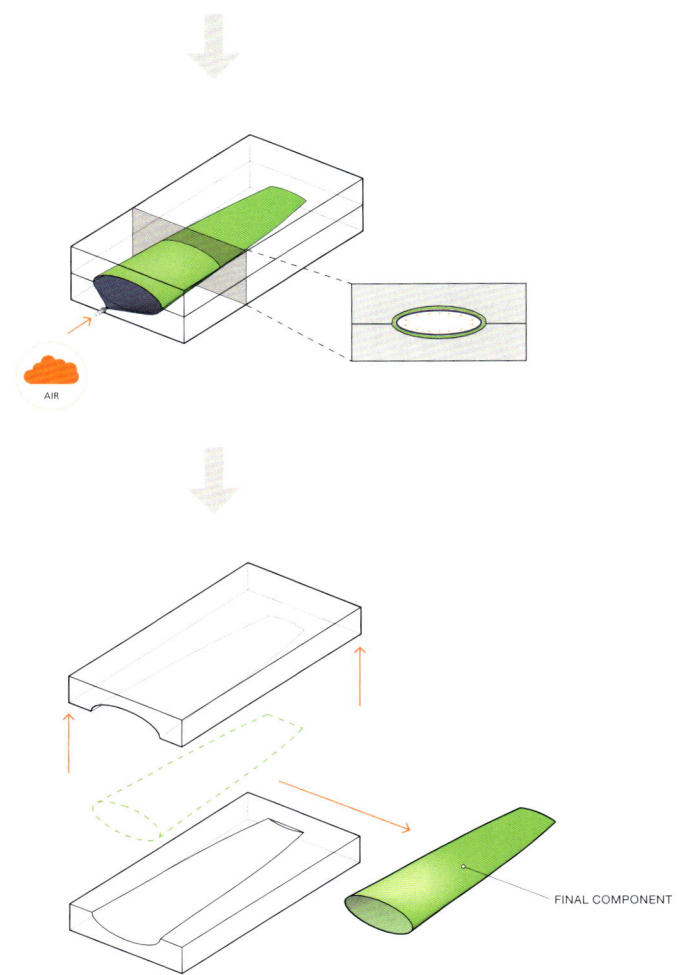

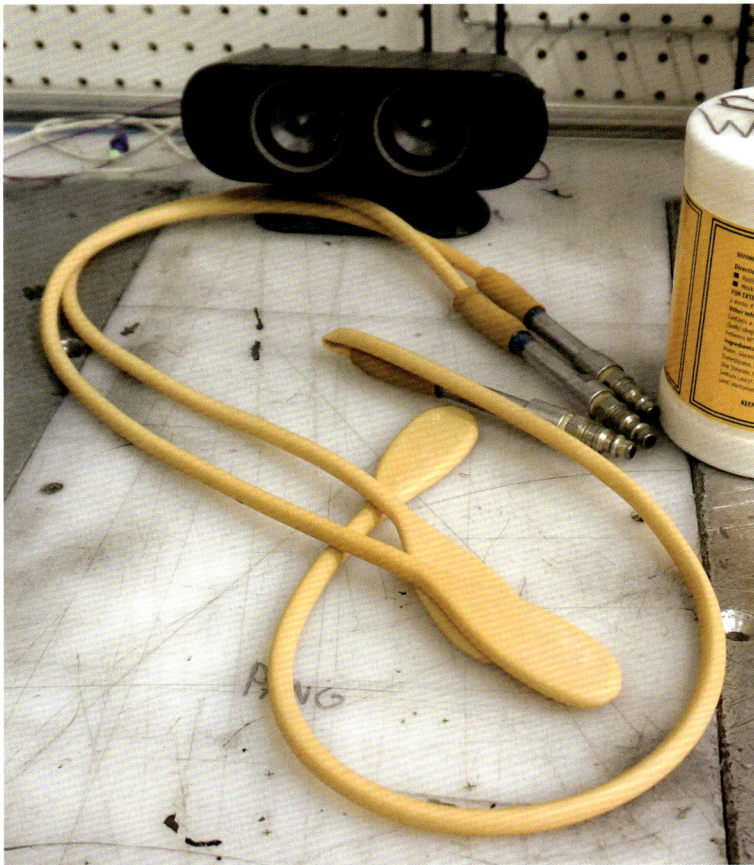

3 Rubber bladders used for the handles' interiors

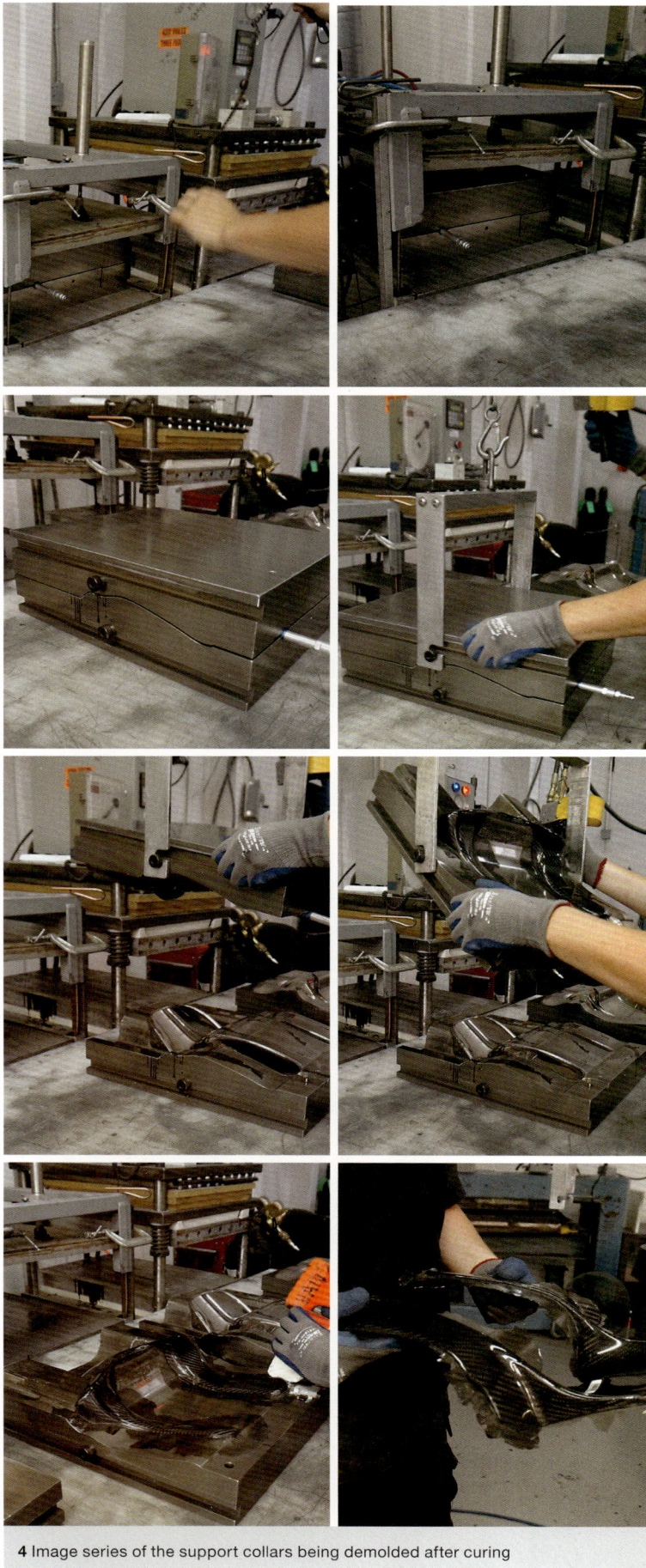

4 Image series of the support collars being demolded after curing

the seam that could not be achieved through a post-production process of mechanically or chemically fusing two separate halves together. [4]

As BIM is not traditionally a highly mechanized process, cycle times can also be long. Typically, resins begin curing approximately 4 hours after mixing. Most manufacturers apply the FRPs during the day and let them cure overnight. To speed up production time, most manufacturers will run multiple molds simultaneously. This allows multiple components to be made each day.

The size limitations with BIM are similar to those associated with contact molding (Chapter 3.1), including resin pot life and the length of workers' arms. In addition, the size of the shop may limit the component size, as BIM requires additional space to close the mold, and to insert and remove the bladder. Larger bladders also require a larger compressor than smaller bladders, but the low pressures associated with BIM do not often require capacities beyond those of shop compressors.

BUILDING PRODUCTS

There are very few commercially available building products made by BIM. Because BIM forms hollow components out of FRP, it is associated with manufacturing elements that have a high strength-to-weight ratio. Because of this, BIM is used to manufacture specialized, large-scale propeller blades, typically used for wind turbines.

TOOLING

Tooling for BIM includes the mold, the optional plug to make the mold, and the bladder. The outside of the BIM object is in contact with the inside face of the mold, so care should be taken to ensure that the mold's inside surface is clean, smooth, and free of defects. Closed molds for BIM can be made of the same materials as for contact molding (Chapter 3.1), including high-density milling foams, fiberglass, wood or wood products, or metals such as aluminum or tool steel. The durability of the mold materials is in direct proportion to the mold's cost. For example, milling foam is the least expensive mold material, but typically it can only support a short production run of ten units or fewer. Conversely, tooling steel is the most expensive, but can support a production run up to one million units. [5]

Bladders can be made of rubber, silicone, or plastic. They can be reused from component to component, deflated after the FRP has cured, and then removed though an opening. Bladders can also be sacrificed and left in the component after curing. This is typically done with inexpensive plastic bladders, or where component openings must be small. [6] Bladders are shaped for

5 Molds for the support collars, machined from tool steel

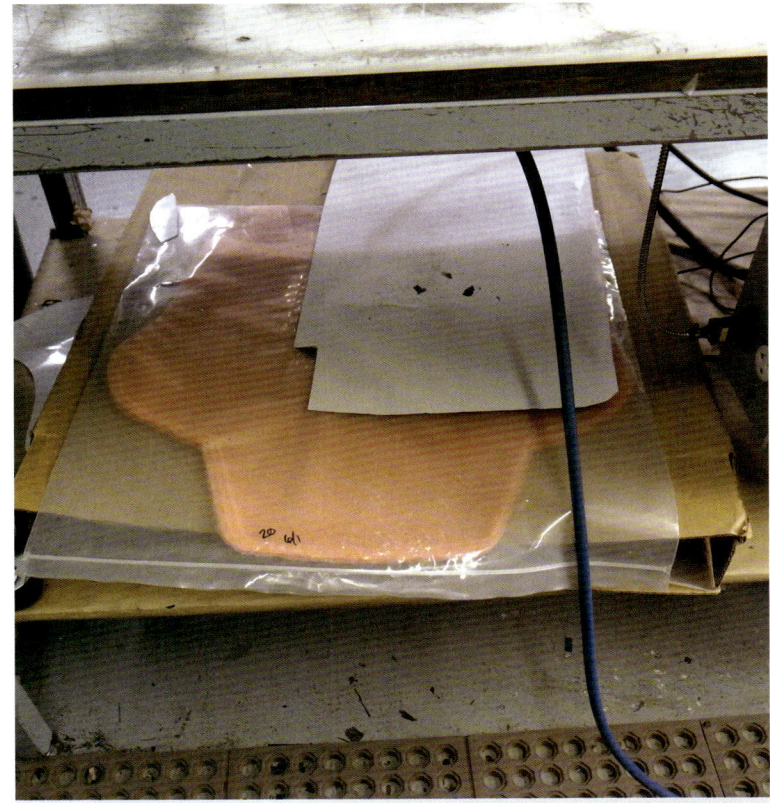

6 A bag of sacrificial plastic bladders, which are left inside the support collars after forming

the component, to ensure that they exert an even pressure on the component.

CNC milling can fabricate foam, wood, or metal tools. Fiberglass tools can be made by contact molding onto CNC-milled plugs. Plywood molds are often fabricated by hand, with some of the more intricate details being made by CNC milling. Metal molds may be cast (Chapter 4.2), fabricated by hand, or machined by EDM.

Generally, BIM tooling is more expensive than that for contact molding. First, because BIM uses a closed mold, costs are double those of a comparable mold for contact molding. Additionally, locator pins will often be placed in the two mold halves so that the mold is properly aligned when it is closed, increasing mold complexity. Finally, there is the added cost of the interior bladder.

ENVIRONMENTAL IMPACT

Little energy is used in this manufacturing process, but it is a labor-intensive process. Generally, there is little manufacturing waste, as only enough composite material is made to fill the mold.

In general, plastic is not environmentally friendly, as it has high amount of embodied energy, and thermoset plastics, specifically, cannot be recycled. As with most plastic manufacturing, BIM releases VOCs, and therefore the process should be carried out in a well-ventilated area. Low-styrene and suppressed-styrene resins, air filters, high-volume/low-pressure spray guns, or pressure infusing can lessen VOCs. After the FRP cures, VOCs can continue to off-gas from the produced components, but this will taper off over time.

MATERIAL CONSIDERATIONS + DESIGN PARAMETERS

BIM is used for composite materials made of reinforcing fibers held in place with a binder or resin. The fibers are typically glass, but can include carbon, steel, or natural fibers such as hemp. Carbon fibers offer the best strength-to-weight ratio but are also the most expensive. Fibers are available in either chop or mat forms for both hand layup and spray-on methods.

FIBER-REINFORCED PLASTIC (FRP)

As a composite, FRP has greater strength and stiffness than plastic alone. The plastic resin is typically a thermoset plastic, but thermoplastics can also be used. Thermoset plastics are less susceptible to heat deformation than thermoplastics. The resins for thermoset plastic come in two parts, which are mixed (sometimes with added heat) to produce a chemical reaction. This permanently bonds the plastics' polymer chains together so that the bonds cannot be broken without reversing the reaction.

With any plastic, there can be issues of creep, ultraviolet (UV)-light degradation, expansion and contraction with changes in temperature and humidity, and susceptibility to fire. The design team should ensure that components are engineered to resist long-term deformation, and that resin additives and coatings are specified to deal with UV light, environmental factors, and to meet flame-spread requirements.

The orientation and thickness of the fibers affects the composite's strength. Woven mats are typically stronger than chopped mats; however, the texture of the mats can transfer to the finished surface of the FRP. Therefore a chopped mat is typically used to as a veil to hide the texture on the finished surface. Typically, for BIM FRPs, the finish is a gel-coat resin, which gives a smooth, glossy finish to the FRP (see figure 3.1.15), and can be matched to any custom color.

SIMILAR PROCESSES

Contact molding (Chapter 3.1) produces thin-walled components, similar to BIM, but in an open mold. Contact-molded components can be joined by chemical welding to make hollow components, but the joint between the two units will be weaker than it would be with BIM. Filament winding (Chapter 3.3) also manufactures hollow components with FRP; however, the finish face is considered the interior of the winding and filament winding's cycle times are longer than with BIM. Rotation molding and blow molding (Chapter 3.5) also produce hollow plastic units similar to BIM, but those processes are limited to thermoplastics rather than FRP.

CORNER RADII

The minimum corner radius is 0.25in (6mm). This process relies on an internal inflatable bladder; therefore the internal bladder must be in contact with the full interior surface of the component. Interior corners are discouraged.

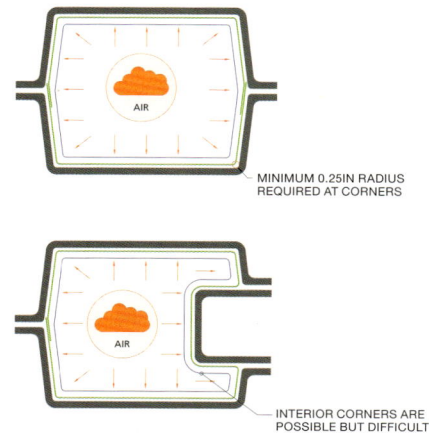

MINIMUM 0.25IN RADIUS
REQUIRED AT CORNERS

INTERIOR CORNERS ARE
POSSIBLE BUT DIFFICULT

DRAFT ANGLES

The draw angle depends on the depth of the draw. In the range of 2–3° is required for shallow draws, and 5° for deeper draws. Shallower draw angles can be used, but they will put additional wear on the molds, therefore decreasing the molds' production run.

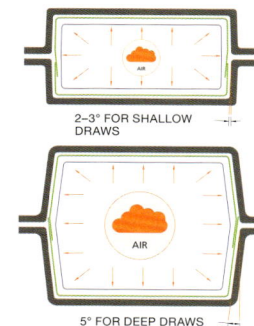

2–3° FOR SHALLOW
DRAWS

5° FOR DEEP DRAWS

FLASHING

Resin often squeezes out between the mold halves and must be knocked off or cut away.

INSERTS

Mechanical fasteners can be integrated into the layup. Because the mold is closed around the layup, it may be difficult to maintain locations.

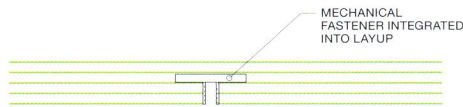

MECHANICAL FASTENER INTEGRATED INTO LAYUP

PARTING LINES

Parting lines between mold parts will be visible on the component.

PRODUCTION SPEED

This process relies on the resin to cure. Production volume can be increased by using multiple molds for parallel productions.

PRODUCTION VOLUME

BIM is not typically used for high-volume productions; it is labor intensive and cycle times are long.

SHAPES

Shapes are typically rounded and symmetrical. There can be a small difference in shape between the two mold halves, but this difference should be minimal to enable consistent pressure to be exerted by the bladder.

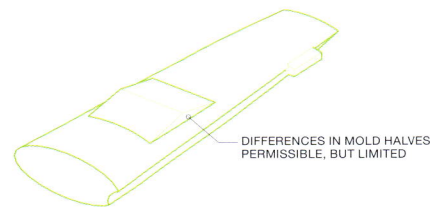

DIFFERENCES IN MOLD HALVES PERMISSIBLE, BUT LIMITED

SHRINKING

Shorter cycles are often accomplished through manufacturing at higher temperatures and early release of components from the mold. Both of these will increase the shrinking of the component.

SIDE-WALL HOLES

This process cannot accommodate side-wall holes. If side-wall holes are required, they must be drilled into the component after it has been removed from the mold. Manufacturers will place small dimples into the mold to help locate holes if necessary.

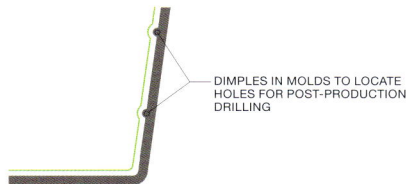

DIMPLES IN MOLDS TO LOCATE HOLES FOR POST-PRODUCTION DRILLING

SINK MARKS AND VOIDS

Sink marks are most likely to occur in thicker sections of the component. Because of the pressure of the internal bladder against the FRP, voids are less frequent in this process when compared with contact molding (Chapter 3.1).

SIZE

There are very few size limitations with this manufacturing process. BIM is slightly more restricted in size compared with contact molding (Chapter 3.1), because it requires additional space to close the mold, and to insert and remove the bladder.

SURFACE TEXTURE

Textures can be added to the mold and can easily be picked up by the gel-coat and the resin.

TOLERANCES

Resins shrink during curing, with each type of resin having different shrinkage rates. If tolerances are tight, the manufacturer may consider making prototypes to verify the final mold size and shape to achieve the requirements.

UNDERCUTS

Undercuts are difficult with this process. BIM results in a shape that is stiffer than traditional contact molding; therefore components formed with this process are not flexible enough to be released from a mold with an undercut. Undercuts are permissible if the mold comes in three or more parts, or if components can be slid lengthwise from the mold rather than lifted out to avoid the

undercut. Keep in mind that both of these options will increase costs and cycle times.

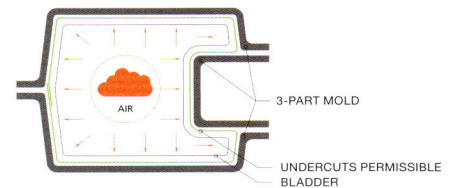

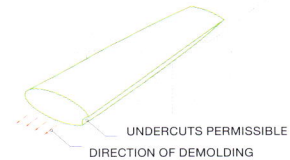

AIR

3-PART MOLD

UNDERCUTS PERMISSIBLE BLADDER

UNDERCUTS PERMISSIBLE

DIRECTION OF DEMOLDING

VENTS

Vent holes are not usually needed. Bladders inflate slowly with this process, so air can escape at the parting line.

WALL THICKNESS

FRP thickness for BIM can range from 0.12in (3mm) up to 1in (25mm). In both hand layup and spray-on methods a consistent cross-sectional thickness may be difficult to achieve.

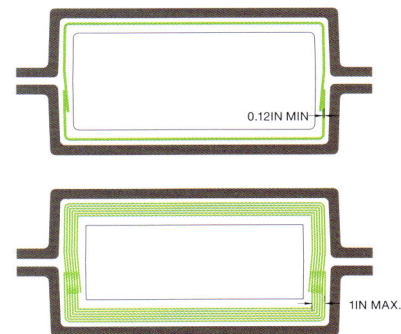

0.12IN MIN

1IN MAX.

WARPING

To control warping, the component should be kept at an even temperature during the curing process. This can be done by layering the composite evenly across the component and allowing air-flow around the mold for cooling. If warping is a particular problem, cooling lines can be embedded in the mold.

FIBER-REINFORCED PLASTIC (FRP)

EXTERIOR LOUVERS | WALBROOK OFFICE BUILDING
Foster + Partners
London, UK

The Walbrook Office Building was built in 2010 for a London-based British developer and property company, Minerva plc. The building includes the headquarters for a major corporation and additional leasable office spaces. The Walbrook is located in London's central, historic core—next to Christopher Wren's St. Stephen Walbrook church, and near St. Paul's Cathedral. **[7, 8, 9, 10]** Because the building is located in a historically sensitive site, it had to adhere to a number of protected view corridors, and the design team needed to be particularly respectful of site context. Foster + Partners designed the project's bays, setbacks, and height so that it fit with surrounding buildings.

The building is over 640,000ft² (60,000m²) and is approximately 165ft (51m) tall. It includes retail and restaurant space on the ground floor, and an enclosed, inner-block courtyard in the back. The building is a series of repeated bays in plan. The bays are articulated with round structural column enclosures and exterior louvers that form gentle convex curves in plan as they span from column to column. The louvers' outer edges are vertically aligned at the base of the building, creating a subtle cornice line that matches its neighbor at 103 Cannon Street. Above the cornice line, the louvers' outer edges are progressively stepped back in plan, creating traditional attic stories for the building's penthouse offices.

The louvers were custom designed and manufactured for this project. In total, there are 7.78 miles (12.53km) of the glass fiber-reinforced plastic (GFRP) louvers on the Walbrook. Individual lengths vary, with the longest measuring approximately 23ft (7m).

DESIGN CONSIDERATIONS

The louvers are spaced over 3ft (1m) apart, which allows for unobstructed horizontal views from the inside. **[11]** The louvers are elliptical and hollow in cross-section. They come in three different widths—approximately 8in, 14in, and 20in (200mm, 350mm, and 500mm).

The horizontal runs of the Walbrook's louvers are made by BIM, while traditional contact molding was used to form the column casing, integrated brackets, and internal bracket connectors. The integrated brackets connect the louvers visually and structurally to the column casings, by an organic, T-shaped, complex curved unit. **[12, 13]** There are additional hidden metal brackets that align with every other glass curtain wall mullion. These hidden brackets are mechanically fastened to the internal bracket connector made from contact-molded GFRP. The connector inside the hollow louver is perpendicular to the louver's curve in plan, and is chemically adhered to the GFRP of the louver's inside face.

7
View down Cannon Street, past the Walbrook Office Building to St. Paul's Cathedral

8
View down Walbrook Street, toward building

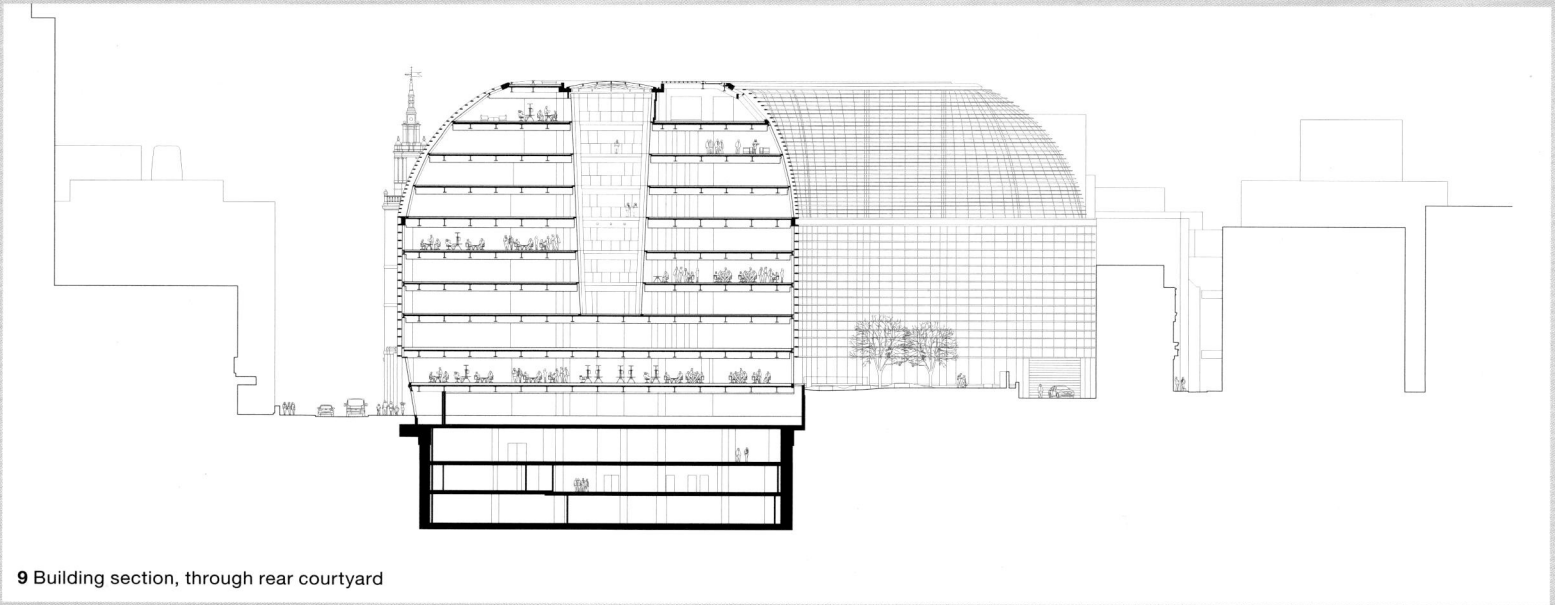

9 Building section, through rear courtyard

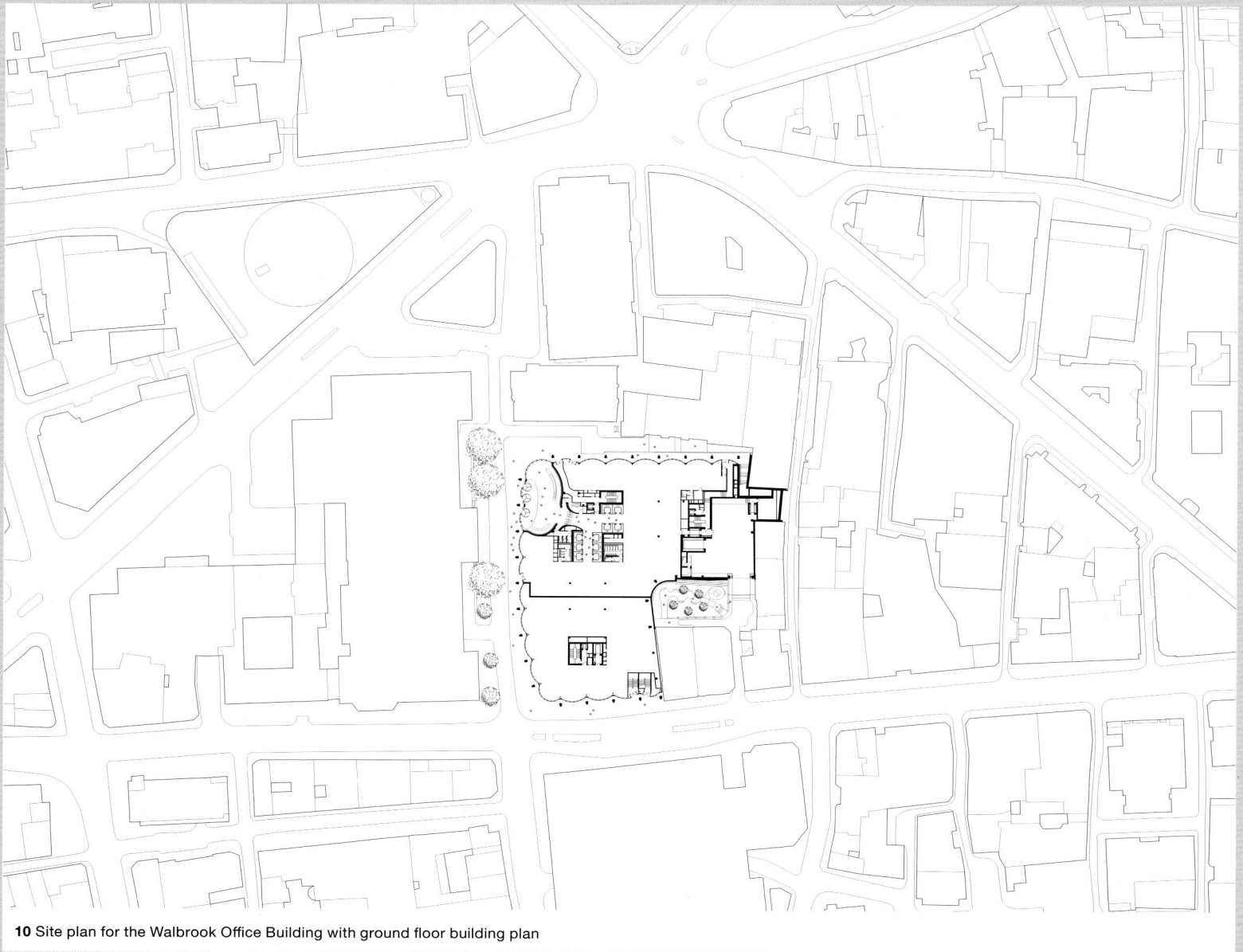

10 Site plan for the Walbrook Office Building with ground floor building plan

GFRP was not the original material choice for Foster + Partners. According to Grant Brooker, senior executive partner for the project, the firm had originally envisioned clear anodized aluminum for the louvers.[1] However, to make the desired shape for the louvers out of aluminum, it would have required a combination of manufacturing processes—casting, extruding, and bending. Extruding and bending would have been used for most of the louver's length, while casting would have been used to connect the louver to the column casing. Using aluminum would have resulted in two problems. First, the cost of producing the louvers was considered too high. Second, the three different manufacturing processes would have required different aluminum alloys and produced different surface finishes. The most notable would have been the difference in the finish between the integrated brackets at the columns and the rest of the louver's length. To achieve a consistent finish in aluminum, the louvers and brackets would therefore have to be painted, an idea rejected by the design team.

The GFRP louvers are painted with a glossy, reflective, metallic gray paint. Because of their painted surface, the louvers both block direct sunlight and reflect light into the building's interior. The louvers were manufactured with a standard gel-coat, typical of most contact-molded GFRP objects. The gel-coat was a high-gloss resin with an integrated color, applied to the mold by a spray gun, with the wet layup applied after the gel-coat had cured. The louvers were then lacquered with three layers, with sanding between each layer. The final finish is a silver, high-gloss finish. The louvers' coating reflects changing light conditions, so that the building can appear glowing orange and pink in the evenings, and blue when reflecting city lights.

MANUFACTURING CONSIDERATIONS

The molds for the Walbrook's louvers were manufactured with a two-step process. A five-axis CNC-milling machine made a plug from high-density foam. FRP molds were then made from the plug via contact molding. The milled plugs were durable enough to produce several FRP molds, and the FRP molds durable enough to produce more than 100 units before needing repair. Two FRP molds were then clamped together to create the closed mold. The ends of the mold were left open to inflate the internal bladder. The louver's FRP was hand-laid on both sides of the mold. The molds with the layered composite were closed around the bladder, and then the bladder was inflated. A hand-laminated process was chosen over spray-on because the design team required a particular material strength and surface quality, which spray-on could not match.

Although a CNC-milling machine was used to make the molds for the louvers, economics did not allow the louvers to be wholly made using CAM technologies. [14] Instead, the design team and manufacturer, FIBER-TECH Group GmbH, designed the louvers so that they balanced the design team's intentions with the reduced costs associated with repetition. This allowed the manufacturer to distribute the cost of fabricating the molds over multiple units.

For the Walbrook, there are only three cross-sections, and those remain consistent along a louver's length. However, each louver's length was customized as it was made. FIBER-TECH would adjust the louver's length by applying different lengths of resin and fibers to the mold before closing it.

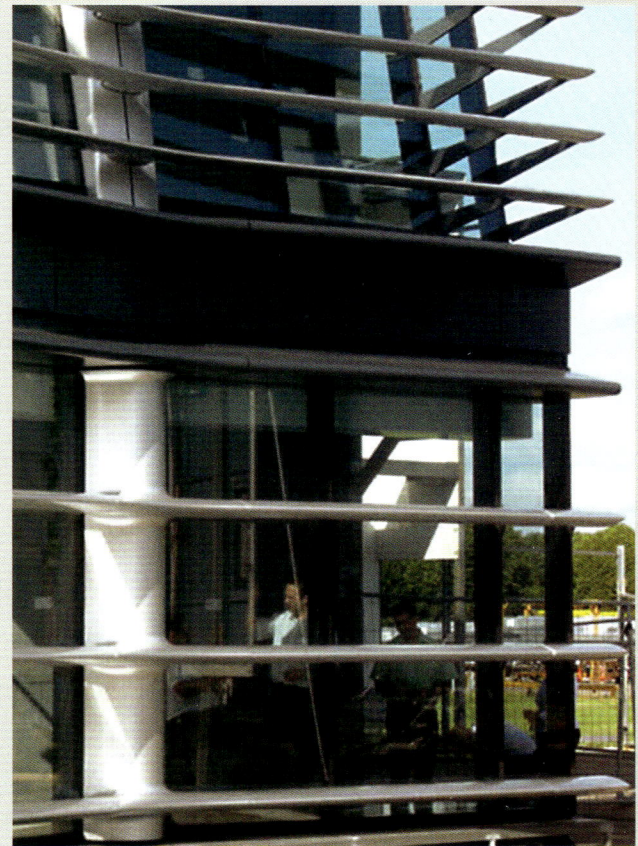

11 Mock-up of building cornice at corner showing louvre spacing

12 The louvers at the manufacturer. The integrated FRP bracket is visible inside the end of the louvers

13 T-shaped components that connect the louvers to the building columns

OTHER CONSIDERATIONS

The louvers' material strength was engineered so that the louvers would be self-supporting and able to bear wind and snow loads. The resin was selected so that the louvers would be fire resistant in accordance with the British Standards system. The louvers' coating was specially developed by FIBER-TECH, with a finish to protect the GFRP from small impact loads that might damage the surface, ultraviolet (UV) light that might degrade the resin, and humidity that might cause warping. The louvers and the exterior building assemblage were tested for performance in various weather conditions, freeze-thaw cycles, temperature fluctuations, and for color quality after 2,000 hours of UV exposure. [15]

LESSONS LEARNED

According to Brooker, there were a number of lessons that Foster + Partners learned through this project that could be applicable to other architects. The first is that if the design intention is paramount, the architect should consider building materials beyond the typical architecture palette. By making the change from the initial selection of aluminum to GFRP, Foster + Partners was able to achieve the desired look for the building within an acceptable cost. [16] Second, they discovered that there are additional advantages to using GFRP on buildings: 1) GFRP is repairable with patching; 2) Because molds costs are low and most FRP manufacturers manufacture small batches, if replacement louvers are ever required, a new louver can be manufactured quite easily.

14 Inserting the FRP bracket into the louver

15 Performance-testing the louvers and exterior wall assembly

16 Detail of louvers

3.3 Filament Winding

aka filament placement

INTRODUCTION

Filament winding is a manufacturing process that wraps resin-impregnated reinforcing strands around a turning mandrel. [1] The mandrel's shape is static while the placement of the reinforcing strands is CNC controlled and can be unique for each winding. The placement of the fibers affects the component's strength and porosity. Traditionally, this process was limited to cylindrical shapes such as tanks, pipes, airplane fuselages, and baseball bats; now it can be used on irregular forms such as T-shaped or elbow pipe fittings, wind turbine blades, and archery bows. Both thermoset and thermoplastic resins can be used in this process, with thermoset being the more common. The reinforcing strands can be of any material; however, glass and carbon are most common.

Surface quality is very good with this process, and tolerances are very high. Size is almost unlimited, as tanks 70ft (21m) in diameter and 50ft (15m) in length have been made with filament winding.[1] [2, 3]

Filament winding is a cyclical process that can be mostly automated. A rotating mandrel can be used, or another tool may be assembled around the mandrel. The filament winder includes the mandrel that spins, the creel that holds the rovings, the winding eye that controls the fiber placement and the carriage that holds the winding eye, rollers to maintain tension, and an optional resin bath if not using pre-impregnated fibers. The filament winder fibers are impregnated with resin and pulled by

1 Small filament winder, winding around three mandrels at once

2 Large metal mandrel, used for filament winding

3 Large filament winder, capable of winding component with a 6ft (1.8m) diameter

MANDREL

RESIN BATH
FIBER

CURE

FINISH CUT

FINAL COMPONENT

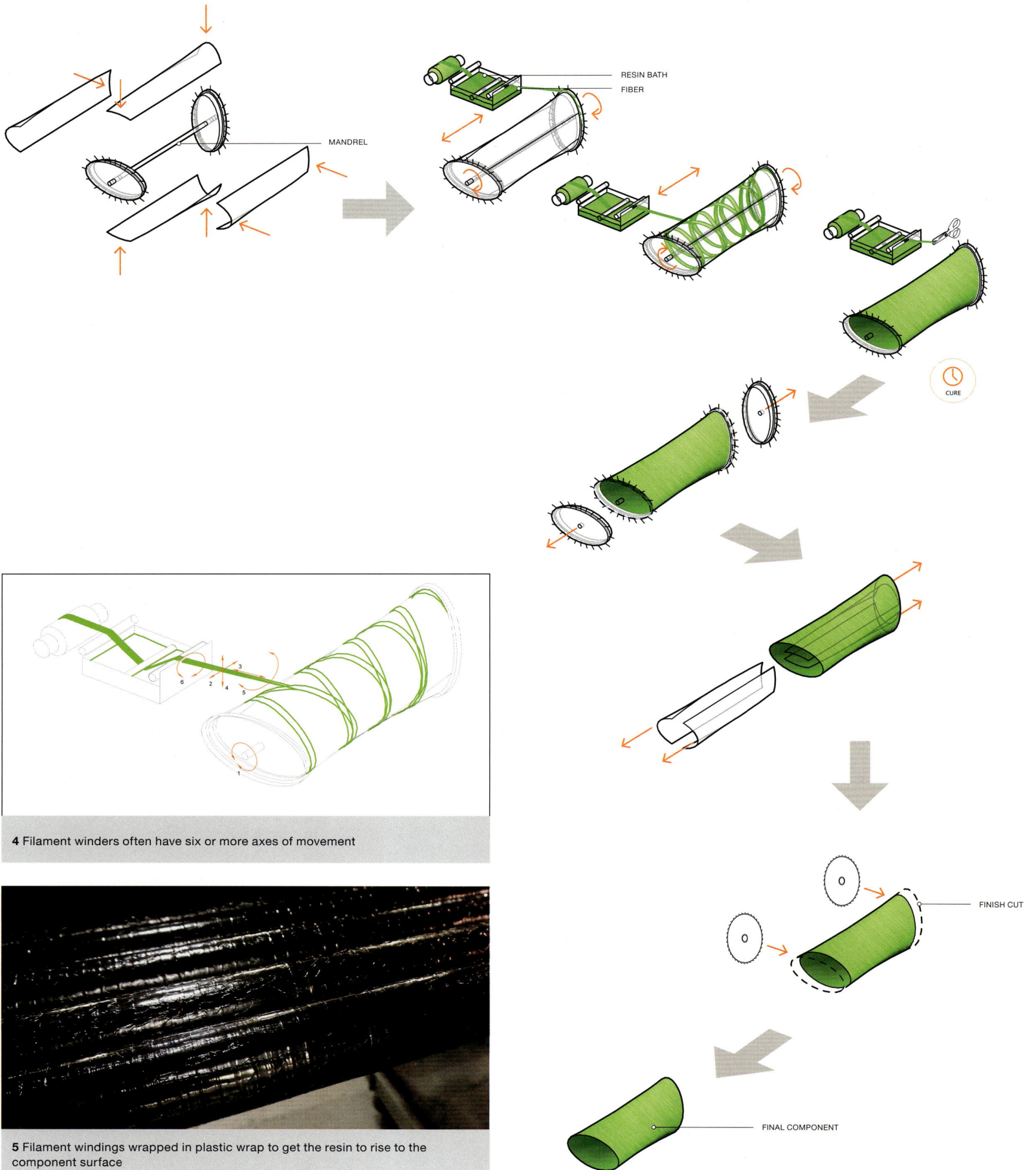

4 Filament winders often have six or more axes of movement

5 Filament windings wrapped in plastic wrap to get the resin to rise to the component surface

the mold and mandrel as they slowly spin. The filament winder carriage then moves so that the fiber and resin mixture covers the mold as required. The fibers are then cut, the resin cures, and the mold is removed. Any post-production trimming or finishing is then done as needed.

At a minimum, the filament winders have two axes of movement: 1) the spinning of the mandrel; 2) the carriage moving along the length of, or parallel to, the mandrel. As most filament winders are now CNC, their movements can be much more complex and can include additional axes of movement. [4] These include: 3) the carriage moving toward and away from the mandrel; 4) the carriage moving up and down; 5) the rotation of the winding eye in plan; 6) the rotation of the winding eye in elevation. More axes of movement have transformed filament winding from a process that traditionally could only wind cylindrical and axisymmetric shapes to one that can wind noncyclical, nonsymmetrical components. Additionally, the CNC placement of the fibers affects their tension, arrangement, and flatness. This, in turn, affects the strength of the component.

The inside face of the component is in contact with the mandrel and is considered to be the finish face. If the component's exterior face is to be finished, the manufacturer will wrap that face in plastic wrap as the resin cures. This causes the resin to rise to the exterior surface of the component, making that face smoother than it would have been without the wrapping. Manufacturers may also grind or sand the component's exterior surface, post-production, to give it a more finished quality. [5, 6]

There are some variants in the filament winding process. First, it is often done horizontally, but components can also be wound vertically. Vertical winding is better for thin-walled, small-diameter, long tubes. For these shapes, the weight of the composite could deform the mandrel, causing a permanent sag to be wound into the component. The disadvantage of vertical winding is that the resin may move during winding, causing there to be more resin at the bottom of the wound component than at the top. Second, some winding machines are set up so that they may wind multiple mandrels simultaneously, speeding up production. [7] Finally, the fiber and resin placement is traditionally flat and solid, but with CNC technology, high-performance fibers, and new roving configurations, filament windings can be twisted together as they are placed on the component's surface.

Generally, filament winding is a manufacturing process that can accommodate customization, because tooling costs are low. Filament winders make a mixture of products and may have standing production orders with their clients. These winders can accommodate small, custom production runs, but may be a little more limited as to when they can start production. Because filament-winding machines are comparatively inexpensive, there are many workshops and job-shops able to produce custom orders.[2] With new research into carbon fibers, robotics, and CNC technology, there are also some research-oriented producers that are testing the limits of what is possible with filament winding.

6 High-gloss or sanded finishes are often available. Sanding is done post-production

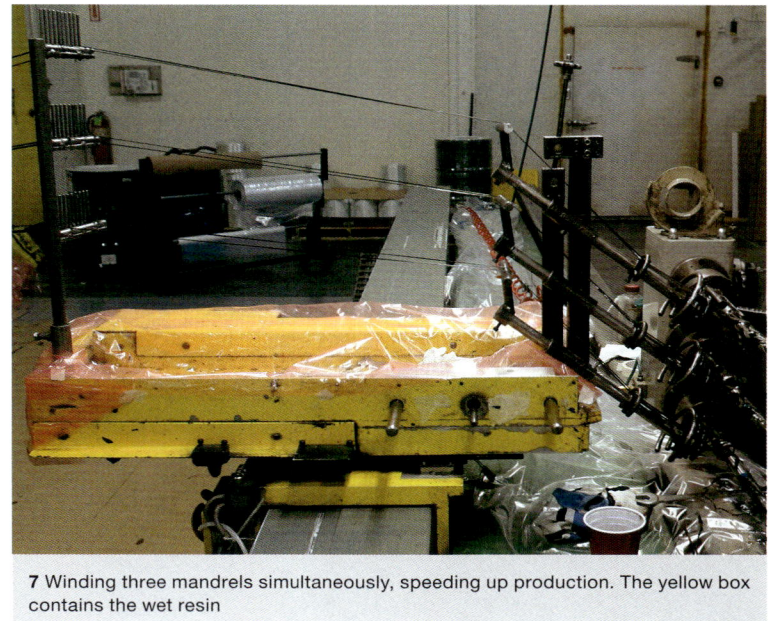

7 Winding three mandrels simultaneously, speeding up production. The yellow box contains the wet resin

BUILDING PRODUCTS

Few standard building products are manufactured by filament winding. When filament winding is used, it tends to be for products that have high-performance requirements, such as composite tubes, pipes, wind turbine blades, tanks, and high-pressure vessels, in which filament winding is used as reinforcement to the vessel's walls.

Not a building product, but designed by an architecture and industrial design firm, is the Filament Wound Stool by Moorhead & Moorhead. This hourglass-shaped stool comes in one shape with three different winding styles. In this way the stool's design makes the most out of a single mold, while making unique wrapping paths aided by the CNC technology.

TOOLING

The tooling required for filament winding is simple, and its cost quickly amortized over the number of units produced. Generally, manufacturing pressures and working temperatures are comparatively low, which allows the tools to be made out of variety of different materials. These may include cardboard, polymers and foam, plaster, balsa and other wood, fiberglass, aluminum, and

8 Large mandrel made of slats, so that it can be disassembled for demolding

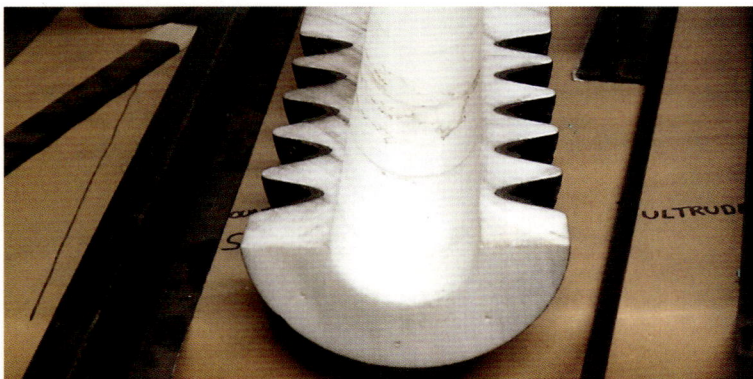

9 A filament-wound component cut in half. Here the mandrel was made of foam and left permanently inside the winding

stainless steel. The material selected for the mandrel will depend on the component's shape and the required production run. It helps if the material can conduct heat away from the resin as it cures and, if winding horizontally, that it does not deflect under its own self-weight.

The mandrel may be solid, or it may be a jig or a frame. The mandrel may come in one piece, or it may disassemble or collapse into smaller pieces for easier removal. [8] Depending on the component's shape and the viscosity of the resin, pins may be used in the mold to help keep the fibers in place during winding. Some mandrels are sacrificial, and are destroyed as they are removed or are permanently left inside the winding.[3] Sacrificial mandrels such as foam [9] or metal liners for high-pressure tanks are left inside the component after it is removed from the filament winder. Some mandrels are made of inflatable or water-soluble materials, which can be removed through small openings in the windings. There are also shape-memory polymers that are hard at room temperature and flexible at elevated temperatures. After curing, the mandrel and component are heated to a higher temperature at which the polymer becomes flexible and can be removed.

With the wide range of materials that can be used for winding mandrels, there is a wide range of methods to fabricate the mandrels. Hand fabrication techniques may be common for mandrels made of cardboard or wood. CNC equipment, such as mills and rapid prototyping (RT) machines, can be used to shape mandrels in polymers, foam, wood, or metal. Other repetitive processes, such as hydroforming (Chapter 1.6) and spinning (Chapter 1.7), may be used for making metal tank liners; and contact molding (Chapter 3.1), bladder inflation molding (Chapter 3.2), and rotational molding may be used to make FRP or plastic mandrels. Each mandrel fabrication process is associated with cost and shaping parameters.

ENVIRONMENTAL IMPACT

Little energy is used in this manufacturing process. Generally, there is little manufacturing waste; however, thermoset plastics are not recyclable, so any manufacturing waste goes to a landfill. Thermoplastics are better, but they are not often used with this process, and long-term durability can be a problem.

In general, plastic is not environmentally friendly, as it has high embodied energy. As with most plastic manufacturing, filament winding releases VOCs, and therefore should be done in a well-ventilated area. Low-styrene and suppressed-styrene resins, air filters, high-volume/low-pressure spray guns, or pressure infusing can lessen VOCs. After the FRP cures, VOCs can continue to off-gas from the produced components, but this will taper off over time. Using FRP or FRC will reduce VOC off-gassing.

MATERIAL CONSIDERATIONS + DESIGN PARAMETERS

Filament winding uses composite materials, made of reinforcing fibers held in place with a plastic resin. The fibers are typically glass, but can include carbon, steel, or natural fibers such as hemp. Fibers are available as rovings, tow, or wovens, and multiple layers can be placed at one time. Fibers can be wetted out during the winding process—this is called wet winding (see figure 3.3.7); or they can use pre-impregnated tow—called dry winding. Pre-impregnated, or prepreg, tow has plastic already impregnated in the strands. After the dry winding is complete, pressure and heat are added to the component to set the plastic. Generally, dry winding is cleaner than wet winding, but material costs are higher.

FIBER-REINFORCED PLASTIC (FRP)

As a composite, FRP has greater strength and stiffness than plastic alone. The resin is typically thermoset plastic, but it can be thermoplastic. Typical thermosets include polyesters and epoxies, but phenolics are good for building applications, as they reduce flame spread. Epoxies are more expensive than polyesters, but are also more resistant to corrosion, tougher, and off-gas less styrene than esters. With any thermoset, a resin's pot life is important because it dictates how long it will take the resin to cure. This will in turn affect the length of time available for filament winding. Thermoset prepregs can eliminate issues associated with pot life and off-gassing.

In filament winding, resins with high viscosities are often selected. This helps keep the fibers in place with little to no slipping as the winding carriage moves back and forth. With any plastic, there can be issues of creep, UV-light degradation, expansion and contraction with changes in temperature and humidity, and susceptibility to fire. The design team should ensure that components are engineered to resist long-term deformation, and that resin additives and coatings are specified to deal with UV light, environmental factors, and to meet flame-spread requirements.

10 Filament-wound glass fibers with a sanded finish. The overlapping layers and wound directions of the fibers are visible

SIMILAR PROCESSES

Bladder inflation molding or BIM (Chapter 3.2) also produces thin-walled, hollow items; however, a BIM-finished face can be coated with a gel-coat and is the component's outside face. BIM produces components faster than filament winding, but without the specialized fiber placement that filament winding's CNC technology can achieve.

When filament winding is used to produce long, linear components, they can be similar to those produced by pultrusion (Chapter 2.2). Pultrusion has higher tooling costs than filament winding and is better suited to high-volume productions.

Carbon fibers have the best strength-to-weight ratio, but are the most expensive. Additionally, the individual strands are brittle; as they are wound, flakes come off and cause static build up and dust to get into the equipment. Winding carbon is more difficult and can cause early wear on the winding equipment. In the winding process, fibers must be available in long, continuous lengths; therefore most fibers are rovings, organized on a creel for continuous supply. Joints between rovings can be aligned or offset between wound plies. Offsetting joints between layers will result in a stronger composite than one that has aligned joints. [10]

Because the filament winder is CNC controlled, it can place and orient the fibers only where required. Generally, filament winding will have the highest strength-to-weight ratio of all of the FRP manufacturing processes, which makes it better than other material manufacturing methods.[4] Fiber placement is measured from the rotating axis of the mandrel. It includes zero degree, or longitudinal wrapping; 90-degree, or hoop wrapping; or helical wrapping, which may include angles ranging from 45 degrees to −45 degrees, or somewhere in between. [11] For most efficient structural performance, fibers are laid so that twists are eliminated. For some specialty weavings, basket windings or other twists can be used as a design feature. Programs such as FiberGrafiX and Cadwind can help predict how a component will behave and propose how to wind the reinforcing strands for particular performance.

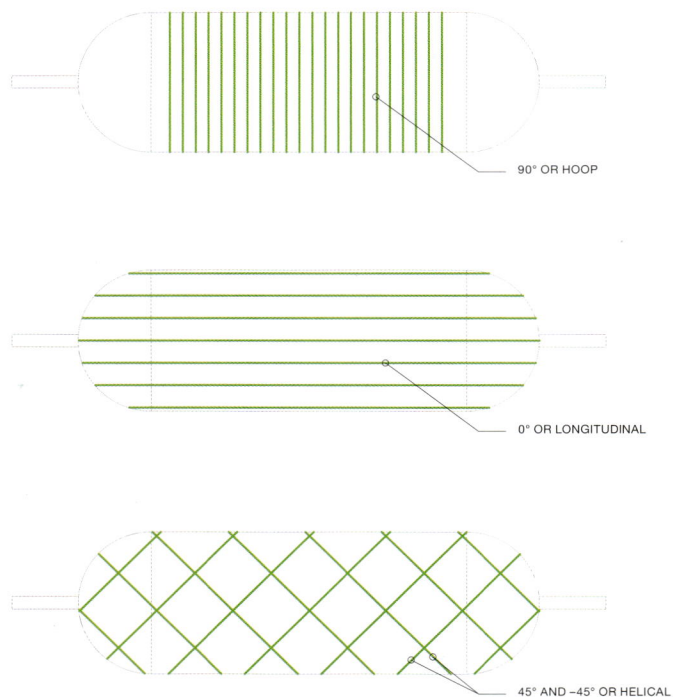

11 Different fiber placements based on CNC technology

ANGLES

Almost any angle can be wound into the component; however, the steeper the angle, the more difficult the winding. Steep angles may require winders with a greater number of axes, or a particular resin.

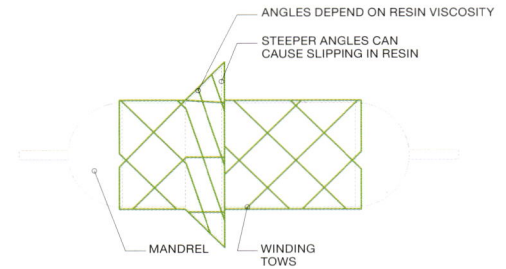

DRAFT ANGLES

Draft angles are not necessary if the mold is sacrificial, collapsible, or if there is little contact area between the mold and the component. If the mold is solid, large, and inflexible, then a draft angle of 0.3° should be sufficient.

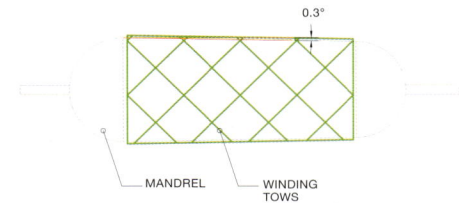

INSERTS

Inserts of other materials, such as metal or plastic, can be placed on the mandrel as the component is wound. The fibers can be placed around the insert so that adequate reinforcing is provided.

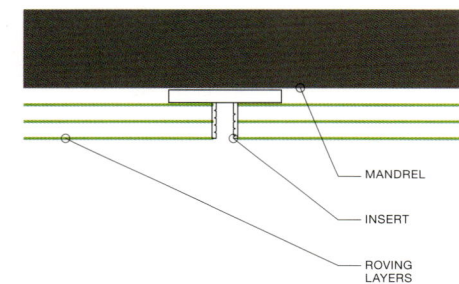

PRODUCTION SPEED

Cycle times are long, depending on shape, thickness, and size. Cycles can range from 20 to 120 minutes for small parts. Curing time is 4–8 hours. Speed can be increased by winding multiple mandrels simultaneously, but this will increase tooling costs.

PRODUCTION VOLUME

Filament winding is best suited to low-volume productions.

SHAPES

Filament-wound components will be hollow. Axisymmetric or cylindrical shapes will be limited to filament winders with fewer axes of movement. Generally, convex curved shapes are easier and less costly than concave shapes; however, due to advancements in robotics, almost any shape can wound.

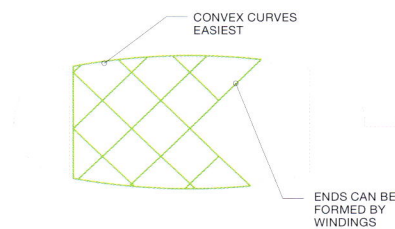

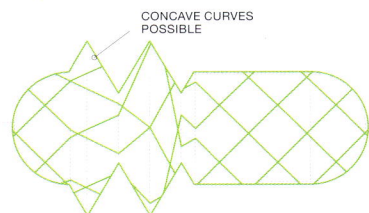

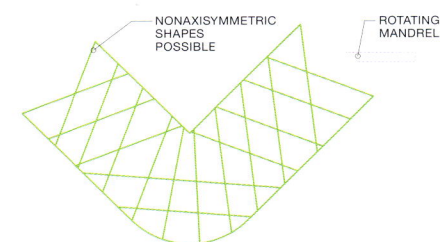

CONVEX CURVES EASIEST
ENDS CAN BE FORMED BY WINDINGS

CONCAVE CURVES POSSIBLE

NONAXISYMMETRIC SHAPES POSSIBLE
ROTATING MANDREL

SHRINKING

There is shrinking due to the resin curing. The actual amount of shrinkage depends on the specific resin and fiber mixture used.

SIDE-WALL HOLES

Side-wall holes can be made during production by programing the filament winder to leave some areas of the mandrel without FRP.

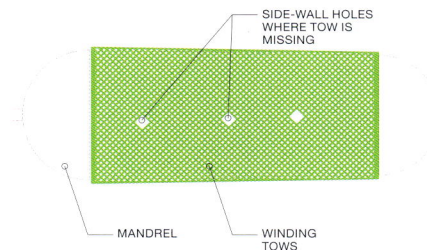

SIDE-WALL HOLES WHERE TOW IS MISSING
MANDREL
WINDING TOWS

SIZE LIMITS

This process has hardly any limit on size. As an example, airplane fuselages are made by filament winding.

TOOLING COSTS

Tooling costs are low, as tools do not need to be solid. (See 2012 ICD/ITKE Research Pavilion on pages 200–203.) The tool's cost will depend on the material used and the method of fabrication.

TOOLING COMPLEXITY

Tooling is simple, with no moving parts.

TOLERANCES

Tolerances for this process can be within 0.004in (0.1mm).

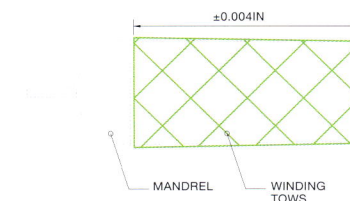

±0.004IN
MANDREL
WINDING TOWS

UNDERCUTS

Undercuts are permissible with this process, if the manufacturer is using a sacrificial mandrel or a multi-part mandrel that can be broken down.

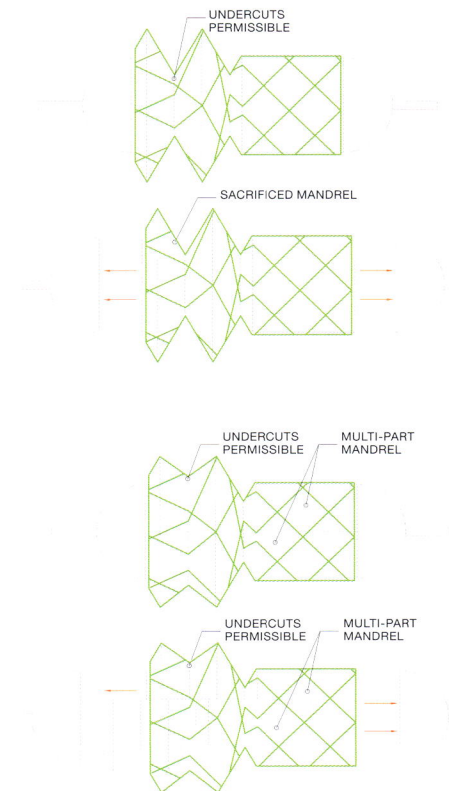

UNDERCUTS PERMISSIBLE
SACRIFICED MANDREL

UNDERCUTS PERMISSIBLE
MULTI-PART MANDREL

UNDERCUTS PERMISSIBLE
MULTI-PART MANDREL

VOIDS

Resin voids for typical fiber windings may range from 3 to 10%. High-performance components can be wound with voids below 1%, but with added cost. With the use of an autoclave, pressure can be added during the curing process, which reduces voids.

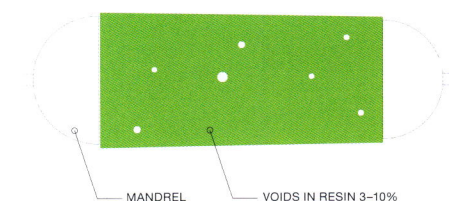

MANDREL
VOIDS IN RESIN 3–10%

WALL THICKNESS

Wall thicknesses can range from only two to three plies of windings to sandwich constructions with FRP on the outer layers and a solid foam center. Because the winding is CNC controlled, wall thickness may be consistent or may vary as needed.

FIBER-REINFORCED PLASTIC (FRP)

2012 ICD | ITKE RESEARCH PAVILION

Institute for Computational Design (ICD) and Institute of Building Structures and Structural Design (ITKE), University of Stuttgart

Stuttgart, Germany

Each year since 2010, the ICD and the ITKE at the University of Stuttgart have designed and constructed temporary research pavilions. Led by professors Achim Menges, ICD director, and Jan Knippers, ITKE director, University of Stuttgart students use the pavilions to test new materials, fabrication methods, and designs. Menges and Knippers provide the general framework that will be explored for that year. In the case of the 2012 pavilion, the research team investigated the architectural implications of filament winding. [13]

There were a number of issues that the ICD/ITKE research team hoped to address with the design and construction of this pavilion. First, filament winding is traditionally used to create discrete elements that would need to be joined together to create a structure, but the team wanted to explore the potential of a large structure without joints. [14] Second, the team wanted to reduce the mold materials necessary to support the winding. Knippers particularly was concerned about the "plastic foam waste" associated with small production runs and prototypes.[5] Third, the team wanted to use the technology associated with filament winding to provide variations within the composite based on performance needs.

The research team designed the pavilion in one semester and constructed it the following semester. The pavilion is made from a combination of glass and carbon fibers with a polyester resin. The pavilion spans over 26ft (8m) and covers an area of 310ft² (29m²). [12] Over 37 miles (60km) of fiber rovings were used in the winding of the pavilion, and yet the pavilion's thickness is only 0.15in (4mm) and it weighs less than 705lb (320kg). Glass and carbon fibers were laid continuously by a robot across a jig that supported the fibers and resin before curing. The jig kept the tooling for this project to a minimum. As Menges wrote of the pavilion, it is the first architectural-scale, load-bearing structure to be produced entirely through robotic, coreless filament winding.[6]

12
Building elevation of the ICD/ITKE Research Pavilion

13
Bird's-eye image of completed pavilion

14
Interior of pavilion

12

13

14

DESIGN CONSIDERATIONS

As the team members began the design process for the pavilion, they investigated filament winding and how composites exist in nature. According to Knippers, all of the ICD/ITKE pavilions are embedded with biometrics; not in a linear or direct way, but always as a background to the design. For this particular pavilion, they studied the exoskeleton of the lobster because it, too, is a composite material, and because the composition of the lobster's composite changes as different performance characteristics are required. For example, sometimes the shell needs to be hard (at it is in a lobster's claws), and sometimes it needs to be flexible (at it is in a lobster's antennae).

The ICD/ITKE research team designed the pavilion form, structure, and winding paths for the robot. The structure of the pavilion was developed with computer simulation under different loading conditions. The team designed the roving pattern to change from helicoidal to unidirectional as structural requirements changed. The team also had to design how the pavilion was to be wound. Because the pavilion's shape and thickness changed during the winding process, the team used computer simulation to predict where the strands were to be located relative to one another.

Inherent in the manufacturing process was a trace of the winding path, but by using the two different fibers, depth and complexity were added. Although embedded in this pavilion are material and manufacturing explorations, there were design considerations. **[15, 16]** For this pavilion, the glass fibers were used as a spatial element and to serve as formwork for subsequent carbon-fiber layers. The carbon fibers were added for strength and stiffness when needed. The quality of the glass fibers provides translucency and light to the space below.

MANUFACTURING CONSIDERATIONS

Different than most of this book's case studies, the ICD/ITKE team was responsible for both the design and the manufacturing. According to Knippers, there were too many unknowns and items being tested, so that he believed it was too soon to work with a contractor for the pavilion's construction. Perhaps after this first iteration, it would have been possible to hire a winder, but this was not something the team was interested in pursuing.

Instead of a full mold, the design team used a jig to support the fibers during winding. The jig edges were made from CNC-milled plywood pieces with cog-like edges. The cogs kept the resin-impregnated strands in place and helped maintain tension on the strands during the winding. The corners of the cogs were rounded so that exact placement by the robot was not necessary, and the strands were eased into place. The edges of the plywood were protected with a plastic foil, so that the resin did not stick to the plywood. The plywood pieces were supported and held in place by a tubular steel frame. After the winding and the resin cures, the jig was deconstructed. Although the pavilion was manufactured as a one-off, the jig was designed to be used repeatedly and could make additional pavilions.

The pavilion had six different winding sequences and took 130 hours to wind. Inside a temporary, weatherproof building, the pavilion was wound

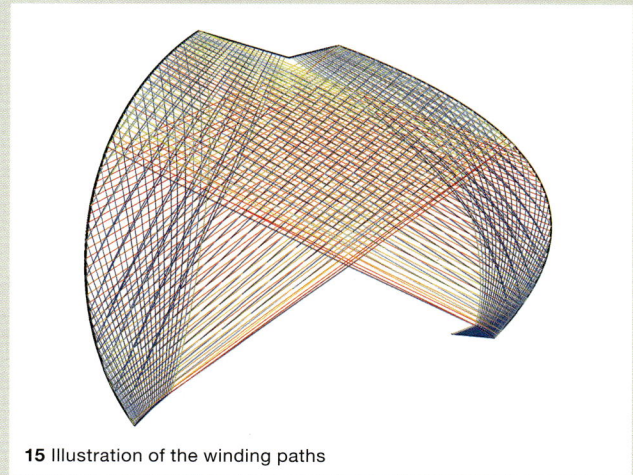

15 Illustration of the winding paths

16 Detail of the pavilion's surface

on-site, but not in place. **[17, 18]** The jig was placed on a CNC-controlled, 6.5ft (2m) high rotating pedestal that spun the jig as a six-axis robot did the winding. The winding was done with a wet layup. In the beginning, winding was slow. The team had to remove the first winding as there were initial problems that would not be fixed with subsequent layers. After winding, heat was added to the temporary building to enable the resin to properly cure.

OTHER CONSIDERATIONS

Because this project was digitally developed, the team members worried that the pavilion would not stand on its own when they removed the jig after curing. In the end, the pavilion stood for six months, from August through February, before being removed. According to Knippers, after the six months, there were no notable changes to the 2012 pavilion or the composite. Knippers did note that the 2014 ICD/ITKE pavilion, also made of glass and carbon-fiber composite, did yellow slightly at the glass fibers; however, the 2014 pavilion was left outside for longer than the 2012 pavilion.

Although the project used biology as a source for design inspiration for composite structures, Blaine Brownell criticized the project's use of energy-intensive and costly carbon fibers.[7] In an article for *Architect Magazine*, Brownell suggests that the use of natural fibers such as hemp, instead of the carbon fibers, would have been more appropriate.

LESSONS LEARNED

Knippers learned a number of lessons with this pavilion. The first was the difficulty of wetting out the strands before they are placed, and the importance of the resin's pot life. Initial investigations into different types of resin made polyester the best choice for this application. Second was the importance of digital modeling. As layers of fibers were added to the pavilion, the geometry of the pavilion changed. The research team recognized this at the beginning of the project and simulated it through digital modeling. In the end, Knippers believed that the 2012 pavilion could not be understood as pure geometry or as digital representation, and that the material properties, the tension within the fibers as they are wound, and the type of resin used all affected how the pavilion ultimately came together.

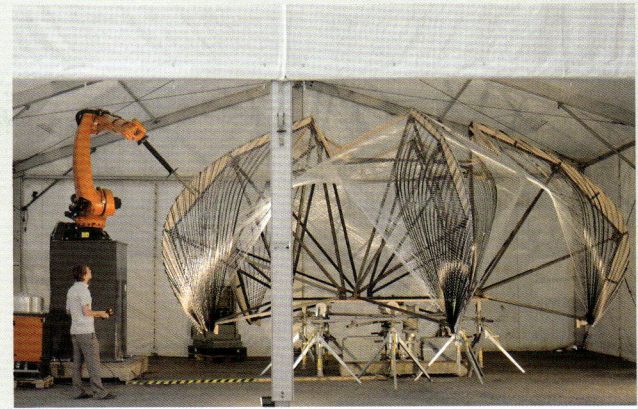

17 Robotic filament winding of pavilion onto a jig, or an open frame

18 Detail of the jig and winding process using the robot

3.4 Centrifugal Casting

aka spin casting

INTRODUCTION

Centrifugal casting is a manufacturing process that spins a round mold at high speed so that centrifugal force pushes the medium against the inside of the mold cavity. [1] Shapes made with this process are hollow in the center and linear in orientation. They can taper along their length and can have a variety of cross-sectional shapes, including circular, oval, octagonal, square, and rectangular. Concrete can be formed in this way, with a lot of manufacturers using high-performance concrete. Exterior surface quality is very good with this process and tolerances are similar to wet-casting concrete. Component lengths can range from 6 to 8ft (1.8–2.4m) up to 130ft (40m). This process results in very little or no post-production work after demolding.

Centrifugal casting can be done vertically or horizontally. In vertical casting, also known as the Stussi process, the mold remains static and the medium is dropped onto a rotating distributor table, which flings the concrete to the sides of the mold. [2] This method is typically used to manufacture drainage pipes from concrete and may result in bug holes on the component surface. In horizontal casting, the mold is rotated fast enough to create the centrifugal force. Horizontal centrifugal casting accommodates a greater variety of lengths and cross-sectional shapes, gives better surface quality than vertical casting, and is the focus of this chapter.

In horizontal centrifugal casting, part of a hollow, linear mold is filled with the concrete to be cast. The mold is then closed with the remaining mold piece or pieces. The closed mold begins to rotate at a speed that creates a centrifugal force about three times the force of gravity. This speed helps to evenly distribute the concrete along the mold cavity surface. Then the rotating speed increases, so that the centrifugal force is 30–40 times the acceleration of gravity. The mold's revolutions per minute (RPM) range from 125 to 400, inversely related to the diameter of the spun component. This centrifugal force eliminates air holes between the concrete and the mold, compacts the concrete, and drives any excess water to the inner face of the concrete, where it drains away. This speed is maintained for 5–10 minutes, depending on the wall thickness of the component. The component is left in the mold

1 Horizontal centrifugal casting. Mold spinning at the Europoles manufacturing facility

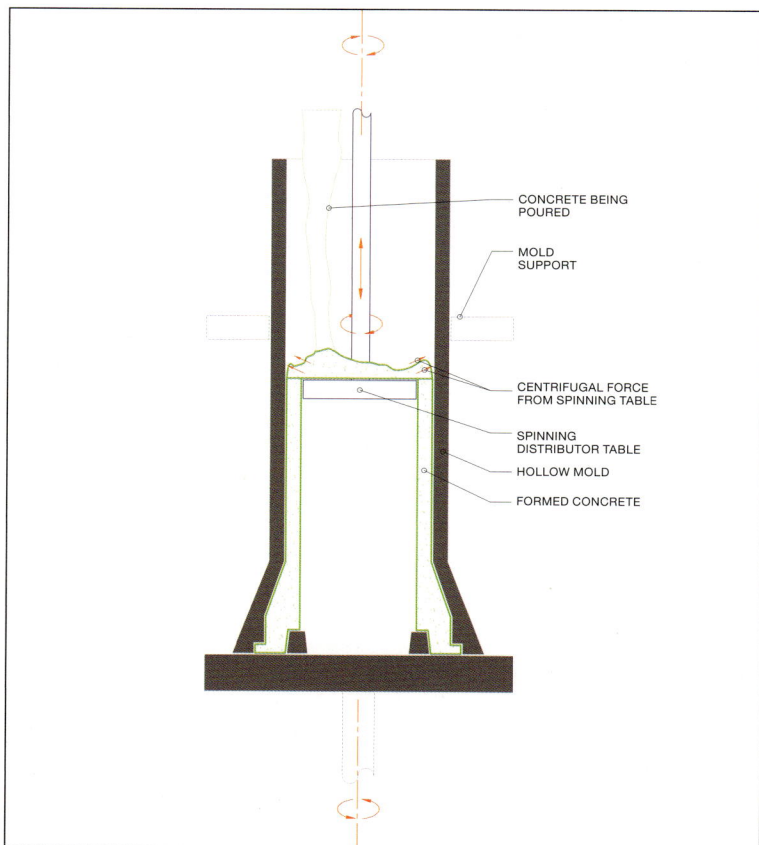

CONCRETE BEING POURED

MOLD SUPPORT

CENTRIFUGAL FORCE FROM SPINNING TABLE

SPINNING DISTRIBUTOR TABLE

HOLLOW MOLD

FORMED CONCRETE

2 Vertical centrifugal casting (also known as the Stussi process). This method limits the concrete component's length and results in a lesser surface quality than with horizontal centrifugal casting

MOLD HALF

MEDIA

MOLD HALF

CENTRIFUGAL
FORCE

CURE

FINAL
COMPONENT

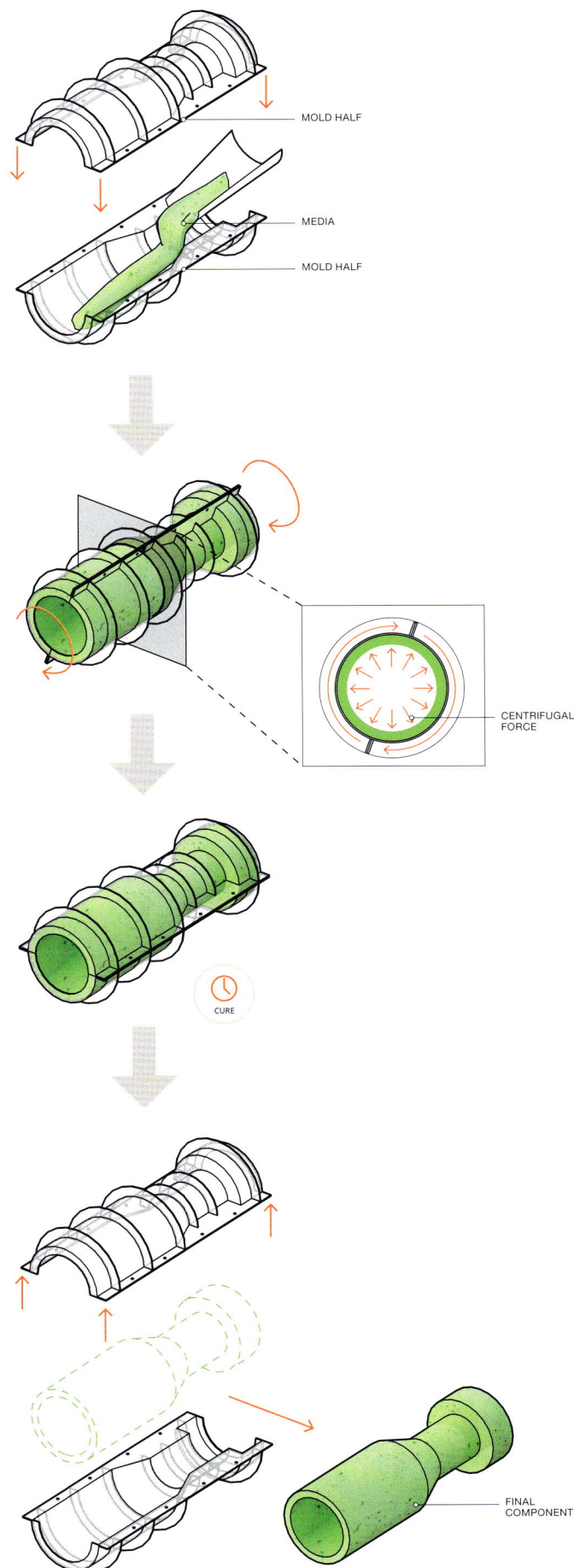

until it has cured enough to be handled without damage. The component is then removed from the mold to cure to its full strength.

The inside face of the mold is in contact with the outside, finished face of the component. Molds are typically fabricated from sheet steel, and the mold finish can range from grit to polished. A grit finish results in a rough finish for the concrete, while a polished surface will give the concrete a glossy sheen. If desired, components can be finished with post-production processes typical with concrete, such as grinding, polishing, acid washing, or grit blasting.

Because centrifugal casting is primarily used to manufacture structural elements—such as building columns, bridge supports, and utility poles and columns—this process can accommodate a variety of structural modifications. First, centrifugal cast concrete can be reinforced with steel. A prefabricated steel reinforcing cage with vertical and spiral steel rebar can be put inside the mold, prior to filling it with concrete, [3, 4] or the rebar can be pre-tensioned. In this case, the rebar will be stretched the length of the mold and held in tension by rings mounted on the ends of the mold during spinning, and will be released after the concrete has cured. Next, perpendicular steel plates welded to the rebar and extending beyond the mold cavity may be formed into the component for structural connections. [5] Finally, parts of the column can be left free of concrete while the internal rebar is continuous. This is done to create a rigid connection between a structural concrete floor and the spun columns. The floor slab's rebar would run through the column's open rebar and the concrete slab would be poured, filling the connection between floor and column. [6]

Generally, centrifugal casting is rather simple without expensive machines, complex molds, or high technical skill required. To spin the mold, it is placed on a set of runners—small wheels that turn the mold at a controlled speed. Concrete is fed into the mold either manually or by conveyor. Additional concrete can be fed into the mold as it is spinning. Molds have no moving parts, and are typically bolted or clamped together by a flange or steel angle at the parting line. Gantry cranes are required to lift the mold and spun component off of the runners for curing, and to remove the component from the mold.

BUILDING PRODUCTS

Centrifugal casting is best used to make building products that benefit from a hollow core. Commercially available spun products include drainage pipes, street lamps and lights (as the open core allows for electrical conduits), and utility poles. Drainpipes often come in standard lengths of 8ft (2.4m), and are manufactured regularly. Street lights and lamps are also manufactured to standard lengths, but are ordered less often; therefore less stock may be immediately available.

TOOLING

The tooling required for centrifugal casting concrete is the mold and the end rings. The mold is made from rolled or bent sheet steel and is reinforced on the outside with steel stiffener plates or steel angles. Depending on the required length of the mold, it may be made of several sheets of steel. To eliminate any joint lines, the sheets should be welded together and the joints ground. The end rings are made from plate or machined steel and are in the shape of the spun cross-section. The end rings help stiffen the ends of the mold and keep the concrete inside the mold, while allowing excess water to escape.

The mold is made in two or three pieces, with the parting line or lines running along its length. This makes demolding easier and places little wear on the mold. The seam between the mold pieces should be externally reinforced with flanges or steel angles. This is for added strength and gives a place where the pieces can be bolted or clamped together before spinning. These molds are fabricated by hand, but can include some CNC processes such as cutting, bending, and welding of stiffeners and angles. [7]

Generally, the inside surface of the mold forms the outside surface of the component; however, there are some possible modifications of the tooling. First, the inside face of the mold can be lined with a rubber form liner. This allows the component to be cast with a decorated or patterned surface. [8, 9] Second, if a manufacturer is spinning a component with a cross-section other than circular, a mold insert will be put inside a circular mold. In this case, the outside of the circular mold is in contact with the runners and will spin as necessary. The inside face of the mold then holds another mold with a noncircular cross-section, which forms the final component. This is how square, rectangular, elliptical, and octagonal cross-sectional shapes are made. [10]

ENVIRONMENTAL IMPACT

Generally, this manufacturing process uses very little energy for production and creates very little waste. This process is not highly mechanized, and heat or steam sources are not necessarily required; therefore the manufacturing facilities tend to use small amounts of energy. The molds are filled only with the concrete that is required to make the component, but there is water waste associated with this process. As the water is extracted from the concrete, it is dirty and full of cement.

The concrete itself has high embodied energy; at the same time, this process results in concrete that is more structurally efficient than conventionally cast concrete. A Life Cycle Assessment

3 Setting the upper shell of the steel form into place, before spinning. The reinforcing steel that runs the length of the component is pre-tensioned

4 Getting ready to demold the concrete by lifting off the top half of the shell

5 Metal connecting plates protruding from rebar cage, and ultimately the component's surface, for on-site, welded connections

6 University of Erlangen-Nuernberg during construction. Concrete is left off of some of the component length so it can be filled with concrete from the site-cast slab

9 Column base for the Great Mosque of Algiers, Algeria. The texture at the bottom has been formed with a rubber form liner

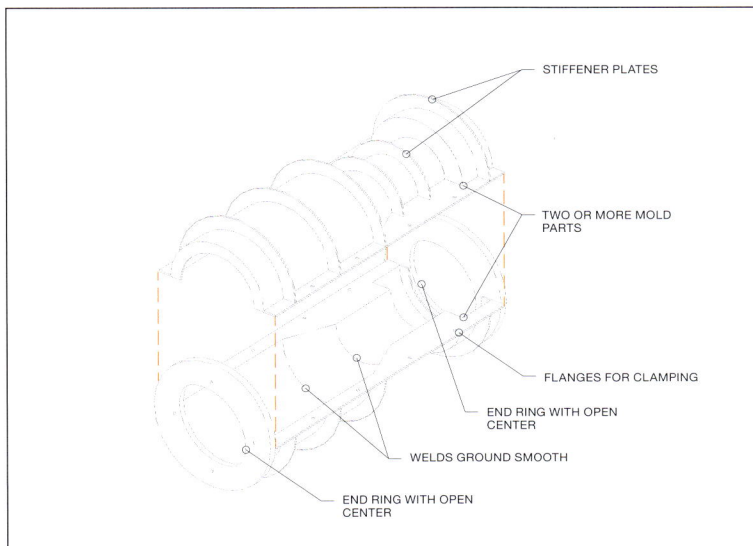

STIFFENER PLATES

TWO OR MORE MOLD PARTS

FLANGES FOR CLAMPING

END RING WITH OPEN CENTER

WELDS GROUND SMOOTH

END RING WITH OPEN CENTER

7 Tooling for this process includes mold parts and end rings with open centers to allow for water to escape during spinning

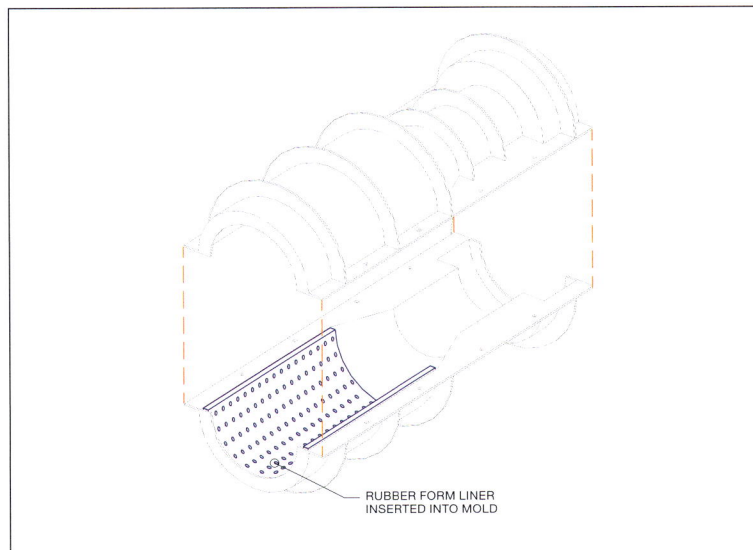

RUBBER FORM LINER INSERTED INTO MOLD

8 Rubber form liners can be added to a mold

10 An oblong oval component centrifugally cast while supported inside a circular mold for ease of rotation

conducted by Life Cycle Engineering Experts GmbH & Company (LCEE) and commissioned by Europoles, a manufacturer of centrifugally cast concrete columns and poles, compared centrifugally cast concrete to a steel composite column over a fifty-year life span. In this assessment, LCEE found that the spun column reduced energy by three-quarters and reduced greenhouse gases by two-thirds, compared to the conventionally cast concrete columns. This was primarily due to less steel reinforcing and the lower maintenance requirements of spun columns.[1]

MATERIAL CONSIDERATIONS + DESIGN PARAMETERS

CONCRETE

Concrete is a mixture of Portland cement, aggregates (course and fine), and water. The color of Portland cement can vary from gray to buff by manufacturer, and by batch. If color is important, consider using a white cement and adding color. Optional admixtures can alter the concrete's properties, including workability, strength, water absorption, ductility, and color. Aggregates can include a wide range of materials including sand, colored rocks, shaped rocks, and glass. The aggregates are exposed when the concrete undergoes post-production finishing such as sand-blasting, acid washing, or face grinding and polishing.

The concrete for spun concrete is different than that for conventional, wet-cast concrete (Chapter 4.1). During spinning, water must be able to move through the concrete to the center of the casting and not carry all of the cement with it. The aggregates should not be able to separate from the mixture; fly ash and other additives can help reduce segregation. Spinning the concrete inside the mold compacts the concrete and expels excess water. [11] Because excess water is expelled during casting, the centrifugal cast concrete is a high early strength concrete, which means that components can be stripped from the molds sooner, thus making production faster with this process than wet-casting.

Typically, spun concrete has less porosity, greater density, higher strength, and increased modulus of elasticity when compared with wet-cast concrete. [12] These characteristics in turn make spun components better able to withstand harsher exterior environments, chemical corrosion, and require less concrete than wet-cast components. Some studies have found that centrifugal cast concrete has the potential to be self-healing and can carry tension loads.[2]

Centrifugal casting can be done with conventional reinforcing or can be combined with pre-tensioned reinforcing strands. Because of the higher density of the concrete, only 0.6in (16mm) of concrete is needed to cover the reinforcing steel. High-performance concrete is more readily used in centrifugal cast products than conventional casting. This is likely due to the structural performance required of these components. Utility poles and bridge columns often have longer unsupported lengths and greater slenderness ratios than building columns.

11 Concrete being placed inside a steel mold

12 Stacked columns after curing

SIMILAR PROCESSES

Centrifugally casting concrete is a unique process. The process most similar to it would be vertical wet-casting concrete (Chapter 4.1); however, centrifugal casting produces hollow components with much better surface quality and structural strength than wet-casting concrete.

DRAFT ANGLES

Draft angles are not necessary. Because molds can be fabricated in two or more pieces, molds can be designed to eliminate draft.

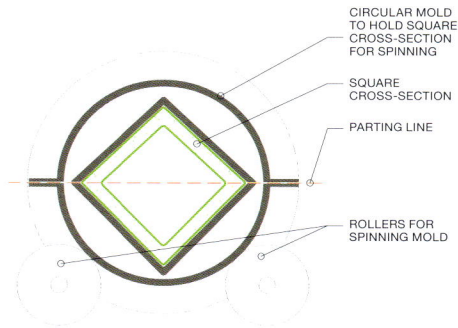

CIRCULAR MOLD TO HOLD SQUARE CROSS-SECTION FOR SPINNING

SQUARE CROSS-SECTION

PARTING LINE

ROLLERS FOR SPINNING MOLD

CORNER RADII

If casting square or rectangular cross-sections, the corners should have a slight radius of 0.12in (3mm).

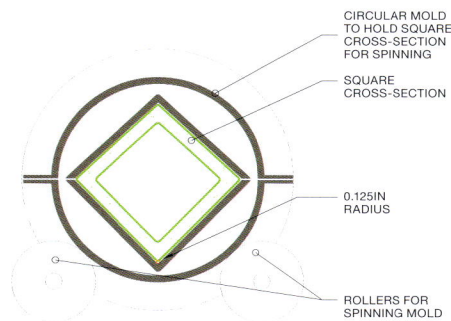

CIRCULAR MOLD TO HOLD SQUARE CROSS-SECTION FOR SPINNING

SQUARE CROSS-SECTION

0.125IN RADIUS

ROLLERS FOR SPINNING MOLD

FLASHING

There is little to no flashing with this process, as the water travels to the center of the component during spinning, keeping cement from the parting line.

FINISH

In-mold finishes can range from matte to satin to glossy. Post-production finishes can include acid washed, grit blasted, ground, or polished.

INSERTS

Centrifugal casting can accommodate metal inserts for connecting spun components to the building. These inserts are often welded to the interior steel reinforcing.

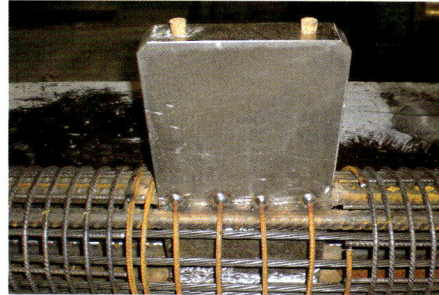

JOINING

Centrifugal cast components can be joined together with site-cast concrete building elements, such as a foundation. When this is done, the exterior surface of the centrifugal casting is textured in the mold with a rubber form liner (see figure 3.4.9). When the column is set into the foundation, concrete is poured into the space between the two. The surface texture of the column helps to mechanically connect the column to the site-poured concrete.

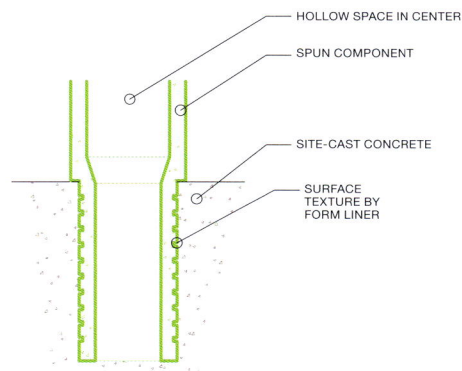

HOLLOW SPACE IN CENTER

SPUN COMPONENT

SITE-CAST CONCRETE

SURFACE TEXTURE BY FORM LINER

PARTING LINES

Parting lines are visible on the component surface.

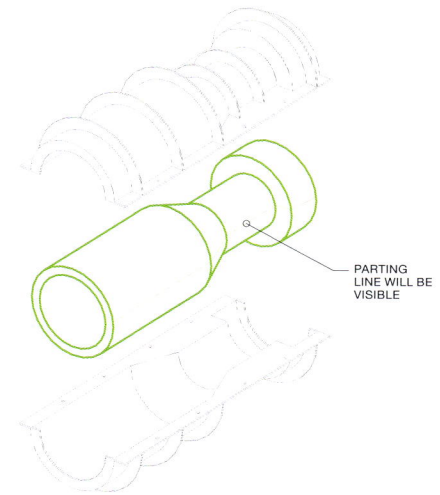

PARTING LINE WILL BE VISIBLE

PRODUCTION SPEED

Generally, centrifugal-cast concrete cures faster than wet-cast concrete. The mold spinning usually takes 5–10 minutes per component. The spun concrete is demolded after approximately 5–6 hours if steam cured, or 20 hours if left to cure in the air. The component is then removed from the mold to finish curing until it reaches full strength.

SHAPES

Linear elements with circular cross-sections are the best to horizontally spin. Cross-sections can also include octagons, squares, rectangles, ellipses, and ovals. For oblong shapes such as rectangles, ellipses, and ovals, the maximum width-to-depth ratio of the cross-section is 1:3.

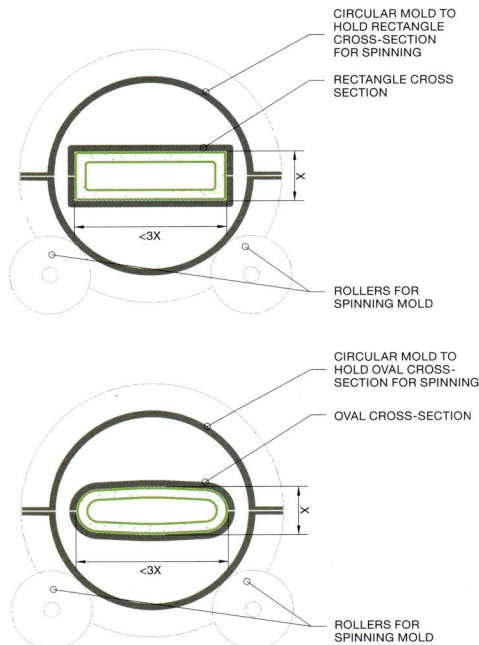

CIRCULAR MOLD TO HOLD RECTANGLE CROSS-SECTION FOR SPINNING

RECTANGLE CROSS SECTION

<3X

ROLLERS FOR SPINNING MOLD

CIRCULAR MOLD TO HOLD OVAL CROSS-SECTION FOR SPINNING

OVAL CROSS-SECTION

<3X

ROLLERS FOR SPINNING MOLD

Castings can get narrower along the length, but sockets or bulges along the length should be avoided. When the concrete is spun, water will rise to the inside surface of the concrete and travel to the open end of the mold. Sockets or bulges will trap water, negatively affecting the concrete in this area.

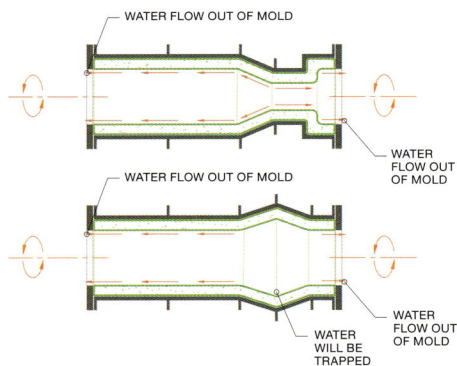

WATER FLOW OUT OF MOLD

WATER FLOW OUT OF MOLD

WATER FLOW OUT OF MOLD

WATER WILL BE TRAPPED

WATER FLOW OUT OF MOLD

SHRINKING

Centrifugally cast concrete shrinks less than conventional wet-cast concrete, because any excess water in the concrete is driven out during the spinning.

SIDE-WALL HOLES

Side-wall holes are possible with this process, and are used to help maneuver the component during erection. If the component is for exterior application, side-wall holes are necessary for air circulation. The position and angle of any side-wall hole may affect demolding.

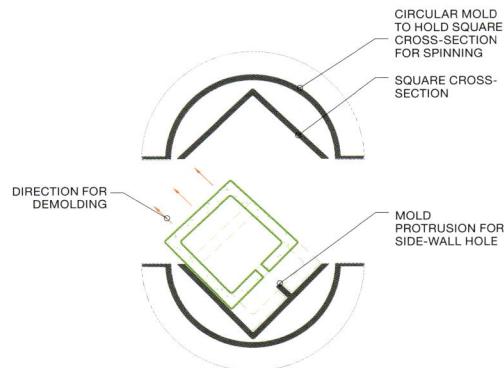

CIRCULAR MOLD TO HOLD SQUARE CROSS-SECTION FOR SPINNING

SQUARE CROSS-SECTION

DIRECTION FOR DEMOLDING

MOLD PROTRUSION FOR SIDE-WALL HOLE

SIZE LIMITS

The cross-sectional diameter is limited to 6ft (1.8m) within the United States, and likely larger in Europe. Lengths up to 130ft (39m) have been made; up to 110ft (35m) is more reasonable. If longer components are required, they can be spun in smaller lengths and spliced together.

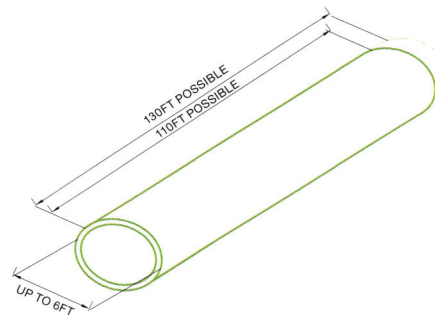

130FT POSSIBLE

110FT POSSIBLE

UP TO 6FT

SURFACE DESIGNS

Surface decorations can be cast into the component with a rubber form liner. Fine detail, 0° draft angles, and undercuts are possible with the rubber form liner.

TOLERANCES

The length tolerance for a spun component is 2in (50mm) and the outside diameter should be within 0.25 in (6mm).

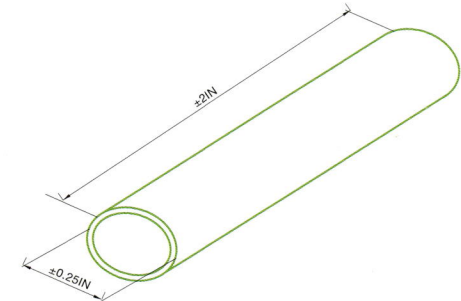

±2IN

±0.25IN

TOOL COMPLEXITY

Molds are very simple and have no moving or active parts.

WALL THICKNESS

Wall thickness is fairly consistent in a spun component, and should vary no more than 0.25in (6mm) for circular cross-sections.

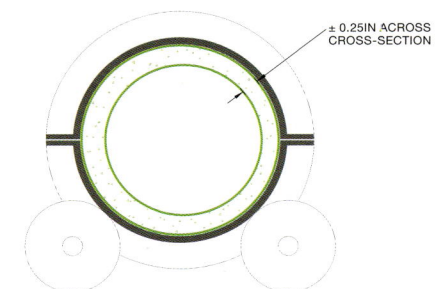

± 0.25IN ACROSS CROSS-SECTION

WARPING

Any linear variation along the length should be less than 0.25in (6mm) per every 10ft (3m).

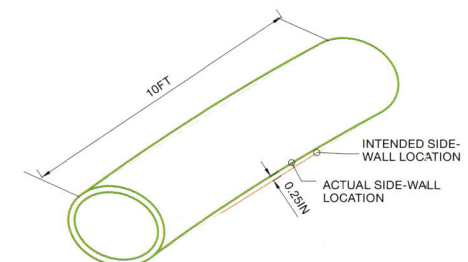

10FT

INTENDED SIDE-WALL LOCATION

0.25IN

ACTUAL SIDE-WALL LOCATION

CONCRETE

HOLLOW TAPERED COLUMNS
FORUM ECKENBERG ACADEMY

Ecker Architekten
Adelsheim, Germany

Eckenberg Academy in Adelsheim, Germany, has an academic focus on science and music. It is located on a hillside surrounded by farmland. Most of the Academy's buildings were completed in the 1960s, providing a mid-century modern context for the new addition. Completed in 2013 by Ecker Architekten, the Forum provides a new campus center and includes an assembly hall, library, café, multipurpose room, and open lounge. [13, 14] The Forum connects an existing gymnasium and cafeteria and serves as a lobby for gym events. The Forum is located at the top edge of the campus and offers an expansive view of the small town of Adelsheim. [15, 16, 17]

According to Ecker Architekten, the project program and plans were fairly established by the client before design began.[3] The Forum measures 85ft (26m) square in plan, is almost 30ft (9m) tall, and has 10,700ft^2 (990m^2) of floor area. The building's materials are primarily concrete and glass, and the floor and ceiling define the architecture. The light color of its concrete

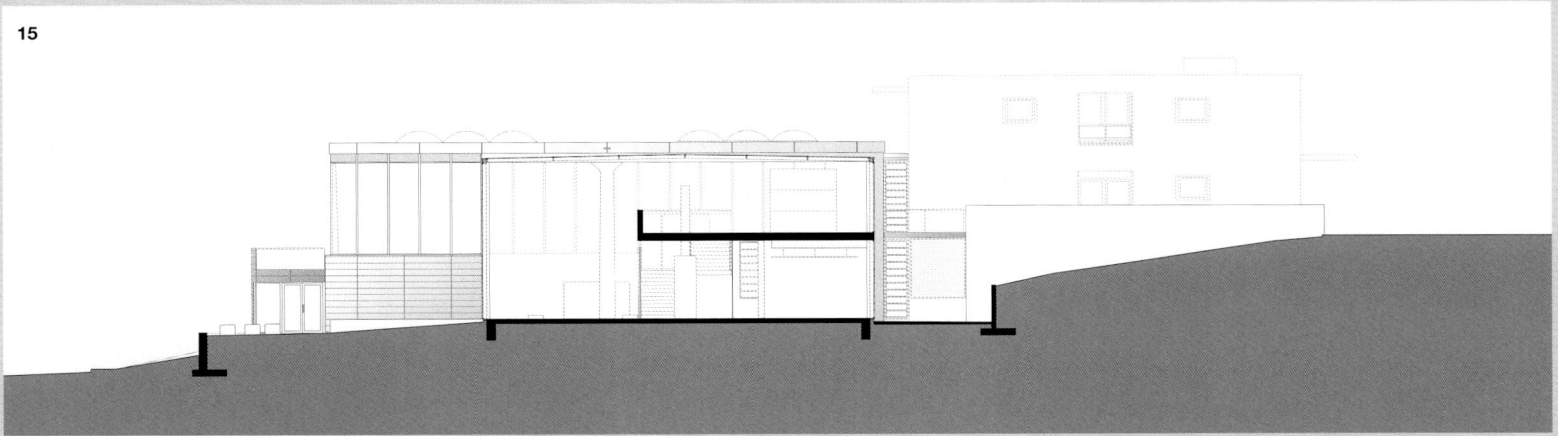

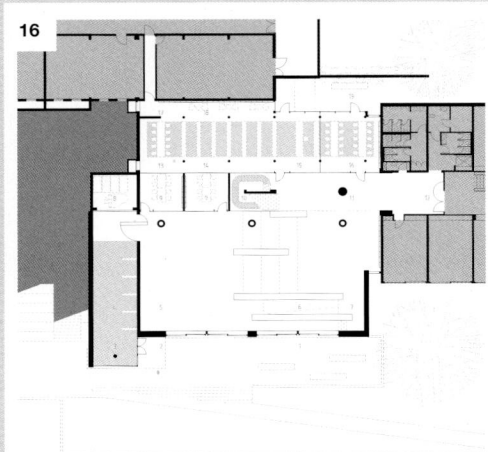

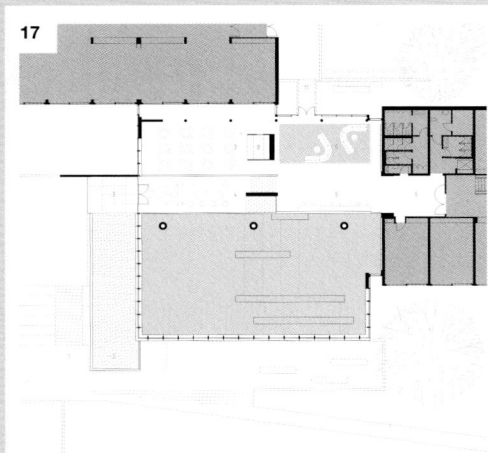

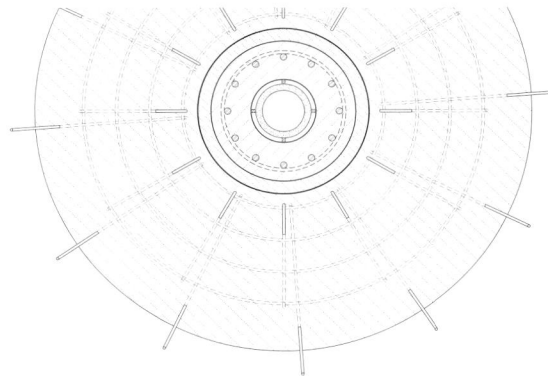

HORIZONTAL SECTION A-A

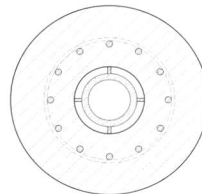

HORIZONTAL SECTION C-C

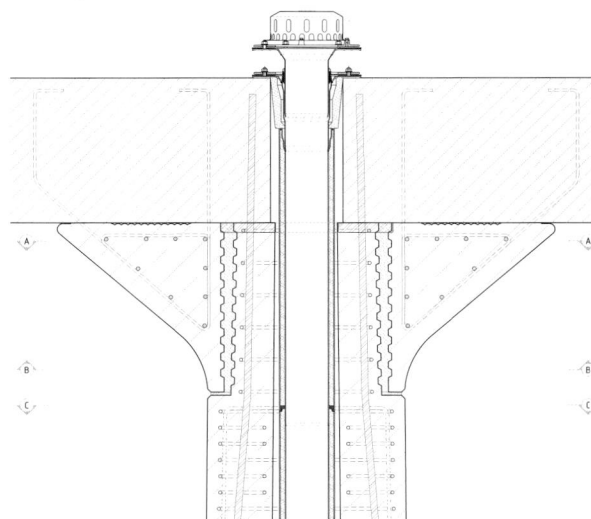

CAPITAL

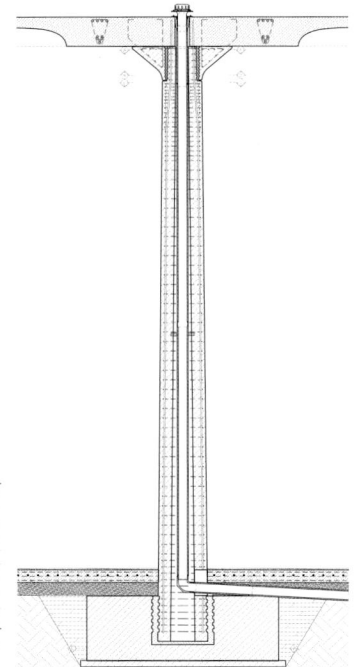

A–A

B–B

C–C

D–D

13
Forum at night

14
Forum interior

15
Transverse building section

16
Lower-level floor plan

17
Upper-level floor plan

18
Technical section through
column with details

comes from a high fly-ash content, and a finish coating added to the concrete's surface. The floors are terrazzo and the ceiling is a coffered, site-cast concrete slab. The concrete for the ceiling was poured in a single session and the molds for the coffers were made by milled Styrofoam set into the formwork. [19] Coffers lighten the slab's dead load and are integrated with artificial lighting, acoustic treatments, and operable skylights.

The primary roof load is carried by three centrifugal cast concrete columns. Europoles GmbH & Company manufactured the columns in three different lengths, with the longest at 26ft 9in (8.15m). All three columns are tapered .025in per foot (18mm per meter) and measure 2ft (600mm) in diameter at the top. [18] The columns are hollow and in the center of each column is a 4in (80mm) diameter stainless steel drainpipe that drains water from the Forum roof to under its building slab. Atop each column is a capital made from traditional, gravity-cast precast concrete. Originally conceived for transferring load from the roof to the column, the capitals are non-load-bearing; however, they do provide a visual transition from the columns to the coffered ceiling. A slight gap between the capital and the column allows the roof slab to deform without damage to the capital. [20]

19 Roof formwork prior to pouring concrete

DESIGN CONSIDERATIONS

Ecker's design objective for the project was to create a structurally expressive roof plane that would span the entire Forum without interruption. This required careful integration of ventilation, fire protection, lighting, and roof drainage. After considering other options during early design, Ecker proposed that the roof drains could be hidden inside hollow columns and that the columns could be engineered to carry the structural loads. [21] Ecker wanted the structure to be visually elegant and to characterize monumentality and permanence. Both the columns and the capitals were finished post-production off-site. The capitals were sand-blasted to a matte, nearly velvety appearance, and the columns were mechanically bush-hammered to expose the aggregate and provide a stone-like haptic quality to the support. Both these treatments eliminated any of the mold marks associated with each process, making both the columns and capitals appear monolithic.

20 Forum during construction, after roof formwork has been stripped

MANUFACTURING CONSIDERATIONS

Primarily, Europoles uses centrifugal casting to manufacture masts and poles for lighting, security, energy, and infrastructure; only a small part of the company is dedicated to architectural applications. When Ecker was working on design, the design team met with a representative from Europoles. With that meeting, the benefits of centrifugal casting were clear to Ecker. In addition to their hollow center, the columns were cast horizontally with one batch of concrete. This eliminated the potential for cold joints and color changes between the lifts associated with vertically cast columns. Ecker found that the design and review process with Europoles was nearly frictionless.

From initial conversations with Europoles, Ecker understood that the project budget could not accommodate the cost of a new steel mold; instead, Ecker designed the columns so that they would make use of existing

21 Forum nearing completion

Europoles molds. Ecker considered that the columns could be manufactured as either a straight-walled cylinder or using Europoles' standard taper for their masts. This limited them to a taper of approximately .005 in per 1ft (18mm per 1m). Ecker reviewed the straight-walled option as well as the options of using the tapered mold either for a taper would be narrower at the top than at the bottom, or for an inverted column. After selecting Europoles' standard taper, Ecker specified the columns' circumferences, lengths, and cast details such as the reveal and shoulder at the column top.

OTHER CONSIDERATIONS

The columns were erected early in the construction sequence, and the rest of the Forum was built around them. [22] Care was taken to protect the columns during construction. The base of the column is embedded into its footing, and the space between the column and the footing is filled with grout. Europoles molded dents into the surface of the column base and top to increase the bonding between the grout and column. [23] The three columns and their capitals were installed by a two-man crew and a crane in less than 8 hours. [24]

The pipes are an insulated, stainless steel modular system, supplied by LORO. To connect the drainpipe in the column to the one in the foundation, the team used a friction-fit sleeve. This allowed for a simple connection between the pipe length and the elbow. Ecker drew and specified wedges along the pipe to keep it centered in the column. Special steel reinforcing for the column was designed where the drainpipe passed through the side wall of the column. The team coordinated between LORO, Europoles, and structural engineers to ensure that column erection and drainage installation would happen on a single day.

According to Ecker, for projects of this size in Germany, it is uncommon to use a general contractor. Most of Ecker's projects are around this size, and so Ecker is often responsible for the process of construction and coordinating the manufacurers. For them, this begins during the design phase, extends through the working drawing and specifications, and ultimately results in intensive site supervision through the important phases of construction. To help with pricing, Ecker has close contact with industries, to help maintain the designs' financial viability. Ecker believes that this practice gives his firm a lot of flexibility with little risk. With this project completed, Ecker has had a continuing relation with Europoles, and are using the company on current projects.

LESSONS LEARNED

With this project, Ecker learned to trust his firm's instincts in construction. As Ecker pointed out, today's architects have available to them an incredible amount of information. One of the firm's most important tasks is to use the richness of this information to explore possibilities in design and construction. According to Ecker, there is "nothing that cannot be constructed, even with tight budgets and demanding clients. It simply requires the determination of the architect, the ability to ask informed questions, and the courage to explore beyond the conventional."[5]

22 Columns were installed early during the construction process

23 Column installation. Note the textured surface at the column base, which provides a mechanical connection between column and foundation

24 Erecting columns

3.5 Blow Molding

INTRODUCTION

Blow molding is a manufacturing process that inflates a heated medium inside a closed mold. [1, 2] When the medium cools and can hold its shape, the mold is opened and the component is removed. Blow molding is a cyclical process, and is primarily limited to plastic and glass. It produces hollow elements with relatively simple shapes and some surface details. Components are typically limited to one large void, but the process can accommodate hollow sub-compartments when necessary. Components can be round, but they may also include faceted, rectangular, or oblong shapes. Blow molding results in good surface quality on the inside and outside of the component. This process typically requires little to no post-production surface refinishing, but flashing needs to be removed.

In blow molding, a heated parison is placed in the mold and a mold is closed around it. Second, air pressure is forced through a blow-hole, inflating the parison against the inside face of the mold, forming the component's shape. Next, the medium is cooled so that it can hold its shape, the mold is opened, and the component is removed. When blow molding plastic, the parison may be separate from the blowing rod, or the parison itself may be inflated. In blow molding glass, the blowpipe is in direct contact with the parison, as the blowpipe is used to gather the glass from the furnace and place the glass in the mold. After the glass cools, the blowpipe is removed, and the blown glass component is finished on the edges that were in contact with the blowpipe.

1 Blow molding plastic for a folding table top. In this image a plastic parison is vertically extruded into the mold and then inflated.

2 Blowing glass (without a mold)

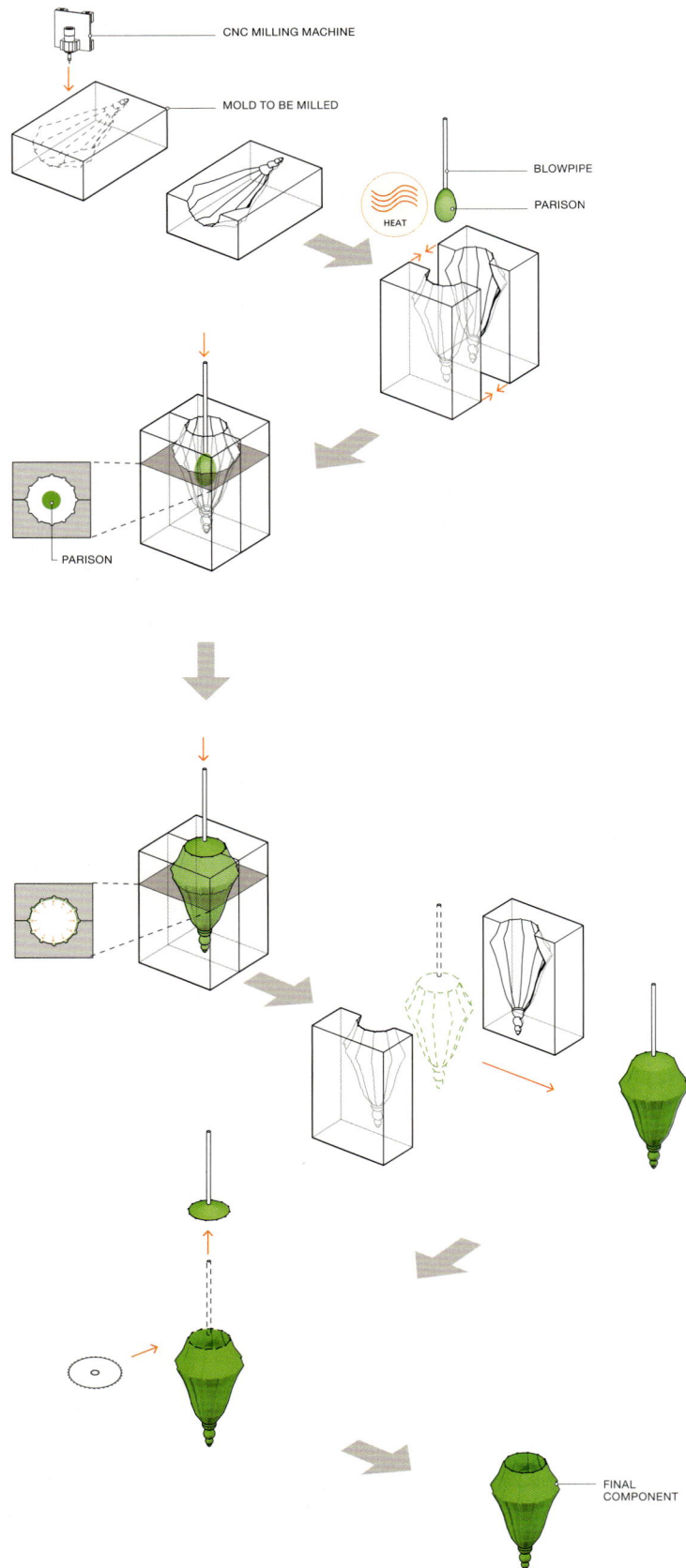

CNC MILLING MACHINE

MOLD TO BE MILLED

HEAT

BLOWPIPE

PARISON

PARISON

PARISON

FINAL
COMPONENT

The parison size is predetermined, based on the amount of surface area and the required wall thickness. There are various ways to form the parison. In plastic blow molding, the parison can be extruded or injection molded. Extruding the parison is more common, and less expensive because less tooling is required. [3] If injection molded, the parison is called a preform and is heated before blow molding. This is done when the blow-molded unit has intricate details, such as the fine threads around the neck of a 2-liter soda bottle. In glass blow molding, the parison can be gathered molten glass from a furnace; or it may be a preformed glass tube typical to lampworking. [4] If glass blow molding a large volume, then molten glass can be pressed into a mold (see Chapter 4.6) to make the parison (also called a blank). The blank is kept hot, and is then placed in a mold for inflating. This method is used to make Mason jars and similar glass containers.

The interior cavity of the component is made by air pressure. It is difficult to accommodate large changes in cavity sizes within the component, but they can be done with an increase in production costs. [5] The size of the components is limited by the size of the molds and how much air pressure is required to inflate the parison against the mold cavity. If the shapes are complex or large, and too much pressure is required, the parison may be pre-inflated to an intermediate size and then heated and inflated again to get to the final component. [6]

3 Plastic parison being vertically extruded

4 Preformed tube used in lampworking

Some details can be included in the process, but they are often limited to surface textures or integrated labels. Examples include the pebble texture on plastic milk jugs, or the company label on Mason jars. Threads for tops can be included without injection molding a preform, but they are not precise and are not suitable for containers with high-pressure contents. The outside of the component, which is in contact with the inside of the mold cavity, is the component's finished face. Wall thickness are difficult to control in this process, so a designer may want to include stiffening ribs to reinforce wall strengths.

Blow molding can be done by highly mechanized manufacturing processes with large production runs, contract manufacturers, or by craftspeople for medium to low production runs. Plastic blow molding is typically limited to highly mechanized or contract facilities, as tooling costs are high and equipment is large. [7] Generally, plastic blow molders will require large production runs to offset those costs. In comparison, glass blow molding can be done through mechanized processes, similar to plastic blow molding, or by craftspeople or workshops. These facilities can accommodate small production runs and prototypes easily and, depending on the size of the workshop, may be able to accommodate medium-sized production runs of fewer than 10,000 units. [8]

BUILDING PRODUCTS

A number of building products are made from plastic blow molding, including large storage tanks, plumbing traps, and light fixture diffusers. The process has been occasionally used to manufacture furniture, including the Sparkling Chair by Marcel Wanders and the Nimrod Chair by Marc Newsom (both made by Magis). Glass blow molding is used to manufacture interior decorative items such as glasses, goblets, vases, and bowls, as well as incandescent light bulbs and light fixtures and shades. [9]

TOOLING

The tooling in blow molding is the mold and an optional trim die for post-production CNC trimming. [10, 11] The mold needs to resist the heat of the parison and to cool down enough between cycles to match the production speed required. To speed up production cycles, cooling lines may be embedded in the mold to draw heat away from the cavity. The mold is typically a two-piece closed mold, with the parting line running vertically. However, in glass blow molding, some craftspeople will use an open mold, called a dip or optic mold, and will control the size and shape of

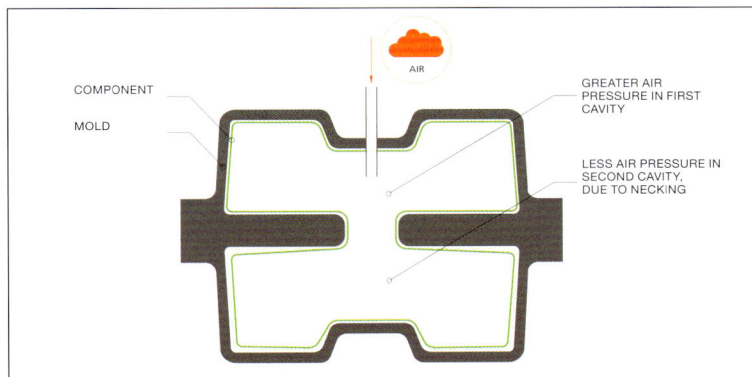

5 Large changes in cavity size may affect air pressure in different areas of the cavity. This results in parts of the component not being fully inflated

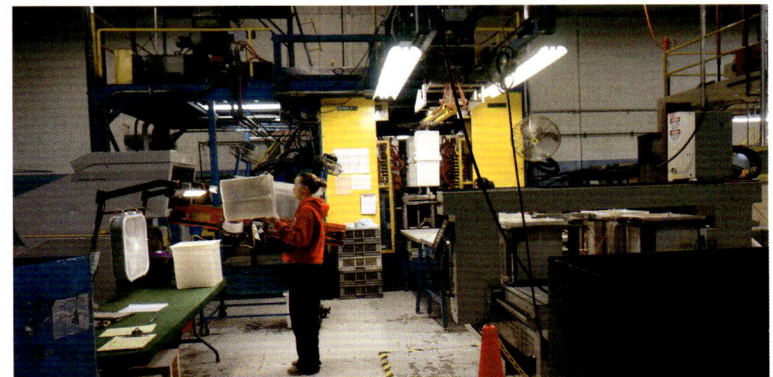

6 Plastic manufacturing will be limited to high-volume or contract manufacturers, as equipment costs are typically too high for small workshops

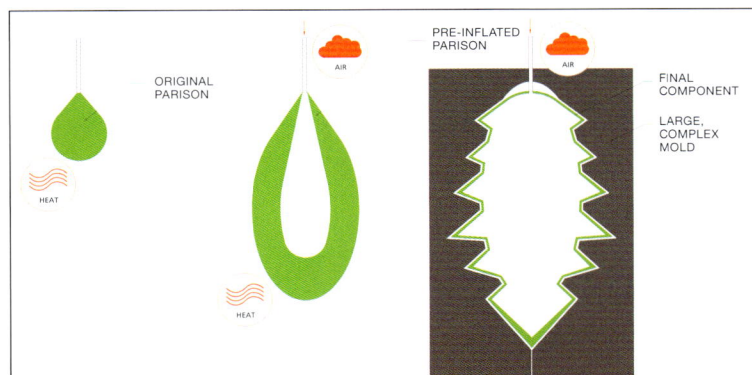

7 Large or complex components may need to be inflated in two or more stages

8 Locally Grown Art is a small lampworking workshop located in Pittsboro, North Carolina

the blown object through air pressure. [14, 15] Multi-part molds, with more than two parts, can also be used, but are better suited to small productions, because of the added time associated with demolding and set-up between cycles.

Unless making a large, complex component, air pressures needed to inflate the parison are fairly low and therefore do not place too much stress on the mold. Molds for plastic blow molding are typically made from machined or cast metals (see Chapter 4.2). FRP has been used for some short-run productions and prototypes, but finding a manufacturer willing to work with FRP molds may be difficult. CNC equipment, such as millers or EDMs, are used to machine metal molds. Cast metal molds are more appropriate for large molds, or if multiple molds are required for parallel productions. Molds can be made from tool or stainless steel, beryllium, copper, or aluminum. Aluminum is not as durable as other mold metals, but is the least expensive. Copper is the most thermally conductive and therefore will speed up production cycles, but is also the most expensive. Molds may be lined with chrome plating to increase their resistance to wear.

The blow-hole is usually located at the top of the closed mold, but for plastic blow molding it can be located on the side of the bottom of the component. [12] For closed molds, with smaller tolerances, vents will need to be placed at the parting line to allow air to escape; this will cause some additional flashing that will need to be trimmed during post-production. To increase cycle times, cooling lines are often embedded in the mold so that the mold and plastic can be quickly cooled and demolded.

Molds for glass blow molding can be made from a wider range of materials than for plastic. For high-volume productions, the mold is made of machined or cast metals, similar to plastic blow molds. For low-volume manufacturers and craftspeople, permanent molds can be made of cast metal (iron or aluminum), water-soaked wood, [13] plaster, graphite, or clay. Plaster molds are easy to make, and inexpensive. Water-soaked wood molds last longer than plaster molds, but tolerances can be difficult to maintain, as the wood expands when soaked in water. Expendable sand molds, similar to those used in metal casting (see Chapter 4.2) can be used. Sand molds are formed against a pattern, which could be made by CNC equipment using plastic, high-density foam, or wood or wood products. If the dimensions and shape of the glasswork are not critical, then a craftsperson may not use a mold at all. Instead, water-soaked pads, tongs, or other shaping tools may be used to form the component's shape. [16]

ENVIRONMENTAL IMPACT

Energy is used to heat both the thermoplastic and glass. Much more energy is spent on heating glass than plastic, as the melting temperature of glass is much higher, as is the time necessary to fully melt the charge. Additional heat is needed for annealing the glass after forming. However, glass blowing usually produces less manufacturing waste than plastic, and the glass is highly recyclable. Thermoplastic, used for plastic blow molding, is also recyclable, but too much recycled content causes inconsistencies in the process (see EcoARK by Miniwiz on pages 232–235). Plastic blow molding with a parison extrudate produces a lot of manufacturing waste with its flashing. The flashing can be reground and then added to virgin material for recycling.

9 Commissioned blown glass components for custom light fixtures. Made by Locally Grown Art

10 Large, closed metal molds for blow molding plastic

11 Trim die for holding components during post-production CNC trimming

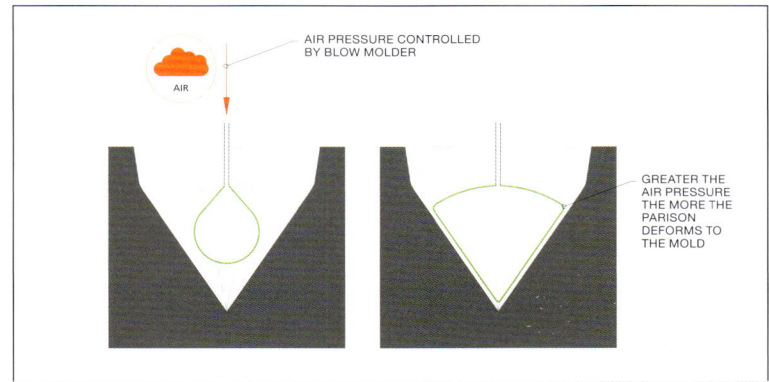

14 With optic molds, the final size and shape of the component is controlled by the blower

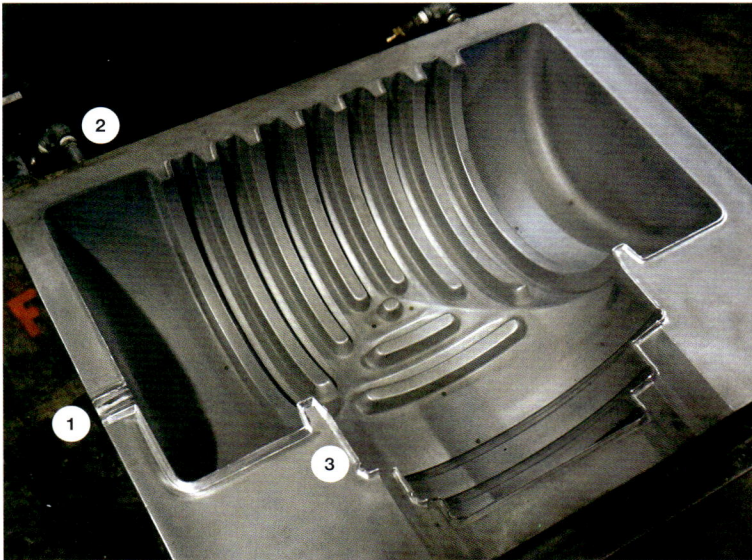

12 Parts of a cast aluminum mold for blow molding plastic: blow-hole [1], cooling lines [2], vents and parting line [3]

15 Cast metal optic mold, also called a dip mold

13 A water-soaked wood mold for glass blowing

16 Additional shaping tools for glass blowing

MATERIAL CONSIDERATIONS + DESIGN PARAMETERS

Materials for blow molding must be viscous enough when heated to deform with air pressure, and yet solidify quickly when cooled to enable fast demolding. This chapter includes glass and plastic blow molding, as those have been used for architectural application. There has been some recent research into blow molding metals (such as superplastic aluminum), but this process is not widely available.[1]

GLASS

The primary starting material for glass is silicon dioxide (SiO_2), which is typically combined with other oxide ceramics to form glass. The mixture and type of oxides affect the properties of the glass. For example, borosilicate glass has boron trioxide and is stronger and more durable than soda lime glass, which has sodium oxide. Glass chips and ceramic powders can be added to the glass charge (see below) to change the overall color of the glass. Additionally, when the glass parison is formed and still molten, it can be rolled in colored glass chips or powders. The chips and powders will adhere to the molten surface of the parison. Then the parison can be further worked to integrate the pieces into it. [17, 18] Be aware that different glass colors contain different metals, ceramics, and other materials, which will in turn affect the density, melting point, viscosity, and ultimately the blowing of the glass.

Glass typically melts around 2,700–3,000°F (1,500–1,650°C), and melting the starting batch of glass, known as a charge, can take 24–48 hours. This is the time for the sand grains to become a clear liquid, for the molten glass to be refined, and for the charge to be cooled to a working temperature. The charge is melted in a furnace, which in workshops and studios is often small—a studio may operate two or more furnaces for production. [19] For high-volume manufacturers, there are continuous-melt furnaces, in which raw materials are placed in one end and molten glass is consistently available at the other.

Glass blow molding can be done either with molten glass gathered in a furnace and kept hot by temporarily placing it in a glory hole; or it can be done with lampworking. Lampworking is working with preformed, solid glass tubes that are kept at room temperature and heated by open gas flames to get the glass to a working temperature. [20] In lampworking, the component size is limited by the size of the original tube, the size of the flame, and the amount of time the piece is kept in the flame. After blow molding, the glass should go through a post-production controlled heating and cooling of the glass to increase its strength. This can be done by annealing or tempering. Annealing can be done in batch kilns [21] or lehrs. The annealing temperatures and timing depends on the thickness of the glass.

SIMILAR PROCESSES

Blow molding glass is a unique process. Pressing glass (Chapter 4.6) can make similar, thin-walled components, but pressing cannot produce closed, hollow components. The wall thickness in glass pressing will be more controlled than with blow molding.

17 Reheating a glass parison in a glory hole at David Goldhagen Art Glass studio

18 Glass chips added to the parison and reheated so they are fully integrated

19 David Goldhagen Art Glass studio. The glory hole is on the left. There is a small furnace in the center for heating the blow rods. On the right is the furnace that holds the charge

20 Lampworking at the Locally Grown Art workshop

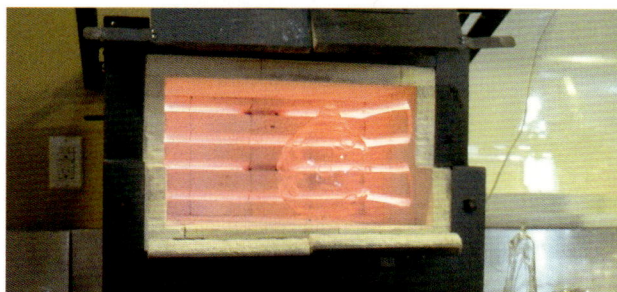
21 A small batch kiln for annealing glass after it is formed

DRAFT ANGLES

Draft angles can be 0° for short distances; generally, most closed molds can be redesigned to eliminate draft—either by rotating the shape, moving the parting line, or making a multi-part mold.

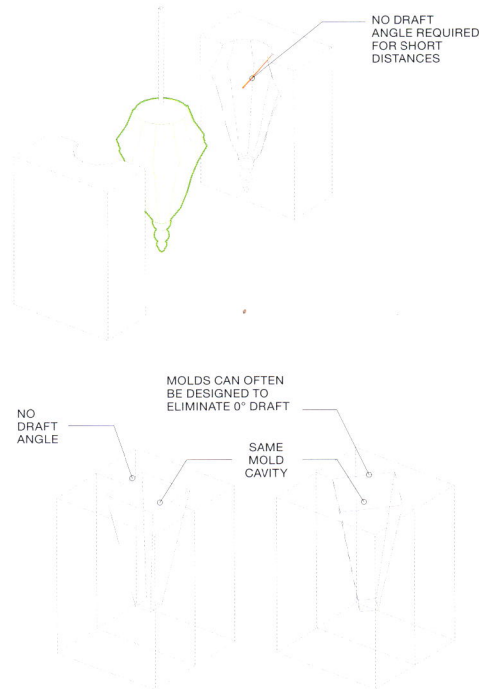

NO DRAFT ANGLE REQUIRED FOR SHORT DISTANCES

NO DRAFT ANGLE

MOLDS CAN OFTEN BE DESIGNED TO ELIMINATE 0° DRAFT

SAME MOLD CAVITY

FLASHING

Molten glass has the consistency of honey, and so flashing is typically not a problem as the glass is too thick to squeeze out of the mold.

INSERTS

Inserts cannot be accommodated by this process.

PARTING LINES

If using a closed mold (as opposed to an optic mold), a parting line will be visible on blow-molded glass. If the parting line is to be removed, the glass can be flame finished, eliminating any lines.

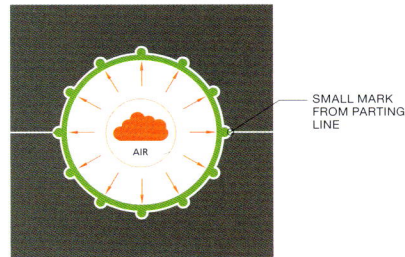

SMALL MARK FROM PARTING LINE

AIR

If the mold is axisymmetric, the glassblower spins the parison while inflating; this eliminates any mark at the parting line.

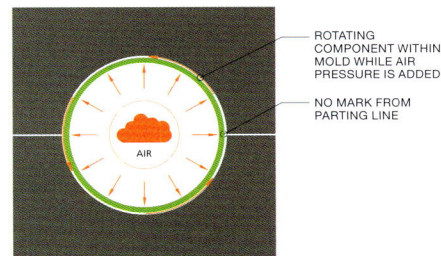

ROTATING COMPONENT WITHIN MOLD WHILE AIR PRESSURE IS ADDED

NO MARK FROM PARTING LINE

AIR

PRODUCTION RUNS

Plaster molds begin to break down within four to eight uses. Wood molds can produce more than 500 units, if properly maintained. Cast and machined metal can produce up to 100,000 units.

SHRINKING

As the glass cools, it will shrink a little. Shrinkage will not be uniform across the component because of the varying wall thicknesses that result from this process.

SURFACE DESIGNS

This process can accommodate surface designs and textures on the outside surface of the glass. Shallow textures will not translate to the inside of the component.

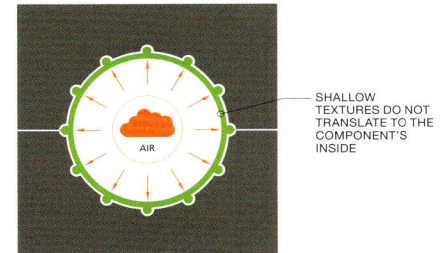

SHALLOW TEXTURES DO NOT TRANSLATE TO THE COMPONENT'S INSIDE

AIR

Surface textures can also be added after molding. The component can be reheated and then pressed or rolled on a flat textured surface. The textured surface can be made of any material that can withstand the temperature of the glass.

TOOLING COMPLEXITY

Molds have no moving parts. Optic molds are very simple and are made from one piece. They are often conical in cross-section, allowing for different-sized parisons to be blown, depending on how deep in the mold they are inserted. Closed molds made from metal, wood, plaster, or clay may be made in multiple parts. Metal molds are typically made in three parts, with two hinged sides and a bottom. More complex molds made from wood, plaster, or clay can easily be made from multiple parts (three or more) and held around the outside by band clamps.

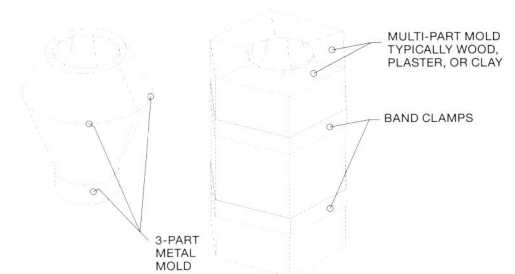

MULTI-PART MOLD TYPICALLY WOOD, PLASTER, OR CLAY

BAND CLAMPS

3-PART METAL MOLD

TOOLING COSTS

Generally tooling costs are low. Optic molds made from cast metal are available off the shelf for less than $500, depending on size. More complicated wood molds may be $1,000. Metal molds may be up to $5,000.

TOOL MARKS

The diameter of the hole in the blowpipe can range from 0.25 to 0.75in (6–19mm). This will leave a natural hole in the component. The hole can be closed post-production.

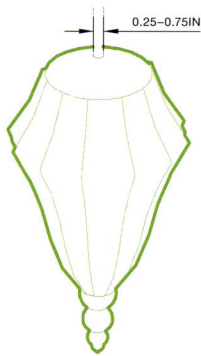

0.25–0.75IN

TWISTING

After forming in the mold, the glassblower can reheat the component and twist it.

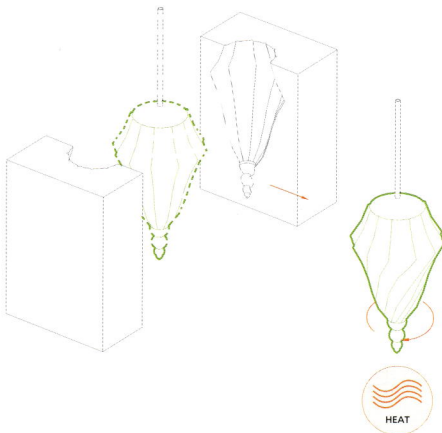

HEAT

UNDERCUTS

Undercuts are possible in glass blowing. For closed molds, the mold can be made in multiple parts to accommodate the undercut. For optic molds, undercuts can be an issue. In this case, after the glassblower inflates the glass to touch the sides of the optic mold, the glass can be slightly deflated by sucking air from the blowpipe. This shrinks the glass bubble from the mold's sides and the glassblower is able to remove the component. After removing the component, the glassblower can add more air to the blowpipe, blowing the piece back to its original size. This takes a lot of skill and can slow production.

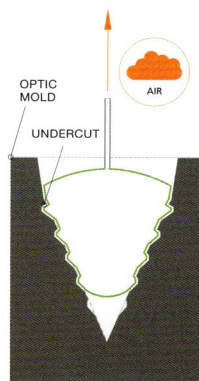

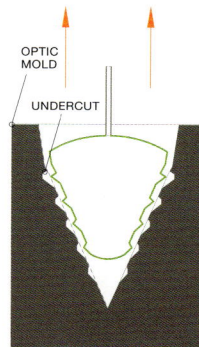

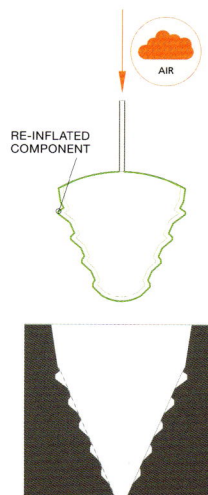

OPTIC MOLD
UNDERCUT
AIR

OPTIC MOLD
UNDERCUT

RE-INFLATED COMPONENT
AIR

VENTS

Vents are necessary so that trapped air can escape as the component is blown into a closed mold cavity. Vents should be located at the bottom of the mold and at any place where the mold protrudes into the cavity. The vent holes can leave small marks in the surface, but they can easily be flame-polished off.

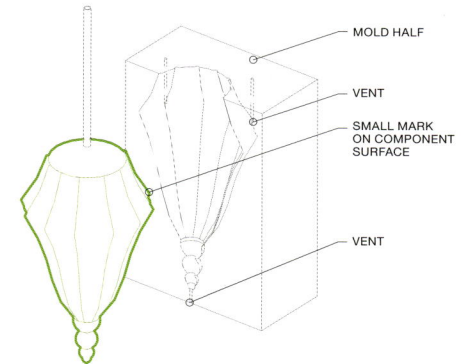

MOLD HALF
VENT
SMALL MARK ON COMPONENT SURFACE
VENT

WALL THICKNESS

Wall thicknesses will vary across the cross-section. The wall thickness at the bottom of the component tends to be thicker than the sides. Mechanized glass blow molding often results in a thinner wall thickness than hand blowing.

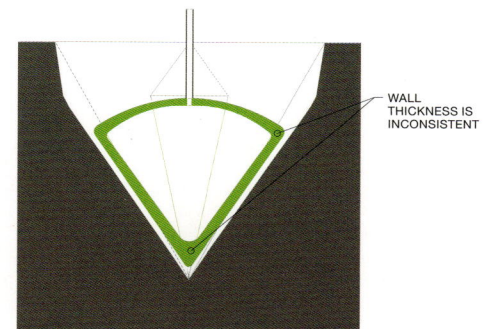

WALL THICKNESS IS INCONSISTENT

GLASS

EXTERIOR SCREEN | HESIODO
Hierve Diseñeria
Mexico City, Mexico

The Hesiodo is a mid-rise condominium building built in 2005, located on a residential street in Mexico City. [22] The building has thirteen apartments covering 27,028ft^2 (2,511m^2) and is organized into two stacks—one at the front of the lot and one in the rear—with an atrium in between. [23, 24] The rear stack faces south and is five stories tall; the front stack faces north and is four stories with a roof terrace that is accessible for all building inhabitants. Both stacks have balconies and open views to either a street or the alley. The building shares two party walls, on the east and west, with its neighbors. There is parking for twenty-four cars, located below grade.

The Hesiodo has a screen that covers the two exposed building faces. The screen creates a visual and protective barrier between the urban street and the apartment balconies and windows. On the north façade, the screen continues up the building and becomes the guardrail for the roof terrace. The screen is made of metal tension cables; hand-blown, wood-molded glass spheres; and ethylene propylene diene monomer (EPDM) rubber disks that support the spheres on the cables. [26, 27, 28] Over 7,700 glass spheres were used for this project. They were manufactured by a craftsman in Guadalajara, less than 350 miles (560km) from the building site.

DESIGN CONSIDERATIONS

Prior to the Hesiodo, Hierve Diseñeria had experience with customized manufacturing and working with manufacturers. The firm has done industrial and furniture design, and designed two different custom concrete blocks (Sistem Arde, first and second generations). According to Alejandro Villarreal, principal of Diseñeria, the inspiration for the Hesiodo's glass spheres came from watching children playing in the plaza and blowing soap bubbles.[2] In order to evaluate the screen, initial prototypes were made. Using these, Diseñeria reviewed the sphere's color and the cable assembly system.

This building itself is highly handcrafted and labor intensive, reinforcing a social component that the firm states is inherent to its work.[3] The sphere's glass thickness is uneven, ranging from 0.4 to 1in (10–25mm) and has air bubbles trapped in the glass. These characteristics are typical of hand-blown glass, and help reinforce how the spheres were manufactured. On-site construction workers strung the spheres, supporting fasteners, and EPDM disks by hand on the cables. According to Villarreal, it was the workers who figured out the best method for then attaching the cables to the building.[4] [29, 30, 31, 32, 33] Finally, the Hesiodo's screen needs to be cleaned by hand every six months or so to remove the dust and smoke residue typical for exposed building elements in Mexico City. It takes about one to three days to properly clean the screen.

22
The Hesiodo by Hierve Diseñeria in Mexico City, Mexico. Condominium primary façade and entrance

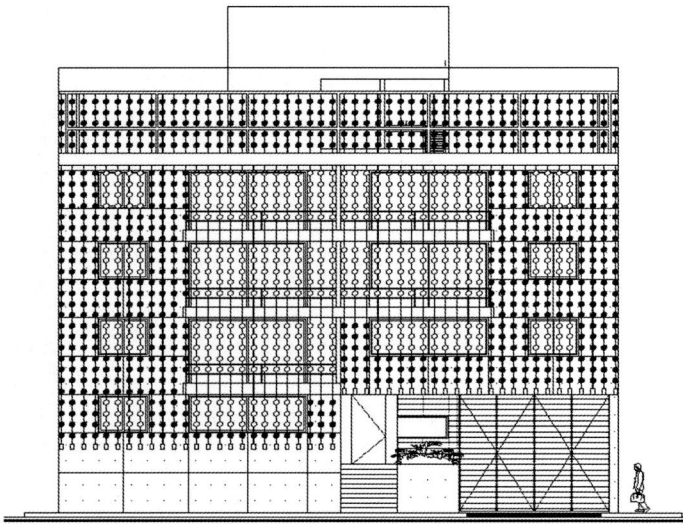

23 Drawing of primary façade

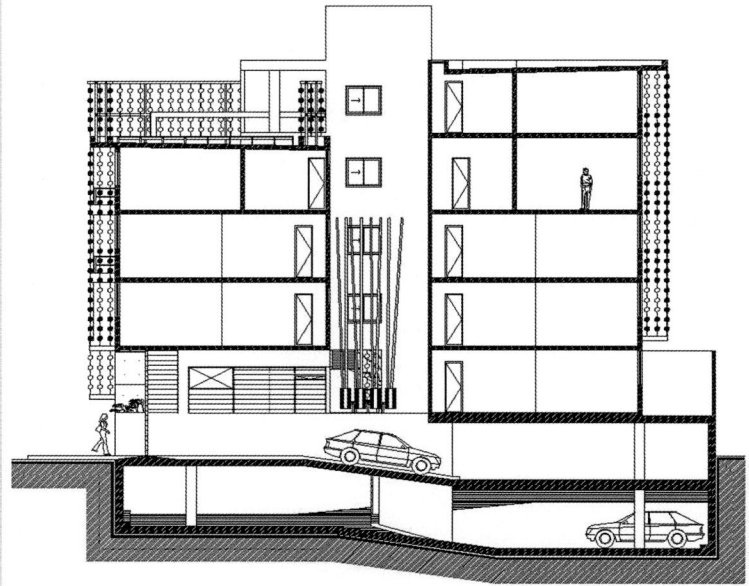

24 Building section through street façade, illustrating the two apartment towers and below-grade parking

INSTALLATION
PROCESS

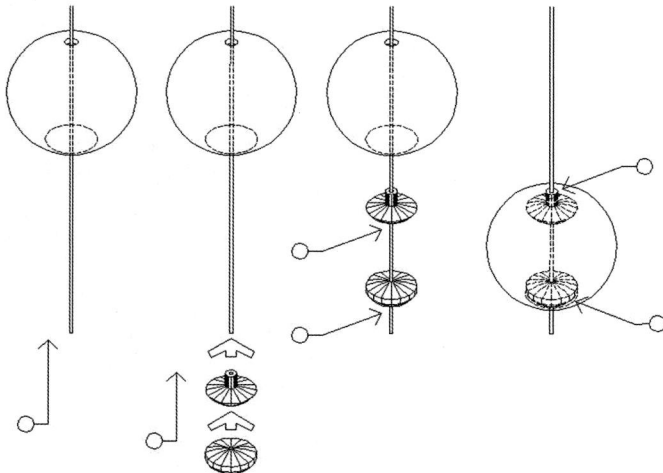

REPLACEMENT
PROCESS

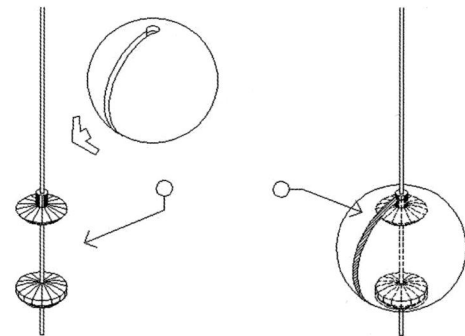

25 Hierve Diseñeria drawings of the installation of the glass spheres on the support (left) and of installing replacement spheres (right)

The design specifics for the glass spheres came from understanding the process for blowing glass. There is a small hole at the top of the sphere where the cable is strung through it. That hole was formed from the blowpipe as the glass was blown. A larger hole at the bottom of the sphere is where the sphere rests on the EPDM washer, and was how the workers on-site were able to access the connectors inside of the sphere. This hole was drilled after the glass was blown and cooled. **[34, 35, 36]**

MANUFACTURING CONSIDERATIONS

Villarreal had researched the possibility of manufacturing the spheres out of plastic rather than glass; however, this was too costly. Plastic blow molding often requires large equipment and is highly industrialized, and therefore would have required a large production volume in order to be cost effective. Conversely, glass blowing can be done by either craftspeople or mechanized manufacturers. According to Villarreal, finding workshops with craftspeople that had the necessary skill set for this project, were willing to take the job, and could handle the required production volume was easy.

Additionally, the EPDM disks, which help attach the spheres to the cables, were custom manufactured for this project. **[25]** Villarreal could not recall how this disks were made (although most likely they were made by injection, transfer, or compression molding), but it was more difficult to find a manufacturer willing to make those than the glass spheres.

26
Blown glass screen

27
Apartment balcony, looking out through screen

28
Close-up of component

29

30

31

32

33

29
Construction workers on building roof

30
Stringing components onto supports

31
Applying sealant between EPDM disks and blown-glass components

32
Screen being hung off of building

33
Building façade from the street

34
The small hole at the top of the component was made by the blow tube; the large hole at the bottom was made by a drill press

35
Glass components in the drill press

36
Detail image of the component in the drill press

OTHER CONSIDERATIONS

In some countries, labor-intensive manufacturing with mid-sized production volumes will cost less and be easier to customize than in more highly industrialized countries. For Villarreal, hand-blown, blow-molded glass cost less than blown plastic, and he was able to find several workshops in Mexico that were willing to undertake the project.

LESSONS LEARNED

The Hesiodo's residents are supposed to pay a maintenance fee to cover the building's upkeep. However, not all of the residents pay, and so the building's exterior, and particularly the spheres, have not been cleaned as required. Smoke and dust have built up on the spheres, and the screen has not aged gracefully.

    Villarreal visited the building approximately ten years after it was completed and only a few spheres had been broken. This is partly due to the thickness, and therefore strength, of the hand-blown glass. Hand-blown glass tends to be stronger than a comparable component made by mechanized glass blowing. The firm had proposed a method for replacing any broken spheres without the need to remove the cable and restring them. This had yet to be done.

MATERIAL CONSIDERATIONS + DESIGN PARAMETERS

THERMOPLASTIC

Plastic blow molding developed from blow molding glass and now is the primary method and material for manufacturing disposable storage containers. [37] Most plastic manufacturing is suited to high-volume productions. Although there is nothing specific about the material and process that restricts it to high-volume productions, most manufacturers are highly mechanized in order to reduce per-unit costs. Most disposable containers are engineered for volume rather than strength, and so most plastic blow molding is for thin-walled components. To meet the high volume requirements, cycle times are kept short by actively cooling the molds to solidify the thermoplastic quickly. [38] However, this increases mold costs and thus increases the production runs necessary to offset these costs.

For plastic blow molding, the parison can be formed by extrusion, either continuous or intermittent, or by injection molding. If continuously extruded, the mold closes around the parison as it is extruded, essentially cutting the parison from the extrudate. The mold is then moved to another station, where a blow-hole is inserted and the parison is inflated. This is typically done for high-volume productions. In intermittent extrusion, the extrusion stops, the mold halves close, and then the parison is inflated. [39] Intermittent extrusion allows for more sophisticated mold actions, such as moving or collapsible cores. Intermittent extrusion does have some inherent difficulties with it, as the extrusion process itself does not lend itself to operating cyclically (see Chapter 2.1); therefore starting and stopping the extrusion to make the parison can cause problems with the extrusion equipment.

Injection molding can be used to create a preform. [40] A preform is a molded shape that is prepared prior to blow molding. Typically, preforms can have pre-threaded necks, which combines the precision of injection molding for the threads with the capabilities of blow molding to make hollow containers with small necks, such as water bottles. The tooling costs for injection blow molding will be significantly more than for extrusion blow molding, particularly since two sets of tools are required—one for the injection molding and one for the blow molding.

Blow molding plastic is limited to thermoplastic. The design parameters given represent an approximation of the parameters for this process. Specific parameters depend on the specific thermoplastic used.

SIMILAR PROCESSES

The advantage of blow molding plastic over other plastic manufacturing processes is its shorter cycle times. Rotational molding, or rotomolding, can produce components similar to those resulting from blow molding plastic; however, tolerances and details are much finer with blow molding than rotomolding. Dual-sheet thermoforming (Chapter 1.2) can also produce components similar to blow molding with a lower tooling cost.

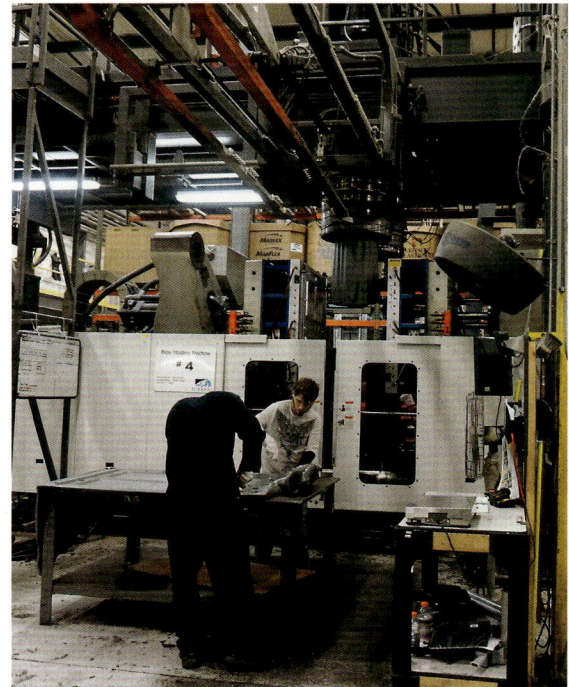

37 Plastic blow molding at Penguin Molding in Sturgis, Michigan

38 Plastic blowing mold with embedded cooling lines for faster cycle times

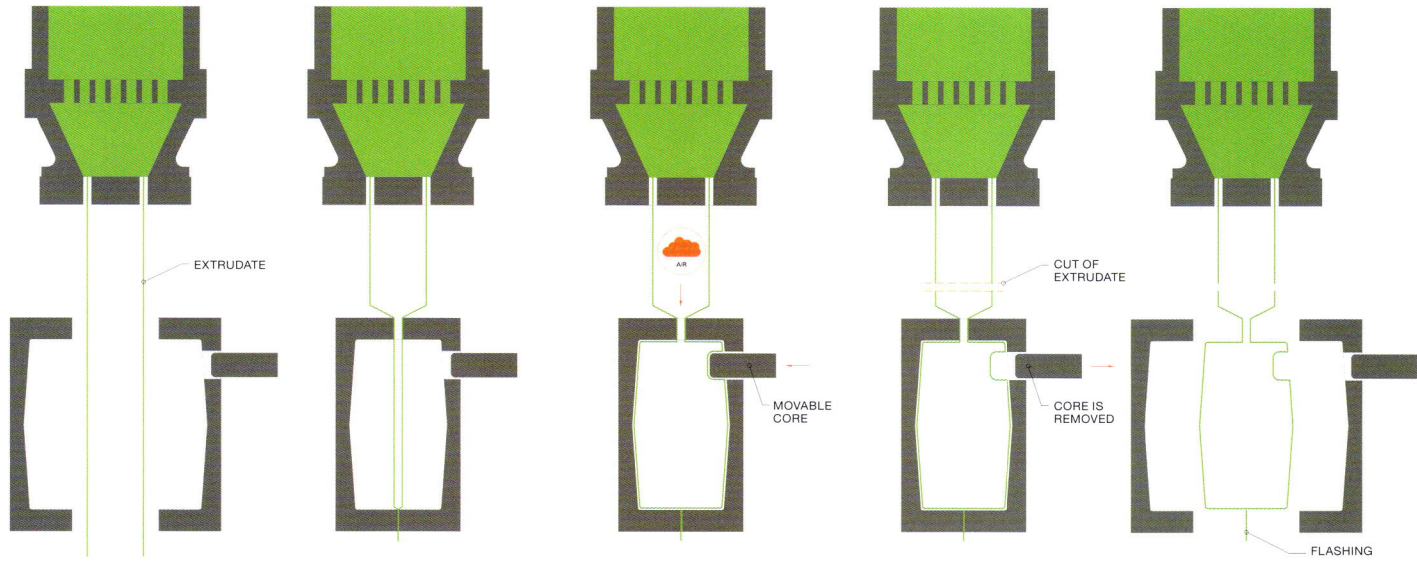

EXTRUDATE

AIR

MOVABLE CORE

CUT OF EXTRUDATE

CORE IS REMOVED

FLASHING

39 Intermittent extrusion blow-molding process

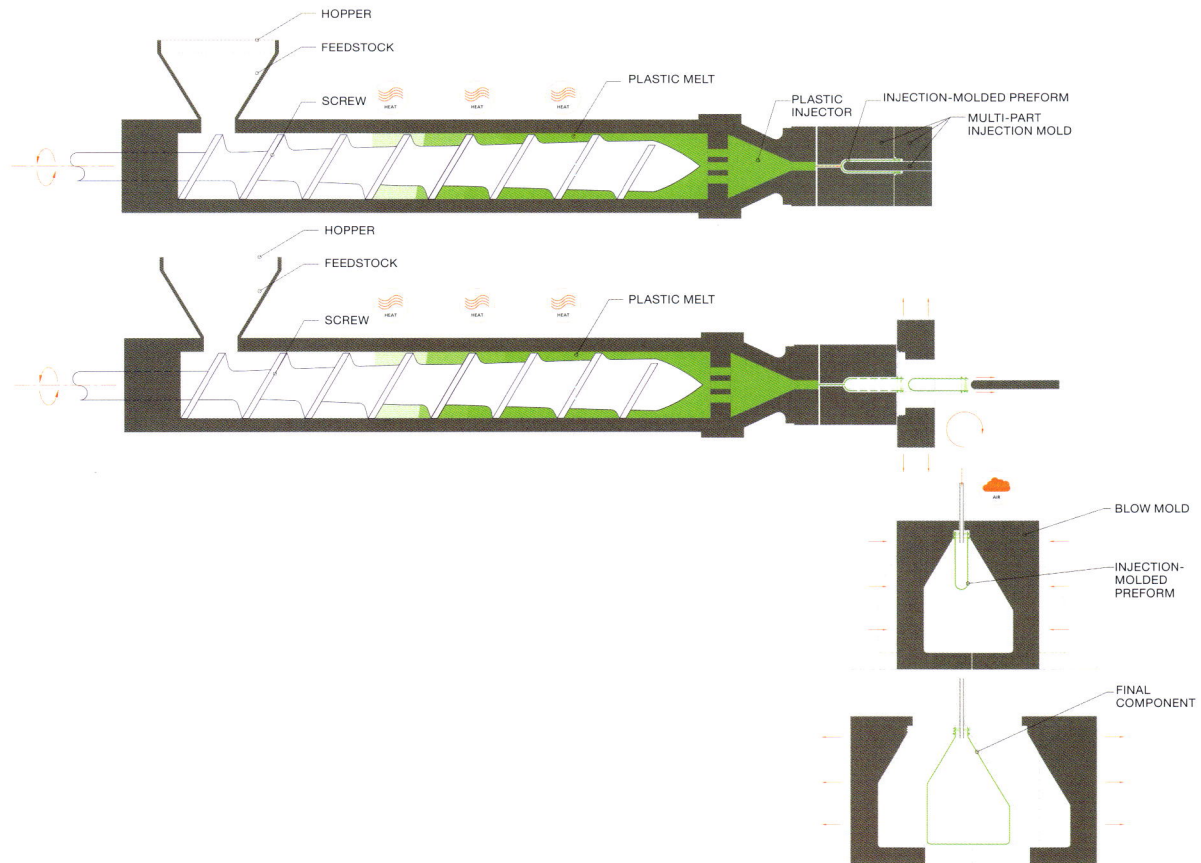

HOPPER

FEEDSTOCK

SCREW

PLASTIC MELT

PLASTIC INJECTOR

INJECTION-MOLDED PREFORM

MULTI-PART INJECTION MOLD

HOPPER

FEEDSTOCK

SCREW

PLASTIC MELT

BLOW MOLD

INJECTION-MOLDED PREFORM

FINAL COMPONENT

40 Injection blow-molding process

CORNER RADII

It is best to design a plastic blow-molded piece with eased corners, to facilitate the stretching of the medium. The corner radii should be greater than 0.25in (6mm). Smaller radii are possible, but they come with added complications, as they can cause tears and thinning of the walls near interior corners.

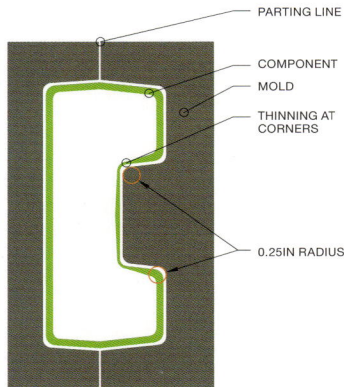

DRAFT ANGLES

Most manufacturing texts claim that because the plastic shrinks as it cools and will pull away from the mold cavity, draft angles are not required. However, unlike injection molding, blow molding does not use injector pins to remove the component from the mold. Therefore it is best practice to include a draft angle of 1° from the parting line. A draft of 3–5° is recommended for any male parts of the mold, as the plastic will shrink around them, making demolding difficult. The draft angle can be adjusted based on the specific thermoplastic and the ability of the manufacturer.

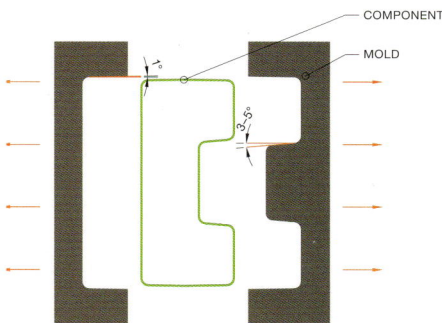

FLASHING

Unless blow molding an injection-molded preform, this process produces flashing that will need to be trimmed. The flashing can be substantial, depending on the size of the mold and the size of the extrudate. Because the flashing is not actively cooled within the mold cavity, it will still be warm when the component has cooled. This allows the flashing to be easily removed.

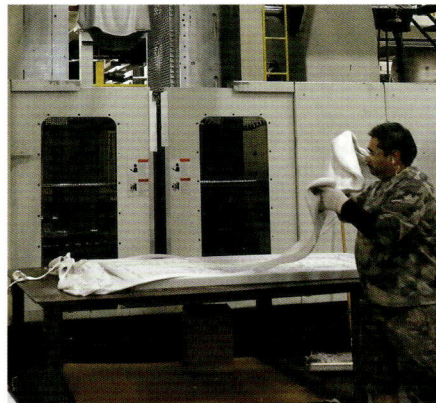

PARTING LINES

There are noticeable parting lines with this process. Parting lines can be flat or can wander as needed.

PRODUCTION RUNS

Volume should be no fewer than 1,000, and can produce up to 500,000 units. Generally, this process is better suited to high-volume production runs.

PRODUCTION SPEED

Production rates are quite high, at 100–2,500 units per hour, depending on size. Speed can be increased by blow molding two components together and cutting them apart post-production, or by dual extrusion, which extrudes two extrudates into two mold cavities during the same cycle.

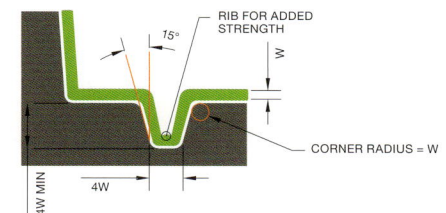

RIBS

If walls are to be thin, stiffening ribs should be added. The ribs will add strength without increasing wall thickness. The depth and width of the ribs will be based on the wall thickness, and the draft should be 15° or greater.

SHRINKING

As the thermoplastic cools, it will shrink. Shrinkage will not be uniform across the component because of the varying wall thicknesses resulting from this process. Shrinking will be less than 0.1% and will depend on the specific plastic used. Based on experience, the mold maker and the manufacturer will determine by how much the mold should be oversized.

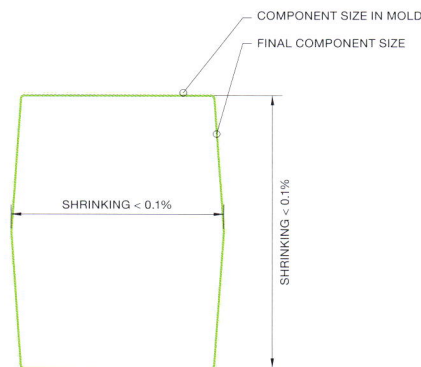
COMPONENT SIZE IN MOLD
FINAL COMPONENT SIZE
SHRINKING < 0.1%
SHRINKING < 0.1%

SIDE-WALL HOLES

It is not possible to mold in side-wall holes with this process. All side-wall holes should be made with post-production machining.

SIZE LIMITS

Various sizes can be achieved with this process, from 0.3in³ (5ml), up to 1,300ft³ (37m³) for storage tanks.

SURFACE DESIGNS

This process can accommodate surface designs, including labels or decorations. Textures in the mold surface require a draft angle of 1° plus an additional draft angle of 1° for each 0.001in (0.3mm) of texture depth.

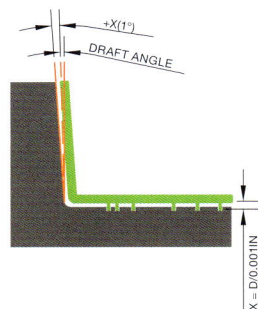
+X(1°)
DRAFT ANGLE
X = D/0.001IN

Because plastic shrinks, male decorations on the mold surface will require a minimum draft angle of 3–5°. Most surface textures will not translate to the inside of the plastic blow-molded component.

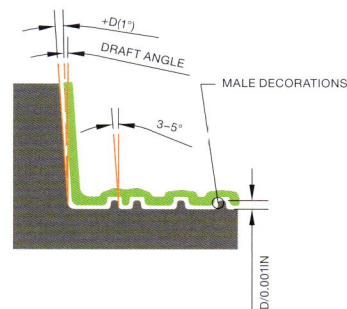
+D(1°)
DRAFT ANGLE
3~5°
MALE DECORATIONS
D/0.001IN

SYMMETRY

Symmetry is not required for component shapes. If the asymmetrical component has only one large inner volume, it can be manufactured with a stationary blow tube. If there are more complex parts, like offset blown handles, than the blow spigot will move inside the component as it is being blown. This added manufacturing complexity will increase costs.

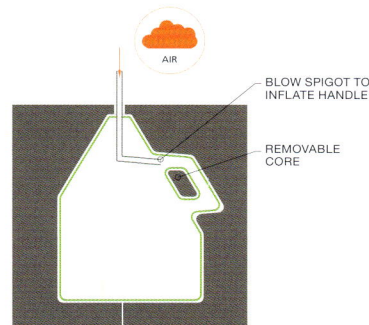
AIR
BLOW SPIGOT TO INFLATE HANDLE
REMOVABLE CORE

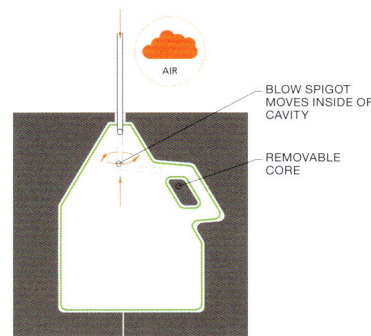
AIR
BLOW SPIGOT MOVES INSIDE OF CAVITY
REMOVABLE CORE

UNDERCUTS

Undercuts that impede demolding in a two-part mold, such as the pushed-up bottom on a soda bottle, are possible with additional moving mold parts; however, this will greatly increase mold costs.

These undercuts are best reserved for high-volume productions.

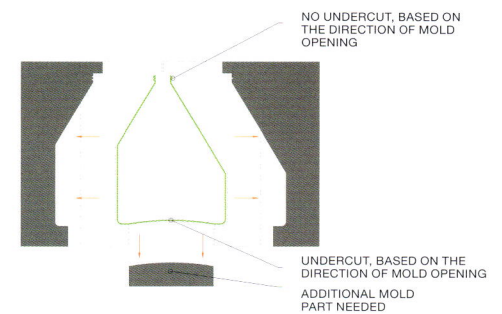
NO UNDERCUT, BASED ON THE DIRECTION OF MOLD OPENING
UNDERCUT, BASED ON THE DIRECTION OF MOLD OPENING
ADDITIONAL MOLD PART NEEDED

VENTS

Vents up to 0.04in (1mm) diameter are used in areas where air entrapment is suspected. This can be at the top of the mold, or at high points away from the parting line. Some plastic will be squeezed into the vents, so they will leave a mark on the component's surface.

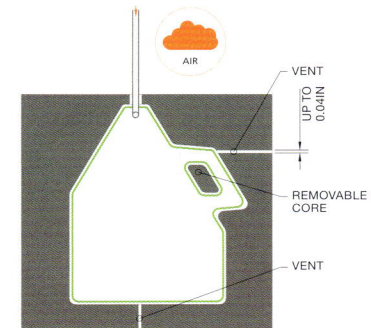
AIR
VENT
UP TO 0.04IN
REMOVABLE CORE
VENT

WALL THICKNESS

Wall thicknesses of blown plastic components can range from a minimum of 0.012in (0.3mm) for beverage bottles to a maximum of 0.5in (13mm) for large, industrial components. If the walls are thick, cooling aids such as carbon dioxide may be required to cool the plastic before it is removed from the mold.

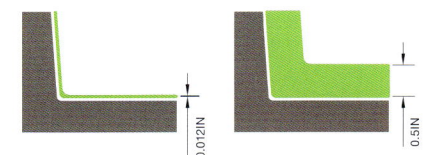
0.012IN
0.5IN

Consistent wall thicknesses can be difficult to achieve with this process. A tolerance of 0.03in (0.8mm) is common, and a tolerance of 0.01in (0.25mm) would be considered a precision tolerance, with an associated increase in cost.

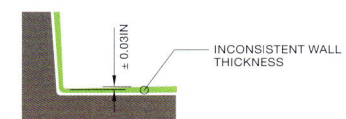
± 0.03IN
INCONSISTENT WALL THICKNESS

THERMOPLASTIC

POLLI-BRICK | ECOARK
Miniwiz
Taipei, Taiwan

The EcoARK is a large pavilion that hosted fashion shows and provided exhibition space for the 2010 Taipei International Flora Exposition, which ran from November 2010 to April 2011. Designed by Miniwiz, the EcoARK has 21,500ft^2 (2,000m^2) of floor area and is nine stories tall. **[41, 42]** It was engineered to withstand earthquakes and typhoons, common in Taipei. In keeping with the inherent nature theme of the exposition, Miniwiz designed the building to be as environmental and sustainable as possible. The building is cooled without air-conditioning and is carbon neutral.

Miniwiz designed the EcoARK's exterior wall with custom plastic blow-molded bottles that interlock with one another. **[44, 45]** The bottles are filled with air, for insulation, but can also be filled with water or sand for thermal mass. The building is about half the weight of a conventional building, which in turn reduces the amount of structure and foundations required. According to a *Wall Street Journal* article about the EcoARK, the building is the least costly of its size ever made.[5] Building construction cost \$250/m^2.

Far Eastern Group, one of the largest plastic producers in Taiwan, commissioned the EcoARK and donated it to the city. Douglas Hsu, group chairman of the Far Eastern Group, supported the project so his company's bottle waste could be upcycled. The EcoARKs bottles are made from recycled polyethylene terephthalate polymer (PET). PET is the plastic typically found in disposable soft drink, water, and juice bottles. Taiwan has a high recycling rate, with 90,000 tons (more than 8 million kilograms) of plastic being recycled every year, so it seemed appropriate for Miniwiz to use this material in its design. In the end, the EcoARK upcycled 1.5 million PET bottles into 480,000 new, plastic blow-molded bottles. **[46]**

Unlike other case studies in this book, the custom-manufactured components were not limited to just the EcoARK. Miniwiz has since developed its blow-molded bottles into a commercially available building product, named the POLLI-Brick. According to the British Broadcasting Corporation (BBC), Miniwiz has gotten requests to use the POLLI-Brick for gymnasiums, military bunkers, and other portable applications.[6] Filled with air, the POLLI-Brick performs almost the same as a triple-layered, vacuum-glass unit, but at a sixth of the cost. It can withstand 68lb/ft^2 (3,255 Pa) of lateral wind force with a fifth of the material weight.[7]

Currently, POLLI-Brick comes in translucent, semi-translucent, and white, but custom colors can be manufactured. POLLI-Bricks are available in three different sizes: 203fl oz, 23.3fl oz, and 13.5fl oz (6,000ml, 690ml, and 400ml), with varying heights of 12in, 7in, and 4.6in (30.8cm, 18cm, and 11.8cm), respectively. The largest size of POLLI-Brick can be used for interior or exterior applications, while the two smaller sizes can only be used for interior applications. POLLI-Bricks are self-extinguishing, fire retardant, and flame retardant, and they meet standards set by ASTM, AAMA, and UL.

DESIGN CONSIDERATIONS

According to Miniwiz, the inspiration for the POLLI-Brick's design was the bee honeycomb, as it is efficient and has natural strength.[8] The bottle shape is based on a hexagon, with the corners either protruding outward or into the bottle. The protrusions snap into one another, locking the bottles together mechanically with minimal adhesive required. POLLI-Bricks are stacked together so that the side-walls connect to one another. They can be stacked unidirectionally, so that all of their caps face the same direction, or in alternating directions, so that their caps face both front and back.

The POLLI-Bricks for the EcoARK are in prefabricated panels that are made from 128 POLLI-Bricks, in a 34ft² (3.2m²) panel, weighing just 40lb (18kg). [47] The POLLI-Bricks are joined together by polycarbonate panels on their front, creating the EcoARK's weather barrier; and welded-wire fabric on their back, providing support in bending. [48] For fire protection, a fireproof laminate was added to the panels' exterior, and a sprinkler system is on the building interior. Miniwiz added LEDs to the inside of some of the EcoARK POLLI-Bricks, lighting up the outside of the building. [43]

Like many exposition buildings, the EcoARK was intended to be a temporary building. Miniwiz's design limited the use of adhesive between the POLLI-Bricks, allowing the panels to be deconstructed and reconstructed. All of the pieces for the building can fit into shipping containers for relocation. However, so far the operators have decided to keep the building where it is and use it as a museum.

MANUFACTURING CONSIDERATIONS

There are a number of steps necessary to manufacture POLLI-Bricks. First the bottles need to be collected. Then they are sorted, the labels are washed off, and they are dried. Next, the bottles are crushed into small flakes of plastic that are then melted into PET pellets. Fourth, the PET pellets are fed into an injection-molding machine that makes the preform. By injection molding the preform first, the quality of the blow-molded plastic will be better than if using an extruded parison. Additionally, the component can have some of the finer design details, such as tight threads on the neck, not typically associated with blow molding. [49] Finally, the preform is heated and inserted into the blow-molding machine, where it is inflated into its final form. It took three months to make all 480,000 POLLI-Bricks for the EcoARK.

The most difficult challenge with blow molding the POLLI-Brick was the plastic itself. Recycled PET bottles come in varying qualities and colors, and have a number of different contaminants, including labels. These problems are compounded when collection is nationwide or even international. Typically, these issues are resolved by adding virgin PET to the recycled PET; however, this would have been against the concept of the EcoARK and therefore was rejected as an option. According to Miniwiz, it was also difficult to maintain the correct temperature for blow molding. If the PET is not hot enough, it is too viscous and will break during blowing; if the PET is too hot, it will be too liquid and will not get hard enough.[9]

If an architect wants to use POLLI-Bricks for a building, current lead time is 1 month and the minimum order is 5,000 units. Miniwiz has

44 POLLI-Bricks

45 POLLI-Bricks stacked together

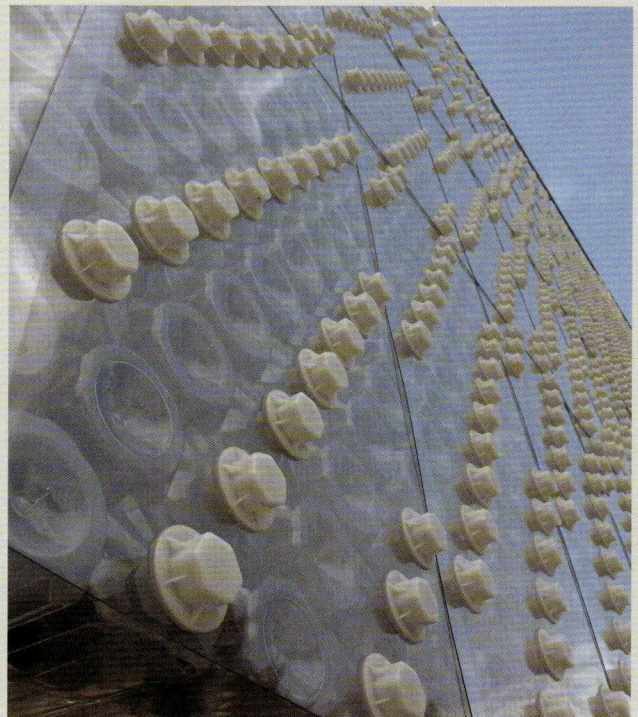

46 Detailed image of the POLLI-Brick wall in the EcoARK

considered the possibility of allowing manufacturing overseas and closer to the building sites. However, it recognizes that there needs to be more demand to make this feasible. As Miniwiz wrote, "A lot of clients concentrated in the same country would justify such [an] operation. But up to now, our clients have been spread worldwide so it didn't justify producing abroad. Yet."[10]

OTHER CONSIDERATIONS

With 128 bricks per panel, and 480,000 bricks in the EcoARK, any dimensional discrepancies get multiplied across all of the bottles. Stresses between the POLLI-Bricks could cause a brick to pop out of the panel, but the polycarbonate sheets helped solve this issue. They were CNC cut with holes to accept the necks of the POLLI-Bricks. This re-aligned the bottles to keep any tolerance errors from accumulating.

Miniwiz did acknowledge the possible degradation of the PET in ultraviolet (UV) light. It estimates that the POLLI-Bricks will last twenty years.

LESSONS LEARNED

With this project's challenges, communication between the designer and manufacturer was paramount. During discussions with the blow molder, Miniwiz realized that the design needed to integrate the technical limits of the equipment. This was particularly important as it seems that not all blow-molding equipment had enough temperature control to work with the 100% recycled PET. According to Miniwiz, the cooperation with the manufacturer enabled the team to reach a better compromise between the structural strength of the POLLI-Bricks and their technical feasibility.[11]

47
The EcoARK during construction

48
Interior of the EcoARK's
POLLI-Brick wall

49
Blow molds for the POLLI-Bricks

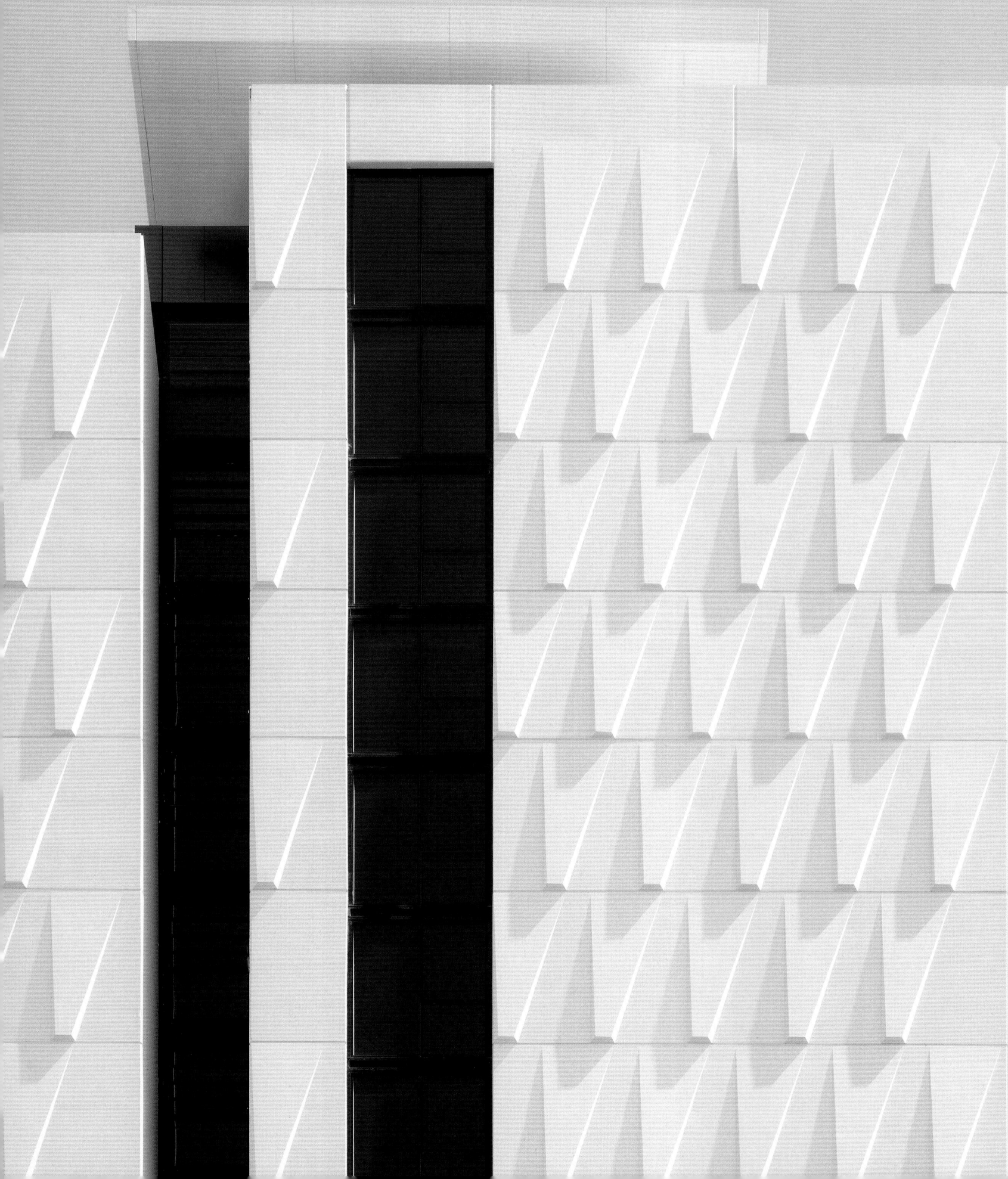

4

Forming Solid

4.1. Casting Concrete / 4.2 Casting Metal
4.3 Casting Glass / 4.4 Vibration-Press Casting
4.5 Vibration-Tamping / 4.6 Pressing

Included in this section are manufacturing processes that take a liquid or malleable medium and let it solidify in a mold, before demolding. Most of the processes in this section form solid or thick-walled components. When forming solid, any side of the component that touches a mold face is considered the finish face. Molds may be open, semi-open, or closed, resulting in five or more finished faces. Because the processes are not mechanized, hinged or multi-part molds are often used, eliminating the concern of undercuts.

Generally, the processes in this section can be done by craftspeople and workshops, or small manufacturers, which can produce custom components. The exception is vibration-press casting (Chapter 4.4), which is used to make concrete masonry units (CMUs). Most CMU manufacturers in industrialized countries are highly mechanized and unable to produce custom shapes. However, changing molds on large equipment is easier than it has ever been. Additionally, there are small manufacturers outside of the United States that are less mechanized and able to produce custom units. Some processes, such as casting metal (Chapter 4.2) and pressing glass (Chapter 4.6), may be produced by small or large-volume manufacturers.

Unlike in the earlier sections of this book, the manufacturing processes in this section range widely based on the manufacturing medium. For example, casting concrete and casting metal are very different, even though both involve pouring a liquid or liquid-like medium into a mold, and so each has its own chapter (4.1 and 4.2, respectively). Similarly, there are differences in the parameters based on tooling materials. For example, when casting concrete (Chapter 4.1), a rubber mold will result in a casting with greater surface detail and with undercuts than will a steel mold. In some of these chapters you will find design parameters given under tooling and material properties, where appropriate.

4.1 Casting Concrete

aka: wet casting concrete, precast concrete,
precast, architectural precast

INTRODUCTION

Casting concrete is a manufacturing process in which a wet mixture of slumping concrete is poured into a mold. [1] Gravity, enough water to enable the concrete to move, additives, and vibration all help to fill the mold entirely with concrete. [2] Depending on the mold material used, casting concrete can be used to create complex geometries with good detail, semi-hollow or solid shapes, and varying cross-sectional thicknesses, and in a variety of colors, aggregates, and finishes. [3] There are almost no size limitations to casting concrete; however, precast concrete sizes are often limited by transportation size limits, such as those established by the United States Department of Transportation. [4] Depending on the cast concrete's size, strength, and reinforcing, precast concrete

has the potential to be used for structural or non-structural architectural applications.

Concrete can be cast in solid or built-up molds. With casting in a solid mold—also known as an envelope mold—the component must be able to be lifted out, leaving the mold intact. With a built-up mold, the sides of the mold are taken apart, allowing for easy removal of the component without damage to the mold. Envelope molds require draft angles, whereas built-up molds require none. After the concrete is poured into the mold, the concrete is vibrated, to help eliminate air pockets and to ensure that the concrete fully fills the mold. Vibrating may be done with a mechanical or pneumatic vibrator inserted into the

1 A wet mixture of slumping concrete being poured into a mold

3 A pneumatic vibrator to help the concrete flow into the mold

2 A range of cast concrete colors, aggregates, and finishes

4 Large components with almost no size limitations, except those imposed by transportation

FORM
LINER

OPTIONAL

FORM
BOARDS

SOLID
MOLD

CONCRETE BUCKET

VIBRATE

SCREED

CURE

OPTIONAL

FINAL
COMPONENT

FINAL COMPONENT

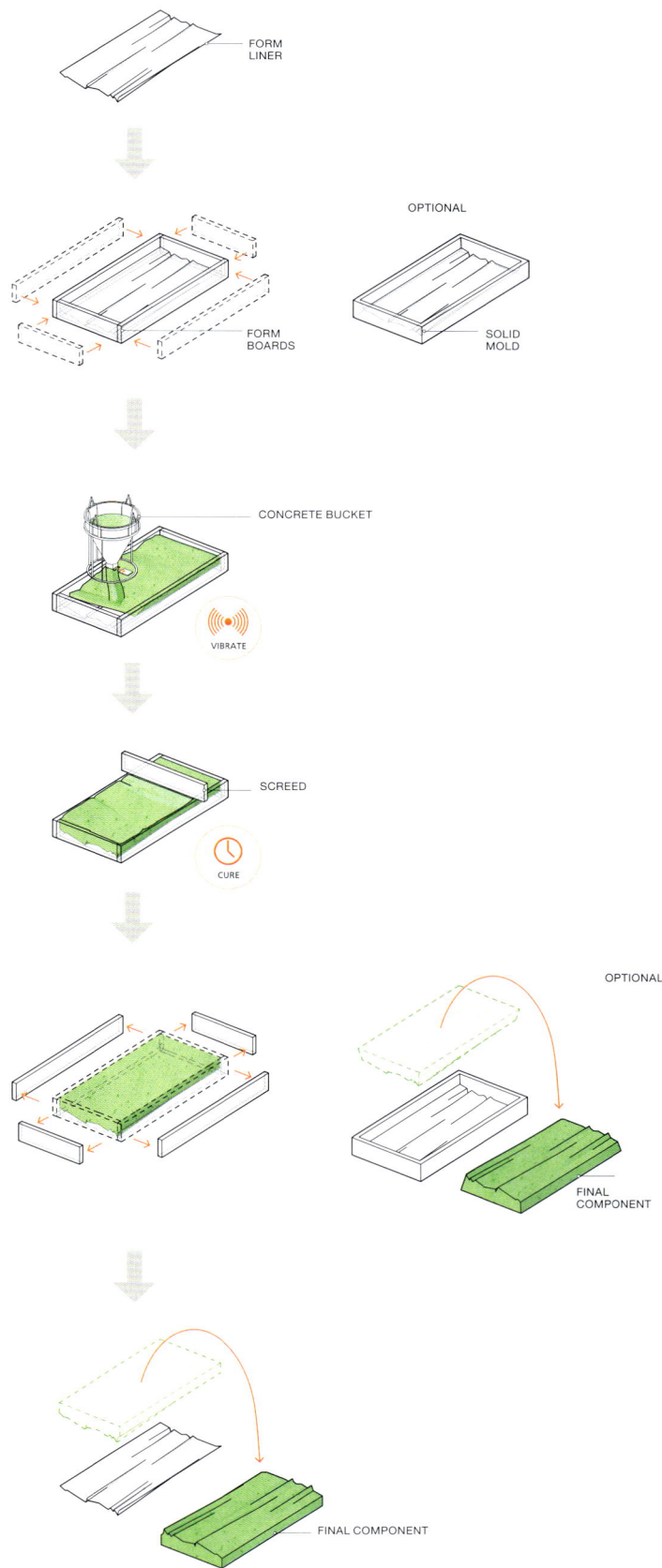

concrete; the mold may be on a vibrating table, where both the mold and the concrete are vibrated; or a vibrator is clamped onto the side of the mold. For open molds, the top of the concrete is leveled with a screed. Within 24 hours the concrete has usually set so that it can be removed from the mold. After demolding, the concrete continues to cure. Depending on the facilities, the ambient temperature and humidity, the project schedule, and the required strength, curing may be carried out in a controlled or semi-controlled environment.

Casting concrete can be used for building structure, architectural concrete, or a combination of the two. This book does not include information about manufacturing standard precast elements, such as hollow-core slabs or double-Ts; instead, it focuses on architectural cast concrete components for both non-structural and structural applications. Architectural concrete has a high standard of uniformity of appearance, surface quality, and color. It can be used to make load-bearing walls, non-load-bearing panels, column covers, and architectural trim details.

Concrete is typically cast in open molds, finish face down. This gives a consistent finish to the surface of the component, as air bubbles will release from the mold surface and travel into the concrete. Casting against vertical sides or with a closed mold increases the likelihood of air voids, also known as bug holes,

5 Concrete casting in a closed mold. Air pockets and bubbles will likely form on the upper face of the mold. This can be repaired with post-production patching

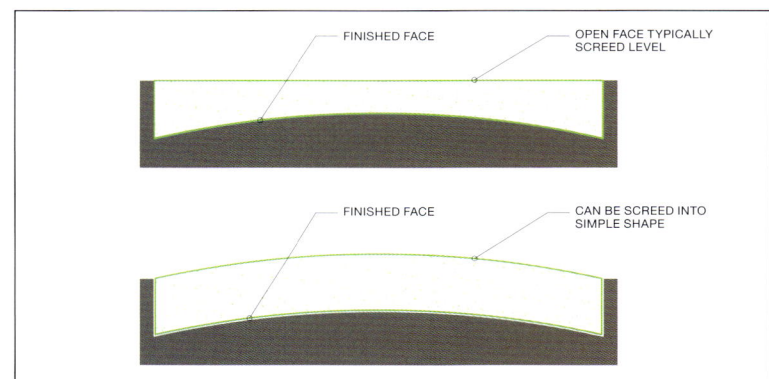

FINISHED FACE   OPEN FACE TYPICALLY SCREED LEVEL

FINISHED FACE   CAN BE SCREED INTO SIMPLE SHAPE

6 When casting in an open mold, the unfinished face is typically screed flat, but can be screed in a gentle curve

forming on the finish face. [5] Generally, tolerances and surface quality are not controlled on the open mold face. Typically, the component's back face is leveled with a screed, however, manufacturers can use the screed to shape the back of the component to form an consistent wall thickness. [6]

Casting concrete is labor intensive, space intensive, and is best suited to prototypes or small production runs. Because precast components are often large, manufacturing facilities require large equipment such as gantries and possibly mobile cranes, interior and exterior storage, and access for concrete mixers. This means that precast manufacturing cannot really be done by craftspeople or in small workshops. Most precast manufacturers can cast small and large production runs, and although there is a cost advantage to larger runs, many precast manufacturers do not require a lot of repeatability with their molds. [7]

BUILDING PRODUCTS

There are commercially available building products made by casting concrete. Because of concrete's durability and scale, products may include urban items such as bollards, planters, street furniture, landscape barriers, and trash containers. [8] A wide range of concrete colors and finishes are available. Because of the size and weight of

these items, they are manufactured to order, and are not available for immediate purchase. Many precast manufacturers that make commercially available building products from architectural precast are also able to manufacture custom architecture components.

NOTES: This book uses the term "tooling" as a manufacturing term, referring to molds, dies, and jigs used to shape repetitively manufactured components. However, specific to precast concrete, "tooling" refers to chisels, needle guns, and bush hammers, used for post-production finishing after the component has been stripped from the mold. For clarity, the term "mold" is throughout this section, rather than "tooling."
–
In casting concrete, because the mold media have as much impact on the design parameters as the concrete material itself, design parameters of molds are listed under Tooling. For universal design parameters for concrete, exclusive of the molds' design, see Material Considerations starting on p. 266.

TOOLING

Although typically cast in open molds, for special shapes and applications, concrete can be cast in closed or semi-closed molds. Closed molds are appropriate for components with front and back finished faces, or for components that require consistent wall thicknesses, but where the walls are too steep to be formed with a screed. For example, precast concrete column covers are

7 Large mold being prepared for casting

8 Steel-hinged molds

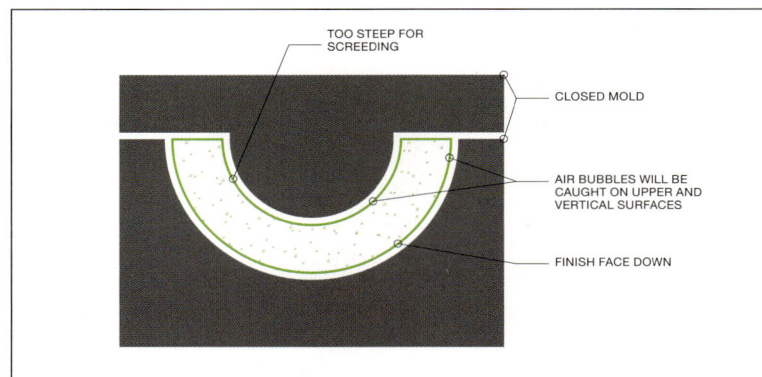

9 Closed molds are used when component walls are too steep to keep the concrete from flowing

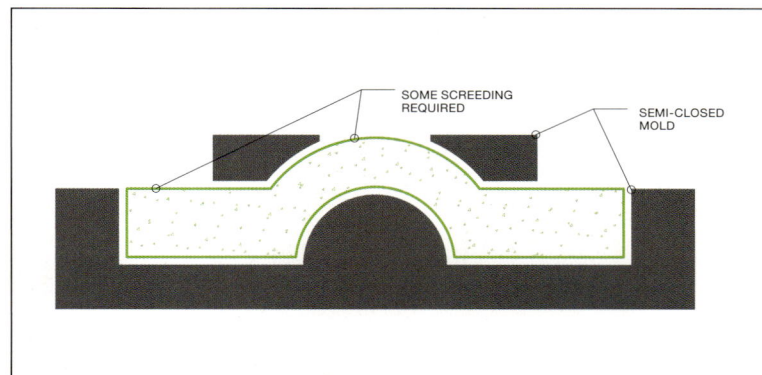

10 Semi-closed mold

best cast in closed molds, as their inner walls may be too steep to prevent concrete slumping into the mold's low point. [9, 10] Semi-closed molds are used for casting components that have projections—such as ribs or corner returns—on their back face. Generally, closed molds are difficult to use for casting concrete. In most cases, air bubbles will rise out of the concrete and collect on the bottom surface of the top of the mold. This will result in a series of bug holes that can only be repaired post-production with patches. In addition, with closed molds, it is difficult to judge whether enough concrete has been placed and if the concrete has enough flow to fill all of the parts of the mold, but not so much that it does not stay in place.

Molds may be envelope molds, for which a single piece of material, such as foam, fiberglass or rubber, is used to form the mold, or they can be built up using multiple pieces that can be broken down. Built-up molds are made from plywood, MDF, or steel and are disassembled to strip the component. Depending on how the mold is disassembled and at what angle the component is removed, built-up molds require no draft angles and can have sharp corners where the mold is disassembled. To keep water and cement from seeping out of a built-up mold, the joints are caulked before each casting.[1] This extra step can increase the labor costs and production schedule for built-up molds when compared to envelope molds. Meanwhile envelope molds are kept intact as the

component is stripped from them, and even if used repeatedly, neither the mold nor the component should be damaged. Depending on the mold material, envelope molds require draft angles on all of the vertical faces. It is also best to provide small radii or chamfers at interior and exterior corners to keep them from breaking. Because envelope molds are kept intact as the component is removed, they have tighter tolerances than built-up molds.

In built-up molds, it is common practice to use mold or form liners. A form liner is a sheet of material placed on the bottom of the mold to form the finished face of the architectural precast. Form liners can be made of any material, but are typically made from thermoformed plastic or rubber. [11] Gravity holds the liner in place during pouring, and form liners can easily be changed between pours. Typically, they are made to fit the mold bed, but they can be made smaller and rearranged to make patterns on the cast concrete. For example, the 656 precast panels on the Perot Museum of Nature and Science by Morphosis (2012) in Dallas, Texas, were made in four different built-up mold boxes with a series of rubber mold inserts, uniquely arranged at the bottom of the built-up mold for each panel. Because the components of a built-up mold are moved between each pour, tolerances can be more difficult to maintain.

Generally, molds for casting concrete have to be strong enough to support the concrete's weight, absorb minimal amounts

11 Built-up mold with a rubber form liner

13 High-gloss concrete surface, cast against a gel-coated, FRP mold

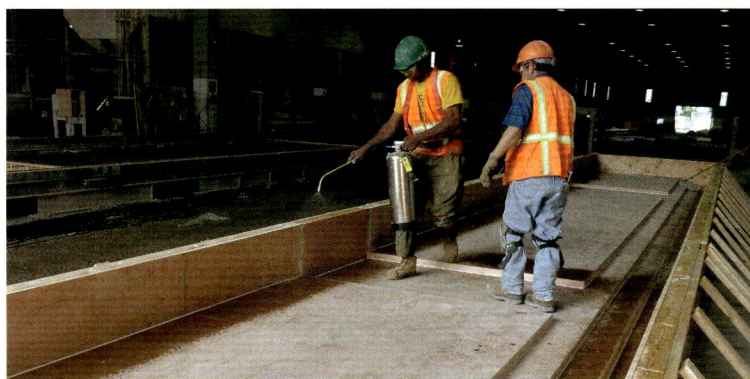

12 Workers coating the mold, prior to concrete pour

14 Post-production finishes available; typically acid washing or grit blasting

of water, and resist leaking. Molds can be made of a variety of different materials, including Styrofoam, thermoplastic, wood or plywood, rubber or elastomerics, FRP, and steel. In casting architectural concrete, the mold material is as important to the component design than are the properties of the concrete. Each of the different mold media results in different component shapes and finishes.

Since water is necessary for the curing of concrete, any water loss or absorption by the mold will affect the concrete performance and finish. This means that molds made from porous materials such as wood and plywood should be sealed. Even with sealing, differences in water absorption rates of the mold will permanently affect the shade and color of the concrete's surface. This results, for example, in wood grains being visible on the concrete's surface after the concrete has been stripped of its mold.

The mold's surface affects the qualities of the face of the concrete cast against it. [12] Typically, the glossier the mold, the shinier the concrete's surface cast against it will be. Gel-coated FRP and polished steel molds can result in satin or gloss finishes, whereas plywood and wood result in a smooth, matte surface. [13, 14] The Precast/Prestressed Concrete Institute (PCI) recommends not using the direct mold finish for concrete; instead it recommends post-production finishing such as sand-blasting or acid washing. Both of these processes remove the weaker laitance layer of the concrete, roughen the surfaces to varying degrees, and expose some of the concrete's aggregate. [15] Generally, color variations and manufacturing defects are more apparent in direct-finish precast components, and this is a particular concern if the panels are large and flat.

Most precast manufacturers have the ability to make their own molds out of wood, plywood, MDF, or melamine-coated particle board. The molds may be coated with a single layer of fiberglass and resin or paint, or coated with polyurethane and caulked at the interior corners. [16] A limited group of precast manufacturers have more specialized mold-making equipment, including CNC mills or CNC wire cutters for foam. In most cases, contact-molded FRP, thermoplastic form liners, and steel molds will be contracted out. Contact-molded FRP molds will be made by a contact molder (Chapter 3.1), thermoplastic molds by a plastic thermoformer (Chapter 1.2) and steel molds by a steel fabricator, perhaps with access to CNC equipment. For mold materials—such as rubber, FRP, and thermoplastic—the design parameters for mold making have to be considered along with the parameters of casting the concrete. That is to say that if an architect is interested in casting against a custom thermoplastic liner, the architect needs to consider both the plastic thermoforming process and the concrete casting process.

Aside from steel molds, most mold materials are relatively inexpensive; however, the labor costs involved in fabricating the molds can be high. Often a manufacturer will modify molds to achieve variation between components rather than fabricate a new mold for each component. For example, form liners can be changed out between pours for surface design variation with little to no added cost. Manufacturers may use dams inside of larger molds, to make smaller variants of larger pieces. [17] This allows for some variety without the costs associated with making more molds. For example, in the Mulberry House apartment building, SHoP Architects (2013) in New York City subdivided a large rubber mold into eight different shapes to form the building's precast composite panels.

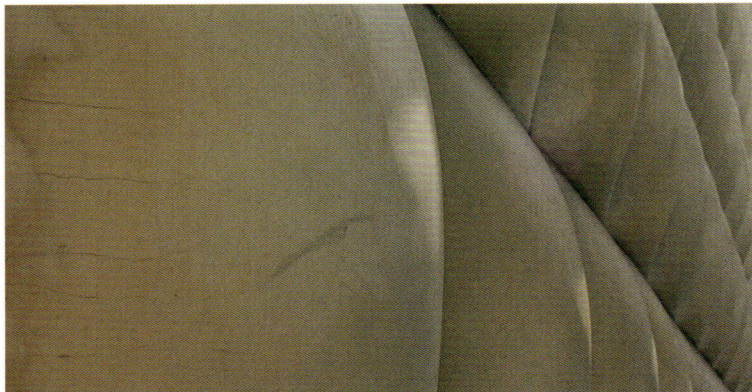

15 The laitance layer of concrete is weak, and likely to crack when exposed to weather

16 Plywood mold coated with a single layer of FRP, for increased durability

17 Temporary dam placed inside a larger mold. This allows the manufacturer to adjust the panels' lengths

FOAM MOLDS

Foam molds tend to be made from inexpensive foams like Styrofoam, rather than the more expensive high-density tool foams used in thermoforming plastic (Chapter 1.2), contact molding (Chapter 3.1), or bladder inflation molding (Chapter 3.2). Foams are also chosen for their ease of shaping, which can be done by hand, CNC mill, or CNC hot-wire foam cutters. The low cost is balanced by very low durability. Foam molds are weak and they often break when the precast concrete is stripped; manufacturers often use foam only once before recycling or disposal. Because foam is a natural insulator, foam molds are not ideal for thick concrete pours. During curing, the concrete that is closest to the foam mold will cure at a higher temperature than the rest. This can cause surface inconsistencies, requiring patching or additional post-production finishing.[2] The larger the pour, the more heat is generated (and the thicker the foam required to support the concrete, thereby adding even more insulation).

SIMILAR PROCESSES

In many ways, casting concrete is a unique process. Compared to other concrete manufacturing processes, such as vibration-press casting (Chapter 4.4) and vibration-tamping (Chapter 4.5), this process uses a wetter mixture that flows into parts of the mold. In this way, casting concrete is more similar to casting metal (Chapter 4.2) or casting glass (Chapter 4.3). This results in concrete components with a denser and smoother surface finish than can be achieved with either concrete blocks (Chapter 4.5) or cast stone (Chapter 4.6).

CORNERS

Internal component corners should have a 0.5in (13mm) radius or chamfer. This will protect the mold when the component is stripped.

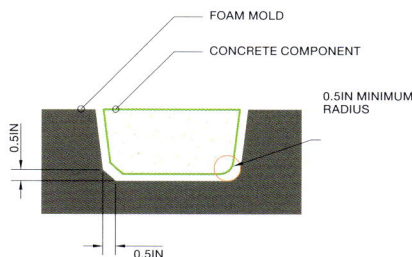

DRAFT ANGLES

The draft angle should be 7° or more for delicate envelope molds. If there is a large surface area (e.g. for ribbed concrete), the draft should be 9.5° or more.

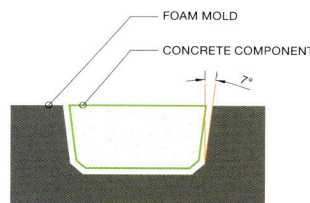

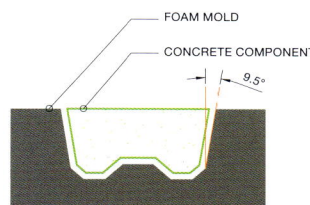

If a steeper draft angle is required, use a slip block, which is temporarily attached to the wall of the mold. As the component is stripped from the mold, the slip block is also removed, and may then be reused.

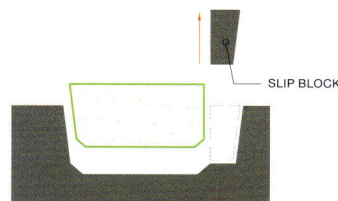

DRAW DEPTH

For envelope molds or deep form liners, limit the draw to 9in (225mm) or less. For built-up molds, there will be no limit to the draw.

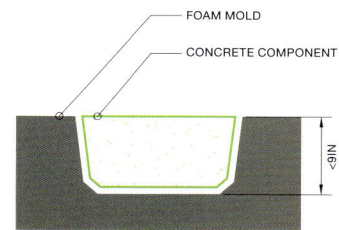

FINISH

The surface quality of foam-cast concrete is low. There will be some flow of the concrete between the cells of the foam, causing some bubble-like roughness on the surface. Post-production finishing such as grit blasting or acid washing is recommended.

PRODUCTION VOLUME

The number of components made from a single foam mold can range from one to fifteen, depending on the foam strength and the component's design parameters (e.g. draw depth, draft angles).

SURFACE TEXTURES

Limit the depth of the design to 0.5–1in (13–25mm), depending on the width of the depression. Surface designs should have a draft angle of 9.5° or more.

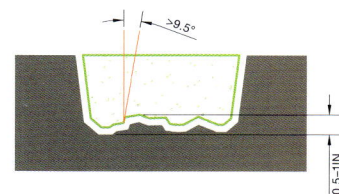

UNDERCUTS

Undercuts are not permissible with foam, unless the mold is sacrificed.

FIBERGLASS MOLDS

Fiberglass molds [18] are made from a composite of glass fibers (woven or mat) and resin. Fiberglass is usually used for envelope molds, but can also be used for lining forms. Typically, the fiberglass mold will have a gel-coat, which gives a high-gloss surface to the fiberglass and a high-gloss finish to the concrete. The advantages of a fiberglass mold are its durability and the finish it gives the concrete.

Making fiberglass molds is a two-step process, similar to making rubber molds. (See Chapter 3.1 for the process of contact molding.) Patterns are usually made from CNC-milled foam that has been gel-coated. Most precast manufacturers will buy their fiberglass molds from contact molders.

18 Fiberglass envelope mold

CORNER RADII

Corners for fiberglass are limited to a 0.25in (6mm) radius.

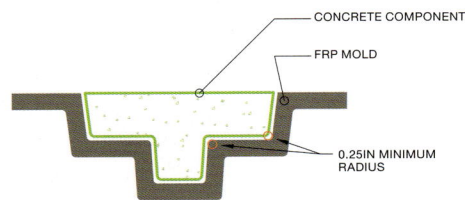

CONCRETE COMPONENT
FRP MOLD
0.25IN MINIMUM RADIUS

DRAFT ANGLES

The draft angle should be 4.5° or more for envelope molds. If there is a lot of surface area (e.g. for ribbed concrete), the draft should be 7° or more. Fiberglass molds are slightly flexible, so a steeper draft angle can be used if the mold is flexible enough to be pulled away from the component.

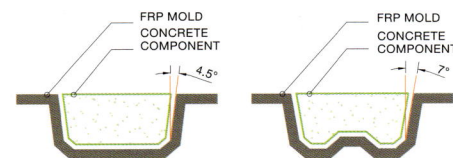

FRP MOLD
CONCRETE COMPONENT
4.5°

FRP MOLD
CONCRETE COMPONENT
7°

FINISH

The surface quality of FRP is very good. It will be a smooth surface, ranging from a satin to a shiny finish. Post-production processes such as acid washing or grit blasting should be used for exterior applications.

PRODUCTION SPEED

Once made, fiberglass molds require little to no preparation prior to pouring concrete.

PRODUCTION VOLUME

Fiberglass molds can produce 200–1,000 components before needing repair.

TOOLING COSTS

Fiberglass molds are more expensive when compared to foam, plastic, wood, and most rubber molds. This cost is offset by their durability.

UNDERCUTS

Undercuts are not permissible.

CASTING CONCRETE IN FIBERGLASS MOLDS

EXTERIOR TILE | 3.1 PHILLIP LIM FLAGSHIP STORE
by Leong Leong Architects
Seoul, South Korea

19
Front façade and details of the
3.1 Phillip Lim Flagship Store

20, 21
Building entrance

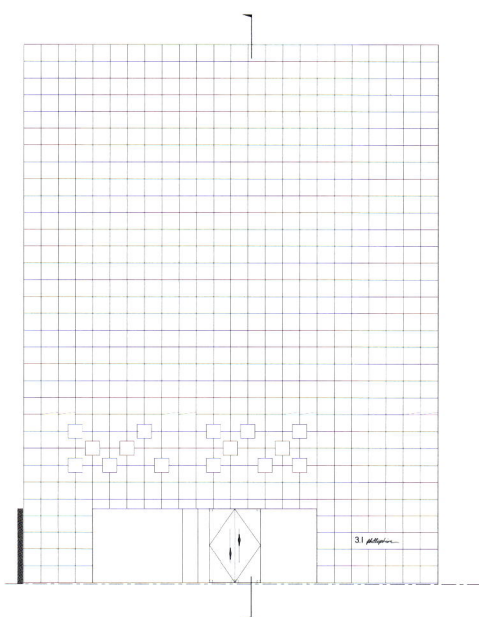

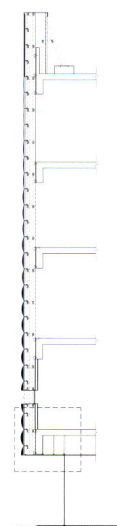

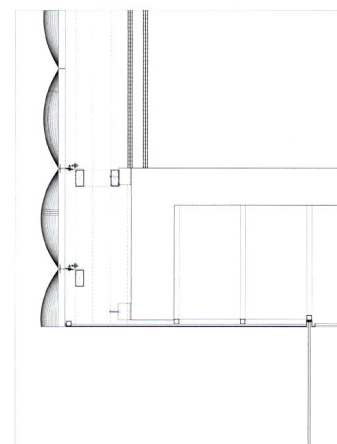

The 3.1 Phillip Lim Flagship Store, completed in 2009, is located on one of the major streets in Seoul's fashion district, called Cheongdam-Dong. [20] Similar to its surrounding buildings, the Phillip Lim store is set back from the wide sidewalk, and provides a few convenient parking spaces at the front. There is a small alley separating the building from the neighboring Armani store, and there is a DKNY store around the corner.

The project was a renovation of an existing four-story building; two floors are dedicated to the store and two floors to office space. [19] It was a design-build project, in which Leong Leong was the project designer and Dadam was both the project's local architect and its contractor. This allowed for the 5,850 ft^2 (550m^2) project to be designed and constructed in only eight months.

DESIGN CONSIDERATIONS

The Seoul flagship store is the second Phillip Lim flagship store that Leong Leong designed. The first was in Los Angeles, California, and was completed earlier in the same year as the Seoul store. According to Dominic Leong, the firm first strove to create an identity and brand for the retailer through both

19 Building elevation, wall section, and entry detail

buildings, and yet at the same time have both buildings stand apart from each another.[3] The façades of both stores are covered in pillowy tiles, giving the buildings a quilt-like look that is reminiscent of the brand's fashion. The Los Angeles store tiles are smaller than those manufactured for the Seoul store. The Los Angeles store was constructed out of aerated concrete, and the architecture office collaborated with a pool tile fabricator in Long Beach to better understand the process.

When designing the Seoul store, the firm wanted to build on its experience with the Los Angeles store and develop the façade further. Because the Seoul building was taller, the firm made the scale of the tile larger. It also designed the building with seven different convexities of tiles, and arranged the tiles as a gradient from most convex at the ground level to flat at the top of the parapet. [21] In the Seoul store, the tile pattern is disrupted by the windows above the entrance. Intentionally, the centers of the windows are located at the intersection of four tiles, allowing the windows to be simultaneously part of and separate from the grid of tiles.

MANUFACTURING CONSIDERATIONS

The tiles were cast individually inside fiberglass molds [22] which left a satin finish on the concrete surface that Leong liked. Leaving that finish on the concrete juxtaposed the smooth surface of the concrete with the quilt-like form of the tiles.

OTHER CONSIDERATIONS

All of the tiles were cast and erected individually, instead of being ganged into larger precast panels. Leong believed that this was done because the individual tiles were easier to handle than larger panels. This is done on construction sites where access is difficult for trucks carrying large precast panels, where cranes are suitable, or where labor costs are low.

LESSONS LEARNED

For this project, Leong Leong learned that it had to accept limitations of control, especially in the context of this project's eight-month design and construction schedule. [23] This was a fast-track project, faster than the firm had initially realized. Leong Leong sent the Rhino model for what it thought was going to be used for making a project mock-up. When visiting the project, expecting to see the mock-up, the firm found that building construction and tile production were already underway. Because of this, there was little to no collaboration between the tile manufacturer and the architect's office.

It was beneficial to the design that the team members had worked on the Los Angeles store prior to the Seoul store. This gave them the opportunity to collaborate with a precast manufacturer first, to see what was possible. Leong believed that without that experience, they may not have tried the tiles on the Seoul store.

22 FRP molds

23 The building during renovation

RUBBER MOLDS

Rubber molds are cast using liquid latex that cures into a flexible rubber mold. [24] The advantage is that the material is flexible, allowing rubber molds to be peeled away from the component. Rubber molds are best for components with steep or negative draft angles, intricate surface details, or undercuts. Rubber can be used as both envelope molds and as form liners in built-up molds. Generally, rubber molds are very durable and can be used for high-volume concrete productions.

Some precast concrete manufacturers have the ability to cast their own rubber molds, but many will buy their molds from another company. Making rubber molds is a two-step process. [25] First, the positive, or pattern, is made; then it is cast against the rubber against the rubber to make the mold. Patterns can be made using CNC-milled foam, plaster, MDF, modeling clay, 3D printed plastic, or almost anything. For example, for the A16 Motorway Toll Booths (1998) in the Picardy region of France, Manuelle Gautrand Architecture arranged leaves and sticks in a mold box, fixed them in place, and poured the rubber over the plants to create the form liner for its precast concrete panels. If the pattern material is durable, multiple rubber molds can be cast on a pattern for parallel production capabilities; if the pattern is not, it can be sacrificed to make the rubber mold.

24 Rubber form liner

25 Making a rubber mold. From closest to furthest away: Pattern, rubber mold, and precast decorative component (not in a frame)

CORNER RADII

Corners do not require a radius or chamfer; however, corners in the concrete will not appear sharp, as the weight of the concrete can soften rubber edges.

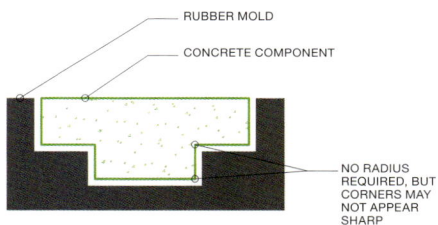

RUBBER MOLD
CONCRETE COMPONENT
NO RADIUS REQUIRED, BUT CORNERS MAY NOT APPEAR SHARP

DRAFT ANGLES

The draft angle can be 0°, with some areas with negative draft. Be aware that vertical sides or negative drafts will trap air against the surface, resulting in bug holes on the concrete's surface.

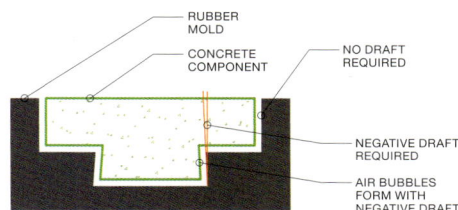

RUBBER MOLD
CONCRETE COMPONENT
NO DRAFT REQUIRED
NEGATIVE DRAFT REQUIRED
AIR BUBBLES FORM WITH NEGATIVE DRAFT

FINISH

The surface quality of rubber-molded cast concrete is high. Depending on the pattern's surface (i.e. the surface on which the rubber was cast), the concrete surface can range from a honed, stone-like finish to a satin-smooth finish.

SURFACE TEXTURES

Rubber molds are particularly useful for panels with delicate textures with fine details.

PRODUCTION SPEED

Concrete should be left in a rubber mold for 24 hours after pouring. Because rubber molds are used with steep draft angles, intricate details, and undercuts, the concrete must be strong enough to be stripped from the mold.

PRODUCTION VOLUME

Rubber molds are durable, and can last 50–100 pulls without damage, depending on the amount and depth of detail.

TOOLING COSTS

Rubber molds typically range from $30 to $40 per square foot of casting. Rubber molds are more expensive when compared to foam, plastic, or wood. This is offset by their durability and ability to form fine details.

UNDERCUTS

Small undercuts are permissible with rubber molds. Bug holes may form at the edge of the undercut.

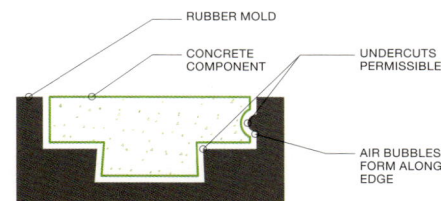

RUBBER MOLD
CONCRETE COMPONENT
UNDERCUTS PERMISSIBLE
AIR BUBBLES FORM ALONG EDGE

CASTING CONCRETE IN RUBBER MOLDS

EXTERIOR CLADDING PANELS | ATHLETES' VILLAGE BLOCK N15
by Niall McLaughlin Architects
London, UK

The Athletes' Village Block N15 is one of the mid-rise residential buildings built in Queen Elizabeth Olympic Park for the 2012 London Olympics. **[26]** Located in Stratford, northeast of Central London, the Athletes' Village is accessible by rail, subway, or bus. As with most Olympic housing units, the London Olympic Village was designed to house athletes during the Olympics and Paralympic Games, and then after the Games concluded the units would be transformed into long-term housing. The units would include one- to four-bedroom apartments; half were to be sold at market rate and the other half were intended to be affordable. The design of the Athletes' Village needed to comply with the standards and regulations set by the Olympic Development Authority (ODA), the needs of a real-estate development group that would manage the long-term residential units, and the expectations of the city of London.

During initial project planning, it was decided that only four architectural practices would design the residential buildings' overall layouts, including plans, interiors, circulation cores, and structure. Because the ODA's standards are complex, limiting the design of the buildings to only four firms was intended to reduce costs and time. At the same time, London wanted a dynamic design for the Athletes' Village that would demonstrate architectural design diversity. Towards that end, twenty-five more experimental firms were hired to design the façades that clad the buildings designed by the other four firms.[4]

Glenn Howells Architects was one of the four firms hired to design the buildings' plans, and Niall McLaughlin Architects was hired as a sub-consultant to design one of Howells' building's façades. During the team's initial meeting, Howells stated that McLaughlin was free to do what he wanted with the façade's design, except syncopated windows. In other words, Howells rejected designs that used sliding windows across the façade, which had become "the ubiquitous answer to cladding nondescript commercial and residential interiors."[5]

McLaughlin established a grid across the building façades so that windows, balconies, and precast concrete panels all aligned. **[27]** Five different mold designs, measuring approximately 7.25ft × 7.25ft (2.2m × 2.2m), were made for this project. Five different widths, measuring approximately 3ft, 4ft, 5.5ft, 6ft, and 7.25ft (0.95m, 1.2m, 1.65m, 1.8m, and 2.2m), were cast on the five mold designs. This gave the design team twenty-five panel variants to randomly disperse throughout the façades' grid. Located in North Lincolnshire, UK, and just over 160 miles (260km) from the Olympic Village, Techrete manufactured over 1,500 panels, covering approximately 147,500ft² (13,700m²).

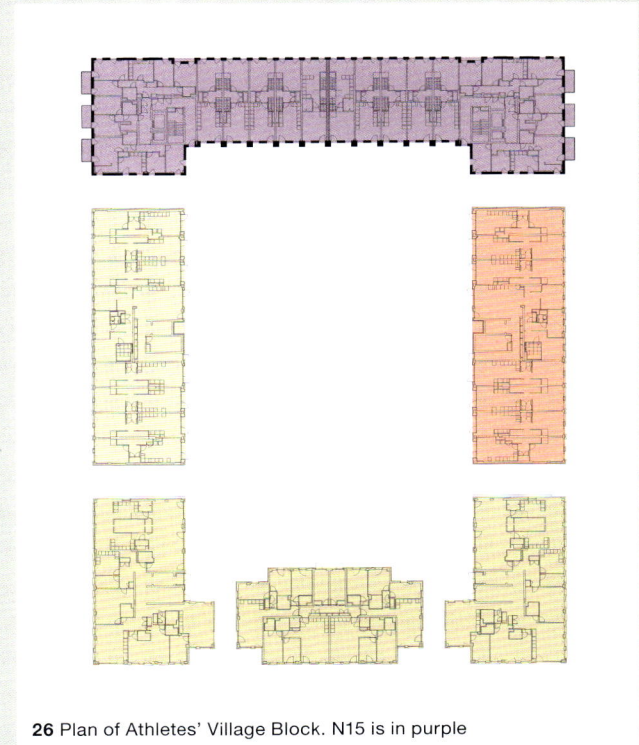
26 Plan of Athletes' Village Block. N15 is in purple

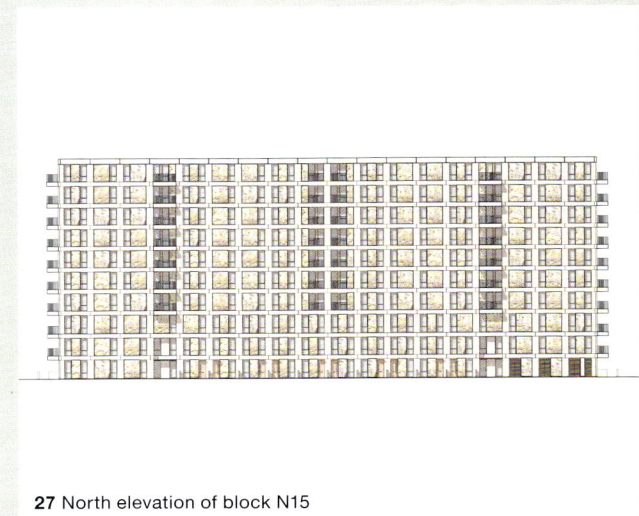
27 North elevation of block N15

28

29

30

DESIGN CONSIDERATIONS

Many architects find separating the architectural design of the building's overall layout from that of the skin uncomfortable at best, and unworthy at worst.[6] However, for Niall McLaughlin, this separation between the two became the leading idea for the project.[7] Influenced by the writings of Gottfried Semper and Karl Bötticher, McLaughlin is interested in ideas of representation in architecture; therefore designing only the façade allowed him to explore this more fully.[8] Toward that end, McLaughlin wanted the façade to have a design relation to history, ornament, representation, and symbolism for a wide audience.

McLaughlin chose to sample the Elgin, or Parthenon, Marbles for his façade, and distributed them randomly in the established grid. [28, 29, 30] Since they hang in the British Museum, the Elgin Marbles have already been removed from their original context in the Pantheon. McLaughlin removed them further by organizing them in a grid on the façade, essentially eliminating the hierarchy between the scenes and negating their original linear organization. Originally, McLaughlin chose five carvings that theoretically related to the notation of representation, including the presentation of the sacred apples to the goddess Athena. However, when the team was laser scanning the Marbles, Ian Jenkins, senior curator of Ancient Greece at the British Museum, gave a lyrical description of the stones. [31, 32] He urged McLaughlin to consider that the Marbles were "all about the horses," so McLaughlin changed his mind, and had other sections of the Marbles scanned. According to McLaughlin, the all-night event in the museum, scanning and talking about the Marbles, is the highlight of his career.[9]

McLaughlin's firm made minor alternations to the sculpted reliefs as they exist on the Marbles. Originally located under the Parthenon's cornice, the Marbles' top edges were not designed to be exposed to precipitation. However, for McLaughlin's application on the building façade, the reliefs would be exposed to London's weather. McLaughlin modified the relief so that the top surfaces of the cast components were no longer undercut and instead sloped slightly away from the panels' surface. This allowed the water to be shed away from the concrete panels' surface. On the underside of the sculpted relief, the original Marbles' undercut was left, creating a natural drip edge for the surface.

28
Finished façade of the Athletes' Village
Block N15

29
Detail of concrete relief panel

30
Detail of façade

31
Panoramic image of 3D scanning of the
Elgin Marbles in the British Museum

32
Detail of 3D scanning of the Elgin
Marbles in the British Museum

PARTHENON NORTH FRIEZE

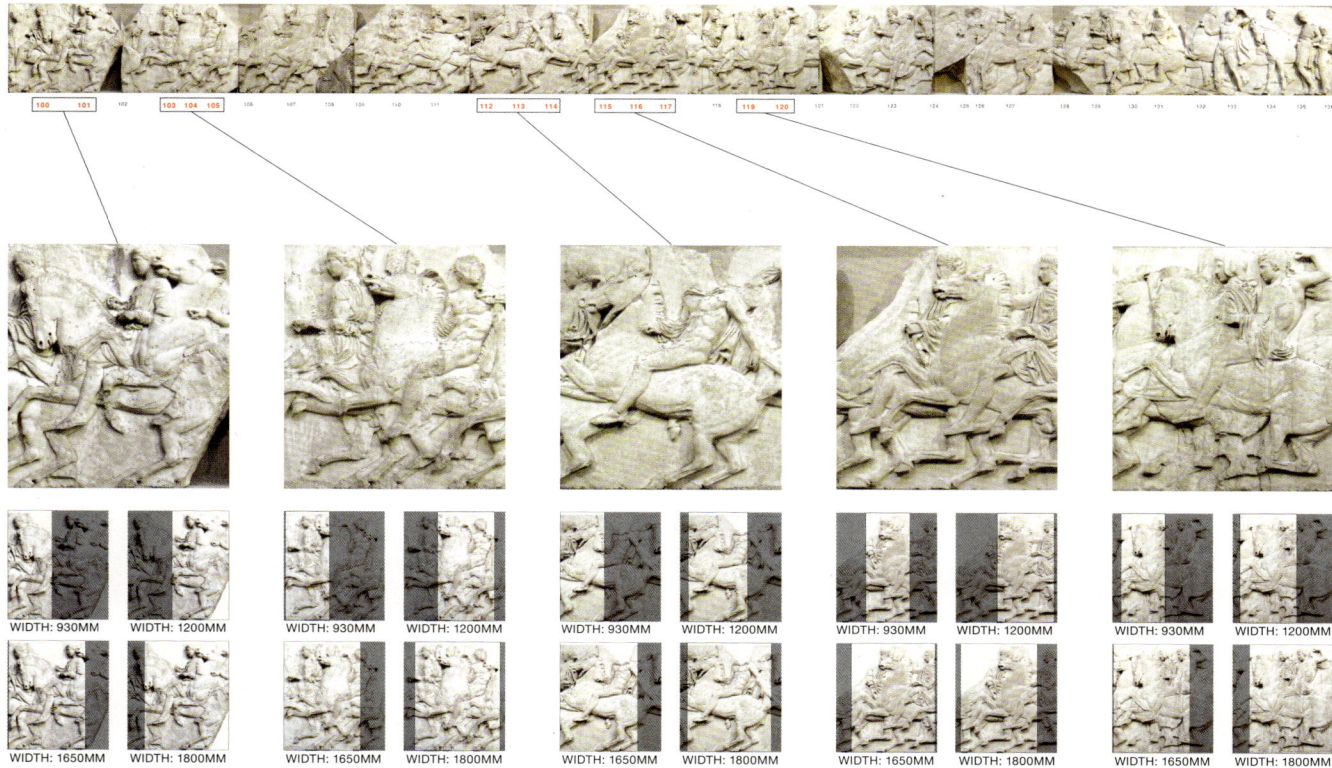

33 Selected panels from the Parthenon frieze with the associated panel widths

The five panels were selected to make the full 7.5ft (2.3m) wide panels, which were then dammed into smaller molds to cast the five narrower widths. **[33, 34]** The placement of the dams within the larger mold was based on the composition of the relief on the smaller pieces. McLaughlin set the cast representations of the Marbles next to flat panels that represent a trabeated system of columns and beams on the façade. The truncated edge of the Marbles cast the shadows of the sculpted images' profiles. False joints were placed between the flat and sculptured panels, to make them look as if they had been made separately. **[35]**

MANUFACTURING CONSIDERATIONS

A five-axis CNC mill was used to fabricate five plugs from high-density polyurethane. **[36]** Typically, Techrete had a particular subcontractor that it used to CNC fabricate plugs; however, this subcontractor only had a three-axis CNC mill and could not fabricate the necessary undercuts. McLaughlin wanted the five-axis mill to replicate the Marble's undercuts. Ultimately, McLaughlin solicited support from London Mayor Boris Johnson to ensure that the five-axis CNC mill would be used.

The plug to make the 7.5ft (2.3m) square panel was too large to fabricate on the five-axis CNC mill. According to McLaughlin, this required that the plug be made of two or three separate sections fitted together. When the sections were joined, the seam between them needed to be finely filled and sanded by hand so that it would not translate to the cast rubber, and ultimately to the concrete.

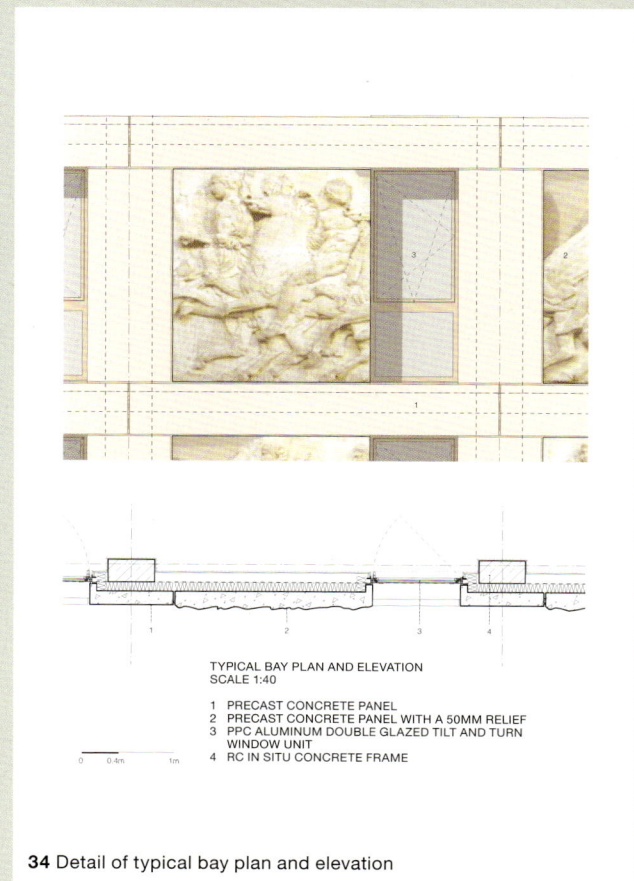

TYPICAL BAY PLAN AND ELEVATION
SCALE 1:40

1 PRECAST CONCRETE PANEL
2 PRECAST CONCRETE PANEL WITH A 50MM RELIEF
3 PPC ALUMINUM DOUBLE GLAZED TILT AND TURN
  WINDOW UNIT
4 RC IN SITU CONCRETE FRAME

34 Detail of typical bay plan and elevation

Techrete cast rubber, or latex, twice against each plug to make the molds for the sculpted surface. [37] Working with ten molds, Techrete could cast many of the components simultaneously, greatly reducing the overall production time. The rubber molds preserved the undercuts inherent to the Marbles and allowed Techrete to easily strip the concrete castings from the mold. Once the full-width molds were made, temporary dams were used to make the smaller widths. The face of the dam was cut to meet the profiled surface of the relief, and caulk was used to temporarily seal the dam so that wet concrete did not seep out during casting. Project costs limited the number of variant rubber molds that could be made, and the number of different widths that could be cast within each panel.

After the panels were stripped from the molds, they were acid etched to expose the aggregate and remove the laitance layer. McLaughlin remembers it taking 2 days to produce each panel, and 100 days to produce all of the panels.

OTHER CONSIDERATIONS

The concrete is made from a white cement; dolomite from Malaga, Spain, and buff sand. This gives the panels a white color that is similar to the Marbles in their current state. Water repellent was never applied to the concrete due to required cost reductions. McLaughlin supported this, as he likes that the panels will age over time, changing slowly while reflecting the natural conditions.

This was a highly political project, with numerous stakeholders. Techrete was supportive of the project and enthusiastic about the castings. When the design team visited Techrete, they saw on the employees' door images of the Marbles' horses. McLaughlin believes that the precasters enjoyed being a part of this project's history and story. This relationship benefited McLaughlin, as there were times when the ODA would schedule a visit to Techrete without the design team being present. When this happened, Techrete contacted McLaughlin so that his office was involved with any architectural decisions.

LESSONS LEARNED

One of the lessons that McLaughlin learned from this project is how to be proactive with value engineering. It seemed that, at many times throughout this project, design decisions were being made without the designers. At one point, McLaughlin recalled being told that his façade would need a base, middle, and top. After arguing that this would be counter to his façade concept, he finally agreed, knowing that he could remove these features during value engineering. The team did a pre-value engineering exercise, running a series of studies, with a schedule, and the completed outcome. They design team also reviewed altering the depth of the relief, the number of plugs and molds required, and the number of different panel widths, as methods for cost reduction.

35 Close-up image of mock-up panel with false joints

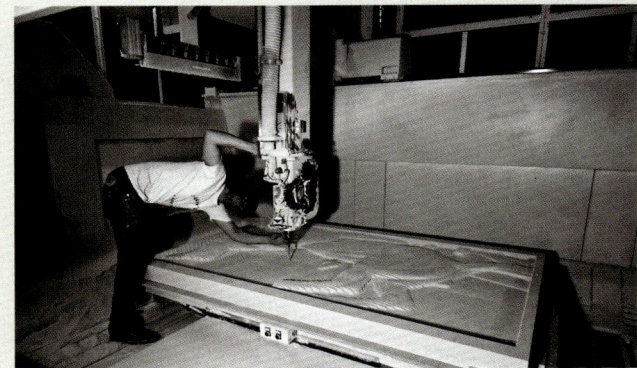

36 Five axis CNC-machining of positive pattern, from which the rubber would be cast to make the mold

37 Rubber form liner

THERMOFORMED PLASTIC MOLDS

Thermoformed plastic is typically used for form liners in built-up molds. [38] It is inexpensive, easily formed, and easily cut to size. The design parameters are limited by the manufacturing processes for both thermoforming plastics (Chapter 1.2) and casting concrete. Depending on the gauge and strength of plastic used, thermoformed plastic molds are slightly more durable than foam molds, but much less durable than wood, FRP, rubber, or steel. Generally, they are best used for productions that exploit the repeatability of a thermoforming plastic mold, but do not rely on using thermoplastic molds repeatedly in casting concrete. Examples could include thermoforming a number of small tiles that are ganged together in large concrete panels, or thermoforming form liners to pour multiple concrete molds for parallel production to increase production speed. Thermoformed plastic works well to hold thin-set bricks for pouring precast concrete composite panels. [39] The precast manufacturer buys these directly from the thermoformer, and often keeps them in stock as jobs come in. These panels are formed with standard brick sizes, joint sizes, and the desired joint profile. For composite panels, the concrete flows between the bricks to the thermoformed plastic surface. After the concrete cures and the panel is removed from the form, the panel is pressure washed with a mild acid. [40] This removes the laitance layer at the joints and any cement that may have seeped between the brick and the form liner.

38 Thermoformed plastic form liner

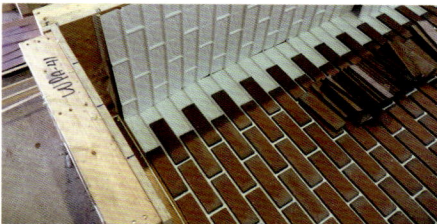

39 Thermoformed plastic form liners, to hold thin-set brick for composite precast panels

40 If cement flows between bricks and form liners, it can be pressure-washed off with acid

CORNERS

Internal component corners should have a 0.5in (13mm) radius or chamfer, or greater. This will protect the mold when the component is stripped. Exterior corners should have a 0.12in (3mm) radius or chamfer to protect the component's corner from breaking.

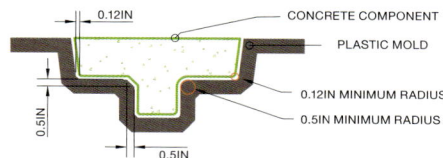

DRAFT ANGLES

The draft angle should be 7° or more. If there are multiple drafts or a lot of surface area (e.g. for ribbed concrete), the draft angle should be 9.5° or more.

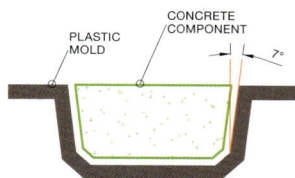

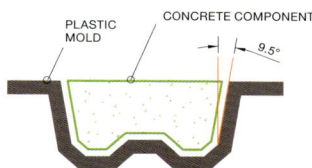

DRAW DEPTH

The draw depth should be limited to 12in (300mm) or less, depending on the plastic's strength.

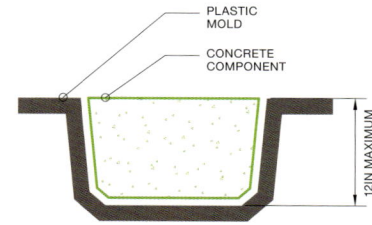

FINISH

The surface quality of plastic-cast concrete is high. For exterior applications, it is recommended to remove the laitance layer with post-production finishing.

PRODUCTION VOLUME

The number of components made from a single foam mold can range from one to thirty, depending on the gauge and strength of the plastic, the draw depth, and the draft angles.

SURFACE TEXTURES

Limit the depth of the design to 0.5–1in (13–25mm), depending on the width of the depression. Surface designs should have a draft of 9.5° or more.

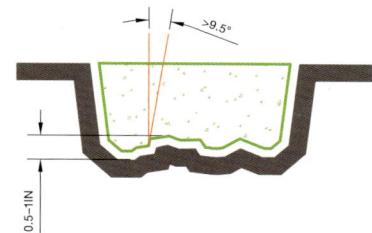

TOOLING COSTS

Thermoformed plastic form liners typically range from $1 to $3 per square foot of casting.

UNDERCUTS

Undercuts are not permissible with plastic, unless the mold is sacrificed.

WOOD MOLDS

Included in this section are molds made from wood, plywood, MDF, melamine-coated particle board, or any combination of these. **[41, 42, 43]** Wood molds are easily built and modified, but can be labor intensive. Most precast manufacturers will build their own wood molds for casting, and many will have access to a CNC mill for specialty work. Generally, wood molds are susceptible to changing dimension and shape with changing moisture and ambient temperature conditions. It is not recommended to use wood molds for production runs over a long period of time.

Wood molds are typically built up from multiple pieces, and will required caulking in between pours to keep cement from seeping into the joints and damaging both the component and the mold. Although built from smaller pieces, wood molds can be either envelope molds or molds that are broken down to the precast. Breaking down a mold each time reduces the required draft, but increases labor costs, wear on the mold, and production time.

The wood is often coated with polyurethane, paint, or other coatings to resist water absorption. Even so, the wood grain may still translate to the concrete surface. If this is not desired, the concrete should be finished post-production with acid washing or grit blasting. The wood can also be textured to change the finish of the concrete. Typical wood textures include sand-blasting the wood or leaving it rough-sawn.

41 A small melamine-coated particle-board mold, with sacrificial wood trim to form a drip edge

42 A large wood mold

43 CNC mill for specialty work

CORNER RADII

Corners can be sharp, but often have a small—0.12 in (3mm)—radius, due to the caulk at the joints.

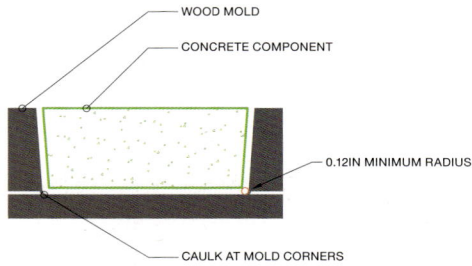

WOOD MOLD
CONCRETE COMPONENT
0.12IN MINIMUM RADIUS
CAULK AT MOLD CORNERS

DRAFT ANGLES

The draft angle should be 4.5°, or more for an envelope mold.

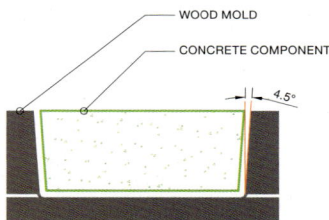

WOOD MOLD
CONCRETE COMPONENT
4.5°

If there is a large surface area (e.g. ribbed concrete), the draft should be 7° or more.

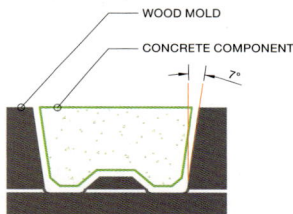

WOOD MOLD
CONCRETE COMPONENT
7°

If a steeper draft angle is required, consider using a slip block.

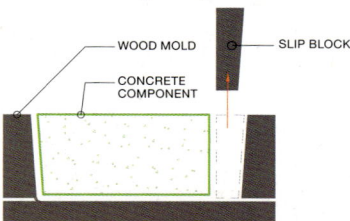

WOOD MOLD
SLIP BLOCK
CONCRETE COMPONENT

Another option for a steeper draft angle is to use a mold with a removable side.

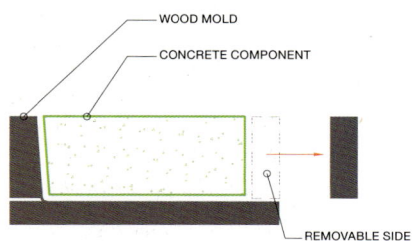

WOOD MOLD
CONCRETE COMPONENT
REMOVABLE SIDE

FINISH

The surface quality of wood-molded cast concrete is moderate, and it may pick up the wood grain of the mold.

PRODUCTION SPEED

Each joint in a wood mold requires caulking prior to casting the concrete. The keeps the water and cement from leaking at the joints and potentially causing damage to both the component and the mold during stripping. After the component is stripped from the mold, any caulk that remains is cleared and replaced with new caulk. Because wood molds are built up from many pieces, there can be many joints, which can greatly decrease the production speed.

PRODUCTION VOLUME

A wood mold can be reused for thirty to forty pulls. For designs with eased draft angles, chamfered or rounded corners, and relatively simple profiles, a mold can be used for up to 100 pulls, but it is likely that the mold will need to be repaired during production.

SURFACE TEXTURES

Surface textures can be intricate. Limit the depth of the design to 0.5–1in (13–25mm), depending on the width of the depression. Surface designs should have a draft angle of 7° or more.

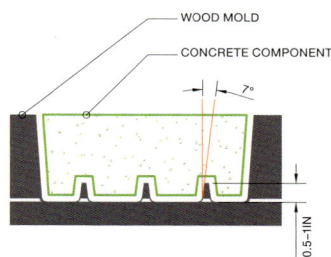

WOOD MOLD
CONCRETE COMPONENT
7°
0.5–1IN

TOOLING COSTS

Wood molds can range from inexpensive to moderately expensive, depending on complexity and size.

UNDERCUTS

Small undercuts such as drip edges can be done with a sacrificial trim piece that is lightly tacked to the sides of the mold (see figure 4.1.41). When the component is stripped, it rips the trim piece from the mold. The trim piece is then pulled out of the component, often breaking in the process.

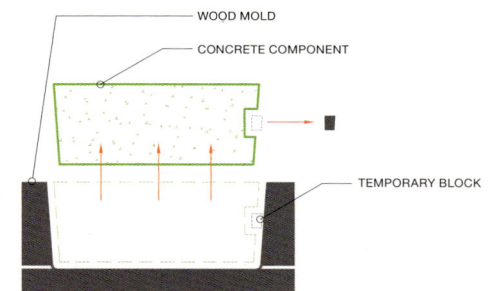

WOOD MOLD
CONCRETE COMPONENT
TEMPORARY BLOCK

CASTING CONCRETE IN WOOD MOLDS

EXTERIOR WALL PANELS | CREMATORIUM HEIMOLEN
KAAN Architecten
Sint-Niklaas, Belgium

The Crematorium Heimolen, completed in 2008, is located on the edge of Sint-Niklaas, in an existing cemetery. **[44, 45, 46]** The project includes two buildings—the Ceremonial Building for quiet thought and reflection, and the Crematorium where cremation happens. The Ceremonial Building is located on the southwest corner of the site, and the Crematorium is at the northeast corner. A small lake separates the two buildings. According to Vincent Panhuysen, founding partner at KAAN Architecten, the Ceremonial Building and the Crematorium are architectural inverses of each other.[10] The Ceremonial Building is a collection of smaller buildings unified by an extended canopy roof. The Crematorium is a single building that is grounded by an extended stereotomic base.

Inside the Crematorium are three cremation ovens as well as inside gathering space for immediate family, while extended observers can gather outside the building on its base. The building is approximately 34,000ft^2 (3,187m^2) and measures 325ft × 130ft (100m × 40m) and 30ft (9m) high. **[47]**

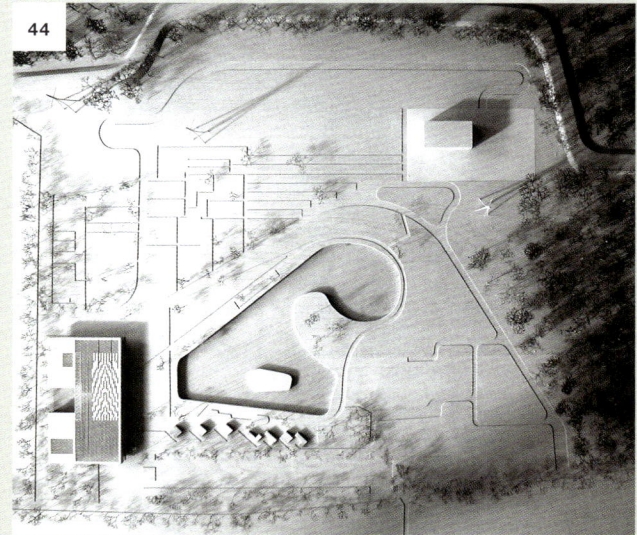

Decorating the surface of the Crematorium are "cassette tiles" that measure 3.25 × 3.25ft (1m × 1m) and have a pattern of concentric, inset squares. The inset squares are offset in elevation from one another by 2in (50mm) and step back into the concrete by 0.5in (13mm). Across the center of the façade, there is a scattering of three different window sizes, the arrangement of which was inspired by a flock of swallows taking flight.[11] The windows are square, centered in the tiles, and measure 5.5in, 9.5in, and 13.4in (140mm, 240mm, and 340mm), matching the dimensions of the tiles' square pattern.

SVK, a precast concrete manufacturer in Sint-Niklaas, won the bid to produce the panels. SVK used stacked painted plywood squares to form the inset-square pattern. The squares were arranged in a grid on the bottom face of the concrete mold. Wood dividers were placed between the squares to create a recessed imitation joint between the cassette tiles. The precast concrete panels are reinforced with steel, and are engineered to support the Crematorium's steel-structured roof. After casting, the panels were acid washed, which softened their surfaces and exposed the natural aggregate. The panels are left exposed on the building's interior. Because of the heat generated by the cremation ovens, no insulation is necessary in the exterior walls.

DESIGN CONSIDERATIONS

The building was designed as a monolithic monument. At 30ft (9m) tall, KAAN could hide the cremation chimneys behind the exterior wall. This gives dignity and a quiet solitude to the building without "the familiar and depressing oven-and-chimney appearance" associated with most crematoriums.[12] **[48]** In the original design, to give the Crematorium a monolithic appearance, the design team had proposed that the building be constructed out of site-cast concrete. The concrete wall was designed with an intricate window pattern that connected the building's interior to its exterior. As the team developed the design, they realized that the wall they were proposing would be cost prohibitive and could not be cast in one lift.

To work within the budget, KAAN made the change from site-cast concrete to precast concrete; however, it wanted to maintain the monolithic appearance of the building by hiding the soft joints between the precast concrete panels. The design team chose to hide the joints by introducing a new surface design more akin to masonry block, or tile construction. Inspired by Frank Lloyd Wright's textile block houses, Panhuysen and his team developed a pattern of the 3.28ft (1m) square cassette tiles with intricate patterns that could be ganged together to form the larger panels associated with precast concrete. **[49, 50]**

There are two advantages to the cassette tiles. **[51, 52]** First, they obscure the soft joints between the precast panels. The precast panels measure 6.5ft (2m) wide and 29.5ft (9m) tall and are made up of the ganged cassette tiles, organized two across and nine high. In between each cassette tile is a 0.75in (19mm) wide and 1.2in (30mm) deep joint between the cassette tiles and at the edges of the precast panel. The deep joint obscures the panel's soft joints in shadow. Second, the inset square geometry of the tiles accommodates the three different window sizes at little to no additional cost.

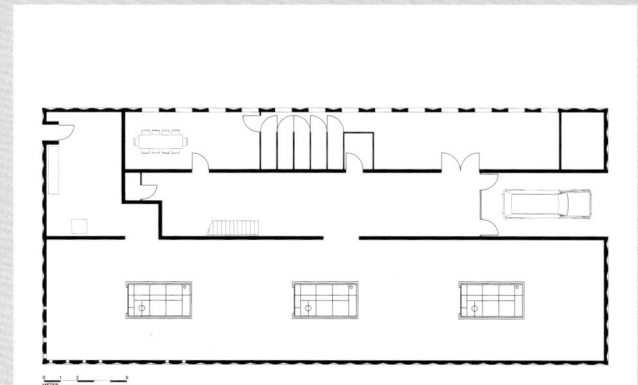

47 Crematorium ground-floor plan

48 Competition concept sketch

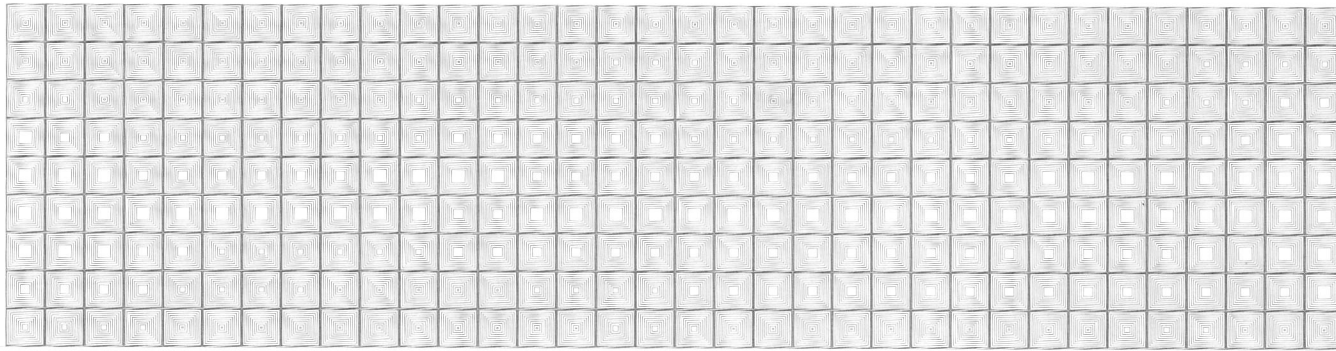

49 Crematorium façade drawing

50 South façade mold type and panel distribution

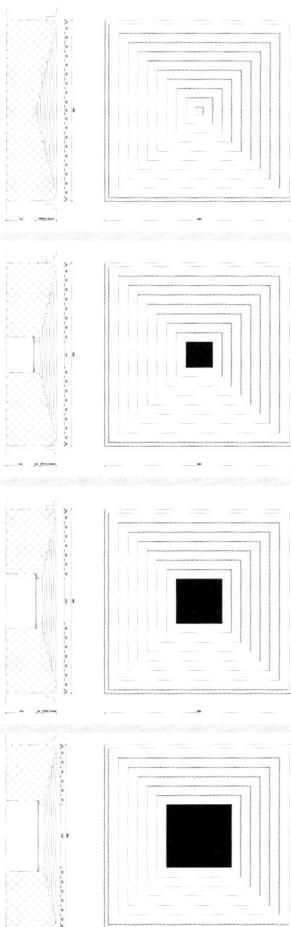

51 Detail of cassette tiles

MANUFACTURING CONSIDERATIONS

KAAN had specific requirements in terms of the quality of the precast concrete. It wanted the concrete to be a natural, light gray with no added colorants. To keep with the overall building concept of a monolith, KAAN also wanted the precast concrete panels to match the building's site-cast base. Because the color of Portland cement varies between batches and is affected by curing, a match between the base and the walls was difficult to achieve. SVK had to produce multiple samples to achieve consistency.

SVK manufactured the corner panels in two separate pours with a cold joint between them. Typically, wet-cast concrete is cast finished side down. This gives the precast a consistent finish, as the aggregate settles to the bottom, and air bubbles are released from the surface (see Material Considerations + Design Parameters on pages 266–267). Once the panel is acid washed, the aggregate will be exposed. If a corner piece is cast with one face down and the other face vertical, the two surfaces will have noticeably different amounts of aggregate and air bubbles. SVK poured one half of the corner panel, finished side down, with a 45° miter joint. After that half cured, SVK turned it vertically and poured the second half against the miter of the first. This allowed both halves to be cast in the same orientation, with the finished side down and the cold joint between the two hidden on the building corner.

The vertical edges of the cassette tile forms had a slight draw angle. This allowed SVK to remove the forms without damage to either the concrete or the form.

52 Close-up of the Crematorium façade. The soft joint, between panels, is the third joint from the left

OTHER CONSIDERATIONS

This project was a design-bid-build project; therefore the design team could not coordinate with the manufacturer of the precast panels until after the construction documents were complete. The design team worked through its assumptions about the manufacturing process without being in contact with a manufacturer. Panhuysen stated that it was beneficial to the project that SVK got the contract. He felt that SVK produced high-quality precast, and being local gave the company a vested interest in this project. **[53, 54]** After SVK was awarded the contract, the design of the cassette tiles developed to accommodate the three different window sizes and their scattered pattern across the façade.

53 Molds by SVK

LESSONS LEARNED

The lesson that Panhuysen learned from this project was the importance of the joint to the overall project design. In this way, KAAN was able to work within the parameters of the manufacturing process, accepting the joints between the panels, and working with them to create a uniform surface pattern. Somehow the joints between the cassette tiles manage the impossible. The need for joints is not denied, and yet simultaneously they are obscured in shadow. Without the investigations of the design team and the commitment of SVK to the project, this might not have been possible.

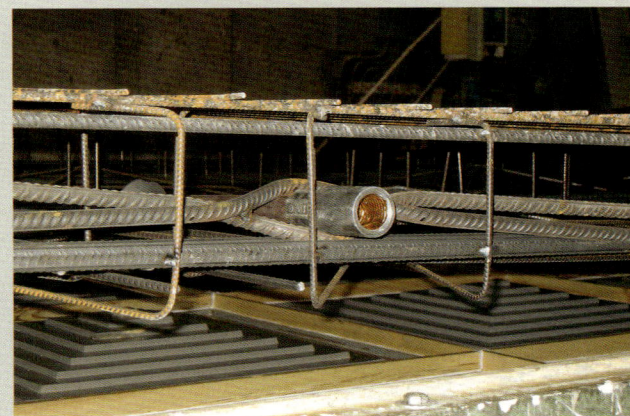

54 Molds by SVK with reinforcing steel

STEEL MOLDS

Steel molds are typically used to cast structural precast, and are less commonly used for custom or architectural precast. Steel is a durable material, and is ideal for large production runs cast over many years. Because of steel's strength, it can be used for vertical pours, that is, for precast components with a lot of depth. Steel is expensive and difficult to shape, and is therefore best used for flat or simple forms without many delicate surface details. Steel molds can be envelope molds or disassembled to strip the component.

Most commonly, steel molds are built up from either flat stock or rolled sheets; the sheets are then supported by a fabricated steel frame. **[55, 56]** The frame helps support a thinner gauge of steel for the mold face, while still allowing the mold to resist the hydrostatic pressure of the concrete. Steel can also be shaped by hand or using CNC milling, but this process takes a lot of time and produces a lot of waste. The corners of the steel can be welded, eliminating the need for caulk, thereby decreasing labor and increasing production speed.

55 Steel bed with pre-tensioned rebar

56 Steel casting bed

CORNER RADII

Corners can be sharp, as the mold will withstand damage. To protect the concrete, there should be a 0.12in (3mm) minimum corner radius or chamfer.

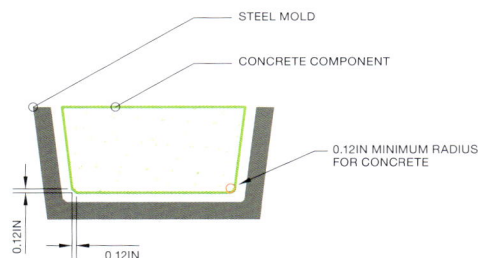

DEPTH

Steel molds are ideal for vertical pours so that components can have two finish faces.

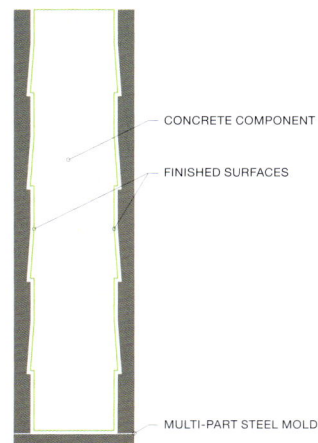

DRAFT ANGLES

The draft angle should be 4.5° or more for envelope molds. If there is a large surface area (e.g. for ribbed concrete), the draft should be 7° or more. No draft angles are required if the sides of the mold can be removed prior to demolding.

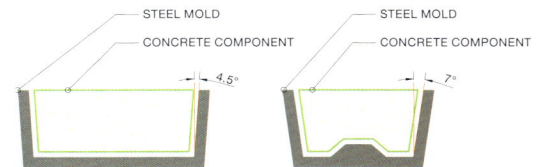

FINISH

Steel molds will produce a smooth surface. The finish can range from matte to glossy, depending on the surface of the steel. For example, if the steel's surface is sand-blasted, the concrete's surface will be similar to a sand-blasted finish; however, if the steel's surface is highly polished, the concrete will be glossy. Because of the time required to polish a steel mold, glossy surfaces are very expensive to produce.

PRODUCTION SPEED

Once made, steel molds require little to no preparation prior to pouring concrete.

PRODUCTION VOLUME

Steel molds can produce 1,000 components or more before requiring repair.

SURFACE TEXTURES

Although surface textures are possible with steel, they are not cost effective. It would be better to use plastic, rubber, or FRP form liners in the steel molds.

TOOLING COSTS

Steel molds are the most expensive molds.

UNDERCUTS

Undercuts are not permissible.

CASTING CONCRETE IN STEEL MOLDS

EXTERIOR WALL | 33 MACKENZIE STREET
Elenberg Fraser
Melbourne, Australia

33 MacKenzie Street, or 33M, is an apartment building located on the edge of Melbourne's central business district. **[57, 58]** The building is thirty-three stories tall and with a gross floor area of 355,000ft² (33,000m²). The building has a mix of one- and two-bedroom apartments and amenities such as parking, ground-floor commercial space, a gym, a pool, terraces, a private dining room, and social spaces. CEL Australia, an international property company, was the project developer, and Brookfield Multiplex, a large, international construction company, was the contractor. Brookfield hired Elenberg Fraser to provide the design and project documents in twelve months. Building construction took eighteen months, and was completed in 2012.

The building massing includes a podium of ground-floor commercial space and three and a half stories of naturally ventilated parking space. Above

57
Exterior view of 33 MacKenzie Street

58
Tower façade detail

the podium are six towers, clad in concrete and glass, ending at various levels to create rooftop terraces. Elenberg Fraser's writing on the design of 33M speaks about the project as a story of ascendance and transcendence, inspired by the angel Metatron.[13] In that spirit, the architect decorated the building in a geometric abstraction of feathers. The feathers stand alone as the open screen for the parking podium and are embedded as surface decoration on the apartment towers' load-bearing precast concrete panels.

The feathers on both the open screen and the six towers are similar and yet different. All of the feathers are trapezoidal in elevation and wedge-shaped in section. Their bottom edge projects 2.4in (60mm) from their top edge, and their edges are eased with a tapered chamfer. The typical feathers on the parking podium are ganged into sets of two, connecting vertically and spanning two stories. [59, 60] Those panels measure just under 19.5ft (6m) tall and 5ft (1.5m) wide. [61] The feathers on the towers are inverted from the ones on the podium. They are embedded in a load-bearing concrete panel that supports the building's floor and spans only one story. For these panels, the feathers are ganged horizontally, typically in groups of three or more. [62]

Advanced Precast, located just over 25 miles (40km) from the project site, manufactured the precast panels, and was selected through an open bid process.

DESIGN CONSIDERATIONS

According to Caleb Smith, project architect for 33M, the design team generated twelve or more design options for the precast components.[14] The design team investigated different patterns using round or punched windows, and different relief designs for the concrete. When evaluating the design of the panel, the team would then put that design into the overall building elevation to see the design result. To better understand how the panel could be made, the design team also visited Advanced Precast. In the yard of the facility, the design team saw precast components that Advance Precast had made for other projects. From that visit, the team felt that it understood the process well enough to improve the design. The team did the detail drawings, which then became the shop drawings.

As the team members developed the design of the feathers, they developed their shape and size to be versatile and rationalized within the overall building design. The feathers are a module across the facade, and their spacing remains consistent and offset from story to story. On the podium, even as the feathers turn the building corner, the feather on top maintains the same overlap relative to the feather below as it does on the flat façade. In this manner, the feathers appear to be marching continuously around the parking garage. On the towers, the feathers do not turn the corners. Instead the vertical edge of the feather is used to terminate the left edge of the panel, and the upper right corner is used to terminate the right edge of the panel.

MANUFACTURING CONSIDERATIONS

According to Smith, Melbourne in particular and Australia in general are known for good-quality precast. The steel molds were made from CNC

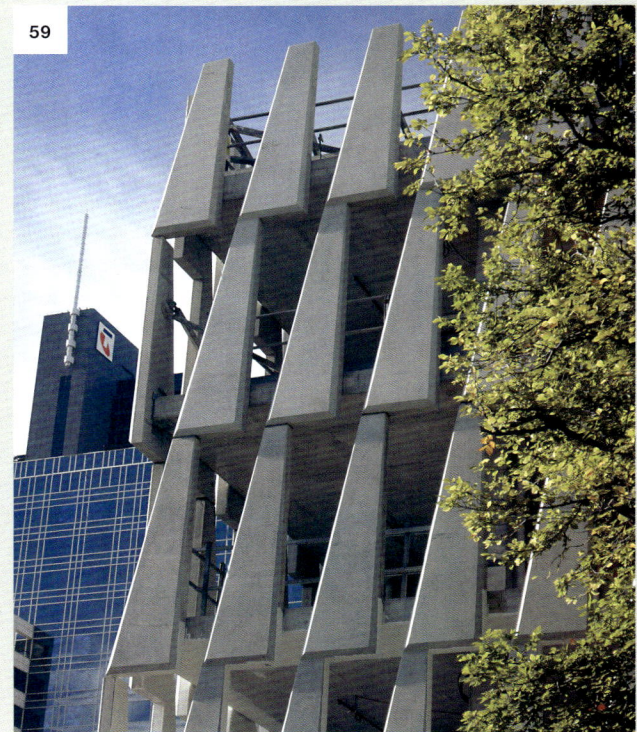

59
Podium panel installation, during construction

60
Installed podium panels, during construction

TYPE 1 PANEL—PLAN DETAIL

RECESSED FIXING OF
POCKETS TO PANELS
AROUND PODIUM
APARTMENTS

TYPE 1 PANEL—SECTION DETAIL

TYPE 1 PANEL—ELEVATION DETAIL

61 Podium precast panel details

TYPICAL TOWER PANEL—DETAIL PLAN

TYPICAL TOWER PANEL—DETAIL PLAN

TYPICAL TOWER PANEL—DETAIL ELEVATION

TYPICAL TOWER PANEL—DETAIL ELEVATION

62 Tower precast panel details

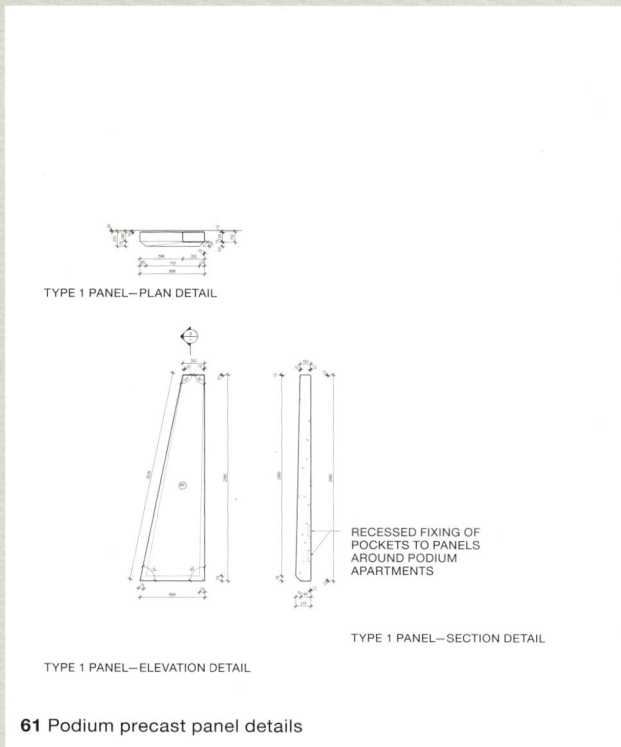

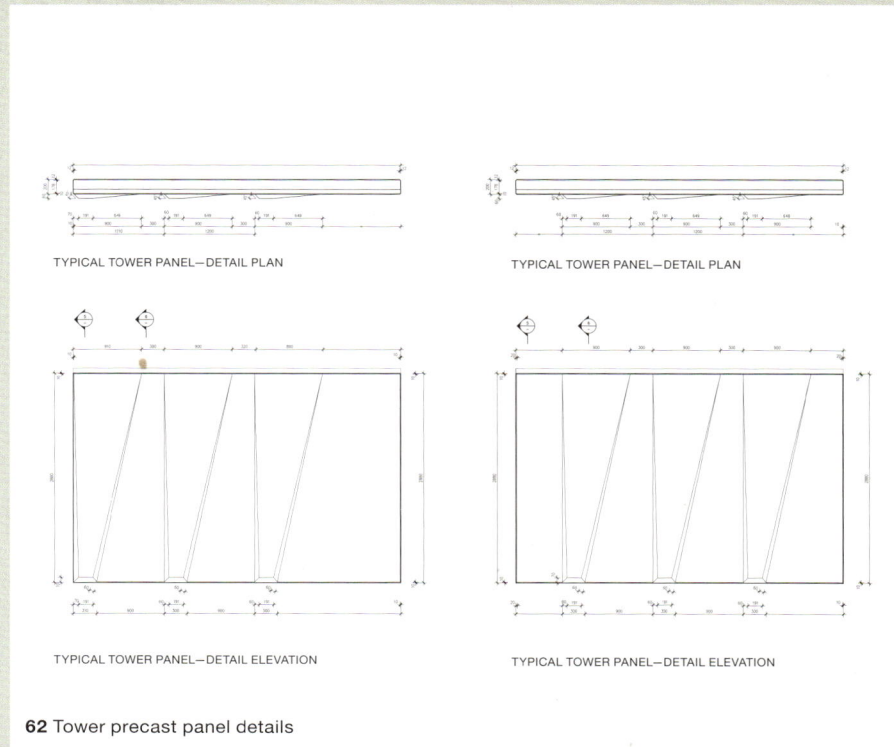

water-jet-cut 0.4in (10mm) steel plates, assembled by a steel fabricator and hand welded. The joints were ground at the corners and the steel was given a shiny finish. As Smith said, the molds were "beautiful—like jewelry." Four molds—two for the podium and two for the tower—were fabricated for parallel productions. **[63, 64]** This allowed one mold to be poured while the other was curing. The molds were made to be oversized and then were dammed with temporary dividers. This allowed the manufacturer to make components with minor modifications without having to make another mold.

Although steel molds are expensive to make, there are a number of benefits to using them. First, 33M's precast panels were manufactured over the course of a year. Unlike wood molds, which tend to break down with moisture and heat over time, the steel mold lasted the required twelve months and ensured that the last panel cast had the same quality as the first panel cast. Second, the mold gave the concrete a clean release with crisp corners, which the architect liked. **[65, 66]** Finally, after the concrete was poured, the mold and the concrete could be vibrated vigorously without damage to the mold. This reduced the air bubbles on the concrete's surface.

Despite the fact that steel can impart sharp corners on the component, Advanced Precast requested that the architect introduce a 0.4in (10mm) chamfer on the edges of the concrete panels. This helped reduce the possibility of damaging the concrete corners when removing the panel from the mold, and allowed production speed to meet the construction schedule. The construction progressed at a rate of five days per floor.

63 Formwork for tower panels

64 Formwork for podium panels

OTHER CONSIDERATIONS

The additional concrete added to the panel surface was small in comparison to the overall budget. The design team worked within parameters set up by the structural engineer, Webber Design. Webber ensured that the added concrete would not increase the amount of reinforcement steel needed in the panels, or drastically increase the dead load of the building. The projection was limited to less than 2.4in (60mm), keeping the total panel width below 10in (250mm).

Additionally, the construction crane was a limiting factor on the panels' design. In order to stay within the crane's lifting capacity, the design team limited the panel size. This meant that the larger of the tower panels were divided into smaller lengths. The seams between the panels were hidden in the shadows of the feathers' vertical edges. Because the feathers offset each floor, this complicated the manufacturing process and required additional time from the design team. Other than the flat section at the building's parapet, joints between panels are well hidden.

The color of Portland cement varies from buff to gray, depending on the batch; the color of the concrete is affected by the curing conditions of the cement. Because the panels were manufactured over twelve months, Elenberg Fraser was concerned about color variations in the panels. For the design team, any color variation was unacceptable. The team researched using white cement instead of Portland cement, as that would maintain a consistent color; however, white cement was rejected due to the added cost. In the end, Elenberg Fraser specified that the panels were to be painted white with a self-cleaning and stain-resistant exterior paint. **[67]** The paint had the added benefit of hiding the concrete patches used to cover the connection between the podium panels and the supporting slab.

LESSONS LEARNED

This was Smith's first project after joining Elenberg Fraser. One of the lessons he learned was that as the design team members developed their initial idea, they also responded to other considerations—such as the structural parameters set by Webber and manufacturing parameters set by Advanced Precast. Before selecting the precast manufacturer, the design team members reviewed other projects that Advanced Precast had produced. They also requested that mock-ups be made, and they inspected the mold before concrete was poured.

Elenberg Fraser works on many commercial projects that are developer driven, and profit is closely tracked. In the project's original conception, the building had more glass. Precast concrete was introduced as a method to lower construction cost. As the pattern was added to the panels, cost did increase. According to Smith, one of the project's challenges was that Elenberg Fraser worked to convince CEL Australia that the added cost would add value to the project. Since the building has been completed, the firm has been tracking the photographs of their buildings on Instagram and following relevant hashtags, and from those has realized that the public notices and appreciates the added design elements. The firm believes that adding a distinct design feature (such as the feathers) does balance the additional cost, because in a developer-driven market, the popularity of a building can add monetary value.

65 Formwork, corner detail

66 Panel corner detail (before painting)

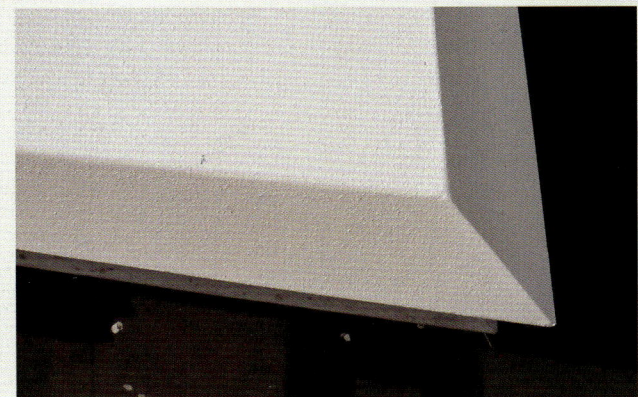

67 Finished panel corner detail (after painting)

ENVIRONMENTAL IMPACT

Generally, casting concrete uses very little energy for production and creates very little manufacturing waste. This process is not highly mechanized, so there are no large machines or moving conveyors, and heat or steam sources are not necessarily required; therefore the manufacturing facilities tend to use low amounts of energy. The manufacturing waste that results from this process is connected with the disposal of the molds themselves. Depending on the material, the type of mold, and how the mold was made, the manufacturer will either throw out the mold or break it down for partial reuse.

However, concrete itself has high embodied energy and requires a lot of water for workability and for curing. The environmental impact of the material can be reduced by replacing some aggregates with recycled content or additives such as fly ash or plasticizers.

MATERIAL CONSIDERATIONS + DESIGN PARAMETERS: CONCRETE

Concrete is a mixture of Portland cement, aggregates (coarse and fine), and water. Optional admixtures can be added to the concrete to alter its properties, including workability, strength, water absorption, ductility, and color. Aggregates can include a wide range of materials, including sand, colored rocks, shaped rocks, and glass. The aggregates are exposed when the concrete undergoes post-production finishing, such as sand-blasting, acid washing, face grinding, and polishing. The color of Portland cement can vary from gray to buff by manufacturer, and by batch. If color is important, use a white cement and add color as desired.

Concrete is made of many ingredients with varying sizes and densities, which affects the casting. [68] First, large aggregates are typically the heaviest, and they naturally settle to the bottom of the pour. This results in more aggregate on a component's finished face, as concrete is cast finished face down. Second, if a component has changing depths, more and larger aggregates will settle to the deeper areas than the shallower areas. Third, aggregates settle against horizontal surfaces, but not vertical surfaces. This, too, will result in an uneven distribution of aggregate that can be particularly noticeable on a component with deep and wide spacing of ribs and other projections. Consider these when specifying a post-production finish such as grit blasting, as it will expose the concrete aggregates.

Air bubbles are trapped as the concrete is poured, and manufacturers will vibrate the concrete to help release them. This works well for horizontal surfaces; however, the air bubbles can get trapped on vertical surfaces and interior corners. [69] This is what causes bug holes and may require patching. If there are a lot of vertical surfaces or interior corners, the manufacturer and architect may consider a self-compacting, high-performance concrete. This minimizes air bubbles and inhibits the segregation naturally associated with concrete and concrete placement but increases costs.

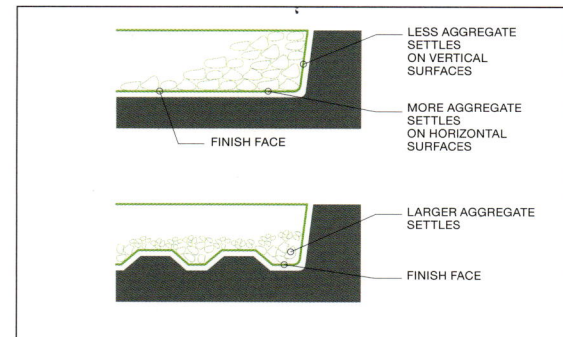

68 Large aggregates settle into the bottom of the pour, resulting in differences on finish faces

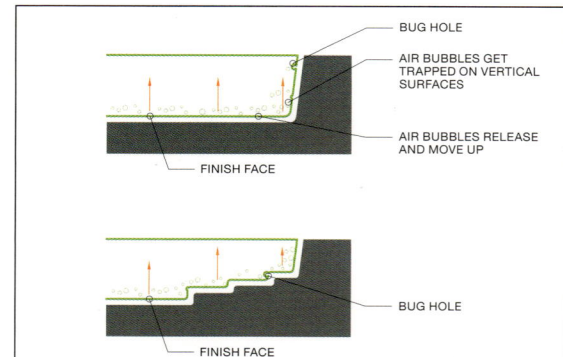

69 Air bubbles release from horizontal surfaces, but get trapped on vertical surfaces and interior corners. This results in bug holes

NOTE: The parameters listed below are inclusive of the material, and do not change based on the mold medium.

CORNERS

To cast concrete panels to turn a building corner, there are two main methods. The first is to cast the component in a single cast with modified formwork to make the return. One face of the panel will be cast horizontally against the mold, and the other vertically. It is recommended to limit the return to 12in (300mm) or less. Note that this method may result in the concrete face being inconsistent due to aggregate settling and trapped air bubbles.

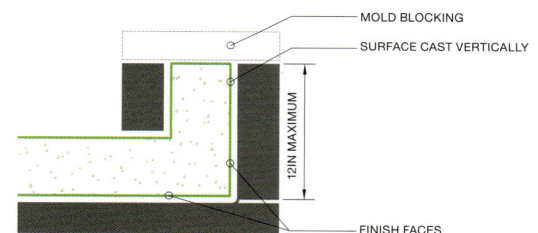

If a consistent finish is required, it is best to make the corner piece in two castings, with a cold joint between (see JOINING).

DRAFT ANGLES

The steeper the angle, the more likely it is that air bubbles will be trapped and bug holes formed.

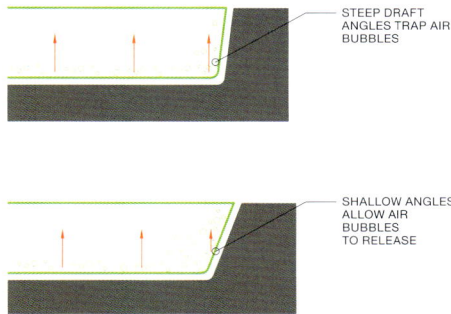

STEEP DRAFT ANGLES TRAP AIR BUBBLES

SHALLOW ANGLES ALLOW AIR BUBBLES TO RELEASE

INSERTS

Concrete can easily be cast around a variety of different materials, including weld plates, reglets, male and female connectors, and handling devices (e.g. eye hooks) to move the components. The tolerance for an insert location for building attachment is within 0.5in (13mm). The tolerance for locating handling devices is within 3in (75mm).

JOINING

Precast concrete can be made with cold joints between concrete pours. In this method, one part of the component is cast finish side down. After it cures, it is stripped and repositioned. New concrete is then poured against the cured concrete, forming a cold joint. Both pours are cast finish face down, ensuring that both finished faces will be of similar quality. This method works particularly well for corner returns (see CORNERS).

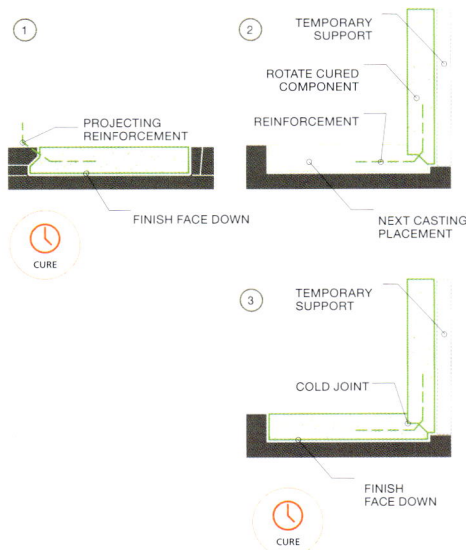

PROJECTING REINFORCEMENT

FINISH FACE DOWN

CURE

TEMPORARY SUPPORT

ROTATE CURED COMPONENT

REINFORCEMENT

NEXT CASTING PLACEMENT

TEMPORARY SUPPORT

COLD JOINT

FINISH FACE DOWN

CURE

PRODUCTION SPEED

Casting concrete is a cyclical manufacturing process with long cycle times. Concrete is typically left in the mold for 24 hours or more before demolding.

RIBS

Ribs may be cast into the panels either for decoration or to add strength without weight. The size and spacing of the ribs will depend on the concrete aggregate. The minimum rib spacing should be 2in (50mm) for a 0.4in (10mm) aggregate.

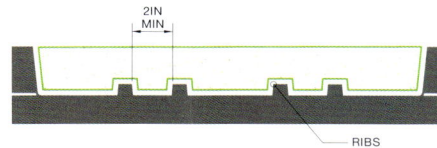

2IN MIN

RIBS

SIZE

Contractors often prefer large or ganged panels so that handling, erection, and on-site labor costs are reduced. The size of the panel is limited by transportation equipment and restrictions. Panels that are 8ft × 8ft × 45ft (2.5m × 2.5m × 13.75m) do not require special permits or equipment. If larger panels are needed, then contractors may use special trailers or purchase permits. Both of these increase costs and production schedules.

SURFACE IMPERFECTIONS

Localized surface imperfections should be limited to 0.25in (6mm) per 10ft (3m). As bug holes are common, a reasonable size for the holes is from 0.12 to 0.25in (3–6mm).

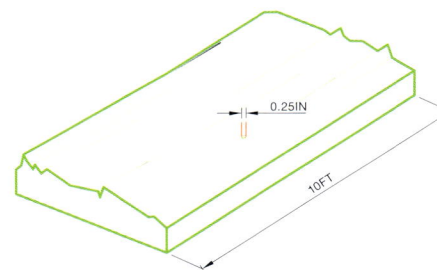

0.25IN

10FT

TOLERANCES

Tolerances will depend on overall precast size, and range from 0.12 to 0.25in (3–6mm) on the finish face. The unfinished face tolerances should be expected to be greater. Ribs and other decoration reliefs have a tolerance of 0.12in (3mm).

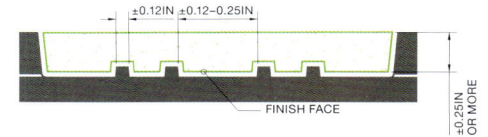

±0.12IN ±0.12–0.25IN

FINISH FACE

±0.25IN OR MORE

WALL THICKNESS

Concrete tends to crack with abrupt changes in geometry. Therefore when designing interior corners it is best to gradually transition from one geometry to the other.

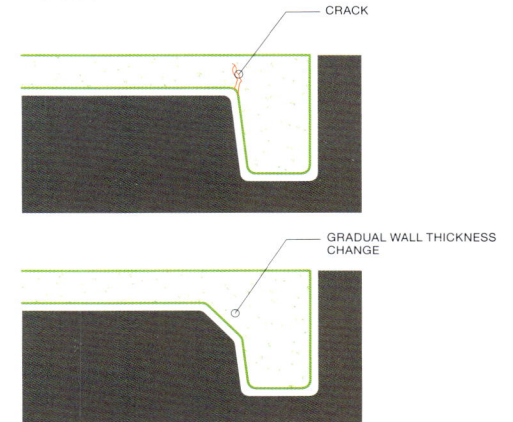

CRACK

GRADUAL WALL THICKNESS CHANGE

WARPING

Components may have a bow length of L/360 up to 1in (25mm). Components may warp up to 0.06in (1.5mm) per foot (300mm).

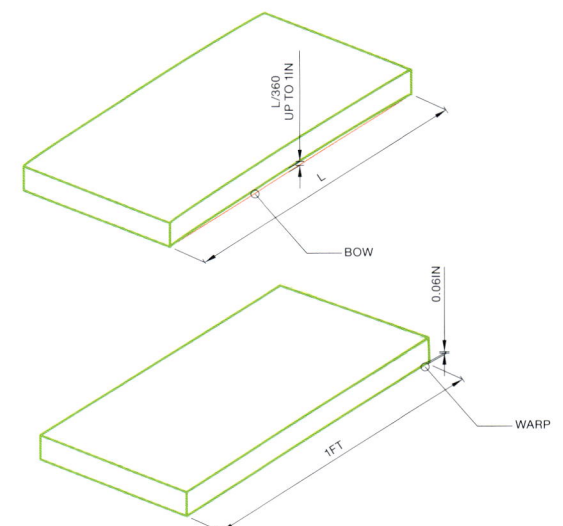

L/360 UP TO 1IN

L

BOW

0.06IN

1FT

WARP

MATERIAL CONSIDERATIONS + DESIGN PARAMETERS: CONCRETE AND BRICK COMPOSITES

Cast concrete components are not limited to a consistent material throughout the casting. Concrete can be cast with brick, ceramic tile, or other facing materials bonded to the concrete, or with one concrete mixture used for the facing material and another concrete mixture used as a back-up material. [70, 71] Using two different concrete mixtures is done when a particular color or aggregate is desired, or if the mold has intricate details that may require a more workable concrete that will flow more easily. The back-up concrete is then selected based on a required structural performance or cost savings.

The predominant composite panel uses brick as the facing material. The benefit of a composite precast panel over that of mason-laid bricks is lower labor and equipment costs. [72] The brick is set into the precast mold by the precast manufacturer, little to no skilled labor is required, and the need for on-site scaffolding and labor is reduced. The brick used for composite panels is a special type that must meet performance specifications set by the PCI. These bricks are manufactured by brick plants (see Chapter 2.1, Stiff mud) and shipped to the precast manufacturer. The composite bricks might have a dedicated die, or the brick manufacturer might take a die for a standard brick and cut it in half to make the thin-set bricks.

The composite bricks range from 0.5 to 1in (13–25mm) in thickness. The face dimensions of the brick are similar to standard available brick sizes such as Modular, Norman, or Utility. Special brick shapes such as corners, edge corners, and end edge corners can also be used for precast concrete corners, sills, and caps. The back surface of the brick may be scored, combed, wire-roughened, ribbed, or dovetailed to ensure a better bond between brick and concrete. Generally, the rougher and deeper the interior surface of the brick, the better its bond to the concrete.

Bricks are set a minimum of 0.4in (10mm) apart to form a joint between the bricks. Form liners or special molds are used to hold the bricks in place as the concrete is poured. [73] The shape of the joint is often formed in the form liner to mimic the tooling joint of a mason. Form liners and molds are typically made from thermoformed plastic or rubber. For composite panels they may be standard to the precast manufacturer and purchased in high quantities from a thermoformer, or they can be custom-made.

Because of the difference in movement between the face material and the back-up concrete, composite panels are often susceptible to bowing; however, the acceptable bowing tolerances are the same between precast concrete and composite panels.

NOTE: The parameter listed here is specific to composite precast concrete panels with a brick facing. For tolerances of the mold medium or concrete, see the previous parameters in this chapter.

70 Composite precast concrete with thin facing brick and colored concrete at face of panel, and structural concrete for panel backing

71 Thin facing brick and precast concrete

72 Thin-set brick in thermoformed plastic form liner, prior to concrete pour

73 Plastic form liner with concave joint profile

TOLERANCES

The tolerance for the mortar joints is 0.12in (3mm).

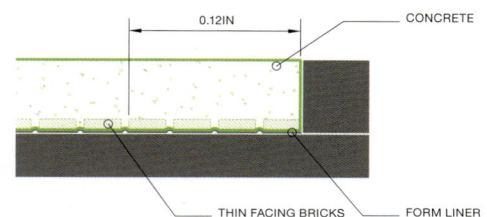

CASTING CONCRETE AND BRICK COMPOSITES

EXTERIOR WALL | VICTORIA GATE ARCADES
ACME
Leeds, UK

The Victoria Gate Arcades is part of a larger development project in Leeds, called Victoria Gate. **[74, 75]** Designed by ACME, Victoria Gate includes a flagship store for John Lewis (a UK-based department store), a parking garage, and the Arcades, which includes multiple stores, cafés, restaurants, and leisure spaces, and is similar to an American shopping mall. The Victoria Gate is located on Leeds City Centre Loop, across the street from the West Yorkshire Playhouse, and in the city's Victorian Quarter. Leeds' Victorian Quarter houses a number of Victorian historic markets like the Kirkgate Market and the Victoria Quarter Arcade. Built for Hammerson Plc, and completed in 2016, the Victoria Gate project includes 381,000ft² (35,400m²) of leasable area, with 301,000ft² (28,000m²) in the Arcades, and parking for up to 800 cars.

According to Catherine Hennessy, ACME project architect for Victoria Arcades, the building materials of the area include black granite, faience (glazed terra cotta), stone, and ornate brickwork.[15] Most of the contextual buildings are highly ornate, with carved stone, cast reconstituted stone, and pressed terra cotta ornament, as well as fine brickwork and corbeling, typical

74
Computer rendering of
Victoria Gate Arcades

74

of Victorian architecture. ACME was interested in having the Victoria Gate project reflect the local context through its materials. The Victoria Arcades has a black, cast-stone plinth; wet-cast, reconstituted stone on the ground floor; and composite, brick-faced, precast concrete panels on the upper floors.

Thorp Precast Ltd. manufactured the reconstituted stone and composite brick panels. There are six different "pleat" designs for the brickwork—P7, P9, P11, P13, P17, P21—ranging from 30in (766mm) wide up to 90in (2,303mm). [76, 77] The numbering of the pleats is based on the number of bricks used to form the pleat's width. The pleats are ganged together to form longer composite precast components in order to reduce erection and crane time. The panels have 6in (150mm) concrete backing at their thinnest depth and up to 16in (400mm) at their thickest. The composite panels are self-supporting, with the lower panels carrying the weight of the panels above. The panels are laterally secured to the building's steel structure via bolted connectors. [78, 79]

DESIGN CONSIDERATIONS

With the ornate Victorian context, ACME believed that with the recent CNC and robot technology, brick would be able to form the three-dimensional exterior wall surface that it wanted. According to Hennessy, ACME explored the idea of using a simple unit with small variations to get a dynamic output with a lot of patterns. ACME produced a number of design options, and then

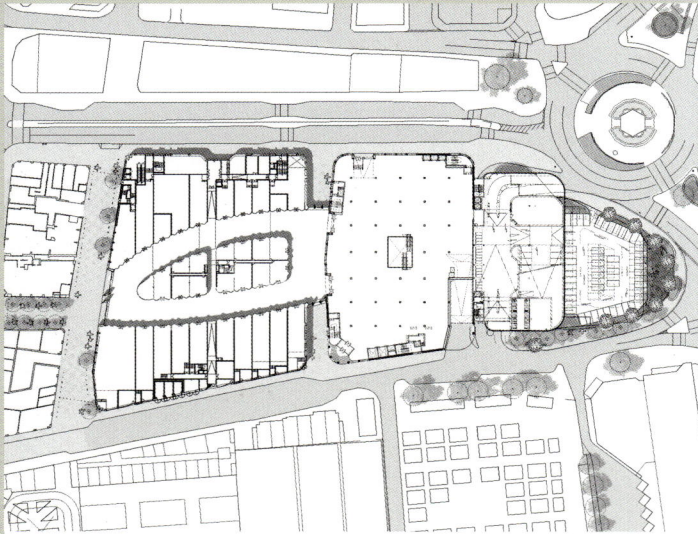

75 Ground-floor plan of Victoria Gate. The Arcades are on the left

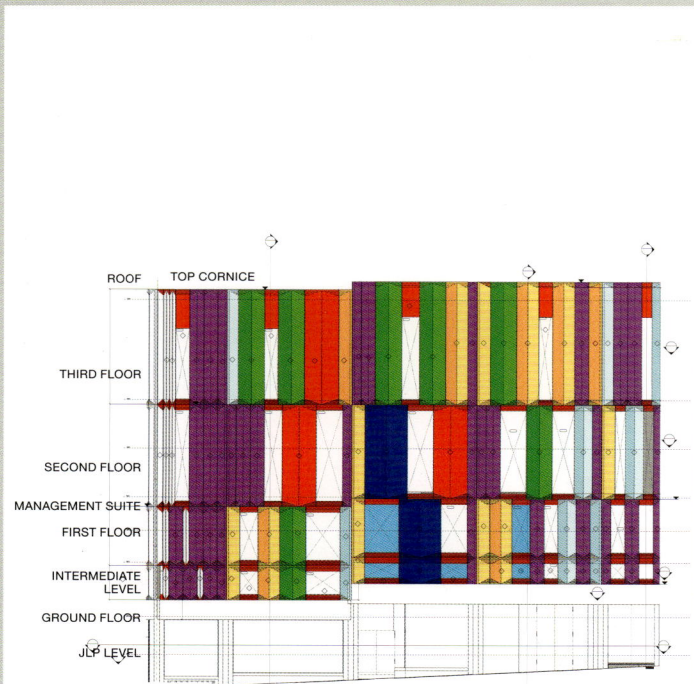

76 Panel types on building façade

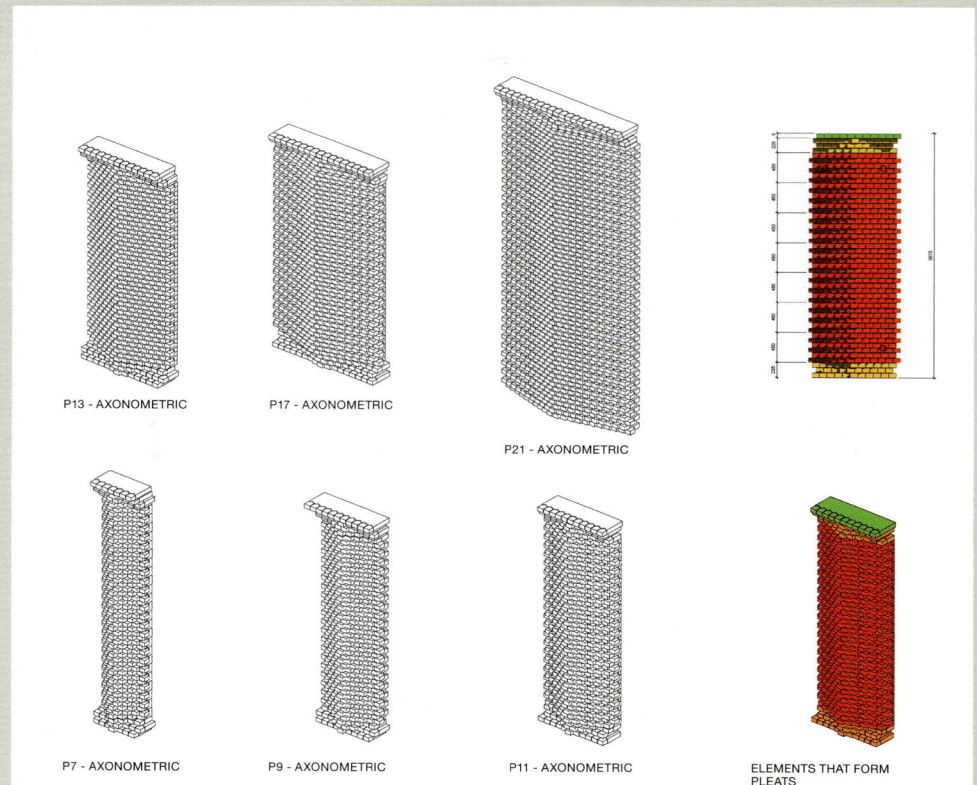

77 Panel types

identified three possibilities of making the walls. The first was by hand and laid by traditional masons; however, ACME thought this would be too labor intensive and ultimately too expensive. The second used a robot to lay the bricks and glue to secure them together. This option was considered through the pricing stage; however, the glue was considered too risky by the firm because of fears around durability.[16] The third was casting the bricks into a precast concrete.

The design team did early investigations into the precast option. They invited Thorp to early design meetings, as Thorp knew more about the manufacturing process than ACME did. According to Hennessy, during the early design meetings Thorp had a good "can-do attitude" and proved how adaptable the manufacturing process could be. Thorp provided to ACME some basic design parameters, such as the amount of stepping for the brick and the minimum amount of concrete required behind the bricks. Hennessy indicated that Thorp's level of confidence and willingness to collaborate with the design team was among the reasons precast composite concrete was chosen for this project.

MANUFACTURING CONSIDERATIONS

Thorp used plywood molds with a modular "cassettes" placed on the bottom of the molds. [80, 81] The brick halves then snapped into the cassettes and concrete was poured onto the back of the bricks.[17] Multiple cassettes would be placed in the bottom of each mold so that the pleats could be ganged together into the larger, ganged panels for erection. Multiple molds and cassettes were made of each pleat design so that up to four panels could be made at any time. The cassettes needed to be replaced often, most likely due to damage during demolding.

Thorp used polystyrene to keep concrete out of the 0.4in (10mm) joints between each brick. Pointing of the bricks was done by traditional masons, after the concrete panels had been stripped from the mold. This allowed the joints to have a hand-laid quality about them, and meant that the mortar profile was more exact than that traditionally afforded by the precast concrete. [82] Initially, ACME was nervous about the quality of the pointing, and requested that test pointing be done on a mock-up panel for approval. Pointing was done indoors, in the precast facility, and at working height. These conditions improved the pointing quality and cost, as it was easier to point in the precast facility than it would have been on-site, outdoors, and on scaffolding. According to Hennessy, an unintended benefit of this method was that if any of the bricks on the precast panels got damaged in transit, the brick could be removed, replaced, and repointed on-site with no visible difference within the panels.

The bricks used for the composite panels were manufactured in the UK. They are a red-blend Class A brick, made in the West Midlands from Etruria Marl clay, which has been used for the past 100 years. The bricks themselves were also custom manufactured for this project. The bricks were cut or broken in half before being placed in the mold. To provide a proper mechanical connection between the brick and the concrete, a custom-shaped key was manufactured into the brick's center. To test the connection between the brick and the concrete, Thorp performed pull-out tests, making sure that the panels would be durable enough for Leeds's freeze-thaw cycles.

78 Panels being installed during construction

79 Panels being installed during construction

80 Precast facility

81 Thin bricks set into molds, prior to concrete being poured

OTHER CONSIDERATIONS

The Victoria Arcades was a design-bid-build project, which meant that during the design phase there was no guarantee as to the precast company that would be awarded the manufacturing contract. Although Thorp provided consulting services for the project, it was not paid for this time. Because of this, initial meetings between ACME and Thorp were not intensive; however, after Thorp was awarded the contract, both ACME and Thorp used bladder inflation molding (BIM) to create the project documents. In the model, every brick was located. With BIM, both teams were able to predict many of the potential project problems before they happened. Hennessy stated, "The role of BIM was significant." Meetings were held every two weeks to update the panels and the building's overall design. Thorp came to the meetings with details that the architecture firm needed to resolve.

As a retail building, Victoria Arcades had its façades updated as tenant leases were being negotiated. In turn, windows were moved or added to meet tenant needs. At the same time, to keep the repetition of the cassettes high, full cassettes were used. This meant that as windows were moved or added, all of the pleats needed to be reorganized across the façade to accommodate the change.

LESSONS LEARNED

One of the lessons Hennessy learned on this project was about the benefits of repetition. For this project, the design team realized that their designs, whether they were manufactured by robot or by precast manufacturer, would be more cost efficient if there were more repetition between panels. With the robot, less repetition resulted in greater programming costs to manage the robot's movements. With the precast process, less repetition resulted in more molds and higher tooling costs. **[83, 84]** To balance repetition with design intention, ACME had internal design reviews looking at how much variety could be achieved within limits.

82 Detail of brick pointing

83 Panels at the precast plant

84 Panels at the precast plant, before pointing

4.2 Casting Metal

INTRODUCTION

Casting metal is a manufacturing process that uses gravity and a phase change to shape molten metal. [1] (For brevity, I will refer to both pure metals and metal alloys as "metal.") Once the casting has solidified and sufficiently cooled, it can be removed from the mold. The term "casting" refers to both the process of pouring the molten metal into a mold and the component that has been cast. Casting metal can be used to create complex geometries with good detail, hollow or solid shapes, and a range of cross-sectional thicknesses. Castings can be done to net shape, where no further manufacturing operations are required to achieve the desired shape; or to near net shape, for which some post-production processes will be required for final shaping. [2, 3] There are almost no

size limitations to this process, and casting metal can manufacture jewelry as well as objects weighing more than 100 tons (90.7Mg).

Casting metal can be done in either open or closed molds, and with permanent or expendable molds. Casting in an expendable sand mold is the most common, can easily accommodate customization, and will be the focus of this chapter, along with some information on permanent mold casting. When sand casting metal in a closed mold, a pattern is made in the component's shape. Often the pattern is attached to a match plate to properly align the parts. A gating system complete with a sprue, runners, and a riser is added to get the molten metal into the mold cavity. Casting sand is compacted in a mold box against each side of the

1 Casting bronze at a small outdoor workshop

2 Net shape, sand-cast, ductile iron components. No post-production work is required of the manufacturer

3 This sand-cast, ductile iron component was cast to a near net shape. Post-production work was required to drill, grind, and polish parts of it to final shape

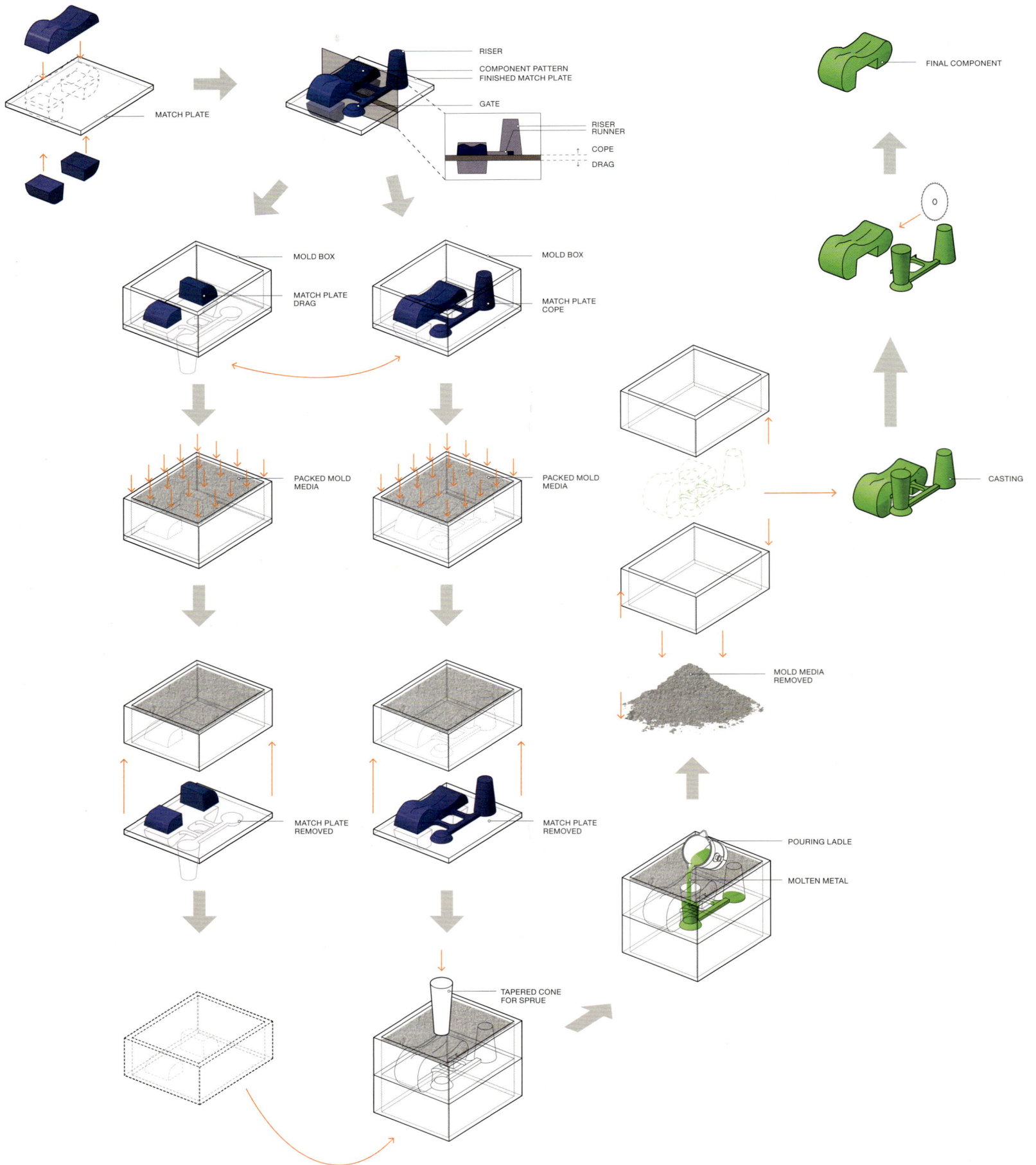

MATCH PLATE

RISER
COMPONENT PATTERN
FINISHED MATCH PLATE
GATE
RISER
RUNNER
COPE
DRAG

FINAL COMPONENT

MOLD BOX
MATCH PLATE
DRAG

MOLD BOX
MATCH PLATE
COPE

CASTING

PACKED MOLD
MEDIA

PACKED MOLD
MEDIA

MOLD MEDIA
REMOVED

MATCH PLATE
REMOVED

MATCH PLATE
REMOVED

POURING LADLE
MOLTEN METAL

TAPERED CONE
FOR SPRUE

pattern, and then both halves are brought together to form the closed mold. A tapered cone is pushed through the sand to reach the sprue. Molten metal is then poured into the mold; the mold remains closed until the metal solidifies. The sand is then broken away from the mold and the gating system is removed. If metal is cast in an open mold, no gating system is required and the metal is poured directly in to the mold cavity. [4] When using open molds, the component is cast finish side down. The part of the casting that is not in contact with the mold is the unfinished face.

Metal casting is a manufacturing process that can be mechanized for large production runs, or is suitable for small production runs or prototypes. A craftsperson can manufacture small to medium production runs, depending on the size and complexity of the component. [5] Most highly mechanized manufacturers can accommodate both large and small production runs. [6, 7] Often manufacturers will cast tests in order to properly develop the manufacturing process for the final production. A manufacturer or a craftsperson will produce components of comparable quality. The primary difference between the two is the opportunities that automation provides, particularly in terms of production speed, potential cost per unit, and equipment. Manufacturers often have access to large equipment such as gantry cranes to move large amounts of dense metals for pouring, and large furnaces that can accommodate large amounts of metal at high temperatures. [8]

BUILDING PRODUCTS

Historically, cast metal has been used for architecture components that require a high degree of ornamental detail, including columns and column capitals; decorative handrails, fences, grilles, and gates; and brackets and cornices. There are a number of commercially available building products made by casting metal, including sidewalk grates, metal grilles, threshold protectors for stair nosings, and handrail and guardrail screens.

NOTE: In casting metal, the mold media have as much impact on the design parameters of cast-metal components as the metal itself; therefore design parameters due to the molds are listed under Tooling. For design parameters of metal, exclusive of mold design, see Material Considerations on p. 290.

TOOLING

Tooling for casting metal may include the mold, the pattern, or both. Molds can be made of a variety of materials, as long as the material can withstand the temperature, weight, and flow of the molten metal without damage. The mold medium affects the surface quality of a cast-metal component. Both open and closed molds can be either permanent or expendable. Permanent molds are used repeatedly for each casting; therefore care must be

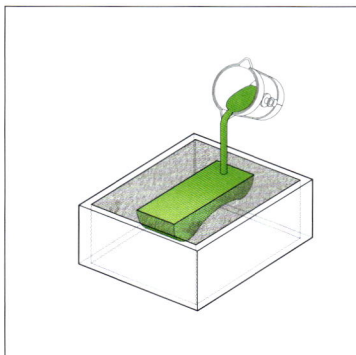

4 Casting in an open mold

5 Workers with molten bronze at a small workshop. The small furnace can be seen in the background

6 Grede Foundry is a highly mechanized facility in Biscoe, North Carolina that makes ductile iron through sand casting. Conveyor belts move sand molds (without mold boxes) to a carousel, where casting occurs

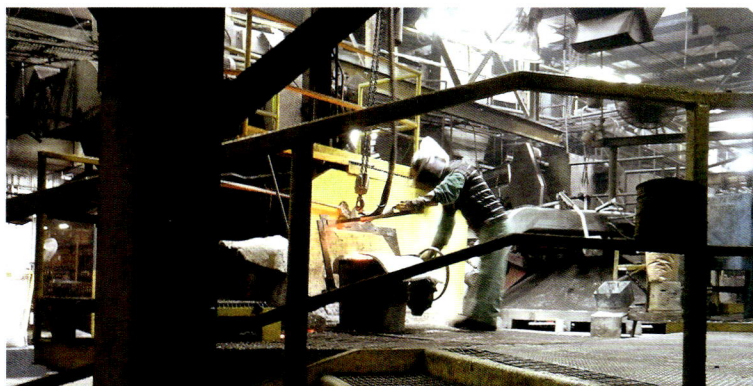

7 The other side of the carousel at Grede, where a worker is casting molten iron

8 Iron is being transferred from the large melting furnace to a crucible at Grede

taken to protect the mold from damage incurred by casting metal or removing the casting from the mold. Conversely, expendable molds are broken each time a casting is removed. To make an expendable mold, typically a pattern is used repeatedly to shape the expendable molds.

For permanent mold casting, care must be taken in selecting the mold material, the casting medium, and the design of the component. Some metals shrink dramatically during the solidification process. This shrinkage can cause stress on the mold, the casting media, or both. Generally, molds needs to be oversized to allow for the metal to shrink to its final dimensions. Each metal shrinks at a particular and predictable rate. If high tolerances must be maintained, the mold should be designed for a particular cast metal.

Permanent molds can be made of plaster, clay, or steel. [9] If the mold is made of steel, it will mostly likely be made by CNC equipment. If it is made of clay or plaster, the mold can be carved or formed by hand, or the clay or plaster can be cast around a pattern. Using a pattern allows multiple molds for parallel productions of the same component shape. [11] If using a clay mold, then it will need to be thoroughly dried, because any residual moisture will quickly vaporize, causing cracks.

Expendable molds are made of sand, plaster, or clay. Before each cycle, a new expendable mold is formed over a reusable pattern. [10] The pattern is made in the shape of the final component, and if using a closed mold, the pattern should include the gating system. For repetitive manufacturing, the pattern is often

9 A small, closed steel mold

11 Parallel castings in open clay molds

10 A cast aluminum match plate with added wood risers, used for sand casting

12 A sand mold, post casting. The sand will be broken away from the casting

13 Video stills of machine forming both sides (cope and drag) of a closed sand mold against a match plate

14 Cast aluminum components. The large circles on top are where the gating system has been removed

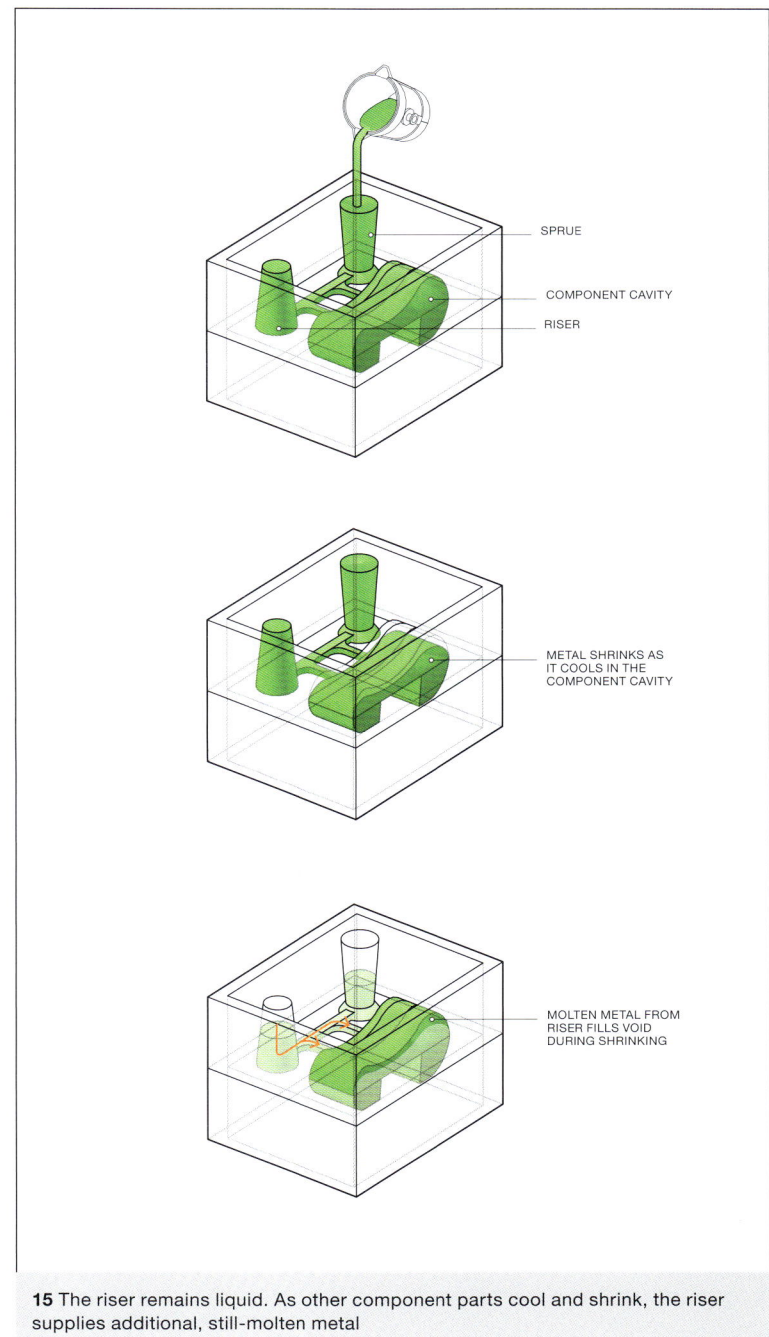

SPRUE

COMPONENT CAVITY

RISER

METAL SHRINKS AS IT COOLS IN THE COMPONENT CAVITY

MOLTEN METAL FROM RISER FILLS VOID DURING SHRINKING

15 The riser remains liquid. As other component parts cool and shrink, the riser supplies additional, still-molten metal

attached to a match plate, so that the pieces of the pattern are placed and aligned properly in the mold. Once the mold medium sets around the pattern, the pattern is removed and the metal is cast in the mold. **[13]** After the metal cools, the mold is broken away from the casting. **[12]** If the mold is made of sand, the sand can be reused to make another expendable mold.

Patterns for expendable molds can be made of a variety of materials, including high-density foam, plastic, wood, or cast aluminum. Typically, the pattern's cost is directly proportional to the potential production run length. For example, an aluminum pattern is the most expensive, but can support production runs of 10,000 units, whereas high-density foam is the least expensive and is often used for production runs of fewer than five units. The expendable mold media will affect the production run length of the pattern. For example, sand is abrasive and will wear down a pattern's surface if made from a soft material.

A gating system is required for closed molds and includes the sprue, gate, runners, and a riser. The gate, runners, and the riser are often attached to the match plate, but can be hand carved into sand molds. The sprue is where the metal is poured, and moves the metal

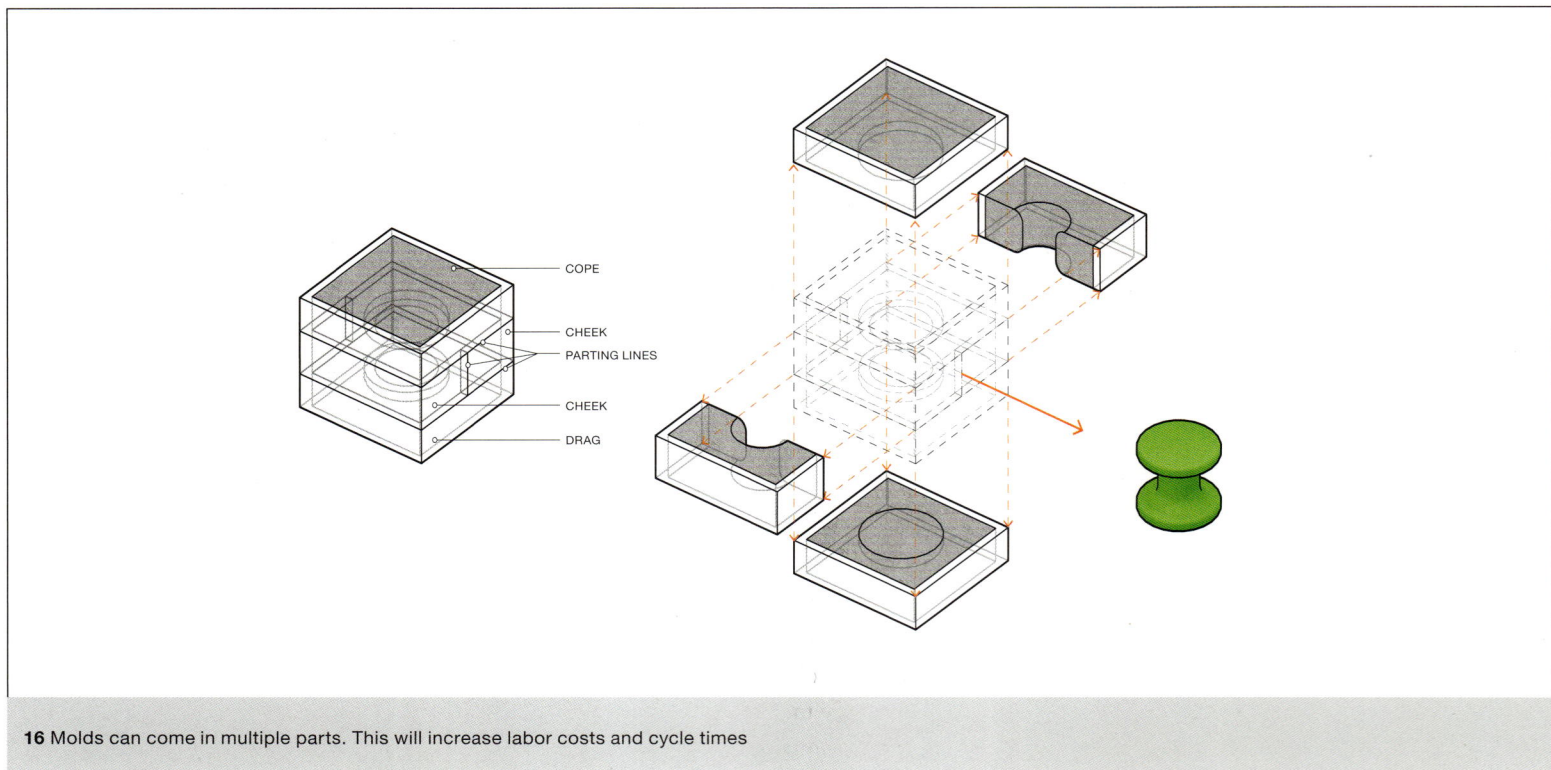

16 Molds can come in multiple parts. This will increase labor costs and cycle times

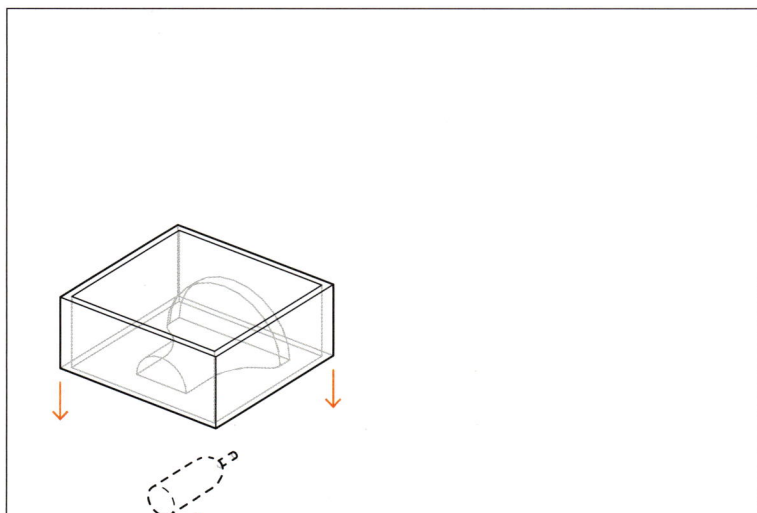

17 Cores can be suspended in casting with a chaplet

from outside the mold to the gate. The sprue is typically inserted after the mold is formed. The runners move the molten metal from the gate to the mold cavity. The riser is an internal reservoir of molten metal, designed to be larger and taller than the main casting. The molten metal in the riser is designed to solidify only after the main casting is finished, so that molten metal can flow from the riser to the casting and fill the voids in the casting that occur when the metal shrinks during cooling. **[15]** Risers are needed to produce parts without voids. The number of sprues, gates, runners, and risers vary based on the size, shape, and number of components to be cast each cycle. When the gating system is removed from the cast component, the surface of the casting will require some post-production finishing. Care must be taken in order to properly place the location of the runners on the cast component. **[14]**

Metal casting molds can be complex and made of multiple pieces, and therefore can have multiple parting lines. This allows cast-metal shapes to have undercuts when using either expendable or permanent molds. **[16]** If using expendable molds, cores may also be added to the casting, and removed with the mold. Cores allow the metal casting to be hollow, and work particularly well with sand casting. The core is placed into a closed mold before pouring the molten metal. If the core is to be suspended within the mold cavity, a chaplet will be used to keep the core in its place. **[17]** The chaplet is made of the same metal as the casting, and as molten metal is poured around it, the chaplet becomes a permanent part of the casting. Generally, the addition of cores and mold pieces increases manufacturing complexity and cost, and decreases production speed.

SAND MOLDS

Sand is the most common expendable mold medium. Sand molds primarily use sand with a binder. The combination of sand grains and binding agents will give the sand molds different finishes, strengths, and thermal capacities. If surface quality of the component is important, a finer face sand is first placed against the pattern and then a rougher backing sand is placed on atop the face sand. This results in a smoother finish for the component. Binders can be oil, clay, or resin. The binder allows the sand to be loose enough to form around a pattern while its cohesion is activated with moisture, pressure, temperature, air, or a combination of these, and is strong enough to hold the mold form during pouring. Green sand is the most common mold sand and includes about 2–3% of water and clay.

There are a number of benefits that sand casting has over other types of metal casting. First, sand casting is a cost-effective process for almost any size of production run. Second, the capital costs are flexible, as patterns can be made of a variety of materials, supporting both small and large production runs. Next, the sand is highly recyclable and can be reused by the foundry. Fourth, internal cores and undercuts can be accommodated because the mold is broken after the casting. Fifth, almost any metal can be cast in a sand mold. Finally, there are almost no size restrictions with this process, as some foundries will pour molten metal in sand pits that have been dug into the earth.

SIMILAR PROCESSES

This process is similar to lost wax or investment casting. The advantages of casting metal over lost wax casting are lower cost, ease of producing repetitive components, faster manufacturing speeds, and larger component sizes. Surface quality of sand-cast components is rough and pitted when compared to lost wax casting; however, sand casting can accommodate undercuts if necessary. Permanent plaster and steel molds can produce components with smooth surfaces.

CORES

Cores can be made of the same sand that the foundry uses, and can be made at the foundry. Cores can also be made from sand with a resin binder from a subcontractor. Cores are often placed by hand into the sand mold.

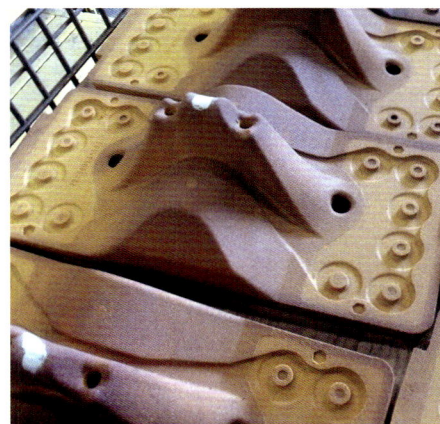

DRAFT ANGLES

Minimum draft angles for the pattern can range from 1 to 5°, depending on the draw depth and surface area. The draft angle is required so that the pattern does not damage the sand as it is removed from the mold. All parts of the pattern, including the gating system, need the draft angle.

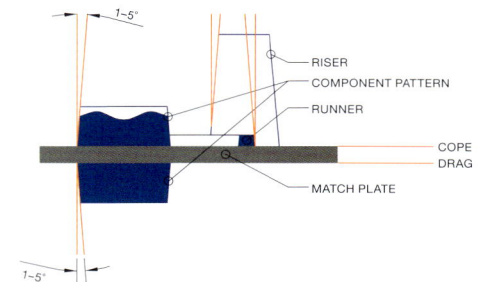

FINISH

As a result of oxidation from casting, the outer layer of the component will be darker than the inside. The sand will also make the surface have a fine grit finish. If a better finish is desired, the casting can be ground, sanded, and polished.

FLASHING

There will be flashing at the parting line that will need to be removed, post-production.

PARTING LINES

Parting lines will be visible on the component. Sometimes, if the mold halves are not properly aligned, there will be a mismatch in geometries across the parting lines. Parting lines are best kept straight, but can wander if required.

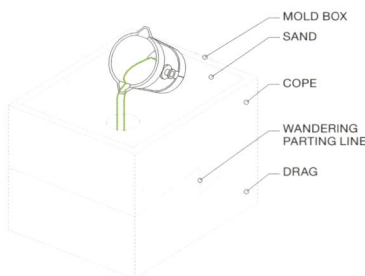

- MOLD BOX
- SAND
- COPE
- WANDERING PARTING LINE
- DRAG

POST-PRODUCTION PROCESSING

The gating system needs to be removed from each casting; this requires post-production cutting and grinding.

PRODUCTION SPEED

Production speeds can reach about 10–15 cycles per hour if done in a workshop. If the foundry is mechanized, production speeds can be up to 50 cycles per hour.

PRODUCTION VOLUME

This process is economical for production runs of fewer than 100 units, and can be used for prototypes. High-volume production is possible, but manufacturing would have to be in a mechanized facility.

SIZE LIMITS

Sand molds offer the largest size range for casting. Sand casting can produce a range of component sizes from small, jewelry-sized components to the largest castings in the metal-casting industry. Large castings are done in sand pits, located in the floor of a foundry. For sand-pit castings, a pattern is often not used, as it is too difficult to manipulate. Instead, a foundry may use a partial pattern, jig, or profile to shape the mold. Repeatability for large castings is difficult to achieve.

SURFACE DESIGNS

Fine surface decorations that are shallower than 0.12in (3mm) are difficult to achieve.

TOOLING COSTS

Depending on the medium, a pattern and optional match plates are fairly inexpensive. A medium-sized pattern made from wood with a moderate complexity would cost around $1,000. If a larger production run (over 1,000 units) is required, an aluminum match plate may be necessary. The aluminum match plate can be directly tooled, but is often cast using a wood or foam pattern. This additional step and the material cost of aluminum can make a comparable aluminum match plate about twelve to fifteen times the cost of a wood match plate.

TOLERANCES

Tolerances can range for this process. It is more difficult to maintain tight tolerances in small components than in large components. Tolerances range from 0.01in per 1in (0.1mm per 10mm) to 0.25in per 3ft (7mm per 1,000mm). Higher tolerances can be maintained with additional cost.

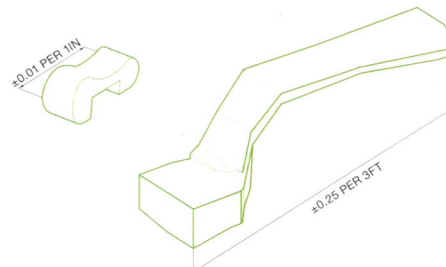

±0.01 PER 1IN

±0.25 PER 3FT

UNDERCUTS

If reusing a pattern to form the mold, undercuts are not allowed. A pattern with an undercut would damage the mold when removing it from the sand. If not reusing a pattern or modifying the mold after the pattern has been removed, an undercut can be cut into the sand. This may disrupt the sand's binding and affect the sand's grain pattern, thus affecting the finish surface of the component.

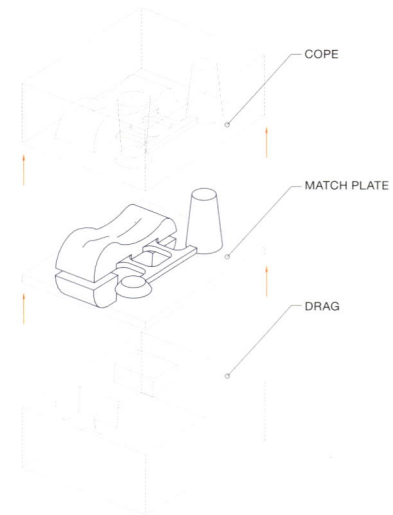

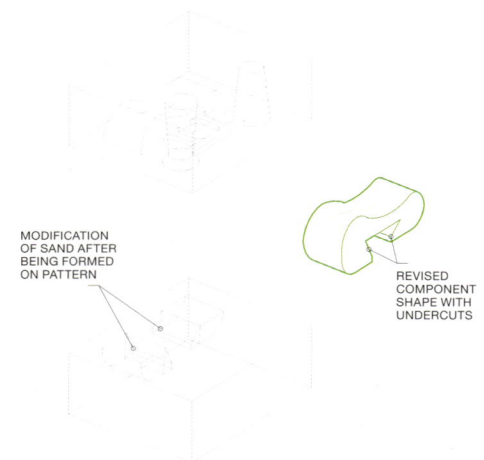

- COPE
- MATCH PLATE
- DRAG

MODIFICATION OF SAND AFTER BEING FORMED ON PATTERN

REVISED COMPONENT SHAPE WITH UNDERCUTS

VENTS

Vents are not needed. Sand molds are porous enough for air to pass through the walls of the mold as the molten metal is being poured.

CASTING METAL IN SAND MOLDS

CAST IRON STOREFRONT | PAUL SMITH STORE
6a architects
London, UK

18
New cast-iron storefront of the Paul
Smith Store by 6a architects

19
Albemarle Street, with the Paul Smith
Store on the left

The Paul Smith Store by 6a architects, completed in 2013, is an expansion of an existing Paul Smith store, located on Albemarle Street in the neighborhood just east of London's Hyde Park. [18, 19] The project included renovating the existing store's neighboring eighteenth-century building to create a new storefront, and connecting the two retail spaces together. Paul Smith invited three architecture practices to produce initial design sketches before selection, and 6a architects was one of those firms. According to John Ross, 6a associate and project architect, during initial meetings, Smith spoke of Paul Smith stores as a global brand, and about their specific location; Smith wanted this store to reference the history of the London shopfront.[1]

Inspired by London's historical uses of cast iron, both for decorative and utilitarian building components, 6a proposed using cast iron for the new Paul Smith storefront. Ductile cast iron was sand cast into large decorative panels that hang off the existing building, to create a new storefront. The pattern is approximately four and a half rows of interlocking circles, spaced evenly across the façade. The circle pattern is used in the majority of the façade's solid panels, for the balustrade for the second-floor windows, and has been carved into a hidden, dark-stained oak door, necessary for accessing the offices above the store.

The cast iron panels range in size from 3.5in (90mm) wide and 14in (359mm) tall to 28.5in (722mm) wide and 108in (2,764mm) tall. [20, 21, 22] The depths of the panels range from 0.25 to 1in (6–24mm) thick, with a 0.5in (12mm) average thickness. The panels were cast with integrated iron hooks on their backs, which hook onto a stainless-steel support structure. [23] Two hooks are located near the top of the panel, which supports the

18

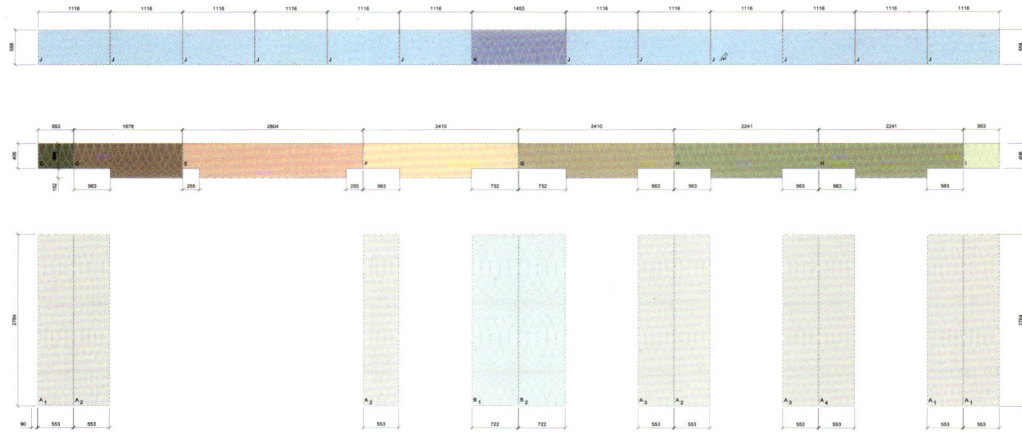

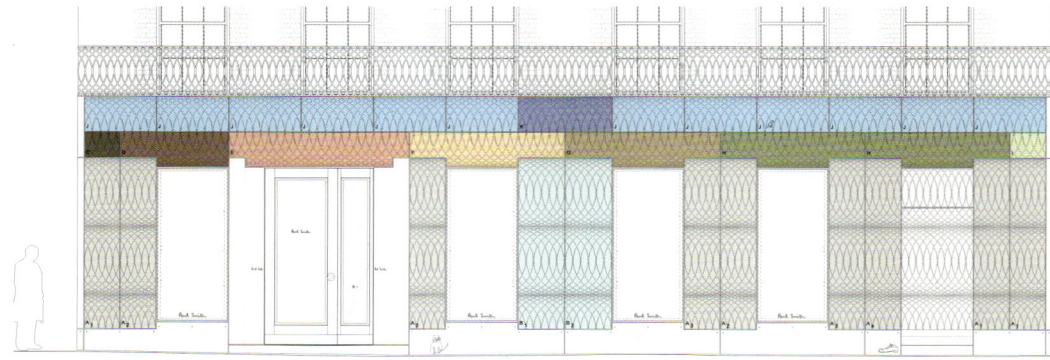

20 Panel layout and sizes for the storefront

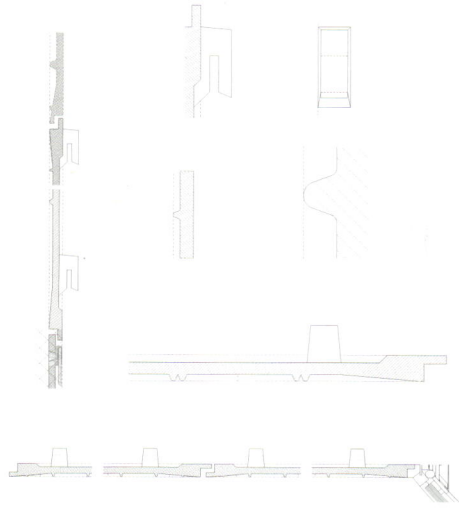

21 Panel detail drawings by **6a**

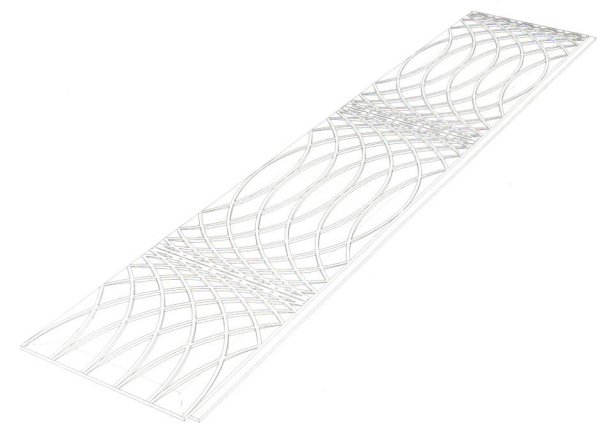

22 Panel detail drawing by **6a**

panels vertically, and two hooks are located near the bottom of the panel to support lateral loads. The panels have a lap joint at their edges, to allow for thermal movement between them.

The architects collaborated with Montresor Partnership, an architecture and façade consultant, to resolve the panels' details and support system, and the curved windows and associated metal fabrication. Finch Seaman Enfield (FSE) Foundry manufactured the sixty-three cast-iron panels for this project, in thirty-four different shapes. [24] Twenty-four panels were cast only once, while one of the spandrel panels was cast twelve times. For each different panel, a new pattern was CNC milled out of high-density polyurethane foam. [25] Because this was a renovation, and there were dimensional inconsistencies with the eighteenth-century building, there were fewer opportunities for repeatability than with new construction.

23 Storefront during construction. Stainless-steel supports hold the integrated cast hooks on the panels' back

DESIGN CONSIDERATIONS

The architects iteratively cast a number of plaster mock-ups to evaluate both the design and making process for the panels. Through these, 6a investigated woven and geometric patterns in relation to different materials and fabrics. Using a clay casting bed and a rudimentary compass made of string and a stick, design team members carved interlocking circles into the clay mold on which they cast a plaster prototype. [26, 27] This pattern of interlocking circles is typical in Regency-period patterns of rails and gates found around London.[2] The fine grain of the circular pattern can be further related to Smith's work, as he is well known for making finely tailored British clothing.

Although the pattern made by the circles gives a refinement to the panels, the actual surface of the panels is pitted and somewhat rough due to the texture of the sand molds. [28] According to Ross, 6a greatly appreciates these marks from the making process, and believes that they enhance the project. For some of the installed panels, there are small pockets into which the metal did not fully flow, and there are visible knit lines, where pours from different sides of the panel meet. As Ross stated, "The nice thing with casting is that you cannot work that stuff out" as it happens naturally as part of the manufacturing process.

To bring some whimsy to the project, three sketches by Paul Smith were cast into the iron panels. [29, 30] There is a cat located near the shop's front door, a bird located in the spandrel panel above a window, and a shoe next to the hidden door to access the upstairs offices. The benefit of the sand molds was that it was easy for 6a to incorporate sketches by Smith directly into the casting. On paper, Smith sketched drawings of a cat, bird, and a shoe. Those sketches were enlarged and the lines cut out of the paper. The paper was then used as a stencil template to transfer the drawing to the sand mold. A small hand-held tool, like a Dremel, was used to carve into the already-formed sand mold. The architects worked with FSE to cast prototypes of the panels, using the sketches to ensure that they would look as intended.

24 The panels at the manufacturer

25 Each pattern was CNC milled from high-density foam

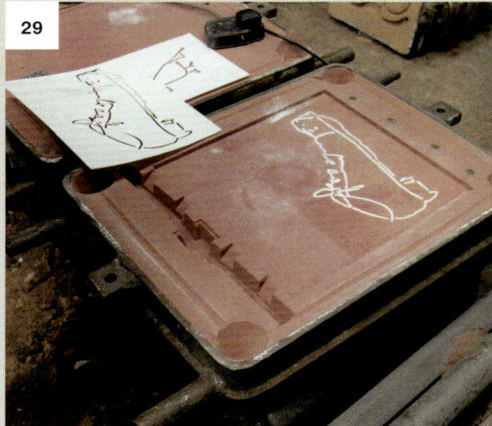

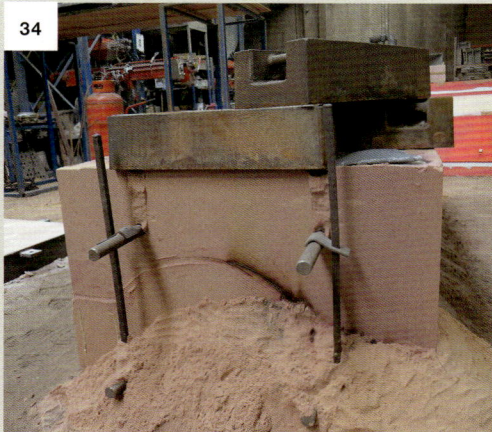

26
Early design studies in cast plaster

27
Clay patterns and plaster cast of the final design idea

28
Casting at Finch Seaman Enfield (FSE) Foundry. Weights are used to hold down the cope so that it does not float due to the hydrostatic pressure of the molten metal

29
Smith's sketches being carved into the sand molds

30
The final result of the sketch

31
Transferring metal at FSE

32
Closed sand mold for large storefront panel. Note the multiple sprues

33
Knit line where molten metal, poured from two different sprues, met

34
Casting the curved panels for the storefront entrance. Note the curved parting line

35
Casting the curved panels

MANUFACTURING CONSIDERATIONS

FSE Foundry is part of a larger management and holding company, FSE Group, which also manages commercially driven product lines, such as staircase nosings and other mass-produced items for the building industry.[3] FSE foundry has an in-house pattern shop and can easily manufacture custom and specialty castings. [31] Prior to the Paul Smith Store, 6a worked with FSE to cast a new iron façade for Raven Row (2009), an addition and renovation for a contemporary art gallery. For Raven Row, FSE cast very large ductile iron panels for the project's rear façade. With this prior experience and working relationship with FSE, 6a approached FSE to discuss the initial design sketches, before making its design pitch to Smith.

According to Ross, team members at FSE had a "can-do attitude" right from the beginning, which allowed them to try manufacturing complicated elements.[4] First, 6a pushed the physical size limits of metal casting panels for the Paul Smith Store. The panels were cast in closed molds, with the sprues and gating systems located on the panels' edges. [32] From the gates, the molten metal flowed to the panel's middle. Where the metal flows met they formed knit lines. [33] Sometimes the metal would begin to chill while casting was still happening, impeding metal flow into remote sections of the mold cavity. In the end, though, only two cast panels were rejected.

Second, FSE was able to cast the two curved panels at the shop's front entrance. [34] These, too, were made in closed molds; however, FSE formed the molds with a curved parting line. [35] Paul Smith's name was to appear on the surface of the curved panel. The team members investigated casting the letters into the panels, but with the curve, they decided against it. In the end, the name was engraved into the panels, post-production, at a facility not far from FSE. [37]

Although FSE used a different pattern for each different panel cast, a separate pattern was used for the panels' lap joints. [38] The lap joints are at the panel edges, and allow the panels to move as a result of thermal expansion and contraction. By separating the lap joint pattern from the surface pattern, FSE was able to use the lap joint pattern repeatedly, lowering tooling costs.

Ross remembered that production was generally fast, and that the panels that took the longest to make were the curved panels at the store entrance. FSE used graphite on the sand mold as a releasing agent, and burned off any excess before pouring. [36] The mold boxes for the closed molds were clamped together before pouring. Weights were placed on the sand of the cope to keep the hydrostatic pressure of the molten metal from lifting the sand during casting.

OTHER CONSIDERATIONS

The design team developed a new method of attaching the panels to the building façade. In Raven Row, self-tapping screws were used from the back to attach the cast iron panels onto the building. This required that the panels for that project be thick enough to accommodate the screw threads. On the Paul Smith Store, FSE cast hooks into the back of each panel. [39] The panels can be unhooked and demounted for fire and smoke ventilation. The hooks allowed the overall panel thickness of the Paul Smith Store to be thinner than those at Raven Row, but it required that the panels be cast in closed molds.

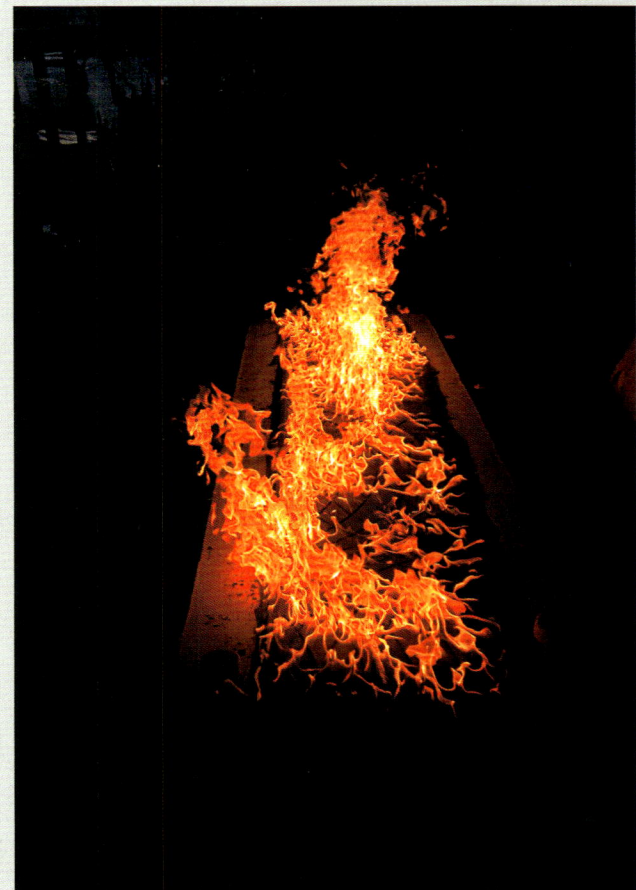

36 Graphite was added to the sand mold as a releasing agent. Any excess graphite was burned off

37 Finished entrance showing Paul Smith's signature

38 A detail of the edge and joint of the panels

The Paul Smith Store has a rusted patina on the panels, similar to the finish for Raven Row. Both projects make use of the natural oxidation of cast iron, and have coated the panels with Kurust by Hammerite, a rust inhibitor. At Raven Row, the panels were installed without the finish. The contractor waited until the panels developed their patina before applying Kurust. For the Paul Smith Store, Smith wanted the panels to be installed in their final, rusted finish. According to Ross, 6a and FSE developed a kind of working recipe—spraying with water, leaving outside, waiting, and applying the inhibitor—to get the desired finish. [40] It took under a week to achieve the desired finish.

LESSONS LEARNED

For this project, one of the lessons that Ross learned was the importance of working with skilled, collaborative people. They need to be enthusiastic and detail-oriented in order to solve potential problems. For him, it is important to cultivate these working relationships, and to work with the manufacturers over multiple projects. Ross suggests that architects tap into other people's knowledge base, so that when you want to do something technically ambitious, it is understood and supported by everyone on the project. Although small in size, the Paul Smith Store had a number of complex elements that had to come together.

39 The back of the panels at FSE

40 Applying a rust inhibitor to the surface for the desired finish

PLASTER MOLDS

The plaster used for casting metal must be able to withstand the temperature of the metal. Generally, casting metals in plaster molds are limited to nonferrous metals, as the high melting temperature of ferrous metals will melt any plaster. Lead should also not be cast in plaster molds, as lead reacts with plaster.

Plaster molds give tighter tolerances, more accuracy, smoother surfaces, better detail, thinner sections, and more complex shapes than sand. Casting in plaster molds may also reduce the necessary post-production work, including machining and finishing. Plaster molds allow the cast metal to cool slowly and uniformly, making it a good medium for manufacturing components with thin walls. However, the slow cooling of the metal negatively affects the metal's grain structure, so that metals cast in plaster molds can lose as much as 25% of their strength compared to the same metals cast in sand or metal molds.

Plaster molds can be cast against patterns made from metal, plaster, wood, plastic, or rubber. Wood is the least preferable pattern medium, as it tends to absorb water from the plaster before the plaster has fully cured.

DRAFT ANGLES

Minimum draft angles should be 0.5–2°, depending on the metal cast. Because the metal shrinks during the freezing process, male mold parts should have a greater draft than female mold cavities.

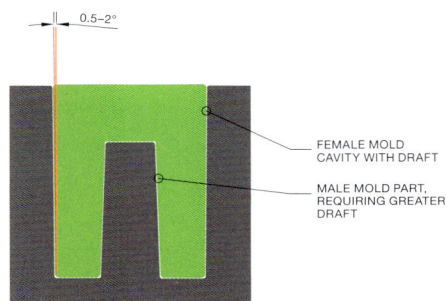

0.5–2°

FEMALE MOLD
CAVITY WITH DRAFT

MALE MOLD PART,
REQUIRING GREATER
DRAFT

FINISH

The metal surface will be smooth, with a matte or satin finish.

FLASHING

If casting in a closed mold, flashing will form at the parting line.

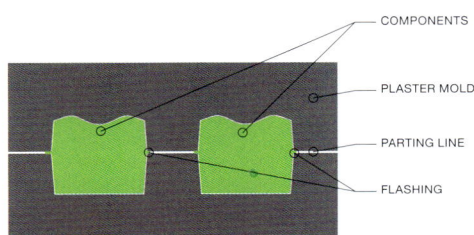

COMPONENTS

PLASTER MOLD

PARTING LINE

FLASHING

PARTING LINES

Parting lines will be visible on the component.

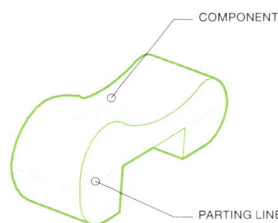

COMPONENT

PARTING LINE

Parting lines are best kept straight, but can wander if required. Generally, it is easier to make wandering parting lines with permanent molds than with sand molds.

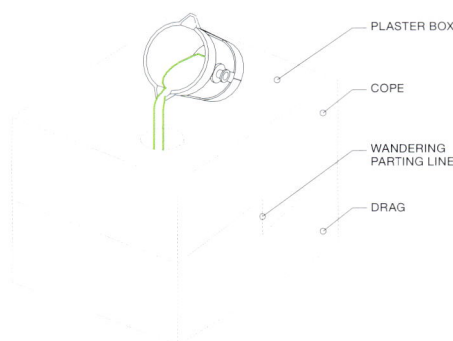

PLASTER BOX

COPE

WANDERING
PARTING LINE

DRAG

PRODUCTION SPEED

Production speed for mechanized manufacturers can range from 40 to 60 cycles per hour. For small workshops, production of about 10 cycles per hour can be done.

PRODUCTION VOLUME

Plaster molds tend to not last for many cycles and are suitable for low production volumes or prototypes.

SIZE LIMITS

Castings can range from 0.4 to 300lb (0.2–140kg).

TOLERANCES

Tolerances are 0.003–0.005in per 1in (0.03–0.05mm per 10mm) and 0.01in (0.25mm) across parting lines for dimensions up to 1in (25mm).

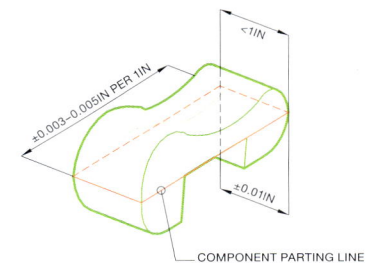

<1IN

±0.003–0.005IN PER 1IN

±0.01IN

COMPONENT PARTING LINE

UNDERCUTS

Undercuts are not permissible, unless using multi-part molds.

WALL THICKNESS

The minimum component wall thickness ranges from 0.03 to 0.25in (0.8–6mm), depending on the casting metal, size, and shape.

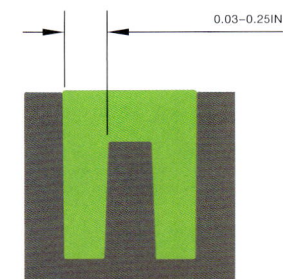

0.03–0.25IN

CERAMIC MOLDS

Ceramic is more heat resistant than plaster, and can be used to make a more durable mold. Both ferrous and nonferrous metals can be poured in a ceramic mold. Generally, mold performance is based on the specific ceramic used. Molds are formed on plaster, wood, metal, or rubber patterns. Ceramic molds can be solid, or slipcast as a slurry with a plaster master-mold. Generally, ceramic is best suited to open molds, as the tight fit at the parting line is difficult to control.

DRAFT ANGLES

Minimum draft angles should be 0.1–1°, depending on the metal cast. Because the metal shrinks during the freezing process, male mold parts should have a greater draft than female mold cavities.

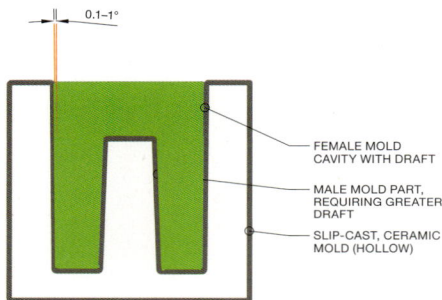

0.1–1°

FEMALE MOLD
CAVITY WITH DRAFT

MALE MOLD PART,
REQUIRING GREATER
DRAFT

SLIP-CAST, CERAMIC
MOLD (HOLLOW)

FINISH

The metal surface will be smooth, with a matte or satin finish.

FLASHING

Molds are most often open. Although not called flashing, pour remnants can be a problem if the metal has been over-poured.

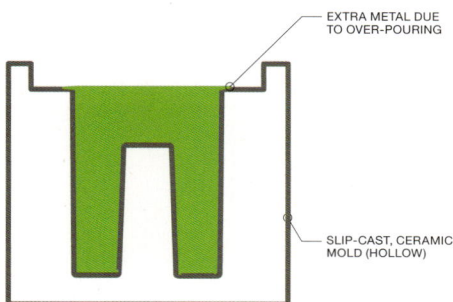

EXTRA METAL DUE
TO OVER-POURING

SLIP-CAST, CERAMIC
MOLD (HOLLOW)

PARTING LINES

Molds are open, without parting lines.

PRODUCTION SPEED

Production speed for mechanized manufacturers can range from 40 to 60 cycles per hour. For small workshops, production of about 10 cycles per hour can be done.

PRODUCTION VOLUME

This process is suitable for small production runs and prototypes.

SINK MARKS

When casting in an open mold, sink marks will likely appear in the middle of the casting on the unfinished side.

SIZE LIMITS

Casting sizes can range from 0.25 to 6,700lb (0.1–3,000kg), but casting less than 110lb (50kg) is typical.

TOLERANCES

Tolerances are 0.06in per 1in (0.6mm per 10mm).

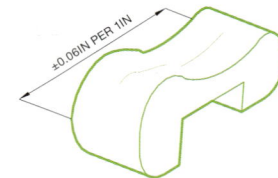

±0.06IN PER 1IN

UNDERCUTS

Undercuts are not permissible, unless using multi-part molds.

STEEL MOLDS

Steel molds are comparable to plaster molds in terms of surface quality and accuracy. Labor costs are often lower with steel molds, but additional equipment is needed to open and close the molds. Molds may often have ejector pins to make demolding faster. Metal molds are the most expensive, and are suitable for high-volume productions to offset costs.

DRAFT ANGLES

Minimum draft angles should be 2–3°, depending on the specific metal cast.

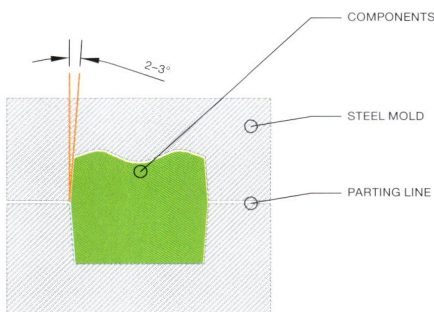

COMPONENTS
STEEL MOLD
PARTING LINE
2–3°

FINISH

The metal surface will be smooth, with a matte or satin finish.

FLASHING

There is little flashing with this process, as molds can be clamped shut. If the flashing is thin enough, it can be knocked off.

INSERTS

Inserts can be placed in the mold prior to casting

PARTING LINES

Parting lines are visible on the component.

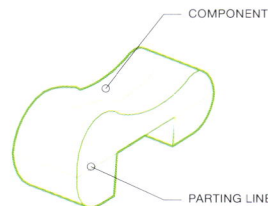

COMPONENT
PARTING LINE

Parting lines are best kept straight, but can wander if required. Generally, it is easier to make wandering parting lines with permanent molds than with sand molds.

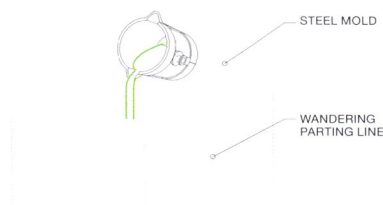

STEEL MOLD
WANDERING PARTING LINE

PRODUCTION SPEED

Production speed is approximately 5–50 cycles per hour, depending on casting size.

PRODUCTION VOLUME

This process is best suited to high-volume productions, but can accommodate small production runs of fewer than 1,000 units. Depending on the metal cast, a steel mold may need to be resurfaced or repaired after several thousand pours.

SIZE LIMITS

Sizes can range from 0.1 to 600lb (0.05–300kg), but the process is most commonly used for castings under 10lb (5kg).

TOLERANCES

Tolerances are 0.1in per 1in (1mm per 10mm)

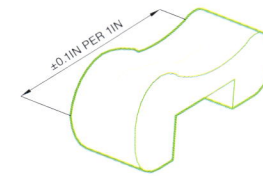

±0.1IN PER 1IN

UNDERCUTS

Undercuts are not permissible.

VENTS

In closed steel molds, vent holes are need at the cavity's high points to allow air to escape as molten metal is being poured into the mold. The air vents may affect the surface quality of the pouring, and the marks they make may need to be removed in a post-production process.

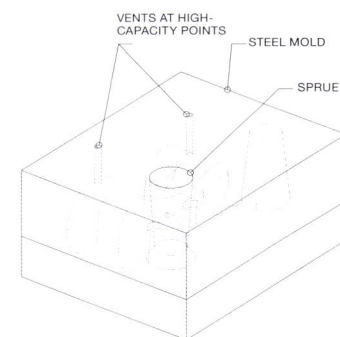

VENTS AT HIGH-CAPACITY POINTS
STEEL MOLD
SPRUE

WALL THICKNESS

The minimum wall thickness is 0.08in (2mm) and the maximum is 2in (50mm).

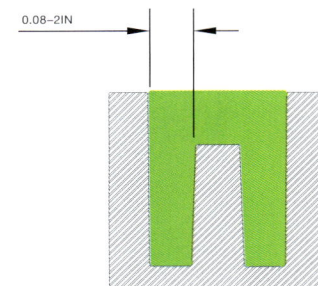

0.08–2IN

ENVIRONMENTAL IMPACT

Generally, casting metal is an energy-intensive process. Most of the energy is spent heating and maintaining the temperature of the molten metal, and temperatures for this process are high. For example, the melting temperature of aluminum is over 1,200°F (650°C). Some metals, such as bronze, are dense and require heavy equipment, such as cranes, to lift, move, and pour the material. At such high temperatures, worker safety should be considered with this process. Casting in open molds produces almost no manufacturing waste, as only the metal that is needed is poured into the mold. Casting in closed molds requires a gating system, which solidifies with each cycle of casting and is removed from the casting. Typically, the gating system is recycled directly by the foundry and placed back into the pot of molten metal. The sand used in expendable mold casting is highly recyclable, with only a little virgin sand being introduced before each cycle.

MATERIAL CONSIDERATIONS + DESIGN PARAMETERS

Casting metal can be done with any metal that is solid at room temperature and can be heated to a liquid state. After casting, the metal goes through a phase change from liquid to solid. Heat is released both as the metal cools and as it changes its phase.

Casting will limit the mechanical properties of metal. When the metal is cast, it solidifies inconsistently across its cross-section. Because the mold wall is cooler than the molten metal, the molten metal that contacts the cavity wall solidifies first and then, as the casting gradually cools, solidification moves toward the casting center. Because of this, cast metals are generally more brittle and have a lower tensile strength than their hot- or cold-worked metal counterparts (formed by stamping, forging, or extruding, for example).

> **NOTE:** The parameters listed below are inclusive of the material, and do not change based on the mold medium.

CORNER RADII

The radii should be less than half of the average wall thickness of pieces that are being joined. Small rounded corners should be added to the interior of corners to improve material flow and reduce concentration of stress during casting.

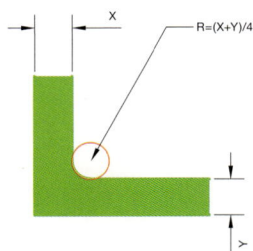

SHRINKING

The shrinkage rates are as follows:

Aluminum and aluminum alloy: 11.5–12.5%
Gray iron: 3–4.7%
Copper: 11.7%
Bronze: 11.2%

Shrinkage is the result of the contraction of the molten metal as it cools. The mold cavities should be oversized to allow for shrinkage.

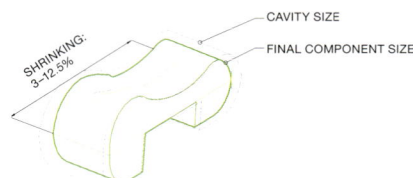

WALL THICKNESS

Cast components should be designed with fairly uniform wall thicknesses to ensure even cooling of the metal. Abrupt changes in cross-section can place internal stresses on the metal and may cause some sections to solidify before the molten metal can get by to a thicker section. Additional runners can be added to solve this problem, or the component can be redesigned with gradual transitions of thicknesses.

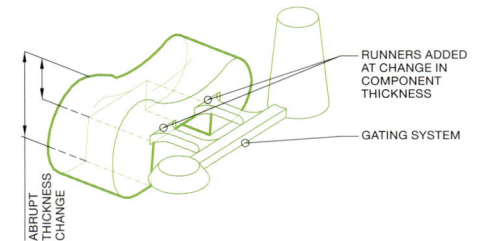

Corners and wall intersections cause inherent changes in wall thickness due to geometry. If material integrity is important at these areas, the casting's design can be improved to reduce internal cavities.

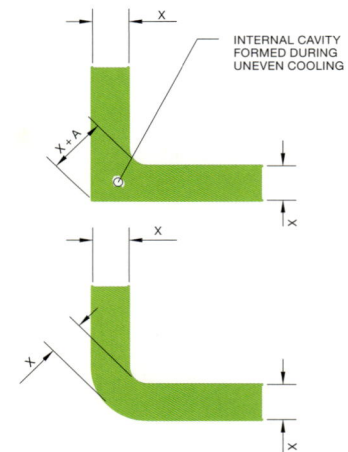

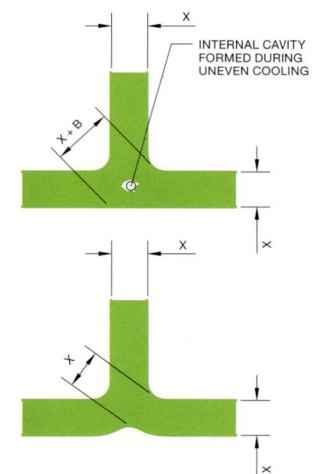

4.3 Casting Glass

INTRODUCTION

Casting glass is a manufacturing process in which glass is heated until it is sufficiently fluid, and then gravity is used to deform the heated glass into the shape of a mold. [1] This process can be done with small to large pieces of glass and inside or outside a kiln. [2] The size of the glass pieces used for the casting will affect the optical quality of the final casting. Small pieces of glass trap air bubbles and will result in opaque castings, whereas larger glass ingots or molten glass poured from a ladle will result in almost transparent castings. Shapes made with this process can be simple or complex. For example, cast glass can be used to form the simple curve of a telescope lens, or to make glass sculptures or figures. Surface quality is high with this process, and the surface finish can range from matte to glossy. Sizes can

1 Pouring molten glass into a sand mold at the Glass Hub, Stowford Manor Farm, Wingfield, Wiltshire, UK

2 Small open molds with broken glass are in a kiln, waiting to be heated

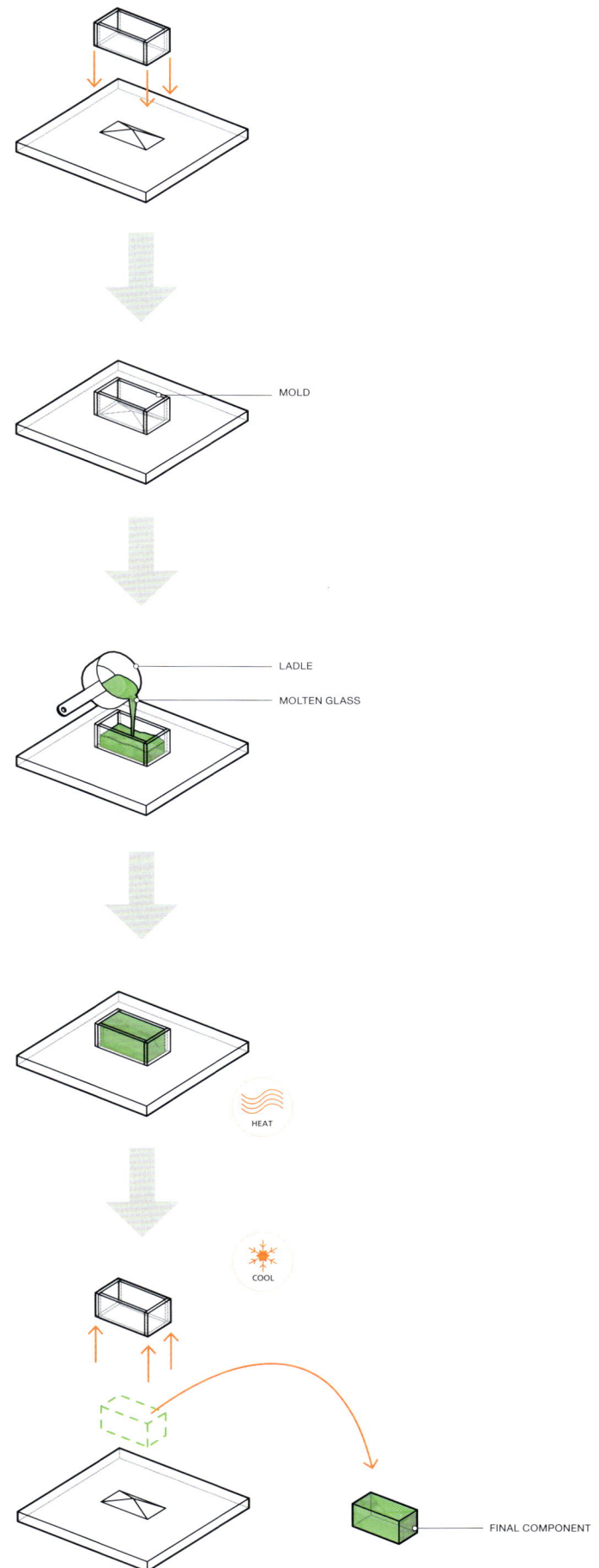

MOLD

LADLE

MOLTEN GLASS

HEAT

COOL

FINAL COMPONENT

range from small glass beads and buttons to castings over 25ft (7.5m) in diameter.

When casting glass, a multi-part mold can be used, as the glass is not fluid enough to seep into the mold joints. Prior to pouring, the mold is heated so that the thermal shock of pouring molten glass does not crack the mold. After the glass has taken the shape of the mold, it is annealed, which means it is kept at an elevated temperature and then cooled in a controlled way. To reduce cracking due to uneven cooling, heat is applied to both the mold and glass to cool it slowly. After the casting has sufficiently solidified, it is removed from the mold. Once the cast glass reaches room temperature, post-production processes such as grinding, cutting, or polishing may be done. Instead of pouring molten glass, an alternative is to fill the mold with pieces of glass and place it in a kiln. [3] The pieces of glass melt together, creating a solid glass casting. This method is called static casting, and results in a translucent to opaque casting.

There are additional alternative methods of glass casting, depending on the glass medium used for casting, and how it fills the mold. Pâte-de-verre is a method that uses finely ground glass pieces, similar to sugar crystals. The glass is brushed, delicately poured, or mixed with a binder paste and painted into the mold. The resulting casting is almost opaque and looks much more like stone than glass. Pâte-de-verre is appropriate for components that are highly detailed, with thin walls, and where color placement is important. [7] Next is slump casting, which takes a large ingot of optical glass that is similar in shape to the casting. In slump casting both the ingot and the mold are fired in the kiln long enough for the ingot to slowly deform to the shape of the mold. Slump casting is best suited to components with simple shapes that require great optical quality. [4] Finally, there is dribble casting. Dribble casting uses a reservoir or crucible to hold large chunks of glass. The molds, reservoir, and glass are then placed into the kiln. As the glass melts into its fluid state, it dribbles into the mold, filling the mold cavity. [5] Dribble casting is good for open or closed molds and will produce components with good optical quality.

Generally, casting glass is not a highly mechanized manufacturing process. It may be appropriate for unique pieces of art, [6] for limited art production runs, or for low-volume manufacturing. Artists and craftspeople may make the glass castings themselves, or they may contract that work to a glass foundry. For example, Cast Glass Forms in Spencer, Iowa is a glass foundry specializing in art glass sculpture work. Casting glass is a time- and labor-intensive manufacturing process. At the same time, because there is little mechanization and most glass foundries do low-volume productions, this process and the associated makers

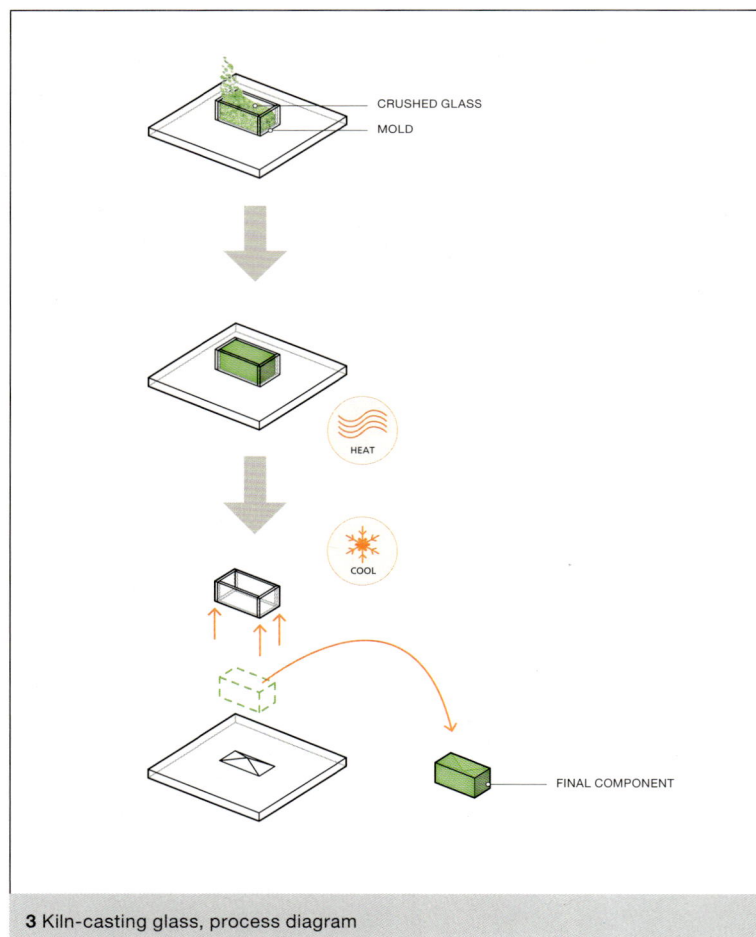

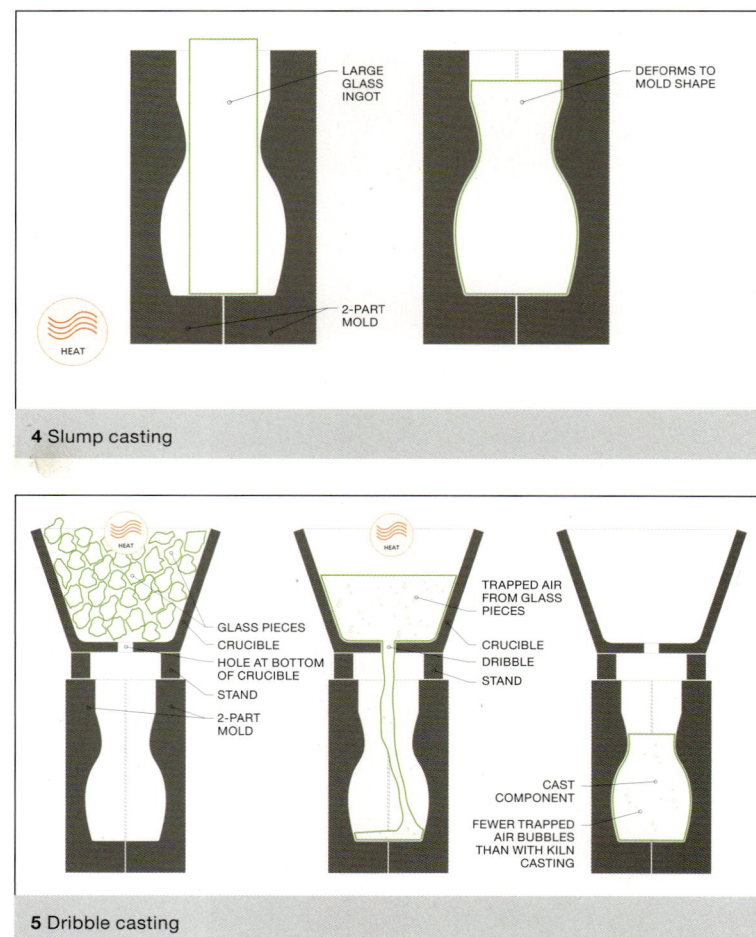

3 Kiln-casting glass, process diagram

4 Slump casting

5 Dribble casting

can usually take on small, custom projects. In addition, because the process is cyclical, it can accommodate different types and colors of glass in each of the castings.

BUILDING PRODUCTS

As this manufacturing process is not highly mechanized, cast glass is used for specialty products such as lenses, large mirrors, or architectural installations. For example, *Ice Falls* is a collaboration between John Lewis Glass, James Carpenter Design Associates, and Foster + Partners for the new lobby of 959 Eighth Avenue in New York City. There are a number of different architectural glass companies and studios that offer glass in particular patterns and can produce custom profiles and designs. There are few commercially available building products manufactured by casting glass as both glass bricks and solid glass blocks are manufactured this way.[1] For architectural glass, the term "cast glass" is used for deeply patterned glass and is similar to slumped glass (Chapter 1.1).

TOOLING

For casting glass, the tooling required is the mold. There are additional tools that the foundry may use in the process, such as crucibles, ladles, and scissors for cutting glass. Generally, molds need to resist heat so that they do not crack on contact with the molten glass or when they are in the kiln while the glass is melting. If the mold is to be filled with molten glass outside the kiln, it can be made of water-soaked wood, graphite, sand, cast iron, or machined steel. If the mold is made of metal, it should be preheated prior to pouring so that the metal does not crack due to the thermal shock. For kiln casting, molds can be made with refractory plaster,[2] graphite, sand, or molded fiber blankets. As these molds are placed into the kiln and heated to the same temperature as the glass, thermal shock is lessened.

The surface of the mold cavity forms the outside surface of the casting. Sand molds will make the surface of the casting textured and slightly pitted. [8] Plaster molds give a matte surface to the glass; additionally, fiberglass may be used to reinforce the plaster molds, and those fibers may leave an imprint on the surface of the glass casting. [9] Generally, metal and graphite molds will leave a shinier surface on the casting than a plaster mold. If a glossy finish is required, the casting should be flame finished before it is annealed.

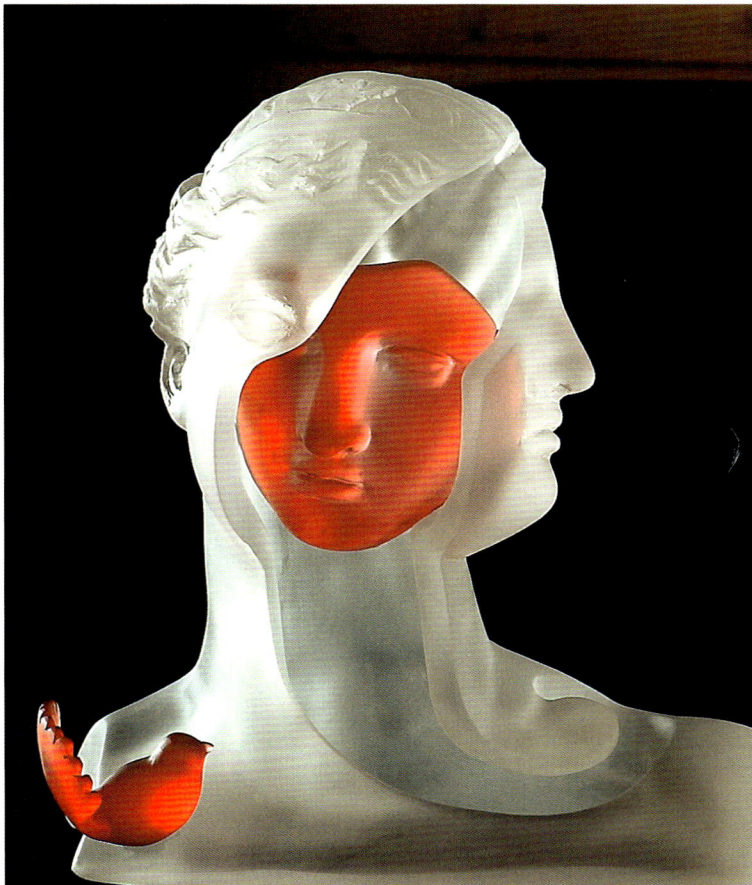
6 Kiln-cast glass sculpture

7 Vessels resulting from the pâte-de-verre technique

8 Surface quality of sand-cast glass

Molds may be open or closed, sacrificial or permanent. Generally, open molds are easier to cast into than closed molds, and can be cast inside or outside of the kiln. Open molds offer better control over glass placement, especially if different types of glass are to be used in the casting (see figure 4.3.2). The drawback is that open molds leave one face of the casting unmolded and unfinished. Due to air exposure, the unmolded face will naturally have a flame finish. If the mold is sacrificed, small undercuts are permissible; however, undercuts cannot be too deep, otherwise the glass casting may be damaged while breaking the mold. Open molds can be made of plaster, graphite, or sand, and can be made in multiple parts.

Closed molds are best for dribble casting, but can also be used when pouring molten glass outside the kiln. The kiln's consistent temperature helps the glass retain its fluidity and gives the glass ample time to fill the mold. The closed mold cavity may be filled directly by the reservoir or crucible, or it may use a sprue system to move the glass from the reservoir to the cavity. The sprue must be wide enough that the glass can flow into the cavity, and is removed from the casting during post-production. [10] Closed molds with small openings must have vents so that trapped air can escape. Placement of glass in the mold cavity is difficult with this process, and this is often where manufacturing problems occur.

Closed molds can be made from one or more pieces. If the mold is made of one piece, it is sacrificed each time the casting is removed. If the mold is made of two or more pieces, it can be made of metal or plaster. For a multi-part mold, no clamping or sealing force is required at the parting line, as the glass is too viscous to flow into the parting line.

Molds for casting glass can be made in a number of different ways. CNC routers can be used for machined steel, carved wood molds, and even to shape plaster. EDM can fabricate steel molds, but is expensive and time consuming, making it more appropriate for high-volume productions. Patterns can also be used to form molds, such those made for sand-cast iron (Chapter 4.2) or cast plaster, or for pressing into sand for shaping. Patterns can be made of wood, resin, clay, or wax and can be CNC milled or three-dimensionally printed.

ENVIRONMENTAL IMPACT

Casting glass is an energy-intensive process. Glass typically melts at around 2,700–3,000°F (1,480–1,650°C) and must be heated slowly to get to the right temperature. After casting, the glass must also be annealed, or cooled slowly in a kiln. Casting often is used to manufacture thick components, and annealing can take 48 hours or more.

Typically, there is little manufacturing waste with this process, as the manufacturer only uses what is needed. Glass is also highly recyclable, and any waste that is created can be melted again or broken and included with other glass pieces.

9 Plaster mold with embedded glass fibers

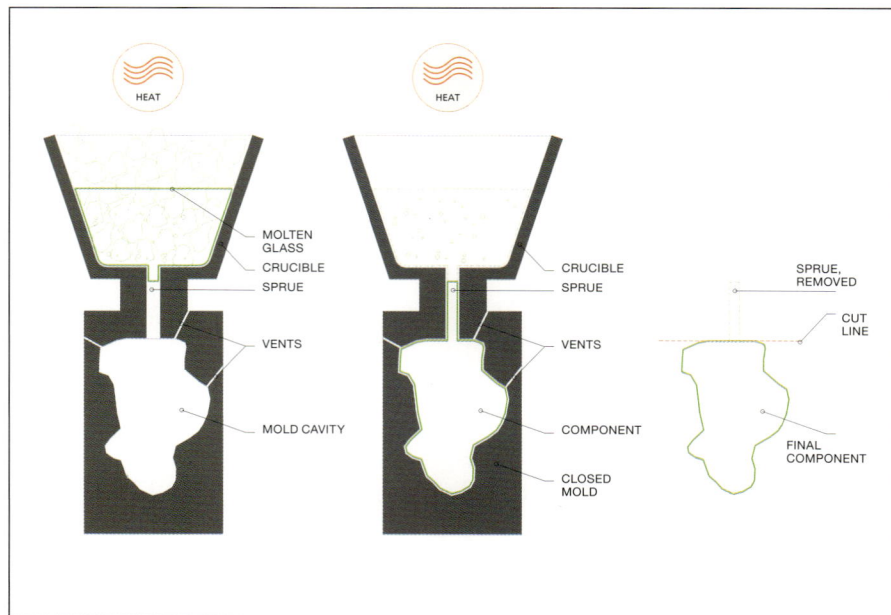

10 Casting glass in a closed mold via a sprue

MATERIAL CONSIDERATIONS + DESIGN PARAMETERS

The primary material for glass is silicon dioxide (SiO_2), which is typically combined with other oxide ceramics. The mixture and type of oxides affect the properties of the glass. For example, borosilicate glass contains boron trioxide and is stronger and more durable, compared with soda lime glass, which contains sodium oxide. Lead can be added so that the glass is more fluid when melted. Lead glass is the easiest to cast, while borosilicate glass is more difficult to work with. Glass can be 100% recycled, although high recycled content may affect its performance. Glass chips, ceramic powders, and metals are added to glass to change its color. These in turn makes the glass expand and contract at different rates, based on its color and composition. Generally, mixing different glass colors is difficult, unless the glass colors are deemed compatible.

Glass does not have a distinct melting point; its melting is a gradual transition rather than a traditional phase change from solid to liquid. In *Kiln Forming Glass*, Helga Watkins-Baker refers to this as the softening of the glass rather than melting it.[3] Molten glass has the fluidity of thick honey.

If glass pieces are used for glass casting, the size of the pieces may range from a single, large glass ingot to millions of small glass granules that are the size of sugar grains. Generally, the smaller the glass pieces used in the casting, the more opaque the resulting casting. This is because the small glass pieces trap air bubbles as they fuse together. When using smaller glass pieces, the mold may need to be over-filled or topped off in the middle of casting. As much as 50% of the glass may settle during the casting process. **[11]**

After casting, the glass should be annealed, meaning it is slowly heated and cooled under controlled conditions so that the temperature differential across the glass's cross-section is negligible. This keeps the glass from cracking during the cooling process. Because cast glass tends to be thicker than pressed or slumped glass, annealing times are long. It is not uncommon for cast glass components to anneal for 48 hours or more.

SIMILAR PROCESSES

Pressing glass (Chapter 4.6) is similar to casting glass. Generally, cast glass is better for thick, solid components whereas pressing glass is better suited for thinner walled components with fine surface detail. Pâte-de-verre can be used for components with thinner walls than pressing, but the process results in opaque glass, whereas pressed glass components can remain clear. Slumping glass (Chapter 1.1) is also similar, as gravity is used to slowly deform the glass against the mold; however, slumping glass is generally used for components which have a surface area larger than their volume.

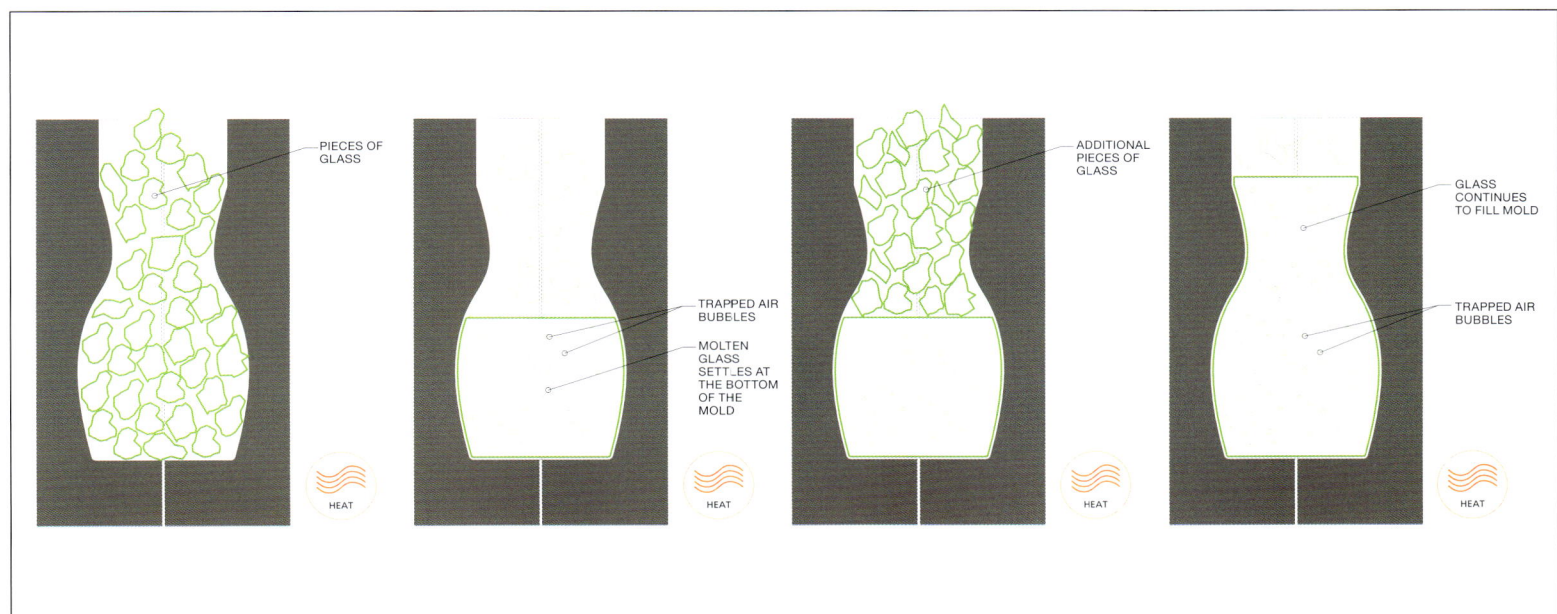

PIECES OF GLASS

TRAPPED AIR BUBELES

MOLTEN GLASS SETTLES AT THE BOTTOM OF THE MOLD

ADDITIONAL PIECES OF GLASS

GLASS CONTINUES TO FILL MOLD

TRAPPED AIR BUBBLES

HEAT   HEAT   HEAT   HEAT

11 Molds may need refilling during kiln casting

CORNER RADII

For permanent molds and sand molds, the radius for interior and exterior corners should be 0.12–0.5in (3–13mm), depending on the size of the casting. For sacrificial molds, no radius is required.

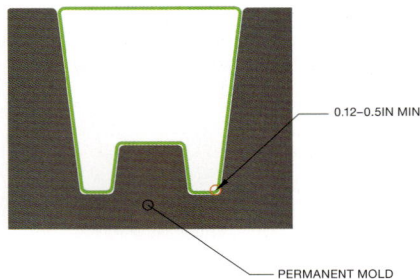

0.12–0.5IN MIN

PERMANENT MOLD

DRAFT ANGLES

For permanent molds, the minimum draft angle should be 5–7°.

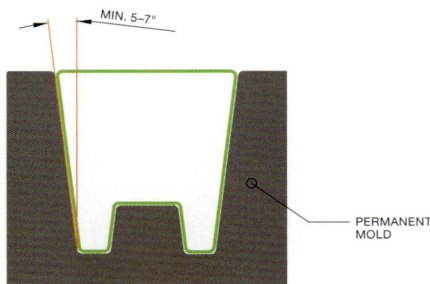

MIN. 5–7°

PERMANENT MOLD

For sacrificial or sand molds, a 0° or negative draft angle of –1–2° is possible.

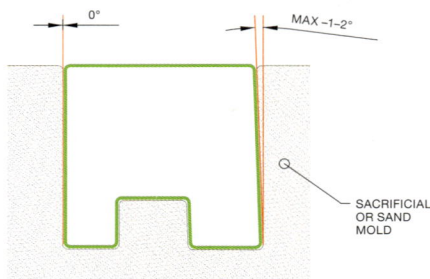

0°

MAX –1–2°

SACRIFICIAL OR SAND MOLD

FINISH

Surface finishes can range from a honed stone to a bright, shiny finish, typical of glass. The finish of the glass casting depends on the mold material or whether the casting is flame finished. The face of the casting that does not touch the mold will be bright and shiny. To get that same finish on the faces that do touch the mold, the casting would need to be removed from the mold and finished in the open air with a flame.

INSERTS

Other materials can be inserted into the glass casting; however, the insert needs to be able to thermally expand and contract at a rate similar to the glass. Inserts can include copper or silver wire or mesh, mica, fired ceramics, or shells.

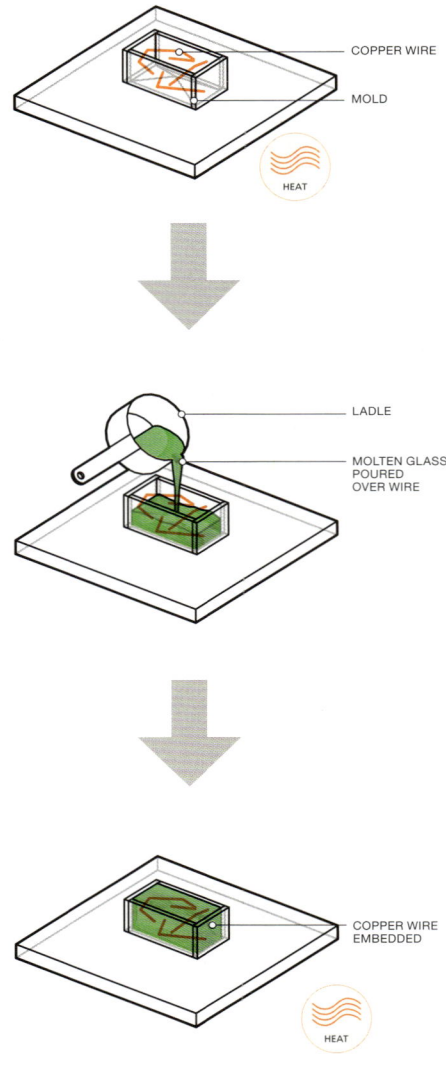

COPPER WIRE

MOLD

HEAT

LADLE

MOLTEN GLASS POURED OVER WIRE

COPPER WIRE EMBEDDED

HEAT

JOINING

Cast glass components can be joined together through heat fusing.

PARTING LINES

Parting lines can wander as necessary to avoid undercuts. Little to no pressure is needed at the parting lines to keep the mold parts together. The parting line may leave a mark on the surface of the glass casting, but this can be easily removed by flame finishing.

PRODUCTION SPEED

Cycle times for this manufacturing process can be long, depending on the thickness of the glass. It is not unusual for cast glass to be in the kiln for days to weeks for proper casting and annealing.

PRODUCTION VOLUME

This process is best suited to low-volume productions. The production volume depends on the shape of the component and the type of mold used. Plaster molds are good for five to ten firings before they are unusable. Cast iron molds may last 500 cycles or longer.

SHAPES

This process is best suited to solid, thick-walled components.

SIZE LIMITS

Sizes range from small, bead-like pieces to large sculptures over 8ft (2.4m) tall, to telescope lenses more than 27ft (8.2m) across. This process is limited only by the size of the kiln and the annealing time.[4]

SURFACE DESIGNS

Cast-glass surfaces can have designs or details. Because gravity is pulling and the glass is thick in is molten state, details at the bottom of the casting may be sharper than details on the casting's side-walls.

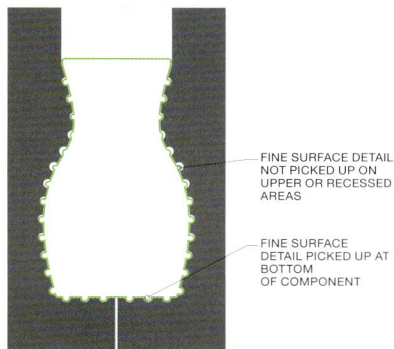

FINE SURFACE DETAIL NOT PICKED UP ON UPPER OR RECESSED AREAS

FINE SURFACE DETAIL PICKED UP AT BOTTOM OF COMPONENT

TOLERANCES

Tolerance for architectural or artisan cast glass will range from 0.06 to 0.12in (1.5–3mm). Tighter tolerances for specialty items can achieved, but at a higher cost.

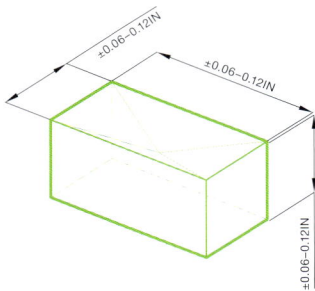

±0.06–0.12IN
±0.06–0.12IN
±0.06–0.12IN

TOOL COMPLEXITY

Tools are simple, with no moving parts.

TOOLING COSTS

Tooling costs for this process are very low, and depend on size and material. A plaster mold can cost less than $50, whereas cast-iron and steel tools may be about $1,000, or more.

UNDERCUTS

If the molds are sacrificed with each casting, undercuts are permissible. If the molds are to be reused, undercuts are not permissible. With closed molds, undercuts can be avoided by using wandering parting lines or multi-part molds.

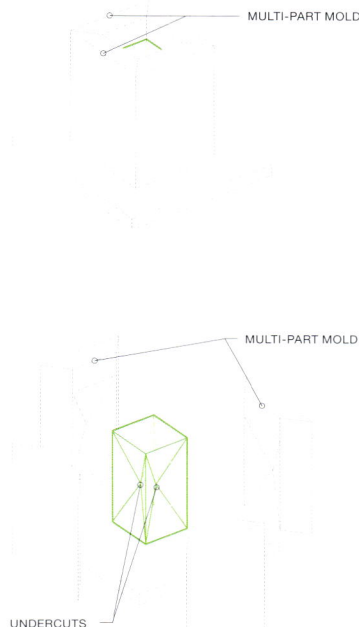

MULTI-PART MOLD

MULTI-PART MOLD

UNDERCUTS

VENTS

In closed molds, with dribble or molten casting, vents are necessary at any cavity overhangs. If using small pieces of glass or an open mold, vents are not necessary.

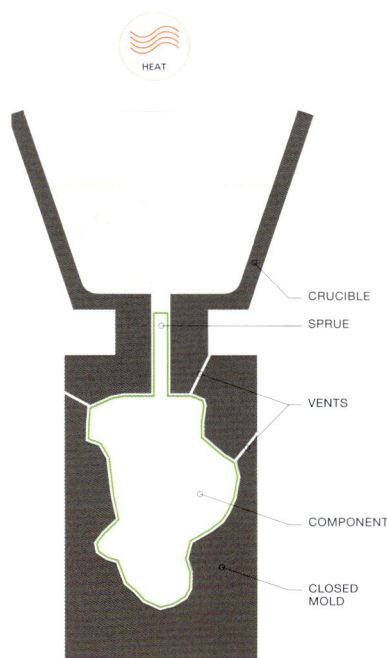

HEAT

CRUCIBLE

SPRUE

VENTS

COMPONENT

CLOSED MOLD

WALL THICKNESS

With static casting or pâte-de-verre, there are no minimum wall thicknesses, as long as the glass pieces can fit in the narrow confines of the mold. For molten or dribble casting, the walls of the component should be thick so that the glass can properly flow. Any changes in wall thickness should be gradual, with the thicker walls closer to the reservoir or sprue, and the thinner walls farther away.

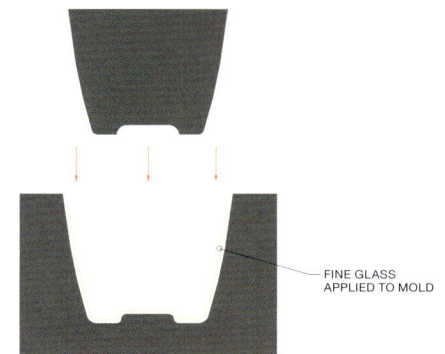

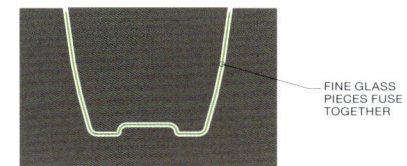

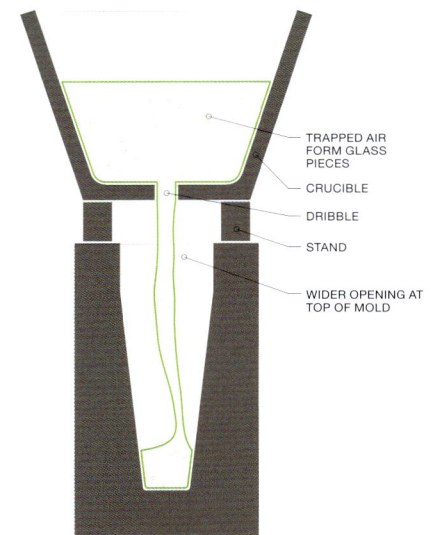

FINE GLASS APPLIED TO MOLD

FINE GLASS PIECES FUSE TOGETHER

HEAT

TRAPPED AIR FORM GLASS PIECES

CRUCIBLE

DRIBBLE

STAND

WIDER OPENING AT TOP OF MOLD

HEAT

CASTING GLASS

EXTERIOR BUILDING SKIN | BAHÁ'Í TEMPLE FOR SOUTH AMERICA
Hariri Pontarini Architects
Santiago, Chile

After a two-stage international design competition, the Bahá'í Community awarded the design commission for its South American Temple to Hariri Pontarini Architects (HPA). The competition was held in 2002 and the building was completed in 2016.[5] **[12, 13]** Bahá'í services can be held in small facilities or members' homes, but the Bahá'í have commissioned large meditative temples for each continent, with the intention that the temples should provide global landmarks for the religion. The Bahá'í believe in the spiritual unity of all people and major religions, with nine being an important number that represents their conception of unity and diversity. All of the built Bahá'í temples have nine sides, a dome, light featuring prominently in the design, and a connection to garden space. **[14]**

HPA worked with the client to find and select the property for the South American Temple. Its site is located just 20 minutes from central Santiago, in the Andean foothills. The total property size is 205 acres (83 hectares)

12
Bahá'í Temple during construction, with the city of Santiago beyond

13
Building during construction

14
Site plan

15
The Temple's custom, kiln-cast slumped glass panel

16
Front view of glass panel

with 15 acres (6 hectares) of gardens. The Temple is 26,000ft^2 (2,400m^2) and holds 600 people. The Temple has nine sails that twist and bend to form the building's dome. The sails are translucent, allowing sunlight to enter through the skin during the day, and the building lights up as a beacon on the foot-hills at night. The interior of the dome is skinned with a thin-cut, translucent marble, and the exterior skin is made from custom kiln-cast glass.

HPA designed the Temple with a mix of flat and slumped glass panels. All of the panels were made from the same size of cast-glass plates. The glass plates were cast by layering two different diameters of drawn borosilicate glass rods into a mold. The rods were broken into random lengths, layered into the mold, and then placed into the kiln. As the kiln reached the correct temperature, the rods fused together, creating a solid glass panel that maintained some of the geometry of the original rods. From there, some of the plates were slumped on a mold. The flat and slumped plates were then CNC trimmed with a water-jet cutter to their final dimensions. [15] Each of the nine sails has 1,129 uniquely shaped glass panels, with 978 flat panels and 151 slumped panels. At the same time the nine sails are repeats of one another, so that each slumped glass form is repetitively manufactured nine times within the project.

HPA collaborated with Jeff Goodman Studio to develop the custom glass for this project. Goodman was a glass artist who primarily works with blown glass, but also does slumping, casting, architectural glass, and commissioned work. Goodman Studio cast all of the glass panels and then sent

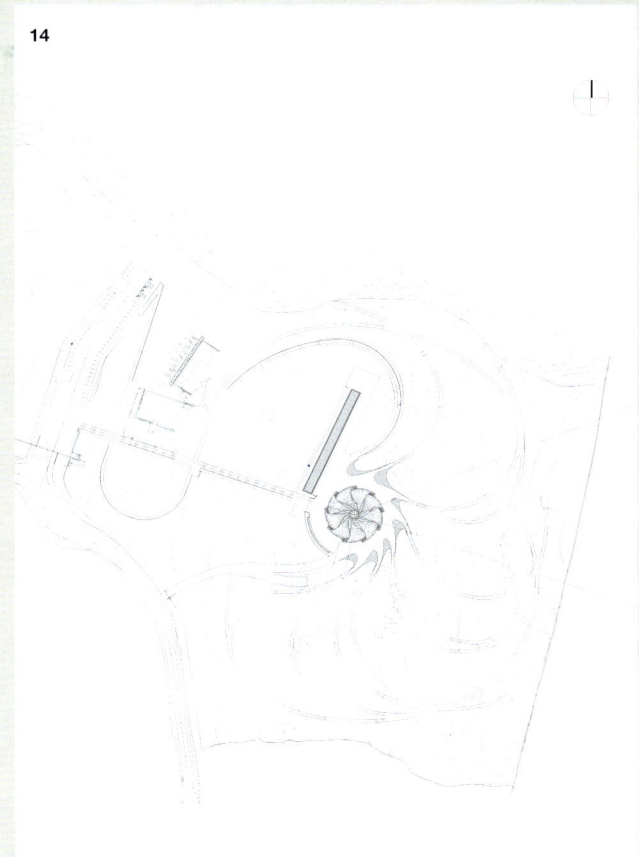

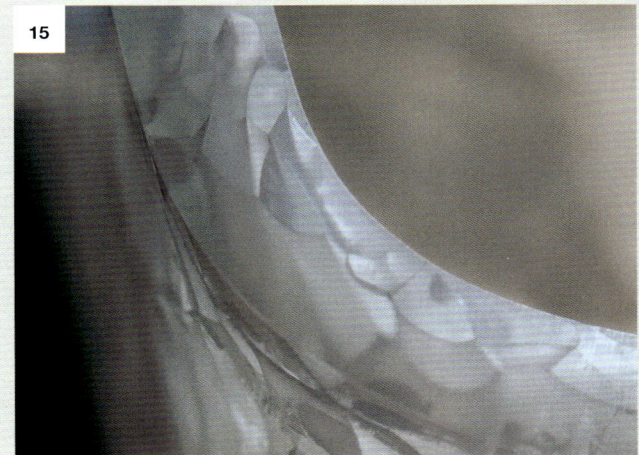

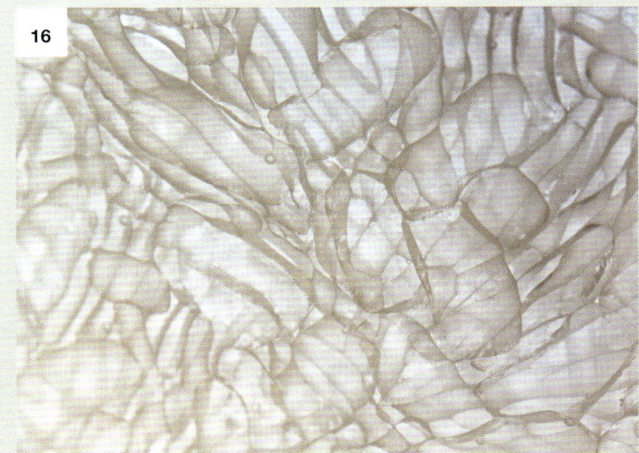

151 cast panels to CBD Glass for slumping. CBD Glass is a Toronto-based glass production facility, so coordination between the architect, artist, and production facility was easily managed. Simpson Gumpertz & Heger (SGH) were the cladding consultants on the project, and Germany-based Josef Gartner GmbH was commissioned to detail and make the Temple's sails, using Goodman Studio's flat cast-glass pieces and CBD's slumped panels.

DESIGN CONSIDERATIONS

According to Justin Ford, HPA's job captain for the Bahá'í Temple, the initial designs proposed that both the exterior and interior skins of the Temple be made with alabaster.[6] Although their initial research had indicated that alabaster could be used for exterior application, the team soon learned that the material would become brittle if exposed to weather, and would turn opaque at temperatures above 86°F (30°C).[7] HPA investigated leaving the alabaster on the building's interior, but that would have required conditioning the building cavity and thereby increasing energy costs. The exterior material was changed to kiln-cast, borosilicate glass, and the interior to marble.

In 2004, HPA approached Goodman Studio to create a glass with similar light qualities to those inherent to alabaster, but with much more durability. [16] According to Ford, Goodman Studio prototyped "many, many samples," experimenting with translucency; rod diameters, lengths, organization, and layering; and glass type. Goodman Studio is located just over 11 miles (18km) from HPA's office, which allowed for many visits, reviews, and discussions between the architect and artist. Over 200 samples were made before the team believed they had the right one.

The glass plates use two different diameters of rod, organized more or less parallel, and laid in two different strata, or layers. [17] The larger diameter rods are placed on the bottom of the glass plate and the narrower rods on the top. This creates a slight shadowing or layering effect in the glass that catches the light from the setting and rising sun. The team selected borosilicate [18, 19] over soda lime glass because of its increased durability, dimensional stability, and strength. However, borosilicate is typically more difficult to work with than the soda lime, and the translucency of the cast glass depends on the temperature cycling of the kiln.

MANUFACTURING CONSIDERATIONS

As an artist, Goodman had a love and a passion for what was being created. According to Ford, his aesthetic desires were aligned with HPA and he was an enthusiastic collaborator. Goodman was closer to a craftsman than a manufacturer. [20, 21] In order to meet the manufacturing schedule associated with the project, Goodman Studio custom-made six kilns to manufacture the cast-glass plates. [22, 23] Because of the size limitations of the kiln, the glass panels were redesigned to be smaller so that they could fit inside the kiln. In the end, HPA was happy with the decision because it gave the project an additional level of detail and reduced the panels to a more human scale.[8] It took two years to make all of the kiln-cast plates, and one and a half years to slump all of the panels.[9] [24]

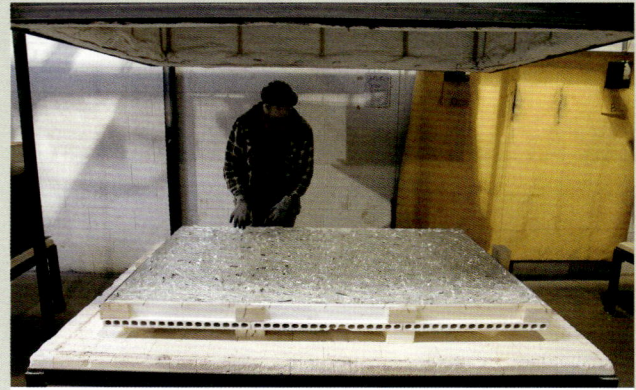

17 Layering glass rods into mold, prior to casting

18 Manufacturing borosilicate rods

19 Manufacturing borosilicate rods

20 Breaking rods at Jeff Goodman Studio

21 Layering glass rods into mold at Goodman Studio prior to casting

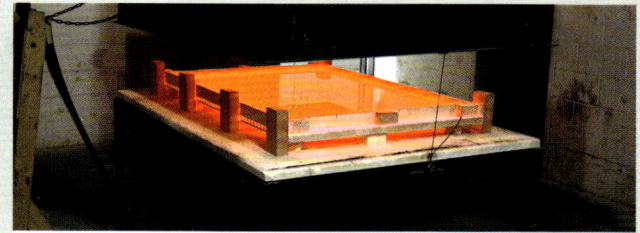

22 During kiln casting

23 Custom kilns were made to fit the glass panels

The casting of the glass plates was repeated in the same shaped mold within each kiln. From there, the flat piece was either cut by CNC or sent to CBD for slumping and then cut. [25] Even though there is little repeatability within each of the glass panels, there is a lot of repetition with the use of the casting molds. This project balances the repetitive use of the mold with the ability of CAM technology to cut custom shapes. The slumping was done on a CNC-milled foam pattern that was then sprayed with a refractory concrete. It is a full mold, with a maximum slumping depth of 12in (300mm). Each slumping mold was used only nine times. After slumping, the glass panels were sent to Germany and cut to size on a five-axis CNC water-jet cutter.

OTHER CONSIDERATIONS

Physical tests were done on the glass, including shooting a ball bearing at it to assess impact loads, and thermal stress tests. This project is located in a seismic zone, so virtual testing was done on the digital model to predict how the structure would behave in an earthquake.

LESSONS LEARNED

One of the lessons that Ford learned though this project is that "it is difficult to make things different." Although the digital technologies can easily produce a lot of variety, fabrication is not necessarily so nimble. Keeping track of each glass panel proved difficult, especially as they were shipped from one manufacturer to another. [26] As HPA developed the design, the firm made decisions to make manufacturing easier. This included reducing the panel size to fit the casting kiln, and reducing the number of slumped glass panels. The initial design had more slumped panels than the 151 different ones made for each sail but, to reduce costs, the design team added more flat pieces to the design.

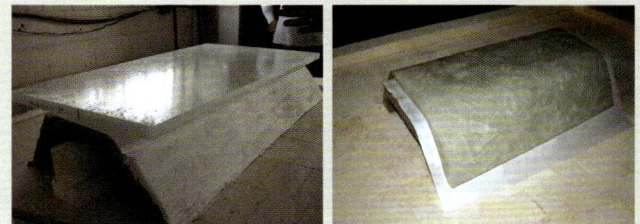

24 Slumping cast-glass panels over molds

25 Numerous slumped glass panels

26 Shipping glass panels

4.4 Vibration-Press Casting
aka vibration casting

INTRODUCTION

Vibration-press casting, or vibration casting, is a manufacturing process that vibrates the mold to help evenly distribute a dry mixture of cementitious binders and small aggregates.[1] The concrete is mixed with just enough water to hold its shape without crumbling and just enough so that the cement can cure. This manufacturing method is used to produce concrete masonry units (CMUs). [1] Varied shapes can be made with vibration casting, based on the type of mold and how mechanized the manufacturing facility is. Vibration casting is used to produce complex shapes with moderate detail and tolerances. It can produce solid or hollow shapes, and various cross-sectional thicknesses. Sizes range from concrete bricks to large landscape components.

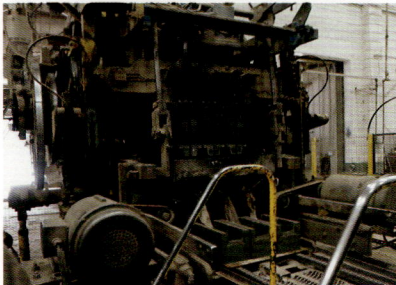

1 U-shaped CMUs being manufactured on a high-volume block machine at Adams Products in Greensboro, North Carolina

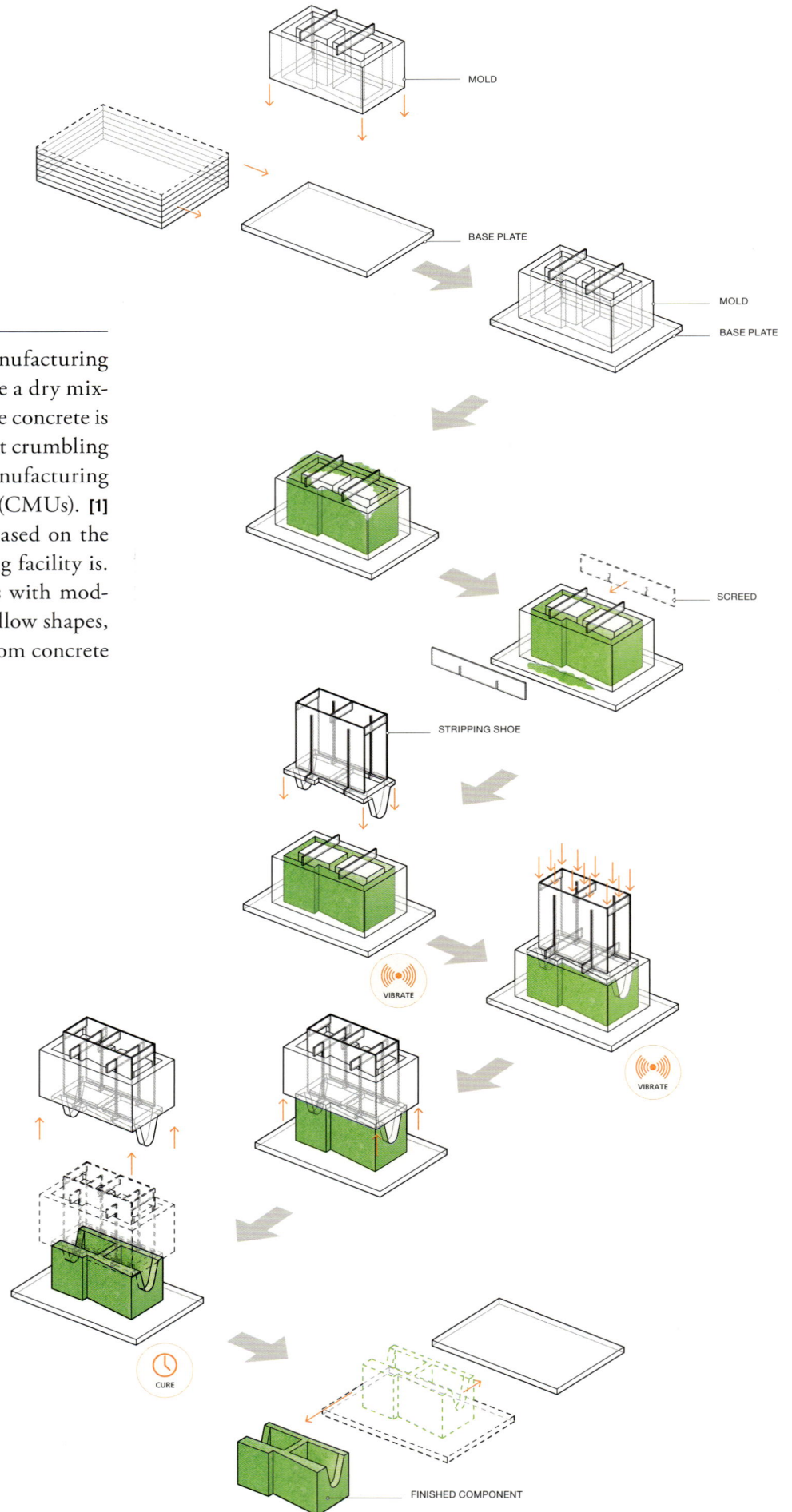

MOLD

BASE PLATE

MOLD

BASE PLATE

SCREED

STRIPPING SHOE

VIBRATE

VIBRATE

CURE

FINISHED COMPONENT

In vibration-press casting, the mold comes down onto a base plate and is filled by the concrete mixture. Any extra concrete is then screed off. The mold is vibrated to move the stiff concrete into the corners as the stripping shoe comes down. The stripping shoe compacts the material to hold its shape, helps to evenly distribute moisture throughout the concrete, and also helps ensure that the concrete fills the bottom of the mold. The mold is then lifted up as the stripping shoe holds the concrete in place on the base plate. The unit, supported by the base plate, is then cured. Once it is strong enough to support itself, the finished component is removed from the base plate.

Although not typical, some manufacturers have the ability to make undercuts with side-wall core pulls. [2] Core pulls move separately from the mold and slide perpendicular to the direction in which the mold moves. Core pulls increase manufacturing cost, complexity, and wear on the mold. As the cores move in and out, they tend to pull cement with them, often binding up the mechanism.

In more industrialized areas, vibration casting is a highly mechanized process, designed for high-volume production of CMUs. CMU manufacturers use large machines to do the castings, a series of conveyors to move products to steam rooms, and conveyors and robots for packaging. [3, 4, 5] Cycle times for this

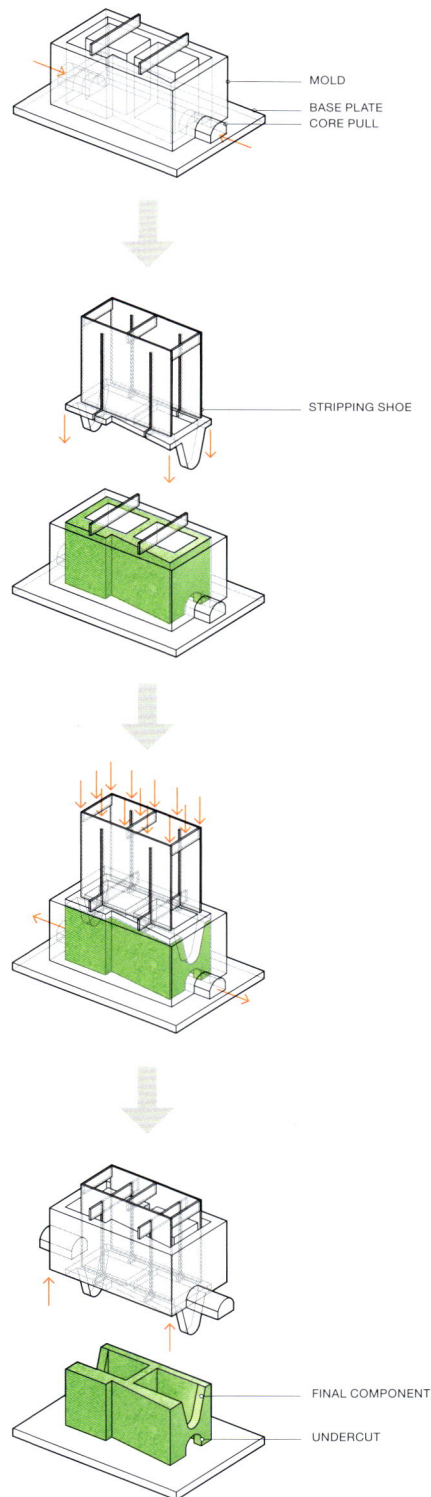

MOLD
BASE PLATE
CORE PULL

STRIPPING SHOE

FINAL COMPONENT

UNDERCUT

2 Use of optional core pulls in process

3 Six solid units being made during each machine cycle

4 Carts with stacked units being automatically loaded into the steam room for curing

process are fairly short, as a machine can cycle every 5–10 seconds. Depending on the size of the CMU, each cycle can make between one and twelve units. Because of the equipment requirements of high-volume production, the size of the CMU will be limited by the size of the mold box that the machines are able to accept. Some manufacturers will have dedicated production lines for smaller production runs, making tooling changes, color changes, and post-production process changes easier to manage. This makes it possible for these manufacturers to take custom orders. Other manufacturers cannot accommodate manufacturing of custom units without disrupting their operations, and therefore will not produce custom units.

In developing nations, vibration casting is a labor-intensive manufacturing process with low capital costs. Manufacturers may use small presses that are operated by hand. In a press, units are formed on a bottom plate that may be made of plywood, wood, metal, or plastic, and the plate may be moved by hand to a place where the CMU can cure. The hand presses can make multiple units simultaneously; however, the units must be light enough to be moved. Another option is manufacturing units on the ground with just the mold and the stripping shoe. Here the four-walled mold is placed on the ground, filled with concrete, and screed. Some molds will vibrate while the stripping shoe presses down on the concrete. Some molds do not vibrate, and instead the

manufacturer rams the stripping shoe into the mold multiple times, compressing the stiff concrete into all corners.[2] The mold is then lifted around the shoe and the whole mechanism is moved to another place on the ground. The formed unit is left on the ground until it cures. This method works well for producing CMUs on-site. Generally, these less-mechanized processes can more easily accommodate custom shapes.

BUILDING PRODUCTS

A number of vibration-cast components are commercially available. Almost all concrete masonry and hardscape units are made by this method, including regular stretchers, solid units, bond beams, concrete caps, pavers, and concrete bricks. [6] There are also some specialty concrete masonry products that are less well known. For example, Omni Block is a new product designed to increase a single-wythe concrete block wall's resistance to heat transfer in order to reduce a building's energy use. [7] It has a reduced height for its internal webs, thereby reducing thermal bridging across the block's cross-section.

In addition to performance, there are also commercially available CMUs designed to improve aesthetics. Some products use single or multiple colored cements, color additives, decorative aggregates, or applications of exterior spray colors. [8] There are

5 Highly mechanized manufacturers using conveyors to move units

7 Omni Block with reduced thermal bridging at the internal webs

6 Storage yard with standard products waiting to be shipped

8 CMU with white cement, decorative aggregates, and a polished face

also slump blocks that use a slightly slumping cement mixture, so that the finish face of the block has a rounded look, decorative screen blocks, and blocks with decorative scoring on the face of the unit. Finally, various kinds of post-production finishing can be done with the block, including tumbling, splitting, grinding, and polishing of the units.

Some of these specialty blocks are proprietary, such as the Omni Block, while others are non-proprietary, such as the split-faced block. Even the non-proprietary options, such as decorative aggregates and spray colors, are only offered by a limited number of manufacturers, so specifying those can limit who can produce them.

TOOLING

The tooling required for vibration-press casting is the mold, the stripping shoe, and optional core pulls. For high-volume productions, the tooling is limited by the size of the block-making machine. These large machines use a mold box, which includes a steel tray attached to a steel frame, with the vibration mechanism also attached. [9] The mold box measures 16in wide by 24in long by 8in high (410 by 610 by 200mm) to fit the machine. Inside the mold box are steel plates that form the vertical faces of the components. [10, 11]

The tooling is typically built up, meaning the tool is made from a series of separate parts and plates. This allows parts of the mold to be replaced as necessary. [12] Because the dry concrete mixture places a lot of friction on the mold faces, the steel plates have to be replaced or repaired often. Inside the mold box are divider bars so that multiple units can be made with each cycle of the press. Optional wear plates can be suspended inside the dividers that alter the shape of the CMU. This is how a stretcher CMU may be turned into a bullnose or a jamb unit. These optional wear plates can be applied to all of the blocks in a mold box, or to only a selection of the blocks. Cores for the blocks are suspended across the top of the mold box by steel bars, but can be removed to make solid units.

The stripper shoe includes a steel plate, a deep frame, and the stripping shoe itself. The plate connects the stripper to the press, and the frame connects the plate to the shoe. [13]. The frame is dimensioned to be taller than the mold box so that it can strip the concrete out through the bottom of the mold onto the plate. The frame must work around any cores, core supports, and divider plates in the mold box. The shoe is shaped to match the shape of the top of the CMU. Typically, the shoe is flat, but it can form the top of the unit into a curved surface, score the unit's top, or make a depression.

Typically, the tools for this process are made with steel, although fiberglass has been used for prototyping molds. For

9 Full tool for a mechanized press. Includes the mold box on the bottom, with frame. Sitting inside of the mold box is the stripping shoe with its supporting frame. Attached to the mold box are the cams for vibrating while pressing

11 Inside a mold box, showing two 10in (250mm) standard stretcher CMU blocks being made.

10 Stripping shoes with frames

12 Molds are typically built up with sheets of tool steel

high-volume manufacturers, the tooling costs are high. The structure for the tooling is typically made from structural-grade steel, while wear plates and stripping shoes will be made from higher-grade tool steel. For smaller production runs, tools may be made from painted steel or aluminum.

Historically, for high-volume manufacturers, it could take anywhere from 2 to 4 hours to change the tooling for a high-volume press. Because the press and the press operators would be idle while the tooling was changed, most high-volume producers would have been reluctant to change tools until a work shift had ended. This, in turn, meant that any customized shapes would have to have enough of a product run to keep an 8–10 hour shift busy. However, there are new presses on the market than can accommodate changing a tool in 15–30 minutes. This means that for manufacturers with newer equipment, there is less pressure to produce a full shift's worth of units. [14]

ENVIRONMENTAL IMPACT

If made by hand or on a hand press, the largest environmental impact of this process is the manufacturing of the Portland cement. Optional steam curing requires some energy, however, energy requirements to make steam are much less than energy required to fire clay in a kiln. In comparison to wet-casting concrete, vibration-press casting uses very little water in the concrete mixture.

Generally, there is little to no manufacturing waste with this process. Most times, any concrete that is screed off is returned back to the hopper and fed into the following cycles. Many high-volume producers can add recycled block as an aggregate into the new block, qualifying the units for LEED credits. Because of the dead load associated with this product, transportation fuel costs can be high; however, this is balanced by the high number of block producers, so that block may be produced close to a construction site.

13 Stripping shoe and frame to make two 12in (300mm) blocks within one mold box

14 Tool storage. On the underside of each tool, the shape of the unit can clearly be seen

MATERIAL CONSIDERATIONS + DESIGN PARAMETERS

STIFF CONCRETE

The concrete used for vibration-press casting is a mixture of Portland cement, aggregates (coarse and fine), and water. The cement itself can be changed from the typical gray Portland cement to a white cement to enable additional color options. The aggregate is a mixture of sand and coarse aggregate with a particle size typically less than 0.4in (10mm). The type of aggregate will affect the density, strength, cost, and potential for recycled content within the CMU. If the block is ground, polished, or split, the aggregate will be exposed. Specialty colors, aggregates, and white cement will increase material costs.

Other additives, such as fly ash, pumice, and furnace slag, may be added to the concrete. This too will affect the performance of the unit, but also could help the unit count toward different sustainability measuring systems (e.g. LEED, Living Building Challenge, etc.). Other additives can also include air-entraining agents, for freeze-thaw applications, and integral water repellents, for exterior applications. Make sure to discuss with your manufacturer where the custom units are to be located, and any specific material performance requirements.

Occasionally, an architect may want a component with a softer or more rounded shape. [15] This can be achieved by using a slightly wetter concrete mixture that will slump after being removed from the mold. This is called a slump block, and it can vary from standard block dimensions by 0.12–0.9in (3–22mm).

For high-volume producers, the units are cured by steam. This can be done with low-pressure steam in a tunnel kiln (see figure 4.4.4). The units are in the kiln for approximately 24 hours, and attain most of their ultimate strength in 2–4 days. Alternatively, a manufacturer may use high-pressure steam, curing the units in autoclaves. There they are steamed for 5–10 hours, after which time the steam and pressure are quickly released from the autoclave, causing a vacuum that pulls any remaining moisture from the units. However, low-volume producers may not have access to steam kilns or autoclaves; for these manufacturers, the concrete may be cured for 28 days without the use of steam or pressure.

SIMILAR PROCESSES

Vibration-press casting is most similar to vibration-tamping (Chapter 4.5), used for making cast stone. The benefits of vibration-press casting over vibration-tamping are faster production speeds, lower per-unit-costs as production volume increases, and that it is more suited to manufacturing load-bearing units. Conversely, vibration-tamping has lower mold costs, produces less porous surfaces, and its finish more closely replicates stone.

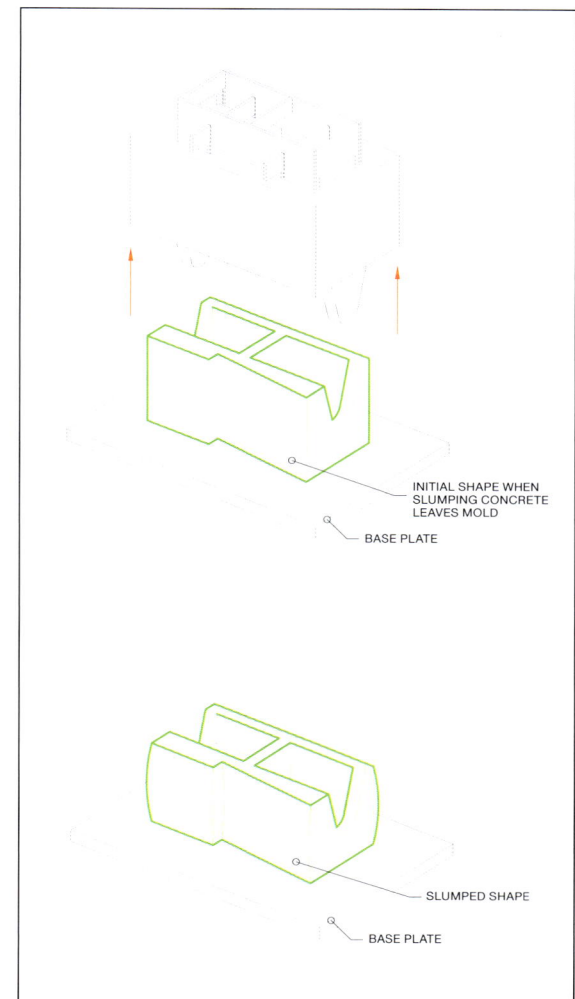

INITIAL SHAPE WHEN SLUMPING CONCRETE LEAVES MOLD

BASE PLATE

SLUMPED SHAPE

BASE PLATE

15 A slumping concrete can be used to make slump block units that have a slightly softened look

ANGLES

Angles in plan should be 60° or greater. Acute angles tend to not be filled in the mold, and are vulnerable to breaking during demolding and transit.

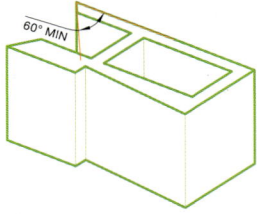

60° MIN

CORES

This process can be used to make either solid or hollow CMUs. The cores can be located in the middle or may engage with the edges of the CMU. Any concrete surrounding the cores must have a minimum thickness of 0.75in (19mm).

Cores are typically rectangular in plan but can take any shape, including triangles, squares, and circles. This is often done if the component is turned on its side to make screen walls.

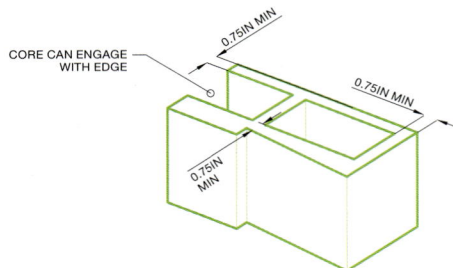

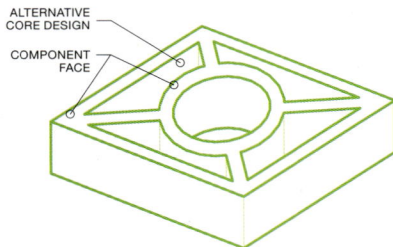

CORE CAN ENGAGE WITH EDGE

0.75IN MIN
0.75IN MIN
0.75IN MIN

ALTERNATIVE CORE DESIGN
COMPONENT FACE

CORNER RADII

No radius is required at the corners.

DRAFT ANGLES

No draft angle is required; however, this process can accommodate a draft angle in the direction of demolding.

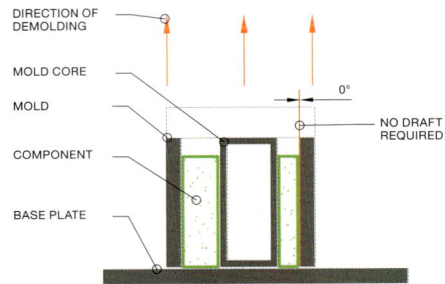

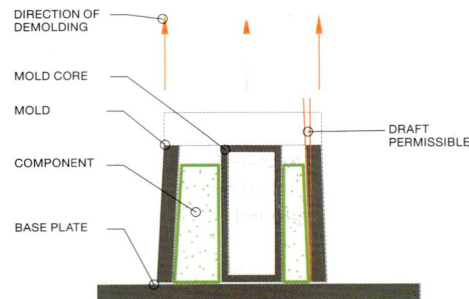

DIRECTION OF DEMOLDING
MOLD CORE
MOLD
COMPONENT
BASE PLATE
0°
NO DRAFT REQUIRED

DIRECTION OF DEMOLDING
MOLD CORE
MOLD
COMPONENT
BASE PLATE
DRAFT PERMISSIBLE

INSERTS

Inserts are not possible with this process.

PRODUCTION SPEED

Highly mechanized presses can cycle every 5–10 seconds. These manufacturing facilities can produce 2,000 or more units per hour. Hand presses can cycle every 25 seconds and can produce 800–1,000 units per hour. Actual production speeds will depend on how many units fit into a mold box and therefore how many units can be produced each machine cycle.

If making the CMUs by hand, using only a mold and a ramming press, the cycle is about 30 seconds or more and typically produces a single block. This would result in 120 blocks produced each hour.

PRODUCTION VOLUME

For high-volume manufacturing, tooling can be used for 50,000–75,000 cycles before needing repair or servicing. For hand presses, or manufacturing blocks by hand, 1,000–10,000 units are possible. Fiberglass molds are good for prototypes and can produce up to 25 units.

SHRINKING

The largest dimension that the units will ever be is in the steam room. After the CMUs steam cure, they lose moisture and shrink. The amount of shrinkage for a 16in (400mm) block is small, and is typically less than 0.01in (0.25mm).

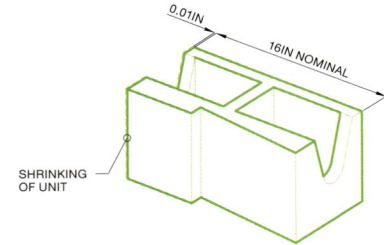

0.01IN
16IN NOMINAL
SHRINKING OF UNIT

SIDE-WALL HOLES

Side-wall holes are possible with core pulls, but it may be more cost effective to drill them post-production.

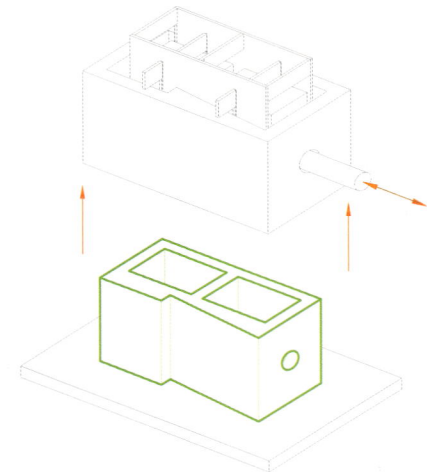

SURFACE DESIGNS

Components' exterior face shells can have surface designs on any four of the mold walls. Both ribs and scores are typically formed this way. They are parallel to the core holes, and their width should be equal to their depth. The face plates of the mold can also be partially shaped, so that the design is not necessarily parallel to the cores. This can result in the addition of pockets, partial bevels, or recessed faces. As long as there are no undercuts, this can easily be accommodated.

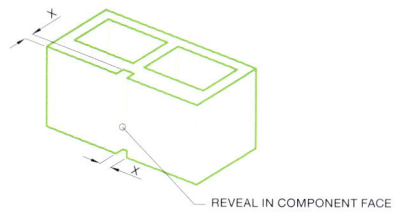

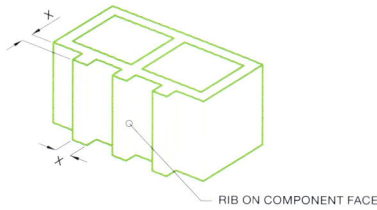

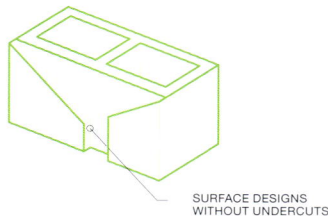

REVEAL IN COMPONENT FACE

RIB ON COMPONENT FACE

SURFACE DESIGNS
WITHOUT UNDERCUTS

Alternatively, the stripping shoe can make a surface design on the top face of the block. In this case, the stripping shoe is shaped or textured.

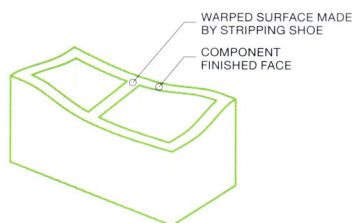

WARPED SURFACE MADE
BY STRIPPING SHOE

COMPONENT
FINISHED FACE

TOLERANCES

Overall dimensions of the CMU will be within 0.12in (3mm) for overall unit width, height, and length. Many manufacturers can hold a tolerance of 0.06in (1.5mm). Tolerance for any molded shell features is 0.06in (1.6mm).

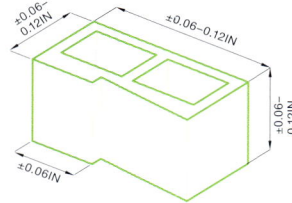

±0.06–0.12IN

±0.06–0.12IN

±0.06–0.12IN

±0.06IN

TOOL COSTS

A new mold, built for high-volume production, can cost $20,000–30,000. For hand presses, painted steel molds will be much less expensive, around $1,500.

UNDERCUTS

Undercuts are permissible with this process, with the use of sliding cores. However, the sliding cores greatly increase production costs and mold wear, and will limit the manufacturer's ability to produce the unit, as not all manufacturers have the necessary technology.

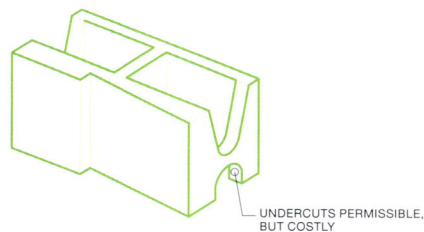

UNDERCUTS PERMISSIBLE,
BUT COSTLY

WALL THICKNESS

For load-bearing units, the exterior CMU face thickness is a minimum of 0.75in (19mm) for a 4in (100mm) block, 1in (25mm) for a 6in (150mm) block, 1.25in (32mm) for an 8in (200mm) block, 1.4in (35mm) for a 10in (25mm) block, and 1.5in (38mm) for a 12in (300mm) block.

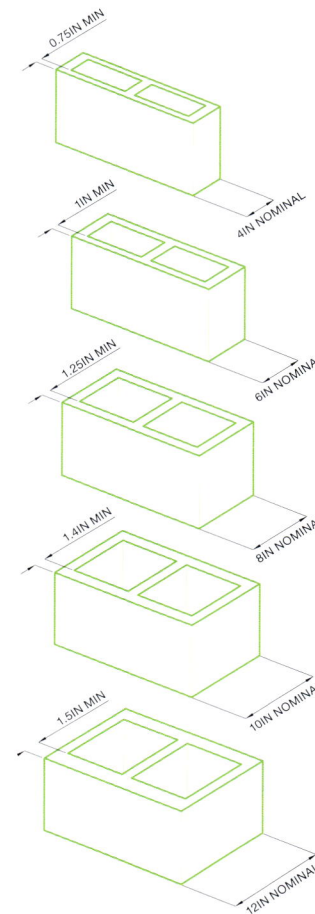

0.75IN MIN

1IN MIN   4IN NOMINAL

1.25IN MIN   6IN NOMINAL

1.4IN MIN   8IN NOMINAL

1.5IN MIN   10IN NOMINAL

12IN NOMINAL

For non-load-bearing block, the minimum exterior shell thickness is 0.75in (19mm).

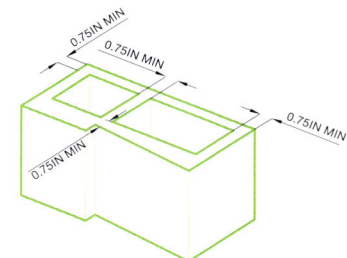

0.75IN MIN   0.75IN MIN

0.75IN MIN

0.75IN MIN

VIBRATION-PRESS CASTING IN STIFF CONCRETE

DECORATIVE SCREEN | MR299
HGR Arquitectos with Ariel Rojo Design Studio
Mexico City, Mexico

MR299 is an apartment building located just south of Mexico City center. **[16]** Completed in 2014, the building is 19,800ft^2 (1835m^2) and is six stories tall. It includes compact parking, a lobby, fifteen apartments with balconies and terraces, and a building garden at the top. A parking garage and the lobby are on the ground floor, and the apartments are above. There are three apartments on each level; the apartment sizes vary from 700 to 1,025ft^2 (65–95m^2) and every apartment looks over a street. The building is located on an urban corner with its two exposed faces perpendicular to one another.

According to Marcos Hagerman, MR299's project architect, the intention of HGR Arquitectos was to design a striking façade for the building while respecting the surrounding buildings.[3] HGR designed the building with site-cast concrete for the upper floors, where the apartments are located. The concrete is almost white in color, smooth, and has refined articulation of organized form ties and expressed joints. In contrast with the site-cast concrete, HGR wanted a concrete lattice to cover the parking area and stairways, while allowing these areas to be naturally ventilated. **[17, 18, 19, 20]**

16
Corner street view of MR299 apartment building

17
Apartment entrances and vertical circulation tower

18
Detail of CMU lattice wall at street level

19
Transverse building section

20
Interior view of CMU lattice wall, showing steel supports

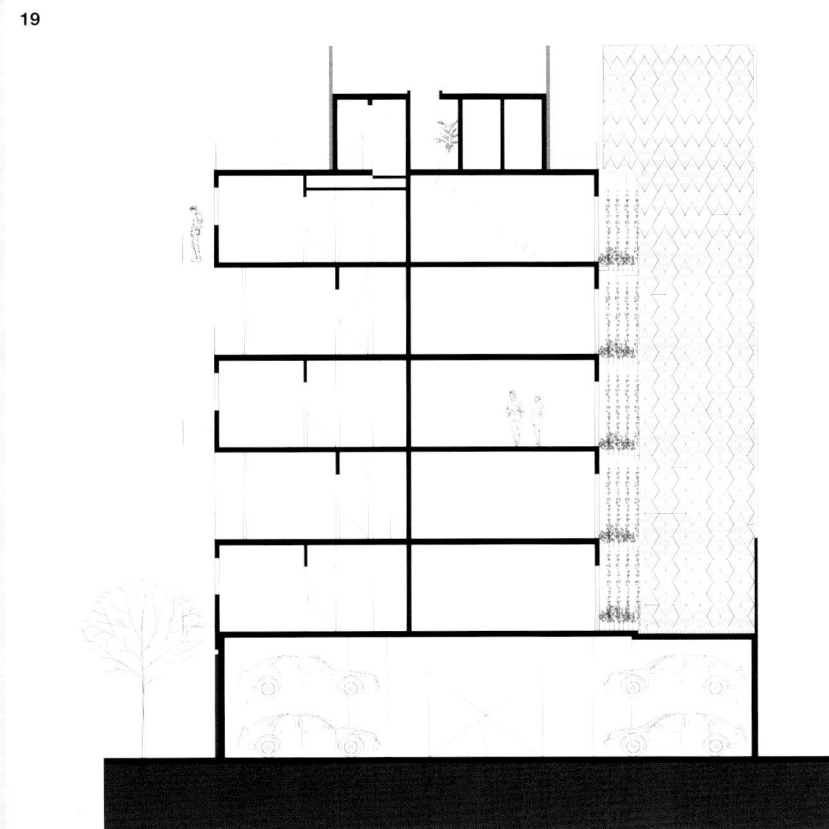

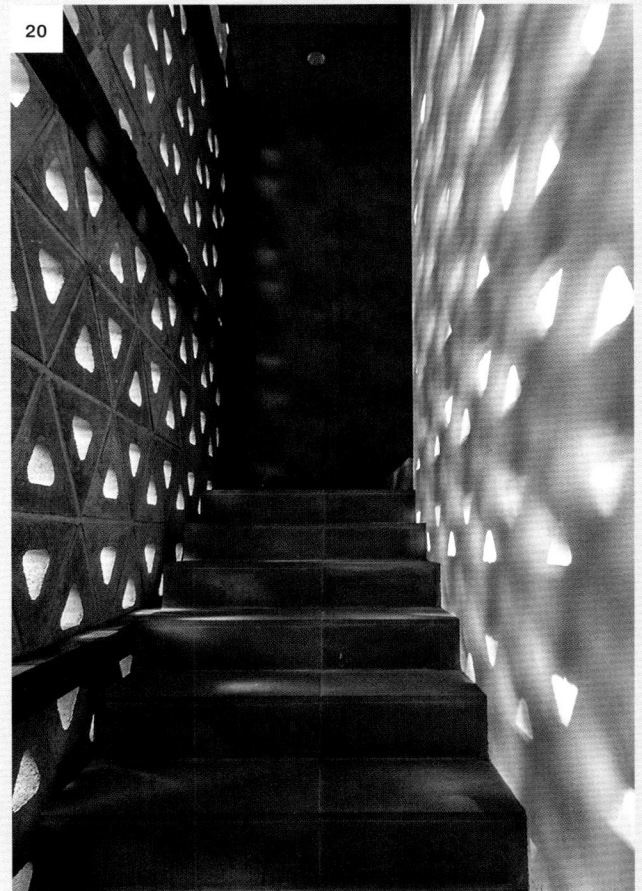

HGR hired Ariel Rojo Design Studio to design a concrete masonry unit to be used in the lattice. **[22]** Rojo's studio does a wide range of projects, including product, furniture, and packaging designs; scene design; architecture; and branding. The studio has prior experience designing custom CMUs, and in 2010 it worked with TAE Arquitectos to design "Multiblok," another custom CMU used for a lattice design. According to Ariel Rojo, he was to comissioned to design the CMU component, while HGR would take care of the manufacturing and correspond directly with the manufacturer.[4]

All of the units are the same equilateral triangular shape, with rounded corners and a hollow center. There is a subtle depression and three score lines on the units' front face. **[23]** Vigueta y Poliestireno Soluciones Arquitectonicas (VYPSA) manufactured the 5,600 units.[5] Each unit is almost 8in (200mm) long on each side, made of dense concrete, and weighs around 44lb (20kg). Each unit is held in place by mortar, and the units are vertically and horizontally supported by a steel structure.

DESIGN CONSIDERATIONS

CMUs are often used for building in Mexico City, and HGR wanted MR299 to continue that tradition. The particular challenge for this project was to design the unit as a module that would be complete as a full unit, but that could also be modified for coursing. To create smaller units, the triangular shape was bisected vertically from its vertex, creating a unit that was 8in

22

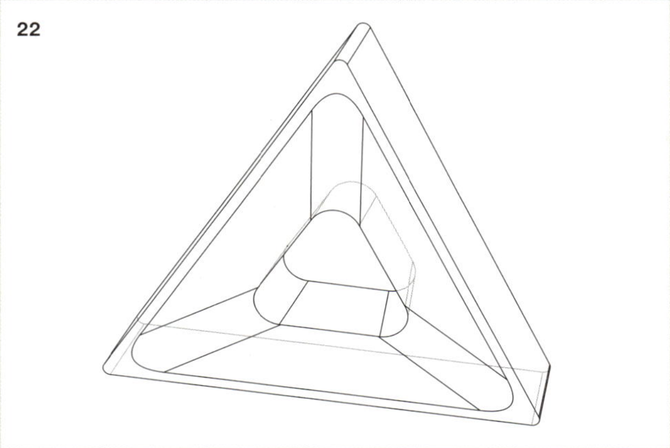

23

21

24

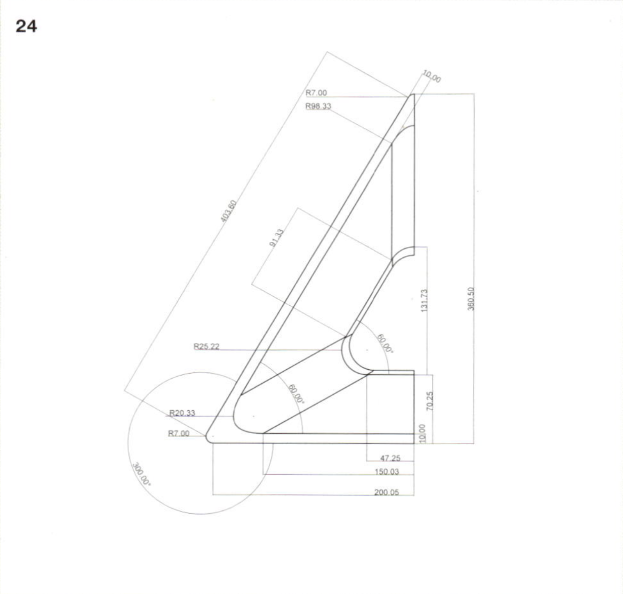

21
Corner detail at street level

22
Ariel Rojo Design Studio drawing of the CMU unit

23
Detail of three units

24
Drawing of the half unit, used at corners and openings

25
Color-testing units at VYPSA

26
Hand-press machine at VYPSA

27
Three units are made each cycle

28
Painted steel mold and tool steel stripping shoe

(200mm) tall by approximately 4in (100mm) wide. The halved units were coursed with the width of the building mass, and around door and window openings. [24] MR299 used a steel angle at the building's corners, giving Rojo more freedom with the units' design, as he was not required to resolve the corner condition. [21]

MANUFACTURING CONSIDERATIONS

According to Rojo, Mexico has a high number of craftsmen available and manufacturing facilities that have not been automated. This allows them to easily produce custom components without much added cost. Additionally, because concrete can be easily shaped it can also be easily customized.

Rojo recommended VYPSA for the manufacturing of the units. VYPSA is located just under 80 miles (130km) from Mexico City, and so Hagerman was able to visit often, before and during the units' production. From those visits, the design team decided on the density, color, and finish of the blocks. [25] VYPSA manufactured the units on a small, hand-operated, mechanical press. The units were formed in a steel mold, three at a time. The steel stripping shoe compacted the units and added an indentation on the block's top surface. [26, 27] The mold lifted away and left the units atop a wooden pallet. The units were then moved by hand away from the press and cured outside. Production took approximately 2 months for all of the units.

The diagonal lines on the surface of the units were a result of the mold-making process. The mold was made so that three steel bars supported the steel for the units' core. The bars were placed low in the mold so that they left their imprint on the units. Rojo decided that it was a nice detail and so this was left on the units. [28]

OTHER CONSIDERATIONS

The design team chose the denser block for its aesthetic properties. As a result, each block weighed 30% more than a standard 4in (100mm) solid CMU. This greater weight, coupled with the project being located in a seismic area, necessitated a substantial steel backing structure to support the units; this required structural coordination and increased construction complexity. On the structural drawings, ladder reinforcing was placed in the bed joints for every second course, and a steel support angle was specified for every four courses.

LESSONS LEARNED

The Rojo Studio works with a number of manufacturers for different product, packaging, furniture, and component designs. As part of that process, the studio tries "to coordinate and supervise the production for each and every design" that it creates.[6] When the Rojo Studio worked on Multiblok for TAE Arquitectos, it worked closely with the blocks' manufacturer to develop the design. According the Rojo, the design team liked the mold marks on the block, although they were unexpected. Rojo hopes to continue to work with manufacturers more closely in future.

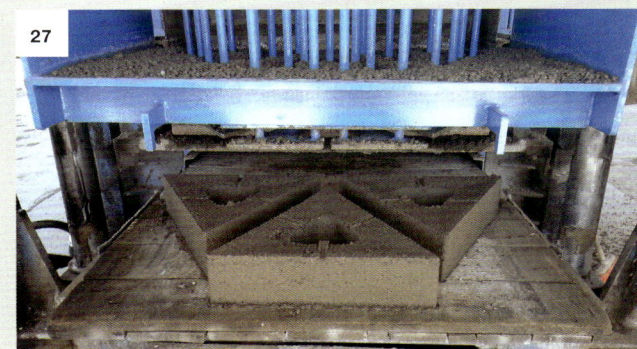

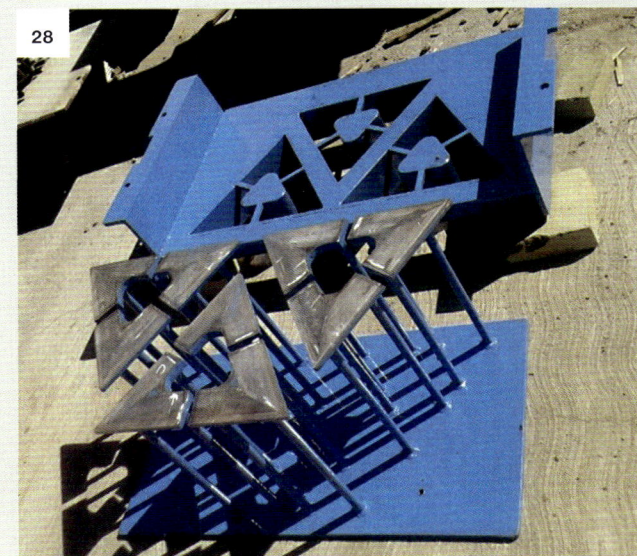

4.5 Vibration-Tamping

aka manufacturing cast stone, vibrant dry tamping (VDT),
vibro-ramming, vibration ram casting

INTRODUCTION

Vibration-tamping is a manufacturing process that places layers (or lifts) of a fairly dry and stiff mixture of cementitious binders and small aggregate, and uses a vibrating tamp to compact the mixture into a mold. This is the manufacturing process used to make architectural cast stone. [1] The shapes that can be made with vibration-tamping are varied and are based on the type of mold and the means of production. The process is used to produce complex shapes with moderate surface detail; it can produce solid or hollow shapes and various cross-sectional thicknesses. Sizes range from bricks to large decorative cast-stone components. [2, 3] As for terminology, vibration-tamping is descriptive of the manufacturing process, but most architects and cast stone manufacturers will refer to it as making or manufacturing cast stone.

When manufacturing cast stone, a stiff or earth-moist concrete mixture is placed into the mold in approximately 2in (50mm) lifts. There is little water in the concrete mixture, and therefore this process does not require built-up molds to have caulking at the joints.[1] This allows the molds to be quickly assembled and disassembled each cycle, as needed. A worker then moves a pneumatic rammer across the back of the lift, compressing it to half of its original depth. Another concrete lift is then added and tamped. This process is repeated until the mold is filled. The component is removed from the mold, set aside to cure, and the tamping starts again. Steam is often used to speed up the curing process.

The finely crushed stone aggregate in the concrete and the dryness of the cement mixture give components the look

1 Vibration-tamping at Cast Stone Systems in Warrenton, North Carolina

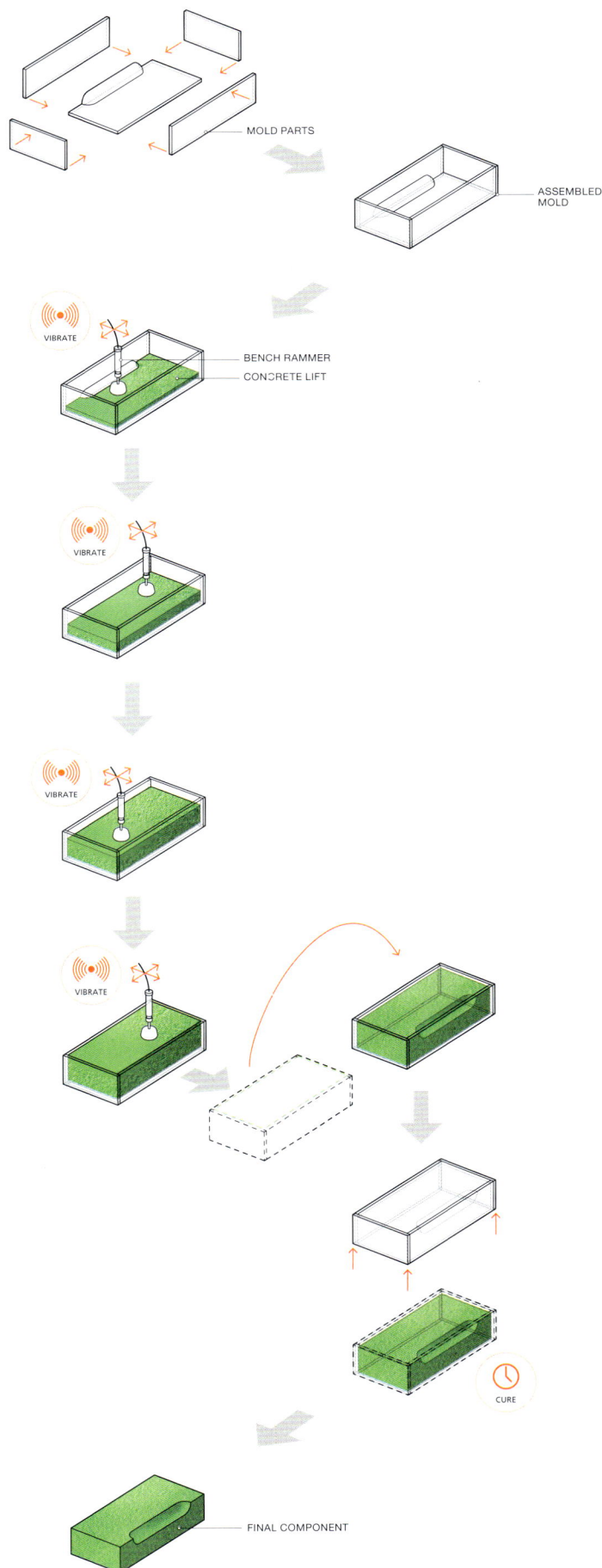

of natural stone. [4] Depending on the mold material used, cast stone can have the look of a sand-blasted, saw-cut, or honed-finished sedimentary rock, such as limestone or sandstone. Although atypical, the manufacturing process can include post-production finishing, such as grit (or sand) blasting, acid etching, or carving. Grit blasting and acid etching are done after the cast stone has cured; carving into the surface can be done before or after curing.

Vibration-tamping is a labor-intensive process that has not yet been effectively mechanized. [5, 6, 7] Cast stone manufacturers' production runs will consist almost entirely of custom manufacturing. There is little incentive for manufacturers to invest in large equipment to mechanize their processes, as automated machines cannot handle the large variety of cast stone shapes and sizes required for most building projects. At the same time, cast stone manufacturers do prefer repeated components in order to reduce the number of molds required. Depending on the size of the component, a typical manufacturer will have one or two molds and one worker at each station. The worker is responsible

MOLD PARTS

ASSEMBLED MOLD

VIBRATE

BENCH RAMMER
CONCRETE LIFT

VIBRATE

VIBRATE

VIBRATE

CURE

FINAL COMPONENT

2 A cast-stone half Corinthian column capital

3 A large cladding component

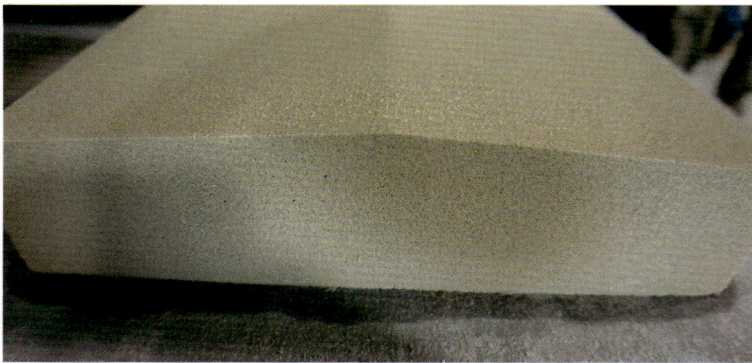
4 Natural cast stone finish, after curing

6 Manufacturing cast stone is a labor-intensive process

5 Hand tamping of molds

7 A pneumatic bench rammer, used for tamping

for placing the lifts, using a rammer for tamping, removing the formed cast stone from the mold (using a crane if necessary), and then preparing the mold for the next cycle.

Despite the labor-intensity of vibration-tamping, the cycle time for this process is much shorter than for casting a similar-sized component in wet concrete (see Chapter 4.1). When manufacturing cast stone, a worker should be able to produce several components per hour from one mold. Because of the high water content in wet concrete, a wet-cast concrete component must remain curing in its mold until it is stable enough to remove, whereas a cast stone component can be removed immediately after tamping. In addition, wet-casting in a built-up mold requires caulking at the mold corners between pours, whereas making cast stone does not. This reduces cycle times.

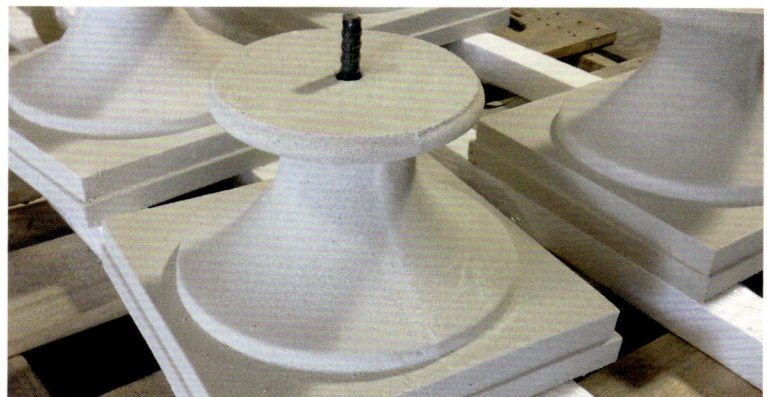
8 A standard cast-stone urn stand

9 A profile with a dam to adjust the length of the molding

BUILDING PRODUCTS

There is a wide range of vibration-tamped cast components commercially available. [8] Building products include column capitals, bases, keystones, brackets, and fireplace surrounds. There are cast stone products for landscape applications too, including planters, urns, and pool caps, as well as standard profiles for window and door jambs, sills and headers, water tables, and cornices. In most cases, cast stone companies can customize the length of their standard profiles by adding a dam in the mold, thereby adding little to no cost for custom lengths. [9]

TOOLING

Molds for vibration-tamping need to be strong enough to resist the forces from the vibration ram. These include molds built from plywood, MDF, and particle board coated with polyurethane or a similar finish. [10, 11] Some manufacturers will use melamine-coated board, as the cast stone will release easily from the plastic. [12] If undercuts or fine details are required, a rubber mold may be used; however, this will increase costs, as making rubber molds is a two-step process. First, a pattern is made and the rubber is cast on the pattern to make the mold. [13] If high production runs are

12 Melamine-coated particle-board mold with CNC-milled profile

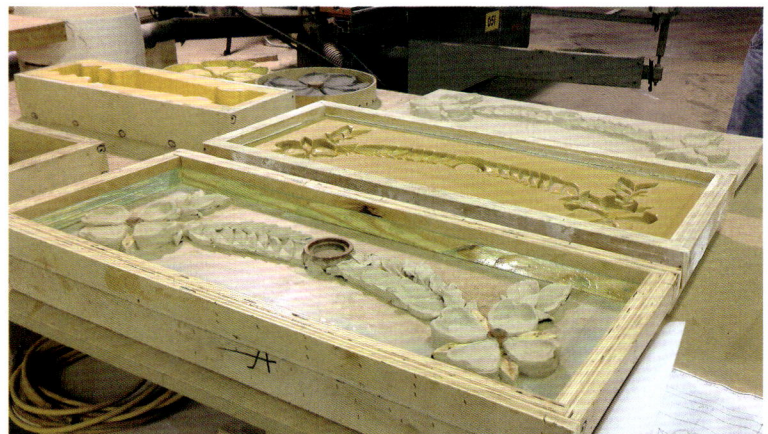

13 Rubber mold. In the foreground is the pattern, in the middle is the rubber mold, and in the background is the cast component

10 A mold made from wood, plywood, and melamine-coated particle board

11 Mold-making materials, with CNC-milled MDF on right

14 The unfinished, or unmolded, side of the cast stone component

15 Carpentry shop at Cast Stone Systems

18 Earth-moist concrete mixture, to be placed in the mold for tamping

16 A CNC mill at Cast Stone Systems, used for specialty molds

17 Rubber mold insert, bought from a rubber-mold maker

19 Steam room for curing cast stone

required, molds can be made from metal. This will increase costs, which may be offset by the molds' durability. Unlike cast wet concrete, the cast stone concrete is so dry that it does not pick up much from the mold surface. For example, the wood grain from a plywood mold will not be visible on a cast stone surface.

Vibration tamping is done in open female molds. The mold opening must be large enough so that the concrete mixture can be added, and to allow the worker to reach all areas of the mold with the vibration tamp. Shallow molds with an opening at least as wide as the component is deep are best. The component is cast so that all of the finished faces are in contact with the mold. The unfinished side is where the worker is able to access the concrete with the vibration ram. It is the same texture as the cast stone, but not as precisely shaped. [14] Typically, the unfinished face is hidden and placed against the building or a mortar joint.

Most cast stone manufacturers make their own molds. In-house carpenters will make simple-shaped molds out of wood or wood products. [15] CNC machines may be used to make custom, complex, or curved mold profiles out of wood or MDF. [16] CNC machines may also be used to make patterns for rubber molds. If the rubber mold is highly detailed, a manufacturer may purchase it from a specialist mold maker. [17]

ENVIRONMENTAL IMPACT

Generally, vibration-tamping has low environmental impact. Because this process still involves manufacture by hand, the largest environmental impact is from the manufacturing of the cement. The earth-moist material has high recycled content and low embodied water. The aggregates are small and are usually the processing waste from cutting and grinding stone. The cast stone components cure in relatively cool, steam-filled rooms that are kept at 100°F (38°C).

There is very little manufacturing waste with this process. There is little to no wasted concrete when the molds are filled. Any excess earth-moist concrete is not vibration-tamped and therefore can be used in the next cycle. The greatest waste associated with the process is the limited use of the molds. As mold costs are fairly low, designers may design components so that a mold is used only a few times. This practice can greatly increase manufacturing waste. To reduce production waste, it is best for designers and manufacturers to limit the number of unique molds.

MATERIAL CONSIDERATIONS + DESIGN PARAMETERS

EARTH-MOIST CONCRETE, AKA SEMI-DRY CONCRETE

The concrete mixture should have the consistency and feel of moist earth. [18] When compressed in the hand, the earth-moist concrete will hold together without crumbling and will not leave any liquid residue. It contains just enough water for the cement to cure, but not so much that the mixture slumps when it is removed from the mold. To ensure that there is enough moisture present for curing the cement, cast stone should be cured in a steam-filled room. [19] The earth-moist concrete includes Portland cement, inorganic pigments, aggregate, and a waterproof admixture. (The waterproof admixture helps make the cast stone less water-absorptive when compared with limestone or other sedimentary rocks.)

The color of the Portland cement ranges from gray to beige. If color is important to the cast stone, white cement should be specified, with added inorganic pigments to change the color. The aggregate is finely crushed stone with dimensions less than 0.25in (6mm), and generally not greater than 0.12in (3mm). Cast stone can be either homogeneous throughout the cross-section, or composite, with a different concrete used for the component face and back. [20] The facing layer will have fine aggregates, and subsequent layers may either be earth-moist concrete with a larger aggregate, or wet-cast concrete. The back of the face layer should be scored, providing a mechanical connection between the two layers.

If required due to component size, proportions, or required material strength, earth-moist concrete can be reinforced with steel rebar and welded wire fabric. Reinforcing will increase the manufacturing difficulty and cost, as workers need to tamp around it. Although cast stone is less absorptive than comparable limestones, components should be designed with proper weather details. This may include a minimum 2% slope away from the building for horizontal surfaces, and drip edges to keep water off of the component face. Similar to other masonry materials, if water gets behind the component, efflorescence may occur. Light colors of cast stone will mask this more effectively than dark colors.

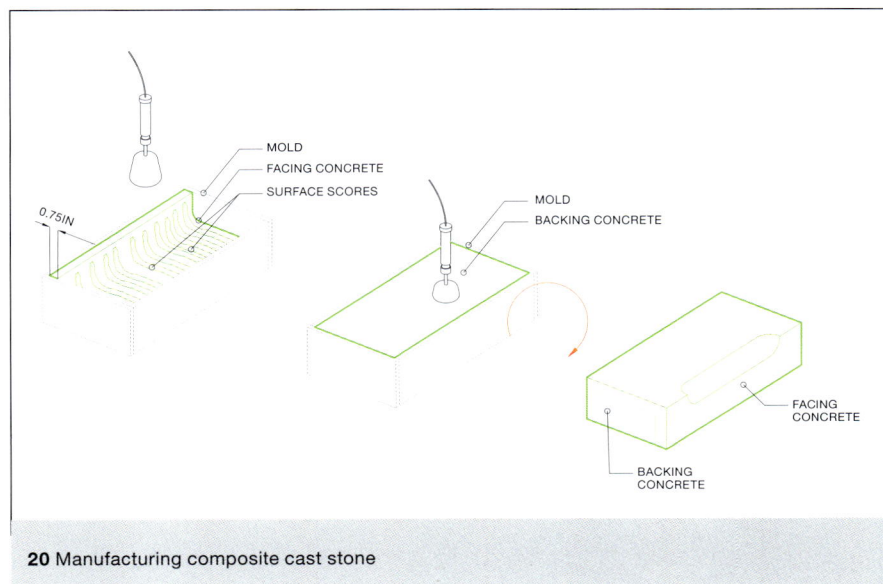

20 Manufacturing composite cast stone

SIMILAR PROCESSES

Vibration tamping is most similar to vibration-press casting (Chapter 4.4), used for making concrete masonry units. The benefits of vibration-tamping over vibration-press casting are the ability to accommodate lower production volumes, lower mold costs, more flexibility in size, and a finish that more closely replicates stone.

CORNER RADII

Corners do not require radii.

DRAFT ANGLES

Draft angles are not required.

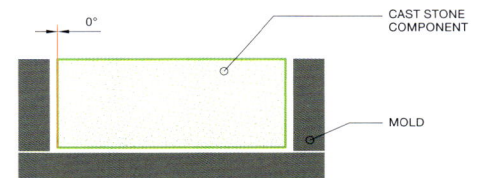

FINISH

The resulting surface of this process is similar to saw-cut natural stone. Post-production finishes, such as acid washing or grit blasting, can be done after the component has cured. A network of small cracks, otherwise known as crazing, often occurs on the surface of the cast stone. This is difficult to control and is considered to be a minor defect in the material that does not warrant rejection.[2]

INSERTS

Inserts can be placed within a tolerance of 0.12in (3mm). Inserts may include reglets, threaded male or female connectors, or grooves.

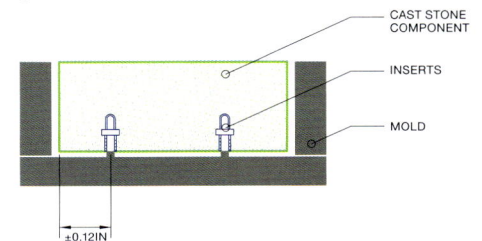

PARTING LINES

When tamping in semi-closed molds, parting lines will be visible.

PRODUCTION SPEED

If the piece is simple, then two to five units are produced per hour, with approximately 20 components produced per day. If the component is large or ornamental with deep surface profiles, the component will be left in the mold for 24 hours to cure.

PRODUCTION VOLUME

Production volumes can vary, from prototypes and small productions to runs of 100,000 units. For large production runs, a manufacturer will often run multiple molds simultaneously. A plywood or melamine-coated particle-board mold will produce 200–300 units.

SIZE LIMITS

Component sizes are typically smaller than with wet-cast concrete. Earth-moist material strength limits will dictate the proportion of the component size to its cross-sectional area. The component's length should be limited to fifteen times its average thickness.

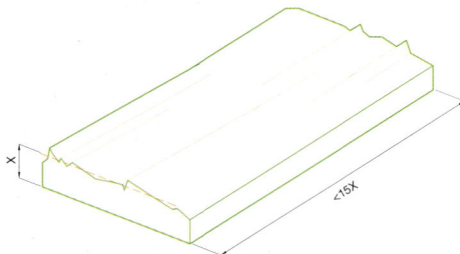

In addition, if the component is larger than 24in × 24in (600mm × 600mm), it will need to be reinforced.

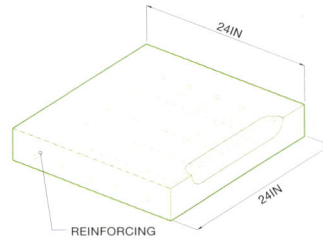

SURFACE DESIGNS

Surfaces can be designed with intricate details such as ornaments, patterns, or lettering. If a consistent detail is required, it is recommended that a rubber mold be used for production. This will allow for easy removal of the component from the mold. Alternatively, a surface pattern can be etched into the surface of the component while it is still green (before the cement has cured). The material is soft then, and almost anything can be used as a carving tool.

SURFACE IMPERFECTIONS

Air voids or pockets on the exterior surface should measure less than 0.06in (1.5mm) in any direction. If there are air pockets, there should be fewer than three in any 1in^2 (25mm^2).

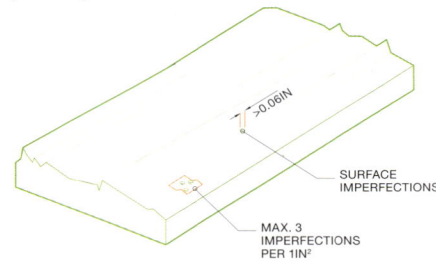

TOLERANCES

Cross-section dimensions should be within 0.12in (3mm) of the prescribed dimensions. Component lengths should be within 0.12–0.25in (3–6mm) of the prescribed dimensions.

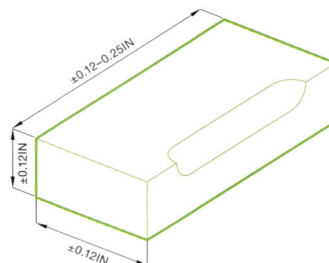

TOOLING COSTS

Tool costs for this manufacturing process are extremely low. Depending on size and complexity, a mold can cost $25–500. Most cast stone manufacturers are equipped to manufacture their own production molds. They will have some carpentry equipment, a CNC miller or router, and rubber casting capabilities.

UNDERCUTS

Undercuts are permissible in either rubber or disassembled wood molds. In a rubber mold, the mold medium is flexible enough that the component can be removed without damage to either the component or the mold. In an assembled wood mold, the manufacturer would need to partially break it down, often by removing a side of the mold. The mold would then be reassembled before the next cycle.

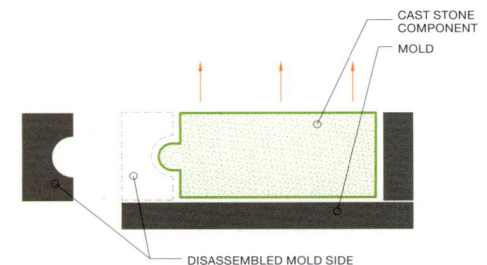

WARPING

Along the length of a cast stone component the component may not be formed straight, and may have a bow, twist, or camber. These are acceptable if they are within L/360.

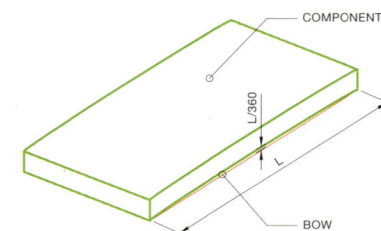

VIBRATION-TAMPING: EARTH-MOIST CONCRETE

CAST STONE MASONRY | MISSISSIPPI LIBRARY COMMISSION HEADQUARTERS
Duvall Decker Architects
Jackson, Mississippi

The Mississippi Library Commission (MLC) Headquarters is both a state library and a service building, serving all of the state's citizens and public libraries. **[21, 22]** The new building, on a heavily wooded lot on a state-owned education and research campus, replaced the existing, 23-year-old facility that had been located in an abandoned Bill's Dollar Store. Completed in 2005, the new MLC building is 60,000ft² (5,600m²) and includes book collections, a public reading room, gallery, computer center, training areas, education support areas, and offices. In 2010, this building was selected for the AIA's Design for the Decades: Civic Buildings initiative.[3]

The MLC exterior walls are a cast-stone clad rainscreen with a concrete block back-up system. According to Roy Decker, partner at Duvall Decker, the rainscreen assembly is better suited to the hot, humid Mississippi climate than traditional masonry cavities, as the rainscreen's vents prevent any trapped moisture in the cavity from turning into steam during Mississippi's steamy summers.[4] The top and left edges of the stone have a step detail to create a labyrinth joint between stones.

The stones are 2ft 3in (685mm) tall, and vary in width as necessary. Duvall Decker designed three different cast stone types: Type A, Type B, and Type C. Type A is flat, varies in width from 1ft 8in (508mm) to 5ft (1,524mm), and occasionally accommodates openings for exterior lights or other needs. Both Type B and Type C accommodate a 1in (25mm) vertical slope on a portion of the stone. Type B's slope is located on the right edge of the stone, while Type C stones have the slope located on the left portion of the stone or across the full stone. The width of the sloped portion and the stone varies as needed. **[23, 24]**

21
East elevation of the Mississippi Library Commission Headquarters, looking through wooded site

22
Site plan showing entry [1], library [2], administration [3] and lawn [4]

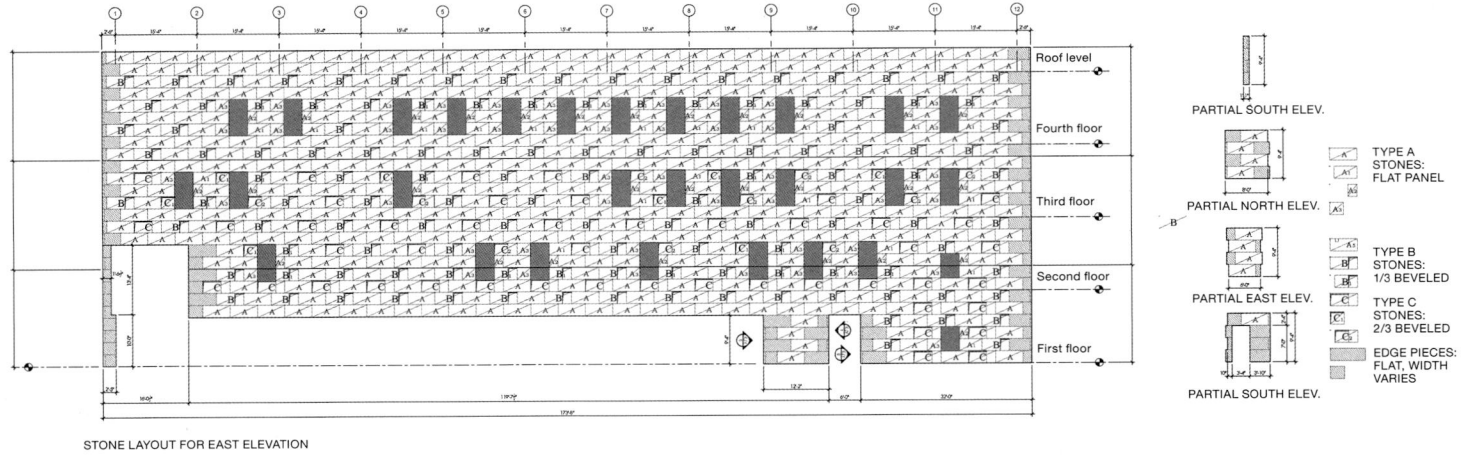

23 Stone panel layouts for east elevation

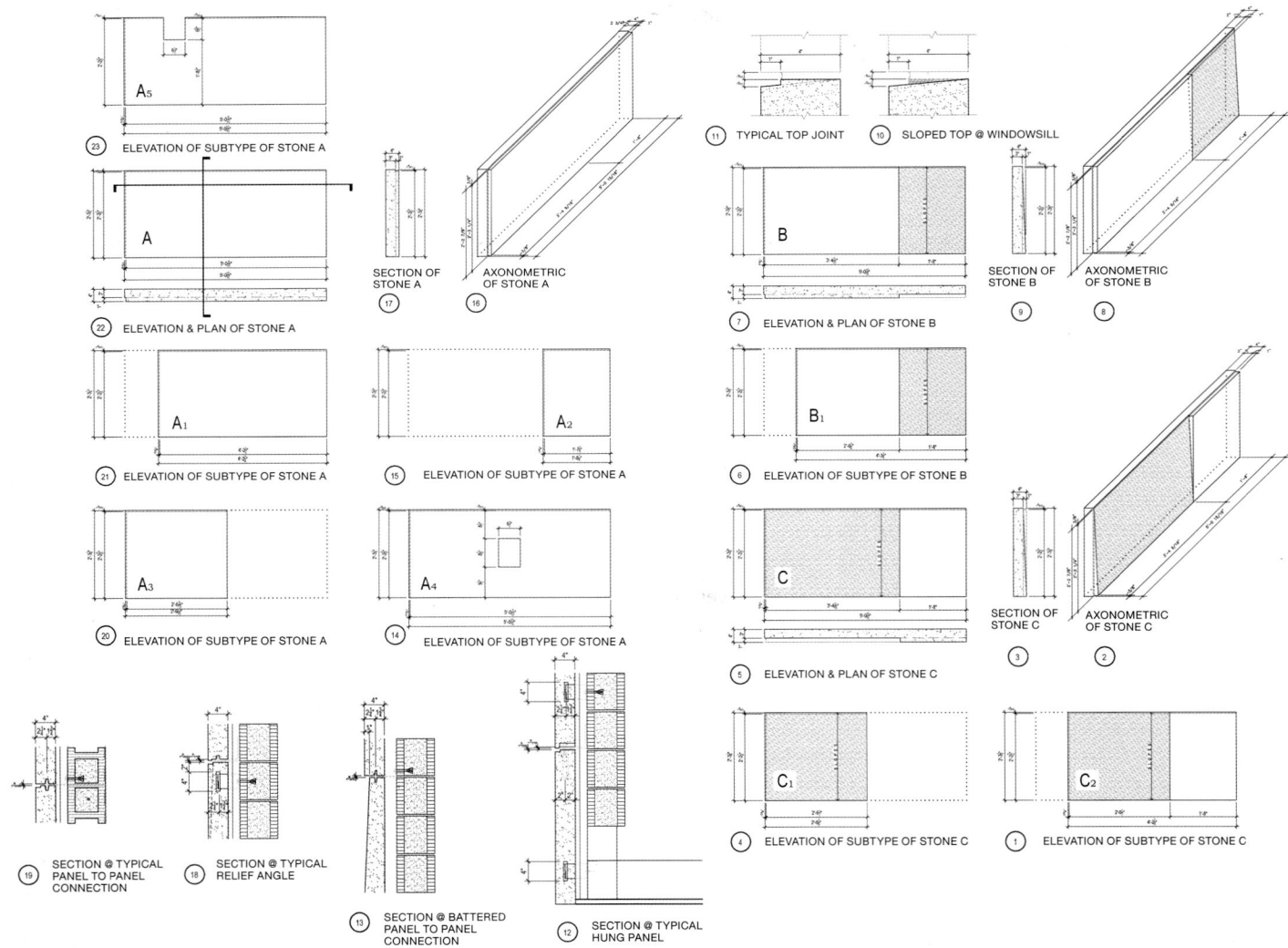

24 Stone panel types and key details

This project was a joint venture of Duvall Decker and Burris/Wagnon Architects. According to Decker, at the time the project was being proposed, both firms were small and so they joined forces to compete against larger, more established firms. Duvall Decker led the design and Burris/Wagnon developed the building details. There were two cast stone manufacturers for this project, Jackson Stone and Precast, which manufactured approximately 20% of the cast stone components required, and United Commercial Cast Stone, which manufactured the rest.

DESIGN CONSIDERATIONS

The building's exterior was a response to its location in the South, and its specific site of a wooded parcel of land. Decker believes that Southern civic buildings use a borrowed set of images and styles, and the firm expected to make the building from red brick with cast stone to emulate limestone. For Decker, using cast stone was a means to work with the materials of the South, and yet establish a new language. Second, Duvall Decker wanted the building to reflect the site's dappled lighting from the surrounding trees. A red brick building would have absorbed the shadows, while a cast stone building would reflect them. The vertical slopes of the stones also cast shadows onto the façade, changing the building's exterior as day turned to night, and with the changing seasons. [25]

A number of studies were done for the amount of inset. In the end, Duvall Decker decided on a 1in (25mm) inset, as deeper insets would make the stone too heavy, and shallower insets were not as apparent. Duvall Decker located the Type B and C stones primarily at the lower levels of the building, where their shadows ground the building and provide rustication to the base. There are fewer cast shadows moving up the building, creating a lightness at the upper levels. The pattern is based on a mathematical or musical relationship developed by Anne Marie Decker, Roy Decker's partner.

MANUFACTURING CONSIDERATIONS

The stones were manufactured in plywood molds. [26] To create the sloped sections, an insert was added into the plywood mold as needed. Inserts allowed the manufacturer to get the most repeatability possible with each mold, and gave flexibility in production. Multiple molds were used simultaneously for parallel productions.

Black quartz grains were thrown into the mold prior to tamping, to give the stones added variety and depth. Duvall Decker did not want the quartz to be evenly distributed across the surface, and appreciated that the quartz was evident of a person's handwork. According to Decker, the manufacturer took some convincing that the imperfections were preferable to a pristine stone, and that the variety offered a richness that would not otherwise be there.

Jackson Stone and Precast and United Commercial Cast Stone manufactured the cast stone components. Jackson was awarded the contract to produce all of the stone for the project, but went bankrupt during production (due to another job) and produced about 10–20% of the total stones required. It was with Jackson that Duvall Decker developed the manufacturing parameters,

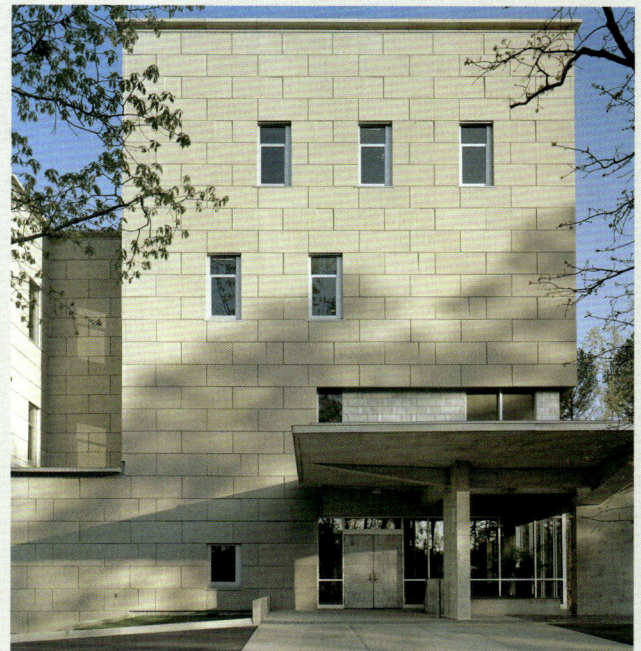

25 South elevation during changing light conditions

26 Cast stone panels being manufactured at Jackson Stone

had engineered the stones and connections, and prototyped about twenty stones for a mock-up.

United Cast Stone was awarded the contract to produce the balance of stones. It worked closely with Duvall Decker to match the color and mix of the Jackson stones. [27] United also made some changes to the details that Jackson had developed. First, it developed a new method of connecting the stones to the façade. Instead of the bolted connection from Jackson, United proposed using a slot connection to connect the stone to the concrete block for adjustability. The slots were cut into the stones after curing. [28] Second, Jackson had proposed field measuring the corner units, and manufacturing the corner stones to the field-verified lengths. United proposed shipping longer stones to the site, and cutting them to length as needed.

27 Matching cast stones on mock-up

OTHER CONSIDERATIONS

Duvall Decker's work is primarily located within Mississippi, where generally, budgets for building are low, most labor is unskilled, and there is little available money and skill for building maintenance. It is within this context that the firm develops its design work. There were multiple reasons why cast stone made the best choice for this project. First, with the heavily wooded site (see figure 4.5.22), there was only one open spot on the site to fit a crane. This mean that using wet-cast or precast concrete (Chapter 4.1) was not possible, as the crane could not be used to lift components into place. Therefore the smaller cast stone components were better, as they could be easily handled by a winch and scaffolding. [29] Second, cast stone's manufacturing process necessitates better consolidation than wet-casting. Third, unlike wet-cast concrete, cast stone requires no secondary procedures such as acid washing or sand-blasting to finish the stones. Unfortunately, with the smaller pieces, the stones were handled a lot during transport and construction, and they tended to break and chip. United patched the stones on site as needed.

28 United Commercial Cast Stone used slots for building attachment

LESSONS LEARNED

The chief lesson learned with this project was the method of connecting the cast stone to the supporting concrete block. The first manufacturer, Jackson, made each of its stones with four female connectors, one near each stone's corner. These connection types left little room for on-site adjustments, so that a connection could line up with the back-up blocks' face or a head joint. Meanwhile United Cast Stone proposed making the stones with a routed slot on the top and bottom of the stone. This allowed the brackets to be adjusted horizontally on-site as needed, and still support the stone.

Not necessarily a lesson learned by the firm, but perhaps a lesson for all architects, is the value of repetition. As the partnership wrote of their practice, "Repetition is one such place; whether in labor or in material, repeating action over and over builds knowledge, efficiency, and skill. This intersection of economy and quality is true in design work, the creation of construction documents, and the process of construction."[5] For Duvall Decker, doing and doing again not only helped the practice but also helped educate the construction workers in Mississippi.

29 Using cast stone required only scaffolding and a small winch to lift the units

4.6 Pressing

INTRODUCTION

Pressing is a manufacturing process that takes a soft medium and presses into a die. After the medium has stiffened and can hold its shape, the component is removed from the mold. Both glass and clay can be pressed and both are included in this chapter. Manual labor can be used to push clay by hand into a mold; [1] mechanical or hydraulic presses can push both glass and clay into a mold. [2, 3] Small pressed components can be solid; if large, then clay components are often semi-hollow to reduce cracking. Pressing results in good surface quality with intricate details. Tooling can be open, semi-open, or closed. Depending on the shape of the component and the mold, all surfaces of a pressed component can be mold-finished. This process typically requires little to no post-production surface refinishing; however, flashing may need to be removed.

Pressing is a cyclical manufacturing process. First, a predetermined amount of softened medium is placed in a die. If the medium is clay, the die will be at room temperature; if the medium is molten glass, the die will be preheated to reduce thermal shock to the tooling and medium. Next, the die closes. Force is then added to press the medium through the mold. The force may be applied by the die half (as shown), by a plunger, or by hand. Next, the medium solidifies in the mold until it can retain its shape for demolding. If glass, solidification is done through cooling, while clay is dehydrated. The component is then removed from the tool for further solidification and processing.

Generally, pressing is appropriate for components with intricate surface details. [4, 5] Historically, pressed glass was used as an inexpensive substitute for etched glass, because almost all of the surface qualities of etched glass could be replicated with pressing.[1] Similar to glass, pressed clay can be used for components with a lot of surface detail, including components used to replicate traditional and classical building features. With a lot of surface detail and potential undercuts, hand pressing is better than mechanical pressing, as more pressure can be applied to the clay where it is needed to fit tight spaces.

There is a limited number of manufacturers that do pressing, however, manufacturers' production capabilities are more diverse. Glass pressing can be highly mechanized, with large production runs done by manufacturers who would otherwise be unwilling to accept contract work. This could include high-volume glassware

2 Ram press for clay at Ceramic Supply Company

1 Hand pressing clay at Boston Valley Terra Cotta in Orchard Park, New York

3 Glass press to make glass blocks at OCMI-OTG SpA in Milan, Italy

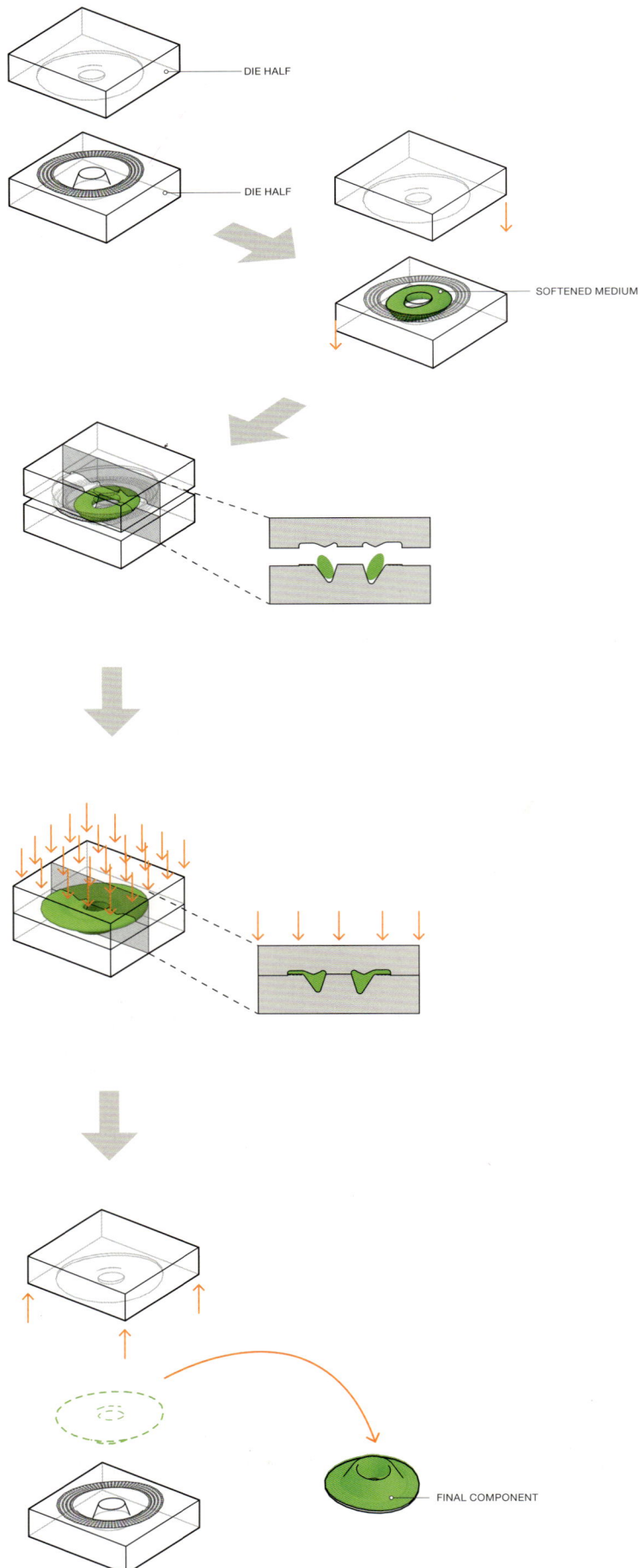

DIE HALF

DIE HALF

SOFTENED MEDIUM

FINAL COMPONENT

and glass block manufacturers [6] with production lines dedicated to particular products. Next, there are mid-sized manufacturers with mechanized equipment that are often flexible enough to accept orders for custom productions. Depending on their facilities, these manufacturers may be able to combine handwork and mechanized pressing. For example—Jeannette Specialty Glass in Jeannette, Pennsylvania, combines pressing and hand forming glass, and Boston Valley Terra Cotta in Orchard Park, New York, does both hand pressing and mechanical pressing of terra cotta. Finally, pressing either glass or clay can also be done by craftspeople in small workshops or artisan studios. Pressing with molds or stamps requires no special equipment and can easily be done by hand or by gravity.

BUILDING PRODUCTS

There are a number of commercially available building products made by pressing. In glass, the most notable are hollow glass blocks. In glass block manufacturing, the halves of the blocks are pressed separately. After the halves are pressed and removed from the mold, their edges are reheated to a molten state. The heated edges are then pressed together to form a full, hollow unit. Other pressed-glass building products include textured glass shapes such

4 Fine surface details in pressed glass

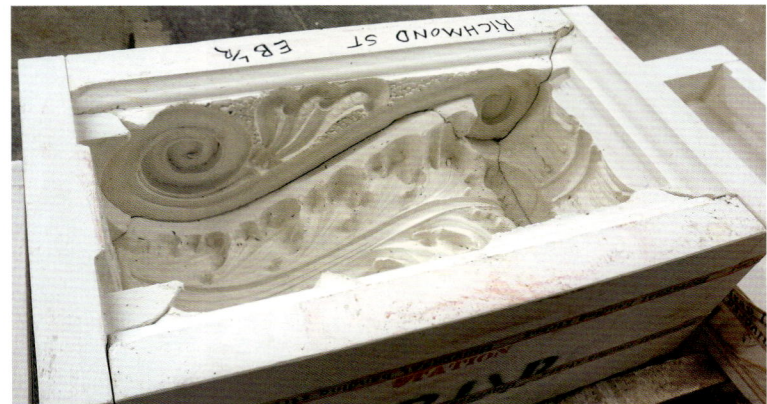

5 Multi-part mold for a decorative clay bracket

as sinks, washbasins, and light fixture refractors, diffusers, and lens covers. [7] For pressed clay, most notable are building products such as roof tiles. Products also include clay tiles, both flat and embossed, and molded bricks.

TOOLING

Tooling for pressing needs to be durable enough to meet the production run and made of materials suited to the manufacturing medium. For example, in glass pressing the tooling will be exposed to high temperatures, and in clay pressing the tooling should draw water away from the clay so it can be demolded quickly. Mechanized glass-pressing molds are made from either cast iron [8] or machined stainless steel. Cast iron is less expensive, but more prone to cracking, and has an inferior surface quality compared with stainless steel. A stainless-steel mold can last approximately 5,000 shots, or cycles, before servicing. Craftspeople will use plaster molds with refractory additives for heat stabilization. A plaster mold may last up to 15 cycles before breaking. Clay pressing tooling can be made from wood, resin, plaster, or metal. Plaster is a good material for clay pressing, as the plaster draws water away from the clay, making the clay stiffen quickly and reducing cycle times. Plaster molds will wear after

producing 50–60 units; resin molds can produce 1,000–2,000 units; and steel molds can last almost indefinitely, but are only cost effective for very large production runs.

In pressing glass, the tooling includes a female mold, a male plunger, and an optional sealing ring. [10] The mold may be solid, or hinged in two or more parts. Hinged molds are opened for demolding and are best for components with undercuts or overall shapes that are narrow, deep, or with steep draft angles. The press moves the plunger, which places pressure on the molten glass, forcing it into its shape. The plunger's shape provides the component's inside surface and governs the wall thickness of the component. The sealing ring guides the plunger as it moves in and out of the mold and provides a stop for the glass so that it does not flow out of the mold.

High-volume pressed glass uses multiple molds with one plunger, and mechanized presses use a turntable for continuous production. As one mold is filled with molten glass, a plunger is pressing into another mold, and cooled pressed glass is being removed from the third. The turntable then rotates, moving the molds to the next station. With this system, one plunger is used for three female molds, allowing each mold to be slightly different, with little added cost.

In pressing clay, the tooling varies, depending on whether the component is hand or machine pressed. Hand pressing uses

6 OCMI-OTG multi-station press to manufacture glass blocks

8 Cast iron molds in the glass press

7 JSG Oceana pressed glass sinks on display

9 Two multi-part plaster molds

an open or semi-open mold, and the maker's hands or hand tools are used to press the clay into the mold. The hand-pressed mold is often made of multiple parts [9] to accommodate undercuts and make demolding easier. In machine pressing, the tooling is a male and female die. In pressing roof tiles, both die halves may be almost identical, as roof tiles have a fairly consistent wall thickness. Conversely, in pressing complex shapes such as cornices or friezes, the male and female halves of the die may have little geometric relationship to each another. [11] To make demolding easier, the male portion of the die is kept stationary and the female portion is moved by the press.

Cast iron molds can be made by casting metal (Chapter 4.2). Machined steel, wood, or resin molds can be fabricated by hand, but are often fabricated by CNC equipment. Plaster tooling can be made by casting against a pattern or directly CNC milling. Patterns for plaster molds can be made from modeling clay, rubber, wood, or plaster. As plaster molds have short cycle times and production runs, some manufacturers will take the time to make a master mold, cast a rubber pattern against the master mold, and then cast multiple manufacturing molds from the pattern. This extra step of using a master mold is mitigated by producing multiple molds for parallel productions, and by small changes that can be made to each pattern (e.g. adding a dam to shorten a component's length) to produce minor modifications without new tooling.

11 Male die half does not fully match the female die half

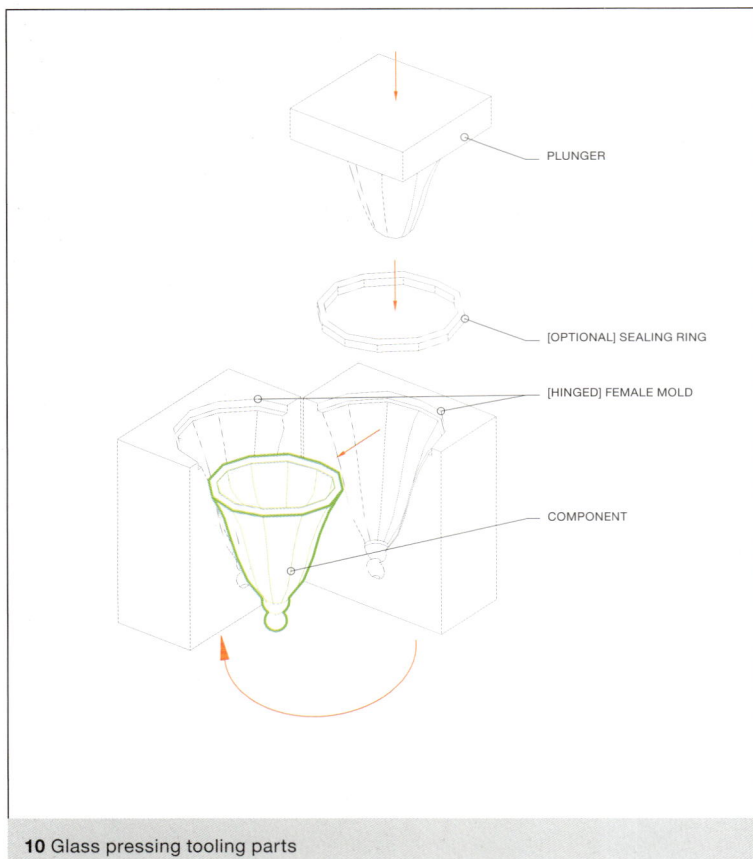

10 Glass pressing tooling parts

PLUNGER

[OPTIONAL] SEALING RING

[HINGED] FEMALE MOLD

COMPONENT

ENVIRONMENTAL IMPACT

Pressing glass is an energy-intensive process. Glass typically melts around 2,700–3,000°F (1,480–1,650°C) and must be heated slowly to reach that temperature. After pressing, the glass must also be annealed, or cooled slowly in a kiln. Typically, there is little manufacturing waste with pressing glass, as the manufacturer only fills the mold cavity with what is needed. Glass is also highly recyclable, and any waste that is created can be melted again with the charge.

Pressing clay is also energy intensive, as high temperatures are needed to fire the clay. Generally, tunnel kilns use less energy than batch kilns of a comparable size, as less energy is spent on reheating. Many clay manufacturers will use residual heat from the kiln to dry the clay components before they go into the kiln. Clay often contains grog, which comes from the manufacturer's production waste, or ceramic, from diverted landfill from dishware or construction debris.

MATERIAL CONSIDERATIONS + DESIGN PARAMETERS

The amount of medium placed in the mold is predetermined, based on the component's surface area and required thickness. When pressing glass, the glass will be in its liquid state, with the consistency of thick honey, and will be measured by weight or volume.[2] When pressing clay, the clay can be extruded into thick slabs, also known as slugs, or green clay scraps can be used on the press. **[13]** Measuring the amount of clay placed in the press is less of an issue than with glass, as any over-press can be easily removed.

GLASS

The primary material for glass is silicon dioxide (SiO_2), which is typically combined with other oxide ceramics. The mixture and type of oxides will affect the properties of the glass. For example, borosilicate glass contains boron trioxide and is stronger and more durable when compared with soda lime glass, which contains sodium oxide. Lead can be added to make the glass more fluid when melted. Lead glass is the easiest to shape, while borosilicate glass is more difficult to work with. Glass can be 100% recycled, although this a high recycled content may affect its performance.

A batch of starting glass materials that are to be melted is known as a charge. Glass typically melts at around 2,700–3,000°F (1,480–1,650°C), and melting a typical charge can take 24–48 hours. In a continuous melt furnace, used for mechanized glass pressing, raw materials are placed in one end of the kiln and molten glass is available at the other. If operating a continuous furnace, the manufacturer most likely will not offer a through-colored glass, as it would be difficult to get the color through the furnace. In this case most color would be added to the component surface in a post-production process with paint or a ceramic powder. **[14]**

After pressing, the glass should go through annealing or tempering, which is post-production controlled heating and cooling of the glass to increase its strength. Annealing is done in batch kilns or lehrs. **[12]**

SIMILAR PROCESSES

Blow molding glass (Chapter 3.5) can produce similar elements with fine surface details; however, blowing results in only one finished surface, while pressing provides two. Because of the pressure that the press exerts, details in pressed glass will be sharper and wall thicknesses will be more precise than with blow molding. Casting glass (Chapter 4.3) is also similar to pressing glass; however, pressed glass typically results in thinner-walled components, taking less time to anneal than cast glass.

13 Green clay scraps are placed in the mold. Any over-press can be easily removed

12 Glass blocks exiting the lehr after annealing

14 Color for pressed glass is added post-production, shown here in detail on the outside of the sink

CORNER RADII

Minimum corner radii range from 0.016 to 0.03in (0.4–0.8mm).

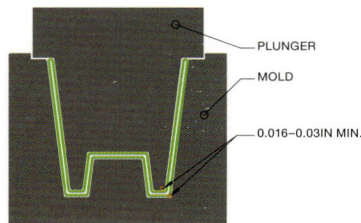

PLUNGER
MOLD
0.016–0.03IN MIN.

DRAW DEPTH

The maximum depth will be from 14 to 18in (355–455mm). The press depth will be affected by the press size, the component size and wall thickness, and the amount of pressure needed to press the glass up the sides of the mold.

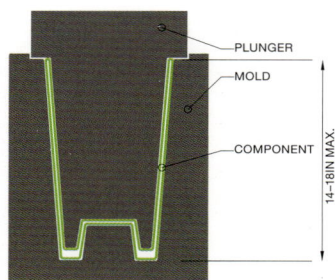

PLUNGER
MOLD
COMPONENT
14–18IN MAX.

DRAFT ANGLES

Draft angles will depend on the depth of the draw and the type of mold. If using a hinged mold, draft angles can be less than 1°.

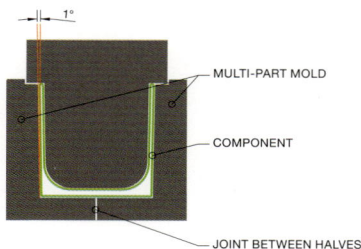

1°
MULTI-PART MOLD
COMPONENT
JOINT BETWEEN HALVES

FINISH

The finish of the glass can be high-gloss, otherwise known as flame polished. Typically, when the glass is removed from the mold, it is passed repeatedly through a flame to remove any marks from the mold or the transfer tools. Other finishes, such as acid etching or sand-blasting, are done post-production.

FLASHING

Flashing with this process is minimal and may occur between the mold and the sealing ring. Any flashing is typically removed by flame finishing.

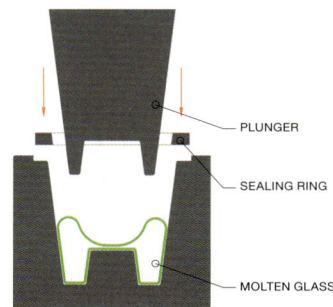

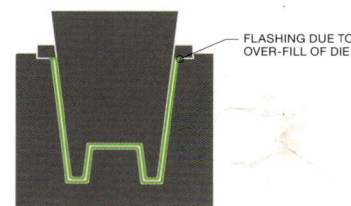

PLUNGER
SEALING RING
MOLTEN GLASS

FLASHING DUE TO OVER-FILL OF DIE

JOINING

Hot, molten glass will stick to other glass with the application of a little pressure. Using a torch for localized heating, two pieces of pressed glass can be fused together without a separate adhesive. This allows for two semi-hollow units to be fused to form a hollow component.

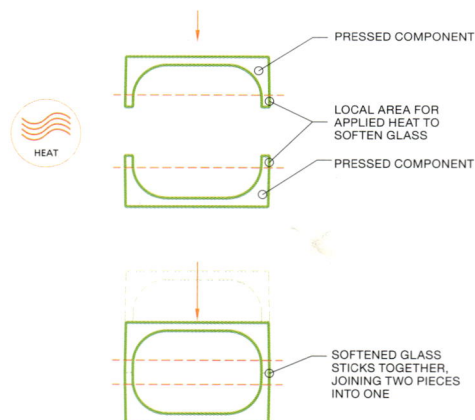

PRESSED COMPONENT
LOCAL AREA FOR APPLIED HEAT TO SOFTEN GLASS
PRESSED COMPONENT
HEAT
SOFTENED GLASS STICKS TOGETHER, JOINING TWO PIECES INTO ONE

PARTING LINES

If using a hinged mold, a parting line will be visible on the pressed glass surface. To remove the parting line, the glass can be flame finished.

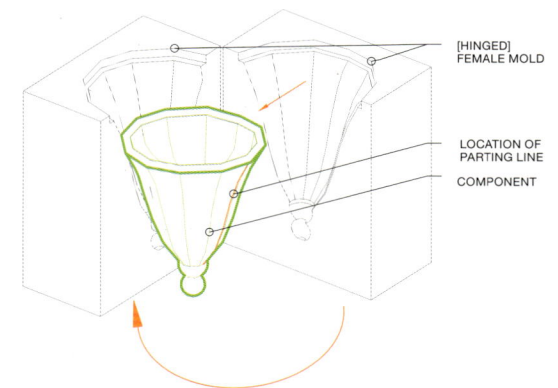

[HINGED] FEMALE MOLD
LOCATION OF PARTING LINE
COMPONENT

POST-PRODUCTION PROCESSING

From the press, the glass can be removed while it is still soft, and modified by hand. Modifications can include folding, bending, slumping, or application of additional surface decoration. Any cuts can be done on a CNC cutter, grinder, or water-jet cutter after the glass has cooled.

PRODUCTION RUNS

Production runs can range from 500 to 20,000 units and larger, depending on the mold medium and the number of molds made for continuous production.

PRODUCTION SPEED

Production speeds can range from 10 to 60 units per hour. The production speed will depend on the type of glass, the mechanization of the manufacturer, and the number of parallel molds being processed.

SHRINKING

As the glass cools it will shrink a little, depending on the component's wall thickness.

SIDE-WALL HOLES

Side-wall holes cannot be molded into the pressed glass. They can be cut into the glass after it is annealed, but before it has been tempered.

SIZE LIMITS

The size limits with this process range from a minimum of 0.25lb (0.1kg), or a volume of approximately 3in³ (50cm³), to a maximum of 50lb (23kg), or a volume of approximately 575in³ (9,420cm³). Smaller components can be made by cutting larger molded units, and larger units can be made by joining smaller units together.

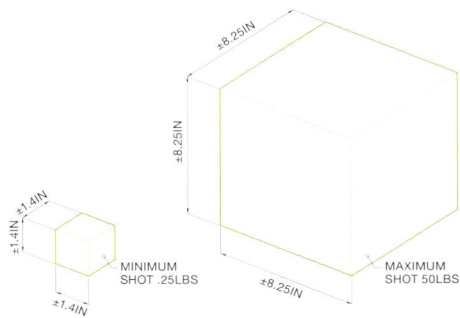

MINIMUM SHOT .25LBS
MAXIMUM SHOT 50LBS

SURFACE DESIGNS

This process can accommodate surface designs on both faces of the component, in contrast to blow molding glass (Chapter 3.5), which only can only make a surface design on the component's exterior face. Generally, surface designs can be deep. If using a single-piece mold, the designs will require more draft than if using a hinged mold.

Surface designs can include textures, lettering, waves, and complex geometric patterns similar to patterns traditionally associated with etched glass (see figure 4.6.4).

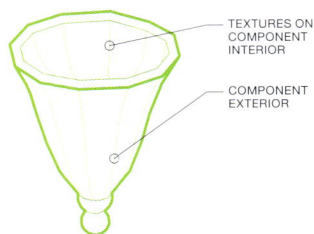

TEXTURES ON COMPONENT INTERIOR
COMPONENT EXTERIOR

TOOLING COMPLEXITY

Generally, tools are simple. Hinged molds may be used, but increase demolding times.

TOOLING COSTS

A tooling package in stainless steel that includes four molds, four sealing rings, and one plunger for high-volume productions can cost $30,000–50,000. Cast iron molds are about half the cost of the steel molds.

UNDERCUTS

Undercuts are possible, but require a hinged mold.

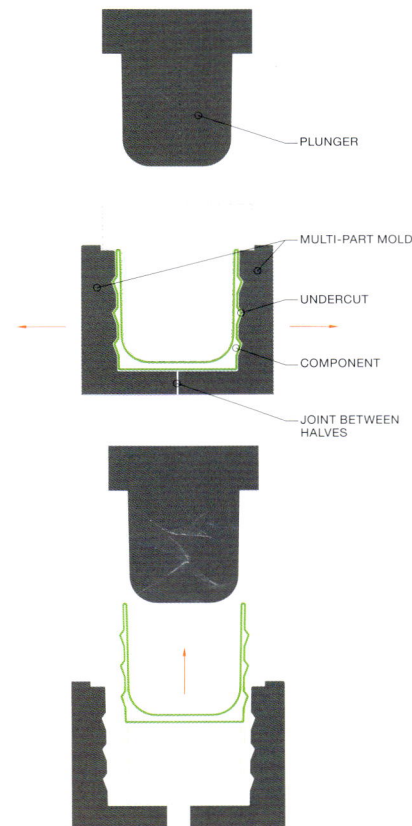

PLUNGER
MULTI-PART MOLD
UNDERCUT
COMPONENT
JOINT BETWEEN HALVES

VENTS

Generally, vents are not necessary, as the molten glass moves from the center of the mold to the exterior, pushing the air out as it moves.

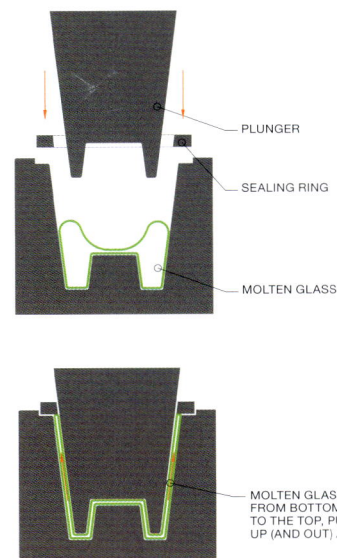

PLUNGER
SEALING RING
MOLTEN GLASS
MOLTEN GLASS MOVES FROM BOTTOM OF CAVITY, TO THE TOP, PUSHING AIR UP (AND OUT) AS IT GOES.

Vents may be necessary at undercuts or overhangs. Typically, vents do not leave a mark on the surface of the glass, but if they do, these can be removed with flame polishing.

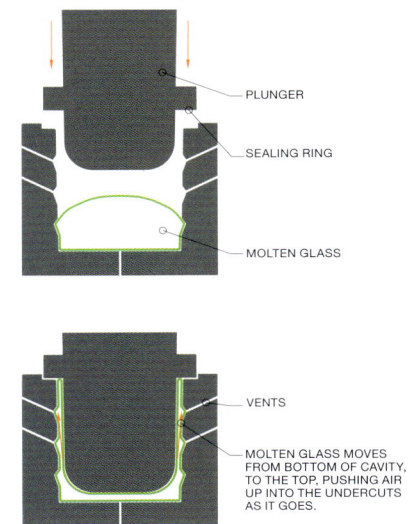

PLUNGER
SEALING RING
MOLTEN GLASS
VENTS
MOLTEN GLASS MOVES FROM BOTTOM OF CAVITY, TO THE TOP, PUSHING AIR UP INTO THE UNDERCUTS AS IT GOES.

WALL THICKNESS

Wall thicknesses can range from 0.25in (6mm) to over 2in (50mm), and can vary across the cross-section. The wall thickness at the bottom of the component tends to be thicker than at the sides.

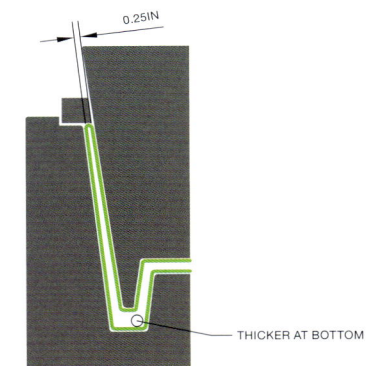

0.25IN
THICKER AT BOTTOM

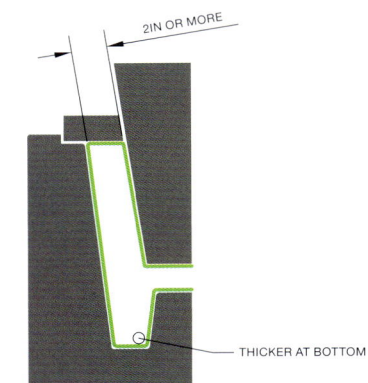

2IN OR MORE
THICKER AT BOTTOM

EXTERIOR GLASS TILE RAINSCREEN | GERRIT RIETVELD ACADEMY ADDITION

Benthem Crouwel Architects
Amsterdam, the Netherlands

The Gerrit Rietveld Academy is a university for fine arts and design that offers a multi-disciplinary bachelor's degree in Fine Arts and Design and four master's degrees. [15, 17] The original building by Gerrit Rietveld was completed in 1966, after his death, and is the architect's largest realized building. The addition by Benthem Crouwel Architects is approximately $70,000ft^2$ ($6,500m^2$), with eight stories above grade and a basement; it includes studios, exhibition space, a library, audiovisual rooms, and offices. The addition, completed in 2004, is located to the south of the original building, and is on the campus edge against a busy street. The addition's north façade has a glass curtain wall, and the south, west, and east faces are clad in a custom pressed-glass tile.

The glass tile manufacturer was commissioned to press 16,000 tiles for this building. The tiles are approximately 14in wide, 13.75in high, and 0.5in thick (360mm, 350mm, and 15mm, respectively). [16] The dimensions of the tiles course out with the building, so that full tiles are used at the corners, at openings, and with the floor heights. There is a small space in the vertical joint between each tile, but the tiles overlap slightly as they cascade down the façade. The tiles were pressed with a relatively large, oval-shaped dimple at the center, a fine surface texture, and an indentation for the fasteners. [18, 20] Pressing allowed all of these details to be done within a single manufacturing cycle, with no post-production processing.

DESIGN CONSIDERATIONS

Making an addition to a building by a well-known and respected architect requires a thoughtful and creative architectural solution. The custom glass tile seemed to offer the solution that Benthem Crouwel wanted. According to Benthem Crouwel team member Peter Kropp, this project was a special solution to a special situation.[3] Others on the building team were also willing to support the custom tile. The building's contractor was open to the idea, and it was supported by Blitta BV, the project's façade consultant.[4]

MANUFACTURING CONSIDERATIONS

Because the Czech Republic is known for its pressed glass, Benthem Crouwel used team member Peter Kropp, who is Czech, to research manufacturers capable of producing the tile. The manufacturer that received the commission had until that point mostly produced beer tankards and ashtrays. It was not a highly automated facility, and therefore it could work with the designers to produce the custom tile. [19] Kropp remembered that the manufacturer was

15
Gerrit Rietveld Academy addition by Benthem Crouwel Architects in Amsterdam, the Netherlands. South façade

16
Detail of glass tile

17
Corner of addition

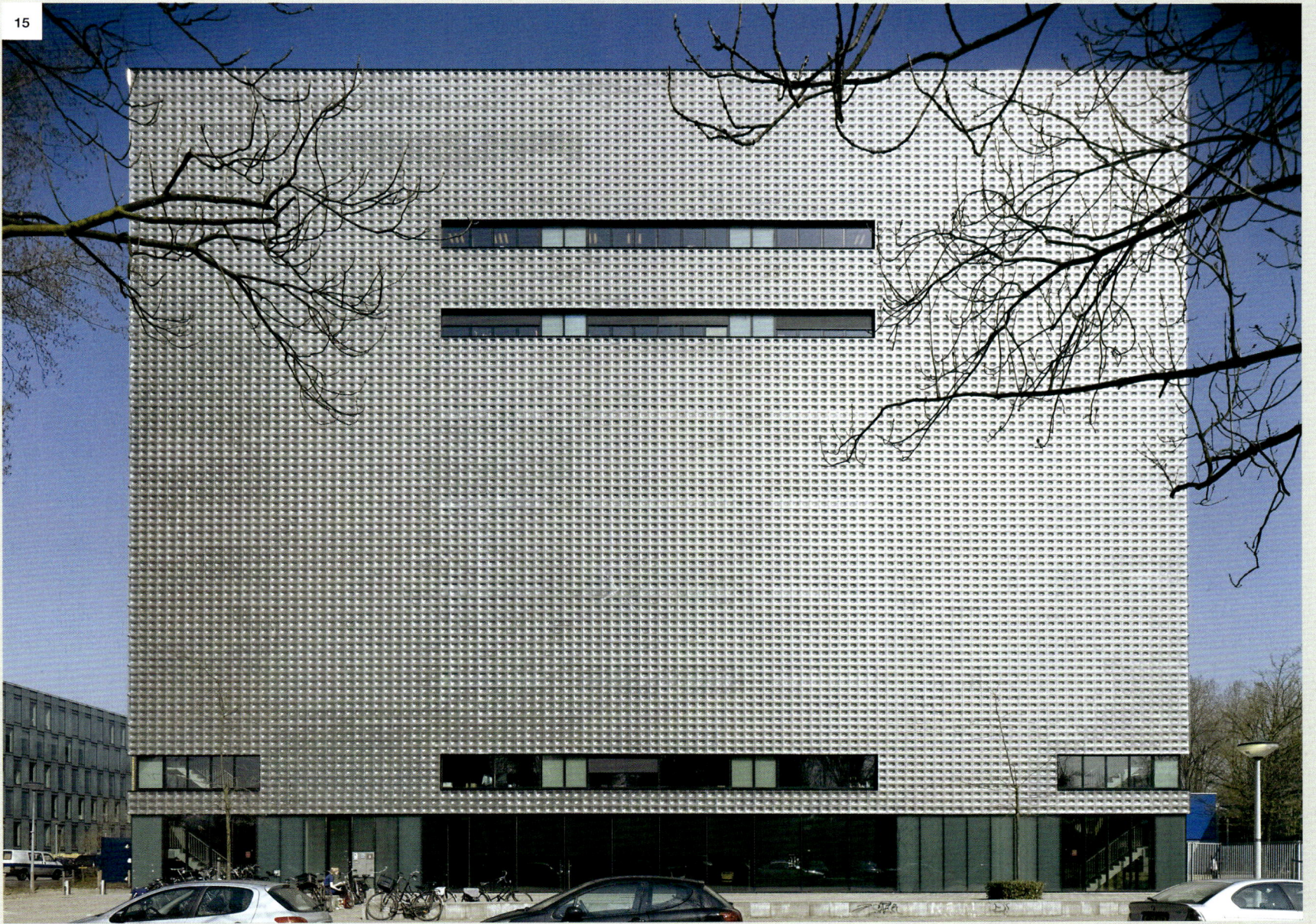

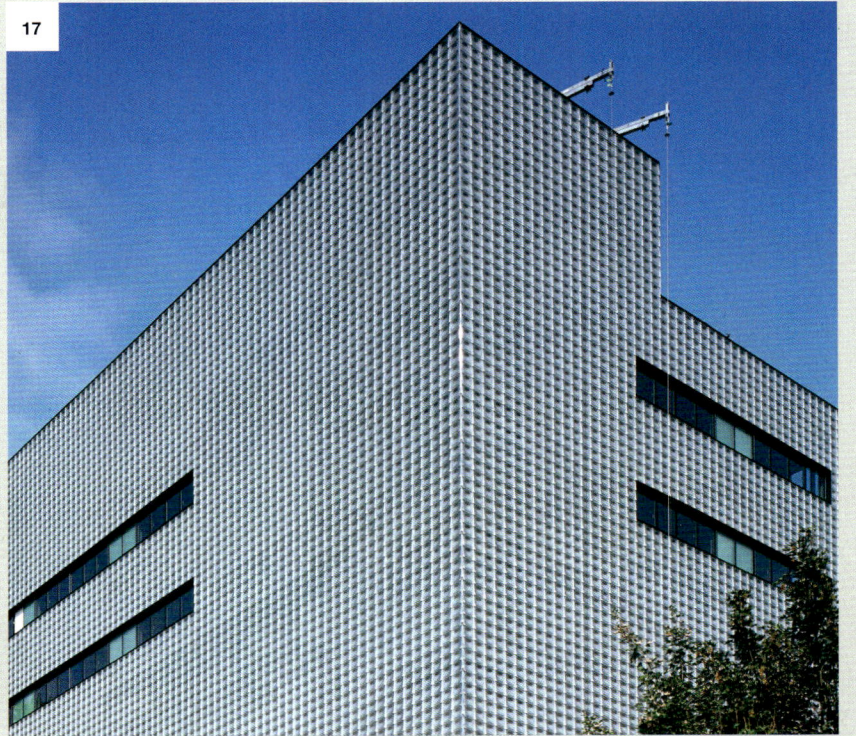

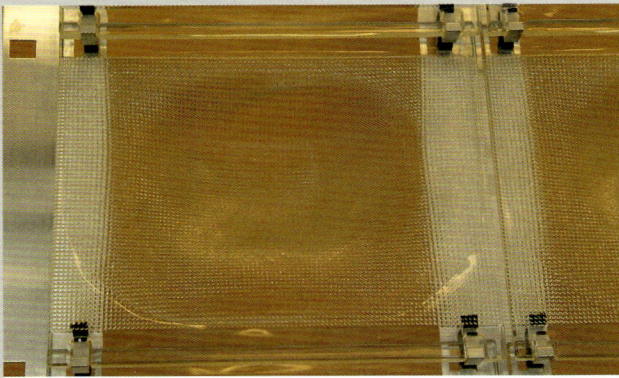

18 Detail of mock-up

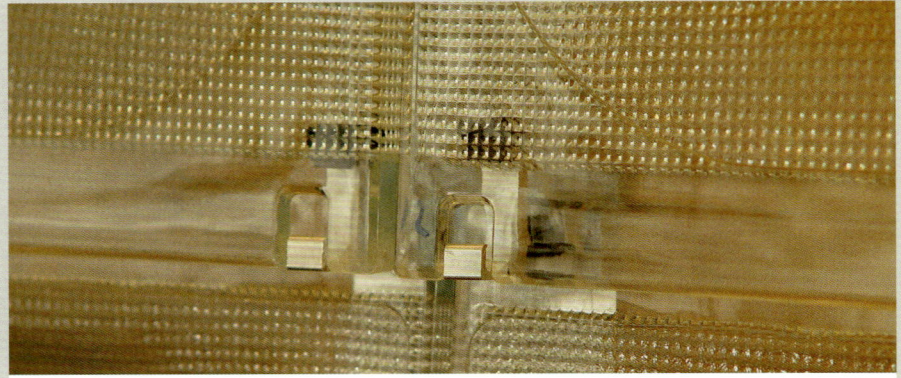

20 Detail of bracket support

19 Manufacturing facility

21 Building under construction

22 Glass tiles being applied during construction

committed to the project and working with the architecture team, but that it struggled to see the potential of pressed glass for additional architecture applications.

Peter Hanen, Blitta managing director, stated that the manufacturer used two CNC-milled, hardened-steel molds with one plunger to press the glass tiles. Each press cycle lasted a few seconds. After the plunger lifted, a worker using tongs would remove the still-glowing glass from the mold.[5]

OTHER CONSIDERATIONS

The glass tiles have held up well over the years, and replacements have not been needed. **[21, 22]**

CLAY

Historically, pressed clay was used as a substitute for carved stone on buildings. [23] Using this process, components could be made faster and lighter than cast or carved stone, but with the same level of detail. Generally, clay used for architectural applications has been shown to be very durable for both interior and exterior applications.[6]

Clay used for pressing can range from dry, which is powder-like and when squeezed in the hand leaves no residue yet can hold a shape, to wet, which is sticky and when squeezed in the hand will leave a wet clay residue. Generally, the dryer the clay, the more force is needed for shaping, and the more delicate the component will be during demolding. [24, 25] Dry-pressed clay has a moisture content of only 12%, and is best for flat pieces that need limited shrinking, whereas wet clays have a moisture range of 25–35%. Little force is needed for shaping wet clay, but it takes longer to dry and has higher shrinking rates than dry clay. To reduce shrinking in wet clay, grog or fired clay particles are added to the clay mixture to stabilize the clay, give it strength, add recycled content, and reduce shrinking. Wet clays can either be hand or mechanically pressed, can have fine details, and because of high shrinking rates are easy to remove from the mold. Because of the shaping advantages of wet clays over dry, this chapter focuses on wet clay for pressing.

Hand pressing uses a wetter clay than mechanical pressing. A hand presser may press or throw small pieces of clay into the mold. Typically, hand pressers will work from the middle of the mold to the outside, helping to eliminate air bubbles. If the mold has a lot of intricate detail, an even wetter slurry mix may be poured into the mold before hand pressing. For mechanical pressing, the clay used in the press is often extruded into slabs, which helps ensure a consistency of material size and thickness, reducing over-flashing and speeding up pressing cycles. If wall thicknesses are important, such as with roof tiles, then the extrusion will be done at a thickness close to the final thickness and cut to the size of the tile, before being placed in the press.

Clay components are designed with fairly even wall thicknesses to reduce shrinking, warping, and the possibility of trapped air bubbles. If a component is large, reinforcing ribs should be added to the inside of the component. These will be placed every 6–8in (150–200mm) and are 1.5–2in (38–50mm) thick. [26] The ribs support the clay during drying and firing, and provide potential anchor points for mechanical fasteners or surfaces for mortar joints. If using mortar between the clay, then the surface of the rib will often be scored and left unglazed, providing a strong mechanical connection between the component and the mortar. [27]

The clay must be dried before firing. If the clay is too wet when placed in the kiln, the trapped moisture will expand at high temperatures, causing the component to break. Drying must be controlled, otherwise the component can warp and crack. Kiln-fired clay is fairly resistant to water absorption and, if oriented vertically, it does not necessarily need to be glazed. Glaze should be considered on horizontal clay surfaces for protection, or for changing the component's color. Glazes can range from matte to glossy, from clear to opaque, and from a single color to multiple colors. Typically, the glaze will be applied to the dried clay prior to firing in the kiln. If the glaze is glossy, it may be fired twice.

SIMILAR PROCESSES
Slumping clay (Chapter 1.1) can produce complex curves that are similar to pressing. However, cycle times are shorter, surface decorations are faster, and wall thicknesses can vary across the cross-section for pressed clay.

23 Components made by hand-pressed clay

24 Dry clay

25 Wet clay

26 Interior supporting walls for component

27 Surface at mortar joint is left unglazed with a texture for mechanical connection

DRAFT ANGLES

For mechanical presses, the draft angle can range from 2 to 4°, depending on draw depth.

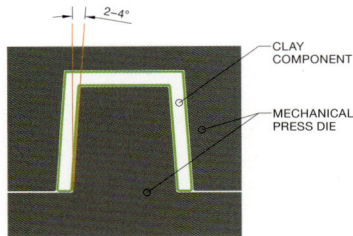

For hand-pressed clay, draft angles can range from 0 to −1° or more, depending on draw depth. This is because the clay can be left in the mold long enough to shrink. If a more negative draft angle is needed, then a multi-part mold will be used.

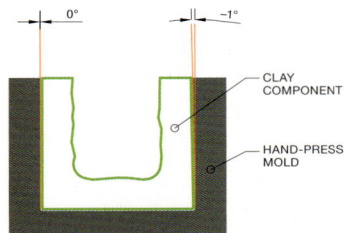

DRAW DEPTH

For mechanical presses, the draw depth will depend on the press, but it is typically limited to 12in (300mm).

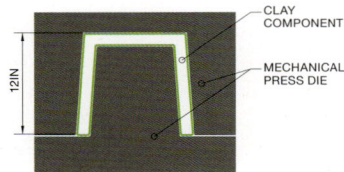

For hand-pressed clay, the draw depends on the hand presser's arm length, and is typically limited to 24in (600mm).

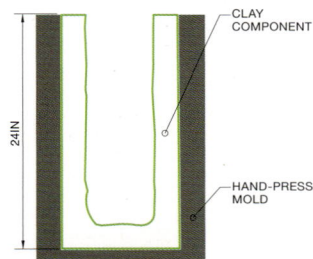

JOINING

Green clay can be fused together with some handwork. This involves scoring the surface of each piece, using clay slip between the pieces, and finishing tools to smooth the joint. This allows complex clay components to be made from existing molds, without making specialty molds. This process is particularly applicable to making components to turn the corner of a building or to fuse two halves together to make hollow components. Although joining pieces together increases labor costs, it can decrease mold costs.

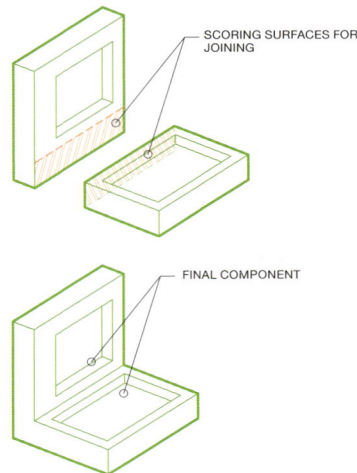

FLASHING

For mechanical pressing, flashing may form between the dies. It is easily removed, and any line from the flashing can be smoothed while the clay is green.

PARTING LINES

For hand pressing in multi-part molds, the parting line will be faint or not visible. Any lines in the component can be smoothed while the clay is green.

POST-PRODUCTION

There are a number of post-production processes that can be done on the clay while it is still green. This can include small changes such as adding surface textures, or making intricate carvings or holes for mechanical fasteners.

PRODUCTION RUNS

Production runs can range from prototypes and small runs of fewer than 200 units, to medium-range productions under 2,000 units, to high productions above 10,000 units. Production runs will depend on the tooling medium and manufacturer equipment. Clay manufacturers can accommodate larger productions, but will use multiple molds for parallel production runs.

PRODUCTION SPEED

Production rates can vary, depending on the size of the component, the stiffness of the clay, and whether it is being pressed by hand or machine. If the clay is brick-sized with limited detail and low water content, 300 units per hour can be pressed. If the clay component is large—approximately the size of two standard concrete blocks—with a lot of moisture and detail, then two units may be produced per hour. Clay may be left in a plaster mold anywhere from 2 to 24 hours, depending on the level of detail.

SHRINKING

Clay will shrink 8–15%. The amount of shrinkage will depend on the clay, the moisture content, and the amount of grog.

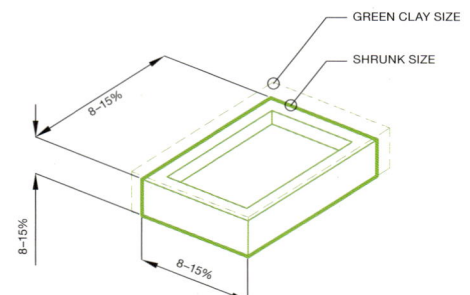

SIDE-WALL HOLES

It is not possible to mold in size-wall holes with this process. All side-wall holes should be made post-production, while the clay is green.

SIZE LIMITS

For mechanical pressing, the size will be limited by the press, and will be less than 24in × 24in (600mm × 600mm). In hand pressing, the size is limited to make handling easier both at the manufacturer and on the construction site. Hand-pressed components should be less than 36in × 36in (915mm × 915mm).

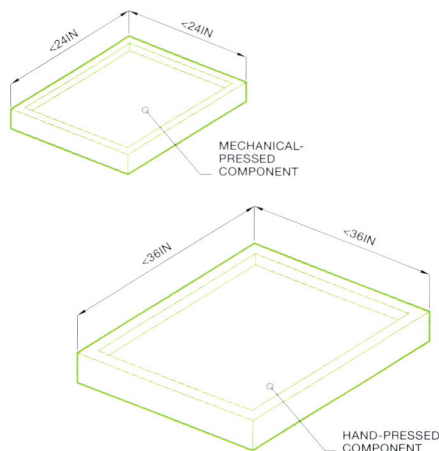

MECHANICAL-PRESSED COMPONENT

HAND-PRESSED COMPONENT

SURFACE DESIGNS

In-mold surface design possibilities are almost unlimited with this process. Designs can include intricate details, ornaments, and undercuts. Fine surface textures can be done in-mold, but are often better done after the component is removed from the mold, but is still green. These textures are done by hand, but could be done by CNC.

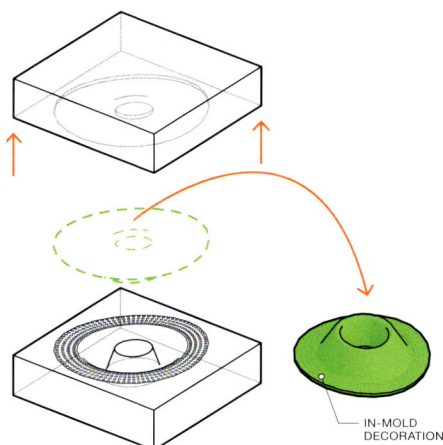

IN-MOLD DECORATION

TOOLING COMPLEXITY

Tools in the process are simple, with no moving parts. Ram presses may use embedded water lines for high-density plaster dies. This forces water to the die's surface, making the clay release from the mold's surface and decreasing cycle times.

TOOLING COSTS

Generally, tooling is inexpensive. For mechanical pressing, tooling will be less than $5,000; for hand pressing, tooling will be less than $500.

TOLERANCES

Pressed clay tolerances will be 0.06–0.12in (1.5–3mm), depending on the component's overall dimensions.

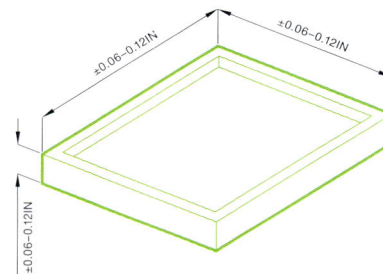

±0.06–0.12IN   ±0.06–0.12IN

±0.06–0.12IN

UNDERCUTS

Undercuts are discouraged in mechanical pressing. Traditionally, this mechanical pressing relies on short cycle times in order to be cost efficient, and the clay must be removed from the mold before the next cycle. Therefore the clay is not left in the mold long enough to shrink away from undercuts.

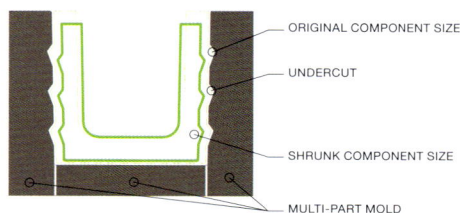

ORIGINAL COMPONENT SIZE

UNDERCUT

SHRUNK COMPONENT SIZE

MULTI-PART MOLD

Undercuts are possible in hand pressing. First, because the clay has a high shrinkage rate, it will shrink away from the mold, making small undercuts possible in a solid mold. Second, because there is hand labor available, the molds can be made of multiple parts so that they can be broken down to remove the component.

VENTS

In mechanical pressing, vents are needed in female cavities to let air escape. Vent holes can be small, and because the clay is green when removed from the press, marks can easily be removed from the clay's surface with a moist sponge.

In hand pressing, vents are not necessary. Pressers should work from the middle of the mold to the exterior, allowing any trapped air to escape at the edges of the clay.

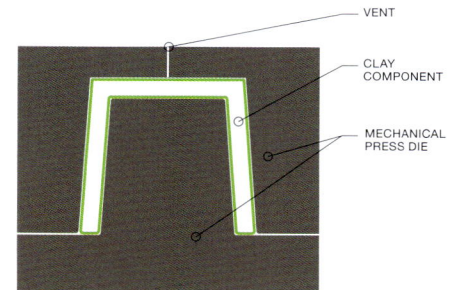

VENT

CLAY COMPONENT

MECHANICAL PRESS DIE

WALL THICKNESS

For large components, wall thickness will be 1.5–2in (40–50mm). Walls are used to provide strength to the component, but cannot be too thick as they limit the possibility of trapped air within the clay. This will reduce the possibility of breaking while the clay is fired in the kiln.

PRESSING: CLAY

EXTERIOR CERAMIC TILE RAINSCREEN | THE ASIAN ART STUDY CENTER AT THE RINGLING MUSEUM OF ART

Machado Silvetti
Sarasota, Florida

28
Building section of the The Asian Art Study Center at the Ringling Museum of Art

29
Design rendering showing aerial view

30
Building plans

The Asian Art Study Center is the newest building located on the John and Mable Ringling Museum of Art campus. **[29, 30]** John, one of five brothers who owned and operated the Ringling Brothers Circus, built with his wife a 36,000ft² (3,350m²) mansion on Sarasota Bay. Shortly after their house was completed, the Ringlings built an art museum for their growing collection of art and art books, and in 1931 it opened to the public. Later, the Circus Museum, Asolo Theater, Visitors Pavilion, and Education Center were added to the campus. The Asian Art Study Center, completed in 2015, includes an 18,000ft² (1,675m²) renovation of the existing Art Museum's West Wing Galleries, and a 7,500ft² (700m²) addition with gallery space, an entry court, a lecture hall, open object storage, study rooms, and a bridge connecting the Study Center to the Art Museum.

According to Craig Mutter, principal at Machado Silvetti and project architect, the donor stipulated that the addition be a modern iconic building on the Ringling campus.[7] The project consists of two parts—the renovation, and an addition to the original building that includes a gallery pavilion. Machado Silvetti kept the form of the addition simple, as an elevated prism atop pilotis that frame an open-air, covered-entry courtyard. **[28]** The simple form allowed the design team to focus its efforts on designing the building skin. **[31, 32]** Most of the buildings on the Ringling campus are of a Venetian style, with architectural ornament made from terra cotta. The design team wanted to keep within the palette of the campus, while meeting the donor's request. The team selected glazed terra cotta panels because of the use of the material on campus, how the material has held up over the years in the Florida climate, and the connection of terra cotta to traditional Asian architecture and its tile roofs.

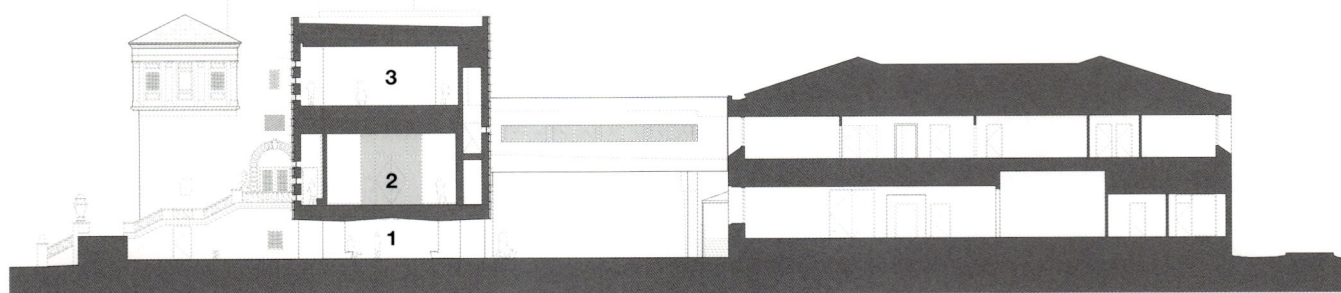

1 ENTRY COURT
2 GALLERY
3 LECTURE HALL

0 10 20 40 100 FEET

31 Main entry of addition

32 Detail of tiles and windows

The tiles were manufactured by Boston Valley Terra Cotta (BVTC), located just south of Buffalo, New York. For this project, BVTC ram-pressed approximately 3,000 tiles and applied a custom green glaze to all of the tiles. [33] The tiles have a curved surface on their outer face, and an almost 90° return to connect to their aluminum support structure. Three primary shapes make up 90% of the building façade, which includes a large square, measuring approximately 24in × 25in × 5.5in (610mm × 630mm × 140mm), the same-sized square with a window cut out, and a smaller square. Each tile weighs approximately 60–70lb (27–31kg). The custom glaze is made from layers of green fired on top of layers of gold. It took 6 months and several hundred batches of samples for the color to be approved by Machado Silvetti. [34]

DESIGN CONSIDERATIONS

The project budget was limited. Machado Silvetti believed that for the project to have the biggest impact, the focus should be on the building's exterior. Project designer Rodolfo Machado was inspired by traditional Asian architecture and garden ornaments, and by the museum's collection of Asian artifacts (particularly those made from carved jade and glazed ceramic, all of which were deep green), as well as by the exuberance of Floridian foliage. As the design team developed the shape of the exterior panels, it also studied color options. Initial concept drawings showed the building as having a green chiseled or pineapple-like texture, in which depth would be revealed by the thickness of the building skin's components.

33 Ram press with tile mold at Boston Valley Terra Cotta

According to Mutter, the design team considered alternative materials and manufacturing processes for the façade panels. The team investigated precast concrete, three-dimensionally formed titanium panels,[8] extruded ceramic, and pressed ceramic. With the intention of revealing thickness on the building's exterior, the design team rejected metal panels, as they would have been a thin material that appeared thick. In the end, ram-pressing was selected to achieve the desired color and shape. The final material selection followed a collaborative process, was approved by both the project donor and the museum director, and became the signature element of the project.

As the design team were making the material and manufacturing selection, they met and toured the BVTC manufacturing facility. Machado Silvetti had previous experience with BVTC. For the Global Center for Academic and Spiritual Life at New York University (2012), Machado Silvetti had considered terra cotta for the building skin, which consisted of a custom perforated rainscreen, but instead selected water-jet-cut stone. Later, for the Wellin Museum of Art at Hamilton College (2012), Machado Silvetti used BVTC to manufacture a custom extruded terra cotta rainscreen. With these experiences, Machado Silvetti was confident of BVTC's capabilities and willingness to collaborate.

The design team did numerous design studies of the tile, the tile pattern and orientation, and optional window layouts. [35] Because the building was small, Machado Silvetti wanted to use large tiles in a repeating pattern to give a scale-less quality to the project. In the end, they selected a checkerboard pattern of alternating large and small tiles. The three-dimensional curve on the face of the tile was done so that two side faces of each tile would be exposed, revealing a depth to the façade. The windows were then grouped together to create a cloud-like arrangement in the pattern. This allowed the tile pattern to continue without being interrupted by a regularized window arrangement.

MANUFACTURING CONSIDERATIONS

Each tile took approximately 28 days, from start to finish, to make. This included pressing, handwork, drying, glazing, firing, re-glazing, re-firing, and packaging. A minimum of twelve pairs of hands touched each component from start to shipping.[9] BVTC hand pressed specialty tiles that were used at the building's corners. It also made the project's molds, by casting large blocks of plaster and then using a five-axis CNC mill to carve out the molds' shapes. (In most cases, some hand finishing was required to remove CNC tool marks so that the finish surface was smooth.)

The molds were designed so that the tiles are hollow on their back side. This helped to reduce wall thickness, both for weight and for reduced breakage during drying and firing. The molds were made so that the parting line was at the back of the tile, reducing the need for post-production finishing. The draft angle required by the press served as a sloped edge on the tile's horizontal surface, shedding water away from the building. A grooved undercut, which was necessary for mounting the tiles to the rainscreen frame, was carved into the tile post-pressing and before drying.

According to Mutter, as Machado Silvetti developed the building design, the firm took into consideration BVTC's capabilities in order to save costs. During its initial BVTC visit, Machado Silvetti learned that BVTC

34 Glaze color samples at BVTC

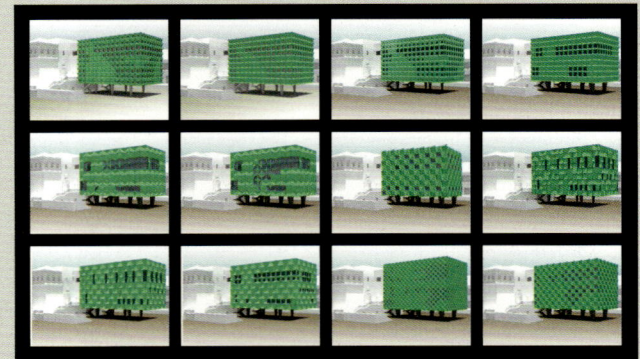
35 Design iterations of tiles and windows

36 Pressed panels drying on a rack

37 Detail of the tile at the manufacturer

had a standard rack that it used to hold the terra cotta pieces during drying and firing. [36] These racks allowed BVTC to efficiently fill the kiln during firing, speeding up production and reducing costs. They realized that by reducing the panels' depth by 1.5in (38mm), more units would fit into a rack, which would greatly shorten BVTC's production time. The design team incorporated these recommendations, and several others from BVTC, as it continued to develop the panel's shape in order to reduce material waste and ease installation. [37]

OTHER CONSIDERATIONS

BVTC is committed to collaborating with architects so that the terra cotta components' manufacturing is in keeping with the design concept. In addition, BVTC has recognized the important role that installation of the terra cotta components has in the overall design. According to BVTC, the quality of the terra cotta is only as good as its installation.[10] To improve installation techniques, BVTC has a list of preferred contractors and does contractor installation training at its factory. [38] BVTC also inspected the installation of the tile at the Asian Art Study Center for additional quality assurance. [39]

    The glaze thickness and color on the Study Center is not consistent across the tile surfaces. Glaze becomes viscous during firing, and gravity moves it over the complexly curved surface of the terra cotta. For this particular tile shape, the glaze pooled at the low points of the tiles' front curved surface, and pulled away from the exterior corners and edges. The variation is subtle, while visually enhancing the curved surface and making the tiles' edges more pronounced. [40] Although manufactured on a ram press, the glaze variation gives the tiles a hand-made quality.

    In case of storm damage, extras of each tile type were manufactured. The extras are kept in the Ringling Museum and at BVTC.

LESSONS LEARNED

The project site is located on the west coast of Florida, on Sarasota Bay, the inland waterway off the Gulf of Mexico, and is subject to local hurricane codes and regulations. Sarasota County has particular requirements to ensure that building assemblies are rated to weather hurricane conditions. Mutter and the design team saw the benefit of combining a custom façade panel with BVTC's standard commercial rainscreen support system. There are a number of rainscreen support systems that have already been approved by Sarasota County for use in new constructions, including BVTC's. By selecting BVTC's standard support system in lieu of a custom support system, the project saved the time and expense related to additional testing and approvals processes. By using BVTC's support system, which had already been approved, the project was able to save money.

38 Installation mock-up for contractor training at BVTC

39 Building corner during construction

40 Design mock-up at BVTC. Note the glaze color variation on the tile face

Endnotes

1.1 SLUMPING

1 Examples of more active sheet manipulation processes include: 1.2 Thermoforming, 1.5 Stamping, and 1.6 Hydroforming.

2 If the depth of the slump is slight, or multiple pieces of glass are placed onto the mold simultaneously, then it may be referred to as kiln-formed glass.

3 Jørgen Markvad. *Kilnformed Glass*. Translated by Elizabeth Anderson. Gedved, Denmark: Apples of Idun, 2006. Print.

4 Cory Taylor, managing principal, Belzberg Architects. Personal interview. 27 April 2015.

5 Ibid.

1.2 THERMOFORMING

1 Steel, brass, or titanium alloys can be used, but these molds are not cost efficient and most likely would outlast their need.

2 SEED stands for Solar Energy Efficient Dwelling.

3 The University of Arizona placed 18th (out of 20) and scored 610.339 points (out of a possible 1,000). The categories in which it did its best were engineering (8th), architecture (7th), and hot water (13th).

4 PET-G is a modification of polyethylene terephthalate (PET), which is typically used for soft-drink containers. The glycol modification lowers the PET's melting temperature, potentially making it easier to thermoform than PET.

5 Dale Clifford. Personal Interview. 27 May 2015.

6 Conventional metals will stretch no more than 120% regardless of temperature or speed of stretching.

7 Gillo Giuliano , ed. *Superplastic Forming of Advanced Metallic Materials: Methods and Applications*. Philadelphia: Woodhead Publishing, 2011. Print.

8 Following the manufacturing parameters of Superform, the students were limited to only using a three-axis CNC router for mold making and post-production trimming. Students were also limited to using only one or two mold forms, as molds for superforming metal are substantially higher than those from thermoforming plastic. Heather Roberge, principal, Murmur. Personal Interview. 12 November 2015.

1.3 EXPLOSIVE FORMING

Other HERF methods include electrohydraulic forming, or electric discharge forming, and electromagnetic forming, or magnetic pulse forming. In electrohydraulic forming, two electrodes are placed in water and a short burst of electrical energy is discharged between them. This process generates less energy, and thus less force, than explosive forming and is suited to small parts. In electromagnetic forming, an energized coil induces an electromagnetic field on the workpiece to cause deformation. With this process, the workpiece needs to be a metal that is a good conductor of electricity.

2 This is called explosive welding (EXW). The explosion disrupts the surface of the metals as they are forced into one another. This creates a wave-shaped joint between the interlocking face, forming a mechanical connection between the metals.

3 Some of the explosives used include trinitrotoluene (TNT), penthrite (PETN), dynamite, and cyclonite (RDX). Detonation velocities range from 12,500ft/s (3,810 m/s) for dynamite to 27,500ft/s (8,380m/s) for RDX. Pressures range from 625ksi (4.3GPa) for dynamite to 3,400ksi (23.4GPa) for RDX. Energy released ranges from 715kJ for dynamite to 1,300kJ for PETN.

4 N.N. Ida. "Explosive-Forming Techniques at Martin-Denver." *Advanced High Energy Rate Forming, Book II*. Detroit: American Society of Tool and Manufacturing Engineers, 1962. Pages 62–84. Print.

5 George F. Schrader and Ahmad K. Elshennawy. *Manufacturing Processes & Materials*. 4th ed. Dearborn, MI: Society of Manufacturing Engineers, 2000. Print.

6 S.A.A. Akbari Mousavi, et al. "Experimental and numerical analyses of explosive free forming." *Journal of Materials Processing Technology*. 2007. Pages 512–516. Print.

7 IAA Architecten. De Grijze Generaal, Eindhoven. http://www.iaa-architecten.nl/projecten/24-de-grijze-generaal/. Accessed 20 November 2015.

8 Klusor Apartment Building by IAA Architecten (2010), Lelystad, the Netherlands.

9 Harry Abels, director, IAA Architecten and Hieke Luik, artist. Personal Interview. 4 November 2015.

10 Test plates were later analyzed using photogrammetry. H.D. Groeneveld. "Photogrammetry Applications For Explosive Forming." *Paton Welding Journal*. 2009. PDF.

1.4 BENDING PLIES

1 The term "bending plywood" refers specifically to creating a simple curved surface. The term "molding plywood" is used to refer to creating a complex curved surface. Generally, simple curved surfaces are easy to form with wood plies, while complex curves are much more difficult. Because the materials used in this process do not have the ability to stretch and shrink, shape making is more limited compared with plastic or metal forming processes. Molding plywood often requires pre-cuts to relieve internal stresses, or is laid in thin strips rather than sheets.

2 Dung Ngo and Eric Pfeiffer. *Bent Ply: The Art of Plywood Furniture*. New York: Princeton Architectural Press, 2003. Page 104.

3 Ibid. Page 16.

4 Ibid. Page 101.

5 In veneering, there is an odd number of layers so that the grain directions on the outside layers are parallel to one another.

6 Todd Zima. Personal interview. 30 April 2015.

7 Jeanne Gang. "The Cook, the Prospector, the Nomad and their Architect." *Re-inventing Construction*. Ed. by Ilka and Andreas Ruby. Zurick: Holcim Foundation, 2010. Page 163.

8 www.upmgrada.com.

9 *UPM Grada—New Thermoformable Wood Material*. Valvefi. Uploaded 19 December 2012. Web. Accessed 24 April 2015. https://www.youtube.com/watch?v=MX-4CdzRrP5E.

10 Samantha Kiljunen, et al. UPM-Kymmene Wood Oy. *Post Formable Plywood Product and Its Manufacturing Method*. US 2011/0091683 A1. United States Patent Application Publication, 21 April 2011. Web. Accessed 24 April 2015.

11 www.tut.fi/en/about-tut/departments/school-of-architecture/research/index.htm. Website. Updated 15 December 2014. Accessed 15 May 2015.

12 Emmi Keskisarja. Email correspondence. 10 March 2015.

13 Emmi Keskisarja, EDGE, and Kristof Crolla, LEAD. Personal interview. 27 May 2015.

14 Laboratory for Explorative Architecture and Design http://1-e-a-d.pro/w/wp-content/uploads/2012/02/DragonSkin-TheMakingOf.m4v. Website. Accessed 15 September 2015.

1.5 STAMPING

1 The specific tooling for metal stamping depends on the action. For example, punching and blanking require only a punch, breaking may require only the break, and drawing often only requires a punch and side-walls to form the walls of the cup shape. This chap-ter focuses on mate dies because of their architectural applications.

2 http://www.seacon-umformtech-nik.de/home/. Accessed 19 June 2015.

3 Cornelius Wens, Benthem Crouwel, project architect. Personal interview. 10 June 2015.

4 Taylan Altan and A. Erman Tekkaya, eds. *Sheet Metal Forming*. Materials Park, OH: ASM International, 2012.

5 This may be attributed to the high cost of tooling associated with metal stamping.

1.6 HYDROFORMING

1 Because it is primarily used for the automobile industry, tube hydroforming is outside of this book's scope.

2 Ed. Atelier d'Architecture et de Design Jim Clemes S.A. *LALUX Neiwisen*. www.jimclemes.com/files/55413.pdf. Downloaded 29 December 2015.

3 All German companies.

4 Ingbert Schilz, Atelier d'Architecture et de Design Jim Clemes S.A. Personal interview. 16 December 2015.

1.7 SPINNING

1 William Ganz, owner, Bill Ganz & Company. Personal interview. 23 June 2015. Bill stated that he could spin oval shapes up to the ratio of 1:2. In the literature on metal spinning, I have not found that others will spin anything other than circular shapes. Check with your spinner before designing this shape.

2 Maple, birch, cherry, or walnut can be used.

3 Metal spinners will work with other metals. Ganz spun galvanized steel; other publications write about spinning pewter and silver. Spinning galvanized steel is not recommended, as spinning may remove some of the galvanized surface.

4 Constantin Iliescu. *Cold-Pressing Technology*. New York: Elsevier, 1990. Page 425.

5 David Keuning. "Dragon Slayer: Neutelings Riedijk Wrapped the Eemhuis in Amersfoort in and Undisguised Reference to George, the City's Patron Saint." *Mark: Another Architecture*. 2014: 108–117. Print.

6 Ibid.

7 Eric Thijssen, cultural house project leader, Neutelings Riedijk Architecten. Personal interview. 9 December 2015.

8 Tim Van der Lee, Leebo Intelligent Building System. Personal email. 13 January 2016.

2.1 EXTRUSION

1 ASCER. About Us. http://www.ascer.es/homeinstitucional/ascerPresentacion.aspx?lang=en-GB&cual=presentacion. Website. Accessed 21 September 2015.

2 Ceramic Cumella. Qui Som (Who We Are). http://www.cumella.cat/quisom.htm. Website. Accessed 21 September 2015.

3 Francisco Mangado, Mangado y Asociados. Personal email correspondence. 9 April 2015.

4 Ibid.

5 Ibid.

6 Francsico Mangado. "The Construction: Project and Execution". *Pabellon de Espana* (Spanish Pavilion Expo Zaragoza 2008).

7 Ibid. Page 65.

8 Interview with Merrill Elam, 6 April 2015. Notes.

9 Progressive Architecture Award, 1988.

10 5468796 Architecture, OMS Stage. http://www.5468796.ca/#oms. Website. Accessed 25 November 2015.

11 Saša Radulović, 5468796 Architecture. Personal interview. 3 December 2015.

12 Victoria Ballard Bell and Patrick Rand. *Materials for Design 2*. New York: Princeton Architectural Press, 2014. Print.

13 I found this relation particularly interesting, as KlarTech is part of a Hutterite colony. Hutterites are communal people living in colonies of approximately fifteen families. The colonies farm, raise livestock, and produce manufactured goods. (www.hutterites.org) Unlike Amish people, Hutterites will use electricity and use digital technology for work, but limit it for personal use. The relationship between a Hutterite manufacturer and a young architecture practice seems particularly enriching—albeit outside of the scope of this book.

14 SK8 by 5468796 Architecture in Winnipeg, Canada.

15 Die swell may be attributed to plastic's change from a liquid to a solid state after it passes through the die. It can also be attributed to plastic's polymer chains. It is thought that the polymer chains become less entangled and more organized when the plastic is compressed through the die, but then reorganize themselves to be more entangled upon exiting the die. This too may cause the swell.

16 selgascano. Personal email. 30 October 2015.

17 selgascano. Personal email. 11 December 2015.

18 Miquel Aliu, Polimer Tecnic SL. Personal email. 14 October 2015.

19 selgascano. Personal email. 11 December 2015.

2.1 PULTRUSION

1 The budget was $165/ft2 (€1,280/m²), in 2010 dollars.

2 Donna Dawson. "Hotel Wrap: Curvilinear Pultrusions." *Composites Technology*. 30 June 2010. www.compositesworld.com/articles/hotel-wrap-curvilinear-pultrusions. Accessed 25 March 2015.

3 Progettazione Costruzione Ricerca website. http://www.pcr-srl.it/about-us/?lang=en. Accessed 30 March 2015.

4 Jeremy King, King Roselli Architetti. Personal interview. 27 March 2015.

3.1 CONTACT MOLDING

1 Gabriel Smith, project architect, Thomas Phifer and Partners. Personal interview. 1 July 2013.

2 Precast/Prestressed Concrete Institute (PCI). *Designing with Precast and Prestressed Concrete*. www.pci.org.

3.2 BLADDER INFLATION MOLDING

1 Grant Brooker, senior executive partner, Foster + Partners. Personal interview. 22 August 2014.

3.3 FILAMENT WINDING

J. Lowrie McLarty. "Filament Winding as a Potential Building Process." *Building Research*. January/March 1969. Print.

2 Glenn L Beall and James L. Thorne. *Hollow Plastic Parts: Design and Manufacture*. Cincinnati: Hanser Gardner Publications, 2004. Page 190. Print.

3 Inflatable mandrels can be made of rubber, silicone, or other plastic. Water-soluble mandrels are made of a mixture of sand and polyvinyl alcohol as the binder.

4 J. Lowrie McLarty. "Control of Filament Winding Parameters". *Composite Filament Winding*. Materials Park, OH: ASM International, 2011. Print.

5 Jan Knippers, director, ITKE. Personal interview. 16 November 2015.

6 Achim Menges and Jan Knippers. "Fibrous Tectonics." *Architectural Design*. September 2015. Online.

7 Blaine Brownell. "Robots Fabricate a Lobster-Inspired Pavilion." *Architect Magazine*. 19 March 2013. Website. www.architectmagazine.com/technology/robots-fabricate-a-lobster-inspired-pavilion_o Accessed 11 November 2015.

3.4 CENTRIFUGAL CASTING

1 N.G. Joshi. *Concrete Pipes and Pipelines: Unreinforced and Reinforced*. Oxford: Alpha Science International Ltd., 2015. Page 33.

2 Life Cycle Engineering Experts GmbH. "Environmental Comparison of Spun-Concrete Columns and Composite Steel." Download. http://www.europoles.com/company-careers/materials/spun-concrete/. Accessed 24 July 2015.

3 Dea Ecker and Robert Piotrowski, Principals, Ecker Architekten. Personal Interview. 29 September 2016.

4 Ecker and Piotrowski. Personal Correspondence. 29 September 2016.

3.5 BLOW MOLDING

1 Jan Schroers et al. "Thermoplastic Blow Molding of Metals". *Materials Today*. Jan–Feb 2011. Online.

2 Alejandro Villarreal, principal of Hierve Diseñeria. Personal interview. 8 April 2015.

3 Statements to the effect can be found on the firm's website. http://www.en.hierve.com/profile/about-us. Accessed 17 April 2015.

4 As a testament to the firm's commitment to social issues, the collection of photographs of the project that Villarreal sent to me included a portrait photograph of the construction workers on the roof of the Hesiodo, stringing the spheres onto the cables.

5 Paul Mozur. "Miniwiz Builds Its Green Presence, Brick by Brick". *The Wall Street Journal*. 6 July 2011. Website. Accessed 5 November 2015.

6 British Broadcasting Corporation. *Rubbish Bin Inspires Taiwan's Plastic Bottle Building*. 15 April 2010. Website. http://news.bbc.co.uk/2/hi/business/8622212.stm. Accessed 5 November 2015.

7 Miniwiz Sustainable Energy Development Ltd. "POLLI-Brick: Your Trash Our Building Material". Brochure. Accessed 30 November 2015.

8 Miniwiz. Personal email correspondence. 19 November 2015.

9 Ibid.

10 Ibid.

11 Ibid.

4.1 CASTING CONCRETE

1 The caulk is often pulled out of the mold each time the concrete is stripped; therefore molds should be recaulked between each pour.

2 The Rice University Library Service Building by Carlos Jimenez Studio (2005) in Houston, Texas, was poured on a Styrofoam mold. In a 2010 interview, Carlos Jimenez stated that the molds caused surface inconsistences on the concrete. The concrete was patched and painted. Dana K. Gulling. "Manufacturing Architecture: Case Studies of Collaborations between Designers and Makers." *Made: Design Education & the Art of Making Proceedings of the 26th National Conference on the Beginning Design Student, Charlotte, NC, 18–21 March, 2010*. Eds Jeffery Balmer and Chris Beokrem. Charlotte, NC: University of North Carolina Charlotte, 2010. Pages 45–52. Print.

3 Dominic Leong, partner, Leong Leong. Personal interview. 17 June 2015.

4 Rob Gregory in *The Architecture Review* referred to the four firms that designed the overall layouts as "established" and twenty-five firms that designed the façades as "up-and-coming." I am not sure those are the best terms for this case study, as Niall McLaughlin and Glenn Howells are considered contemporaries of each other. Rob Gregory. "Skill." *The Architectural Review*. April 2011. Pages 82–83. Print.

5 Gregory, page 83.

6 Gregory, page 83.

7 Niall McLaughlin, principal, Niall McLaughlin Architects. Personal interview. 23 September 2015.

8 McLaughlin has embraced the separation of the façade from the building design; so much so that he has yet to go inside of the building where his design ends and Howells' begins. McLaughlin, interview.

9 McLaughlin, interview.

10 Vincent Panhuysen, partner, KAAN Architecten. Personal interview. 18 June 2015.

11 Ibid.

12 Catherine Slessor. "Heimolen Crematorium." *Architectural Review*. April 2009. Pages 84–86. Print.

13 Elenberg Fraser. "0810 33M Media Kit". Ibid. http://elenbergfraser.com/#!/project/0810_33m. Website. Accessed 21 July 2015.

14 Caleb Smith, project architect, Elenberg Fraser. Personal interview. 29 June 2015.

15 Catherine Hennessy, project architect, ACME. Personal interview. 4 November 2015.

15 Ibid.

17 The cassettes are proprietary to Thorp. Thorp would not share photographs of the cassettes or allow ACME to discuss them in detail.

4.2 CASTING METAL

1 John Ross, associate and Paul Smith Store project architect, 6a architects. Personal interview. 30 September 2015.

2 Nick Compton. "Iron Will." *Wallpaper*. September 2015. Print.

3 The mass-production company is called Antislip Antiwear Treads International (AATi Ltd.) "Current Group Structure," FSE Group. www.fsegroup.co.uk. Website. Accessed 13 October 2015.

4 John Ross, interview.

4.3 CASTING GLASS

1 Hollow glass blocks are made by welding together two pressed halves.

2 Refractories, such as silica, diatomite (diatomaceous earth), alumina hydrate, or dried clay, are added to stabilize the plaster mold against high kiln temperatures. Optional additives include grog, which lowers the expansion and contraction rates of the mold; and fiberglass, which increases the mold's strength at lower temperatures.

3 Helga Watkins-Baker. *Kiln Forming Glass*. Ramsbury, Marlborough: The Crowood Press Ltd., 2010. Page 29.

4 In 1936, a 17ft (5.2m) diameter by 3ft (0.9m) thick glass mirror lens was cast for the Hale telescope, located in San Diego, California. Scientists estimated that the casting would take 11 months to anneal in a custom kiln. Watkins-Baker, page 39.

5 Justin Ford, Hariri Pontarini Architects (HPA), attributes the overall project length to site selection issues, finding the correct contractor, material changes, and working in another country with a different language.

6 Justin Ford, Hariri Pontarini Architects. Personal interview. 2 November 2015.

7 Ibid.

8 Ibid.

9 Although outside of this chapter's scope, according to Ford, any difficulty in making these panels was in their slumping. Early in the manufacturing process, cracks would form in the slumped panels. CBD experimented with the temperature cycles to lessen breakage. Some cracks were due to the uneven heating of the glass, as the heating elements were located on the top of the kiln, causing the top of the glass to heat faster than the bottom. Ford estimated that at the beginning one out of five glass sheets broke during slumping.

4.4 VIBRATION-PRESS CASTING

1 Typically, the concrete mixture is stiff and has zero slump, as measured by a concrete slump test. If one is manufacturing slump block (discussed later in the chapter) a slumping concrete may be used.

2 An example is the Doubell Brick Machines. www.makebricks.co.za.

3 Marcos Hagerman, project architect for HGR Arquitectos. Personal email correspondence. 16 June 2015.

4 Ariel Rojo. Personal email correspondence. 11 June 2015.

5 The translated company name is Polystyrene Beam and Architectural Solutions.

6 Rojo, email correspondence, 11 June 2015.

4.5 VIBRATION-TAMPING

1 This is in contrast to casting concrete (Chapter 4.1), which requires caulking at joints before each cycle, slowing down production speed.

2 The ASTM states that crazing "shall not constitute a cause for rejection" of a cast stone component. ASTM International, "Designation: C1364—10b Standard Specification for Architectural Cast Stone".

3 "Design for the Decades: Civic Buildings." *Architect*. 16 December 2010. Website. www.architectmagazine.com/aia-architect/design-for-decades/design-for-decades-civic-buildings_o. Accessed 29 December 2015.

4 Roy Decker, partner, Decker Duvall Architects. Personal interview 22 December 2015.

5 Roy T. Decker and Anne Marie Duvall Decker. "Inquiry in Practice and Experience." *Journal of Architectural Education*. September 2007. Print.

4.6 PRESSING

1 The differences between etched and pressed glass are in the slight radius of the corners that pressed glass requires. This means the edges do not feel as crisp and the light refraction is a little duller in pressed glass when compared to etched glass.

2 If the glass pressing is done in a mechanized facility, the amount of glass can be measured accurately by CNC equipment.

3 Peter Kropp, team member, Benthem Crouwel Architects. Personal interview. 13 April 2015.

4 Blitta was responsible for the glass tiles and their hanging system. Blitta BV Website: http://www.blitta.nl/en/references/its_ref/special-facade-systems/single/0/2/Gerrit-Rietveld-Academie-Amsterdam.html. Accessed 17 April 2015.

5 Peter Hanen, managing director, Blitta. Personal email. 9 June 2015.

6 According to the *Thames & Hudson Manual of Architectural Ceramics*, "the best terracotta has survived more than 150 years without deteriorating." David Hamilton. *Thames & Hudson Manual of Architectural Ceramics*. London: Thames and Hudson, 1978. Page 64. Print.

7   Craig Mutter, principal, Machado Silvetti. Personal interview. 25 August 2015.

8   Mutter did not indicate what forming process was investigated, but it most likely would have included stamping, hydroforming, or explosive forming.

9   Craig Mutter, email correspondence, 9 September 2015.

10 Tricia Herby, sales administrator, Boston Valley Terra Cotta. Personal interview and factory tour. 1 June 2015.

Glossary

ACID WASHING
A post-production finishing process for cast concrete, in which the manufacturer sprays diluted acid over the cured concrete to remove its cement surface, or laitance layer. Generally, the acid wash does not expose the aggregate, and gives the concrete a finish similar to cast stone.

AMERICAN SOCIETY OF TESTING AND MATERIALS (ASTM)
An organization that sets international, voluntary technical standards for a range of materials, products, systems, and services. www.astm.org

ANISOTROPY
The property of a material to behave differently along different axes. Most notable anisotropy is wood's greater compression strength for loads applied parallel rather than perpendicular to its grain.

ANNEALING
Glass: Annealing glass is a post-forming process, necessary to relieve internal stresses that form during shaping. When annealing glass, it is heated and then cooled slowly. Annealed glass is more durable, stronger, and less prone to cracking when exposed to temperature changes or mechanical stress than glass that has not been annealed.

Metal: Annealing metals may be done before, during, or after forming the metal workpiece. The metal is heated and then some metals are cooled slowly, while others are quenched in water. Annealed metal is more ductile and easier to form than metal that has not been annealed.

AXISYMMETRIC
A symmetry along a rotated axis.

BAND CLAMP
An adjustable clamp that encircles the item or items being clamped.

BATCH KILNS
Kilns that operate in cycles. They turn on and off between loading and unloading.

BENDING METAL
Use of a brake press to create a bend in a localized area of a metal blank or workpiece.

BENDY PLYWOOD
Laminated wood-veneer sheet products that are made to bend.

BENT PLYWOOD
Plywood with simple, or unidirectional, curves.

BLADDER
A flexible membrane that can apply even pressure.

BLANK
A sheet material, not yet in its final shape.

Metal: For metal-sheet forming (e.g. stamping, spinning, or hydroforming), a blank is a precut sheet of metal that has not been formed.

Plywood: In bending plywood, a blank is the bent plywood form that has not yet been trimmed.

BLANK HOLDER
In metal forming, it holds the blank in place during forming.

BLANKING
Cutting a piece of sheet metal from a larger sheet of metal. The metal that is cut away is the piece kept, while the remainder of the sheet is scrap.

BLOWPIPE
Hollow tube for blow molding glass. Typically, there is a mouthpiece on one end for blowing and an opening at the other end for the workpiece.

BOSSES
A solid circular feature added to the wall of a component. Bosses give a self-tapping screw a place where it can be drilled without damaging the component.

BOWING
Out-of-plane curvature, along the component's length.

BRITISH STANDARDS (BS)
Set by the British Standards Institution (BSI), voluntary technical standards for a range of materials, products, systems, and services. www.bsigroup.com

BUG HOLES
Small holes on a cast concrete surface due to air bubbles trapped during casting.

BUSH HAMMERING
Fracturing the surface of concrete (or masonry) with a mechanically or pneumatically driven hammer so that the interior aggregate is exposed.

CALENDARING
A manufacturing process in which a material is passed through a series of rollers to form long, thin sheets. Calendaring is used to manufacture rolls of paper, textiles, rubber, or plastic.

CAPITAL COSTS
Fixed, one-time expenses associated with production. They can include the cost of land, buildings, equipment and machinery, and molds.

CASTING
Noun: The object resulting from the casting process. This term particularly refers to cast metal components.

Verb: Pouring a liquid medium into a mold.

CATENARY CURVE
The draped shape that a material forms naturally, due to gravity and self-weight.

CHARGE
Explosive forming: The explosive material used for each explosion or cycle.

Glass: The starting batch of molten glass.

CHOPPED STRAND MATS (CSM)
Fiber mats made from short, chopped fibers held together by a resin-soluble binder.

CLAY
Natural, fine-grained earth that can be plastically shaped when wet.

CLAY SLIP
Clay that is suspended in water.

CLOSED MOLDS
Molds that have limited openings to access their inner cavity. Generally, closed molds produce components with all faces finished.

COMPUTER-AIDED MANUFACTURING (CAM)
Manufacturing that relies on CNC equipment (see below).

COMPUTER-NUMERIC CONTROL (CNC)
Computer-controlled electronics and motors that operate a machine's production in a precise and reproducible manner.

COEFFICIENT OF THERMAL EXPANSION
The fractional change in material size per degree temperature change.

COLD WORKING
Working metal at room temperature.

COMPLEX CURVE
A shape in which two or more curves intersect one another.

COMPOUND DIE
A metal stamping die that can perform more than one operation in a single stroke.

CONTINUOUS FILAMENT MAT (CFM)
A non-woven mat that has random, swirled, and indefinitely long fibers held together by a resin-soluble binder.

CONTINUOUS KILNS
Kilns that are kept continuously at an elevated temperature.

CONTINUOUS MANUFACTURING
Manufacturing processes that operate continuously, rather than in cycles.

CONTRACT MANUFACTURERS
Manufacturers that make items to fill a contracted order, and do not produce their own final products.

COPE
The upper half of a closed mold.

CRAZING
Fine cracks that appear on a surface.

CREEL
In pultrusion or filament winding, a rack or collection of fiber strands.

CULLET
Recycled glass.

CYCLE TIME
The amount of time it takes for a full cycle to be completed.

CYCLICAL MANUFACTURING
Manufacturing processes that operate in repeatable cycles. Components are removed from the tooling before the cycle begins again.

DEMOLD
Removing a component from a mold.

DIE
A tool that impresses a shape onto a material.

DIE ANGLE
In extrusion, the die angle is on the die's upstream side, which funnels the medium toward the die opening. The steeper the die angle, the more pushing force needed to move the medium through the die.

DIE CLEARANCE
In metal stamping, the distance between two die halves. The die clearance affects the wall thickness of the component.

DIE SWELL
In plastic extrusion, the property of plastic to change shape when exiting the die. The amount of die swell is specific to the type of plastic being extruded.

DIP MOLD
See optic mold.

DO IT YOURSELF (DIY)
The term for doing work without the direct help of professionals or experts. Ability can vary greatly.

DRAFT ANGLE
The angle needed to remove the component from its mold without damaging either the component or mold. Also called draw angle.

DRAG
The bottom half of a closed mold.

DRAPE FORMING
In thermoforming, this is forming the component over a male mold.

DRAW ANGLE
See draft angle.

DRAW BEAD
In metal stamping, a rib-like projection along die edges that locks the blank in place and controls its flow rate into the die.

DRAW RADIUS
The radius needed on the exterior corners of the die cavity entrance to keep the medium from tearing on entry.

DRAW DEPTH
The depth that sheet material can deform out of its original plane.

DRAW RATIO
The ratio of the surface area of a deformed workpiece to the surface area of the original blank.

DUCTILITY
The ability of a material to stretch plastically, without damage.

EARTH-MOIST
For clay or concrete: when the earth-moist medium is squeezed in the hand, no water residue is left behind; however, there is just enough moisture for the medium to hold its shape during demolding.

EJECTOR PINS
Movable pins as part of a tool that help with demolding.

ELASTIC BEHAVIOR
A material's behavior if stressed below its yield point. When the stress or load is removed, the deformed material returns to its original shape.

ELECTRONIC DISCHARGE MACHINE (EDM)
A CNC machine that uses electronic discharge to cut or shape metal.

ENVELOPE MOLDS
In casting concrete, a five-sided mold that is left intact when demolding.

EXPENDABLE MOLD
A mold that is temporary and not reusable from one cycle to the next.

EXTRUSION RATIO
In metal extrusion, the ratio of a billet's cross-sectional area to the cross-sectional area of the extruded profile.

EXTRUDATE
The material as it comes out of an extrusion die.

FAIENCE
Glazed clay.

FEEDSTOCK
Loose medium (e.g. pellets or flakes) that is fed into a hopper.

FEMALE MOLDS
Molds with an interior cavity, in which the component is formed.

FERROUS ALLOYS
Metal alloys that contain iron.

FIBER FABRIC MAT
Fibers that are woven together to create a fabric.

FIBER-REINFORCED COMPOSITE (FRC)
A material with fibers that are embedded in a matrix, typically plastic. The fibers carry most of the loading while the matrix holds the fibers in place.

FIVE-AXIS CNC
A CNC mill with five directions of movement, typically able to produce undercuts.

FLAME FINISH
See flame polished.

FLAME POLISH
The natural finish for glass when it is exposed to high temperatures. Flame-polished glass will be smooth, shiny, and—if the glass is transparent—clear. Also called flame finish.

FLANGE
In metal stamping, the part of the blank that does not enter the die cavity. Typically removed during post-production.

FLASHING
Excess medium that squeezes out between mold or die parts. Typically removed during post-production.

FLASK
In sand casting, the box that holds the compressed sand mold.

FOLLOWER/FOLLOWING BLOCK
In metal spinning, the block that clamps the blank into place and forms the component bottom.

FORMABILITY
The ability of a metal to undergo plastic deformation without tearing.

GAUGE
Sheet material thickness.

GATING SYSTEM
The network of channels through which molten media flows into a closed-mold cavity.

GLORY HOLE
A reheating chamber for working glass, typically in a glass studio setting.

GRAIN ORIENTATION
The direction of the crystalline structure within a metal alloy. Affects the direction in which the metal can be bent.

GREEN CLAY
Clay that just has been removed from the mold. Green clay is stiff enough to hold its shape and can easily be carved with hand tools and little pressure.

GROG
Fired clay scraps that are ground into small pieces.

HYBRID COMPOSITE
A fiber-reinforced composite (FRC) with two or more different fibers.

INJECTION MOLDING
A manufacturing process that uses pressure to force a medium (e.g. plastic) through a gating system into a closed mold.

ISOTROPY
The property of a material to behave the same along different axes. The opposite of anisotropy.

KIRKSITE
A zinc alloy that can be cast at a relatively low melting temperature.

LAITANCE
A layer of fine sand and hydrated cement that appears on the surface of concrete. It is weaker than the interior of the concrete and is prone to cracking.

LAMPWORKING
Using a concentrated flame to heat glass to a working temperature.

LAYUP
FRC: The method of applying fibers and resin onto a mold.

Plywood: A stack of plywood veneers and wet adhesive.

LEATHER-HARD
Clay that has dried to a similar stiffness as leather, if the leather were the same thickness as the clay. Leather-hard clay can be handled without damage and trimmed or gouged with pressure and hand tools.

LEADERSHIP IN ENERGY AND ENVIRONMENTAL DESIGN (LEED)
A third-party certification program to measure the environmental impact of buildings.

LEHR
A temperature-controlled tunnel or continuous kiln to anneal glass.

LIFT
For casting concrete, a layer of poured concrete.

MALE MOLDS
Positive molds on which components are formed.

MASTER
A mold used to make a pattern that is then used to make the mold used in manufacturing.

MATCH PLATE
Two sides of a pattern attached on opposite sides of a plate.

MODEL
Similar to a pattern.

MOLDED PLYWOOD
Plywood shaped into a complex curve.

MOLD SIDE
The face of the component that is or was in direct contact with the mold.

NEAR NET SHAPE
A manufactured component that required little post-production work, such as cutting, trimming, or milling.

NET SHAPE
A manufactured component that requires no post-production work.

NONFERROUS ALLOY
An alloy without iron.

OPEN MOLDS
Molds with large openings to access the mold cavity. Generally, open molds produce components with one unfinished face.

OPTIC MOLD
In glass blowing, a partial or open mold used to shape glass. The molten glass is dipped into the mold, inflated, and then removed from the mold.

OVER-PRESS
Extra medium that is squeezed out of the press because too much was put in the mold or the die. Over-press should be removed with post-production finishing.

PARALLEL PRODUCTIONS
Running two or more simultaneous productions on similar or the same molds. Parallel productions are done to speed up production schedules when mold costs are low.

PARISON
Molten glass or plastic that is to be inflated inside a mold.

PARTING AGENT
A material or coating between the mold and the workpiece that allows the workpiece to be easily demolded.

PARTING LINE
The seam between mold parts.

PATTERN
Tooling used to repeatedly form expendable molds.

PERMANENT MOLD
A mold that is to last multiple cycles.

PLASTICITY
Clay: When the clay can be rolled and bent without cracking.

Metal: When metal is stressed above its yield point but below its strain-hardening phase. Little to no additional loading is placed on the material, but it permanently deforms.

POST-PRODUCTION
Secondary processes that are required after manufacturing.

POT LIFE
The amount of time that a thermoset resin will remain viscous before setting.

PREFORM
In blow molding, a semi-shaped pieced that has been formed in a mold, prior to being heated and blown into a mold cavity.

PREPREG
Reinforcing tow or mat that has been pre-impregnated with resin to make FRC.

PRODUCTION RUN
The number of components that are to be produced for a particular job.

PRODUCTION TIME
The amount of time it takes to produce all the components for a particular job.

PRODUCTION VOLUME
The number of components that are to be produced for a particular job or from a particular tool.

PROGRESSIVE DIE
In metal stamping, a die with multiple steps that work in sequence to shape sheet metal.

PUNCH DIE
In metal stamping, the male part of the die.

PUNCHING
In metal stamping, cutting a piece of metal from a blank, in which the metal that is cut away is scrap (aka slug), and what is left of the blank is kept.

QUENCHING
Quickly cooling a material after heating—typically done in water, but can be done in oil.

REFRACTORY
Additive ingredients in a mold medium so that it can withstand high temperatures.

REGLET
A small notch in a material.

RESTRIKING
In metal stamping, after a workpiece is trimmed it is placed into the die to be stamped again.

RIB
A feature used to strengthen the component's wall without adding the wall thickness.

RISER
In metal casting, a riser stores molten metal so that as the metal shrinks during cooling, molten metal from the riser will flow into any resulting cavities.

SAG
The drooping of material over time.

SCREED
The straight-edged tool used to level concrete, or the act of leveling concrete with a straight-edged tool.

SHOT
The amount of media that is placed in the mold for each cycle.

SINK MARKS
Localized surface depressions caused by material shrinkage while cooling.

SLIP BLOCK
In concrete casting, a mold part that is sacrificed or removed as the component is demolded.

SLUG
In metal stamping, the scrap metal resulting from a punching operation.

SLUMP TEST
A test to measure the workability of newly mixed concrete.

SPRINGBACK
The elastic behavior in sheet metal forming, in which a newly deformed metal sheet partially returns to its original shape.

STRIPPING
Removing concrete from a mold.

STROKE
Each cycle of a metal stamping press.

SUPERPLASTICITY
Unusual capacity of a material to withstand large amounts of uniform strain without necking or rupturing.

TEMPERING (GLASS)
Reheating annealed glass to a high temperature, and then quickly cooling the glass surface.

THERMOPLASTIC
Type of plastic with no bonds between polymer chains. Thermoplastics are shaped by heating them to a prescribed temperature.

THERMOSET PLASTIC
Type of plastic with chemical bonds between polymer chains. Thermoset plastics are shaped before the bonds form; after bonds form, they can only be reshaped by breaking the bonds.

TOLERANCE
The allowable variation of a component's dimensions.

TOOLING
Manufacturing: Tools, such as patterns, molds, dies, and jigs, used to form the component.

Precast concrete: Post-production finishing tools, such as chisels, needle guns, and bush hammers, which change the cast surface of the concrete.

TUNNEL KILN
Large kiln that runs continuously. Room-temperature components are fed into one end of the kiln and emerge at the other end, having been elevated to their required temperature.

UNDERCUT
A recess in the component's surface that makes demolding difficult or impossible.

VEIL
For a composite, the outer layer that provides a smooth, finished surface.

VENTS
Small holes in tooling that allow for air-flow.

VISCOSITY
The resistance of a liquid to flow, due to internal friction.

WANDERING PARTING LINE
A seam between mold parts, not in a singular, geometric plane.

WARM WORKING
Working a material above room temperature but below hot-working temperature. For metal, this is below its recrystallization temperature.

WARPING
Twisting of a member so that two corners do not fall in the same plane.

WOOD PRODUCTS
Manufactured materials made from wood or wood waste. These include oriented strand board (OSB), plywood, and particle board.

WORKPIECE
The piece that is in the process of being manufactured. It is in an in-between state—neither the medium, blank, nor final component.

WYTHE
A vertical layer of masonry unit or product.

Index

Illustration references are indicated in *italic*; page ranges in **bold** indicate main subject entries

Image credits

Image are listed by figure number except where indicated. Images not listed below were provided by the author.

Cover Courtesy Machado and Silvetti Associates LLC (for more information see pages 338–341)

page 6 Christian Richters

page 7 Courtesy KAAN Architecten - Vincent Panhuysen

intro 4 Terri Meyer Boake

intro 5 David Hill

intro 6 Terri Meyer Boake

intro 7 © Nigel Young/ Foster + Partners

intro 8 Courtesy of Hierve Diseñera

intro 9 Scagliola/Brakkee © Neutelings Riedijk Architects

intro 11 Photo Vanessa Guillen. © Hariri Pontarini Architects (left)Jeff Goodman Studio (right)

intro 12 Emmi Keskisarja (EDGE), Pekka Tynkkynen (EDGE), Kristof Crolla (LEAD), Sebastien Delagrange (LEAD)

Intro 13 Michael Zaretsky, 2004

page 22 (section 1 opening image) Emmi Keskisarja (EDGE), Pekka Tynkkynen (EDGE), Kristof Crolla (LEAD), Sebastien Delagrange(LEAD)

1.1.1 Glass Images & Creations Inc

1.1.3–1.1.4 Will Crocker Photography

1.1.5 Laurel Porcari

1.1.6 Wendy Kershaw

1.1.8 Glass Images & Creations Inc

1.1.13–1.1.14 Bruce Damonte

1.1.15–1.1.24 Courtesy of Belzberg Architects

1.2.12–1.2.22 Courtesy Dale Clifford, Jason Vollen, Matt Gindlesparger, Eddie Hall and Professor William Katavalo (University of Arizona)

1.2.26 Image courtesy of SuperformUSA

1.2.27–1.2.29 image courtesy of Murmur

1.2.30 Drawing by Murmur

1.2.31–1.2.37 image courtesy of SuperformUSA

1.3.1–1.3.2 PA&E Bonded Metals Division

1.3.5 CSULB Special Collections & University Archives

1.3.9 CSULB Special Collections & University Archives

1.3.10–1.3.13 IAA Archiecten NL IR. Harry Abels

1.3.14–1.3.16 Photo Hieke Luik

1.3.17 IAA Archiecten NL IR. Harry Abels

1.4.10–1.4.22 Courtesy Studio Gang Architects

1.4.27–1.4.29 Photograph by Emmi Keskisarja (EDGE)

1.4.30 Design team: Emmi Keskisarja (EDGE), Pekka Tynkkynen (EDGE), Kristof Crolla (LEAD), Sebastien Delagrange(LEAD

1.4.31 Photograph by Sebastien Delagrange(LEAD)

1.4.32 Photographed by Dennis Lo Designs

1.4.33 Photograph by Sebastien Delagrange(LEAD)

1.4.34 Photographed by Dennis Lo Designs

1.4.35–1.4.36 Photograph by Pekka Tynkkynen (EDGE)

1.4.37 Photograph by Emmi Keskisarja (EDGE)

1.4.38 Photograph by Pekka Tynkkynen (EDGE)

1.5.16 Photo © Dirk Laubner

1.5.17–1.5.19 Photo © Jens Kirchner

1.5.20–1.5.29 Photo courtesy Benthem Crouwel Architects

1.6.14 Courtesy Jim Clemes Associates

1.6.15 Robert Sprang

1.6.16 Ferdinand Grafvon Luckner

1.6.17 Werner Huthmacher

1.6.18 Courtesy Jim Clemes Associates

1.6.19 Ferdinand Grafvon Luckner

1.6.20–1.6.22 Fielitz

1.6.23–1.6.24 Courtesy Jim Clemes Associates

1.7.10 Photograph by Peter Mallet, courtesy Heatherwick Studio

1.7.15–1.7.16 © Neutelings Riedijk Architects

1.7.17–1.7.23 Scagliola/Brakkee © Neutelings Riedijk Architects

1.7.24–1.7.25 LEEBO Intelligent Building Systems

page 120 (section 2 opening image) © Mangado y Asociados

2.1.23–2.1.24 © Mangado y Asociados

2.1.25 © Pedro Pegenaute

2.1.26–2.1.33 © Mangado y Asociados

2.1.39 Photograph by Timothy Hursley

2.1.40 Mack Scogin Merrill Elam Architects

2.1.41 Photograph by Timothy Hursley

2.1.42–2.1.44 Mack Scogin Merrill Elam Architects

2.1.48–2.1.60 Courtesy 5468796 Architecture

2.1.65 Courtesy selgascano

2.1.66–2.1.67 Photo IwanBaan

2.1.68–2.1.75 Courtesy selgascano

2.2.12 King Roselli Architetti

2.2.13–2.2.14 © Santi Caleca

2.2.15 King Roselli Architetti

2.2.16–2.2.17 King Roselli Architetti & PCR

2.2.18–2.2.21 King Roselli Architetti

page 166 (section 3 opening image) © Nigel Young/ Foster + Partners

3.1.25–3.1.34 Courtesy Tim Wilson, Wilson Composites, LLC

3.2.7–3.2.8 © Nigel Young/Foster + Partners

3.2.9–3.2.16 © Foster + Partners

3.3.12–3.3.18 Courtesy ICD/ITKE, University of Stuttgart

3.4.1–3.4.12 © Europoles GmbH & Co. KG

3.4.13–3.4.24 Photographs by Brigida González, courtesy Ecker Architekten

3.5.22 © Fernando Cordero. Courtesy Hierve-Diseñería

3.5.23–3.5.36 Courtesy Hierve-Diseñería

3.5.41–3.5.49 Miniwiz Co., Ltd

page 236 (section 4 opening image) Peter Clarke Photography

4.1.19 © Leong Leong

4.1.20–4.1.21 © Iwan Baan

4.1.22–4.1.22 © Dadam

4.1.23 © Leong Leong

4.1.26–4.1.37 Courtesy Niall McLaughlin

4.1.44 Photo © Christian Richters

4.1.45 KAAN Architecten

4.1.46 Photo © Christian Richters

4.1.47–4.1.51 KAAN Architecten

4.1.52 Courtesy KAAN Architecten - Vincent Panhuysen

4.1.53–4.1.54 Photo SVK

4.1.57–4.1.58 Peter Clarke Photography

4.1.59–4.1.67 Elenberg Fraser

4.1.74–4.1.84 Courtesy Acme

4.2.18–4.2.19 Photo © David Grandorge

4.2.20–4.2.24 © 6a Architects

4.2.25 © Data2Pattern

4.2.26–4.2.29 © 6a Architects

4.2.30 © Paul Smith

4.2.31 © 6a Architects

4.2.32 © FSE Foundry

4.2.33–4.2.35 © 6a Architects

4.2.36 © FSE Foundry

4.2.37 Photo © David Grandorge

4.2.38–4.2.40 © 6a Architects

4.3.1 Patricia Piggott

4.3.2 Photo glass.h0uses

4.3.6–4.3.7 Sculpture by Sue Hawker. Photo Kaiwhakahaere via Wikimedia Commons

4.3.8 Photo narissa's ring

4.3.12–4.3.13 Photo Justin Ford. Courtesy Hariri Pontarini Architects

4.3.14 Courtesy Hariri Pontarini Architects

4.3.15–4.3.16 Photo Vanessa Guillen. Courtesy Hariri Pontarini Architects

4.3.18–4.3.19 Courtesy Hariri Pontarini Architects

4.3.20–4.3.22 Photo Jeff Goodman Studio

4.3.23 Courtesy Hariri Pontarini Architects

4.3.24 Photo Jeff Goodman Studio

4.3.25 Courtesy Hariri Pontarini Architects

4.3.26 Photo Jeff Goodman Studio

4.4.16–4.4.18 Photo Diana Arnau. Courtesy HGR Arquitectos

4.4.19 Courtesy HGR Arquitectos

4.4.20–4.4.21 Photo Diana Arnau. Courtesy HGR Arquitectos

4.4.22 Ariel Rojo Design Studio

4.4.23 Photo Ponxo Tenorio. Courtesy HGR Arquitectos

4.4.24 Ariel Rojo Design Studio

4.4.25 Photograph taken by Marcos Hagerman, courtesy of HGR Arquitectos

4.4.26–4.4.27 Photo Ponxo Tenorio. Courtesy HGR Arquitectos

4.4.28 Photo Marcos Hagerman. Courtesy HGR Arquitectos

4.5.21 Photo Timothy Hursley

4.5.22–4.5.24 Courtesy Duvall Decker Architects, P.A.

4.5.25 Photo Timothy Hursley

4.5.26–4.5.29 Courtesy Duvall Decker Architects, P.A.

4.6.3–4.6.8 Courtesy OCMI-OTG S.p.A.

4.6.15–4.6.17 © Jannes Linders

4.6.18–4.6.22 © Benthem Crouwel Architects

4.6.28–4.6.30 Courtesy Machado and Silvetti Associates LLC

4.6.33 Photo Craig Mutter

4.6.34 Photo Jamie Setzler

4.6.35 Courtesy Machado and Silvetti Associates LLC

4.6.36 Photo Jamie Setzler

4.6.37 Photo Craig Mutter

4.6.38–4.6.39 Photo Jamie Setzler

Acknowledgements

I would like to thank my colleagues and the administration at NCSU College of Design. Without the release time, teaching seminars and studios that helped shaped this work, and funding for travel, I could not have done this. I particularly want to thank David Hill for reading very (very) early drafts of chapters, and helping to shape the book even before it was written.

Thank you to all of the manufacturers who opened their doors to me. It was through this access that I better understood what was possible with each process and at each facility.

Thank you to my NCSU students. Through my seminar and studios you gathered many of manufacturing process, materials, and case studies that have made it into this book. Thank you particularly to Dylan Impink for helping gather research and Mason Lehman for generating the process diagrams.

Thank you to my former colleagues and students at University of New Mexico and Savannah College of Art and Design. You were there at the beginning, when I was being to explore the value of manufacturing to architecture.

Thank you to my editors, for your patience as I finished.

Thank you to my parents, as I would not be where I am without you.

Thank you to my family: My husband, Sean Tobin, who bared most of the parenting on weekends and nights as I worked—your love and support was everything to me; and my daughter, Adele Tobin-Gulling, who at many times told me that my working "was boring", but was always happy for me when I reached a milestone. I love you both.

Imperial Units

in	inch or inches
fl oz	fluid ounces
ft	foot or feet
ft²	square foot or feet
k/in²	kip or kips per square inch (equals 1,000lb/in²)
lb	pound or pounds
lb/in²	pound or pounds per square inch
lb/ft²	pound or pounds per square foot
°F	degrees Fahrenheit

SI Units

kPa	kilo Pascal or Pascals (equals 1,000 Pa)
mm	millimeter or millimeters
cm	centimeter or centimeters
m	meter or meters
m²	square meter or meters
mL	milliliter or milliliters
L	liter or liter
Pa	Pascals
km	kilometer or kilometers
kg	kilogram or kilograms
°C	degrees Celsius

Acronyms & Abbreviations

AAMA	Asia America Multi-technology Association
APA	American Plywood Association
ASTM	American Society of Testing and Materials
BIM	building information modeling
BS	British Standards
CAM	computer-aided manufacturing
CAD	computer-aided design/computer-aided drafting
CNC	computer numeric controlled
CLT	cross-laminated timber
DIY	do it yourself
EDM	electronic discharge machine
FRP	fiber-reinforced plastic
LED	light-emitting diode
LEED	Leadership in Energy and Environmental Design
MDF	medium-density fiberboard
PET	polyethylene terephthalate polymer (plastic)
PET-G	polyethylene terephthalate glycol-modified polymer
PVB	polyvinyl butyral
SPF	superplastic forming
UK	United Kingdom
UL	Underwriters Laboratory
US	United States (of America)
USD	United States dollar
UV	ultraviolet light
VOC	volatile organic compound